Feature Paper Collection in the Section 'Electrical, Electronics and Communications Engineering'

Feature Paper Collection in the Section 'Electrical, Electronics and Communications Engineering'

Guest Editors

Alexander Barkalov
Larysa Titarenko
Kazimierz Krzywicki

MDPI

Basel • Beijing • Wuhan • Barcelona • Belgrade • Novi Sad • Cluj • Manchester

Guest Editors

Alexander Barkalov
Institute of Metrology,
Electronics and Computer
Science
University of Zielona Gora
Zielona Gora
Poland

Larysa Titarenko
Institute of Metrology,
Electronics and Computer
Science
University of Zielona Gora
Zielona Gora
Poland

Kazimierz Krzywicki
Department of Technology
The Jacob of Paradies
University
Gorzow Wielkopolski
Poland

Editorial Office

MDPI AG
Grosspeteranlage 5
4052 Basel, Switzerland

This is a reprint of the Special Issue, published open access by the journal *Applied Sciences* (ISSN 2076-3417), freely accessible at: https://www.mdpi.com/journal/applsci/special_issues/T9967EV084.

For citation purposes, cite each article independently as indicated on the article page online and as indicated below:

Lastname, A.A.; Lastname, B.B. Article Title. *Journal Name* **Year**, *Volume Number*, Page Range.

ISBN 978-3-7258-7579-5 (Hbk)
ISBN 978-3-7258-7580-1 (PDF)
https://doi.org/10.3390/books978-3-7258-7580-1

Contents

About the Editors

Alexander Barkalov

Alexander Barkalov (member of HiPEAC) received an M.Sc. degree in Computer Engineering from the Donetsk Politechnical Institute (currently Donetsk National Technical University), Ukraine, in 1976, and a Ph.D. degree in Computer Science from the Leningrad Institute of Precise Mechanics and Optics, Russia, in 1983. In 1995 he received a Doctor of Technical Sciences degree in Computer Science from the Institute of Cybernetics named after V. M. Glushkov (Kiev, Ukraine). He has been an Assistant Professor (since 1976), an Associate Professor (since 1984) and a Professor (since 1996) at the Institute of Computers, Donetsk National Technical University. From 2003 he is a Professor of Computer Engineering at the Institute of Informatics and Electronics, University of Zielona Gora, Poland, while remaining a Professor at the Institute of Computers, Donetsk National Technical University. His current research interests include theory of digital automata, especially the methods of synthesis and optimization of control units implemented with field programmable logic devices. He has taken part in the realization of a number of research projects sponsored by different institutions of the former USSR aimed at the development of computer-aided design tools for implementation of control units. Alexander Barkalov has published more than 750 papers in international journals and conference proceedings. He is an author of two and co-author of 27 monographs and 2 book chapters.

Larysa Titarenko

Larysa Titarenko (member of HiPEAC) received an M.Sc. (1993), a PhD (1996) and a Doctor of Technical Sciences (2005) degree in Telecommunications from Kharkov National University of Radioelectronics, Ukraine. She has been an Assistant Professor (from 1993), an Associate Professor (from 1996) and a Professor of telecommunications at the Institute of Telecommunication Systems, Kharkov National University of Radioelectronics, Ukraine. From 2007 she is a Professor of Telecommunications at the Institute of Informatics and Electronics, University of Zielona Gora, Poland, while remaining a Professor of telecommunications at the Institute of Infocommunication Engineering, Kharkov National University of Radioelectronics, Ukraine. Her current research interests include theory of telecommunication systems, theory of antennas and theory of digital automata and its applications. She has taken part in the realization of a number of research projects sponsored by the Ministry of Science and Higher Education of Ukraine (1993, 2005). Larysa Titarenko has published more than 350 papers in international journals and conference proceedings. She is an author of two and co-author of 23 monographs and three book chapters.

Kazimierz Krzywicki

Kazimierz Krzywicki was born in Zielona Gora, Poland, in 1985. He obtained a PhD in Computer Science from the University of Zielona Gora in 2019. In 2010, he founded and became the head of the KGK Pro company, which creates software and hardware solutions. The main areas of its activity are embedded systems and Internet of Things, especially animal tracking devices. Over 12 years, he was a court expert and computer forensics investigator. Furthermore, he is a member of PTI (Polish Information Processing Society). His research interests include design and implementation of distributed embedded systems and hardware synthesis for reprogrammable devices. He published over 60 papers in international journals and conference proceedings.

Preface

This Reprint was prepared in order to present a focused yet diverse collection of recent studies in electrical, electronics, and communications engineering. Its scope reflects on the broad and evolving character of the field by bringing together contributions devoted to programmable hardware and digital design; embedded and wearable systems; communication and networking solutions; signal processing, antenna, and microwave engineering; cybersecurity and intelligent computational methods. Although these topics are varied, they are connected by a shared interest in practical implementation system performance reliability and relevance to current engineering challenges.

The purpose of this Reprint is to provide readers with an integrated view of ongoing developments across areas that increasingly interact in contemporary research and applications. The motivation for preparing this Reprint was the opportunity to gather contributions that illustrate both methodological advances and real-world engineering perspectives within a single volume. In this way the Reprint highlights not only progress within individual subfields but also the growing convergence of hardware, software, communications, and data-driven approaches.

This Reprint is addressed to researchers, engineers, academics, and advanced students interested in current directions, future challenges, and interdisciplinary connections in modern electrical electronics and communications engineering.

Alexander Barkalov, Larysa Titarenko, and Kazimierz Krzywicki
Guest Editors

applied sciences

Editorial

Advances and Outlook in Electrical, Electronics and Communications Engineering

Alexander Barkalov [1,*], Larysa Titarenko [1,2] and Kazimierz Krzywicki [3,*]

1 Institute of Metrology, Electronics and Computer Science, University of Zielona Gora, ul. Licealna 9, 65-417 Zielona Gora, Poland; l.titarenko@imei.uz.zgora.pl
2 Department of Infocommunication Engineering, Faculty of Infocommunications, Kharkiv National University of Radio Electronics, Nauky Avenue 14, 61166 Kharkiv, Ukraine
3 Department of Technology, The Jacob of Paradies University, ul. Fryderyka Chopina 52/b.7, 66-400 Gorzow Wielkopolski, Poland
* Correspondence: a.barkalov@imei.uz.zgora.pl (A.B.); kkrzywicki@ajp.edu.pl (K.K.)

1. Introduction

Electrical, electronics, and communications engineering continue to play a central role in modern technological development, underpinning the digital infrastructure that enables computation, connectivity, sensing, and control across virtually all sectors. Over the last decade, progress in semiconductor integration, programmable and heterogeneous computing, and advanced signal processing has accelerated the pace at which complex systems can be designed and deployed [1]. In particular, programmable hardware platforms (including FPGA-based and other reconfigurable architectures) remain essential where low latency, deterministic behavior, and energy-efficient processing are required, while modern design flows increasingly combine high-level abstractions with implementation-aware optimization [2].

In parallel, communications engineering is being reshaped by growing demands for high-throughput and low-latency services, as well as by the need to provide reliable connectivity for a large number of devices. The evolution toward next-generation mobile networks and converged access/backhaul architectures has highlighted the importance of end-to-end performance modeling, traffic engineering, and resilient operation under dynamic conditions [3]. A further major trend is the adoption of data-driven techniques and machine learning to support network management, resource allocation, and signal processing tasks, offering improved adaptivity but also creating new requirements related to robustness, interpretability, and validation [4]. These developments are closely linked to a broad shift toward edge and fog computing paradigms, where computation is distributed closer to data sources to reduce latency and bandwidth usage, often under strict energy constraints [5].

At the system level, increasing complexity presents persistent challenges in design, implementation efficiency, reliability, and integration. Modern electronic systems frequently blend hardware and software components, incorporate distributed sensing/actuation, and operate under safety, security, and maintainability constraints that must be addressed throughout the life cycle [6]. Reliability and fault tolerance remain crucial in safety- and mission-critical deployments, motivating continued research into redundancy strategies, runtime monitoring, and practical fault models [7]. In addition, the expanding attack surface of interconnected systems has made security-by-design and trusted operation—including authentication, integrity, and supply-chain assurance—an increasingly important engineering objective [8]. Across all these topics, energy efficiency has become a primary optimization target, driven by sustainability considerations and by the practical limitations of mobile, wearable, and distributed embedded devices [9].

Against this background, the Special Issue entitled "Feature Paper Collection in the Section 'Electrical, Electronics and Communications Engineering'" brings together fourteen peer-reviewed articles that reflect current advances across programmable hardware, communication networks, signal processing, embedded systems, antennas and microwave structures, and emerging interdisciplinary applications. Collectively, the contributions highlight how progress in the field increasingly depends on cross-layer thinking—linking algorithms, architectures, and implementation decisions with realistic deployment constraints and measurable performance outcomes [10].

2. Overview of Contributions

Several contributions focus on programmable hardware and digital system implementation. Salauyou et al. demonstrated an efficient FPGA implementation technique using ASMD-FSMD methods, achieving significant performance improvements in digital devices (contribution 1). Similarly, Kubica and Czerwinski analyzed triple modular redundancy mitigation techniques in FPGA systems, addressing reliability challenges in critical applications (contribution 2).

Communication systems and signal processing are another major research area represented in this Special Issue. Klinkowski and Więcek analyzed latency prediction models in packet-switched Xhaul networks, demonstrating improved performance using data-driven approaches (contribution 3). Datta et al. proposed a neural beamforming method for multi-channel speech enhancement, improving speech quality in complex acoustic environments (contribution 4). Lee et al. presented a secure authentication scheme for fog-based vehicular networks, improving both performance and security (contribution 5). Lee et al. also introduced a denoising autoencoder-based localization method, improving connectivity-based localization accuracy (contribution 6).

Research on antennas and microwave systems is represented by several important contributions. Madji et al. presented a novel antenna design capable of generating circularly polarized beams with improved performance characteristics (contribution 7). Negri et al. provided a comprehensive review of two-dimensional leaky-wave antennas and their design techniques (contribution 8). Çolak and Ertay proposed an efficient design method for glide-symmetric waveguide structures, improving microwave system design efficiency (contribution 9). Karkanis et al. presented a comparative study of microwave ablation applicators, providing insights into electromagnetic and thermal performance optimization (contribution 10).

Embedded systems and electronic measurement techniques were addressed in several contributions. Suchorolski et al. analyzed analogue and digital methods for magnetic flux estimation in voltage transformers, demonstrating effective implementation approaches (contribution 11). Januszkiewicz and Nowak introduced textile-based microwave transmission lines for wearable electronic systems, providing new possibilities for wearable communication technologies (contribution 12).

In addition, system-level and interdisciplinary contributions highlight emerging applications and design methodologies. Lew et al. proposed a distributed software build assurance framework using blockchain to improve software supply chain integrity (contribution 13). Łukaniszyn et al. reviewed the use of artificial intelligence and digital twins in personalized healthcare, demonstrating the growing importance of intelligent systems integration (contribution 14).

https://doi.org/10.3390/app16062736

Taken together, these contributions reflect current trends in electrical, electronics, and communications engineering and demonstrate the continued development of advanced electronic and communication systems.

3. Research Challenges and Future Directions

Despite significant advances, several important research challenges remain. Improving hardware efficiency, reliability, and scalability continues to be essential, particularly in programmable logic systems and embedded platforms (contributions 1 and 2).

Communication systems must support increasing performance requirements while maintaining reliability and efficiency. Advances in communication protocols, signal processing, and network optimization will remain critical research areas (contributions 3–6).

Antenna and microwave system design continues to evolve, supporting new applications in wireless communication, sensing, and medical technologies (contributions 7–10).

Embedded systems, wearable electronics, and intelligent integrated systems represent another important research direction, requiring efficient hardware–software integration and innovative system architectures (contributions 11–14).

4. Conclusions

This Special Issue presents a diverse collection of research contributions addressing key challenges and emerging trends in electrical, electronics, and communications engineering. The published papers demonstrate advances in programmable hardware, communication systems, signal processing, antenna design, embedded systems, and intelligent applications.

We would like to thank all of the authors for their valuable contributions, the reviewers for their careful evaluations, and the editorial staff of *Applied Sciences* for their support throughout the publication process.

We hope that this Special Issue will contribute to further advances in electrical, electronics, and communications engineering and inspire future research in these important areas.

Author Contributions: Conceptualization, A.B., L.T. and K.K.; validation, A.B., L.T. and K.K.; formal analysis, A.B., L.T. and K.K.; investigation, A.B., L.T. and K.K.; writing—original draft preparation, A.B., L.T., K.K.; supervision, A.B. All authors have read and agreed to the published version of the manuscript.

Conflicts of Interest: The authors declare no conflicts of interest.

List of Contributions:

1. Salauyou, V.; Klimowicz, A.; Grzes, T. High-Performance Digital Devices Design by the ASMD-FSMD Technique for Implementation in FPGA. *Appl. Sci.* **2025**, *15*, 410. https://doi.org/10.3390/app15010410.
2. Kubica, M.; Czerwinski, R. Performance Testing of the Triple Modular Redundancy Mitigation Circuit Test Environment Implementation in FPGA Structures. *Appl. Sci.* **2024**, *14*, 8604. https://doi.org/10.3390/app14198604.
3. Klinkowski, M.; Więcek, D. Performance Analysis of Data-Driven and Deterministic Latency Models in Dynamic Packet-Switched Xhaul Networks. *Appl. Sci.* **2025**, *15*, 12487. https://doi.org/10.3390/app152312487.
4. Datta, J.; Firoozabadi, A.D.; Zabala-Blanco, D.; Castillo-Soria, F.R. Multi-Channel Speech Enhancement Using Labelled Random Finite Sets and a Neural Beamformer. *Appl. Sci.* **2025**, *15*, 2944. https://doi.org/10.3390/app15062944.
5. Lee, S.; Son, S.; Kwon, D.; Park, Y.; Park, Y. A Secure and Efficient Authentication Scheme for Fog-Based Vehicular Ad Hoc Networks. *Appl. Sci.* **2025**, *15*, 1229. https://doi.org/10.3390/app15031229.

 https://doi.org/10.3390/app16062736

6. Lee, W.H.; Ozger, M.; Challita, U.; Song, T. Denoising-Autoencoder-Aided Euclidean Distance Matrix Reconstruction for Connectivity-Based Localization. *Appl. Sci.* **2025**, *15*, 2656. https://doi.org/10.3390/app15052656.
7. Madji, M.; Negri, E.; Fuscaldo, W.; Comite, D.; Galli, A.; Burghignoli, P. Two-Dimensional Scanning of Circularly Polarized Beams via Array-Fed Fabry–Perot Cavity Antennas. *Appl. Sci.* **2024**, *14*, 12058.
8. Negri, E.; Fuscaldo, W.; Burghignoli, P.; Galli, A. An Overview of Design Techniques for Two-Dimensional Leaky-Wave Antennas. *Appl. Sci.* **2025**, *15*, 1854.
9. Çolak, F.; Ertay, A.O. A Fast, Simple, and Approximate Method for Minimal Unit Cell Design of Glide-Symmetric Waveguides. *Appl. Sci.* **2025**, *15*, 5876.
10. Karkanis, N.; Kaifas, T.; Samaras, T.; Kyriacou, G. Comparative Study of Minimally Invasive Microwave Ablation Applicators. *Appl. Sci.* **2025**, *15*, 2142.
11. Suchorolski, P.; Smolarczyk, A.; Łukaszewski, P.; Łapczyński, S.; Szulborski, M.; Owsiński, M.; Łukaszewski, A.; Kolimas, Ł.; Nogal, Ł. Comparative Analysis of Analogue and Digital Methods for Magnetic Flux Estimation. *Appl. Sci.* **2024**, *14*, 11304.
12. Januszkiewicz, Ł.; Nowak, I. Knitted Microwave Transmission Line for Wearable Electronics. *Appl. Sci.* **2024**, *14*, 10798.
13. Lew, K.; Sarker, A.; Wuthier, S.; Kim, J.; Kim, J.; Chang, S. Distributed Software Build Assurance for Software Supply Chain Integrity. *Appl. Sci.* **2024**, *14*, 9262.
14. Łukaniszyn, M.; Majka, Ł.; Grochowicz, B.; Mikołajewski, D.; Kawala-Sterniuk, A. Digital Twins Generated by Artificial Intelligence in Personalized Healthcare. *Appl. Sci.* **2024**, *14*, 9404.

References

1. Mii, Y.J. Semiconductor industry outlook and new technology frontiers. In *Proceedings of the 2024 IEEE International Electron Devices Meeting (IEDM)*; IEEE: New York, NY, USA, 2024; pp. 1–6.
2. Barkalov, A.; Titarenko, L.; Krzywicki, K. *Logic Synthesis for FPGA-Based Mealy Finite State Machines: Structural Decomposition in Logic Design*, 1st ed.; CRC Press: Boca Raton, FL, USA, 2024. [CrossRef]
3. Fayad, A.; Cinkler, T.; Rak, J. Toward 6G optical fronthaul: A survey on enabling technologies and research perspectives. *IEEE Commun. Surv. Tutor.* **2024**, *27*, 629–666. [CrossRef]
4. Pivoto, D.G.S.; de Figueiredo, F.A.P.; Cavdar, C.; Tejerina, G.R.d.L.; Mendes, L.L. A comprehensive survey of machine learning applied to resource allocation in wireless communications. *IEEE Commun. Surv. Tutor.* **2025**, *28*, 1986–2053. [CrossRef]
5. Kong, L.; Tan, J.; Huang, J.; Chen, G.; Wang, S.; Jin, X.; Zeng, P.; Khan, M.; Das, S.K. Edge-computing-driven internet of things: A survey. *ACM Comput. Surv.* **2022**, *55*, 1–41. [CrossRef]
6. Segovia-Ferreira, M.; Rubio-Hernan, J.; Cavalli, A.; Garcia-Alfaro, J. A survey on cyber-resilience approaches for cyber-physical systems. *ACM Comput. Surv.* **2024**, *56*, 1–37. [CrossRef]
7. Solouki, M.A.; Angizi, S.; Violante, M. Dependability in embedded systems: A survey of fault tolerance methods and software-based mitigation techniques. *IEEE Access* **2024**, *12*, 180939–180967. [CrossRef]
8. Alsheavi, A.N.; Hawbani, A.; Othman, W.; Wang, X.; Qaid, G.; Zhao, L.; Al-Dubai, A.; Zhi, L.; Ismail, A.; Jhaveri, R.; et al. Iot authentication protocols: Challenges, and comparative analysis. *ACM Comput. Surv.* **2025**, *57*, 1–43. [CrossRef]
9. He, P.; Zhou, Y.; Qin, X. A survey on energy-aware security mechanisms for the internet of things. *Future Internet* **2024**, *16*, 128. [CrossRef]
10. Lin, P.; Liu, L.; Li, Y. Cross-layer design approaches for wireless systems. In *Proceedings of the International Conference on Information Processing and Network Provisioning*; Springer Nature: Singapore, 2024; pp. 15–28.

https://doi.org/10.3390/app16062736

applied sciences

MDPI

Article

Performance Testing of the Triple Modular Redundancy Mitigation Circuit Test Environment Implementation in Field Programmable Gate Array Structures

Marcin Kubica [1,2] **and Robert Czerwinski** [1,2,*]

[1] Department of Digital Systems, Silesian University of Technology, ul. Akademicka 2A, 44-100 Gliwice, Poland; mkubica@polsl.pl
[2] KP Labs, Bojkowska 37J, 44-100 Gliwice, Poland
* Correspondence: rczerwinski@polsl.pl; Tel.: +48-32-237-17-20

Abstract: The logic structures implemented in Field Programmable Gate Arrays (FPGAs) are often critical and their correct operation is vital. FPGA devices are often used in areas where there is increased ionising radiation (space, medical diagnostics, aviation or nuclear power). There is therefore a need for mechanisms to correct radiation-induced errors. A common approach is the redundant implementation of particularly critical parts of the logic structure. By triplicating selected fragments, it is possible not only to detect potential errors but also to correct them. Such an approach is called triple modular redundancy (TMR), and its essence lies in the use of specialised voting circuits called voters, which allow the erroneous results of individual subcircuits to be eliminated by voting. The triplicate circuit under consideration, together with the voter, constitutes the mitigation structure. It becomes necessary to develop a test environment to assess the correct operation of these circuits. Also key is the efficiency of the implementation of these structures, which can be related to the occupation of logical resources or the power consumption of a given implementation. This paper demonstrates the essence of implementing a test environment to test the correctness of the mitigation of logic structures using TMR voters. An error injector mechanism using the Pseudo-Random Bit Sequence (PRBS) register is proposed, which introduces an element of randomness into the testing process. The aim of this research is to determine the implementation efficiency of the proposed test environment. In the experimental part, the implementation costs of the proposed solution were examined. The results indicate that between 66 and 109 LUT blocks were required to implement the error injector, corresponding to a relatively small increase in dynamic power consumption: by 22% for combinational circuits and by 37% for sequential circuits.

Keywords: TMR; voter; mitigation; technology mapping

1. Introduction

Designing complex digital systems implemented in FPGA (Field Programmable Gate Array) devices is a challenging task. In most cases, there are a number of constraints to consider. As a rule, these constraints may relate to power consumption [1–5], the availability of logic resources [6–8] or speed of operation [9]. In many cases, it is also necessary to consider in the design process the specific characteristics of the environment in which the device will operate. It is often the case that an FPGA device is exposed to ionising radiation, which can lead to a number of errors in the operation of the implemented functionality. Application areas where increased levels of radiation can be expected include aerospace, medical diagnostics, nuclear power plants and most importantly, space applications.

FPGA devices are often used in space missions [10,11]. A deeper analysis of this environment therefore becomes necessary. As shown in [12], three main sources of radiation for space missions within the solar system can be distinguished, and these are galactic cosmic rays, solar radiation and radiation belts. Galactic cosmic rays are high-energy protons from interstellar space that reach the solar system. Solar radiation is a stream of plasma emitted in all directions by the sun. This emission can be quite violent during Coronal Mass Ejections (CMEs). The last source of radiation is radiation belts. These are areas of increased radiation resulting from accumulations of energetic particles in the magnetic field of planets.

From a technological point of view, an FPGA device is a semiconductor device. Radiation effects impact semiconductors in the following ways: Single-Event Effects (SEEs) and Dose effects. Dose effects correspond to a permanent change in selected parameters due to prolonged exposure to radiation. SEEs are associated with phenomena resulting from the impact of a single particle on a logic structure. Such an event is random and instantaneous. It can cause a change in the value of individual bits. The work [13] divides SEEs into Soft Error (no physical damage) and Hard Error (physical damage) phenomena.

Soft Errors are upsets to the device operation. The most important types of Soft Errors are single-event transients (SETs), single-event upsets (SEUs) and single-event function interrupts (SEFIs). A SET event corresponds to the generation of additional pulses in combinational logic that can be propagated throughout the logic structure. SEU-type events correspond to a change in the state of a memory element due to the impact of a high-energy particle. SEFIs, on the other hand, correspond to a change in the normal functioning of the device (a change in the circuit functionality).

Also in the case of Hard Errors, several types of events can be distinguished. These can be distinguished as a single-event latch-up (SEL), which is a circuit latch-up induced by radiation; single-event burnout (SEB), which is short-circuiting caused when a high-energy ion impacts a transistor source; and single-event gate rupture (SEGR), which involves physical damage to the gate oxide insulation in a silicon structure.

The main contribution of this paper is a novel test circuit for mitigation circuits using TMR (triple modular redundancy) voters, based on the PRBS (Pseudo-Random Bit Sequence) register. The solution proposed in this paper will allow for more efficient testing of the mitigation capability of TMR circuits with a slight increase in the number of logic resources and power consumption required. This is of particular importance in space applications where such limitations are particularly relevant. Section 2 discusses the mitigation methods used in FPGA devices. Particular attention is paid here to triple redundancy. The design of different voter models is also discussed. Section 3 presents the concepts of a test environment for mitigation circuits using the PRBS. The focus is on the efficiency problem of implementing these circuits in FPGA devices. Section 4 addresses the practical implementation problems of the test environment in projects. Section 5 presents the experimental results obtained. This paper is concluded with a summary.

2. Theoretical Background

There are many mitigation methods to reduce the impact of radiation on the performance of a digital device [11,12,14]. Of course, technological methods, such as the appropriate doping of silicon, can be discussed to improve the mitigation properties [15]. Naturally, it is also crucial to ensure the adequate shielding of digital devices. Unfortunately, in many cases, these methods are insufficient and SEEs can still occur. In this situation, it is crucial that the digital system is properly designed to resist these phenomena.

In many space missions, key digital-system elements are implemented in FPGA devices (telemetry systems, onboard computers and AI systems) [16–20]. This raises the question of mitigation methods targeting FPGA devices. An extremely important component of FPGA devices is the configuration memory. This is most often SRAM (Static Random-Access Memory), which stores information on how to configure and interconnect the available resources of the FPGA device in the logical structure. As a result of SEUs, the values of selected configuration bits in the configuration memory can be swapped, which will affect the resulting logical structure. This problem is illustrated in Figure 1.

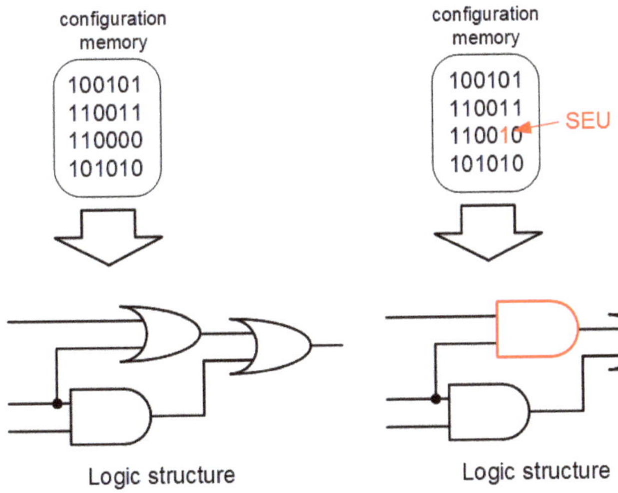

Figure 1. Impact of SEUs on configuration memory.

The primary mitigation method in this case is scrubbing, which involves 'refreshing' configuration memory from an external source. Scrubbing techniques are the subject of many research papers [21–24].

Radiation can also affect the logical structure itself. In this case, there are also mitigation techniques. The primary technique is the use of systems using Error Checking and Correction (ECC) [25]. Correction coding most commonly uses the Hamming code [26] or the Reed–Solomon code [27].

An extremely important method of mitigation is redundancy. The use of redundancy in mitigation processes involves replicating selected functional blocks or circuits several times in order to perform exactly the same task. In extreme cases, where the space mission is specifically exposed to significant radiation, entire units are duplicated. If the duplicated modules, at the same time, function in exactly the same way (the state of their outputs is the same), this means that there have been no SEE-induced errors in the operation of the modules. If, however, the signals on their outputs are different, this means that a fault must have occurred in one of the duplicated modules. Naturally, duplicating parts of a circuit, modules or entire devices several times is expensive. This raises the question of how many times a circuit fragment should be duplicated to ensure effective mitigation. It turns out that replicating the circuit twice only allows statements to be made that an SEE phenomenon has occurred but without the possibility of error correction. For this reason, triple redundancy (TMR, triple modular redundancy) is commonly used. In this approach, three identical and independent modules perform the same functionality. If one of them malfunctions due to an SEE, by comparing the state of the outputs of all three modules, the expected (correct) state of the module's outputs can be unambiguously determined by a voting process. Of course, a single fault is assumed. Thus, in order to realise TMR, it is necessary to have a voter comparing the outputs of the individual modules and realising the voting. The essence of TMR is illustrated in Figure 2.

TMR is one of the basic mitigation techniques. It is the subject of many scientific papers [28–32]. It should be noted that one of the main drawbacks of this approach is the significant growth of the logical structure obtained. The use of TMR significantly increases the number of logical resources used. There are methods to reduce them [33,34]. Naturally, it is also extremely important to adopt a strategy for using TMR in a project [35].

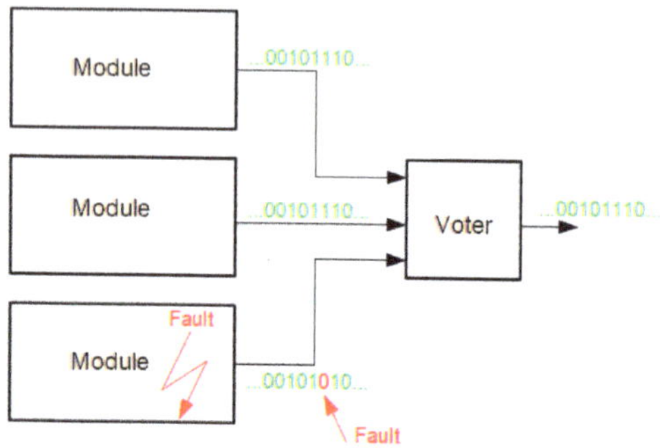

Figure 2. The idea of TMR operation.

As already mentioned, a key element of TMR is the voters. Voters in the voting process select the majority answer from triplicated modules. Most often, these are fairly simple combinatorial arrangements. There are a number of voter designs. These are summarised in the work [36]. Some of the more important constructions include the classical voter [37], the Kshirsagar voter [38], the Ban and Naviner voter [39], the Balasubramanian voter [40] or the Mux-based voter [36]. The structures of the individual voters are shown in Figure 3.

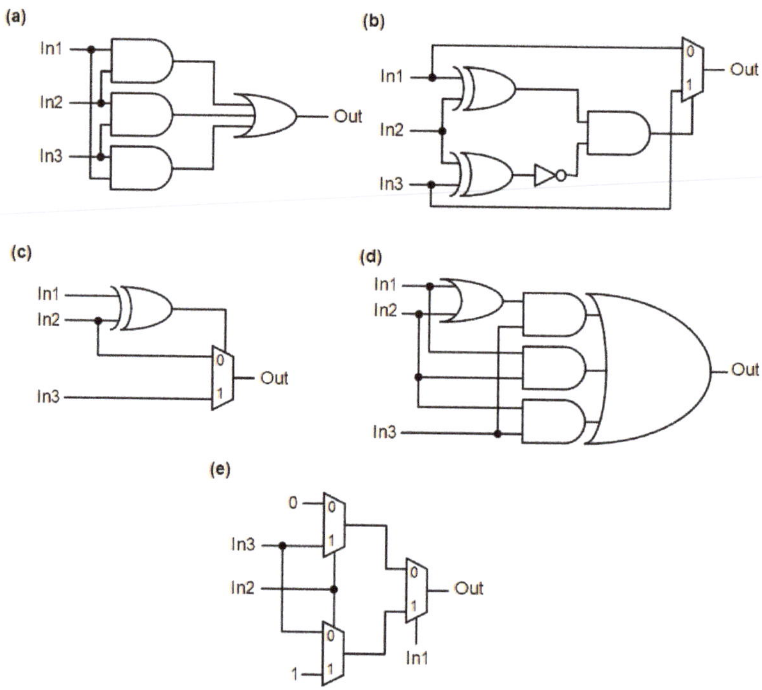

Figure 3. Examples of voter constructions: classical voter (**a**), Kshirsagar voter (**b**), Ban and Naviner voter (**c**), Balasubramanian voter (**d**) or Mux-based voter (**e**).

The classic voter is a design based on an AND–OR structure. This type of solution fit well into older PLD (Programmable Logic Device) circuit architectures such as CPLDs (Complex Programmable Logic Devices), where the core of the circuits were PAL (Programmable Array Logic) cells [41,42]. Of course, there is nothing to prevent these voters from also being used in FPGAs. In the case of the Kshirsagar voter or Naviner voter, the designs are based on XOR gates, leading to more reliable fault tolerance. A certain modification of the classical voter is the Balasubramanian voter, where the AND–OR structure is implemented in the form of a logic cell. It is also possible to implement the voter using only multiplexers (the Mux-based voter).

The work [36] is limited to a power and area analysis of transistor structures corresponding to individual voter designs. In the case of FPGA devices, voters are implemented either as IP (Intellectual Property) cores or in the form of HDL (Hardware Description Language) descriptions. Of course, the HDL description itself can take different forms: an array description, a structural description or a description in the form of equations. Often, FPGA device chip manufacturers provide their voter solutions [43,44]. Independent companies offering synthesis tools also support high-reliability designs [45]. In many cases, the inputs as well as the outputs from the voter are complex interfaces, e.g., AXIS (Advanced eXtensible Interface; Stream protocol) [43]. Taking all this into account, it is crucial to efficiently map the voter along with redundant modules (mitigation circuits) into LUT (Look-up Table) blocks, which form the basis of the FPGA chip architecture. LUT blocks are simple memories in which logic functions with a limited number of inputs are implemented. Of course, at the appropriate stages of logic synthesis, complex designs are split (function decomposition) and mapped into these resources [8].

Let us therefore consider the concepts of a test environment implemented in a real FPGA chip to test the correctness of error correction by TMR mitigation circuits.

3. Test Environment for TMR Mitigation Structures

Assessing the effectiveness of the implementation of mitigation mechanisms using TMR voters is a difficult task. It is possible to imagine a whole range of factors on which effectiveness should depend, such as the occupation of logical resources necessary for their implementation and power consumption.

From a logic-resource-occupation point of view, more efficient solutions are those that use less logic resources (a smaller silicon area). In the classical approach, the aim is to minimise transistors or gates. In the case of FPGAs, the problem is more complicated because the implemented logic functions are mapped in LUT blocks. These blocks implement simple logic functions with a small number of variables (e.g., 6). Logic functions in a larger number of variables have to be decomposed and then mapped into several suitably interconnected logic blocks [8]. Obviously, looking at the TMR voter, it is apparent that these structures are simple enough that, in theory, a single LUT block should be sufficient to implement them. The resource utilisation of the redundant modules attached to the voter inputs remains an open question. It turns out that synthesis tools can in some cases produce results far from optimal, which can result in a significant growth of the logic structure. In addition, it should be noted that TMR voter inputs are not necessarily single-bit. Each input can be an n-bit bus, making the voter itself much more complex. It is also possible to imagine much more complex voter designs, e.g., using a golden model (a priority model) or designs in which individual inputs are assigned appropriate weights. Theoretically, a voter can have more voting inputs (of course, this is no longer TMR), and the process of selecting the correct data is then more complex, involving a significantly higher number of necessary logic resources. From the point of view of FPGAs, it is also important how the voter and the circuits attached to its inputs are described in the HDL language. It turns out that a combinational circuit can be described in many ways (by arrays, equations and structural descriptions), which often leads to solutions using a different number of logic resources. Taking all this into account, evaluating the effectiveness of mitigation structures in terms of the use of logical resources is an extremely important issue.

Of considerable importance from the point of view of mitigation structures using TMR is their power consumption. The power consumed by a digital circuit is the sum of static and dynamic power. Static power depends on the technology in which the circuit is made. Mitigation circuits are not separate ICs, so a comparison in terms of static power makes no sense. The situation is different for dynamic power, which depends on the switching frequency of the digital circuit. The dynamic power P_{dyn} of an n-vertex logic network can be expressed by (1):

$$P_{dyn} = \frac{1}{2} V_{dd}^2 f \sum_{i=1}^{n} C_i SW_i \quad (1)$$

where V_{dd} is the supply voltage of the digital circuit and f is the frequency of the clock signal. Additionally, this power depends on the product of the connection capacitance between the nodes of the logic network C_i and the switching activity SW_i. In the classical case, the vertices of the logic network are the individual gates, while in the case of FPGAs, they are the LUT blocks. The key parameter from the perspective of power reduction is the switching activity (SW). The switching activity SW_i is related to the probability of 'switching' the considered ith node to the opposite state, i.e., the transition from 0 to 1 or the transition from 1 to 0. The switching activity can be expressed by (2):

$$SW_i = 2P(x)(1 - P(x)) \quad (2)$$

where $P(x)$ is the probability of the variable x taking the value one. In the case of mapping in logic gates, knowing the probability at the inputs $P(x)$, one can determine the probability of the value one at their output $P(y)$; for example, NOT: $P(y) = 1 - P(x)$, two-input AND: $P(y) = P(a)P(b)$, two-input OR: $P(y) = 1 - (1 - P(a))(1 - P(b))$. Of course, such an analysis can be applied to more complex gate structures such as TMR voters. This means that for different voter designs, different SW values can be obtained depending on the logic structure, and similarly for the circuits connected to the voter inputs. This means that the dynamic power consumed for equivalent mitigation structures may differ. A circuit will be more efficient if it has a lower switching activity. It is naturally open to determine the value of $P(x)$ for the individual inputs of the implemented circuits. As a rule, for the analysis, it is assumed that the probability of 0 appearing is the same as the probability of 1 appearing at the input $P(1) = P(0) = P(x) = 0.5$. In the case of mapping the logic network in LUT blocks, such an analysis in terms of the SW would be very difficult to carry out. As a rule, FPGA manufacturers provide suitable simulators to estimate dynamic power. There are also academic tools to determine the power of ABC [46] or PowerdekBDD [2,3]. In such an analysis, care should be taken to ensure that the probabilities of 0 and 1 are the same for the inputs to a given mitigation structure. In this situation, a good solution may be to attach a clock signal of a certain frequency to the individual inputs, as shown in Figure 4.

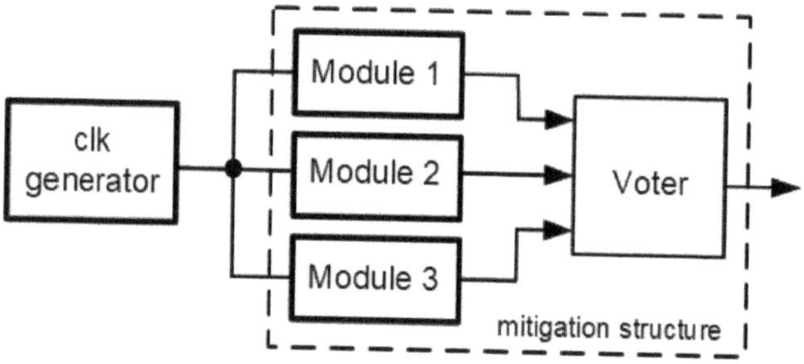

Figure 4. Connecting input signals to the voter to determine dynamic power.

Extremely important from the perspective of studying mitigation circuits using TMR is to assess their error-correction capability. Naturally, under simulation conditions, a TMR voter will perform as expected. This may be slightly different in a real hardware implementation, where the performance of the voter may depend on the dynamic properties of the implemented circuits. In the case of FPGAs, this verification will involve implementing the mitigation circuit under a test in a hardware-test environment implemented in an FPGA device.

It is often the case that synthesis tools, in the process of optimising a circuit in terms of the number of blocks, realise the sharing of logic resources between selected logic functions. The common parts (the subfunction) of several selected functions are only realised once in a single shared subcircuit. Then, the result of this subfunction is delivered to the selected functions. From the point of view of reducing the number of logic blocks and power, this is an advantageous phenomenon (a given section of the circuit can be realised only once, rather than several times for the selected functions separately). Unfortunately, from the point of view of TMR mitigation, it is a very unfavourable phenomenon. The individual circuits attached to the voter should not have parts in common. Let us imagine a situation in which individual modules A, B and C have a part of the circuit in common, implementing a specific subfunction. If an error occurs in this part of the circuit, the error will be propagated through all three modules in exactly the same way. This means that the voter will not detect any differences in its inputs and will not correct the error. Such a case is shown in Figure 5. Thus, it can be seen that optimising the implementation in terms of the number of resources can, in some cases, lead to a degradation of the mitigation properties of the circuit.

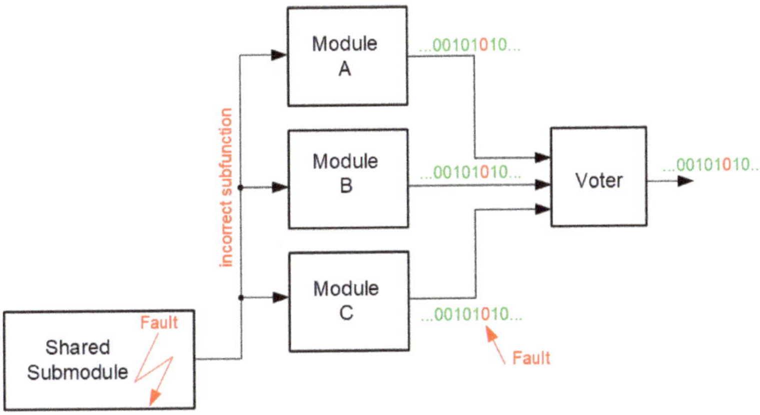

Figure 5. Impact of resource sharing on the mitigation properties of TMR.

A key component of the hardware-test environment is the error injector. Under normal operating conditions, the same signal is present on all inputs of the voter. In order to test the voter's ability to correct an error, it is necessary to replace one of the input signals with an erroneous one (an error injection into the voter). In the general case, the error injector consists of two blocks: an error-sequence generator and an error selector, as shown in Figure 6.

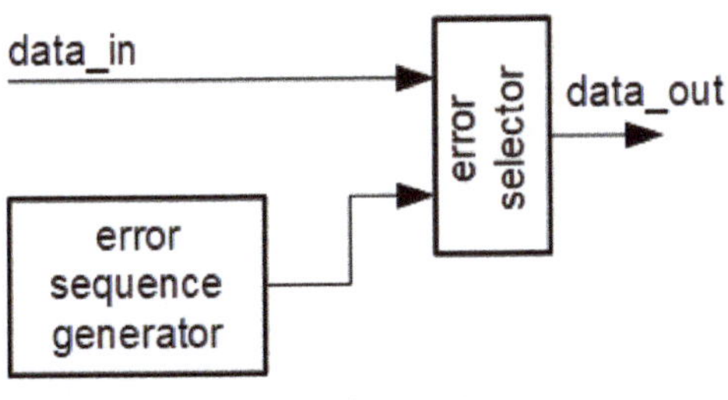

Figure 6. Block diagram of the error injector.

In the simplest case, the selector can be implemented based on OR, AND or XOR gates. In the case of the OR function, the values for which the injector has generated a high state are blocked in the high state; in the case of the AND function, those for which the injector has generated a low state will be blocked in the low state. In the case of an XOR function, those values for which the injector has generated a high state are negated.

In the case of the error-sequence generator, two concepts can be distinguished: a concept in which the error is triggered at fixed cyclic and specified intervals, and a concept in which the error is triggered at random. The concept with randomness seems to better reflect SEU phenomena, which is why the authors focus on it later in this article.

There are various forms and possibilities for building such an error-sequence generator. One solution may be to use a module that generates a Pseudo-Random Bit Sequence (PRBS). To generate the PRBS, a shift register with feedback implemented by an XOR-type logic gate is usually used. Each shift register is associated with some polynomial over a finite body. The maximum length is for shifting registers associated with primitive (non-decomposable) polynomials over the body. Such registers include the polynomial $X^{15} + X^{14} + 1$, which is associated with the sequence denoted PRBS15. It uses a 15-bit ring register and involves $2^{15} - 1$ combinations (32,767 combinations). Since the polynomial is prime, the number of states includes all but zero. The micro-architecture of the error injector using the XOR function and the PRBS15 module is shown in Figure 7. When PRBS[15] returns a high state, the data bits are negated and thus an error is injected into the data stream.

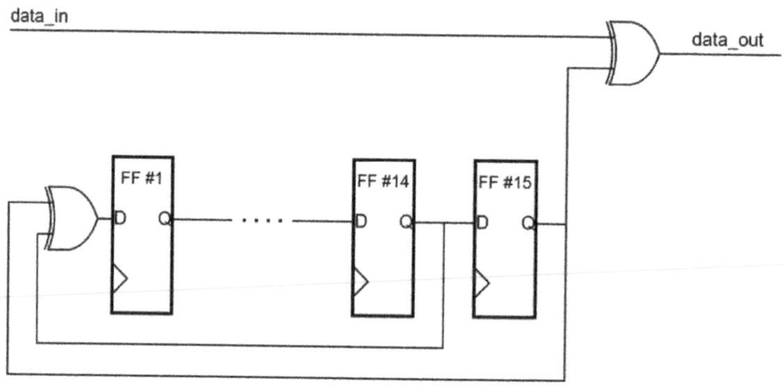

Figure 7. Micro-architecture of a fault injector module using PRBS for a single channel.

An injection circuit built in this way provides a very high error rate because the distribution of zeros and ones is practically comparable in the output stream of the PRBS block (all possible states from the 15-bit space without the 0..00 state).

It is very common that a single voter input (the input channel) corresponds to an n-bit vector (bus) rather than a single bit. In this situation, the error injector should provide randomness when injecting an error with respect to both the channel and the bus bit. This type of operation is provided by the circuit shown in Figure 8. An input demultiplexer redirects a single PRBS15 stream to one of the channels, while a second layer of demultiplexers ensures that this stream is redirected to a specific bit on the k-bit bus. XOR gates ensure that the specified bit is negated, thus infecting the channel at that point in time. Such an architecture ensures that an error is injected into a randomly selected bit of a randomly selected channel. In this case, only one PRBS15 module is implemented, from whose output the stream for error injection is taken. Naturally, the demultiplexers are also controlled from individual registers (PRBS[1]-PRBS[15]). The error injector presented in Figure 8 ensures that a single error is injected into a randomly selected bit of a randomly selected channel.

The error injector is a key component of the hardware-test environment and can be used in the process of testing the correctness of the mitigation of a design using TMR, implemented in FPGAs. This concept is discussed in Section 4.

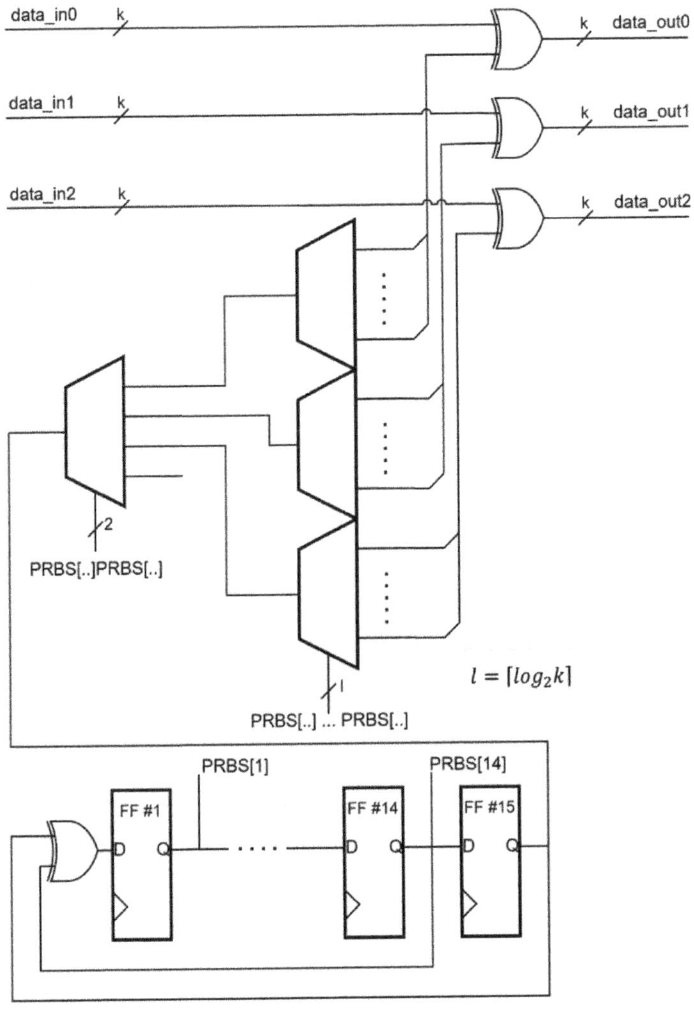

Figure 8. Micro-architecture of the error injector module for buses.

4. The Essence of Using a Hardware-Test Environment Based on an Error Injector to Test the Correctness of Design Mitigation

From a mitigation point of view, it is crucial to identify the circuit locations where TMR voters should be placed. It is extremely important to secure the memory elements appropriately. In the most elementary case, the individual registers can be triplicated as in Figure 9a. However, it must be remembered that the voter is then built into each set of registers. Although this kind of protection seems best, the disadvantage is the overhead resulting from the use of multiple voters. Therefore, in practical applications, triple modular redundancy is considered for the entire module performing a specific function, as shown in Figure 9b. This approach leads to a significant reduction in the number of voters required.

However, the question remains open as to how to test such a circuit, or more precisely, where to inject the errors. Well, attaching an error injector to the output of a module performing a specific function will have a different purpose than attaching an error injector to the input of such a circuit. In the former, it will be possible to analyse SEU-type error corrections, and in the latter also SEFI-type errors. This is because a change in the input state in the module can lead to a malfunction of this circuit (for example, the sequential automaton will go to the wrong state). At the same time, the individual modules of a given block subject to TMR may have different numbers of input and output ports. The error injector circuit will then be attached to each input and output, as shown in Figure 10.

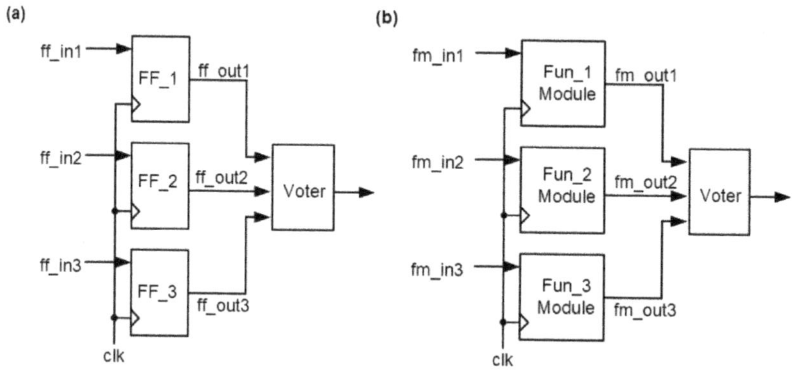

Figure 9. Triple modular redundancy system: applied to registers (**a**) and applied to modules performing a specific function (**b**).

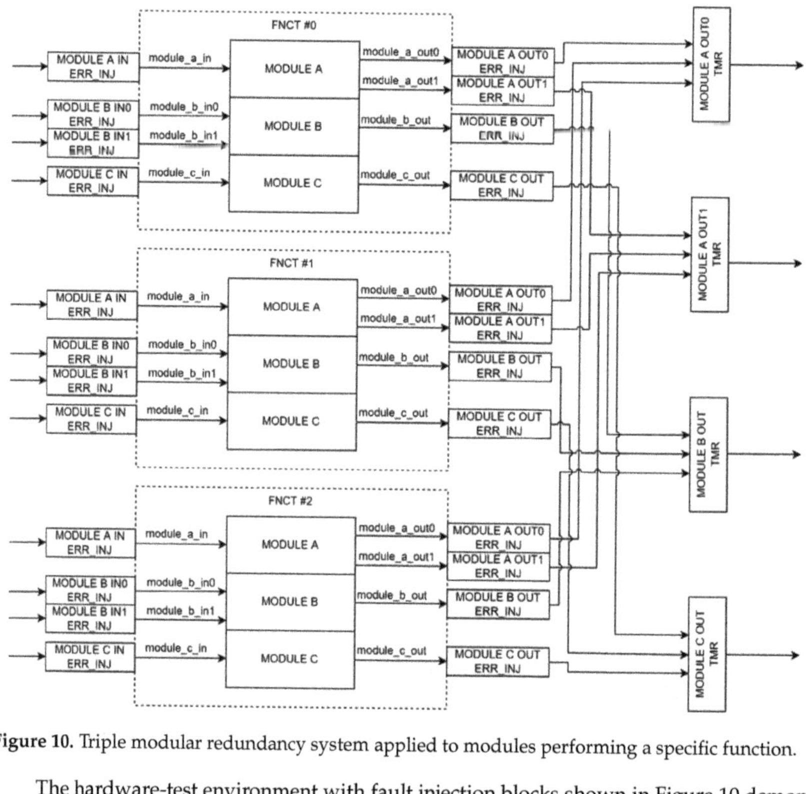

Figure 10. Triple modular redundancy system applied to modules performing a specific function.

The hardware-test environment with fault injection blocks shown in Figure 10 demonstrates the need for a flexible approach to testing. The FNCT block contains three modules (MODULE A, B and C). Each has a slightly different configuration of input and output ports: MODULE A has one input and two output ports, MODULE B has two input and one output and MODULE C has one input and one output. In the general case, the ports are multibit and the use of an error injector as in Figure 8 is appropriate here, with the injector module shown here broken down into three FNCT blocks. For example, MODULE A IN ERR_INJ at the input of MODULE A in FNCT block #0, FNCT #1 and FNCT #2 are one and the same injector enabling the generation of errors at the inputs of the individual modules. Of course, testing the correctness of the mitigation in the TMR circuit shown in Figure 10 only makes sense for injecting errors into one channel, i.e., into one of the three inputs. Secondly, as errors are injected at the input of a given module, errors are not injected at their output, in line with the very idea of TMR, which says that two misrepresentations are not corrected. In contrast, the testing of MODULE A, MODULE B and MODULE C can be carried out in parallel if there is no data flow between these modules, i.e., they perform functions independent of each other.

The error injector proposed by the authors was used in a mitigation study of the Quasar project carried out by KP Labs for the ESA (European Space Agency) [47]. This shows that the proposed solutions are scalable. This project uses an AMD Kintex UltraSacle+ FPGA device (XCKU035-2SFVA784I). The use of a device with such significant resources is necessary due to the need to implement a complex design (a radio channel for telemetry modules, telecommand, encryption, etc.). In general, in space missions, the implemented designs are most often so large that it is necessary to use FPGA devices with significant logical resources. Naturally, a TMR-based mitigation process is therefore often used for large-scale projects. The experimental section presents the results of mitigation in this project.

5. Experimental Results

A key element in assessing the effectiveness of a test-environment implementation is to evaluate that implementation in terms of the occupation of logic resources and the dynamic power consumption of the corresponding logic structures. The method of determining both the number of logic resources required and the dynamic power consumption boils down to synthesising appropriately described circuits in HDL languages (Verilog HDL) in selected synthesis tools. In this paper, both commercial tools (Vivado from AMD) and the academic ABC [46] were used for synthesis.

In order to carry out the experiments, it is necessary to identify the circuits that will be mitigated. A popular set of benchmarks [48] was chosen, which contains both combinational and sequential circuits. The individual benchmarks contain a description of the function in Verilog, which was subjected to an initial minimisation targeting multioutput function.

Before proceeding to the actual experiments, it is extremely important to determine the occupancy of the logical resources and to determine the dynamic power of a single voter. Various voter designs were considered (described in Section 2). After synthesis in the Vivado tool targeting seven-series FPGAs, as expected, each voter can be realised on a single LUT block regardless of the solutions presented in Section 2. Similarly, the dynamic power in each case was 0.086 W. Taking this into account, a classical voter design was used in further experiments in the mitigation circuits (Figure 3a).

The first series of experiments was carried out in the ABC academic system. The synthesis was targeted at LUT blocks with four inputs. We decided to choose blocks with as few inputs as possible in order to highlight the differences between the different series of experiments as clearly as possible. The approaches without mitigation (Bench. column) and with mitigation (Bench.+vot. column) were compared. The results for the combinatorial systems are summarised in Table 1 and for the sequential systems in Table 2.

In both tables, the first columns describe each benchmark: the name of the benchmark (Name), the number of inputs (IN), the number of outputs (OUT) and, in the case of sequential circuits, the number of internal FSM states (ST). For each series, the number of vertices of the logic network (nd) is specified. This number directly corresponds to the number of LUT blocks with four inputs. In addition, the switching activity value (SW), which is directly related to the dynamic power, was specified. The last row is the sum of the individual values, as shown as graphs in Figure 11.

Table 1. Results of the synthesis of combinatorial circuits in the ABC system.

Name	IN	OUT	Bench.		Bench.+vot.	
			nd	SW	nd	SW
9sym	9	1	118	48.47	118	46.99
alu2	10	8	43	18.62	43	19.59
alu4	14	8	756	251.86	759	253
b12	15	9	26	12.18	26	11.65
clip	9	5	156	57.39	162	59.56
cm162a	14	5	13	6.79	13	6.57
cm163a	16	5	13	6.31	13	5.98
cm85a	11	3	14	6.85	14	6.55
con1	7	2	5	2.97	5	2.91
ex1010	10	10	748	219.01	751	227.31
f51m	8	8	55	25.38	55	24.85
rd53	5	3	21	10.81	21	10.49
rd73	7	3	67	27	76	28.72
rd84	8	4	272	93.02	268	89.72
sao2	10	4	80	29.59	82	29.35
sqrt8	8	4	26	11.24	22	10.39
t481	16	1	72	23.52	72	22.6
x2	10	7	18	7.57	18	7.65
xor5	5	1	2	1.28	2	1.2
	Sum		2505	859.86	2520	865.08

Table 2. Results of the synthesis of sequential circuits in the ABC system.

Name	IN	OUT	ST	Bench.		Bench.+vot.	
				nd	SW	nd	SW
bbtas	2	2	6	6	3.22	15	8.47
beecount	3	4	7	18	6.48	53	19.77
dk14	3	5	7	40	28.23	118	78.04
dk15	3	5	4	26	15.3	77	46.67
keyb	7	2	10	124	41.01	313	96.9
lion	2	1	4	3	1.13	10	3.79
lion9	2	1	9	5	1.77	16	6.29
mc	3	5	4	8	4.54	23	14.03
train4	2	1	11	3	1.46	8	4.41
train11	2	1	4	17	4.76	50	14.39
	Sum			250	107.90	683	292.76

Looking at the graphs in Figure 11a,b, it can be seen that the results obtained are practically the same regardless of whether triple redundancy was implemented or not. The expected result is a situation where the number of blocks and the dynamic power will be about three times higher in the approach where there is TMR (Bench.+Vot.) than for the approach without TMR (Bench.). Such a relationship can be observed for sequential systems. For the number of blocks (Figure 11c), the growth of the logic structure due to the implementation of TMR is 2.73 times. In the case of power, on the other hand, it is 2.71 times. Looking at combinational circuits, it can be seen that the expected redundancy was removed in the optimisation process during the synthesis process. In this situation, the question of methods for describing mitigating systems remains open. In the case of sequential circuits, the relationship between the number of blocks in the cases is less than three, indicating that the synthesis process was carried out in such a way that there must be resource sharing between the individual modules attached to the voter inputs. Given the nature of TMR, it is an open question whether this is a beneficial phenomenon. The *SW* relationship in Figure 11d directly reflects the relationship of the number of resources used, so it is difficult to speak of power optimisation.

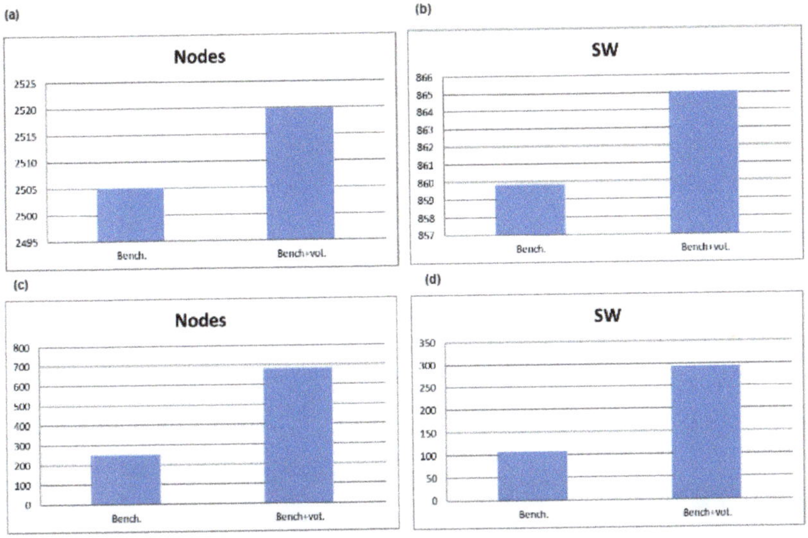

Figure 11. Summary results of the synthesis in ABC: for combinational circuits, number of logic network vertices (**a**) and *SW* value (**b**); for sequential circuits, number of logic network vertices (**c**) and *SW* value (**d**).

Having analysed the effects of the implementation of the mitigation circuits, it is possible to move on to an analysis of the implementation of the test environment, of which the error injector (EI) is a major component. A comparison was made between the benchmarks given the mitigation (Bench.+Vot.) and the benchmarks to which the test environment containing the error injector (EI) was additionally added. Due to the complex description of the EI, the synthesis for both series was realised in the Vivado system for the logic blocks contained in the seven-series FPGAs. The results obtained are shown in Table 3 for the combinational circuits and Table 4 for the sequential circuits.

In both tables, the number of LUT blocks (LUT) was determined for each series. In addition, the dynamic power (Power) value is specified. The last row is the sum of the individual values, as shown as graphs in Figure 12.

Analysing the graphs in terms of the number of blocks used, it can be seen that for the considered set of benchmarks, the implementation of a test environment containing an error injector significantly increases the number of LUT blocks used (3.6 times for combinational circuits and almost 10 times for sequential circuits). However, it should be noted here that the benchmarks considered describe very small test circuits, so the relationships described are not entirely reliable for describing the implementation efficiency. It is worth noting that between 66 and 109 LUT blocks are required to implement the error injector, so the more complex the circuit, the lower the potential cost of EI implementation.

It is very interesting to compare the dynamic power in both cases (Figure 12b,d). Despite the significant growth of the logic structure in the case with the EI, the dynamic power increases only slightly (by 22% for combinational circuits and by 37% for sequential circuits). This indicates a good implementation efficiency of the test environment, even for small circuits.

Comparing the power consumption results between Bench. and Bench.+vot., it can be seen that the results obtained are practically the same. Minor differences are due to the nature of the synthesis tool in the placement and routing stages.

Table 3. Results of the synthesis of combinatorial circuits in the Vivado system.

Name	IN	OUT	Bench.		Bench.+vot.		Bench.+vot.+El	
			LUT	POWER	LUT	POWER	LUT	POWER
9sym	9	1	6	0.441	6	0.442	73	0.851
alu2	10	8	14	2.703	14	2.702	103	3.26
alu4	14	8	286	5.978	286	5.978	373	6.493
b12	15	9	14	2.29	13	2.305	110	2.817
clip	9	5	20	2.924	27	3.083	110	3.547
cm162a	14	5	7	1.435	7	1.433	91	1.944
cm163a	16	5	7	1.351	7	1.349	93	1.85
cm85a	11	3	6	0.793	6	0.793	81	1.29
con1	7	2	2	0.799	2	0.799	74	1.236
ex1010	10	10	170	8.11	170	8.121	279	8.95
f51m	8	8	10	3.925	10	3.923	99	4.487
inc	7	9	10	2.963	10	2.963	105	3.533
rd53	5	3	2	1.491	2	1.491	77	1.946
rd73	7	3	6	1.953	6	1.953	81	2.423
rd84	8	4	11	2.11	11	2.115	94	2.578
sao2	10	4	30	1.182	34	1.251	110	1.667
sqrt8	8	4	6	1.536	6	1.535	87	2.025
t481	16	1	5	0.721	5	0.721	72	1.135
x2	10	7	8	1.671	8	1.639	94	2.146
xor5	5	1	1	0.776	1	0.776	68	1.191
	Sum		621	45.152	631	45.372	2274	55.369

Table 4. Results of the synthesis of sequential circuits in the Vivado system.

Name	IN	OUT	ST	Bench.		Bench.+vot.		Bench.+vot.+El	
				LUT	POWER	LUT	POWER	LUT	POWER
bbtas	2	2	6	3	0.473	3	0.467	74	0.878
beecount	3	4	7	7	1.074	7	1.072	88	1.546
dk14	3	5	7	7	2.885	7	2.89	91	3.383
dk15	3	5	4	4	2.475	4	2.475	88	2.985
keyb	7	2	10	48	0.774	48	0.774	121	1.207
lion	2	1	4	2	0.245	2	0.245	69	0.636
lion9	2	1	9	2	0.265	2	0.265	69	0.636
mc	3	5	4	4	2.481	4	2.481	86	2.775
train11	2	1	11	4	0.265	4	0.263	71	0.662
train4	2	1	4	2	0.183	2	0.183	68	0.567
	Sum			83	11.12	83	11.115	825	15.275

As written in the previous chapter, the proposed solutions were used in a project of considerable complexity (the Quasar project [47]). The synthesis targeting the XCKU035-2SFVA784I chip was realised in the Vivado tool (due to the support of the FPGA chip manufacturer, AMD). In this vendor's devices, LUT blocks are grouped into more advanced CLB (Configurable Logic Block) cells, which can operate in well-defined configurations. In the first instance, synthesis was carried out without any mitigation. This led to the use of 113,347 LUT blocks, representing 55.80% of all blocks (corresponding to 26,027 complex CLB blocks (85.90%)). The described TMR mitigation was then carried out in the report of the encryption modules. This led to the use of 137761 LUT blocks, representing 67.82% of the total blocks (corresponding to 30,300 complex CLB blocks (99.49%)). It should be noted here that the system had to perform resynthesis several times for the synthesis to be successful. The bitstream was then generated and the FPGA device was programmed and tested using prototype DPU. This shows that the solutions proposed in this paper can be applied to practical applications of considerable complexity, which is crucial when designing devices aimed at space missions.

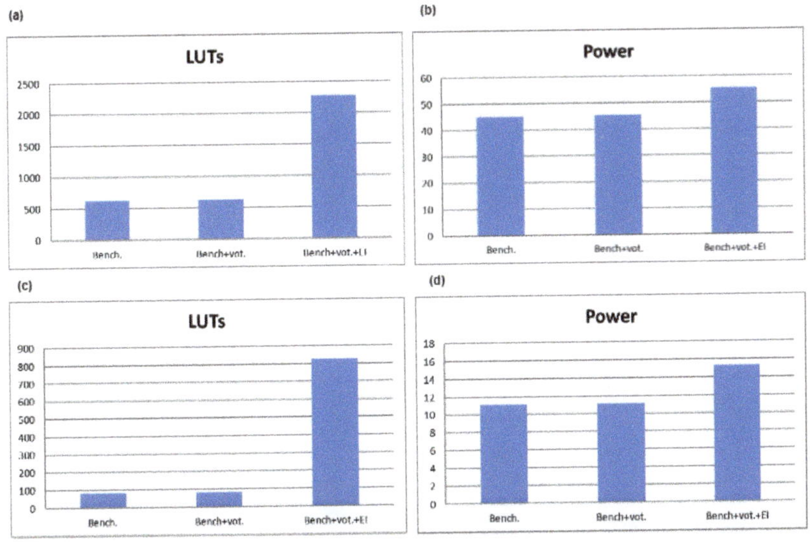

Figure 12. Summary results of synthesis in Vivado: for combinational circuits, number of LUT blocks (**a**) and dynamic power value (**b**); for sequential circuits, number of LUT blocks (**c**) and dynamic power value (**d**).

6. Conclusions

The aim of this paper was to demonstrate the efficiency of the implementation (measured by the number of logic resources used and dynamic power consumption) of the TMR mitigation circuit test environment. A novel element was the introduction of an 'element of randomness' into this environment through the use of the PRBS register in the error injectors. The testing performed revealed a number of observations.

The first observation is the issue of the synthesis of mitigation circuits. It is clear that the synthesis algorithms are focused on circuit optimisation, which, in extreme cases, can limit the robustness of the circuit to radiation errors (e.g., sharing logic resources). The second observation concerns the number of resources used by the error injector. It can be seen that in this case, it is inefficient to apply mitigation to small circuits. The last observation concerns dynamic power and shows that the implementation of the test environment does not significantly affect its consumption. All these observations lead to the conclusion that it is worthwhile to implement this environment provided that we have sufficient logic resources in the FPGA.

The efficient synthesis of mitigation circuits has proven to be of great importance. It is becoming necessary to develop algorithms that, on the one hand, provide suitably efficient logic structures and, on the other hand, do not degrade the mitigation properties of circuits. The authors plan to address the problem of mitigation-oriented synthesis in the future.

Author Contributions: Conceptualisation, M.K. and R.C.; methodology, M.K. and R.C.; software, M.K.; formal analysis, M.K. and R.C.; investigation, M.K. and R.C.; resources, M.K. and R.C.; data curation, M.K.; writing—original draft preparation, M.K. and R.C.; writing—review and editing, M.K. and R.C.; visualisation, M.K. and R.C.; supervision, M.K.; funding acquisition, M.K. and R.C. All authors have read and agreed to the published version of the manuscript.

Funding: This research was partially supported by European Space Agency (ESA Contract No. 4000132609/20/NL/FE), and by the Polish Ministry of Science and Higher Education funding for statutory activities.

Institutional Review Board Statement: Not applicable.

Informed Consent Statement: Not applicable.

Data Availability Statement: The original contributions presented in the study are included in the article, further inquiries can be directed to the corresponding author.

Acknowledgments: Thank you for the invitation from Academic editor.

Conflicts of Interest: Authors Marcin Kubica and Robert Czerwinski were employed by the company KP Labs. The remaining authors declare that the research was conducted in the absence of any commercial or financial relationships that could be construed as a potential conflict of interest.

Abbreviations

The following abbreviations are used in this manuscript:

AXI	Advanced eXtensible Interface
AXIS	Advanced eXtensible Interface; Stream protocol
CME	Coronal Mass Ejection
CPLD	Complex Programmable Logic Device
CLB	Configurable Logic Block
ECC	Error Checking and Correction
ESA	European Space Agency
FPGA	Field Programmable Gate Arrays
HDL	Hardware Description Language
LUT	Look-up Table
PAL	Programmable Array Block
PRBS	Pseudo-Random Bit Sequence
SEB	Single-event burnout
SEE	Single-Event Effect
SEFI	Single-event function interrupts
SEGR	Single-event gate rupture
SEL	Single-event latch-up
SET	Single-event transient
SEU	Single-event upset
SRAM	Static Random-Access Memory
TMR	Triple modular redundancy

References

1. Kubica, M.; Opara, A.; Kania, D. Logic Synthesis Strategy Oriented to Low Power Optimization. *Appl. Sci.* **2021**, *11*, *8797*, 1–15. [CrossRef]
2. Opara, A.; Kubica, M.; Kania, D. Decomposition Approaches for Power Reduction. *IEEE Access* **2023**, *11*, 29417–29429. [CrossRef]
3. Opara, A.; Kubica, M. Technology mapping of multi–output functions leading to the reduction of dynamic power consumption in FPGAs. *Int. J. Appl. Math. Comput. Sci.* **2023**, *33*, 267–284. [CrossRef]
4. Chattopadhyay, S.; Yadav, P.; Singh, R. Multiplexer Targeted Finite State Machine Encoding for Area and Power Minimization. In Proceedings of the IEEE INDICON, India Annual Conference, Kharagpur, India, 20–22 December 2004.
5. Kajstura, K.; Kania, D. Binary Tree-based Low Power State Assignment Algorithm. In Proceedings of the 12-th International Conference of Computational Methods in Science and Engineering, ICCMSE 2016, Athens, Grece, 17–20 March 2016.
6. Barkalov, A.; Titarenko, L.; Chmielewski, S. Improving characteristics of LUT-based Moore FSMs. *IEEE Access* **2020**, *8*, 155306–155318. [CrossRef]
7. Barkalov, A.; Titarenko, L.; Mielcarek, K. Improving characteristic of LUT-based Mealy FSMs. *Int. J. Appl. Math. Comput. Sci.* **2020**, *30*, 745–759. [CrossRef]
8. Kubica, M.; Opara, A.; Kania, D. *Technology Mapping for LUT-Based FPGA*; Springer: Berlin/Heidelberg, Germany, 2021.
9. Cheng, L.; Chen, D.; Wong, M.D.F. DDBDD: Delay-Driven BDD Synthesis for FPGAs. In Proceedings of the 44th ACM/IEEE Design Automation Conference, Athens, Grece, 4–8 June 2007; pp. 910–915.
10. Berg, M. *Field Programmable Gate Array (FPGA) Single Event Effect (SEE) Radiation Testing*; Technical Report; MEI Technologies in Support of NASA/Goddard Space Flight Center; NASA: Washington, DC, USA, 2012.

11. Hall, F. Fault Tolerant Design Implementation on Radiation Hardened by Design SRAM-Based FPGAs. Master's Thesis, Massachusetts Institute of Technology, Cambridge, MA, USA, 2013. Available online: https://dspace.mit.edu/handle/1721.1/82490 (accessed on 18 September 2024).
12. Baumann, R.; Kruckmeyer, K. *Radiation Handbook for Electronics*; Texas Instruments: Dallas, TX, USA, 2020.
13. White, D. *Considerations Surrounding Single Event Effects in FPGAs, ASICs, and Processors*, v1.0.1 ed.; Xilinx Inc.: San Jose, CA, USA, 2012.
14. Adell, P.; Allen, G. *Assessing and Mitigating Radiation Effects in Xilinx FPGAs*; Technical Report; Jet Propulsion Laboratory 08-92/08; Jet Propulsion Laboratory: La Cañada Flintridge, CA, USA, 2008.
15. Actel. *Radiation-Tolerant ProASIC3 FPGAs Radiation Effects*; Actel: Aliso Viejo, CA, USA, 2010.
16. Benelli, G.; Giuffrida, G.; Ciardi, R.; Davalle, D.; Todaro, G.; Fanucci, L. GPU@SAT, the AI enabling ecosystem for on-board satellite applications. In Proceedings of the 2023 European Data Handling & Data Processing Conference (EDHPC), Juan Les Pins, France, 2–6 October 2023; pp. 1–4. [CrossRef]
17. Coca, M.; Datcu, M. FPGA Accelerator for Meta-Recognition Anomaly Detection: Case of Burned Area Detection. *IEEE J. Sel. Top. Appl. Earth Obs. Remote. Sens.* **2023**, *16*, 5247–5259. [CrossRef]
18. Shendy, R.; Nalepa, J. Few-shot satellite image classification for bringing deep learning on board OPS-SAT. *Expert Syst. Appl.* **2024**, *251*, 123984. [CrossRef]
19. Miroszewski, A.; Mielczarek, J.; Czelusta, G.; Szczepanek, F.; Grabowski, B.; Le Saux, B.; Nalepa, J. Detecting Clouds in Multispectral Satellite Images Using Quantum-Kernel Support Vector Machines. *IEEE J. Sel. Top. Appl. Earth Obs. Remote. Sens.* **2023**, *16*, 7601–7613. [CrossRef]
20. Wijata, A.M.; Foulon, M.F.; Bobichon, Y.; Vitulli, R.; Celesti, M.; Camarero, R.; Di Cosimo, G.; Gascon, F.; Longépé, N.; Nieke, J.; et al. Taking Artificial Intelligence Into Space Through Objective Selection of Hyperspectral Earth Observation Applications: To bring the "brain" close to the "eyes" of satellite missions. *IEEE Geosci. Remote. Sens. Mag.* **2023**, *11*, 10–39. [CrossRef]
21. Zheng, S.; You, H.; He, G.; Wang, Q.; Si, T.; Jiang, J.; Jin, J.; Jing, N. A Rapid Scrubbing Technique for SEU Mitigation on SRAM-Based FPGAs. In Proceedings of the IEEE International Symposium on Circuits and Systems (ISCAS), Sapporo, Japan, 26–29 May 2019; pp. 1–5. [CrossRef]
22. Kumar, M.; Digdarsini, D.; Misra, N.; Ram, T.V.S. SEU mitigation of Rad-Tolerant Xilinx FPGA using external scrubbing for geostationary mission. In Proceedings of the 4th International Conference on Signal Processing and Integrated Networks (SPIN), Noida, India, 2–3 February 2017; pp. 414–418. [CrossRef]
23. Ruano, Ó.; García-Herrero, F.; Aranda, L.; Sánchez-Macián, A.; Rodriguez, L.; Maestro, J. Fault Injection Emulation for Systems in FPGAs: Tools, Techniques and Methodology, a Tutorial. *Sensors* **2021**, *21*, 1392. [CrossRef] [PubMed]
24. He, W.; Wang, Y.; Xing, K.; Chen, L. SEU readback interval strategy of SRAM-based FPGA for space application. In Proceedings of the IEEE International Conference on Computer Science and Automation Engineering, Shanghai, China, 10–12 June 2011; pp. 238–241. [CrossRef]
25. Alacchi, A.; Giacomin, E.; Temple, S.; Gauchi, R.; Wirthlin, M.; Gaillardon, P. Low Latency SEU Detection in FPGA CRAM With In-Memory ECC Checking. *IEEE Trans. Circuits Syst. I Regul. Pap.* **2023**, *70*, 2028–2036. [CrossRef]
26. Hamming, R.W. Error detecting and error correcting codes. *Bell Syst. Tech. J.* **1950**, *29*, 147–160. [CrossRef]
27. Reed, I.S.; Solomon, G. Polynomial Codes Over Certain Finite Fields. *J. Soc. Ind. Appl. Math.* **1960**, *8*, 300–304. [CrossRef]
28. Mahmoud, D.G.; Alkady, G.I.; Amer, H.H.; Daoud, R.M.; Adly, I.; Essam, Y.; Ismail, H.A.; Sorour, K.N. Fault secure FPGA-based TMR voter. In Proceedings of the 7th Mediterranean Conference on Embedded Computing (MECO), Budva, Montenegro, 10–14 June 2018; pp. 1–4. [CrossRef]
29. Benites, L.A.C.; Kastensmidt, F.L. Automated design flow for applying Triple Modular Redundancy (TMR) in complex digital circuits. In Proceedings of the IEEE 19th Latin-American Test Symposium (LATS), Sao Paulo, Brazil, 12–14 March 2018; pp. 1–4. [CrossRef]
30. Tan, C.; Li, Y.; Cheng, X.; Han, J.; Zeng, X. General Efficient TMR for Combinational Circuit Hardening Against Soft Errors and Improved Multi-Objective Optimization Framework. *IEEE Trans. Circuits Syst. I Regul. Pap.* **2021**, *68*, 3044–3057. [CrossRef]
31. Ruano, O.; Maestro, J.A.; Reviriego, P. Validation and optimization of TMR protections for circuits in radiation environments. In Proceedings of the 14th IEEE International Symposium on Design and Diagnostics of Electronic Circuits and Systems, Cottbus, Germany, 13–15 April 2011; pp. 399–400. [CrossRef]
32. Wilson, A.E.; Wirthlin, M.; Baker, N.G. Neutron Radiation Testing of RISC-V TMR Soft Processors on SRAM-Based FPGAs. *IEEE Trans. Nucl. Sci.* **2021**, *70*, 603–610. [CrossRef]
33. Liu, J.; Li, X.; Zhang, J.; Li, J. An Area-Efficient Design of Enhanced Space-Time Redundant DFF (IEST_TMR DFF). In Proceedings of the 7th International Conference on Computer and Communication Systems (ICCCS), Wuhan, China, 22–25 April 2022; pp. 721–726. [CrossRef]
34. Gomes, I.A.C.; Martins, M.; Reis, A.; Kastensmidt, F.L. Using only redundant modules with approximate logic to reduce drastically area overhead in TMR. In Proceedings of the 16th Latin-American Test Symposium (LATS), Puerto Vallarta, Mexico, 25–27 March 2015; pp. 1–6. [CrossRef]
35. Hamamatsu, M.; Tsuchiya, T.; Kikuno, T. Finding the Optimal Configuration of a Cascading TMR System. In Proceedings of the 2008 14th IEEE Pacific Rim International Symposium on Dependable Computing, Taipei, Taiwan, 15–17 December 2008; pp. 349–350. [CrossRef]

36. Deepa, M.; Augusta Sophy Beulet, P. An Improvised Voter Architecture For TMR With Reduced Area Overhead. In Proceedings of the 2022 Third International Conference on Intelligent Computing Instrumentation and Control Technologies (ICICICT), Kannur, India, 11–12 August 2022; pp. 1001–1007. [CrossRef]
37. Wang, J. Radiation effects in FPGAs. In Proceedings of the 9th Workshop on Electronics for LHC Experiments, Amsterdam, The Netherlands, 29 September–3 October 2003; pp. 34–43. [CrossRef]
38. Kshirsagar, R.; Patrikar, R. Design of a novel fault-tolerant voter circuit for TMR implementation to improve reliability in digital circuits. *Microelectron. Reliab.* **2009**, *49*, 1573–1577. [CrossRef]
39. Ban, T.; de Barros Naviner, L.A. A simple fault-tolerant digital voter circuit in TMR nanoarchitectures. In Proceedings of the 8th IEEE International NEWCAS Conference 2010, Montreal, QC, Canada, 20–23 June 2010; pp. 269–272. [CrossRef]
40. Balasubramanian, P.; Prasad, K. A Fault Tolerance Improved Majority Voter for TMR System Architectures. *arXiv* **2017**, arXiv:1605.03771.
41. Kubica, M.; Kania, D.; Kulisz, J. A Technology Mapping of FSMs Based on a Graph of Excitations and Outputs. *IEEE Access* **2019**, *7*, 16123–16131. [CrossRef]
42. Kubica, M.; Kania, D. Graph of Outputs in the Process of Synthesis Directed at CPLDs. *Mathematics* **2019**, *7*, 1171. [CrossRef]
43. AMD. *Triple Modular Redundancy (TMR) v1.0 LogiCORE IP Product Guide (PG268)*; AMD: Santa Clara, CA, USA, 2022.
44. INTEL. *Intel Agilex® 7 SEU Mitigation User Guide, UG-20253*; INTEL: Santa Clara, CA, USA, 2024.
45. White, M.A. *An Automated Method for Adding Resiliency to Mission-Critical SoC Designs*; SYNOPSYS White Paper; SYNOPSYS: Sunnyvale, CA, USA, 2023.
46. Berkeley Logic Synthesis Group. *ABC: A System for Sequential Synthesis and Verification*; Berkeley Logic Synthesis Group: Berkeley, CA, USA, 2005.
47. KP Labs. QUAntum-SAfe Reprogrammability of Critical Avionics Functions. Available online: https://kplabs.space/quasar/ (accessed on 18 September 2024).
48. *Collaborative Benchmarking and Experimental Algorythmics Laboratory*; LGSynth93 Benchmarks; NC State University: Raleigh, NC, USA, 2008.

applied sciences

MDPI

Article

Distributed Software Build Assurance for Software Supply Chain Integrity

Ken Lew [1,*], Arijet Sarker [2], Simeon Wuthier [1], Jinoh Kim [3], Jonghyun Kim [4] and Sang-Yoon Chang [1,*]

1 Department of Computer Science, University of Colorado Colorado Springs, Colorado Springs, CO 80918, USA; swuthier@uccs.edu
2 Department of Computer Science, Florida Polytechnic University, Lakeland, FL 33805, USA; asarker@floridapoly.edu
3 Department of Computer Science and Information Systems, Texas A&M University-Commerce, Commerce, TX 75428, USA; jinoh.kim@tamuc.edu
4 Electronics and Telecommunications Research Institute, Daejeon 34129, Republic of Korea; ikkim21@etri.re.kr
* Correspondence: klew2@uccs.edu (K.L.); schang2@uccs.edu (S.-Y.C.)

Abstract: Computing and networking are increasingly implemented in software. We design and build a software build assurance scheme detecting if there have been injections or modifications in the various steps in the software supply chain, including the source code, compiling, and distribution. Building on the reproducible build and software bill of materials (SBOM), our work is distinguished from previous research in assuring multiple software artifacts across the software supply chain. Reproducible build, in particular, enables our scheme, as our scheme requires the software materials/artifacts to be consistent across machines with the same operating system/specifications. Furthermore, we use blockchain to deliver the proof reference, which enables our scheme to be distributed so that the assurance beneficiary and verifier are the same, i.e., the node downloading the software verifies its own materials, artifacts, and outputs. Blockchain also significantly improves the assurance efficiency. We first describe and explain our scheme using abstraction and then implement our scheme to assure Ethereum as the target software to provide concrete proof-of-concept implementation, validation, and experimental analyses. Our scheme enables more significant performance gains than relying on a centralized server thanks to the use of blockchain (e.g., two to three orders of magnitude quicker in verification) and adds small overheads (e.g., generating and verifying proof have an overhead of approximately one second, which is two orders of magnitude smaller than the software download or build processes).

Keywords: software supply chain; assurance; software integrity; applied cryptography; blockchain

1. Introduction

We use computer software products in our everyday lives from digital information transfer to sensor implementations to machine control. Due to our heavy reliance on software products, securing software development and its supply chain has become of paramount importance. Malicious modifications or injections, such as malware and backdoors, can compromise software, yielding vulnerabilities for applications and operations building on the software. Software development trends, such as open-source software projects, an increasing number of software repositories, and collective software developments, have resulted in even greater security risks, as they contribute to having more diverse, dynamic, and complex software supply chain involving many actors and contributors to software development.

Previous and ongoing research and development contribute toward securing software development and its supply chain. Such research and development includes the Software Bill of Materials (SBOM) and reproducible build. SBOM generates a record of software supply chain components to enable transparency, accountability, and tracking of the software development process. SBOM has been mandated for software products in commerce in the US by an executive order [1]. Reproducible build, on the other hand, is also known as deterministic verifiable build because, given the source code and the build condition, it generates an identical build. Reproducible build can detect a compromise (malicious change, such as a backdoor or malware insertion at the compiler) in the build condition. Instead of advancing SBOM and reproducible build technologies themselves, we build on previous research and development for these technologies to secure their outputs.

We secure the software supply chain against malicious compromise or injections in various steps in the supply chain. More specifically, we build a software build assurance scheme to detect the following compromises [2,3]: there has been a compromise and a change/insertion in the build or distribution process, the source code has been modified, or the download repository provides a different/modified code. The user downloading the software can detect such changes and verify the software integrity confirming that the software has not been modified from that by the legitimate source. To achieve such goals, the user generates a proof based on the software artifacts (code, compiler outputs, SBOM outputs) and compares it with a reference proof. We rely on the security-robust cryptographic hash function to generate the proof so that a malicious adversary cannot manipulate the proof or avoid detection, e.g., the adversary's injection or change in the software, which can occur in different parts of the software download and build processes, changes the pseudo-random proof.

We use blockchain to serve as the trusted authority to provide the reference proof for verification on the user machine. Blockchain is appropriate for such purpose because it has high security in payload integrity (cannot change or modify the payload content on the blockchain ledger), resistance to a single point of failure (as long as the majority of the distributed participants follow the protocol), and high visibility and accountability (thanks to the distributed storage and easy read-access). We also utilize blockchain's strength in automatic broadcasting and distributed storage to distribute the proof offline, i.e., the reference proof can be shared any time before the software build assurance proof verification.

Our work applies generally to all software projects in principle. We thus describe our scheme in the abstract using variables in Section 4 to highlight the general applicability. For synergy and to provide a concrete implementation instance of our scheme for validations and system-based analyses, we implement our scheme in Section 5 targeting the Ethereum cryptocurrency software (developed by a collective group of developers, while implementing the operations to process transactions of approximately tens of billions of dollars market capitalization magnitude). We implement the blockchain, serving as a decentralized trusted authority for our scheme using Ethereum Smart Contract, which can be used to build various digital decentralized applications.

In this paper, we build on reproducible build and blockchain and apply them to achieve the following research contributions beyond the state of the art.

- We assure the software artifacts, including but beyond the source code.
- We make the software assurance distributed so that the assurance beneficiary and verifier align, i.e., the node downloading and using the software verifies its materials and artifacts.
- We achieve significant performance gains compared to the approach based on a centralized server.

2. Software Supply Chain Background

Generic Software Supply Chain Paths: The software supply chain starts with the developer who stores and shares the source code (s) in a repository. The source code, along with the dependencies, will then be used in the build process involving compiling the source code into machine-readable code. The build/compilation process outputs the software build (b) and the documentation (d).

There are two popular paths to download and build software. First, the user can download the source code and the dependencies from the source code repository and the dependencies repositories, respectively, and then build/compile the software themself. Second, a distribution platform can facilitate the download by providing the pre-build packages to the user. The user then compiles and builds the software from those packages.

Our work focuses on these two paths as they are the most typical paths for software download/build.

SBOM and Reproducible Build: More recent software download and build processes involve reproducible build for b and the software bill of materials (SBOM) for d. SBOM is mandated for the software for commerce and generates a record and documentation of the software supply chain components to enable transparency, accountability, and tracking of the software development process. Reproducible build, also known as deterministic verifiable build, provides an identical build output given the source code and the build condition to detect a compromise in the compiler or in the build condition. Major open-source software projects, such as Debian for Linux distribution, Tor for anonymous routing, and cryptocurrency blockchain (including Bitcoin Core and Ethereum), support reproducible build; we discuss the relevant recent research in Section 7.2. We also describe the concrete implementation of SBOM using Syft and reproducible build for Ethereum Archanes in greater detail in Section 5.

3. Problem Statement and Our Contribution

3.1. Problem Statement: Threats against Software Supply Chain

In this section, we describe the threats against the software supply chain that motivate our work. More specifically, we describe the threats residing within the main components and entities, described in Section 2 and illustrated in Figure 1.

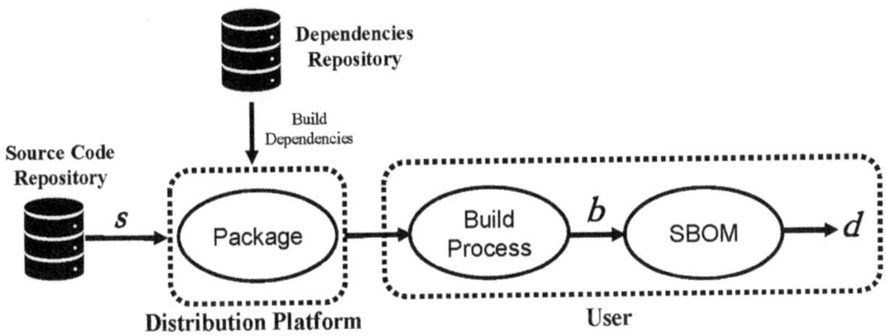

Figure 1. Software supply chain involving SBOM and reproducible build. This diagram illustrates the distribution-platform path, while the other user-direct path without the distribution is not illustrated due to space constraint.

Source Code Repository: Malicious actors can create an entirely new repository that is malicious from the creation. By doing so, victims will be downloading from a malicious repository. If it is an existing repository, malicious actors can also submit malicious merge requests that will turn into a backdoor or be exploitable by hiding the malicious intent via control characters, intentional concealing, and masking code differences [4]. This would effectively conceal malicious intent within the source code in the repository and hence compromise it. Another threat could also be to utilize configuration errors like leaked API keys in repositories and social engineering techniques that can empower a malicious actor to gain control of the source code or repository [5]. Once gaining control, malicious actors can modify the repository to carry out malicious intent.

Dependencies Repository and Build Process: Similar to source code repositories, the build process involves retrieving dependencies from designated repositories. This is facilitated by the utilization of package managers like npm and pip. This, however, could also lead to vulnerabilities like injections of malicious code from repositories into the dependency tree [6] that would affect the build process. Another type of threat that is not related to compromise of the dependencies repository but is related to the build process would be typosquatting or package confusion [7]. This technique is where malicious actors rely on and exploit common typing errors of users based on misspelling, character substitution, and pluralization of package names to carry out the attack. As examples, 'ethereum-go' vs. 'etheruem-go', 'backdoor-pkg' vs. 'backdoor-pkgs', and many more.

Distribution Platform: While malicious actors can attempt to inject malicious code into the source code repository, which would compromise the software supply chain, the distribution platform may also often rely on third-party dependencies and if these dependencies have vulnerabilities, it is another attack vector that malicious actors may choose to exploit.

SBOM: CISA suggests various types of SBOM, but in our case, we are focusing on the build type [8]. This means the SBOM creates a list of all the components needed for our project from the build process (b). If both the dependencies repository and the build process are compromised, it puts the accuracy of the SBOM at risk.

3.2. Our Contributions: Assurance Targets Across Software Supply Chain and Blockchain for Distributed Authority

We build a software build assurance scheme to check and assure the integrity of the various steps in the supply chain to defend against the active modification and malicious threats described in Section 3.1, More specifically, we use the software artifacts generated from the supply chain, namely, the source code (s), the build output including compilation (b), and the SBOM documentation (d), as the inputs and targets of our software assurance. We describe and explain these software artifacts as well as the software build assurance scheme in greater detail in Section 4.

In addition to assuring the software in multiple stages in the supply chain, our work advances beyond the approaches requiring a centralized authority and real-time protocol interactions with the centralized server, c.f., remote code attestation. Our scheme does not involve such centralized authority and instead uses blockchain to replace the centralized server authority. We also build on recent software development technologies of reproducible build and SBOM to enable our scheme; the reproducible build, in particular, enables our use of blockchain because it generates a deterministic software artifact in b to enable multiple recipients.

Our software build assurance is agnostic to the software applications, and our work can apply to any software in principle. However, our work requires reproducible build so that the software artifacts/compiler outputs are consistent across different machines If the software artifacts (the inputs of our assurance scheme) are not consistent and vary across machines, the verification does not work due to our scheme's use of the hash function (which produces a different output if using different inputs). While we provide a concrete validation using one software application for the Ethereum blockchain, we leave further validation and demonstration of other software applications to show the general applicability for future work. Previous research, however, has applied similar techniques as ours on other software applications, e.g., Bitcoin [9] and in cellular networking [10], although these assure only the software codes (which tends to be more consistent, e.g., a legitimate software source provides the same set of source code files).

4. Our Scheme

We build on SBOM and reproducible build, described in Section 2. We provide *assurance* of the software artifacts so that any changes and modifications of the software artifacts are detected. We thus take the outputs and the artifacts of the software supply chain, including those from SBOM d and reproducible build b, and input them into our scheme. The user of the software development, and the entity downloading the software conduct the software build assurance.

We present our scheme using abstraction and variables in this section while providing a more concrete implementation instance in Section 5.

4.1. Our Protocol Overview

The software supply chain makes use of the source code s and builds/compiles the software to generate b and the documentation d, as described in Section 2. Our scheme uses the SBOM to generate d and reproducible build to generate b so that b, given the user's compiler and the build conditions, provides the same b. Thanks to the use of reproducible build, other entities, given the same build condition and environment, also produce the same b. Our scheme, described in Figures 2 & 3 executed by the user, takes these software artifacts, i.e., s, b, d, to construct a proof p. Table 1 lists these variables used in our paper, and the rest of the section describes our scheme in greater detail.

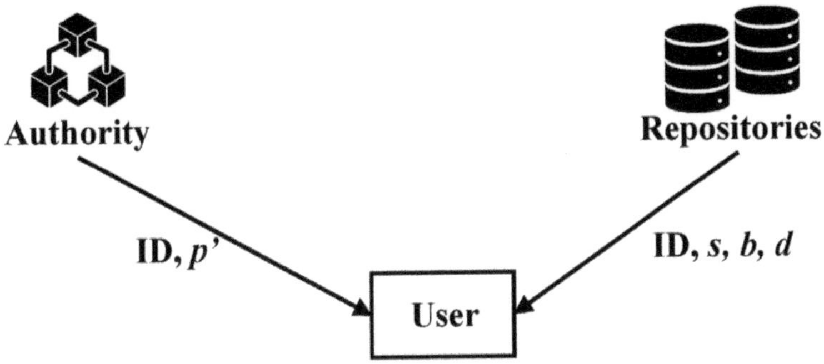

Figure 2. Our scheme overview, including information sources and inputs from the authority (providing the assurance reference) and the repository ecosystem. The authority's reference information delivery is implemented in blockchain in our scheme, while the centralized server approach relies on the online, real-time networking with a remote centralized server.

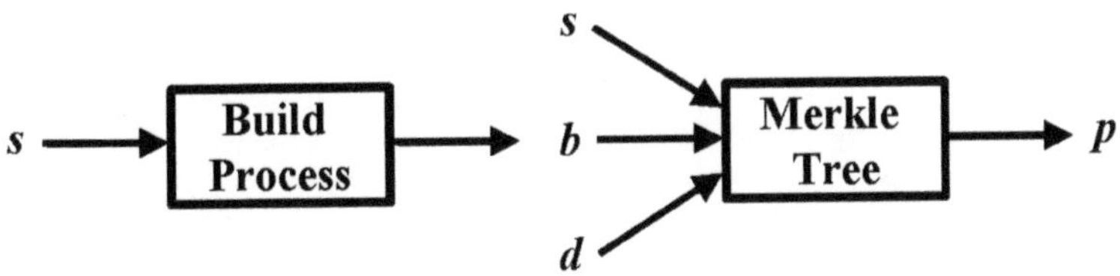

Figure 3. Online process from source code s to build/compilation b to the generation of proof p.

Table 1. Variable descriptions (Section 4) and assignments for implementation (Section 5).

Variable	Description	Our Implementation
s	Source code files of the specific version of the target software downloaded by user	Source code files of the latest Ethereum software, Archanes (v1.13.4)
b	Reproducible build compiler output from user	Geth of Archanes (v1.13.4) stored in the Ethereum repository [11]
d	SBOM documentation of the specific version of the target software generated by user	SBOM documentation of the Ethereum software, Archanes (v1.13.4)
p	Proof for the target software generated by the user	Proof for Archanes (v1.13.4) generated by the user
s'	Source code files of the specific version of the target software from authority	Source code files of the latest Ethereum software, Archanes (v1.13.4)
b'	Reproducible build compiler output from infrastructure from authority	Geth of Archanes (v1.13.4) stored in the Ethereum repository [11]
d'	SBOM documentation of the specific version of the target software from authority	SBOM documentation of the Ethereum software, Archanes (v1.13.4)
p'	Proof reference from blockchain	Proof stored in the Ethereum blockchain and centralized server
ID	Index of Proof	Index of Proof, p' in the Ethereum blockchain
H	Hash function	SHA-256

The authority is a logical entity that provides the information to the user about what the software artifacts and the proof should be, which we call the references and use the prime variables in Table 1. The authority can be implemented in many ways as long as it is an entity that has ownership over the source code in terms of storing or distributing it to users, for example, the software vendor who developed it. The authority provides the reference build (b'), the reference documentation (d'), the software ID and the reference proof (p') to the user. p' is generated in the same way as p but only from the authority. p' is computed by the authority and is a deterministic function of s', b', d', similarly to how p is computed by the authority and is a deterministic function of s, b, d. Thus, if $s = s'$, $b = b'$, and $d = d'$ and there has been no unauthorized modifications and changes in s', b', d', then $p = p'$. The user assures that the software artifacts have been unmodified and the software supply chain integrity by comparing p and p'; if $p \neq p'$, then the breach is detected.

4.2. Authority Implementation and Offline vs. Online

For the authority implementation, we compare our scheme against the centralized server approach. In the centralized server approach, the authority providing the reference inputs for software build assurance is a centralized remote server and requires real-time networking between the server and the user, c.f., remote code attestation discussed in Section 7.

Our distributed scheme, in contrast, implements the authority using blockchain. We use blockchain to replace the centralized server and to provide the proof reference p'. The use of blockchain enables the user to forgo networking beyond its own node for software assurance verification. We describe the blockchain design and application for our assurance scheme to implement the distributed authority in greater detail in Section 4.5.

We define online vs. offline to better explain the overhead differences. The online operations occur at the time of the software download, while the offline operations can occur before the software download and build. The offline overheads and costs are lower than the online overheads because the offline activity can occur any time before the time of the software download and build. Our work specifically enables the delivery of the authority-reference inputs offline by using blockchain. Blockchain automatically synchronizes and delivers the reference information offline at the time when the software updates are available in the repositories, which is in advance of the online software update to the user.

4.3. Building Blocks: Hash Function, Merkle Tree, and Blockchain

The cryptographic hash function is a mathematical algorithm that turns input into a fixed-size string of characters, known as a hash value. It ensures data integrity by generating unique hash values for different inputs and exhibiting properties like collision and pre-image resistance, making it challenging for adversaries to tamper with or to reverse-engineer the data.

Merkle trees, building on the cryptographic hash functions themselves, utilize these properties to create a hierarchical structure. Building the tree starts with a set of leaf node values $x_1, x_2, \ldots, x_n$, where each node x_i would contain hash value $H(x_i)$. In the next level of the tree moving up would be the parent node that would contain the hash value of the concatenation of two of the children nodes, for example, $H_{12} = H(H(x_1)||H(x_2))$. The process will continue to build on the next level until a root hash is formed. This root hash represents the entire dataset concisely. A Merkle tree [12] based on a hash function is known to be efficient for verification and is popularly used in many computing applications, as described in Section 7.3.

Blockchain provides a cryptographic system with robust security properties using the likes of the hash function, the Merkle tree, and the public-key digital signature. It provides a digital ledger with high integrity where one can securely track who wrote the transaction on the ledger. Specifically, blockchain utilizes the public-key digital signature to provide authenticity, non-repudiation, and data integrity [13]. Such robust security properties enable the blockchain to be applied to high-risk security applications. One notable example is the cryptocurrency blockchains processing digital financial transactions. However, while we use similar cryptographic construction for the ledger security as the cryptocurrency, our blockchain application environment having the software authorities (e.g., known software sources which are more reputable than the others) enables the use of a permissioned consensus protocol (e.g., as opposed to a permissionless protocol, such as that based on proof of work), providing significantly more efficient processing.

4.4. Proof Generations for p and p' Using Merkle Tree for Setting Up Assurance

In Figure 4, we use ID, s, b, and d as the leaf nodes (which are the nodes on the bottom of the tree) highlighted in gold color. As the source file inputs (s) contain multiple files, we denote each individual file as F_i, where i indicates the source code file index. With the use of a one-way hash function, the Merkle tree computation propagates from bottom to top. The final Root computation yields the Root, which serves as the proof p. The same computation occurs from the authority side providing the reference but using ID, s', b', and d' to generate p', as described in Section 4.5. The Merkle tree is used in both offline blockchain and online user-side computing, which are described in greater detail in the following sections.

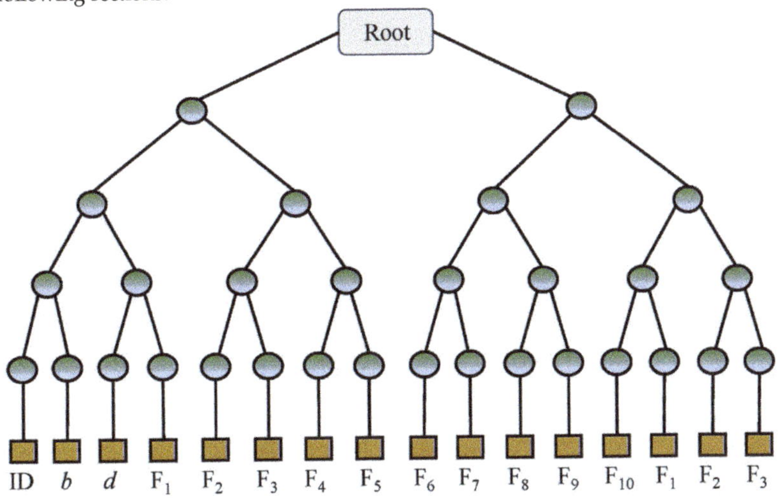

Figure 4. Merkle tree application for our scheme, where F_i are the source code s files and the Root is the proof p.

4.5. Blockchain for Authority: Reference Distribution in Offline and Access in Online

We use blockchain to serve as the authority to provide the reference information to enable the online user-side verification, in contrast to the centralized server approach implementing the logical authority on a physical remote server machine, as described in Section 4.2. In addition to having high payload integrity (cannot change or modify the payload content on the blockchain ledger) and high visibility and accountability (thanks to the distributed storage and easy read-access), we apply blockchain to implement the authority because blockchain supports automatic broadcasting and distributed storage to distribute the proof offline.

In our scheme, blockchain enables the reference proof to be distributed to the prospective downloading users offline (i.e., any time before the software download, build, and the build assurance verification). The networking and sharing of the proof reference information of p' (s', b', d' are used to compute p' but do not get networked) are offline so that they are stored within the user machine before the software download and build. In online, i.e., when downloading and building the software, the user simply accesses the blockchain database stored within its machine (computing only). In contrast, the centralized server approach involves the p' delivery and networking online (networking and computing). Because the networking and distribution of the reference information of p' are offloaded to before the software download/build, our scheme is significantly more efficient than the centralized server approach. without the explicit networking with another node, as this information is already stored in the local database provided by the blockchain.

We build the authority using a permissioned blockchain, which controls the entities who can write on the blockchain and require registration. These entities generate the references s', b', d', p' and distribute them to write on the blockchain database, the database being locally stored and distributed to many other nodes. The entities can vary, including the software developers who write/commit/upload on the repositories or a third-party entity dedicated for software build assurance, in our scheme implementation. blockchain monitors and tracks the s', b', d', p' for accountability, so such entity control can be dynamic, i.e., an entity can be revoked. In our work, we focus on the scheme framework itself as opposed to making strong recommendations about the ecosystem when implementing our scheme framework, including who can generate the blockchain payloads and who has the write-access on the blockchain and the trade-off analyses (e.g., third-party entity outside of the developers themselves or the source-code repository can provide the separation, which can be useful in some software applications). While our scheme supports different ecosystem models and can support various entities who can contribute to writing/uploading s', b', d', p', in our concrete implementation instance in Section 5, we introduce a third-party entity to write and upload the s', b', d', p' on the blockchain data. Because of the permissioned blockchain, we use proof-of-authority for our consensus protocol, which is significantly more efficient and transaction-scalable (generating more transactions) than the permissionless blockchains, such as those for cryptocurrency (e.g., Bitcoin and Ethereum).

4.6. User-Side Verification (Online)

In online, i.e., during the software development, including the download of s and the build of b and d, the user computes and generates the proof p described in Section 4.4. In user-side computing, a user first downloads the ID and s of the target software from the repository and compiles s in their machine to obtain b and d. Then, it is involved in the proof generation process by constructing the Merkle tree using s, b, and d to calculate its proof, p, for the target software version. The proof verification process involves retrieving the respective ID and p' from the blockchain and comparing p with p'. If both p and p' match then it assures the user about the s, b, and d, i.e., all the software artifacts correspond to the authority-references and $s = s'$, $b = b'$, and $d = d'$.

5. Our Scheme Implementation to Assure the Ethereum Software Chain

While Section 4 describes our scheme using abstraction and the variables which are generally applicable across software projects and cryptographic function choices, we provide an implementation instance of our scheme in this section to provide a proof-of-concept and provide concrete analyses. Our implementation consists of the generation of proof on both the blockchain side and the user side. In this section, we focus on the user-side, computing p using s, b, d, but the same applies to the authority (blockchain in our scheme), with p' depending on s', b', d' and thus omits the prime variables on the authority.

5.1. Authority Implementation For Our Scheme (Blockchain) vs. Centralized Server Approach (Remote Server)

Our scheme uses blockchain to distribute the authority-reference information offline, and the user can use this reference information to check the software artifacts of s, b, d online at the time of software download and build, as described in Section 4. The use of blockchain enables the user to access and retrieve the relevant reference information within its device, as blockchain provides distributed storage on the user. In contrast, the centralized server approach requires the user to communicate with the remote server authority to retrieve the reference information.

To demonstrate the efficiency of our scheme's proof verification enabled by the blockchain use, we implement the centralized server approach described in Section 4.2 and implement a remote server as the centralized authority to provide the references for software build assurance. We implement the remote servers in various locations and, more specifically, in four distinct locations in the world (two in the United States and two overseas) through the Google Cloud Platform. More specifically, the remote servers are located in "Iowa", "California", "Singapore", and "London". We use these geographical locations to label and identify the distinct remote authority servers for the centralized authority.

5.2. Target Software for s

Our target software is the Ethereum cryptocurrency software. More specifically, the source code s is the latest Ethereum software version, Archanes (v1.13.4). Our work is generally applicable to any software project in principle. However, we chose the Ethereum cryptocurrency software because it is highly relevant to our work. Ethereum cryptocurrency is highly relevant because of its high-security risk. Ethereum cryptocurrency is developed by a collective group of developers, making it highly vulnerable to software compromise. Cryptocurrency is also very popular with its operations to process transactions (the market capitalization is in tens of billions of dollars), and thus compromising the integrity of the software has a high breach impact.

5.3. Building Blocks for Our Scheme for b and d

5.3.1. b Using Reproducible Build

The current Ethereum builds and supports reproducible build in popular OSs, such as Linux, Windows, and MacOS [11]. In our implementation, we focus on the reproducible build for the Linux 64-bit processor. The reproducible build output b (which becomes one of the inputs to our proof generation in our scheme) is the compilation output, which is the geth (Archanes (v1.13.4)) running the Ethereum node and wallet. This b is stored in the official Ethereum repository.

5.3.2. d Using SBOM

We use an open-source SBOM generator tool called Syft [14] for our implementation. Using Syft, the SBOM includes information on geth for Archanes (v1.13.4), 91 packages as dependencies, and its relationships (total 181) between packages. The generated SBOM will then be used as d in our implementation. We chose Syft as it can convert between SBOM formats easily and works well with another tool called 'Grype', which is a vulnerability scanner that can scan for any common vulnerability and exposure (CVE). This would be particularly helpful to incorporate in a future proof of concept.

5.4. Proof Generation Using Merkle Tree and Hash

Based on the overview of the Merkle tree in Section 4.3 and Figure 4, we build Proof generation with the Merkle tree construction using the open-source implementation of Merkle tree [15] and Proof verification functionalities using C++, OpenSSL SHA-256 hash implementation and recursive directory iterator, and a regular expression to retrieve all relevant files of the Ethereum latest version, Archanes (v1.13.4) (excluding dynamic user-specific and configuration files) associated with C, C++, and shell. The ID, s, b, and d of Archanes (v1.13.4) are the inputs of the Merkle tree for proof generation. We have a total of 1350 inputs of the Merkle tree with s containing 1347 inputs and 1 input each from ID, b, and d. However, we use cyclic extension of these files till 2048 inputs as discussed in [9] to make it a balanced Merkle tree with the number of leaf nodes equal to the power of two.

5.5. Blockchain for Reference Proof Delivery

We build a smart contract using Solidity v0.8.21 to upload the ID and its respective p (as a form of key-value pair) on the local private Ethereum blockchain. As a proof-of-concept (PoC) implementation, we do not upload ID and p in the Ethereum Mainnet to avoid transaction fees. Our smart contract design enables the maintainers of the smart contract to add new nodes with write permission. We use two mappings in our smart contract: authorization mapping (maps the address to a Boolean value specifying the authorization of the address to modify the ledger) and key-value pair mapping (maps the Proof with the respective ID). It can also verify whether a node has the write privilege using the authorization map before granting permission to upload an ID with the p on the blockchain. A user can retrieve p for the respective ID from the blockchain for proof verification.

5.6. Hardware and Experimental Setup

Our experiment consisted of two main pieces of hardware that we used for user and remote servers. The remote servers are only used in the centralized server approach. For user hardware, we use Intel Xeon CPU E5-1650 v2 with 32GB RAM. We use the Google Cloud Platform (GCP) for our remote server that has 2 vCPU with 8GB RAM. While the power of a processor (CPU) is important, the memory specification on the random access memory (RAM) provides information on the capability of a computer to access and process data. We also implemented an in-memory data store using the Redis open-source database [16] for higher efficiency in data storage access.

6. Experimental Analyses

We implement our scheme and empirically verify the correctness of our scheme in implementation, i.e., correctly detect the modifications of the software artifact inputs to our scheme in Section 6.1. After verifying that our scheme correctly detects the changes and modifications of the software artifacts, we analyze the performances. Our performance measurements and analyses include the online user-side computing for proof generation and verification (compared with the software download/build latencies) in Section 6.2. For our performance analyses, we measure latency, storage/memory, and processing. Furthermore, to highlight the efficiency of the authority delivering the references of s', b', d', p', we implement and compare the performances of our blockchain-based scheme vs. the approach based on a centralized server.

6.1. Verification Correctness

We observe that a change in s, b or d changes the proof p so that it becomes $p \neq p'$ due to the pseudo-random hash functions used in our implementation. More specifically, in our implementation, omission of a file, addition of a new file, and even a single bit flip in s, b or d changes p so that $p \neq p'$, failing the integrity check and verification, and detecting the changes in the software supply chain in s, b or d.

6.2. Computing Performances

Computational Latency: A user needs to perform leaf node construction (hashing all the files of the Ethereum software, compiler output, and SBOM document) and then finally generate the non-leaf nodes up to the Merkle root to generate a proof using the Merkle tree in Figure 4. The leaf-node construction corresponds to the bottom lines for the hash computations of the leaf nodes (ID, b, d, and the source files F) in Figure 4, while the non-leaf node construction takes the preceding hash outputs as the inputs to progress upward. The leaf-node construction is the dominant factor of the computing overhead because of the longer sizes and the processing for ID, b, d, and the source files F. In our measurements, the leaf nodes construction and the non-leaf nodes construction take 1082 ms or 1.082 s and 14.48 ms, respectively, resulting in a proof generation latency of 1096 ms or 1.096 s. On the other hand, the proof verification takes only 0.4254 ms. Therefore, the computing overhead including the proof generation and verification is 1097 ms or 1.097 s for the software build assurance of the Ethereum software artifacts. To compare, the Ethereum software download takes 157 s and 371 s for compilation, which are two orders of magnitude greater than our online scheme overhead of 1.097 s. Both the software download/build and the user-side proof generation and verification occur online.

Storage, Memory, and Processing: Though each Ethereum software version can have different b values (thus different p) based on the operating systems and processors, a user needs to store the Merkle tree of only the Ethereum software version it is using. For the latest Ethereum software version (Archanes (v1.13.4)), the Merkle tree size is 197.42 kilobytes with a total of 1972 files, including the SBOM document and compiler output. Moreover, in our experiment, it takes only 3–5% RAM and 1–2% CPU usage for Proof generation and verification.

6.3. Authority Delivering References: Our Scheme vs. Centralized Server Approach

As described in Section 4.5, our scheme utilizing blockchain enables the networking and distribution of the reference information of p' offline, in contrast to the centralized server approach which relies on a server and the online networking and sharing of p'. The proof verification process online (more specifically, after the software download/build and the proof generation for p) operates very differently between our scheme vs. the centralized server approach. In this section, we focus on the online software build assurance verification process. We also analyze how the efficiency of the verification affects the bandwidth of the assurance operations (the number/rate of assurances supported by our scheme vs. the centralized server approach).

Online Proof Verification For Our Scheme vs. Centralized Server Approach: Because our scheme only involves computing while the centralized server approach involves both networking and computing (computing and verification based on the communication receiving results of p'), our scheme is significantly more efficient in the online proof verification operation. Figure 5 shows the empirical measurement distribution in CDF and identifies the average values in dotted vertical lines. The proof verification takes 0.4254 ms, while the centralized server approach takes at least 91.42 times more, depending on the locations. Among the distinct remote servers serving as the authority to our scheme, the Iowa server is the quickest at 38.89 ms (91.42 times slower than our use of blockchain for the authority) and the London server is 370.9 (871.9 times slower). In general, the remote servers in the US nation (the user is also in the US) perform much better than the ones outside, because they go through a smaller number of distinct internet service providers (ISPs). In our experiments, our scheme based on the blockchain-authority performs two to three orders of magnitude quicker than having a centralized, remote authority.

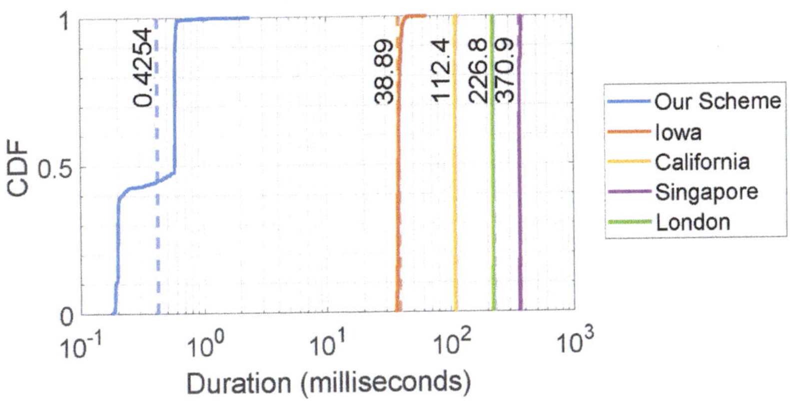

Figure 5. The proof verification time between our scheme using distributed blockchain vs. centralized remote servers.

Assurance Bandwidth For Our Scheme vs. Centralized Server Approach: Using blockchain as the authority for our scheme as opposed to the centralized server approach also provides significant improvement in the rate support. We define the bandwidth here to be the number of assurance resolutions that can be supported using our scheme. We experimented using 1000 requests per second and observed how many of those requests were resolved, including the final verification. As shown in Figure 6, if using the blockchain as the authority, our scheme can support 905.9 assurance resolutions per second. If using a remote centralized server as the authority for our scheme, the bandwidth is limited to between 17.90 (London with the worst performance) and 63.78 (Iowa with the best performance). Comparing between the distinct remote-server simulations, similarly to the above latency measurements, the remote servers in the US perform much better than the authority servers outside.

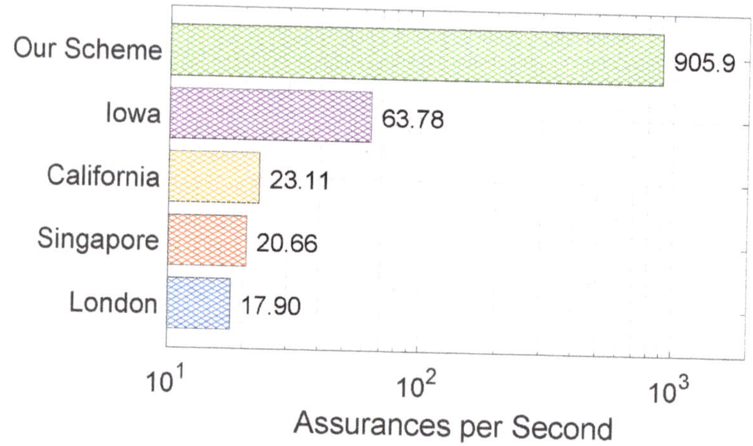

Figure 6. Bandwidth performance in assurance resolutions per second in comparison between our scheme and remote server locations.

6.4. Supports Software Assurance Requirements

Our scheme is applied for the software build assurance. New software versions, which are the new inputs of our software assurances, only occur when the software is updated. For Ethereum cryptocurrency, which is our target software for assurance, there have been 22 version updates since 2014 [17], so 2.2 version updates per year. The current Ethereum stable build [11] supports three different operating systems of Linux, Mac OS, and Windows, so 6.6 updates per year. Our scheme bandwidth performance of 905.9 assurance resolutions per second in Section 6.3 is enough to support our software build assurance application for Ethereum, as a 6.6 assurance resolutions *per year* requirement is significantly smaller than the 905.9 assurance resolutions per second our scheme supports.

The blockchain ledger also grows according to the software build assurance requirement to support new software version updates. The 6.6 version updates per year requirement results in the blockchain ledger growing 1.3030 kB = 6.6 × 197.42 kB per year if storing the entire Merkle tree nodes, where 197.42 kB is for each software build version as empirically analyzed in Section 6.2. This blockchain storage requirement is significantly less than most applications, such as the global financial transaction processing in cryptocurrency, whose ledger sizes are typically of the order of tens of GB, and, for more popular cryptocurrencies, such as Bitcoin and Ethereum, of the order of hundreds of GB. As the ledger's storage requirements remain minimal, even with multiple updates, the overall storage overhead is negligible, given the relatively small size of each update.

7. Related Work

7.1. Remote Code Attestation

Our work is related to remote code attestation that verifies the integrity of the running code on the users' system, adopting several hardware-based, software-based, and hybrid techniques. Hardware-based attestation techniques [18–20] involve hardware components, e.g., trusted platform module (TPM), software guard extensions (SGX), and software-based attestation techniques [21–24], that involve a challenge and response protocol in real-time, time synchronization, empty memory space filling, etc. An advancement of these techniques, hybrid attestation techniques [25–27], integrates both hardware-based and software-based techniques, minimizing the hardware cost with embedded processing components, e.g., field-programmable gate array (FPGA), memory protection unit (MPU) and micro-controller unit (MCU), etc. Our scheme goes beyond the research in remote code attestation in two ways: first, our scheme verifies the integrity of a software in different stages of the supply chain; second, our scheme does not rely on the centralized authority by using a distributed blockchain.

7.2. Reproducible Build

Reproducible build yields a deterministic build which achieves reproducibility when, with identical source code, build environment, and build instructions, any entity can recreate precise, bit-for-bit copies of all specified artifacts. [28] Projects and development efforts, such as Debian packages [29], Gitian [30], and other Linux distribution [31,32], focus on the reproducibility and verifiable build where there will be involvement using a virtual environment that would fix non-deterministic variables. Some other methods also include removing embedded timestamps from binary and making changes to the CFLAGS variable to produce a deterministic output [33]. It is also worth mentioning that [34] suggested that having a deterministic build for close-source software proves to be difficult due to lack of documentation and many other compilation processes that are susceptible to non-deterministic output [35]. Our work assumes, builds on, and uses the reproducible build technology.

7.3. Hash and Merkle Tree Applications for Securing Integrity

Our work builds on the Merkle tree and hash function to construct our scheme for software integrity. Previous research has utilized the Merkle tree and hash function for integrity in other applications and purposes than ours, including in over-the-air vehicular software updates [36,37], vehicular firmware updates [38,39], transactions, blocks, and the consensus mechanism in blockchain [40,41], cryptocurrency and cellular networking software assurance [9,10]. Version control systems (VCSs) used for project collaborations include Git [42], Subversion [43], and Mercurial [44]. Our work uses the Merkle tree to achieve different goals than these previous works, i.e., we use it to assure software integrity.

7.4. Blockchain for Security

Blockchain provides security for many types of systems, e.g., identity management [45], electronic voting [46], decentralized cryptocurrencies [47], supply chain management [48], healthcare [49], public key infrastructure (PKI) [50,51], cellular networking [52], the Internet of Things (IoT) [53], and vehicular networking [54], etc. The use of blockchain in these systems mitigates several types of security risks and attacks, e.g., single point of failure, data tampering, unauthorized access control, users' identity and data breach, distributed denial-of-service (DDoS) attacks, Sybil attacks, replay attacks, injection attacks, and man-in-the-middle (MITM) attacks, etc. with its properties such as decentralization, anonymity, immutability, transparency, and automatic synchronization, etc. In our scheme, we use these properties of blockchain to preserve the software supply chain integrity, which has a different goal from that of the previous research.

8. Conclusions

In this paper, we design and build a software build assurance scheme assuming reproducible build (for deterministic build output) and SBOM (for documentation, recording, and tracking of the software development). Our software build assurance scheme checks the integrity against (unauthorized or unintentional) changes and modifications in multiple software artifacts generated in the software supply chain. More specifically, it checks the integrity of the software artifacts of the source code (s or F, the latter of which corresponds to the source code in multiple files), build or compilation output (b), and the documentation or record (d). Computing on these inputs and using cryptographic hash and Merkle tree yields the proof p in our scheme. We further use blockchain to serve as the authority providing the reference information for our scheme; this information provides the comparison reference and corresponds to what the software artifacts should be. In addition to the blockchain providing high integrity and control on the write-access, the distributed storage and automatic broadcasting strengths of the blockchain provide significant performance advancements in the online software build assurance verification processes by offloading the reference delivery to offline before the time of the software download/build.

In addition to describing our scheme using abstraction and variables, we empirically implement our scheme targeting the Ethereum software as the object of assurance to show the correctness of our scheme (i.e., changes are detected). Our empirical performance analyses based on our implementation also show that our scheme is appropriate and provides small and manageable costs in the software download/build process, e.g., our scheme's online overhead is two orders of magnitude smaller than both the download and build/compilation duration. Furthermore, the blockchain-based authority is also two to three orders of magnitude quicker than the authority based on a centralized remote server.

Author Contributions: Conceptualization, K.L. and S.-Y.C.; Methodology, K.L. and S.-Y.C.; Software, K.L.; Validation, K.L. and S.-Y.C.; Formal analysis, K.L, A.S. (Arijet Sarker), S.W. (Simeon Wuthier); Investigation, K.L. and S.-Y.C.; Resources, J.K. (Jinoh Kim), J.K. (Jonghyun Kim) and S.-Y.C.; Data curation, S.W.; Writing—original draft, K.L. and S.-Y.C.; Writing—review & editing, K.L., A.S. (Arijet Sarker), S.W. (Simeon Wuthier), J.K. (Jinoh Kim), J.K. (Jonghyun Kim) and S.-Y.C.; Visualization, K.L. and S.W. (Simeon Wuthier); Supervision, J.K. (Jinoh Kim) and S.-Y.C.; Project administration, J.K. (Jinoh Kim), J.K. (Jonghyun Kim) and S.-Y.C.; Funding acquisition, J.K. (Jinoh Kim), J.K. (Jonghyun Kim) and S.-Y.C. All authors have read and agreed to the published version of the manuscript.

Funding: This work was supported in part by the National Science Foundation under Grant No. 1922410 (50%) and by an Institute of Information and Communications Technology Planning and Evaluation (IITP) grant funded by the Korean government (MSIT) (No. 2021-0-02107, with collaborative research on element Technologies for 6G Security-by-Design and standardization-based International cooperation, 50%).

Data Availability Statement: The raw data supporting the conclusions of this article will be made available by the authors on request.

Conflicts of Interest: The authors declare no conflicts of interest. The funders had no role in the design of the study; in the collection, analyses, or interpretation of data; in the writing of the manuscript; or in the decision to publish the results.

References

1. The United States Government. The White House. 2023. Available online: https://www.whitehouse.gov/briefing-room/presidential-actions/2021/05/12/executive-order-on-improving-the-nations-cybersecurity/ (accessed on 29 October 2023).
2. SolarWinds Supply Chain Attack | Fortinet. Available online: https://www.fortinet.com/resources/cyberglossary/solarwinds-cyber-attack (accessed on 29 September 2024)
3. Advanced Persistent Threat Compromise of Government Agencies, Critical Infrastructure, and Private Sector Organizations | CISA. Available online: https://www.cisa.gov/news-events/cybersecurity-advisories/aa20-352a. (accessed on 29 September 2024).
4. Wu, Q.; Lu, K. On the Feasibility of Stealthily Introducing Vulnerabilities in Open-Source Software via Hypocrite Commits 2021 Available online: https://api.semanticscholar.org/CorpusID:233479632 (accessed on 11 August 2024).
5. Meli, M.; McNiece, M.R.; Reaves, B. How Bad Can It Git? Characterizing Secret Leakage in Public GitHub Repositories. In Proceedings of the Network and Distributed System Security Symposium 2019, San Diego, CA, USA, 24–27 February 2019. [CrossRef]
6. Liu, C.; Chen, S.; Fan, L.; Chen, B.; Liu, Y.; Peng, X. Demystifying the vulnerability propagation and its evolution via dependency trees in the NPM ecosystem. In Proceedings of the 44th International Conference on Software Engineering, Pittsburgh, PA, USA, 25–27 May 2022. [CrossRef]
7. Neupane, S.; Holmes, G.; Wyss, E.; Davidson, D.; Carli, L.D. Beyond Typosquatting: An In-depth Look at Package Confusion. In Proceedings of the 32nd USENIX Security Symposium (USENIX Security 23), Anaheim, CA, USA, 9–11 August 2023; pp. 3439–3456.
8. Cybersecurity and Infrastructure Security Agency (CISA). Types of Software Bill of Material (SBOM) Documents. Available online: https://www.cisa.gov/sites/default/files/2023-04/sbom-types-document-508c.pdf (accessed on 11 August 2024).
9. Sarker, A.; Wuthier, S.; Kim, J.; Kim, J.; Chang, S.Y. Version++: Cryptocurrency Blockchain Handshaking with Software Assurance. In Proceedings of the 2023 IEEE 20th Consumer Communications & Networking Conference (CCNC), IEEE, Las Vegas, NV, USA, 8–11 January 2023; pp. 804–809.
10. Purification, S.; Kim, J.; Kim, J.; Kim, I.; Chang, S.Y. Distributed and Lightweight Software Assurance in Cellular Broadcasting Handshake and Connection Establishment. *Electronics* **2023**, 12, 3782. [CrossRef]
11. The Go-Ethereum Authors. Stable Releases. 2023. Available online: https://geth.ethereum.org/downloads (accessed on 29 October 2023).
12. Merkle, R.C. A digital signature based on a conventional encryption function. In *Advances in Cryptology—CRYPTO '87*; Lecture Notes in Computer Science; Springer: Berlin/Heidelberg, Germany, 1988; pp. 369–378. [CrossRef]
13. Bitcoin.org. Available online: https://bitcoin.org/bitcoin.pdf (accessed on 1 October 2024).
14. GitHub—Anchore/Syft: CLI Tool and Library for Generating a Software Bill of Materials from Container Images and Filesystems. Available online: https://github.com/anchore/syft. (accessed on 10 November 2023).
15. Microsoft. Microsoft/Merklecpp: A C++ Library for Creation and Manipulation of Merkle Trees. 2023. Available online: https://github.com/microsoft/merklecpp (accessed on 20 October 2023).

16. Redis. Available online: https://redis.io/ (accessed on 29 January 2024).
17. Ethereum.org. The History of Ethereum. 2024. Available online: https://ethereum.org/en/history/ (accessed on 6 August 2024).
18. Trusted Computing Group. Trusted Platform Module (TPM). 2023. Available online: https://trustedcomputinggroup.org/work-groups/trusted-platform-module/ (accessed on 26 May 2023).
19. Intel. Intel Software Guard Extensions. 2023. Available online: https://www.intel.com/content/www/us/en/developer/tools/software-guard-extensions/overview.html (accessed on 26 May 2023).
20. ARM. Layered Security for Your Next SoC. 2023. Available online: https://www.arm.com/products/silicon-ip-security (accessed on 26 May 2023).
21. Armknecht, F.; Sadeghi, A.R.; Schulz, S.; Wachsmann, C. A security framework for the analysis and design of software attestation. In Proceedings of the 2013 ACM SIGSAC Conference on COMPUTER & Communications Security, Berlin, Germany, 4–8 November 2013; pp. 1–12.
22. Kovah, X.; Kallenberg, C.; Weathers, C.; Herzog, A.; Albin, M.; Butterworth, J. New results for timing-based attestation. In Proceedings of the 2012 IEEE Symposium on Security and Privacy, IEEE, San Francisco, CA USA, 20–23 May 2012; pp. 239–253.
23. Gardner, R.W.; Garera, S.; Rubin, A.D. Detecting code alteration by creating a temporary memory bottleneck. *IEEE Trans. Inf. Forensics Secur.* **2009**, *4*, 638–650. [CrossRef]
24. Castelluccia, C.; Francillon, A.; Perito, D.; Soriente, C. On the difficulty of software-based attestation of embedded devices. In Proceedings of the 16th ACM Conference on Computer and Communications Security, Chicago, IL, USA, 9–13 November 2009; pp. 400–409.
25. Nunes, I.D.O.; Eldefrawy, K.; Rattanavipanon, N.; Tsudik, G. APEX: A Verified Architecture for Proofs of Execution on Remote Devices under Full Software Compromise. In Proceedings of the USENIX Security Symposium, Boston, MA, USA, 12–14 August 2020; pp. 771–788.
26. Ammar, M.; Crispo, B.; De Oliveira Nunes, I.; Tsudik, G. Delegated attestation: Scalable remote attestation of commodity CPS by blending proofs of execution with software attestation. In Proceedings of the 14th ACM Conference on Security and Privacy in Wireless and Mobile Networks, Abu Dhabi, United Arab Emirates, 28 June–2 July 2021; pp. 37–47.
27. Eldefrawy, K.; Rattanavipanon, N.; Tsudik, G. HYDRA: Hybrid design for remote attestation (using a formally verified microkernel). In Proceedings of the 10th ACM Conference on Security and Privacy in wireless and Mobile Networks, Boston, MA, USA, 18–20 July 2017; pp. 99–110.
28. Reproducible Builds. A Set of Software Development Practices That Create an Independently-Verifiable Path from Source to Binary Code. Available online: https://reproducible-builds.org/ (accessed on 10 November 2023).
29. ReproducibleBuilds—Debian Wiki. Available online: https://wiki.debian.org/ReproducibleBuilds (accessed on 10 November 2023).
30. GitHub—Devrandom/Gitian-Builder: Build Packages in a Secure Deterministic Fashion Inside a VM. Available online: https://github.com/devrandom/gitian-builder (accessed on 10 November 2023).
31. Build Result Compare Script. Available online: https://build.opensuse.org/package/show/openSUSE:Factory/build-compare (accessed on 10 November 2023).
32. GitHub—Kholia/ReproducibleBuilds: Reproducible Builds in Fedora ("Remock"). Updated for Fedora 23, and Rawhide. Available online: https://github.com/kholia/ReproducibleBuilds (accessed on 10 November 2023).
33. FOSDEM 2014—Reproducible Builds for Debian. Available online: https://archive.fosdem.org/2014/schedule/event/reproducibledebian/ (accessed on 10 November 2023).
34. de Carné de Carnavalet, X.; Mannan, M. Challenges and implications of verifiable builds for security-critical open-source software. In Proceedings of the 30th Annual Computer Security Applications Conference, ACM, New Orleans, LA, USA, 8–12 December 2014. [CrossRef]
35. Fourné, M.; Wermke, D.; Enck, W.; Fahl, S.; Acar, Y. It's like flossing your teeth: On the Importance and Challenges of Reproducible Builds for Software Supply Chain Security. In Proceedings of the 2023 IEEE Symposium on Security and Privacy (SP), IEEE, San Francisco, CA, USA, 22–25 May 2023. [CrossRef]
36. Bazzi, A.; Shaout, A.; Ma, D. MT-SOTA: A Merkle-Tree-Based Approach for Secure Software Updates over the Air in Automotive Systems. *Appl. Sci.* **2023**, *13*, 9397. [CrossRef]
37. Ghosal, A.; Halder, S.; Conti, M. STRIDE: Scalable and secure over-the-air software update scheme for autonomous vehicles. In Proceedings of the ICC 2020-2020 IEEE International Conference on Communications (ICC), IEEE, Dublin, Ireland, 7–11 June 2020; pp. 1–6.
38. Nilsson, D.K.; Sun, L.; Nakajima, T. A framework for self-verification of firmware updates over the air in vehicle ECUs. In Proceedings of the 2008 IEEE Globecom Workshops, IEEE, New Orleans, LA, USA, 30 November–4 December 2008; pp. 1–5.
39. Ghosal, A.; Halder, S.; Conti, M. Secure over-the-air software update for connected vehicles. *Comput. Netw.* **2022**, *218*, 109394. [CrossRef]
40. Nakamoto, S. Bitcoin: A peer-to-peer electronic cash system. *Decentralized Bus. Rev.* **2008**. [CrossRef]
41. Buterin, V. A next-generation smart contract and decentralized application platform. *White Paper* **2014**, 3, 2-1.
42. Git. Git—Distributed-Even-If-Your-Workflow-Isnt. 2023. Available online: https://git-scm.com/ (accessed on 10 January 2023).
43. Apache Subversion. Apache Subversion. 2023. Available online: https://subversion.apache.org/ (accessed on 10 January 2023).
44. Mercurial. Work Easier Work Faster. 2023. Available online: https://www.mercurial-scm.org/ (accessed on 10 January 2023).
45. Liu, Y.; He, D.; Obaidat, M.S.; Kumar, N.; Khan, M.K.; Choo, K.K.R. Blockchain-based identity management systems: A review. *J. Netw. Comput. Appl.* **2020**, *166*, 102731. [CrossRef]

46. Benabdallah, A.; Audras, A.; Coudert, L.; El Madhoun, N.; Badra, M. Analysis of blockchain solutions for E-voting: A systematic literature review. *IEEE Access* **2022**, *10*, 70746–70759. [CrossRef]
47. Ghosh, A.; Gupta, S.; Dua, A.; Kumar, N. Security of Cryptocurrencies in blockchain technology: State-of-art, challenges and future prospects. *J. Netw. Comput. Appl.* **2020**, *163*, 102635. [CrossRef]
48. Lim, M.K.; Li, Y.; Wang, C.; Tseng, M.L. A literature review of blockchain technology applications in supply chains: A comprehensive analysis of themes, methodologies and industries. *Comput. Ind. Eng.* **2021**, *154*, 107133. [CrossRef]
49. Villarreal, E.R.D.; García-Alonso, J.; Moguel, E.; Alegría, J.A.H. Blockchain for healthcare management systems: A survey on interoperability and security. *IEEE Access* **2023**, *11*, 5629–5652. [CrossRef]
50. Matsumoto, S.; Reischuk, R.M. IKP: Turning a PKI around with decentralized automated incentives. In Proceedings of the 2017 IEEE Symposium on Security and Privacy (SP), IEEE, San Jose, CA, USA, 22–26 May 2017; pp. 410–426.
51. Sarker, A.; Byun, S.; Fan, W.; Chang, S.Y. Blockchain-based root of trust management in security credential management system for vehicular communications. In Proceedings of the 36th Annual ACM Symposium on Applied Computing, Virtual, 22–26 March 2021; pp. 223–231.
52. Nguyen, D.C.; Pathirana, P.N.; Ding, M.; Seneviratne, A. Blockchain for 5G and beyond networks: A state of the art survey. *J. Netw. Comput. Appl.* **2020**, *166*, 102693. [CrossRef]
53. Huo, R.; Zeng, S.; Wang, Z.; Shang, J.; Chen, W.; Huang, T.; Wang, S.; Yu, F.R.; Liu, Y. A comprehensive survey on blockchain in industrial internet of things: Motivations, research progresses, and future challenges. *IEEE Commun. Surv. Tutor.* **2022**, *24*, 88–122. [CrossRef]
54. Alladi, T.; Chamola, V.; Sahu, N.; Venkatesh, V.; Goyal, A.; Guizani, M. A comprehensive survey on the applications of blockchain for securing vehicular networks. *IEEE Commun. Surv. Tutor.* **2022**, *24*, 1212–1239. [CrossRef]

applied sciences

MDPI

Review

Digital Twins Generated by Artificial Intelligence in Personalized Healthcare

Marian Łukaniszyn [1,*], Łukasz Majka [2,*], Barbara Grochowicz [1], Dariusz Mikołajewski [3,4] and Aleksandra Kawala-Sterniuk [5,*]

1 Faculty of Electrical Engineering, Automation and Computer Science, Opole University of Technology, 45-758 Opole, Poland; b.grochowicz@po.edu.pl
2 Faculty of Electrical Engineering, Silesian University of Technology, 44-100 Gliwice, Poland
3 Faculty of Computer Science, Kazimierz Wielki University in Bydgoszcz, 85-064 Bydgoszcz, Poland; dariusz.mikolajewski@ukw.edu.pl
4 Laboratory of Neurophysiological Research, Medical University in Lublin, 20-124 Lublin, Poland
5 Department of Artificial Intelligence, Faculty of Information and Communication Technology, Wroclaw University of Science and Technology, Wyb. Wyspiańskiego 27, 50-370 Wroclaw, Poland
* Correspondence: m.lukaniszyn@po.edu.pl (M.Ł.); lukasz.majka@polsl.pl (Ł.M.); aleksandra.kawala-sterniuk@pwr.edu.pl (A.K.-S.)

Featured Application: Featured Application: The potential application of the work relates to novel digital twins of patients or their organs based on artificial intelligence.

Abstract: Digital society strategies in healthcare include the rapid development of digital twins (DTs) for patients and human organs in medical research and the use of artificial intelligence (AI) in clinical practice to develop effective treatments in a cheaper, quicker, and more effective manner. This is facilitated by the availability of large historical datasets from previous clinical trials and other real-world data sources (e.g., patient biometrics collected from wearable devices). DTs can use AI models to create predictions of future health outcomes for an individual patient in the form of an AI-generated digital twin to support the rapid assessment of in silico intervention strategies. DTs are gaining the ability to update in real time in relation to their corresponding physical patients and connect to multiple diagnostic and therapeutic devices. Support for this form of personalized medicine is necessary due to the complex technological challenges, regulatory perspectives, and complex issues of security and trust in this approach. The challenge is also to combine different datasets and omics to quickly interpret large datasets in order to generate health and disease indicators and to improve sampling and longitudinal analysis. It is possible to improve patient care through various means (simulated clinical trials, disease prediction, the remote monitoring of apatient's condition, treatment progress, and adjustments to the treatment plan), especially in the environments of smart cities and smart territories and through the wider use of 6G, blockchain (and soon maybe quantum cryptography), and the Internet of Things (IoT), as well as through medical technologies, such as multiomics. From a practical point of view, this requires not only efficient validation but also seamless integration with the existing healthcare infrastructure.

Keywords: artificial intelligence; machine learning; medical engineering; personalized medicine; digital twin; DT; AI-based DT; omics

1. Introduction

The concept of digital twins as virtual representations of physical objects or systems has a history dating back several decades [1,2]. Although the term "digital twin" only gained popularity 20 years ago, its basic concepts have been around for over 60 years. Key milestones in the history of digital twins include:

1. Early foundations (1960s–1980s);

2. Development of the digital twin concept (1990s–2000s);
3. Technological advances (2010s);
4. Modern applications (2020s) [2–4].

The concept of using computers to simulate physical systems began in the 1960s and 1970s with the development of computer-aided design (CAD) systems that allowed the creation of digital models of physical objects. The early concept of DTs is believed to be partially related to NASA's use of pairing technology to create mirror systems during the Apollo missions, which created physical and digital replicas of spacecraft on Earth, enabling the monitoring and troubleshooting of space missions. In the 1990s, the development of product lifecycle management (PLM) systems integrated product lifecycle data and processes into digital models for design, manufacturing, and maintenance. The term "digital twin" was first used by Dr. Michael Grieves at the University of Michigan in 2002 as a virtual representation—a real-time digital equivalent of a physical object or process. The development of the Internet of Things in the 2010s extended the capabilities of DTs to include sensors embedded in physical objects. These enabled real-time data collection and communication with their digital counterparts. During this period, digital twins have been implemented in many industries, including healthcare, as discussed later. Subsequently, the integration of AI and machine learning (ML) with DTs has enabled more sophisticated analysis and predictive capabilities. As a result, DTs have evolved from static models to dynamic systems capable of simulating complex behaviours and scenarios. In 2020, the Digital Twin Consortium was established to promote best practices and standardize digital twin technologies across technology companies, government agencies, and academic institutions. The further development of AI-based DTs by 2030 will be based on emerging technologies, including those based on 6G (Figure 1) [4–6].

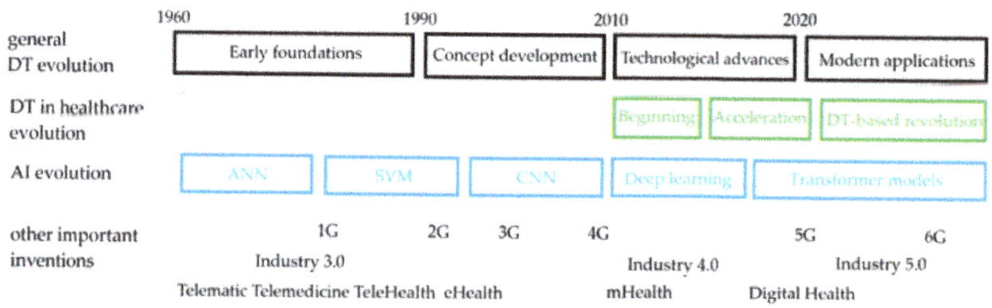

Figure 1. DTs development against the background of AI development (own version).

The story of digital twins in healthcare began to gather momentum in the 2010s, with the rise of the Internet of Things and artificial intelligence (AI)-based data analytics enabling the real-time monitoring of patient health through wearable devices. Early applications focused on creating digital replicas of organs, such as the heart, to simulate conditions and optimize treatment plans. The concept has been further developed through the integration of AI and machine learning, enabling personalized medicine through predictive modelling of patient outcomes. By the mid-2010s, digital twins were being used in surgical planning, where virtual models of a patient's anatomy helped surgeons practice and refine procedures before actual surgeries. The COVID-19 pandemic has accelerated interest in digital twins as a tool to manage and predict the spread of the virus and assess the impact of public health interventions. Advances in genomics have also enabled the creation of digital twins at the cellular level, facilitating more targeted therapies. Hospitals began implementing digital twins of entire facilities to optimize patient flow and resource management, improving overall efficiency. This concept extended to drug development, where virtual models of human physiology were used to simulate drug interactions, reducing the time and cost of clinical trials. The increasing availability of high-quality medical data and advanced computing power have made digital twins more accessible and accurate, driving their widespread adoption. From the 2020s, AI-based DT technologies in healthcare are poised to revolutionize patient care, offering unprecedented levels of personalization and predictive power (Figure 2) [7–11].

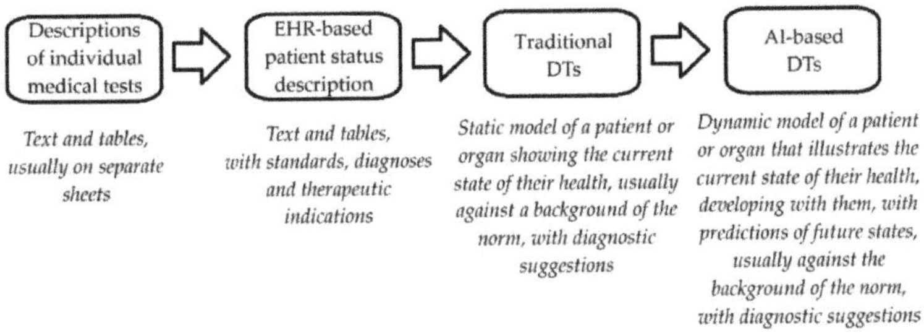

Figure 2. Evolution of AI-based DTs in healthcare [12–15].

2. Materials and Methods

2.1. Dataset and Devices

In developing the bibliometric analysis methods for this review, we focused on exploring the research landscape in the area of parameter selection strategies and development of AI-based DTs and possible innovations and clinical applications in this research area. For this purpose, we used bibliometric methods as analytical tools to review scientific publications. To better guide our review and selection of publications, we formulated research questions that help us discover key aspects of the research area, concerning research question 1 (RQ1)—the evolution of research topics/problems over time; RQ2—the geographical distribution of studies/publications, authors, scientific institutions, and publications with the highest impact; and RQ3—topics that may shape future research agendas. To achieve the above objectives, it was crucial to fully understand the current state of research, industry practices (connecting science and engineering, manufacturing and clinical applications), efforts, and future research directions in the pursuit of the optimal selection of AI-based DTs for a specific clinical application. Here, the analysis and interpretation of bibliometric data can make a key contribution to the ongoing discussion and build a more solid foundation for further analysis and research (Figure 3).

The criterion for selecting articles for review was also that we mainly wanted to use open sources in order to select not only new but also studies that are easily accessible for people from different fields, showing a broader perspective on AI-based DT. It is worth noting that not all publications were in English, and results published in national languages in India, China, South Korea, and Arab countries may not be available in other languages.

2.2. Methods

The study followed some of the points in the PRISMA 2020 guidelines [16] for creating a review with bibliographic analysis, namely point #3—rationale; point #4—objectives, point #5—eligibility criteria; point #6—sources of information; point #7—search strategy; point #8—selection process; point #9—data collection process; point #13a—synthesis methods; point #20b—synthesis results; and point #23a—discussion. In the review, we used the tools built into the Web of Science (WoS), Scopus, and PubMed databases, as well as the Biblioshiny tool from the Bibliometrics Rv.4.1.3 package for bibliometric analysis. This approach is better suited for bibliometric and scientometric studies, sometimes offering more precise categorization into conceptual/area/branch structures, authors, documents, and sources, and the different results are presented using graphs and information tables with a choice of analysis and visualization. Due to the complexity and interdisciplinary nature of the topic, we summarized the results of the review in a table.

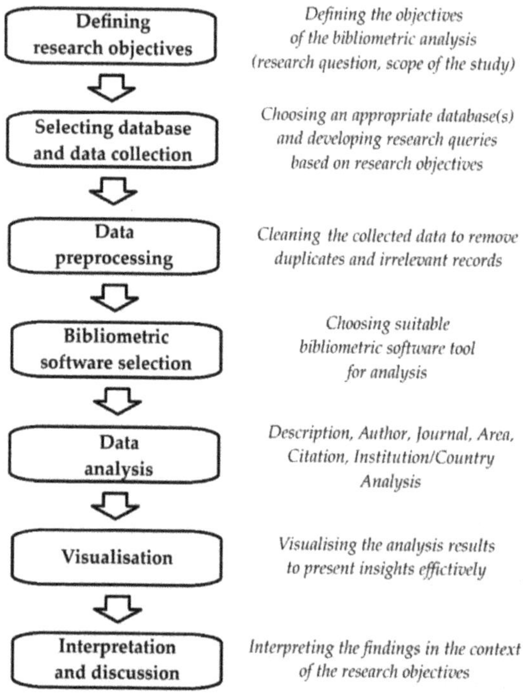

Figure 3. Bibliometric analysis procedure.

3. Results

After analysing the content of the main databases in the field of AI-based DT, we searched for research articles in three main databases: WoS, Scopus, and PubMed. This choice was dictated by the wide scope of research results they contained and the detailed data and analytical tools that allow for comprehensive analyses, which is particularly beneficial when conducting interdisciplinary bibliometric analyses and assessing the impact of research results, as was the case in our study. When creating advanced queries tailored to our research goals, we applied filters to select relevant publications. In this way, we limited our search to articles in English. Later in the study, we manually reviewed the articles again, excluding some of them (including duplicates) to match our research goals, which resulted in the final sample size (Figure 4). The WoS search was performed using "Topic" (the search was carried out using the set: title, abstract, keyword plus, and other keywords); the Scopus search was performed using the following set: article title, abstract, and keywords; and the PubMed search was performed using manual keyword sets.

Three databases were searched using the keywords "artificial intelligence" or "machine learning", "digital twin" and "healthcare". The obtained publications were subjected to further selection (Figure 4).

We started the bibliometric analysis with descriptive statistics to understand the characteristics of the dataset of the selected group of scientific publications, including leading authors, research institutions, topic areas, and emerging trends in the topic area under study (Figure 5). This allows us to identify evolving vocabulary and major research achievements. Examining changes in trends over time allows us to note changes in the focus/mainstream of research over time and the type and dynamics of the area, including the categorization of publications into topic clusters and a picture of the connections between research topics. This enabled the easier further identification of key topics and subdomains, including emerging research directions.

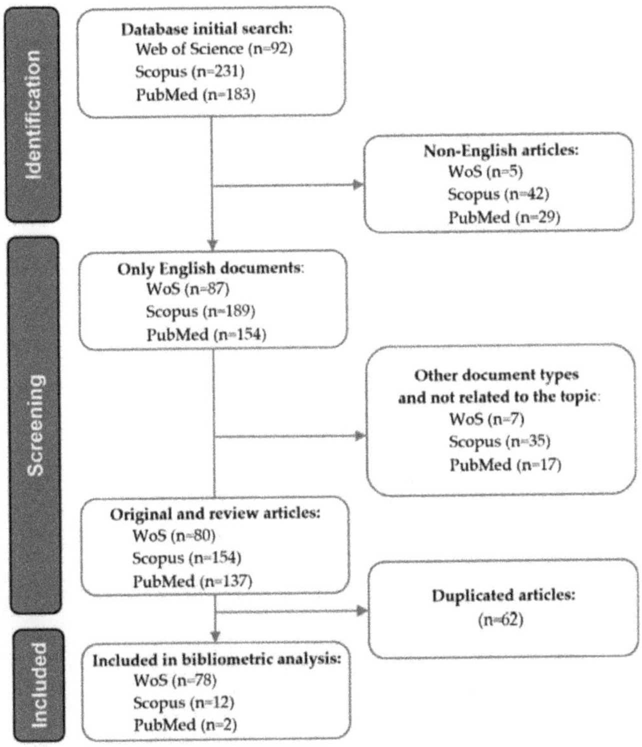

Figure 4. A PRISMA flow diagram of the review process using selected PRISMA 2020 guidelines [16]. Partial PRISMA 2020 checklist is added as Supplementary Materials.

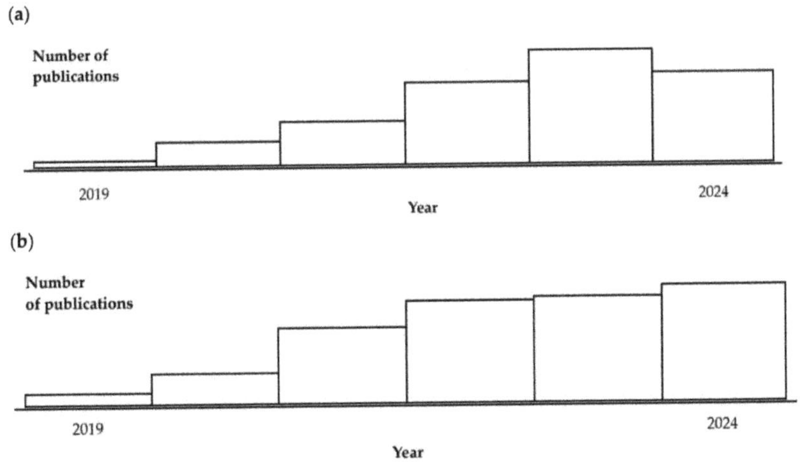

Figure 5. Review results: (**a**) AI + DT (183 publications, 2019–2024); (**b**) ML + DT (134 publications, 2019–2024).

The summary of the bibliographic analysis results is presented in Table 1. The largest number of research articles and almost three times fewer reviews were observed. A significant part of all publications were conference papers and book chapters. Most of the publications were works in the field of computer science and engineering, with medicine only in third place. More than half of the leading topics were technological issues, and a smaller part was medicine. The table presents details of diseases and patient conditions that were addressed by the developed AI-based DTs. The leading countries conducting and financing research turned out to be large countries of Asia, North America, and Europe, which is also reflected in the leading affiliations and names of the leading researchers.

Table 1. Summary of results of bibliographic analysis (WoS, Scopus, PubMed).

Parameter/Feature	Value
Leading types of publication	Article (35.9%), conference paper (25.1%), book chapter (15.2%), review (13.9%)
Leading areas of science	Computer science (31.0%), Engineering (20.4%), Medicine (10.6%)
Leading topics	Industrial: design and manufacturing, telecommunications, security systems, human–computer interactions
	Medical: cardiac arrhythmia, neuromuscular disorders, nursing, tuberculosis and leprosy, wounds and ulcers, ECK, multiple sclerosis, high-level disinfection
Leading countries	India, USA, China, UK, Italy, Canada, Germany
Leading scientists	N. Wickramsinghe, A. Athar, J. Cai, T. Huynh-The, H.C. Kim, N. Ulapane, C. Yi, J. Zelcer
Leading affiliations	Swinburne University of Technology, Galgotias University, Mohamed Bun Zayed University of Artificial Intelligence
Leading funders (where information available)	National Natural Science Foundation of China, Horizon 2020 Framework Programme/European Commission, Ministry of Science and ICT of South Korea, Ministry of Science and Technology of China

3.1. Sources of Data for AI-Based DTs

The creation and maintenance of AI-based DTs in healthcare is facilitated by the availability of large historical datasets from previous clinical trials and other real-world data sources (e.g., patient biometrics collected from mobile devices). AI-based DTs in healthcare rely on a diverse set of data sources to accurately model a patient's health status. Electronic health records (EHRs) provide a structured medical history, including diagnoses, treatments, and laboratory test results. Mobile devices and remote monitoring systems provide real-time physiological data such as heart rate, blood pressure, and activity levels. Medical imaging (e.g., MRI, CT scans) offers detailed anatomical and functional information that is crucial for creating accurate models of organs and systems. Genomic data provide personalized insights into a patient's genetic predispositions and potential responses to treatment. Patient-reported outcomes and data from mobile health apps capture subjective experiences, symptoms, and lifestyle factors that impact health. Environmental and social determinants of health provide context about external factors, such as air quality and socioeconomic status, that affect a patient's well-being. Pharmacy records provide information on medication adherence and potential interactions. Finally, clinical notes and unstructured data from healthcare professionals add valuable narrative information, often processed using natural language processing (NLP) techniques to help others understand a patient's condition. There is also the challenge of combining disparate datasets and omics to quickly interpret large datasets to generate health and disease indicators to improve sampling and longitudinal analysis [17–20].

Multiomics in AI-based DTs involves integrating data from multiple "omics" disciplines—genomics, proteomics, transcriptomics, metabolomics, and epigenomics—to create a comprehensive and personalized model of a patient's biological processes.

Genomics provides information about a patient's DNA sequence and genetic variants, helping to predict disease risk and response to treatment. Proteomics analyses the proteins expressed by genes, offering insight into cellular function and disease mechanisms. Transcriptomics examines RNA transcripts to understand patterns of gene expression that can indicate how genes are activated or repressed under specific conditions. Metabolomics focuses on metabolites, small molecules produced during metabolic processes, revealing real-time physiological states and treatment responses. Epigenomics examines DNA modifications that affect gene expression without changing sequence, providing information on how environmental factors affect genetic activity. By integrating these omics layers, AI-based DTs can model the complex interplay of biological processes with unprecedented precision. This holistic approach allows for the more accurate prediction of disease progression, treatment efficacy, and personalized healthcare strategies, ultimately improving patient outcomes [21–24].

3.2. AI-Based DT Architecture

An AI-powered patient DT is a virtual replica that dynamically reflects a patient's physiological, psychological, and behavioural states in real time. The architecture typically integrates data from multiple sources, such as EHRs, wearable devices, and imaging systems, to create a comprehensive patient model. The system uses advanced machine learning algorithms to continuously update and refine the twin, ensuring it accurately reflects the patient's current health status. A key component is a predictive analytics engine that can simulate potential outcomes based on different treatment scenarios, helping clinicians make informed decisions. The architecture often includes a feedback loop in which the AI analyses real-time data, predicts changes, and recommends interventions that are then validated and implemented in the real world. Interoperability is key, enabling the digital twin to integrate with various healthcare systems and devices, ensuring a seamless flow of data. Privacy and security measures, such as encryption and anonymization, are integral to protecting sensitive patient data. DT models also include a user interface that provides visualizations and insights for medical professionals, enabling them to more effectively monitor and manage patient health. In advanced implementations, the twin can incorporate natural language processing (NLP) to interpret unstructured data from clinical notes and patient communications, further enriching the model. Finally, continuous learning capabilities ensure that the DT model evolves over time, adapting to new medical knowledge and the changing the health profile of an individual patient [22–27].

DTs represent a virtual model of a physical system, object, or process in real time, which is why their accuracy and functionality rely heavily on advanced AI models and ML methods and the accuracy of the data learned and used later for model honing. At the core of DTs are AI-based models such as deep learning, reinforcement learning, and generative models, which are used to predict and optimise the performance of physical/physiological entities. In healthcare applications, neural networks, such as convolutional neural networks (CNNs) and recurrent neural networks (RNNs), enable DTs to process sensor data, identify patterns, and predict future patient behaviour. These models are trained using large datasets that record historical performance, often relying on supervised learning methods to map inputs to specific outputs, such as predicting failures/illnesses or optimising operations. Unsupervised learning techniques such as clustering and anomaly detection are key in identifying patterns in unlabelled data, enabling DTs to detect unusual body system behaviour or emerging faults in real time. As a particularly effective method for decision-making in dynamic environments, reinforcement learning (RL) enables DTs to autonomously optimise processes such as autonomous systems, where the DT continuously improves its performance by interacting with its environment. Physics-based neural networks (PINNs) are also being used to embed physical laws directly into AI models, ensuring that predictions are consistent with known physical constraints, which is crucial in areas such as healthcare, aerospace, or energy systems, where deviations from physical laws can lead to dangerous consequences. The integration of generative models, such as variational autoencoders (VAEs) and generative adversarial networks (GANs), enables the creation of virtual simulations that mimic the performance of a physical twin under different conditions, helping to proactively maintain or test new configurations without affecting actual operations. In addition, transfer learning allows DTs to quickly adapt to new environments or conditions, using knowledge from one model or system to optimise another. Real-time feedback loops between a physical entity and its digital counterpart are facilitated by AI models that process continuous streams of data, often involving complex sensor fusion techniques to combine data from different sources. A growing trend is the implementation of federated learning in DTs, where multiple twins collaborate to improve their models without sharing raw data, thus protecting privacy and reducing data transfer needs. DTs are evolving to use hybrid AI models that combine data-driven machine learning approaches with traditional physics-based simulations to provide more accurate, reliable, and interpretable results. These AI models allow digital twins to move from mere simulations to fully autonomous systems capable of self-adaptation, prediction, and decision-making in complex and changing environments.

There is no single formalized framework for AI-based DTs; moreover, depending on the application, the patient–organ model itself may not be the final result, but only an intermediate link for the further development of personalized medicines or implants (Figures 6–9) [28–32].

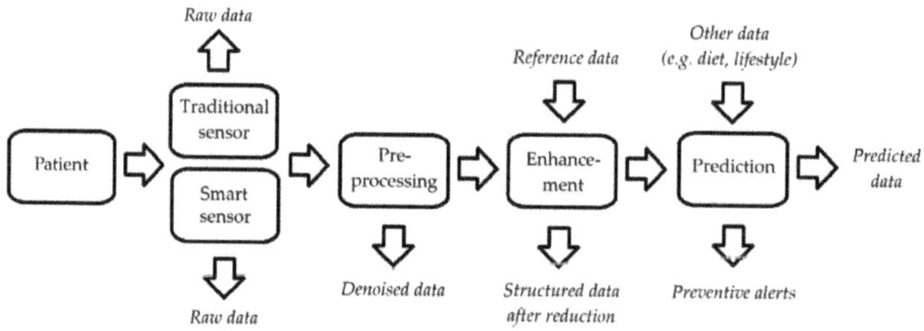

Figure 6. AI-based DT architecture (own version based on [22–27]).

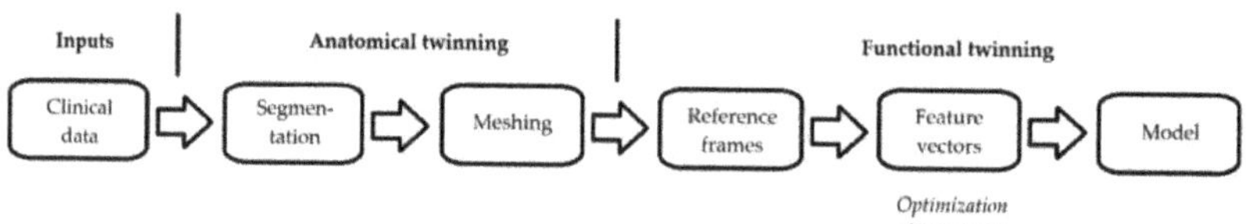

Figure 7. Example of basic workflow for AI-based DTs (own version based on [22–27]).

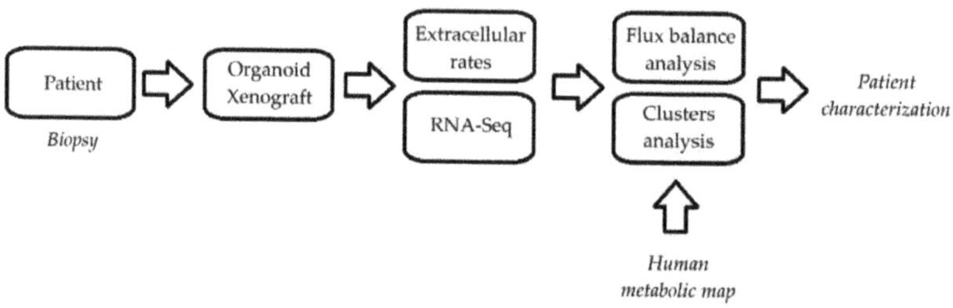

Figure 8. Example of advanced workflow for AI-based DTs (own version based on [22–27]).

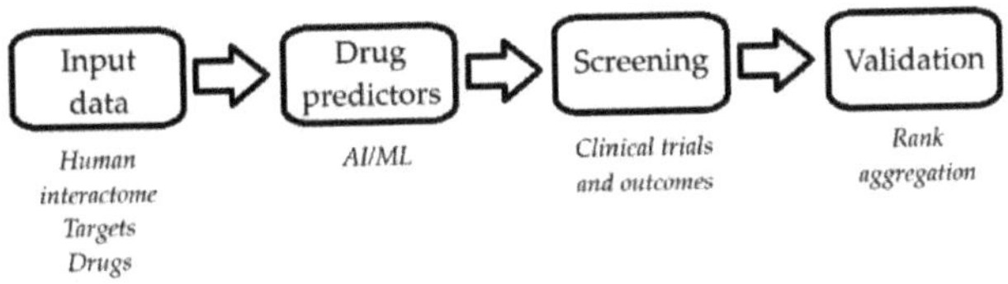

Figure 9. Example of pharmaceutical workflow for AI-based DTs for personalized drugs (own version based on [22–27]).

3.3. AI-Based DT Building

The proposed steps for building AI-generated DTs in personalized healthcare are as follows (Table 2). For the purposes of this study, it was assumed that DTs can be applied to both a sick patient and a healthy person (e.g., an athlete) in the context of preventive medicine [33,34]. Therefore, DTs must reflect both physiological and pathological processes/states.

Table 2. Stages of building AI-generated DTs in personalized healthcare (own version based on [33–39]).

Stage Number	Stage Name	Tasks
1	Data collection	Collecting comprehensive and diverse patient data, including electronic health records, genetic information, lifestyle data, and real-time data from wearable devices, to create a detailed foundation for the digital twin.
2	Data integration and preprocessing	The collected data undergoes integration and pre-processing, where data from different sources is standardized, cleaned, and organized (e.g., normalized, balanced) to ensure consistency and readiness for modelling.
3	Model/algorithm selection and development	AI algorithms and ML models are selected and developed to represent the patient's physiological systems, health status, and potential responses to treatment. This can be carried out based on pre-prepared initial templates for easier initialization.
4	Simulation and calibration	The DT is simulated using the processed data, and the model is calibrated to reflect the patient's actual current health status by adjusting parameters to ensure that the DT accurately reflects the patient's unique characteristics important for clinical diagnosis. Also, the directions and degree of their changes should be the same as those of the patient.
5	Validation and testing	The constructed DT undergoes rigorous validation and testing against real-world outcomes to ensure that it accurately predicts the patient's health trajectory and response to various interventions.
6	Personalization and adaptation	The DT is then personalized by incorporating patient-specific factors and continually updating the model with new data to reflect any changes in the patient's health over time and to keep the DT current (concurrent with the physical original).
7	Integration into clinical processes	The DT is integrated with clinical processes, providing healthcare providers with a tool for real-time decision support, treatment planning, and monitoring patient progress. Initially, this may be carried out using the infrastructure of medical simulation centres.
8	Feedback and refinement	As a DT is used in clinical practice, continuous feedback is collected from medical professionals and healthcare providers and results are monitored, leading to the continuous refinement and improvement of the model (both the technology itself, its engine and templates, and the specific DT of a healthy patient or one with specific conditions).
9	Ethical and regulatory compliance	Ensuring DT compliance with ethical standards and regulatory requirements is key, with attention paid to patient consent, data privacy, and legal issues.
10	Implementation and monitoring	Finally, the DT is implemented for use in personalized healthcare, with continuous monitoring to track its performance and effectiveness and to make further changes if necessary.
11	Continuous improvement	The DT is never finished; it constantly evolves with changes in technology and the patient's health, and after the patient dies and is anonymized, it serves as a basis for the teaching, learning, simulation, and development of the next generation of DTs.

The integrated digital twin model in personalised healthcare, generated by AI, is a dynamic, virtual representation of a patient's physiological and medical state. It is constantly evolving, reflecting real-time input from wearables, EHRs, and genetic information.

Artificial intelligence ensures model convergence by optimising algorithms that adapt and improve based on a variety of biomedical data, ensuring high quality and accurate simulations. Machine learning models dynamically adapt as new data are introduced, providing a personalised profile that becomes increasingly accurate over time. To systematically populate the model, artificial intelligence integrates structured (clinical data, lab results) and unstructured data (doctors' notes, imaging) using NLP and other AI techniques. The model predicts individual responses to treatment and medical conditions by simulating complex interactions in the patient's biological systems. Using patient-specific data helps doctors make more informed decisions about diagnosis, treatment plans, and disease prevention. The AI system continuously monitors convergence rates, ensuring that as the digital twin develops, its simulations are consistent with the patient's actual physiological responses. As more patients submit data, the AI learns from the larger dataset, further refining predictions and personalised care recommendations. Finally, the convergence of the model relies on a feedback loop between data collection, AI-based insights, and actual clinical outcomes, ensuring both the precision and accuracy of personalised healthcare.

The structure of such an integrated digital twin model in personalised healthcare consists of several interconnected layers: data acquisition, data processing, AI-based modelling, simulation, and feedback. Data acquisition includes the continuous collection of biomedical data from wearables, EHRs, and genetic databases, ensuring the capture of both real-time and historical data. The data processing layer cleans, organises, and standardises the incoming data, enabling consistent input for AI algorithms. AI-based modelling uses ML and deep learning techniques to interpret the data and generate personalised health models that adapt as more information becomes available. Layers of simulation then predict patient-specific outcomes, such as disease progression, response to treatment, or physiological changes.

3.4. AI-Based DT Clinical Use

DTs can use AI models to predict future health outcomes for individual patients in the form of an AI-generated digital twin to support the rapid assessment of intervention strategies in silico. We gain the ability to update real-time data from our physical patients and connect to multiple diagnostic and therapeutic devices. To date, at least several methods have been defined for the use of AI-generated DTs in personalized healthcare. By analysing a patient's DT, physicians can predict the onset of diseases or complications before they manifest in various scenarios, enabling early intervention and potentially preventing adverse health events and reducing the invasiveness and cost of therapeutic interventions. DTs can be used to simulate a patient's response to different treatment options, allowing healthcare providers to tailor treatments based on DT predictions, thereby optimizing outcomes for the individual. DTs can be used to model a patient's response to different medications, helping to identify the most effective medications and doses while minimizing side effects, especially in cases where personalized drug therapy is crucial. Surgeons can use DTs to plan complex surgeries by simulating different procedural approaches and predicting outcomes, thereby reducing risk and improving surgical precision. DTs enable the continuous monitoring of a patient's health through real-time data analysis, allowing for timely adjustments to treatment plans and the management of chronic conditions. Interestingly, patients can interact with their DTs to better understand their health status, the impact of lifestyle choices, and the potential outcomes of different treatments, allowing them to make more informed decisions.

With improved diagnostics and prognosis, AI has the potential to revolutionize various fields of medicine by supporting medical professionals for AI-cased DTs. The implementation of omni-channel engagement in digital health interventions and digital twins allows the flexibility of personalization that can increase and sustain patient engagement in digital health interventions and, ultimately, the quality of care and patient outcomes [40,41]. Yada et al. proposed to supplement structured cancer patient data with clinical concepts extracted from unstructured text (e.g., hospital discharge notes) using NLP techniques to extract disease and drug names and link them to medical concepts using medical dictionaries. These data included richer information on patient symptoms than tabulated diagnosis records and could be a useful supplement, further enhanced by a drug safety module that captures suspected adverse drug reactions caused by the concomitant use of anticancer drug pairs [42]. In the study by Khan et al., DTs support the monitoring of respiratory failure, accelerating necessary interventions, helping to personalize treatment plans, and providing decision support to healthcare professionals. Respiratory data were collected using an ESP32 Wi-Fi Channel State Information (CSI) sensor and statistically augmented with time-series data to generate larger synthetic respiratory data with the comparative analysis of the experimental and synthetic datasets. These data were then denoised (smoothed and filtered) and dimensionality reduced using principal component analysis (PCA). The patient's breaths per minute (BPM) were estimated from the raw patient data with an accuracy of 92.3% from the raw respiratory data and an accuracy of 89.2% and 83.7% from the combined real and synthetic respiratory datasets with the larger synthetic dataset, respectively [43]. The study by Avanzato et al. demonstrates an approach to the diagnosis and treatment of chest diseases known as Lung-DT, which is based on IoT sensors and AI algorithms and is used to establish a digital representation of a patient's respiratory health. Based on the YOLOv8 neural network, this system classifies chest X-rays into five distinct lung disease categories (normal, COVID-19, lung opacity, pneumonia, and tuberculosis) with an average accuracy of 96.8%, a precision of 92%, a recall of 97%, and an F1 score of 94%.This not only allows for the real-time monitoring of lung health through continuous data collection from IoT sensors, facilitating early diagnosis and intervention, but also the automated and objective evaluation of chest X-rays, reducing the dependence on subjective human interpretation and combining multiple data streams for personalized treatment plans [44]. Maglogiannis et al. presented the AI4Work project approach to using digital twin technology to improve work environments where AI and robots seamlessly collaborate with humans in a human–machine task division across six domains. DTs can help occupational physicians and psychologists create a sustainable work environment, e.g., by monitoring the physical and mental health of hospital staff to predict burnout symptoms. In education, AI4Work can help maintain the mental health of teachers and students and a sustainable learning environment [45]. Kuriakose et al. showed that most of the research on DTs in healthcare has been carried out since 2018, with significant contributions from the interdisciplinary fields of AI, ML, and data science. It enables data interoperability and privacy protection and primarily represents an opportunity for chronic disease management, predictive analysis, drug discovery, and surgery planning [46]. Adibi et al. have shown that sensor-driven digital twins can further extend the capabilities of location-based services (LBS) in smart environments to meet both healthcare needs and patient requirements. The broader use of wearable medical devices, AI-based health analytics, and digital twin applications will help improve personalized healthcare interventions and emergency response capabilities. This demonstrates the potential of mobile DTs with patients [47]. In telemedicine, DTs can be used to deliver personalized care plans and real-time health monitoring to remote patients, ensuring that they receive high-quality care regardless of their location [46,47]. DTs enable virtual clinical trials, where multiple scenarios can be tested in a model before actual human trials, improving design and reducing risk in developing new therapies. By simulating multiple risk factors and their interactions, digital twins can provide personalized health risk assessments, helping to identify and mitigate potential threats to a patient's health. In post-operative or chronic care settings, DTs can be used to track a patient's rehabilitation progress, providing insight into the recovery process and adjusting care plans as needed to support optimal recovery. These benefits of AI-based DTs will see them dominate the healthcare market, displacing competing solutions [48–52].

It is possible to improve patient care through various means (simulated clinical trials, disease prediction, the remote monitoring of the patient's condition, treatment progress, treatment plan adjustments), especially in the environment of smart cities and smart territories and through the wider use of 6G, blockchain (and soon maybe quantum cryptography), and the Internet of Things (IoT), as well as in the field of medical technologies, such as multiomics. From a practical point of view, this requires not only efficient validation but also seamless integration with the existing healthcare infrastructure [53–58].

AI-based DTs in preventive medicine are used to proactively monitor and manage a patient's health, with the goal of preventing diseases before they occur. By continuously analysing real-time data from sources such as wearable devices and electronic health records, DTs can identify early warning signs and subtle changes in a patient's health. Predictive analytics within a twin model can predict the likelihood of developing specific conditions based on personalized risk factors such as genetics, lifestyle, and environmental influences. This includes early signs of aging or differences in fitness (but also risk) in athletes. These insights allow medical professionals to implement targeted interventions, such as lifestyle modifications or preventive treatments, to mitigate potential health risks. DTs can simulate the effects of different preventive strategies, helping clinicians choose the most effective approach for each person. It also supports personalized health education, providing patients with tailored recommendations to maintain optimal health. Overall, AI-based DTs enable a shift from reactive to proactive healthcare, significantly increasing efforts to prevent disease and maintain health [56–60].

3.5. User Interfaces

AI-based DTs in healthcare are characterized by user interfaces that are highly intuitive and visually engaging, designed to present complex data in an easily understandable format. They often include 3D representations of the human body, where clinicians can interact with different organs or systems, gaining real-time insight into the patient's condition. Interactive dashboards display a wealth of information, from vital signs to predictive analytics, using clear graphs, tables, and color-coded alerts to highlight critical issues. Interfaces are typically responsive, adapting to different devices such as tablets or desktops, ensuring accessibility in a variety of clinical environments. Advanced features can include simulation controls that allow healthcare providers to predict the outcomes of potential treatments by manipulating variables in the digital twin. Natural language processing capabilities are often integrated, allowing users to search the system using conversational language, making the technology more accessible to non-specialists. The interfaces also emphasize data privacy and security, with multi-layered authentication and encrypted data streams to protect patient information. Collaboration tools are embedded, allowing multiple healthcare providers to simultaneously view and interact with the DT, supporting a collaborative approach to patient care. Additionally, these interfaces are designed to be highly configurable, allowing clinicians to tailor the display to their specific needs, whether focusing on a specific organ system or integrating a specific patient history. They also offer real-time updates and notifications, informing users of any significant changes in a patient's condition or new insights generated by the AI algorithms. Finally, the interfaces often include educational modules, providing training and support to healthcare providers, ensuring they can effectively use the advanced features of the digital twin [61,62].

3.6. Interoperability

Interoperability between AI-based healthcare DT systems and other eHealth systems is key to seamless data exchange and integration. These systems are typically designed to communicate with EHRs, allowing DT systems to automatically retrieve patient data such as medical history, lab results, and imaging studies. Standard protocols such as HL7 and FHIR are often used to ensure consistent and accurate data exchange between the digital twin and various healthcare systems. AI-based DT systems are also capable of integrating with clinical decision support systems (CDSSs), enabling real-time insights to be incorporated into clinical workflows. Interoperability extends to mobile devices and remote monitoring tools, enabling the continuous transfer of patient data, which is then processed and visualized in the digital twin interface. These systems often include application programming interfaces (APIs) that enable connections to other healthcare applications, facilitating the creation of a comprehensive and connected ecosystem. Data interoperability ensures that digital twins can be used across healthcare settings, from hospitals to outpatient clinics, ensuring continuity of care. They are also designed to meet regulatory standards such as HIPAA and GDPR, ensuring secure data exchange between systems and protecting patient privacy. Furthermore, AI-powered DTs can integrate with public health databases and research platforms, providing anonymized data for large-scale research and epidemiological tracking. Finally, interoperability with telehealth platforms enables the use of digital twins during remote consultations, providing clinicians with detailed patient information regardless of location [61–64].

4. Discussion

Previous studies and publications indicate that AI-generated DTs will play a key role in personalized healthcare by creating dynamic, real-time models of individual patients (or their organs), enabling precise and tailored flexible treatment plans. In a smart city environment, they will facilitate continuous monitoring and proactive health management, seamlessly integrating with digital health infrastructures such as IoT devices, telemedicine platforms, and entire eHealth systems. These AI-based models will enable the predictive diagnosis, early intervention, and optimization of healthcare resources, improving overall public health outcomes. In addition, DTs provide patients with personalized insights about their health, promoting informed decision-making and better engagement in their own care. In this way, DTs are a transformative tool in the transition towards more personalized, efficient, and proactive healthcare systems [63,64].

4.1. Current State of the Art Limitations

Healthcare DTs require diverse data from different sources, such as electronic health records, wearable devices, and genetic information. Integrating these different types of data into a coherent model remains a significant challenge. While AI can generate DTs, ensuring that they adapt (including through self-learning) in real time to reflect the changing condition of the patient remains difficult, especially in the case of unpredictable health events. Using sensitive personal data (including health data) to generate DTs raises privacy concerns. Ensuring that patient data are securely managed and compliant with regulations such as the EU GDPR is a critical limitation. The accuracy of AI-generated DTs depends on the quality and quantity of the data used. Inaccurate or incomplete data can lead to unreliable models, potentially resulting in incorrect diagnoses or health prognoses. Creating and maintaining complex DTs, especially those that simulate entire physiological systems, requires significant computing power that may not be readily available in all healthcare settings. In addition, there is no universal standard for how DTs should be built or used in healthcare, especially in the case of AI/ML, leading to inconsistencies in their development and application across organizations and systems. The use of DTs in healthcare raises ethical questions, such as who is liable if a DT makes an incorrect prediction and how to ensure equitable access to this technology. While DTs may work well at a small scale or for specific use cases, scaling these models to widespread use across patient populations is challenging due to the variability of individual health profiles. The complex algorithms behind AI-based digital twins can be difficult to interpret, making it difficult for healthcare providers to trust and act on the predictions and insights generated by these models. The regulatory framework for AI-based digital twins in healthcare is still evolving, and the approval processes, accountability, and long-term validation of these technologies are uncertain [65–67].

4.2. Directions for Further Research

Future research should focus on developing methods for the seamless (automatic) integration of different data sources, including standard formats and protocols, to improve the interoperability and consistency of DTs across healthcare systems. Exploring advanced

AI techniques for real-time data processing and dynamically updating DTs (reflecting the patient's current health status) will be critical to ensuring that these models accurately reflect the patient's current health status. Exploring ways to increase the accuracy of digital twins through improved data quality, more comprehensive datasets, and improved AI algorithms will be essential for reliable health predictions and interventions. Research should prioritize the development of robust privacy-preserving technologies such as federated learning, blockchain, and advanced encryption methods to protect sensitive patient data while enabling the generation of effective, reliable DTs. Exploring scalable, cost-effective computational methods, including the use of cloud computing and edge computing, will be critical to making DTs more accessible and feasible at all levels of healthcare. Research should delve into the ethical implications of digital twins, including establishing clear guidelines for accountability, transparency, and fairness in the use of AI-generated models in healthcare. Developing methodologies to scale digital twins to serve diverse and large patient populations, accounting for differences in genetics, lifestyle, and environmental factors, is a key area for future research. There is a need for research into explainable AI (XAI) approaches that can make digital twin models more understandable to healthcare providers, enabling them to trust and effectively use these tools in clinical decision-making. Conducting long-term studies to confirm the efficacy and safety of DTs in various clinical scenarios will be important for regulatory approval and widespread adoption. The ultimate goal is to explore how to effectively integrate DTs into existing clinical processes, including developing user-friendly interfaces and decision support systems that streamline rather than disrupt healthcare delivery [67–71].

The future of AI-based DTs is linked to emerging technologies such as ML, 6G, IoT, edge computing and augmented reality (AR), and the growing awareness of AI-based DTs among healthcare professionals and their patients. The development of legal medicine (health medicine) can have a major impact here. This future means even greater precision, speed, and accessibility of DTs, making it an integral part of eHealth and smart city and smart territory environments.

5. Conclusions

Digital society strategies in healthcare include the rapid development of digital twins (DTs) of patients and of human organs in medical research and clinical practice to more effectively, quickly, and cheaply use artificial intelligence (AI) to develop effective treatments. The evolution of digital twins from basic computer simulations to advanced, AI-based, real-time virtual representations has been driven by advances in computer science, data analysis, and data transmission and collection. Digital twins are now an essential tool in modern healthcare and are poised to play a key role in future clinical advances. Support for this form of personalized medicine is necessary due to the complex technological challenges, regulatory perspectives, and complex security and trust issues in this approach.

Supplementary Materials: The following supporting information can be downloaded at: https://www.mdpi.com/article/10.3390/app14209404/s1. Partial PRISMA 2020 checklist.

Author Contributions: Conceptualization, M.Ł., Ł.M., B.G., D.M. and A.K.-S.; methodology, M.Ł., Ł.M., B.G., D.M. and A.K.-S.; software, B.G., D.M. and A.K.-S.; validation, B.G., D.M. and A.K.-S.; formal analysis, Ł.M., B.G., D.M. and A.K.-S.; investigation, D.M. and A.K.-S.; resources, D.M. and A.K.-S.; data curation, D.M. and A.K.-S.; writing—original draft preparation, B.G., D.M. and A.K.-S.; writing—review and editing, M.Ł., Ł.M., D.M. and A.K.-S.; visualization, Ł.M., B.G., D.M. and A.K.-S.; supervision, M.Ł.; project administration, A.K.-S.; funding acquisition, M.Ł. All authors have read and agreed to the published version of the manuscript.

Funding: This research received no external funding.

Institutional Review Board Statement: Not applicable.

Informed Consent Statement: Not applicable.

Data Availability Statement: Data is contained within the article or Supplementary Material.

Conflicts of Interest: The authors declare no conflicts of interest.

References

1. Rojek, I.; Mikołajewski, D.; Dostatni, E. Digital Twins in Product Lifecycle for Sustainability in Manufacturing and Maintenance. *Appl. Sci.* **2021**, *11*, 31. [CrossRef]
2. Menaguale, O. Digital twin and cultural heritage—The future of society built on history and art. In *The Digital Twin*; Springer International Publishing: Cham, Switzerland, 2023; pp. 1081–1111.
3. Hawkinson, E. Automation in Education with Digital Twins: Trends and Issues. *Int. J. Open Distance e-Learn.* **2022**, *8*. [CrossRef]
4. Sel, K.; Osman, D.; Zare, F.; Masoumi Shahrbabak, S.; Brattain, L.; Hahn, J.O.; Inan, O.T.; Mukkamala, R.; Palmer, J.; Paydarfar, D.; et al. Building Digital Twins for Cardiovascular Health: From Principles to Clinical Impact. *J. Am. Heart Assoc.* **2024**, *13*, e031981. [CrossRef] [PubMed]
5. Meijer, C.; Uh, H.W.; El Bouhaddani, S. Digital Twins in Healthcare: Methodological Challenges and Opportunities. *J. Pers. Med.* **2023**, *13*, 1522. [CrossRef]
6. Dihan, M.S.; Akash, A.I.; Tasneem, Z.; Das, P.; Das, S.K.; Islam, M.R.; Islam, M.M.; Badal, F.R.; Ali, M.F.; Ahamed, M.H.; et al. Digital twin: Data exploration, architecture, implementation and future. *Heliyon* **2024**, *10*, e26503. [CrossRef]
7. Pesapane, F.; Rotili, A.; Penco, S.; Nicosia, L.; Cassano, E. Digital Twins in Radiology. *J. Clin. Med.* **2022**, *11*, 6553. [CrossRef]
8. Gazerani, P. Intelligent Digital Twins for Personalized Migraine Care. *J. Pers. Med.* **2024**, *13*, 1255. [CrossRef]
9. Vallée, A. Challenges and directions for digital twin implementation in otorhinolaryngology. *Eur. Arch. Oto-Rhino-Laryngol.* **2024**. [CrossRef]
10. Voigt, I.; Inojosa, H.; Dillenseger, A.; Haase, R.; Akgün, K.; Ziemssen, T. Digital Twins for Multiple Sclerosis. *Front. Immunol.* **2021**, *12*, 669811. [CrossRef]
11. Mikołajewski, D.; Rojek, I.; Kotlarz, P.; Dorożyński, J.; Kopowski, J. Personalization of the 3D-Printed Upper Limb Exoskeleton Design—Mechanical and IT Aspects. *Appl. Sci.* **2023**, *13*, 7236. [CrossRef]
12. Paul, G.; Abele, N.D.; Kluth, K. A Review and Qualitative Meta-Analysis of Digital Human Modeling and Cyber-Physical-Systems in Ergonomics 4.0. *IISE Trans. Occup. Ergon. Hum. Factors* **2021**, *9*, 111–123. [CrossRef] [PubMed]
13. Segovia, M.; Garcia-Alfaro, J. Design, Modeling and Implementation of Digital Twins. *Sensors* **2022**, *22*, 5396. [CrossRef]
14. Vallée, A. Envisioning the Future of Personalized Medicine: Role and Realities of Digital Twins. *J. Med. Internet Res.* **2024**, *26*, e50204. [CrossRef] [PubMed]
15. Vallée, A. Digital twin for healthcare systems. *Front. Digit. Health* **2023**, *5*, 1253050. [CrossRef] [PubMed]
16. Page, M.J.; McKenzie, J.E.; Bossuyt, P.M.; Boutron, I.; Hoffmann, T.C.; Mulrow, C.D.; Shamseer, L.; Tetzlaff, J.M.; Akl, E.A.; Brennan, S.E.; et al. The PRISMA 2020 statement: An updated guideline for reporting systematic reviews. *BMJ* **2021**, *372*, n71. [CrossRef]
17. Martinek, R.; Ladrova, M.; Sidikova, M.; Jaros, R.; Behbehani, K.; Kahankova, R.; Kawala-Sterniuk, A. Advanced Bioelectrical Signal Processing Methods: Past, Present and Future Approach—Part I: Cardiac Signals. *Sensors* **2021**, *21*, 5186. [CrossRef]
18. Martinek, R.; Ladrova, M.; Sidikova, M.; Jaros, R.; Behbehani, K.; Kahankova, R.; Kawala-Sterniuk, A. Advanced Bioelectrical Signal Processing Methods: Past, Present, and Future Approach—Part III: Other Biosignals. *Sensors* **2021**, *21*, 6064. [CrossRef]
19. Xiao, B.; Zhong, J.; Bao, X.; Chen, L.; Bao, J.; Zheng, Y. Digital twin-driven prognostics and health management for industrial assets. *Sci. Rep.* **2024**, *14*, 13443. [CrossRef]
20. Mikolajewska, E.; Prokopowicz, P.; Mikolajewski, D. Computational gait analysis using fuzzy logic for everyday clinical purposes–preliminary findings. *Bio-Algorithms Med-Syst.* **2017**, *13*, 37–42. [CrossRef]
21. Prokopowicz, P.; Mikołajewski, D.; Mikołajewska, E.; Kotlarz, P. Fuzzy System as an Assessment Tool for Analysis of the Health-Related Quality of Life for the People After Stroke. In Proceedings of the Artificial Intelligence and Soft Computing: 16th International Conference, ICAISC 2017, Zakopane, Poland, 11–15 June 2017; Proceedings, Part I 16. Springer International Publishing: Cham, Switzerland, 2017; Volume 10245, pp. 710–721.
22. Qiu, C.; Zhou, S.; Liu, Z.; Gao, Q.; Tan, J. Digital assembly technology based on augmented reality and digital twins: A review. *Virtual Real. Intell. Hardw.* **2019**, *1*, 597–610. [CrossRef]
23. Gürses, A.; Reddy, G.; Masrur, S.; Özdemir, Ö.; Güvenç, I.; Sichitiu, M.L.; Sahin, A.; Alkhateeb, A.; Dutta, R. Digital Twins for Supporting AI Research with Autonomous Vehicle Networks. *arXiv* **2024**, arXiv:2404.00954.
24. Zhu, Z.; Liu, C.; Xu, X. Visualisation of the digital twin data in manufacturing by using augmented reality. *Procedia Cirp* **2019**, *81*, 898–903. [CrossRef]
25. Rojek, I.; Kowal, M.; Stoic, A. Predictive compensation of thermal deformations of ball screws in cnc machines using neural networks. *Teh. Vjesn./Tech. Gaz.* **2017**, *24*, 1697–1703.
26. Wang, H.; Arulraj, T.; Ippolito, A.; Popel, A.S. From virtual patients to digital twins in immuno-oncology: Lessons learned from mechanistic quantitative systems pharmacology modeling. *NPJ Digit. Med.* **2024**, *7*, 189. [CrossRef]
27. Boje, C.; Guerriero, A.; Kubicki, S.; Rezgui, Y. Towards a semantic Construction Digital Twin: Directions for future research. *Autom. Constr.* **2020**, *114*, 103179. [CrossRef]
28. Sieczkowski, K.; Sondej, T.; Dobrowolski, A.; Olszewski, R. Autocorrelation algorithm for determining a pulse wave delay. In Proceedings of the 2016 Signal Processing: Algorithms, Architectures, Arrangements, and Applications (SPA), Poznan, Poland, 21–23 September 2016; pp. 321–326.

29. Rojek, I. Neural networks as prediction models for water intake in water supply system. In Proceedings of the Artificial Intelligence and Soft Computing–ICAISC 2008: 9th International Conference, Zakopane, Poland, 22–26 June 2008; Proceedings 9. Rutkowski, L., Tadeusiewicz, R., Zadeh, L.A., Zurada, J.M., Eds.; Springer: Berlin/Heidelberg, Gemany, 2008; pp. 1109–1119.
30. Jain, M.J.; Akbari, G.G.; Umraniya, Y.N.; Nagar, S.M.; Patel, N.R.; Shah, R.H.; Patel, C.B.; Undhad, R.P. Healthcare in the Dynamism of Metaverse After COVID-19: A Systematic Review of Literature. *Cureus* **2024**, *16*, e57554. [CrossRef]
31. Murawski, K.; Sondej, T.; Różanowski, K.; Macander, M.; Macander, L. The contactless active optical sensor for vehicled driver fatigue detection. In Proceedings of the SENSORS, 2013 IEEE, Baltimore, MD, USA, 3–6 November 2013.
32. Rojek, I. Models for Better Environmental Intelligent Management within Water Supply Systems. *Water Resour. Manag.* **2014**, *28*, 3875–3890. [CrossRef]
33. Różanowski, K.; Piotrowski, Z.; Ciołek, M. Mobile application for driver's health status remote monitoring. In Proceedings of the 2013 9th International Wireless Communications and Mobile Computing Conference (IWCMC), Sardinia, Italy, 1–5 July 2013; pp. 1738–1743.
34. Rojek, I.; Jasiulewicz-Kaczmarek, M.; Piechowski, M.; Mikołajewski, D. An Artificial Intelligence Approach for Improving Maintenance to Supervise Machine Failures and Support Their Repair. *Appl. Sci.* **2023**, *13*, 4971. [CrossRef]
35. Piras, G.; Agostinelli, S.; Muzi, F. Digital Twin Framework for Built Environment: A Review of Key Enablers. *Energies* **2024**, *17*, 436. [CrossRef]
36. Rojek, I. Neural networks as performance improvement models in intelligent CAPP systems. *Control. Cybern.* **2010**, *39*, 55–68.
37. Pawlicka, A.; Pawlicki, M.; Tomaszewska, R.; Choraś, M.; Gerlach, R. Innovative machine learning approach and evaluation campaign for predicting the subjective feeling of work-life balance among employees. *PLoS ONE* **2020**, *15*, e0232771. [CrossRef] [PubMed]
38. Rojek, I. Classifier models in intelligent CAPP systems. In *Man-Machine Interactions, Advances in Intelligent and Soft Computing*; Cyran, K.A., Kozielski, S., Peters, J.F., Stanczyk, U., Wakulicz-Deja, A., Eds.; Springer: Berlin/Heidelberg, Germany, 2009; pp. 311–319.
39. Wojcik, G.M.; Kamiński, W.A. Self-organised criticality as a function of connections' number in the model of the rat somatosensory cortex. In Proceedings of the Computational Science–ICCS 2008: 8th International Conference, Kraków, Poland, 23–25 June 2008; Proceedings, Part I 8. Springer: Berlin/Heidelberg, Germany, 2008; pp. 620–629.
40. Bhattad, P.B.; Jain, V. Artificial Intelligence in Modern Medicine—The Evolving Necessity of the Present and Role in Transforming the Future of Medical Care. *Cureus* **2020**, *12*, e8041. [CrossRef] [PubMed]
41. Blasiak, A.; Sapanel, Y.; Leitman, D.; Ng, W.Y.; De Nicola, R.; Lee, V.V.; Todorov, A.; Ho, D. Omnichannel Communication to Boost Patient Engagement and Behavioral Change With Digital Health Interventions. *J. Med. Internet Res.* **2022**, *24*, e41463. [CrossRef] [PubMed]
42. Yada, S.; Nishiyama, T.; Wakamiya, S.; Kawazoe, Y.; Imai, S.; Hori, S.; Aramaki, E. Utility analysis and demonstration of real-world clinical texts: A case study on Japanese cancer-related EHRs. *PLoS ONE* **2024**, *19*, e0310432. [CrossRef] [PubMed]
43. Khan, S.; Alzaabi, A.; Ratnarajah, T.; Arslan, T. Novel statistical time series data augmentation and machine learning based classification of unobtrusive respiration data for respiration Digital Twin model. *Comput. Biol. Med.* **2024**, *168*, 107825. [CrossRef] [PubMed]
44. Avanzato, R.; Beritelli, F.; Lombardo, A.; Ricci, C. Lung-DT: An AI-Powered Digital Twin Framework for Thoracic Health Monitoring and Diagnosis. *Sensors* **2024**, *24*, 958. [CrossRef]
45. Maglogiannis, I.; Trastelis, F.; Kalogeropoulos, M.; Khan, A.; Gallos, P.; Menychtas, A.; Panagopoulos, C.; Papachristou, P.; Islam, N.; Wolff, A.; et al. AI4Work Project: Human-Centric Digital Twin Approaches to Trustworthy AI and Robotics for Improved Working Conditions in Healthcare and Education Sectors. *Stud. Health Technol. Inform.* **2024**, *316*, 1013–1017. [CrossRef]
46. Kuriakose, S.M.; Joseph, J.; Rajimol, A.; Kollinal, R. The Rise of Digital Twins in Healthcare: A Mapping of the Research Landscape. *Cureus* **2024**, *16*, e65358. [CrossRef]
47. Adibi, S.; Rajabifard, A.; Shojaei, D.; Wickramasinghe, N. Enhancing Healthcare through Sensor-Enabled Digital Twins in Smart Environments: A Comprehensive Analysis. *Sensors* **2024**, *24*, 2793. [CrossRef]
48. Krittanawong, C.; Rogers, A.J.; Aydar, M.; Choi, E.; Johnson, K.W.; Wang, Z.; Narayan, S.M. Integrating blockchain technology with artificial intelligence for cardiovascular medicine. *Nat. Rev. Cardiol.* **2020**, *17*, 1–3. [CrossRef]
49. Wojcik, G.M.; Kamiński, W.A.; Matejanka, P. Self-organised criticality in a model of the rat somatosensory cortex. In Proceedings of the Parallel Computing Technologies: 9th International Conference, PaCT 2007, Pereslavl-Zalessky, Russia, 3–7 September 2007; Proceedings 9. Springer: Berlin/Heidelberg, Germany, 2007; pp. 468–476.
50. Sondej, T.; Piotrowski, Z.; Sawicki, K. Architecture of car measurement system for driver monitoring. In Proceedings of the Communication Technologies for Vehicles: 4th International Workshop, Nets4Cars/Nets4Trains 2012, Vilnius, Lithuania, 25–27 April 2012; Proceedings 4. Springer: Berlin/Heidelberg, Germany, 2012; pp. 68–79.
51. Kawarase, M.A., IV; Anjankar, A. Dynamics of Metaverse and Medicine: A Review Article. *Cureus* **2022**, *14*, e31232. [CrossRef] [PubMed]
52. Lewis, K.O.; Popov, V.; Fatima, S.S. From static web to metaverse: Reinventing medical education in the post-pandemic era. *Ann. Med.* **2024**, *56*, 2305694. [CrossRef] [PubMed]
53. Wang, Y.; Li, C.; Qu, L.; Cai, H.; Ge, Y. Application and challenges of a metaverse in medicine. *Front. Robot. AI* **2023**, *10*, 1291199. [CrossRef] [PubMed]

54. Matwala, K.; Shakir, T.; Bhan, C.; Chand, M. The surgical metaverse. *Cir. Esp.* **2024**, *102* (Suppl. 1), S61–S65. [CrossRef]
55. Hulsen, T. Applications of the metaverse in medicine and healthcare. *Adv. Lab. Med.* **2024**, *5*, 159–165. [CrossRef]
56. Pressman, S.M.; Borna, S.; Gomez-Cabello, C.A.; Haider, S.A.; Haider, C.; Forte, A.J. AI and Ethics: A Systematic Review of the Ethical Considerations of Large Language Model Use in Surgery Research. *Healthcare* **2024**, *12*, 825. [CrossRef]
57. Hamet, P.; Tremblay, J. Artificial intelligence in medicine. *Metabolism* **2017**, *69*, S36–S40. [CrossRef]
58. Laird, J.E.; Lebiere, C.; Rosenbloom, P.S. A Standard Model of the Mind: Toward a Common Computational Framework across Artificial Intelligence, Cognitive Science, Neuroscience, and Robotics. *AI Mag.* **2017**, *38*, 13–26. [CrossRef]
59. Jin, Z. Analysis of the Technical Principles of ChatGPT and Prospects for Pre-trained Large Models. In Proceedings of the 2023 IEEE 3rd International Conference on Information Technology, Big Data and Artificial Intelligence (ICIBA), Chongqing, China, 26–28 May 2023; pp. 1755–1758.
60. Albujeer, A.; Khoshnevisan, M. Metaverse and oral health promotion. *Br. Dent. J.* **2022**, *232*, 587. [CrossRef]
61. Ayoub, A.; Pulijala, Y. The application of virtual reality and augmented reality in Oral & Maxillofacial Surgery. *BMC Oral Health* **2019**, *19*, 238. [CrossRef]
62. Bamakan, S.M.H.; Nezhadsistani, N.; Bodaghi, O.; Qu, Q. Patents and intellectual property assets as non-fungible tokens; key technologies and challenges. *Sci. Rep.* **2022**, *12*, 2178. [CrossRef] [PubMed]
63. Guze, P.A. Using technology to meet the challenges of medical education. *Trans. Am. Clin. Climatol. Assoc.* **2015**, *126*, 260–270. [PubMed]
64. Lee, J.; Kim, H.; Kim, K.H. Effective virtual patient simulators for medical communication training: A systematic review. *Med. Educ.* **2020**, *54*, 786–795. [CrossRef] [PubMed]
65. Wong, C.H.; Siah, K.W.; Lo, A.W. Estimation of clinical trial success rates and related parameters. *Biostatistics* **2019**, *20*, 273–286. [CrossRef] [PubMed]
66. Madabushi, R.; Seo, P.; Zhao, L.; Tegenge, M.; Zhu, H. Review: Role of model-informed drug development approaches in the life cycle of drug development and regulatory decision-making. *Pharm. Res.* **2022**, *39*, 1669–1680. [CrossRef]
67. Azer, K. History and future perspectives on the discipline of quantitative systems pharmacology modeling and its applications. *Front. Physiol.* **2021**, *12*, 637999. [CrossRef]
68. Bai, J.P.F. Quantitative systems pharmacology: Landscape analysis of regulatory submissions to the US Food and Drug Administration. *CPT Pharm. Syst. Pharma.* **2021**, *10*, 1479–1484. [CrossRef]
69. Wu, C.; Lorenzo, G.; Hormuth, D.A., II; Lima, E.A.B.F.; Slavkova, K.P.; Di Carlo, J.C.; Virostko, J.; Phillips, C.M.; Patt, D.; Chung, C.; et al. Integrating mechanism-based modeling with biomedical imaging to build practical digital twins for clinical oncology. *Biophys. Rev.* **2022**, *3*, 021304. [CrossRef]
70. Arulraj, T.; Wang, H.; Ippolito, A.; Zhang, S.; Fertig, E.J.; Popel, A.S. Leveraging multi-omics data to empower quantitative systems pharmacology in immuno-oncology. *Brief. Bioinform.* **2024**, *25*, bbae131. [CrossRef]
71. Pawłowski, T.; Bokota, G.; Lazarou, G.; Kierzek, A.M.; Sroka, J. Emulation of Quantitative Systems Pharmacology models to accelerate virtual population inference in immuno-oncology. *Methods* **2024**, *223*, 118–126. [CrossRef]

applied sciences

MDPI

Article

Knitted Microwave Transmission Line for Wearable Electronics

Łukasz Januszkiewicz [1,*] and Iwona Nowak [2]

1 Institute of Electronics, Faculty of Electrical, Electronic, Computer and Control Engineering, Lodz University of Technology, 90-924 Lodz, Poland
2 Textile Institute, Faculty of Material Technologies and Textile Design, Lodz University of Technology, 90-924 Lodz, Poland; iwona.nowak@p.lodz.pl
* Correspondence: lukasz.januszkiewicz@p.lodz.pl; Tel.: +48-42-631-2614

Featured Application: The research results described in the article will find applications in modern systems that integrate electronic devices with textiles in the form of e-textiles and intelligent clothing.

Abstract: This paper introduces a novel approach to fabricating textile microwave transmission lines through knitting techniques. These textile-based transmission lines, capable of transmitting high-frequency signals between wearable transceivers and antennas, offer significant potential for the development of advanced wearable electronics. By leveraging a single technological process, our proposed method enables the creation of flexible and wearable devices. To demonstrate the feasibility of this approach, we present the design and numerical modeling of a microstrip line operating within the gigahertz frequency range. A prototype structure was fabricated and experimentally characterized, revealing moderate attenuation of less than 5 dB for frequencies below 2.5 GHz. However, a major challenge in the field of wearable electronics is the real-time applicability of such devices. Our work aims to address this challenge by providing a flexible and scalable solution for integrating wireless communication capabilities into wearable systems. Future research will focus on further optimizing the design and fabrication processes to enhance performance and minimize signal loss, ultimately enabling the realization of practical and user-friendly wearable devices.

Keywords: e-textiles; knitted fabric; wearable electronics; microwave elements

1. Introduction

Wearable systems are made of electronic devices designed to be worn on the body, often integrated into clothing or accessories. These systems leverage advancements in technology to provide a wide range of functionalities, enhancing various aspects of daily life [1]. Wearable systems can be used for health monitoring, tracking vital signs, detecting anomalies, and providing early warnings for potential health issues [2]. They can also be used for fitness and activity tracking, measuring steps, heart rate, sleep patterns, and calorie consumption to support fitness goals [3]. Additionally, wearable systems can be employed for environmental sensing, monitoring air quality, noise levels, and other environmental factors to assess exposure and inform decision-making [4]. Furthermore, wearable systems can enhance personal safety by detecting falls, emergencies, or threats, and providing immediate assistance or alerting designated contacts [5]. They can also offer augmented reality experiences, enhancing the physical world with digital information and providing immersive interfaces [6]. Wearable systems can be used for data transmission, collecting and transmitting data for analysis, research, or communication purposes [7–11]. Finally, they can provide entertainment and gaming experiences, offering interactive content and social connectivity [12]. The versatility of wearable systems enables them to cater to diverse needs and preferences, making them a growing and influential segment of the technology landscape.

Wearable electronics benefits from technology development, especially the miniaturization of integrated circuits and improvement of power density available from rechargeable batteries. Since high-frequency transceivers have become a one-chip solution, high-frequency wireless transmission has become available for wearable systems. This, however, requires textile antennas and textile transmission lines to connect them with electronic devices. The development of textile-based microwave transmission lines is essential for the realization of fully integrated wearable electronic systems, as presented in Figure 1. Microwave transmission lines serve as crucial conduits for delivering radio frequency (RF) signals from transceivers to antennas and need to have a fixed impedance (usually 50 Ω) and low signal attenuation in high-frequency ranges. In the context of wearable devices, where antennas are often fabricated from textile materials [13–16], the use of textile transmission lines offers significant advantages. By employing a fully textile-based structure, the entire system becomes inherently flexible and lightweight, ensuring comfort and ease of wearability [15–17]. This integration of textile components not only enhances the aesthetic appeal of wearable devices, but also facilitates seamless integration with clothing and other textiles, providing a more natural and unobtrusive user experience.

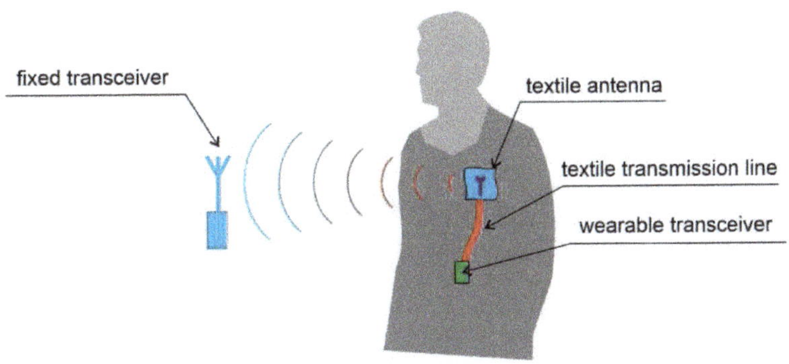

Figure 1. Schematic view of the wearable wireless system with textile antenna and textile transmission line.

Textile transmission lines can be fabricated with different technologies. The embroidery of conductive yarn into dielectric textile substrate was used in [18]; however, the limited precision of the embroidery process affected the performance of the structure. Another paper presents textile lines that were made by sewing electro-conductive strips onto a non-conductive textile substrate for the composition of textile materials [19]. This approach, however, requires a precise positioning of the upper and lower layers relative to each other and their stabilization during the stitching process. Also, screen-printing technology has been applied for textile transmission line fabrication [20]. Using this technology, the minimal feature size depends not only on the paste, the stencil, and the number of printing passes, but also on the textile substrate; it has been shown that wide geometrical tolerances are not suitable for microwave structures. Textile transmission lines were fabricated using conductive yarns and ultrasonic welding technology [21]; however, this technology influences the thickness of the dielectric layers, melting the yarns, and may not be suitable for high-frequency applications.

The technology of spacer knitted fabrics, also known as layered knitted fabrics or 3D knitted fabrics, has been known for many years and is widely used in many industries. Products manufactured in this way can be found on a daily basis in the furniture industry (as upholstery for office furniture, sofas, and headboards), automotive industry (seats, covers, filters), footwear (specialized insoles for footwear, upper part of shoes), and clothing (protective clothing, sportswear), but new development opportunities are constantly emerging for manufacturers of this type of knitted fabric [22–26]. Recently, distance knitted fabrics have been used in wound dressings, compression products, channel mats, and composite products [27–30]. Three-dimensional knitted products can be made of classic knitting yarns made of staple or filament fibers, natural, artificial or synthetic fibers, threads with special electrically conductive properties, technical threads with increased mechanical or thermal strength, or waterproof or luminescent yarns [27–31].

Spacer knitted fabrics differ from classic knitted fabrics in that they are mostly made of two layers [31–34], but there are also known works where a three-layer weft product has been obtained [35]. It is worth emphasizing that these layers are not dependent on each other and are often even separated by a certain distance, defined at the production stage. This distance can be achieved in three ways: connections through stitches, through intermediate yarn, or by scooping. The connections between the decks in 3D knitted fabric are extremely important because they determine the subsequent physical properties of the material. Depending on needs, spacing between the layers of 2 to 65 mm can be achieved [36].

Innovative knitted commodities based on weft distance knitted fabrics are created on special machines called crochet machines; flat crochet machines or cylindrical machines can be used for this purpose [37]. The spacer knitted fabric technology allows for the production of textile materials with unique properties that cannot be obtained by any other methods (low specific gravity, high elasticity, appropriate thermoregulatory properties). It is worth noting that it is possible to design a layered structure in which each layer has different properties; these properties can be completely independent of each other or even divergent (e.g., one side of the material can absorb moisture and the other be hydrophobic) [38,39]. In one preparation stage, a material is made from three or more coils, which makes the manufacturing process itself relatively cheap and simple compared to other methods of creating spatial textiles.

A single-process fabrication method for textile transmission lines offers significant advantages for wearable electronics. By seamlessly integrating conductive and insulating elements within a textile structure, this approach enhances mechanical integrity, electrical performance, and scalability. This leads to improved durability, consistent impedance matching, reduced interference, and efficient production. Furthermore, the resulting devices are highly flexible, lightweight, and comfortable to wear. This enables the creation of complex and multifunctional wearable electronic systems, such as smart clothing, health monitoring devices, and interactive garments. By seamlessly integrating transmission lines into clothing, we can create truly functional and stylish wearable devices that blend seamlessly into our everyday lives. In this paper, a microwave transmission line is presented that was fabricated with knitting technology. In one technological process, a 3D structure was fabricated that consists of a conducting strip on top of a dielectric structure that separates it from the conducting ground plane. The following sections present the transmission line design and preliminary computer simulations. This is followed by a detailed description of the knitting technology that was used for the prototype fabrication. Later, the results of measurements obtained with the prototype transmission line are presented and compared to the results of simulations. It is shown that the proposed structure can be used for microwave wearable systems that operate below 2.4 GHz ISM band.

2. Materials and Methods

2.1. Microstrip Transmission Line Model

Microwave transmission lines enable the transmission of high-frequency signals from a source to the load. In the case of wearable wireless systems, the signal source is the transmitter output and the load is the textile antenna, as presented in Figure 1. Each of these elements is characterized by its impedance, as shown for the case of the microstrip line in Figure 2, where the source of the signal a_1 is connected to port 1 of the line, while the output signal b_2 at port 2 is connected to the load (textile antenna, potentially).

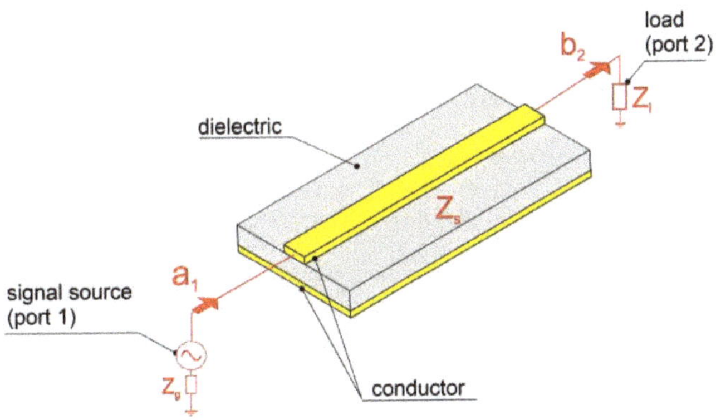

Figure 2. Microstrip transmission line impedances and signal definition.

To avoid reflection losses, the transmitter output impedance Z_g should be equal to the characteristic impedance of the line Z_s, and this should be equal to the antenna input impedance Z_l. Typically, high-frequency elements have an impedance aimed at the reference value Z_0 = 50 Ω, and any component of the system, such as the transmission line, should have a very similar value of impedance. In high-frequency systems, where unbalanced transmission lines (such as the microstrip line discussed herein) are predominantly used, the characteristic impedance is standardized to a value previously common in coaxial lines. Except for the 75 Ω cable used in television systems, the majority of coaxial cables and connections in everyday use have a 50 Ω characteristic impedance. These decisions are justified by the fact that an air-filled coaxial line has maximum power capacity at a characteristic impedance of roughly 30 Ω and minimum attenuation at a characteristic impedance of roughly 77 Ω. Therefore, a 50 Ω characteristic impedance is a trade-off between highest power capacity and least attenuation [40]. The measure of impedance matching that is used in this paper is the S_{11} element of the scattering matrix, defined in logarithmic scale (in dB) as follows (1) [41]:

$$|S_{11}| = 20 \cdot log_{10}\left(\frac{Z_s - Z_0}{Z_s + Z_0}\right), \quad (1)$$

where

Z_s is line impedance;
Z_0 is the reference impedance of the system (50 Ω).

In the case where the impedance of the elements is equal to the reference impedance Z_0, there is no signal reflection and the value of the S_{11} module approaches minus infinity. The greater the impedance mismatch, the greater the signal reflection and the value of the S_{11} module. In extreme cases (short circuit or open circuit), the value of this parameter is 0. It is desired then for the transmission line to have as small an S_{11} module as possible; however, practically, values below −10 dB are acceptable, since this corresponds to the case when the reflected signal power is 10 times smaller than the power of the inserted signal.

Another important parameter describing the transmission line is signal attenuation. Referring to Figure 2, it is the ratio of the output signal b_2 at port 2 to the input signal a_1 at port 1. It can be described by the parameter S_{21} of the scattering matrix, which is the transmittance from port 1 to port 2, and is defined in logarithmic measure as follows (2) [41]:

$$|S_{21}| = 20 \cdot log_{10}\left(\frac{b_2}{a_1}\right), \quad (2)$$

where

a_1 is the signal inserted at port 1;

b_2 is the signal leaving port 2.

The value of the S_{21} parameter should be as high as possible, ideally being 0 for a lossless line, for which $b_2 = a_1$. In practice, lines with attenuation not exceeding a few decibels are acceptable.

The microstrip line, which has been extensively studied, is a widely used form of planar transmission line due to its easy miniaturization and integration with passive and active microwave devices, as well as its ability to be made using photolithographic methods [40].

Figure 3 illustrates a microstrip line's geometry. A thin layer of conducting material, of thickness h_g, is placed on the lower surface of a dielectric material of thickness h_d and permittivity ε_r. On the upper surface of the dielectric, there is a thin strip of conducting material of width w_s and thickness h_s, while L is the length of the line.

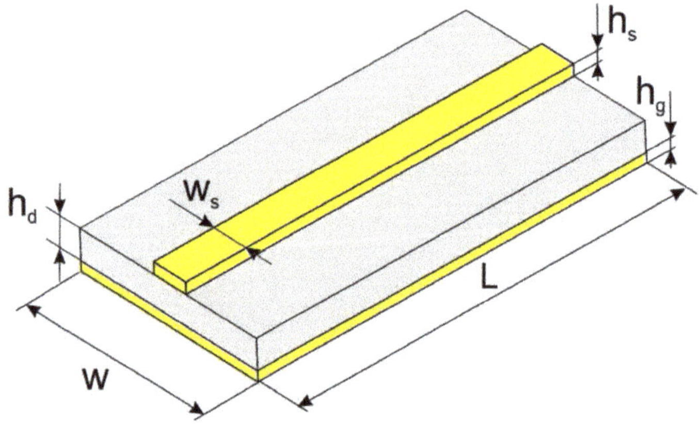

Figure 3. Microstrip transmission line dimensions.

The microstrip transmission line is an unsymmetrical quasi-TEM waveguide that requires the connection of the conducting layer (that is located on the bottom surface of the dielectric) to the ground potential, as presented in Figure 2. It is then compatible with the transceivers, which often have unsymmetric output, and with antennas with unsymmetric feeding; it is especially compatible with microstrip antennas that also have a dielectric backed with a grounded conductor layer [42].

In the literature, there are analytical relations used both for designing and analyzing the microstrip transmission line [41,42]. The first approach allows the determination of the dimensions of the line, assuming the required characteristic impedance. The second approach assumes knowledge of the structure geometry and material properties. On this basis, the line input impedance and other parameters, such as attenuation or the velocity of signal propagation, are calculated. A significant limitation of this approach is that the analytical formulas are derived assuming that the thickness of the conductive strip is many times smaller than the thickness of the dielectric. It is then possible to ignore the edge effects associated with the complex distribution of the electric field at the boundary of the strip and the dielectric. In the case of the textile transmission line presented here, such an assumption is not met because in knitting technologies it is impossible to obtain very thin conductive layers. Knowing the parameters of this technology, it was assumed that strip thickness would be approximately h_s = 0.5 mm and substrate thickness would be h_d = 3.5 mm. For this structure, h_s is 1/7 of the substrate thickness, and in such a case the analytical approach cannot be applied.

To design a knitted microstrip transmission line that operates in a 2.4 GHz band, computer simulations were applied in the CST Studio Suite program (2022.05 release). Simulations were made in a time domain using the Finite Integration Technique (FIT) [43].

This allowed us to include in the simulations the significant thickness of the strip in relation to the dielectric. Figure 4 shows a cross-sectional view of the line model in which a complex structure of knitwear is approximated as the homogenous material. The knitted dielectric substrate is modeled as a lossy dielectric and characterized by a relative permittivity ε_r and loss tangent tan (δ). The conducting surfaces at the bottom of the dielectric and the strip are modeled as perfect conductors. In this model, hexahedral mesh was used, the size of which was automatically adjusted to the geometry of the model. The shortest edge of the mesh was 0.1 mm (in the region of the ground conductor) and the largest was 2.5 mm (in the free space region). The distribution of the module of electric field intensity in this structure is presented in Figure 5. In this case, the complex nature of this distribution in the area of the side walls of the strip, near the dielectric, is visible.

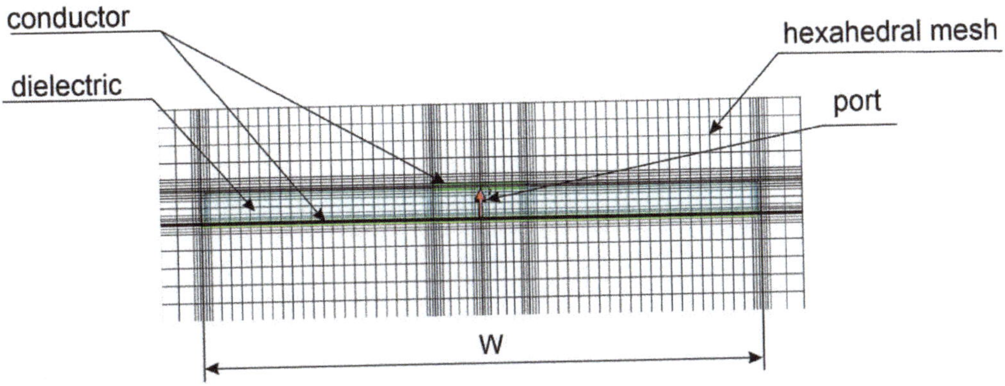

Figure 4. Numerical model of microstrip transmission line (cross-section).

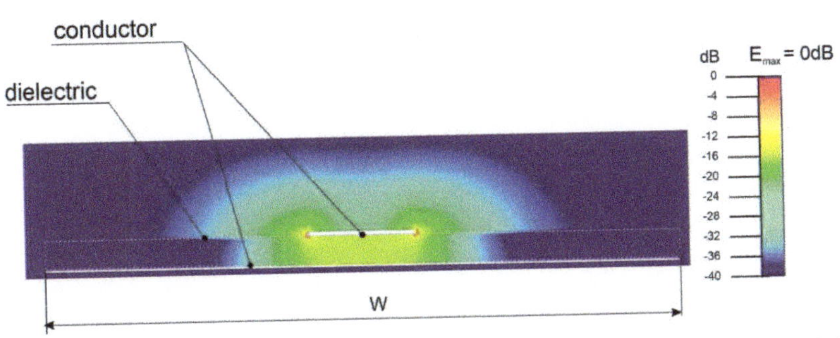

Figure 5. The electric field intensity in the cross-section of the transmission line model at 2.5 GHz.

The geometrical parameters of the microstrip line were selected considering the limitations of the available equipment and the knitting technology employed for its fabrication. This necessitated the use of a 3.5 mm thick dielectric substrate. The strip height that could be obtained in the considered technology was equal to 0.5 mm, while its width was chosen to be significantly smaller than the substrate; however, this parameter could not be varied over a wide range. The final geometrical parameters of the line that could be realized using the available equipment are presented in Table 1.

To investigate the behavior of the textile transmission line, a series of numerical simulations were conducted using a transmission line model. Given the inherent uncertainty in the electrical properties of textile substrates, a parametric approach was adopted to explore the impact of varying relative permittivity (ε_r) and loss tangent (tan (δ)) on the line's performance. Simulations were carried out for ε_r values ranging from 1 to 4 and tan (δ) values from 0 to 0.2. For clarity, only the results corresponding to three representative values of each parameter are presented in Figures 6 and 7. Figure 6 illustrates the S_{11} parameter for different ε_r values and tan (δ) = 0.05, while Figure 7 depicts the S_{21} parameter for varying tan (δ) values and ε_r = 1.5. The comprehensive simulation dataset was instrumental in identifying the optimal material properties for the fabricated prototype line. By comparing the simulation results to the experimental measurements, the actual values of ε_r and tan (δ) were determined.

Table 1. Parameters of the transmission line.

Parameter	Value (mm)
Line length, L	115
Line width, W	65
Strip width, W_s	11
Thickness of dielectric, h_d	3.5
Thickness of the strip, h_s	0.5
Thickness of the ground plane, h_g	0.2

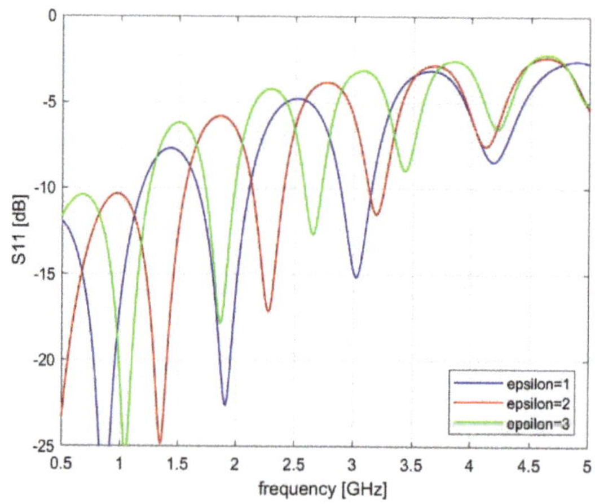

Figure 6. S_{11} obtained from simulations for tan (δ) = 0.05 and various ε_r parameters.

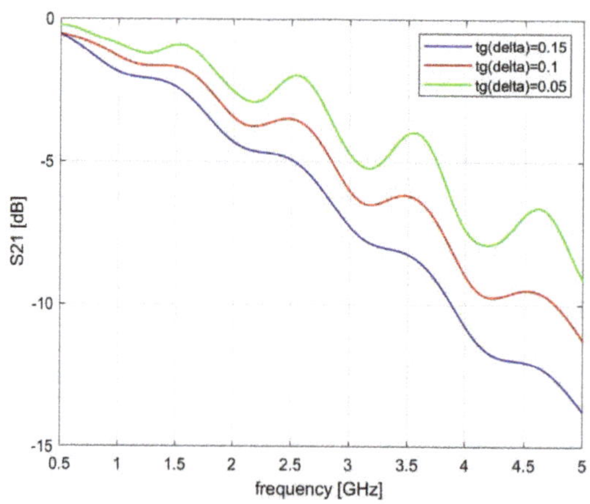

Figure 7. S_{21} obtained from simulations for ε_r = 1.5 and various values of the tg(δ) parameter.

2.2. Microstrip Transmission Line Fabrication Technology

To fabricate the knitted transmission line, weft spacer knitted fabric technology was selected, as it provides the possibility of making the product using a small amount of raw material, directly from the coil, bypassing the processes of yarn preparation before production, such as rewinding or weaving. A model of 3D weft knitted fabric is made of two outer layers made with a basic weave (usually shaker stitch), bonded with a monofilament thread (separates the outer layers). The monofilament thread does not form loops: it is knitted in the form of take-up, keeping the outer layers at a distance from each other. The construction of the classic spacer knitted fabric is shown in Figure 8.

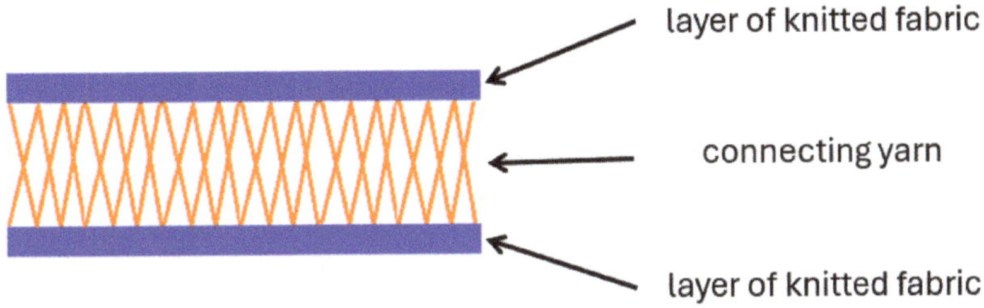

Figure 8. Spacer knitted fabric structure.

The microstrip transmission line was made using spacer weft knitting technology on a Mayer & Cie cylindrical crochet machine (Mayer & Cie, Albstadt, Germany), type OVJA 36. The machine had a needle number of 20 (E20), a cylinder with a diameter of 30 inches, and a needle pitch of 1.27 mm (Figure 9).

Figure 9. The Mayer & Co knitting machine used in the work to create a transmission line.

This knitted fabric consists of two outer layers made of basic weaves and an inner layer made of sections of threads running between the outer layers of the knitted fabric.

The outer layers of the knitted fabric are created with a plain stitch, using two types of yarns: Shieldex Z100HB yarn (Shieldex, Bremen, Germany) with a linear mass of 117/17 dtex (transmission path and mass plane) and polypropylene monofilament with a diameter of 0.08 mm (the remaining area of the upper layer of the knitted fabric surrounding the electroconductive path). The inner layer, called the spacer, is made of monofilament polypropylene thread. The selection of materials for the textile transmission line was primarily influenced by the capabilities of the crochet machine. This machine, typically used for producing flat structures, was adapted to create 3D structures by adjusting the cylinder position. The needle count of the machine determined the suitable yarn diameter, with 0.08 mm threads proving optimal for smooth operation and precise stitch formation. Extensive experimentation with different yarn types revealed that this particular diameter minimized yarn stress, preventing errors in the knitted fabric. While the type of yarn did not significantly affect production capacity, factors such as machine speed and weave pattern influenced the overall performance.

All the component weaves forming the spacer knitted fabric are shown in Figure 10, while Figure 11 shows the produced sample taken using an OPTA-TECH SN series stereoscopic microscope (OPTA-TECH, London, UK) in cooperation with the Opta View Version 4.3.0.6001 software. A spatial knitted fabric in the form of the so-called sleeve was obtained. The parameters of the knitted fabric forming the transmission line are presented in Table 2.

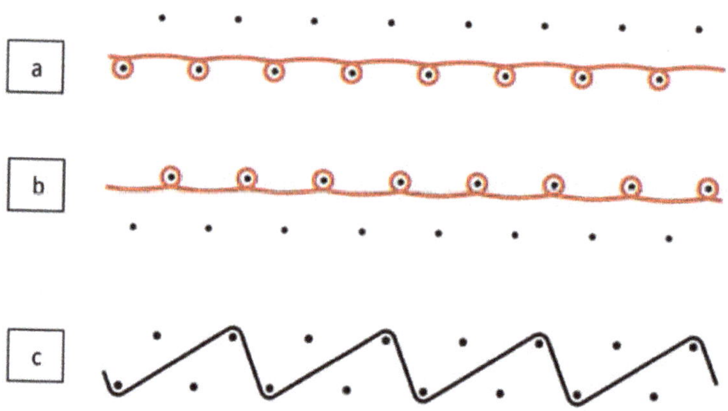

Figure 10. Spacer knitted weaves: (**a**,**b**) plain stitch; (**c**) monofilament providing distance (not forming the knitted mesh).

Table 2. Parameters of the knitted fabric forming the transmission line.

Parameter	Value
Fabric Thickness (mm)	0.47
Surface Mass, Mp (g/m^2)	423
Course Density, Pr (course/10 cm)	202
Wale Density, Pk (wales/10 cm)	94
Loop Shape Factor, C	0.46

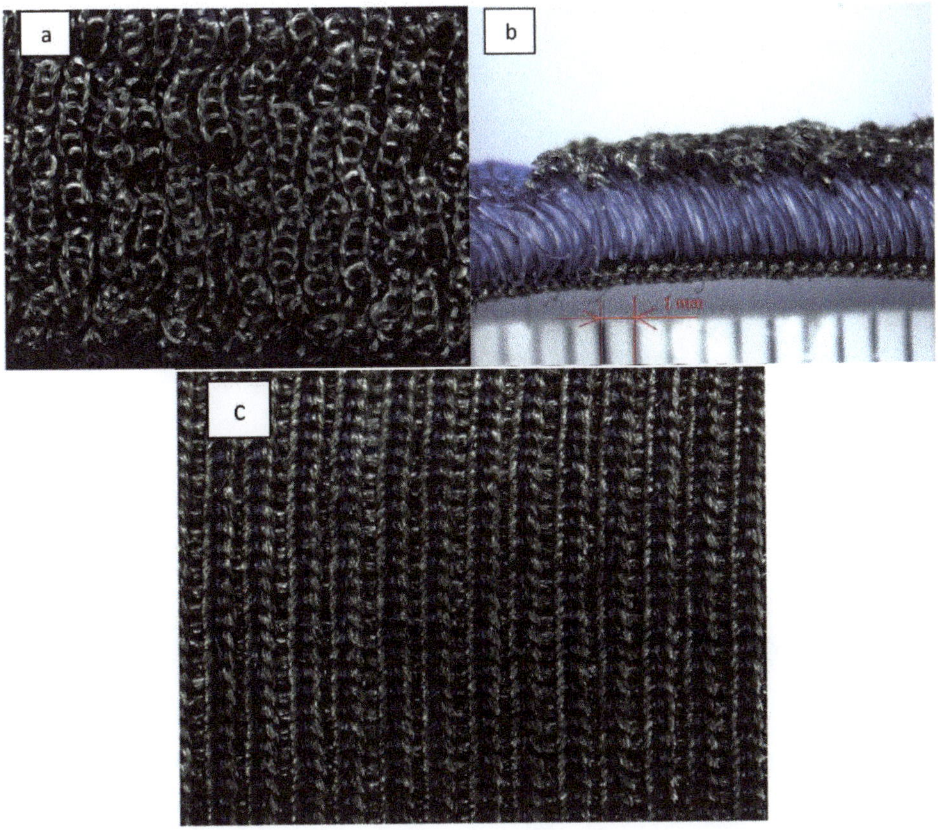

Figure 11. The knitted fabric: (**a**) top view showing the transmission path weave (top of the sample); (**b**) cross-section; (**c**) view of the bottom layer (ground plane).

3. Results

The technology described above enabled the fabrication of a prototype textile microstrip line. A visual representation of the prototype line is provided in Figure 12. This prototype was subsequently employed in the next phase of research to conduct measurements of the transmission line's characteristic parameters. For this purpose, a measurement setup, illustrated in Figure 13, was utilized. This comprised a vector network analyzer (Anritsu MS4647B, Atsugi-shi, Japan) and measurement probes in the form of open-ended coaxial cables (Huber+Suhner Multiflex 86, Herisau, Switzerland), which were connected to the transmission line for testing. Prior to the measurements, the analyzer was calibrated, and the calibration plane was shifted to the connection point between the coaxial probe and the tested line.

Using the measurement setup described above, the parameters characterizing the textile transmission line were measured. Figure 14 presents the measurement results of the S_{11} parameter module (in red). The corresponding simulation result (in blue), which exhibited the closest match, is superimposed on the measurement data. The best agreement was obtained for simulations with a substrate relative permittivity of $\varepsilon_r = 1.5$ and a dielectric loss tangent of $\tan(\delta) = 0.15$. Figure 15 shows the measurement results for the S_{21} parameter of the prototype line. In this case, as well, the closest simulation result, obtained for the same material parameters as for the S_{11} parameter, was superimposed on the measurement data.

(a) (b)

Figure 12. Prototype of the knitted transmission line: (a) top side; (b) bottom side (ground plane).

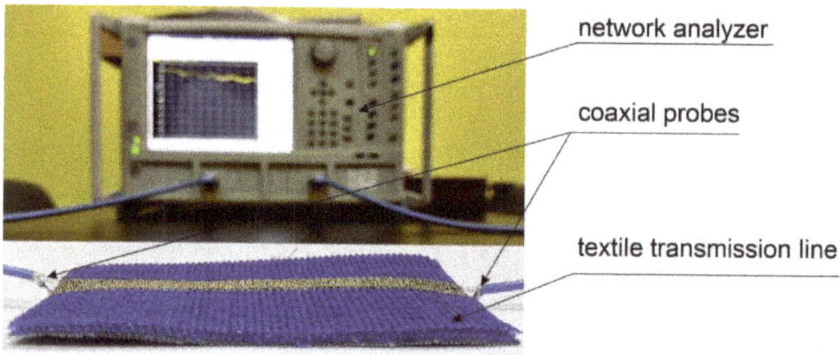

Figure 13. Measurement setup for transmission line characterization.

The transmission line presented in our paper is intended for wearable applications, where it may be subjected to bending due to the curvature of the human body. While twisting is less likely, bending along the longitudinal axis is a significant concern. To evaluate this, we conducted bending tests on a cylindrical surface with a 100 mm radius. The experimental setups for convex and concave bending are depicted in Figures 16 and 17. A Styrofoam form was utilized to introduce deformation into the prototype textile line. This choice of material was based on the need to minimize measurement artifacts. Styrofoam's electrical properties (at 3 GHz, $\varepsilon_r = 1.03$, $\tan(\delta) = 0.0001$ [40]), being comparable to those of air, ensured that the fixture would have a negligible impact on the measured parameters. The results of these measurements, specifically the impact on the S_{11} and S_{21} parameters, are presented in Figures 18 and 19.

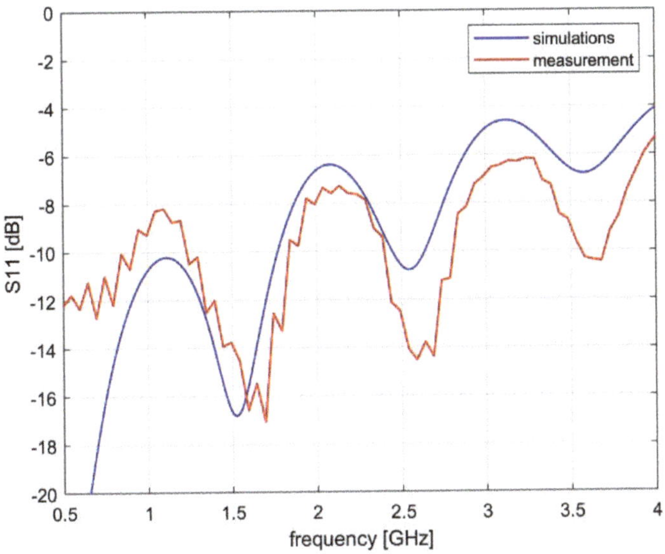

Figure 14. S_{11} obtained from measurements of prototype line compared with results of simulations for ε_r = 1.5 and tg(δ) = 1.5.

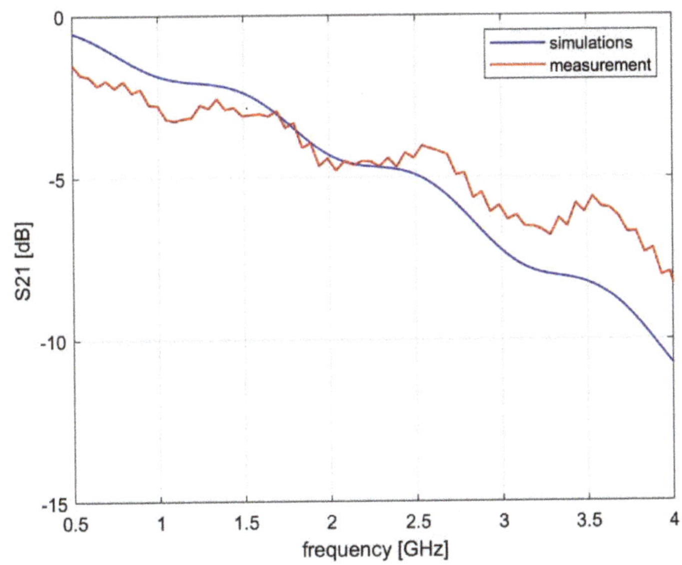

Figure 15. S_{21} obtained from measurements of prototype line compared with results of simulations for ε_r = 1.5 and tg(δ) = 1.5.

Air permeability is a crucial characteristic of wearable devices as it ensures user comfort. The developed prototype line underwent air permeability testing. The air permeability of the knitted structure shown in this work gave an average result of 861 $dm^3/(m^2{\cdot}s)$. This is similar to other knitted fabrics of this kind. Several knitted fabrics with similar structural parameters (tightness, surface mass, thickness) made of polyester and cotton yarns were analyzed, and average results were obtained for them in the range of 814–901 $dm^3/(m^2{\cdot}s)$.

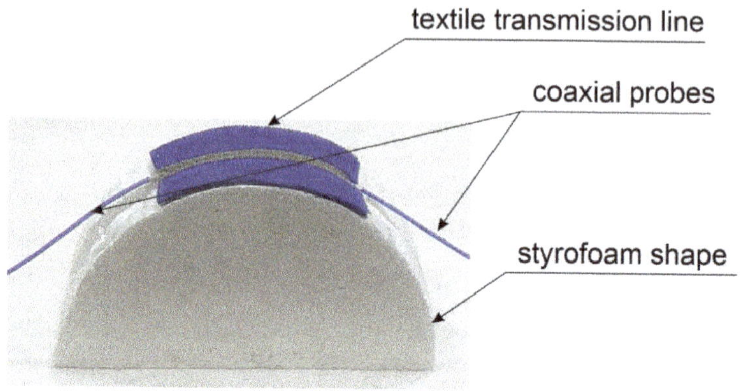

Figure 16. The experimental setup for convex bending.

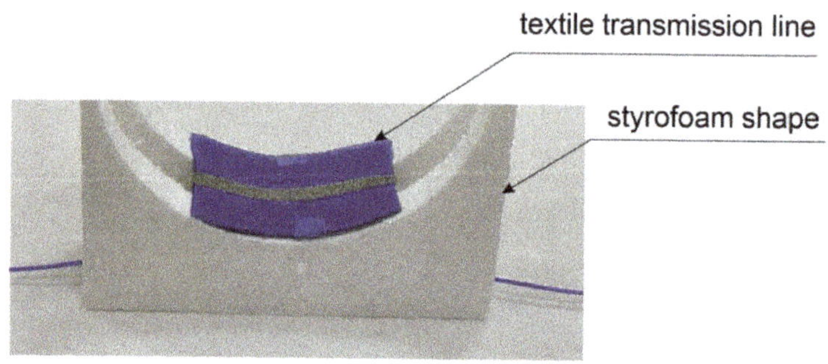

Figure 17. The experimental setup for concave bending.

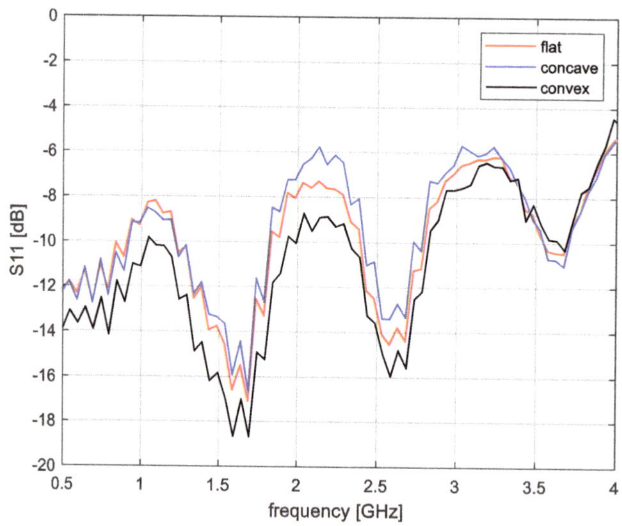

Figure 18. Measurement results of S_{11} parameter for bent transmission lines compared with a straight line.

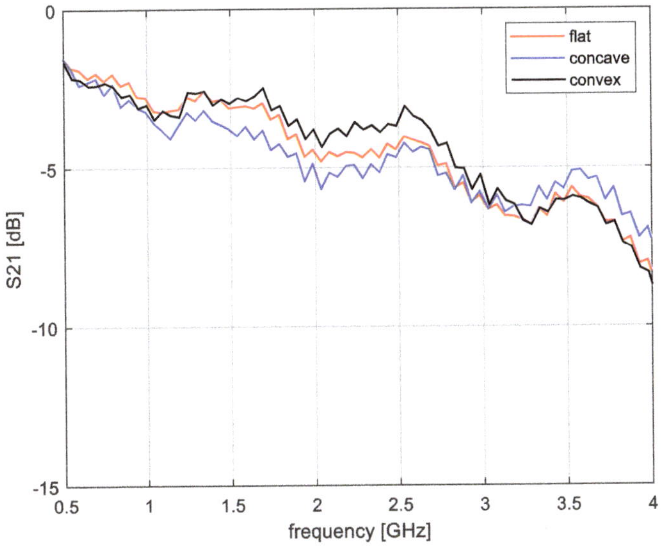

Figure 19. Measurement results of S_{21} parameter for bent transmission lines compared with a straight line.

4. Discussion

Based on the analysis of the measurement results for the prototype line, it can be concluded that the textile technology that was used in this research enabled the fabrication of a transmission line whose parameters allow its application in the transmission of high-frequency signals in the 2.4 GHz band. In this frequency range, the line exhibits good impedance, matching a reference impedance of $Z_0 = 50\ \Omega$. For the center frequency of this band, the value of the S_{11} parameter does not exceed -10 dB.

The developed transmission line section, 115 mm in length, exhibits an acceptable level of signal attenuation in the considered band (i.e., frequencies below 2.5 GHz). The value of the S_{21} parameter is not less than -5 dB. This may result both from dielectric losses in the textile insulating material and from the limited conductance of the conductive fiber layers. Dielectric loss is a crucial factor affecting the performance of high-frequency transmission lines. Excessive dielectric loss can result in significant signal attenuation and distortion, particularly at higher frequencies. To mitigate these effects, several strategies can be employed, including the careful selection of low-loss textile materials, the optimization of transmission line design, and the utilization of precise fabrication techniques.

Previous research has explored various approaches to address dielectric losses in textile-based transmission lines. These include the use of low-loss dielectric materials, the optimization of line geometries, and the development of advanced fabrication techniques. However, at this stage of the research, the transmission line is not optimized in terms of selecting materials with the lowest possible loss. In further research, it will be verified to what extent the selection of fiber material will affect the line attenuation and what effect the parameters of the technological process (such as the density of spacer fibers) have on this phenomenon.

In a simplified numerical model of the line, as shown in Figure 7, the attenuation of the line (S_{21} parameter) depends on the dielectric losses of the insulating material. Assuming a tan (δ) value of 0.15, the simulation results were found to be in agreement with the measurement results. This value can be adopted for the design of lines of this type in order to account for energy losses in both the dielectric and in the conductive layers.

As shown in Figures 14 and 15, a fairly good agreement between the simulation and measurement results was obtained. The slight discrepancies between them may be attributed to the influence of the open-ended coaxial probe on the measurement result. This point introduces a discontinuity in the measurement setup structure and can be a source of additional errors. Nevertheless, the overall good agreement between the measurements and simulations indicates that the proposed method allows for the effective determination of material parameters of a complex structure such as spacer fabric. The simplification of the composition of fibers and air to a homogeneous material characterized by permittivity and dielectric loss appears to be a sufficient approximation for engineering applications.

Figures 18 and 19 demonstrate that bending the transmission line with a radius of curvature of 100 mm has a negligible impact on its electrical performance. Interestingly, when using a convex fixture, a minor improvement in impedance matching and a reduction in attenuation were observed at 2.4 GHz. This phenomenon could be attributed to a slight reduction in the thickness of the dielectric substrate. These results indicate that further optimization of the transmission line design by varying the dielectric substrate thickness may yield beneficial outcomes.

Further work on textile transmission lines of the considered type will focus on the selection of materials and process parameters to minimize line attenuation. Studies will also be conducted to develop a method of connecting the considered type of line to a coaxial guide in order to facilitate the realization of connections for both measurement purposes and the implementation of target microwave systems.

5. Conclusions

The presented research demonstrates the feasibility of knitting technology for fabricating textile-based transmission lines suitable for high-frequency applications in the 2.4 GHz band. The fabricated line exhibits good impedance matching and acceptable attenuation levels, despite the inherent dielectric losses associated with textile materials. The simulation results align well with the measured performance, validating the proposed modeling approach. Importantly, bending the line with a 100 mm radius of curvature has a minimal impact on its electrical characteristics.

The proposed method offers a unique advantage by eliminating the need for post-processing techniques like sewing or gluing, thereby simplifying the manufacturing process and enhancing the overall reliability of fabricated structures. The precise control over line geometry and the close agreement between theoretical predictions and experimental results underscore the potential of this approach.

However, challenges remain in terms of scalability, cost-effectiveness, and long-term durability. Future research will focus on addressing these limitations by exploring advanced knitting techniques, optimizing material selection, and implementing robust packaging strategies. Additionally, investigating the integration of these lines with various antenna types and developing techniques for efficient signal transmission and reception will be crucial for practical applications.

Author Contributions: Conceptualization, I.N. and Ł.J.; methodology, I.N. and Ł.J.; software, Ł.J.; validation, I.N. and Ł.J.; formal analysis, I.N. and Ł.J.; investigation, I.N. and Ł.J.; resources, I.N.; data curation, I.N. and Ł.J.; writing—original draft preparation, I.N. and Ł.J.; writing—review and editing, I.N. and Ł.J.; visualization, I.N. and Ł.J.; supervision, Ł.J.; project administration, I.N. All authors have read and agreed to the published version of the manuscript.

Funding: This research received no external funding.

Institutional Review Board Statement: Not applicable.

Informed Consent Statement: Not applicable.

Data Availability Statement: The original contributions presented in the study are included in the article, further inquiries can be directed to the corresponding author.

Conflicts of Interest: The authors declare no conflicts of interest.

References

1. Pekas, D.; Radaš, J.; Baić, M.; Barković, I.; Čolakovac, I. The Use of Wearable Monitoring Devices in Sports Sciences in COVID Years (2020–2022): A Systematic Review. *Appl. Sci.* **2023**, *13*, 12212. [CrossRef]
2. Escobar-Linero, E.; Muñoz-Saavedra, L.; Luna-Perejón, F.; Sevillano, J.L.; Domínguez-Morales, M. Wearable Health Devices for Diagnosis Support: Evolution and Future Tendencies. *Sensors* **2023**, *23*, 1678. [CrossRef]
3. Seçkin, A.Ç.; Ateş, B.; Seçkin, M. Review on Wearable Technology in Sports: Concepts, Challenges and Opportunities. *Appl. Sci.* **2023**, *13*, 10399. [CrossRef]
4. Bernasconi, S.; Angelucci, A.; Aliverti, A. A Scoping Review on Wearable Devices for Environmental Monitoring and Their Application for Health and Wellness. *Sensors* **2022**, *22*, 5994. [CrossRef]
5. Newaz, N.T.; Hanada, E. The Methods of Fall Detection: A Literature Review. *Sensors* **2023**, *23*, 5212. [CrossRef]
6. Ibiş, A.; Çakici Alp, N. Augmented Reality and Wearable Technology for Cultural Heritage Preservation. *Sustainability* **2024**, *16*, 4007. [CrossRef]
7. Sun, X.; Zhao, C.; Li, H.; Yu, H.; Zhang, J.; Qiu, H.; Liang, J.; Wu, J.; Su, M.; Shi, Y.; et al. Wearable Near-Field Communication Sensors for Healthcare: Materials, Fabrication and Application. *Micromachines* **2022**, *13*, 784. [CrossRef]
8. Jing, L.; Zhou, J.; Zhang, Z. Wearable Sensing Devices and Technology. *Electronics* **2024**, *13*, 2951. [CrossRef]
9. Liu, L.; Cai, Y.; Jiang, X.; Wang, J.; Wang, C.; Duan, J. A Versatile Surface Micro Structure Design Strategy for Porous-Based Pressure Sensors to Enhance Electromechanical Performance. *Chem. Eng. J.* **2024**, *490*, 151529. [CrossRef]
10. Cao, P.; Wang, C.; Niu, S.; Han, Z.; Liu, L.; Duan, J. An Ultrasensitive Flexible Force Sensor with Nature-Inspired Minimalistic Architecture to Achieve a Detection Resolution and Threshold of 1 mN for Underwater Applications. *Mater. Sci. Eng. R Rep.* **2024**, *161*, 100862. [CrossRef]
11. Wu, H.; Wang, C.; Liu, L.; Liu, Z.; He, J.; Zhang, C.; Duan, J. Bioinspired Stretchable Strain Sensor with High Linearity and Superhydrophobicity for Underwater Applications. *Adv. Funct. Mater.* **2024**, 2413552. [CrossRef]
12. Nalepa, G.J.; Kutt, K.; Giżycka, B.; Jemioło, P.; Bobek, S. Analysis and Use of the Emotional Context with Wearable Devices for Games and Intelligent Assistants. *Sensors* **2019**, *19*, 2509. [CrossRef]
13. Del-Rio-Ruiz, R.; Lopez-Garde, J.-M.; Legarda, J. Planar Textile Off-Body Communication Antennas: A Survey. *Electronics* **2019**, *8*, 714. [CrossRef]
14. Tsolis, A.; Bakogianni, S.; Angelaki, C.; Alexandridis, A.A. A Review of Clothing Components in the Development of Wearable Textile Antennas: Design and Experimental Procedure. *Sensors* **2023**, *23*, 3289. [CrossRef]
15. Veeramuthu, L.; Cho, C.-J.; Venkatesan, M.; Kumar, G.R.; Hsu, H.-Y.; Zhuo, B.-X.; Kau, L.-J.; Chung, M.-A.; Lee, W.-Y.; Kuo, C.-C. Muscle Fibers Inspired Electrospun Nanostructures Reinforced Conductive Fibers for Smart Wearable Optoelectronics and Energy Generators. *Nano Energy* **2022**, *101*, 107592. [CrossRef]
16. Sharma, D.; Kumar, S.; Tiwari, R.N.; Choi, H.C.; Kim, K.W. On Body and off Body Communication Using a Compact Wideband and High Gain Wearable Textile Antenna. *Sci. Rep.* **2024**, *14*, 14493. [CrossRef]
17. Wagih, M.; Weddell, A.S.; Beeby, S. Overcoming the Efficiency Barrier of Textile Antennas: A Transmission Lines Approach. *Proceedings* **2019**, *32*, 18. [CrossRef]
18. Moradi, B.; Fernández-García, R.; Gil, I. E-Textile Embroidered Metamaterial Transmission Line for Signal Propagation Control. *Materials* **2018**, *11*, 955. [CrossRef]
19. Leśnikowski, J. Effect of Cyclical Bending and Rubbing on the Characteristic Impedance of Textile Signal Lines. *Materials* **2021**, *14*, 6013. [CrossRef]
20. Locher, I.; Tröster, G. Screen-Printed Textile Transmission Lines. *Text. Res. J.* **2007**, *77*, 837–842. [CrossRef]
21. Atalay, O.; Kalaoglu, F.; Kursun Bahadir, S. Development of Textile-Based Transmission Lines Using Conductive Yarns and Ultrasonic Welding Technology for e-Textile Applications. *J. Eng. Fibers Fabr.* **2019**, *14*, 155892501985660. [CrossRef]
22. Gries, T.; Bettermann, I.; Blaurock, C.; Bündgens, A.; Dittel, G.; Emonts, C.; Gesché, V.; Glimpel, N.; Kolloch, M.; Grigat, N.; et al. Aachen technology overview of 3D textile materials and recent innovation and applications. *Appl. Compos. Mater.* **2022**, *29*, 43–64. [CrossRef]
23. Li, N.-W.; Yick, K.-L.; Yu, A.; Ning, S. Mechanical and Thermal Behaviours of Weft-Knitted Spacer Fabric Structure with Inlays for Insole Applications. *Polymers* **2022**, *14*, 619. [CrossRef]
24. Asayesh, A.; Ehsanpour, S.; Latifi, M. Prototyping and analyzing physical properties of Weft knitted spacer fabrics as a substitute for wound dressings. *J. Text. Inst.* **2021**, *110*, 1–11. [CrossRef]
25. Chen, F.; Wang, J.; Gao, S.; Ning, X.; Yan, P.; Tian, M. An experimental study on the vibration behavior and the physical properties of weft-knitted spacer fabrics manufactured using flat knitting technology. *Text. Res. J.* **2023**, *93*, 615–631. [CrossRef]
26. Hamedi, M.; Salimi, P.; Jamshidi, N. Improving cushioning properties of a 3D weft knitted spacer fabric in a novel design with NiTi monofilaments. *J. Ind. Text.* **2020**, *49*, 1389–1410. [CrossRef]
27. Wardiningsih, W.; Rudy, R.; Permana, M.; Sinuraya, D.; Munandar, T. Study of Structural Parameters of Weft Knitted Spacer Fabrics on Wound Dressing Performance. *Text. Leather Rev.* **2024**, *7*, 644–669. [CrossRef]
28. Kowalski, K.; Włodarczyk, B. Modification of External Layers of Distance Knitted Fabrics with Elastomeric Threads and Its Effect on the Structural Parameters. *Fibres Text. East. Eur.* **2012**, *20*, 62–66.
29. Pieklak, K.; Mikołajczyk, Z. Strength Tests of 3D Warp-Knitted Composites with the Use of the Thermovision Technique. *Fibres Text. East. Eur.* **2011**, *19*, 100–105.

30. Mikołajczyk, Z.; Szałek, A. Analysis of newborn thermal comfort in a textile incubator. *J. Text. Inst.* **2021**, *113*, 1521–1530. [CrossRef]
31. Zhao, T.; Long, H.; Yang, T.; Liu, Y. Cushioning properties of weft-knitted spacer fabrics. *Text. Res. J.* **2018**, *88*, 1628–1640. [CrossRef]
32. Kumar, N.M.; Thilagavathi, G.; Periasamy, S. Development and characterization of warp knitted spacer fabrics for helmet comfort liner application. *J. Ind. Text.* **2020**, *51*, 152808372093921.
33. Yu, A.; Sukigara, S.; Shirakihara, M. Effect of Silicone Inlaid Materials on Reinforcing Compressive Strength of Weft-Knitted Spacer Fabric for Cushioning Applications. *Polymers* **2021**, *13*, 3645. [CrossRef]
34. Chen, C.; Du, Z.; Yu, W.; Dias, T. Analysis of physical properties and structure design of weft-knitted spacer fabric with high porosity. *Text. Res. J.* **2018**, *88*, 59–68. [CrossRef]
35. Włodarczyk, B.; Kowalski, K. Technology and Properties of Distance Five-layered Double-Weft-Knitted Fabrics with Elastomeric Threads. *Fibres Text. East. Eur.* **2014**, *22*, 68–73.
36. Dejene, B.; Abtew, M.; Birlie, A.; Woldeab, M. Three-dimensional (3D) knitted spacer textile materials for advanced healthcare solutions: A comprehensive review. *J. Ind. Text.* **2024**, *54*, 15280837241290169. [CrossRef]
37. Dejene, B.; Gudayu, A. Exploring the potential of 3D woven and knitted spacer fabrics in technical textiles: A critical review. *J. Ind. Text.* **2024**, *54*, 15280837241253614. [CrossRef]
38. Huang, Y.; Song, X. Study on an innovative knitting technology of spacer fabrics and the low-velocity impact properties of its composites. *Text. Res. J.* **2023**, *93*, 004051752211280. [CrossRef]
39. Kopias, K. *Technology of Weft Knitted Fabrics*; Lodz University of Technology Publishing House: Lodz, Poland, 2013.
40. Pozar, D.M. *Microwave Engineering*, 4th ed.; John Wiley & Sons Inc.: Hoboken, NJ, USA, 2012; pp. 147–150.
41. Gustrau, F. *RF and Microwave Engineering: Fundamentals of Wireless Communications*; John Wiley & Sons Ltd.: Chichester, UK, 2012; pp. 157–162.
42. Balanis, C.A. *Antenna Theory Analysis and Design*, 4th ed.; John Wiley & Sons Inc.: Hoboken, NJ, USA, 2016; pp. 783–815.
43. Schuhmann, R.; Weiland, T. Recent Advances in Finite Integration Technique for High Frequency Applications. In *Scientific Computing in Electrical Engineering*; Schilders, W.H.A., ter Maten, E.J.W., Houben, S.H.M.J., Eds.; Mathematics in Industry; Springer: Berlin/Heidelberg, Germany, 2004; Volume 4. [CrossRef]

applied sciences

MDPI

Article

Comparative Analysis of Analogue and Digital Methods for Magnetic Flux Estimation in the Core of a Medium-Voltage Voltage Transformer Operating Under Ferroresonance Conditions

Piotr Suchorolski [1], Adam Smolarczyk [1], Piotr Łukaszewski [1], Sebastian Łapczyński [1], Michał Szulborski [1], Maciej Owsiński [2], Artur Łukaszewski [1], Łukasz Kolimas [1] and Łukasz Nogal [1,*]

1 Electrical Power Engineering Institute, Warsaw University of Technology, 75 Koszykowa Street, 00-662 Warsaw, Poland; piotr.suchorolski.dokt@pw.edu.pl (P.S.); adam.smolarczyk@pw.edu.pl (A.S.); piotr.lukaszewski.dokt@pw.edu.pl (P.Ł.); sebastian.lapczynski.dokt@pw.edu.pl (S.Ł.); michal.szulborski.dokt@pw.edu.pl (M.S.); lukasz.kolimas@pw.edu.pl (Ł.K.)

2 The Institute of Power Engineering—National Research Institute, 8 Mory Street, 01-330 Warsaw, Poland; maciej.owsinski@ien.com.pl

* Correspondence: lukasz.nogal@pw.edu.pl

Abstract: The main objective of the research described in the article was to determine the following: Is it possible to estimate the magnetic flux linkage in the core of a voltage transformer using analogue or digital methods? Will it be possible to estimate it approximately both in the normal state and in the state of deep core saturation (ferroresonant state)? The research aimed to identify the advantages and disadvantages of both proposed estimation methods. As part of the research described in this paper, a simulation model was developed and executed in the MATLAB/Simulink environment to generate a series of secondary voltage and flux waveforms in voltage transformers. The secondary voltage and flux waveforms were modelled under ground fault conditions, initiating ferroresonance oscillations in the medium-voltage network. To determine the associated flux from the simulated secondary voltages of the voltage transformers, an analogue integration circuit, a voltage analogue input circuit and a numerical integration algorithm with offset elimination were developed and implemented in an STM32 microcontroller. The obtained reference flux waveforms were used to verify the accuracy of the estimation of flux waveforms obtained using the analogue and digital methods. As a result, it was determined that both methods allow for a relatively accurate estimation of the periodic component of the magnetic flux. It also presented how both methods respond to the presence of slowly changing (aperiodic) components. Possible applications were proposed in order to create an innovative criterion for detecting ferroresonance oscillations.

Keywords: magnetic flux; voltage transformer; ferroresonance; medium voltage networks; integrating circuit; trapezoidal integration method; STM32 microcontroller; MATLAB/Simulink

1. Introduction

Despite the increasing usage of voltage and current sensors in today's electric power industry, conventional inductive voltage transformers are still widely used. The use of ferromagnetic-core voltage transformers means that ferroresonance in medium-voltage networks is still an ongoing problem.

Ferroresonance of (parallel) currents, occurring mostly in medium-voltage networks with an isolated neutral point, is characterised by the appearance of sub-harmonics, harmonics or, in general, non-linear zero-order voltage oscillations. For this reason, the most common methods of detecting ferroresonance in medium-voltage networks are based on the observation of the secondary neutral voltage $3u_0$ of the transformer. This voltage can be measured in an open triangle voltage transformer system or calculated digitally by summing samples of the individual phase waveforms. Nevertheless, there is an alternative method, which consists of observing the waveform of the resultant flux associated with the primary and secondary windings, which induces a voltage in the secondary windings of the voltage transformer. Having the core magnetisation characteristics (obtained, e.g., by measurements) and having information on the shape of the resultant associated flux waveform, it is possible to approximately determine the saturation of the core. The proposed method is an innovative approach, as it is an attempt to estimate the associated magnetic flux in order to determine the state of the transformer core, and is not widely undertaken. The proposed approach is inclined to observe the mechanism causing ferroresonance oscillations and not to observe only its effects—the secondary voltage of the zero sequence.

To obtain the waveform of the resultant flux associated with the primary and secondary windings, the time integral must be calculated from the secondary voltage waveform (and then converted to the primary side). A voltage transformer is essentially a transformer in an idle state [1].

According to the simplified equivalent diagram of an ideal transformer shown in Figure 1, we can write the equation describing the current distribution in a voltage transformer:

$$i_1 = i_2' + i_\mu = \frac{1}{\vartheta} \cdot i_2 + i_\mu \tag{1}$$

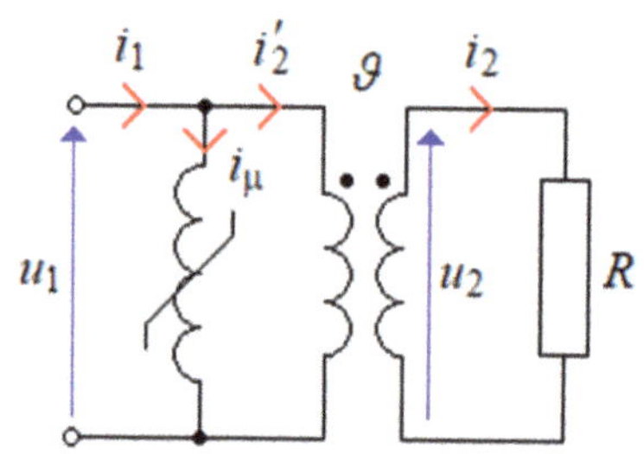

Figure 1. Simplified equivalent circuit of a transformer (winding leakage resistances and inductances omitted).

Due to the relatively high value of the load resistance R of the transformer, we can write that the secondary current i_2', converted to the primary side, is much smaller than the magnetising current i_μ:

$$i_2' \ll i_\mu \tag{2}$$

Therefore, Formula (1) takes the form:

$$i_\mu = i_1 - i_2' \tag{3}$$

Assuming that the inequality (2) is valid, we obtain the approximation (4), according to which the magnetising current i_μ is approximately equal to the primary current i_1 of the voltage transformer:

$$i_\mu \approx i_1 \tag{4}$$

The individual currents i_1, i_2' and i_μ are associated with the flux linkages Ψ_1, Ψ_2' and $\Psi_\mu = \Psi_{12}$. The linkage in the primary and secondary windings Ψ_{12} is the resultant linkage according to the following formula:

$$\Psi_{12} = \Psi_1 - \Psi_2' = \Psi_1 - \vartheta \cdot \Psi_2 \tag{5}$$

Relationship (5) is illustrated in Figure 2, which shows the distribution of linkages in the core of a transformer.

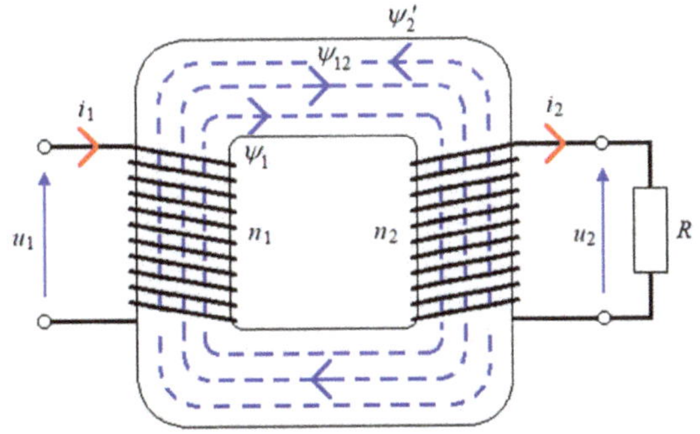

Figure 2. Illustrative drawing of a transformer with a ferromagnetic core with marked linkages Ψ_1 and Ψ_2' from individual windings n_1 and n_2, as well as the resultant associated flux Ψ_{12} from both windings (leakage fluxes not taken into account).

Similarly to the current in Equation (2), for a magnetic circuit, we can write the inequality resulting from the state of the voltage transformer, which is close to the no-load state:

$$\Psi_2' \ll \Psi_{12} \tag{6}$$

As a consequence, approximation (7) is true, according to which the mutual flux linkage Ψ_{12} is approximately equal to the flux linkage in the primary winding Ψ_1.

$$\Psi_2' \ll \Psi_{12} \tag{7}$$

Differentiating on both sides of approximation (7) with respect to time, we obtain the following approximation:

$$u_1 = \frac{d\Psi_1}{dt} \approx \frac{d\Psi_{12}}{dt} = \vartheta \cdot u_2 \tag{8}$$

Omitting the left-hand side of the approximation (8), we obtain the following equation:

$$\frac{d\Psi_{12}}{dt} = \vartheta \cdot u_2 \tag{9}$$

Then, integrating both sides of Equation (9) with respect to time, we obtain the following equation:

$$\int \frac{d\Psi_{12}}{dt} dt = \int \vartheta \cdot u_2 dt \tag{10}$$

After rearranging Equation (10), we obtain integral Equation (11), which is the dependence of the flux linkage associated with both windings (converted to the primary winding side), and therefore the magnetising flux linkage in the core, on the time integral of the secondary voltage of the voltage transformer:

$$\Psi_{12} = \vartheta \cdot \int u_2 dt + C \tag{11}$$

In Equation (11), which contains the indeterminate integral, there is also an integration constant C, the value of which is calculated from the knowledge of the initial conditions (12), i.e., the value of the resultant flux linkage Ψ_{12} at the first moment of integration of the secondary voltage waveform u_2.

$$\Psi_{12}(0) = \Psi_0 \tag{12}$$

In practice, the initial condition, i.e., the exact value of the linkage Ψ_0, is not known (or even available to determine). More about the problem of determining the initial conditions in the practical implementation of the numerical integration algorithm is described in Section 5.3.

Stable ferroresonance oscillations occurring in medium voltage networks are mostly sub-harmonic oscillations with frequencies close to 25 Hz [2]. They are initiated by transients accompanying the elimination of ground faults or switching processes (voltage switching). Under specific conditions, ferroresonance subharmonic oscillations of approximately 12.5 Hz, harmonic oscillations of approximately 50 Hz, quasi-periodic oscillations or chaotic oscillations may also be induced. Each of these types of oscillations has a characteristic resultant flux linkage waveform.

If, therefore, it is assumed that a method based on observation of the resultant magnetic flux waveform is to be used for ferroresonance detection, the problem of selecting an appropriate method for estimating this waveform becomes fundamental. This is because the chosen estimation method should allow us to reproduce as accurately as possible the shape of the flux waveform compared to the real waveform (which is the reference waveform in this case).

2. State-of-the-Art

The phenomenon of series ferroresonance of voltages in high-voltage networks, as well as parallel ferroresonance of currents in medium-voltage networks, has been widely described in [2–6]. In these studies, the authors presented a qualitative analysis of the phenomenon and attempted to explain the mechanism of ferroresonance excitation. They pointed to a number of factors, such as saturation of the magnetic core of the voltage transformer or power transformer, the operation of the network under no-load conditions, the network topology and associated switching processes. This included short-circuit tripping, recloser cycles, switching, or, finally, the transverse and reciprocal parameters of the network: the capacitances of the cable lines, the capacitances of the overhead lines, or the capacitive coupling of adjacent lines between their tracks.

Issues narrowed down to ferroresonance in medium-voltage networks with an isolated neutral point have been analysed by means of computer simulation studies on the models developed in [7–14].

The results of simulation studies conducted on a ferroresonance detection method based on the measurement of magnetic flux in the core of a voltage transformer are presented in [15]. In that paper, a detection method is proposed in which the secondary waveform of the zero-sequence component voltage ($3u_0$), measured in an open triangle voltage transformer system, is integrated. This voltage is filtered using a first-order Walsh filter, which, being a low-pass filter, simultaneously performs an integration operation and filters out the 25 Hz sub-harmonic component of the neutral flux ($3\Psi_0$). However, the integration method used is imperfect, as it has a strongly non-linear frequency response (total attenuation of frequencies that are multiples of 50 Hz). This approach, although sufficient for the chosen application, is nevertheless insufficient when the aim is to perform the integration over a wide frequency band while keeping the frequency response as linear as possible.

In addition, a large collection of publications [16] focused on detection methods related to the measurement and analysis of zero voltage ($3u_0$). One can indicate other detection methods based on the use of neural networks and artificial intelligence [17,18], in which a suitably trained algorithm is tasked with selectively identifying the waveform as ferroresonance oscillations. Other, less frequently used, methods include vibroacoustic methods [19], based on the analysis of recorded sound waves.

The analogue integration method used in the research described in this paper is based on a prepared electronic circuit. It is a solution well-known and described in the literature on the fundamentals of analogue electronics [20–22]. Similarly, the proposed discrete signal integration method, which was implemented in a microcontroller, is one of the basic numerical integration methods widely described in the literature on this topic [23].

3. Voltage Transformer Model

This chapter presents the developed electrical model of a conventional (inductive) voltage transformer. The description of the prepared simulation model has been narrowed down only to the model of the voltage transformer, given its key role in the problem of testing simulation systems with ferroresonance oscillations in medium voltage networks.

Figure 3 shows an electrical equivalent model of a voltage transformer in the form of a T-type quadrupole with two secondary windings, whose terminals are labelled a-n and da-dn [24]. The primary winding, with terminals marked a-n, is used to obtain a secondary three-phase system connected in a full star arrangement. The secondary winding, with terminals marked da-dn, is designed to be connected in a secondary open-triangle arrangement to measure the zero-sequence voltage (triple zero voltage $3u_0$). The equivalent circuit diagram shown is for a voltage transformer in one phase only (phase L1) [25,26].

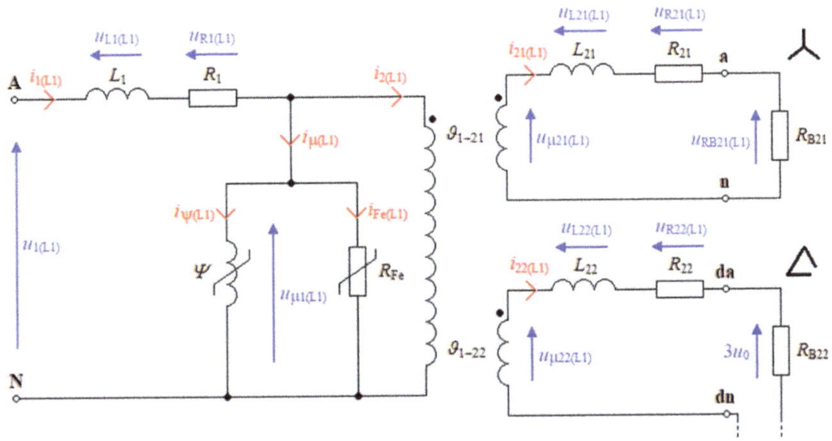

Figure 3. Equivalent diagram of the T-type voltage transformer (phase L1) with secondary circuits (terminals da-dn connected in an open delta configuration).

The developed mathematical model includes voltage transformers operating on all three phases. This procedure is necessary because the phenomenon of parallel ferroresonance (currents) occurs in medium-voltage networks only as a disturbance of a three-phase nature (which, it should be noted, is not necessarily of a symmetrical nature).

The primary circuit of a single-phase voltage transformer for phase L1 (terminals on the left side of the figure marked A-N) is described by the voltage equation:

$$u_1 = u_{L1} + u_{R1} + u_{\mu 1} \tag{13}$$

The flow of currents in the primary circuit, on the other hand, is described by following the equation:

$$i_1 = i_\mu + i_2 = (i_\Psi(\Psi) + i_{Fe}) + i_2 \tag{14}$$

Assuming that the two secondary circuits are connected to the secondary circuit via an idealised air transformer with winding ratios ϑ_{1-21} and ϑ_{1-22}, the current, i_2, can be described by the following equation:

$$i_2 = \frac{i_{21}}{\vartheta_{1-21}} + \frac{i_{22}}{\vartheta_{1-22}} \tag{15}$$

Current i_2 is the total load current of the voltage transformer, fed to the primary side of the transformer, and resulting from the individual values of secondary currents i_{21} and

i_{22}. According to the equivalent diagram shown in Figure 3, Equation (13) can be expanded to the form of the following equation:

$$u_1 = L_1 \frac{di_1}{dt} + R_1 i_1 + R_{Fe}(i_{Fe}) i_{Fe} \tag{16}$$

After substituting Equation (14) into Equation (16), the following equation was obtained:

$$u_1 = L_1 \frac{di_1}{dt} + R_1 i_1 + R_{Fe}(i_{Fe})(i_1 - i_\Psi(\Psi) - i_2) \tag{17}$$

Equation (17) can then be transformed to form (18) which is a first-order non-linear differential equation.

$$\frac{di_1}{dt} = \frac{1}{L_1}(u_1 - R_1 i_1 - R_{Fe}(i_{Fe})(i_1 - i_\Psi(\Psi) - i_2)) \tag{18}$$

The non-linearity of the differential Equation (18) results from the non-linearity of the function describing the magnetisation curve of the non-linear coil (in the form of the dependence of the magnetising current on the associated flux $i_\Psi(\Psi)$) and from the non-linearity of the function describing the total core loss curve (in the form of the dependence of the loss resistance on the core loss current $R_{Fe}(i_{Fe})$).

The voltage $u_{\mu 21}$, representing the electromotive force (induced voltage) in the primary secondary circuits, forms a voltage equation of the form with the other voltage drops:

$$u_{\mu 21} = u_{L21} + u_{R21} + u_{RB21} \tag{19}$$

Knowing that $u_{\mu 21}$ is equal to the following:

$$u_{\mu 21} = \frac{u_{\mu 1}}{\vartheta_{1-21}} \tag{20}$$

The voltage Equation (19) can be developed into an equation based on the equivalent diagram from Figure 3:

$$u_{\mu_{21}} = L_{21} \frac{di_{21}}{dt} + R_{21} i_{21} + R_{B21} i_{21} \tag{21}$$

After substituting Relation (20) into Equation (21) and performing the transformation, the following equation was obtained:

$$\frac{u_{\mu_1}}{\vartheta_{1-21}} = L_{21} \frac{di_{21}}{dt} + (R_{21} + R_{B21}) i_{21} \tag{22}$$

By performing a further transformation of Equation (22), a first-order differential equation of the form was obtained:

$$\frac{di_{21}}{dt} = \frac{1}{L_{21}} \left[\frac{u_\mu}{\vartheta_{1-21}} - (R_{21} + R_{B21}) i_{21} \right] \tag{23}$$

According to Ohm's law, the voltage drop $u_{R_{B21}(L1)}$ across the load resistance R_{B21} in phase L1 is as follows:

$$u_{R_{B21}(L1)} = R_{B21} i_{21} \tag{24}$$

According to the electrical equivalent circuit diagram in Figure 3, the secondary circuit, connected in an open triangle arrangement, forms a series connection of all three secondary winding leads of the auxiliary windings together with the series connected load resistance. This circuit can be described by a voltage equation of the following form:

$$u_{\mu_{22}(L1)} + u_{\mu_{22}(L2)} + u_{\mu_{22}(L3)} = 3u_{L_{22}} + 3u_{R_{22}} + u_{R_{B22}} \tag{25}$$

Equation (25) can be developed and transformed to the following form:

$$\frac{1}{\vartheta_{1-22}}\sum_{p=1}^{3}u_{\mu(p)} = 3L_{22}\frac{di_{22}}{dt} + 3R_{22}i_{22} + R_{B22}i_{22} = 3L_{22}\frac{di_{22}}{dt} + (3R_{22} + R_{B22})i_{22} \quad (26)$$

After further transformations, Equation (26) takes the form (27), which is a first-order differential equation.

$$\frac{\mathrm{d}i_{22}}{\mathrm{d}t} = \frac{1}{3L_{22}}\left[\frac{1}{\vartheta_{1-22}}\sum_{p=1}^{3}u_{\mu(p)} - (3R_{22} + R_{B22})i_{22}\right] \quad (27)$$

According to Ohm's law, the voltage drop $u_{R_{B22}}$ across the load resistance R_{B22} is as follows:

$$3u_0 = u_{R_{B22}} = R_{B22}i_{22} \quad (28)$$

The voltage $u_{R_{B22}}$ is equal in value to the tripled secondary voltage of the zero order.

The voltage drops across the transverse elements visible in the primary winding circuit in Figure 3—the voltage drop across the non-linear coil, the voltage drop across the non-linear resistance and the voltage drop across the primary winding of an air-perfect transformer—are equal to each other, as expressed in the following equation:

$$u_{\mu_1} = u_{\Psi} = u_{R_{\mathrm{Fe}}} \quad (29)$$

After appropriate substitutions and transformations, Equation (29) can be developed into an equation of the following form:

$$u_{\Psi} = \frac{\mathrm{d}\Psi}{\mathrm{d}t} = R_{Fe}(i_{Fe})i_{Fe} = R_{Fe}(i_{Fe})(i_1 - i_{\Psi}(\Psi) - i_2) \quad (30)$$

The above Equation (30) is a non-linear differential equation of the first order.

The function describing the non-linear ferromagnetic core coil is expressed in terms of an incomplete power polynomial to approximate the magnetisation curve of the modelled voltage transformer. The function describing the non-linear coil takes the form of the following equation:

$$i_{\Psi}(\Psi) = a_1\Psi + a_5\Psi^5 + a_7\Psi^7 \quad (31)$$

The values of the coefficients of the incomplete power polynomial appearing in Equation (31) are taken in turn:

$$\begin{aligned} a_1 &= 6{\cdot}10^{-4} \\ a_5 &= 1.5{\cdot}10^{-8} \\ a_7 &= 3{\cdot}10^{-12} \end{aligned} \quad (32)$$

By performing the substitution of Equation (31) into Equation (30), the flux Ψ was obtained, which is a first-order non-linear differential equation of the following form:

$$\frac{d\Psi}{dt} = R_{Fe}(i_{Fe})\left[i_1 - \left(a_1\Psi + a_5\Psi^5 + a_7\Psi^7\right) - i_2\right] \quad (33)$$

Figure 4 shows the non-linear magnetising current characteristics of a non-linear ferromagnetic core coil $i_{\Psi}(\Psi)$, depending on the magnetic flux associated with the primary winding Ψ.

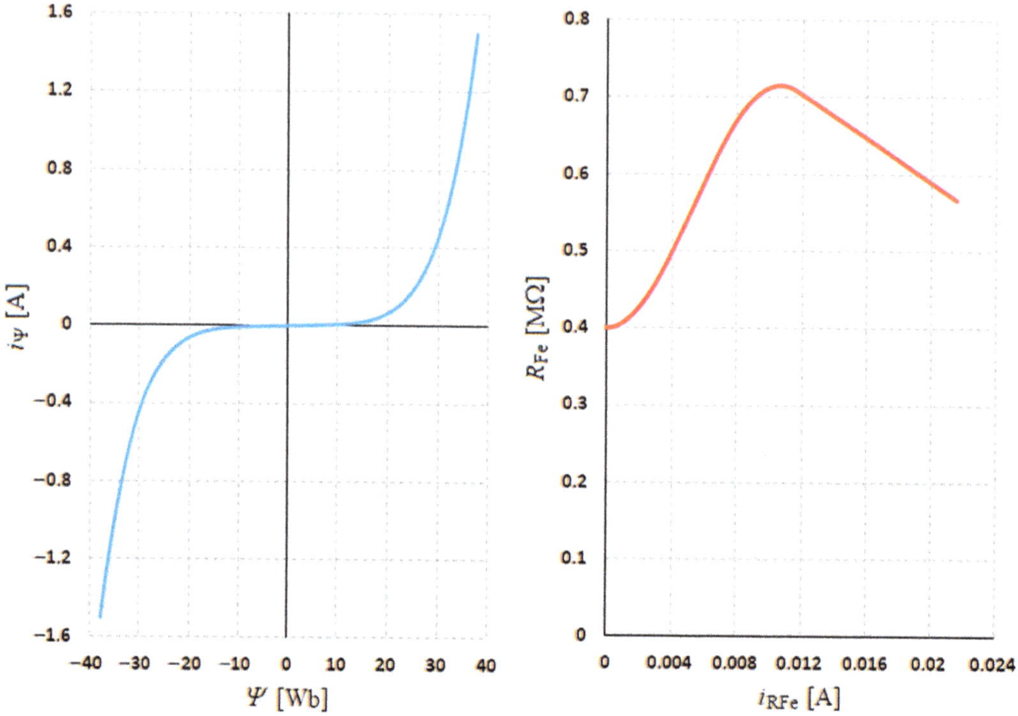

(a) (b)

Figure 4. Nonlinear function describing: (**a**) nonlinear coil with ferromagnetic core, (**b**) nonlinear resistance representing total losses in the core.

The characteristic shown in Figure 4 was approximated by a folded function with two functions: for i_{Fe} between 0 and I_{RFe_1}

$$R_{\mathrm{Fe}} = \frac{R_{\mathrm{Fe\_max}} + R_{\mathrm{Fe\_min}}}{2} - \frac{R_{\mathrm{Fe\_max}} - R_{\mathrm{Fe\_min}}}{2} \cdot \cos\left(\frac{\pi \cdot |i_{\mathrm{Fe}}|}{I_{\mathrm{RFe\_max}}}\right) \tag{34}$$

and for i_{Fe} greater than I_{RFe2}

$$R_{\mathrm{Fe}} = a \cdot |i_{\mathrm{Fe}}| + b \tag{35}$$

where, for the individual constants appearing in Equation (34), values were used as follows:

$$\begin{gathered} R_{\mathrm{Fe\_2}} = 574000\ \Omega \\ R_{\mathrm{Fe\_min}} = 400000\ \Omega \\ I_{\mathrm{RFe\_max}} = 0.0107\ \mathrm{A} \\ I_{\mathrm{RFe\_1}} = 0.0116\ \mathrm{A} \\ I_{\mathrm{RFe\_2}} = 0.0212\ \mathrm{A} \\ I_{\mathrm{RFe\_2}} = 715700\ \mathrm{A} \end{gathered} \tag{36}$$

The value of the constant R_{Fe_1}, which defines the range for the first component of the folding function, is calculated from the following formula:

$$R_{\mathrm{Fe}_1} = \frac{R_{\mathrm{Fe\_max}} + R_{\mathrm{Fe\_min}}}{2} - \frac{R_{\mathrm{Fe\_max}} - R_{\mathrm{Fe\_min}}}{2} \cos\left(\frac{\pi \cdot I_{\mathrm{RFe\_1}}}{I_{\mathrm{RFe\_max}}}\right) \tag{37}$$

The constants a and b, appearing in Equation (35), were calculated from the following equation:

$$\begin{aligned} a &= (R_{Fe\_2} - R_{Fe\_1})/(I_{RFe\_2} - I_{RFe\_1}) \\ b &= -(a \cdot I_{RFe\_1}) + R_{Fe\_1} \end{aligned} \tag{38}$$

On the right-hand side of Figure 4, one can see the non-linear characteristic of the resistance of the total losses in the core of the voltage transformer R_{Fe} depending on the active current of the losses in the core i_{Fe}. Equations (34)–(38) were developed by the authors of the paper and represent a proposed approximation of the non-linear resistance function R_{Fe}.

The composite of the non-linear characteristics described by Equations (31), (34) and (35) (shown in Figure 4) together form an electrical representation of the static hysteresis loops. The equations allow the shape of the static hysteresis loops to be reproduced for the entire range over which they were measured. The static hysteresis loops obtained by modelling are shown in Figure 5.

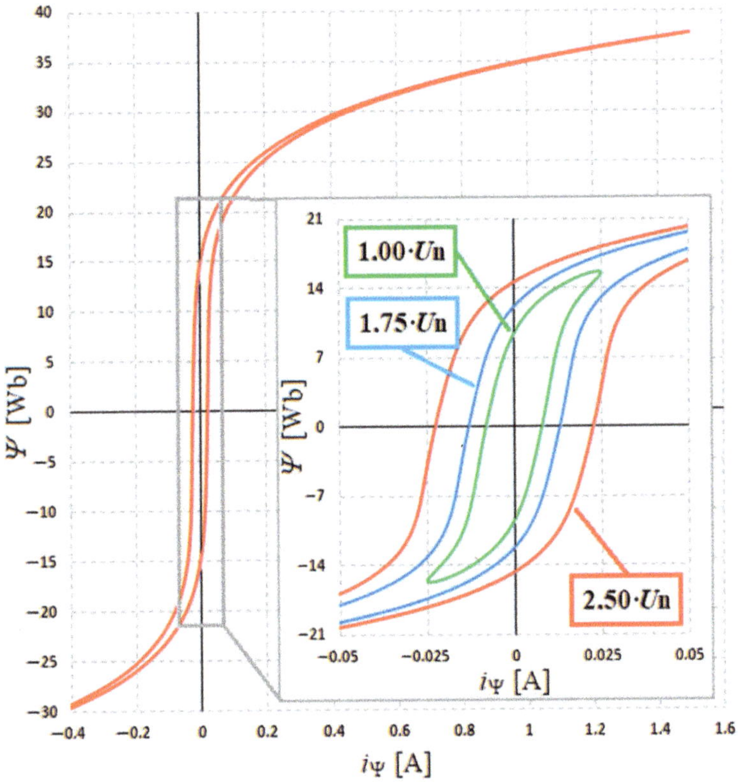

Figure 5. Static hysteresis loops modelled by nonlinear equations: static loop in the deep saturation state of the modelled voltage transformer (below), superimposed static hysteresis loops for different values of the measured voltage (on top).

It is worth noting at this point that the modelled static hysteresis loops are, in fact, a composite of the averaged trajectories along which the peak value point of the current and associated flux waveforms move. The resulting static loops are, therefore, only an electrical representation of the active and reactive components of the current drawn by the magnetising branch. This has consequences because, in dynamic states, the proposed hysteresis loop model will behave differently from what the real waveforms would suggest.

The inconsistency of the simulated waveforms with the real waveforms will be smaller the deeper the core saturation is simulated. In the case of modelling ferroresonance oscillations, the transformers operate in a deeply saturated state, which is conducive to reducing the relative error of the simulation results.

It should, therefore, be borne in mind that the proposed model, based on the representation of static hysteresis loops, is only an approximation of the behaviour of the actual hysteresis loop. However, it is a more accurate approximation than a constant value of the loss resistance R_{Fe} is assumed. Nevertheless, the developed model has some limitations and imperfections. The most important of these are:

1. Only averaged modelling of flux and magnetising current waveforms in transient (dynamic) states.
2. Incorrect modelling of the magnetic remanent in the case of long short-circuit durations in the L1 phase, where a metallic short has occurred. In the model, the magnetic remanent disappears slowly with a certain time constant.
3. The shape of the modelled hysteresis loop does not depend on the frequency, temperature or dynamics of the magnetising current change.

However, despite the mentioned limitations and imperfections, the developed model is sufficient for the purpose of the simulation studies performed.

4. Simulation-Generated Reference Flux Waveforms

The developed simulation model of a medium-voltage network with an isolated neutral point, together with a prepared model of a set of voltage transformers for each phase in the network, was used to generate reference core flux waveforms in phase L1.

The simulation model of the medium voltage network with an isolated neutral point was developed in the MATLAB/Simulink simulation environment. However, a detailed presentation of the simulation model was not presented and described in this paper due to its extensiveness. Nevertheless, the prepared three-phase simulation model consisted of an equivalent model of the power supply system, the network earth capacitance and the previously described voltage transformer model. Ferroresonance oscillations in the model were initiated by eliminating the earth fault in phase L1 (by making a step change in the phase-to-earth resistance). The simulation parameters are presented in Table 1.

Table 1. Simulation parameters set in MATLAB/Simulink program for the developed medium voltage network model.

Parameter:	Value:
Start time:	0.0 s
Stop time:	0.5 s
Type:	Variable step
Solver:	ode23 (stiff/Mod. Rosenbrock)
Max step size:	1×10^{-5}
Min step size:	1×10^{-7}
Initial step size:	1×10^{-6}
Relative tolerance:	1×10^{-5}
Absolute tolerance:	Auto

The simulation-generated flux waveforms acted as a reference for the waveforms obtained using the chosen phase-voltage integration methods, analogue and digital, were compared. The following waveforms were generated for the specified simulation conditions and the specified value of the grid earth capacitance: secondary zero-sequence voltage $3u_0$, the secondary voltage of the L1 phase voltage transformer $u_{21(L1)}$ and the linkage in the core of the L1 phase voltage transformer $\Psi_{12(L1)}$.

The generated waveform of the secondary zero-sequence voltage $3u_0$ was used to determine which kind of ferroresonance oscillations (no oscillations, self-damped, steady-state) occurred for the adopted network earth capacitance and to identify the type of induced ferroresonance oscillations (sub-harmonic, harmonic, quasi-periodic, chaotic). The secondary voltage waveform of the voltage transformer for the L1 phase $u_{21(L1)}$ served as the signal fed to the input of the analogue (electronic) integration circuit or to the input of the system performing numerical integration in the microcontroller after prior discretisation of the signal. For this purpose, the waveforms of the secondary voltages $u_{21(L1)}$ were saved to *.mat files and converted to COMTRADE format files. The prepared COMTRADE files were loaded and forced as actual voltage waveforms using an Omicron CMC-type tester. Finally, the magnetic linkage waveform Ψ_{12} served as a reference waveform (instantaneous expected value waveform), to which the flux waveforms obtained using analogue and digital integration were then compared.

In each of the simulations carried out, the factor intended to initiate ferroresonance oscillations was the elimination of a metallic ground fault. The short circuit was switched on when the flux in the core reached its maximum value (the maximum flux remanent value during the short circuit). The short circuit was eliminated after a time of 95 ms, at the moment when the short circuit current passed through zero.

Figure 6 summarises the waveforms of secondary voltage $3u_0$, voltage $u_{21(L1)}$ and flux $\Psi_{12(L1)}$, for a network, the earth capacitance of $C_0 = 17.5$ μF. On the left, the waveforms are sequentially t over the time interval from 0 s to 0.5 s. On the right, there is an enlarged section of the left waveform in the time interval from 0.14 s to 0.34 s.

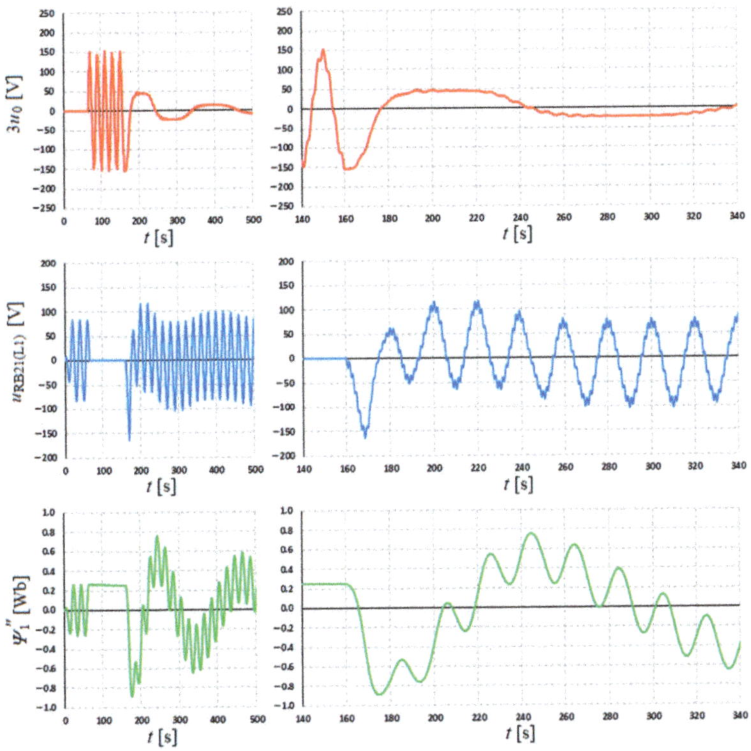

Figure 6. Waveforms (from top): secondary voltage $3u_0$, phase secondary voltage $u_{21(L1)}$ of phase L1, associated flux $\Psi_{12(L1)}$ of phase L1 for the assumed value of the network capacitance to earth equal to $C_0 = 17.5$ μF.

For the adopted value of the earth capacitance ($C_0 = 17.5$ μF), no ferroresonance occurred as a result of the elimination of the earth fault, but only a slowly varying oscillation that faded over time.

Figure 7 summarises the waveforms of secondary voltage $3u_0$, voltage $u_{21(L1)}$ and flux $\Psi_{12(L1)}$, for a network ground capacitance of $C_0 = 1.85\ \mu F$.

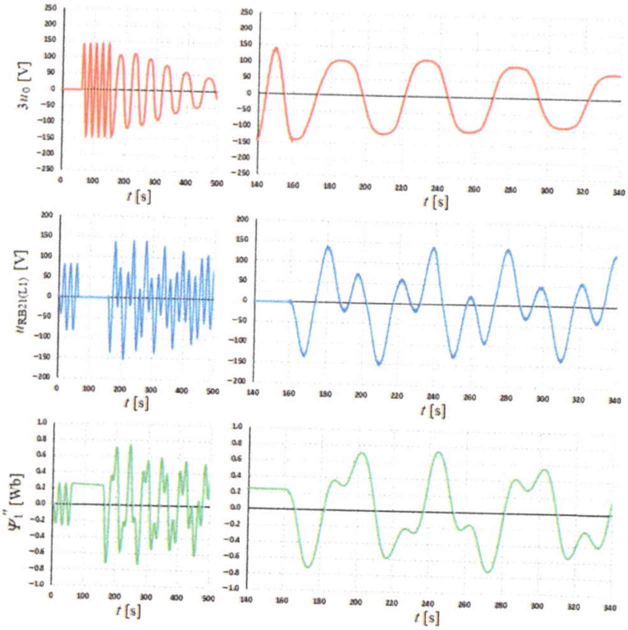

Figure 7. Waveforms (from top): secondary voltage $3u_0$, phase secondary voltage $u_{21(L1)}$ of phase L1, associated flux $\Psi_{12(L1)}$ of phase L1 for the assumed value of the network capacitance to earth equal to $C_0 = 1.85\ \mu F$.

For the adopted value of the ground capacitance ($C_0 = 1.85\ \mu F$), the elimination of the ground fault resulted in a sub-harmonic self-damped ferroresonance, with an oscillation frequency close to 25 Hz.

Figure 8 summarises the waveforms of secondary voltage $3u_0$, voltage $u_{21(L1)}$ and flux $\Psi_{12(L1)}$, for a network ground capacitance of $C_0 = 1.5\ \mu F$.

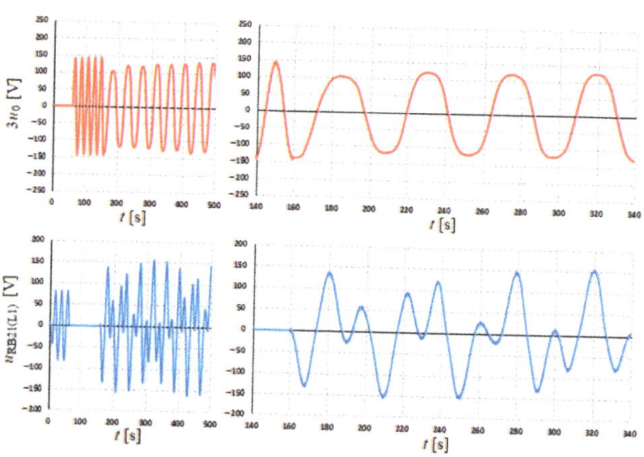

Figure 8. *Cont.*

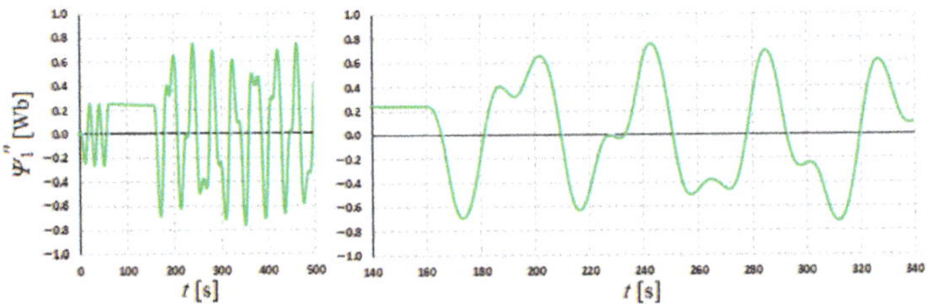

Figure 8. Waveforms (from top): secondary voltage $3u_0$, phase secondary voltage $u_{21(L1)}$ of phase L1, associated flux $\Psi_{12(L1)}$ of phase L1 for the assumed value of the network capacitance to earth equal to $C_0 = 1.5$ μF.

For the adopted value of the ground capacitance ($C_0 = 1.5$ μF), the elimination of the ground fault resulted in a sub-harmonic steady-state ferroresonance, with an oscillation frequency close to 25 Hz.

Figure 9 summarises the waveforms of secondary voltage $3u_0$, voltage $u_{21(L1)}$ and flux $\Psi_{12(L1)}$, for a network ground capacitance of $C_0 = 0.1$ μF.

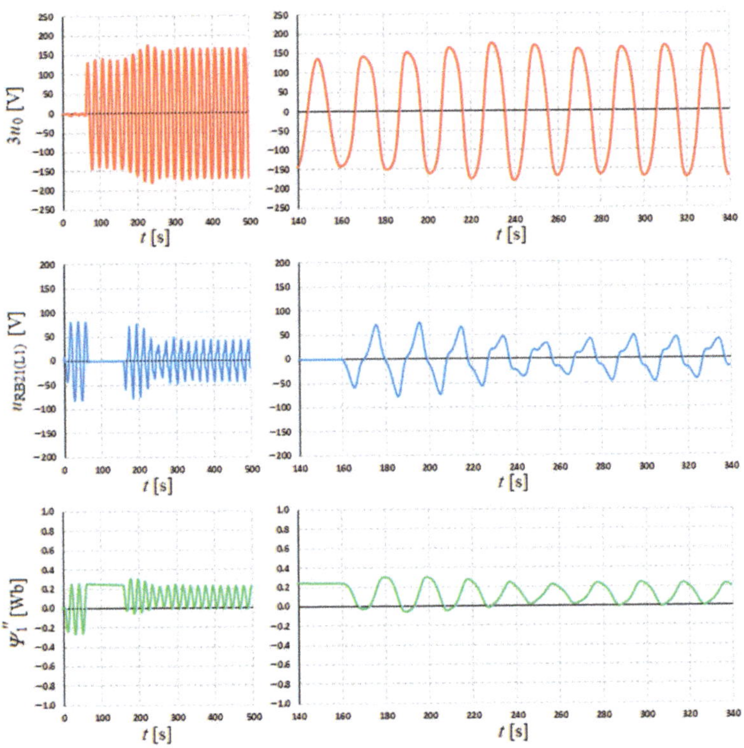

Figure 9. Waveforms (from top): secondary voltage $3u_0$, phase secondary voltage $u_{21(L1)}$ of phase L1, associated flux $\Psi_{12(L1)}$ of phase L1 for the assumed value of the network capacitance to earth equal to $C_0 = 100$ nF.

For the adopted value of the earth capacitance ($C_0 = 0.1$ μF), the elimination of the earth fault resulted in a harmonic steady-state ferroresonance, with an oscillation frequency close to 50 Hz (oscillation close to the mains frequency).

Figure 10 summarizes the waveforms of secondary voltage $3u_0$, voltage $u_{21(L1)}$ and flux $\Psi_{12(L1)}$, for a network ground capacitance of $C_0 = 0.009$ μF.

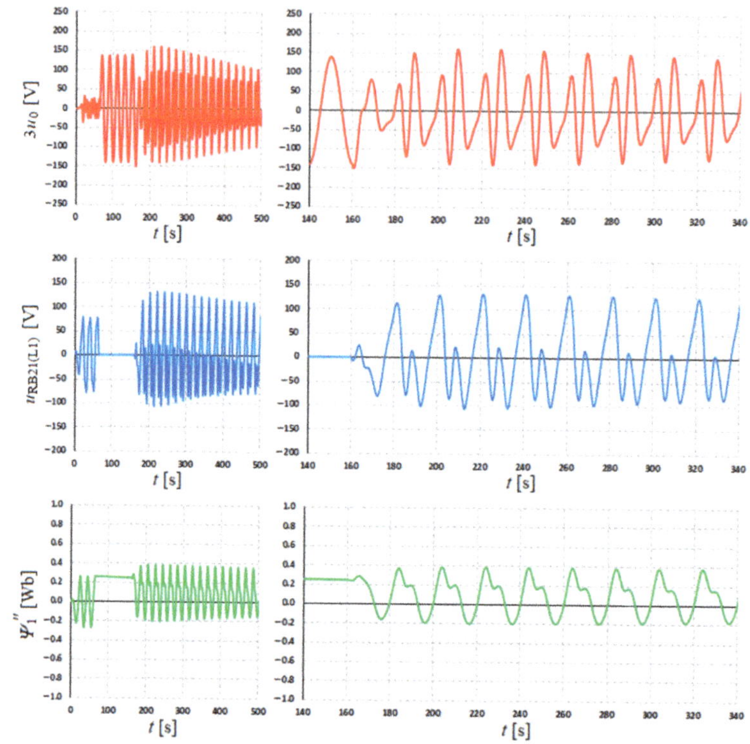

Figure 10. Waveforms (from top): red color is secondary voltage $3u_0$, blue color is phase secondary voltage $u_{21(L1)}$ of phase L1, green color is associated flux $\Psi_{12(L1)}$ of phase L1 for the assumed value of the network capacitance to earth equal to $C_0 = 9$ nF.

For the adopted value of the earth capacitance ($C_0 = 9$ nF), a quasi-periodic self-damped ferroresonance, characterised by strong oscillation nonlinearity, occurred as a result of the elimination of the ground fault.

5. Applied Magnetic Linkage Estimation Methods

In order to carry out tests aimed at comparing the analogue and numerical integration methods, it was necessary to construct a suitable measuring system. An electronic circuit implementing the analogue integration operation on the input voltage signal, an analogue input circuit implementing the conditioning of the input voltage signal and a development board of the NUCLEO H7A3ZI Q type with an integrated STM32 microcontroller were developed and manufactured. An overview photo of the prepared measurement system is shown in Figure 11.

5.1. Input of Analogue Circuit

The voltage signal generated by the Omicron CMC-type tester was fed to the input of an analogue conditioning circuit. This circuit adjusts the measured voltage signal so that it can be fed to the input of the analogue-to-digital converter in the STM32 microcontroller. An electronic schematic of the analogue voltage input circuit implementing the signal conditioning is shown in Figure 12.

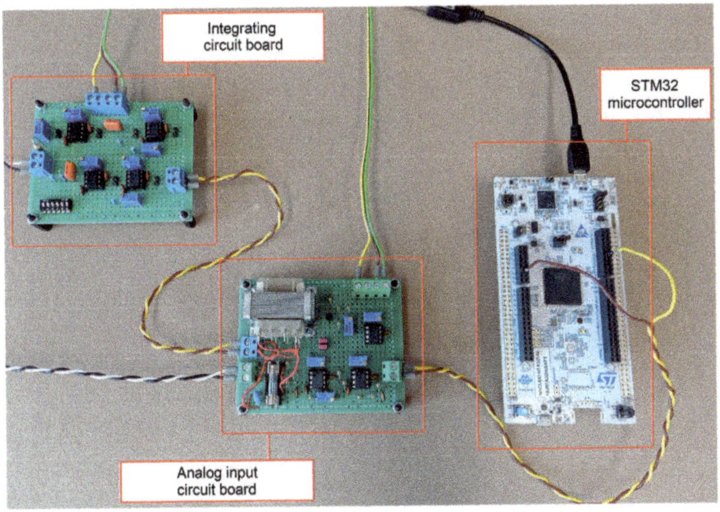

Figure 11. Prepared measurement system consisting of an analogue integrator, analogue voltage input and a NUCLEO-H7A3ZI-Q development board.

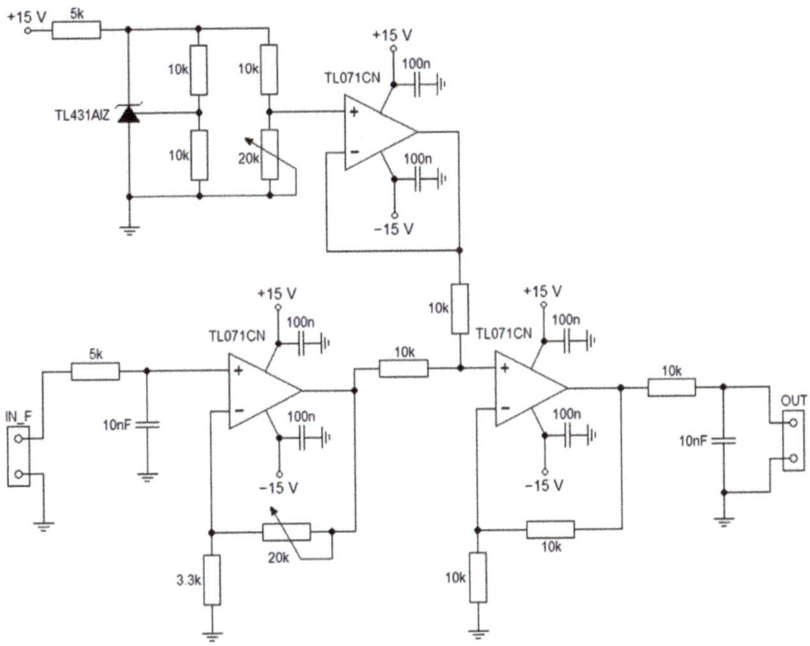

Figure 12. Schematic diagram of the analogue voltage input electronic circuit that performs input signal conditioning.

The analogue voltage input circuit has two pairs of input terminals:

1. Galvanically isolated input terminals IN_Tr, isolated by a voltage reduction transformer. This input is not marked on the diagram as it was not used;
2. Input terminals without galvanic isolation IN_F, connected directly to the low-pass filter. This input is dedicated to the connection of a voltage divider with a buffer. The

described divider mediated the signal exchange between the voltage output of the Omicron CMC-type tester and the IN_F input terminals.

In addition, the analogue voltage input circuit consists of five subcircuits:

1. Input a low-pass filter with a cut-off frequency equal to the following:

$$f_{c\_IN} = \frac{1}{2\cdot\pi\cdot(R_{f\_IN}\cdot C_{f\_IN})} = \frac{1}{2\cdot\pi\cdot(5\ \text{k}\Omega\cdot 10\ \text{nF})} = 3183\ \text{Hz} \quad (39)$$

This filter provides pre-filtering of the voltage input signal, suppressing high-frequency noise.

2. Non-inverting active amplifier with adjustable voltage gain in the following range:

$$G_{u1} = 1 + \frac{R_f}{R} = 1 + \frac{(0 \div 20)\ \text{k}\Omega}{3.3\ \text{k}\Omega} = (1 \div 7.06) \quad (40)$$

3. DC voltage source (offset) separated by a buffer, with adjustable voltage gain in the following range:

$$U_{\text{offset}} = U_{\text{Ref}}\cdot\left(1 + \frac{R_1}{R_2}\right)\cdot\frac{R_4}{R_3 + R_{4\_max}} = 2.495\ \text{V}\cdot\left(1 + \frac{10\ \text{k}\Omega}{10\ \text{k}\Omega}\right)\cdot\frac{(0 \div 20)\ \text{k}\Omega}{10\ \text{k}\Omega + 20\ \text{k}\Omega} = (0 \div 3.33)\ \text{V} \quad (41)$$

The preset fixed voltage U_{offset} is used to artificially raise the AC voltage of the input signal so that it can be applied to the input of the analogue-to-digital converter, which processes voltages in the range of 0 V to 3.3 V. The preset DC voltage is as follows:

$$U_{\text{offset}} = 1.65\ \text{V} \quad (42)$$

4. Non-inverting summing active amplifier with constant voltage gain equal to the following:

$$G_{u2} = 1 \quad (43)$$

This circuit sums a voltage input signal (alternating) and a fixed voltage U_{offset}, creating a variable positive voltage signal.

5. An output low-pass filter with a cut-off frequency is equal to the following:

$$f_{c\_OUT} = \frac{1}{2\cdot\pi\cdot(R_{f\_OUT}\cdot C_{f\_OUT})} = \frac{1}{2\cdot\pi\cdot(10\ \text{k}\Omega\cdot 10\ \text{nF})} = 1592\ \text{Hz} \quad (44)$$

This filter provides final filtration of the output voltage signal, suppressing fast-changing interference (noise) from the electronic circuit. The cut-off frequency f_{c_OUT} has been selected in such a way as to suppress signals with a frequency higher than that defined by the sampling theorem, also known as the Nyquist–Shannon theorem [27,28], for the assumed sampling frequency f_p:

$$f_{c\_OUT} \leq \frac{f_p}{2} \quad (45)$$

The adjusted output signal is finally passed to the input of the analogue-to-digital converter of the STM32 microcontroller on the NUCLEO-H7A3ZI Q development board.

5.2. The Used Analogue Method

The electronic diagram of the developed analogue integrating circuit is shown in Figure 13. The analogue integrator consists of six subcircuits:

1. Input resistive voltage divider with an adjustable ratio in the following range:

$$\vartheta_{d\_IN} = \frac{R_2}{R_1 + R_{2\_max}} = \frac{(0 \div 20)\ \text{k}\Omega}{300\ \text{k}\Omega + 20\ \text{k}\Omega} = (0 \div 0.0625) \quad (46)$$

The divider provides an initial adjustment (reduction) of the input signal amplitude.

2. A voltage buffer with a voltage gain equal to the following:

$$G_{u1} = 1 \tag{47}$$

3. High-pass filter with a cut-off frequency as follows:

$$f_{c\_1} = \frac{1}{2 \cdot \pi \cdot (R_{f\_1} \cdot C_{f\_1})} = \frac{1}{2 \cdot \pi \cdot (330\ \mathrm{k\Omega} \cdot 330\ \mathrm{nF})} = 1.46\ \mathrm{Hz} \tag{48}$$

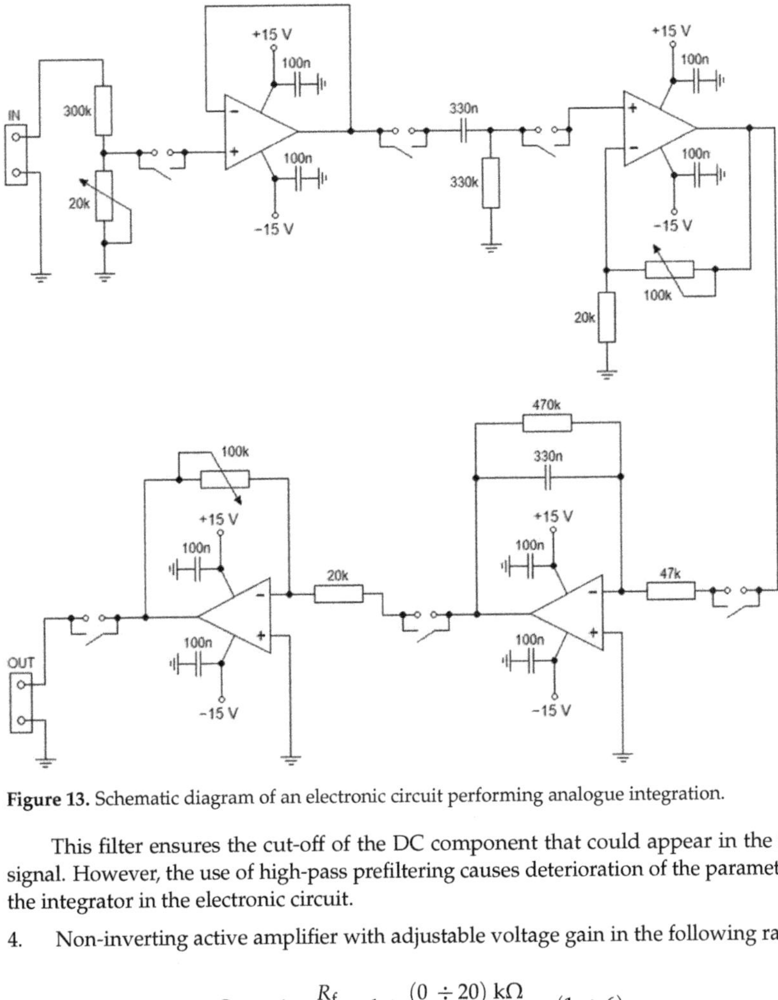

Figure 13. Schematic diagram of an electronic circuit performing analogue integration.

This filter ensures the cut-off of the DC component that could appear in the input signal. However, the use of high-pass prefiltering causes deterioration of the parameters of the integrator in the electronic circuit.

4. Non-inverting active amplifier with adjustable voltage gain in the following range:

$$G_{u2} = 1 + \frac{R_f}{R} = 1 + \frac{(0 \div 20)\ \mathrm{k\Omega}}{100\ \mathrm{k\Omega}} = (1 \div 6) \tag{49}$$

5. Inverting integrator (low-pass filter), with additional parallel connected resistance R_{f_INT} in the feedback loop, with the following cut-off frequency:

$$f_{c\_INT} = \frac{1}{2 \cdot \pi \cdot (R_{f\_INT} \cdot C_{f\_INT})} = \frac{1}{2 \cdot \pi \cdot (470\ \mathrm{k\Omega} \cdot 330\ \mathrm{nF})} = 1.03\ \mathrm{Hz} \tag{50}$$

And the blocking frequency:

$$f_{0\_INT} = \frac{1}{2 \cdot \pi \cdot (R_{1\_INT} \cdot C_{f\_INT})} = \frac{1}{2 \cdot \pi \cdot (47\ \text{k}\Omega \cdot 330\ \text{nF})} = 10.26\ \text{Hz} \tag{51}$$

The cut-off frequency f_{c_INT} and the stop frequency f_{0_INT} selected in this way for the expected input signal with a frequency of 25 Hz allows for relatively accurate integration of the waveform. The phase shift (delay) of the output signal relative to the input signal with a frequency of 25 Hz is −83.93°, and for a frequency of 50 Hz, it is −87.30°. This value takes into account the initial signal shift (lead) introduced by the high-pass filter (differentiator). An additional parallel resistor R_{f_INT} in the feedback loop ensures gradual discharge of the capacitor C_{f_INT}, due to which the system suppresses the DC component in the output signal with a time constant equal to the following:

$$f_{0\_INT} = \frac{1}{2 \cdot \pi \cdot (R_{1\_INT} \cdot C_{f\_INT})} = \frac{1}{2 \cdot \pi \cdot (47\ \text{k}\Omega \cdot 330\ \text{nF})} = 10.26\ \text{Hz} \tag{52}$$

6. Inverting active amplifier with adjustable voltage gain in the following range:

$$G_{u3} = -\frac{R_f}{R} = \frac{(0 \div 100)\ \text{k}\Omega}{20\ \text{k}\Omega} = (-5 \div 0) \tag{53}$$

The voltage signal generated by the Omicron CMC tester was fed to the input of the analogue integrator, while the output signal of the analogue integrator was finally transmitted to the input of the analogue voltage input system (IN_F input terminals without galvanic isolation).

5.3. The Used Digital Method

To implement the digital integration of the phase waveform of the secondary voltage, a numerical method known as the trapezoidal method (sometimes also called the modified Euler method, which can also be interpreted as a variant of the Heun method) was used. The trapezoidal method is an implicit second-order method. The basic implicit Forward Euler method with next-value prediction can be derived from the Formula (54), which is a formula for the derivative of a function.

$$\frac{\text{d}y}{\text{d}t} = \lim_{\Delta t \to 0} \frac{y(t + \Delta t) - y(t)}{\Delta t} \tag{54}$$

The differential expression contained in formula (54) was converted into the form of a function:

$$\frac{\text{d}y}{\text{d}t} = \text{f}(t, y) \tag{55}$$

The time interval Δt contained in Formula (54) is replaced by a constant and finite step size h:

$$\Delta t = h \tag{56}$$

Assuming a constant and finite step h, the limit for Δt tending to zero was eliminated from Formula (54) and an approximation of the form (56) was obtained. The obtained result is more accurate in relation to the analytical solution, with the smaller the value of step h.

$$\text{f}(t, y) \approx \frac{y(t + h) - y(t)}{h} \tag{57}$$

Formula (56) is written in discrete form:

$$\text{f}(t_n, y_n) = \frac{y_{n+1} - y_n}{h} \tag{58}$$

After transformation, Equation (58) was obtained, which expresses the implicit Euler method with the prediction of the next value:

$$y_{n+1} = y_n + h{\cdot}\mathrm{f}(t_n, y_n) \tag{59}$$

For the continuous form of the input signal of the measured secondary voltage, we can write the following:

$$\frac{\mathrm{d}y}{\mathrm{d}t} = \mathrm{f}(t, y) = u_2(t) \tag{60}$$

For the discrete form of the input signal of the measured secondary voltage, we can write the following:

$$\mathrm{f}(t_n, y_n) = u_2(n) \tag{61}$$

Assuming that

$$n = m - 1 \tag{62}$$

then, by substituting expression (62) into the indices in Formula (59), the prediction was shifted to the current step:

$$y_{(m-1)+1} = y_{m-1} + h{\cdot}f(t_{m-1}, y_{m-1}) \tag{63}$$

By arranging Equation (59) and transforming it into the discrete form of the flux path, the following equation was obtained:

$$\Psi(m) = \Psi(m-1) + h{\cdot}u_2(m-1) \tag{64}$$

Similarly, the basic implicit Backward Euler Method can be derived from Formula (65) for the derivative of a function. This time, however, the derivative is determined from the current value and one step back (the earlier value):

$$\frac{\mathrm{d}y}{\mathrm{d}t} \approx \frac{y(t) - y(t-h)}{h} \tag{65}$$

Formula (65) was written for a discrete signal in the following form:

$$\mathrm{f}(t_n, y_n) = \frac{y_n - y_{n-1}}{h} \tag{66}$$

Formula (66) was transformed into the following form:

$$y_n = y_{n-1} + h{\cdot}\mathrm{f}(t_n, y_n) \tag{67}$$

To move one step forward, Formula (67) is modified to the following:

$$y_{n+1} = y_n + h{\cdot}\mathrm{f}(t_{n+1}, y_{n+1}) \tag{68}$$

Assuming that

$$n = m \tag{69}$$

then, by substituting expression (67) into the indices in Formula (69), the following equation was finally obtained for the flow course:

$$\Psi(m) = \Psi(m-1) + h{\cdot}u_2(n) \tag{70}$$

The modified Euler method used in the numerical integration algorithm is, in fact, a combination of the two basic Euler methods described earlier. The modification introduced, however, consists in the fact that two values of the voltage waveform from two moments of time are used to perform the integration operation, and then they are averaged, which is expressed by the following equation:

$$y_{n+1} = y_n + \frac{h}{2} \cdot [\mathrm{f}(t_n, y_n) + \mathrm{f}(t_{n+1}, y_{n+1})] \tag{71}$$

assuming that

$$n = m - 1 \tag{72}$$

Finally, Equation (71), after substituting Equation (72) for subscripts, was transformed into (73) in such a way that it expresses the current value of the flux curve determined on the basis of the previous value of the flux curve (initial value) and the average of the current and previous values of the integrated voltage curve:

$$\Psi(m) = \Psi(m-1) + \frac{h}{2} \cdot [u_2(m-1) + u_2(m)] \tag{73}$$

Equation (73) expresses the implicit modified Euler method of the second order. This form is almost identical to the form of the equation used in the Heun method. However, in the case of the adopted method, it is necessary to perform the prediction of the function value for the next step using the basic Euler method because after shifting (delaying) the algorithm by one step, the algorithm is calculated based on the measured value of the integrated voltage. The advantage of the chosen numerical integration method is the improvement of the accuracy of the obtained results in comparison with the previously presented basic Euler methods. Figure 14 shows a pictorial comparison of the accuracy of numerical methods (basic Euler methods and the applied modified Euler method) with respect to the exact solution.

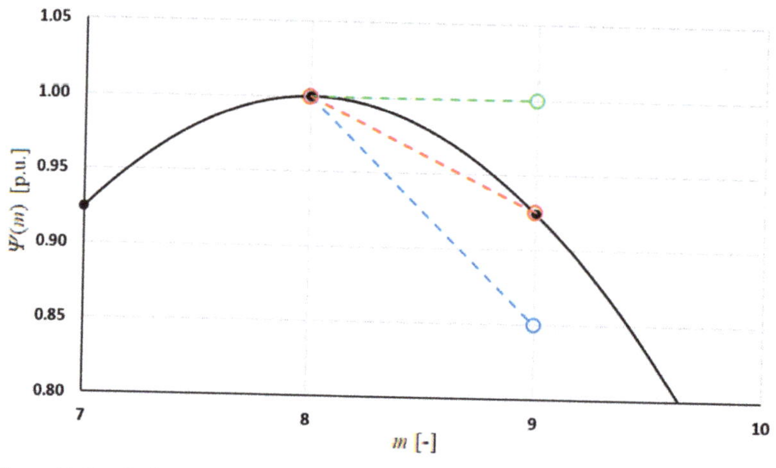

Figure 14. Graph illustrating integration errors for the considered numerical integration methods (green section—forward Euler, blue section—backward Euler, red section—modified Euler, black section—analytical solution).

As can be seen from the above figure, the modified Euler method, with averaging, provides a much more accurate solution compared to both basic methods. As mentioned in the introduction (Section 1), the indefinite integral Equation (11) contains an integration constant C, the value of which is calculated based on the knowledge of the initial conditions, i.e., the initial value of the linkage Ψ_0; however, this value is not known. Therefore, in practical applications of the numerical integration algorithm, it is assumed that for the first iteration, when $m = 1$, the initial value of the associated flux is equal to zero:

$$\Psi(m-1) = \Psi(0) = 0 \quad (74)$$

This assumption, although convenient, is, however, false. Assuming zero initial conditions means that in the case of integration of a sinusoidal waveform, an additional constant component will appear in the solution, the value of which will depend on the initial phase angle of the integrated waveform (in practice, until the integration begins).

$$\int A \cdot \sin(\omega t)dt = -\frac{1}{\omega} \cdot A \cdot cos(\omega t) + C \quad (75)$$

Assuming zero initial conditions for solving Equation (75), we obtain the following equation:

$$-\frac{1}{\omega} \cdot A \cdot cos(\omega t) + C = 0 \quad (76)$$

Equation (76) has been rearranged to determine the value of the integration constant C:

$$C = 0 + \frac{1}{\omega} \cdot A \cdot cos(\omega t) \quad (77)$$

Equation (77) is calculated for time $t = 0$:

$$C = \frac{1}{\omega} \cdot A \cdot cos(\omega \cdot 0) = \frac{1}{\omega} \cdot A \quad (78)$$

Finally, substituting the result of Equation (78) into Equation (75), we obtain Equation (79), which is true for assumed zero initial conditions:

$$\int A \cdot \sin(\omega t)dt = -\frac{1}{\omega} \cdot A \cdot cos(\omega t) + \frac{1}{\omega} \cdot A = \frac{1}{\omega} \cdot A \cdot (-cos(\omega t) + 1) = \frac{1}{\omega} \cdot (-A \cdot cos(\omega t) + A) \quad (79)$$

According to Formula (79), the value of the integration constant depends on the amplitude A and on the value of ωt, i.e., on the initial phase angle of the integrated waveform. Furthermore, according to the basic Formula (80) for the indefinite integral of the constant a, the solution is a linear function whose slope is equal to the constant a:

$$\int a dx = a \cdot x + C \quad (80)$$

This means that the integration operation is sensitive to the presence of a constant component in the input signal. Considering technical limitations, it is necessary to modify the numerical integration algorithm in such a way that during subsequent iterations, both the constant component in the input signal and the constant component (offset) in the output signal resulting from the assumed zero initial conditions are eliminated. A simplified block diagram of the proposed integration algorithm with offset elimination is shown in Figure 15.

The algorithm uses Walsh filters of order 0 (rectangular filters of the average value with a window width of 25 Hz). Subtracting the average value calculated from the input signal eliminates the problem of the presence of a constant component of the input signal, resulting in a linear rise/fall of the solution. The elimination of the constant component at the output is ensured by filtering the constant component from the solution, the value of which is then subtracted in the feedback loop from the signal entering the integrator. The calculated average value is also multiplied by an appropriately selected gain/attenuation coefficient β. This coefficient should always be less than 0.5. Otherwise, in certain conditions, problems with the obtained stability (convergence) of the solution may occur. Adopting values of the β coefficient closer to 0.5 results in faster elimination of the constant component but at the cost of increasing the decaying oscillations of the solution. The adoption of smaller values, closer to 0.1, extends the elimination time of the DC component but allows obtaining an asymptotically stabilising solution. In the proposed algorithm, the value of the gain/attenuation coefficient was assumed to be $\beta = 0.25$. The sampling frequency of the analogue signal was $f_p = 3200$ Hz.

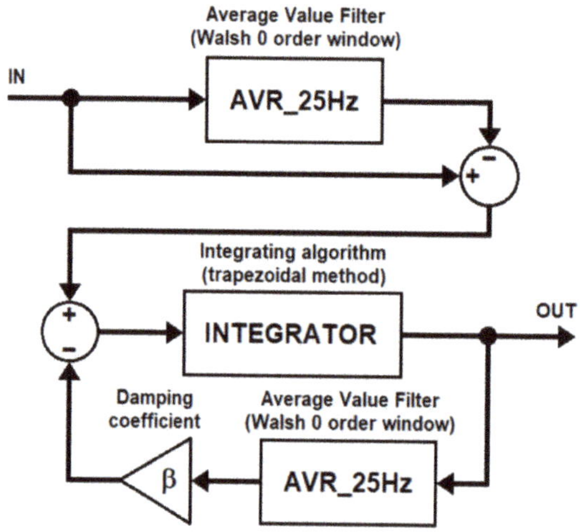

Figure 15. Simplified block diagram illustrating the idea of the applied numerical integration algorithm with elimination of the constant component at the input and output of the integrator.

6. Results

Using the analogue and numerical (digital) methods of integrating phase voltage waveforms, the estimated associated flux waveforms in the core of the simulated voltage transformer were obtained. For both integration methods, the obtained flux waveforms were superimposed on the reference waveforms generated by the simulation model.

6.1. Results of the Analogue Method

Figure 16 shows a comparison of the reference flux curve and the curve estimated using an analogue integrator for the network capacitance to earth $C_0 = 17.5$ μF.

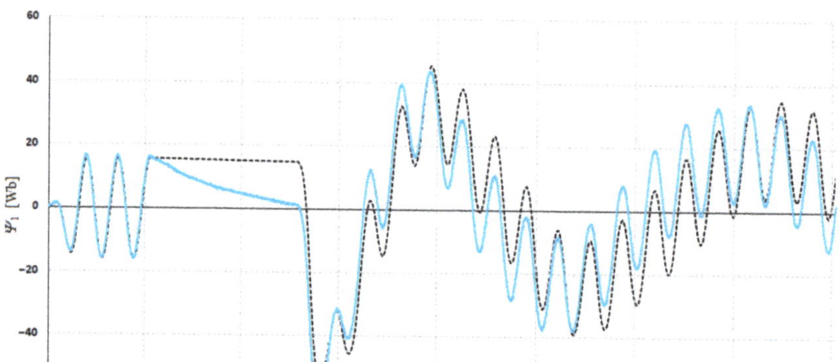

Figure 16. Comparison of the reference flux curve (grey, dashed) and the curve estimated by the analogue integration system (blue) for the capacitance $C_0 = 17.5$ μF.

Figure 17 shows a comparison of the reference flux curve and the curve estimated using an analogue integrator for the network capacitance to earth C_0 = 1.85 μF.

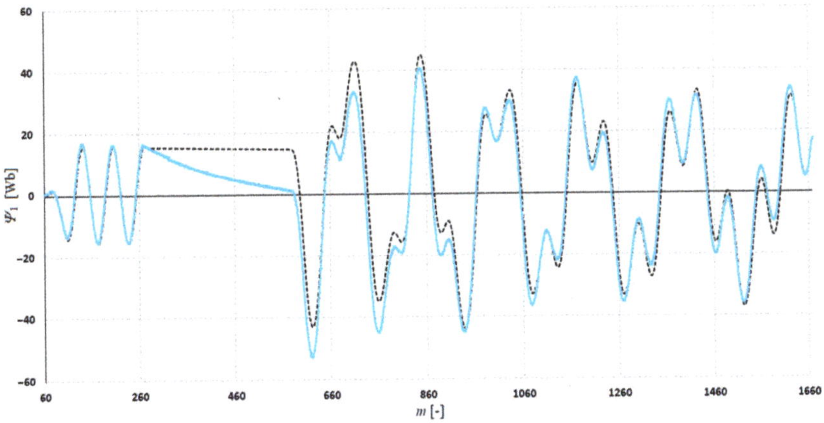

Figure 17. Comparison of the reference flux curve (grey, dashed) and the curve estimated by the analogue integration system (blue) for the capacitance C_0 = 1.85 μF.

Figure 18 shows a comparison of the reference flux curve and the curve estimated using an analogue integrator for the network capacitance to earth C_0 = 1.5 μF.

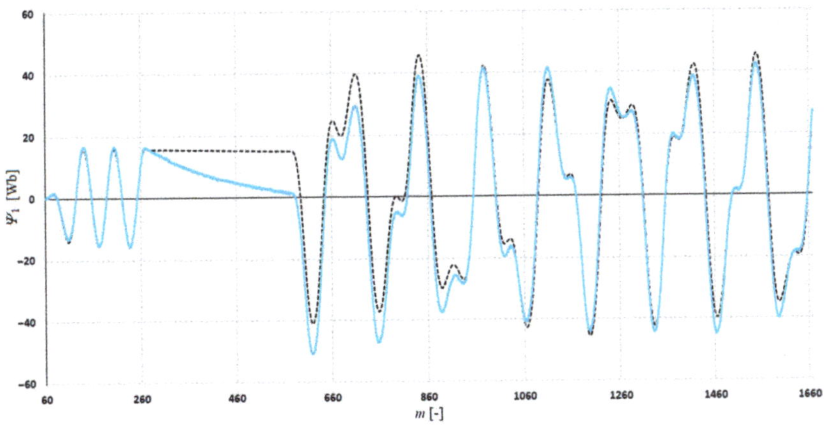

Figure 18. Comparison of the reference flux curve (grey, dashed) and the curve estimated by the analogue integration system (blue) for the capacitance C_0 = 1.5 μF.

Figure 19 shows a comparison of the reference flux curve and the curve estimated using an analogue integrator for the network capacitance to earth C_0 = 100 nF.

Figure 20 shows a comparison of the reference flux curve and the curve estimated using an analogue integrator for the network capacitance to earth C_0 = 9 nF.

For all flux patterns (Figures 16–20) obtained by using the analogue method, an aperiodic decay of the associated flux pattern in phase L1 was observed during the short circuit. If a constant component occurred in the reference ferroresonance oscillation patterns (Figures 19 and 20), it was damped. This means that the analogue method used does not allow for the estimation of the magnetic remanence in the core or the constant component in the flux pattern. The oscillating, slowly changing component occurred in the reference pattern (Figure 16) and was represented less accurately when the rate of its change was the highest. For all flux patterns, after damping the constant component, the periodic components were represented with relatively high accuracy.

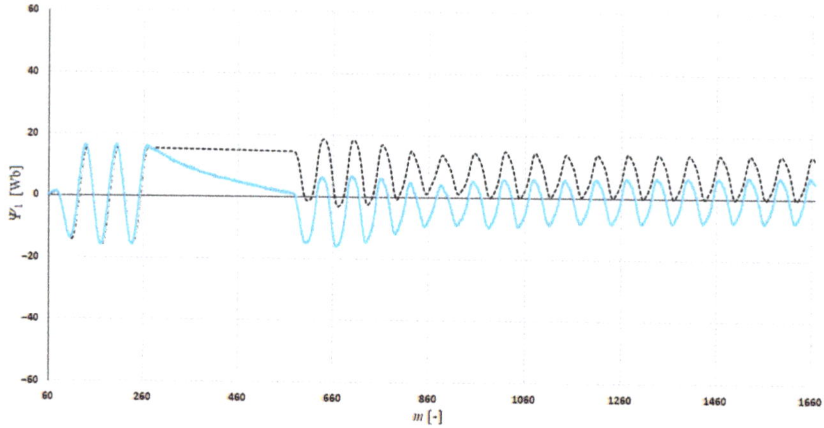

Figure 19. Comparison of the reference flux curve (grey, dashed) and the curve estimated by the analogue integration system (blue) for the capacitance $C_0 = 100$ nF.

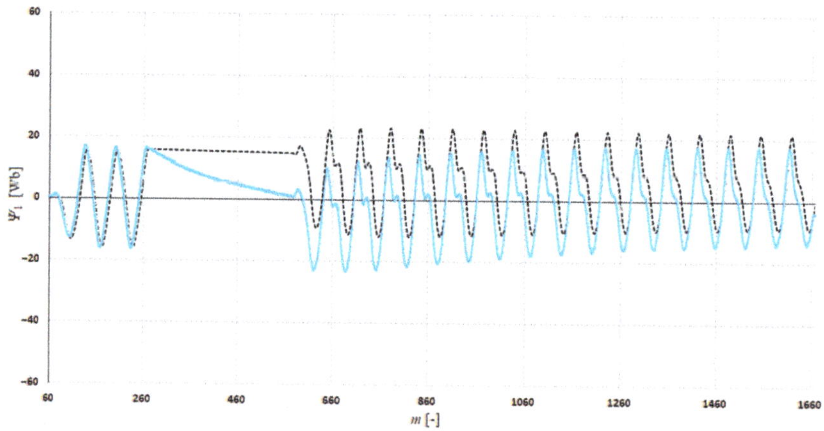

Figure 20. Comparison of the reference flux curve (grey, dashed) and the curve estimated by the analogue integration system (blue) for the capacitance $C_0 = 9$ nF.

6.2. Results of the Digital Method

Figure 21 shows a comparison of the reference flux curve and the curve estimated using the proposed numerical integration algorithm with offset elimination for the network capacitance to earth $C_0 = 17.5$ μF.

Figure 22 shows a comparison of the reference flux curve and the curve estimated using the proposed numerical integration algorithm with offset elimination for the network capacitance to earth $C_0 = 1.85$ μF.

Figure 23 shows a comparison of the reference flux curve and the curve estimated using the proposed numerical integration algorithm with offset elimination for the network capacitance to earth $C_0 = 1.5$ μF.

Figure 24 shows a comparison of the reference flux curve and the curve estimated using the proposed numerical integration algorithm with offset elimination for the network capacitance to earth $C_0 = 100$ nF.

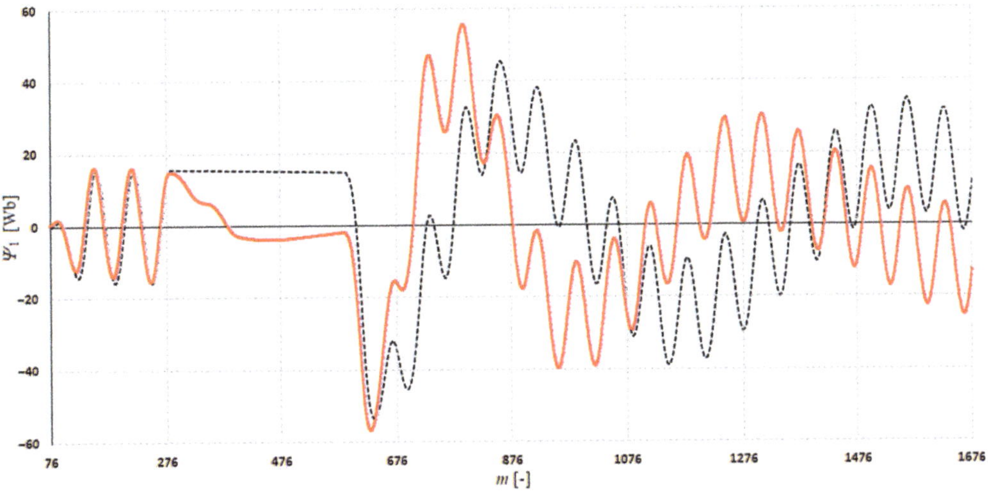

Figure 21. Comparison of the reference flux curve (grey, dashed) and the curve estimated with the proposed numerical integration algorithm with offset elimination (red) for the capacitance $C_0 = 17.5$ μF.

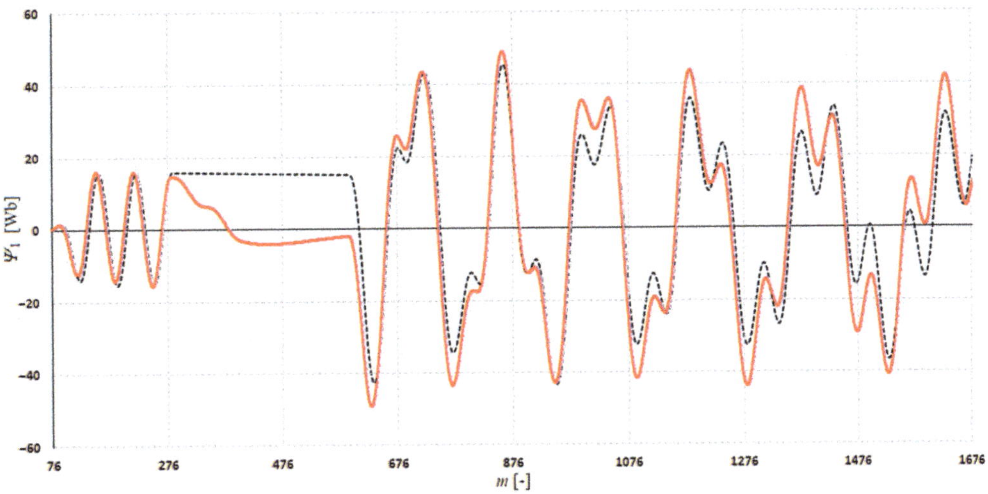

Figure 22. Comparison of the reference flux curve (grey, dashed) and the curve estimated with the proposed numerical integration algorithm with offset elimination (red) for the capacitance $C_0 = 1.85$ μF.

Figure 25 shows a comparison of the reference flux curve and the curve estimated using the proposed numerical integration algorithm with offset elimination for the network capacitance to earth $C_0 = 9$ nF.

For all flux courses (Figures 21–25) obtained by using the proposed digital method, a nonlinear, oscillatory-like decay of the flux course was observed in the voltage-free interval range. If a constant component occurred in the reference ferroresonance oscillations courses (Figures 24 and 25), it was damped. This means that the proposed digital method does not allow for the estimation of the magnetic remanence in the core or the constant component in the flux course. The oscillating, slowly changing component occurred in the reference course (Figure 21) and was represented incorrectly, with a relatively large error. For all flux courses, after damping the constant component, the periodic components were represented with relatively high accuracy.

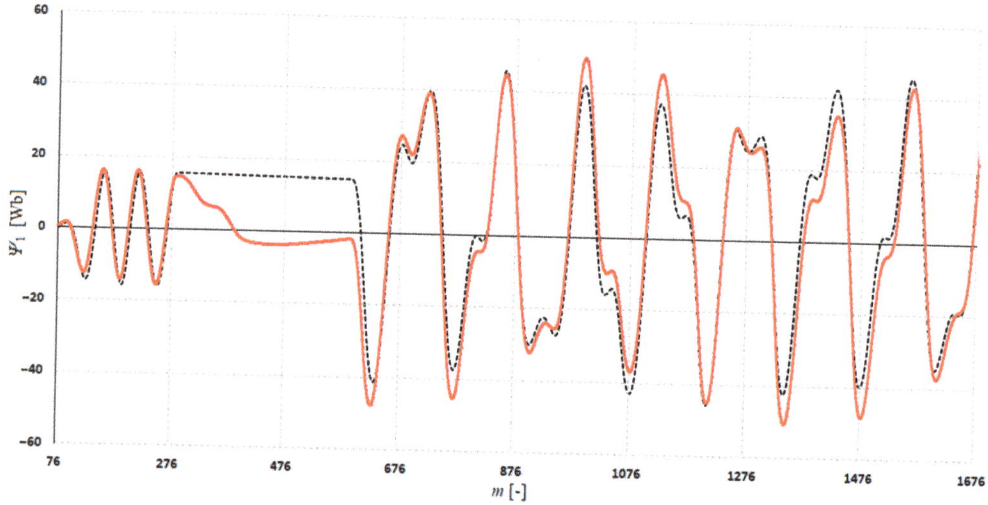

Figure 23. Comparison of the reference flux curve (grey, dashed) and the curve estimated with the proposed numerical integration algorithm with offset elimination (red) for the capacitance $C_0 = 1.5$ μF.

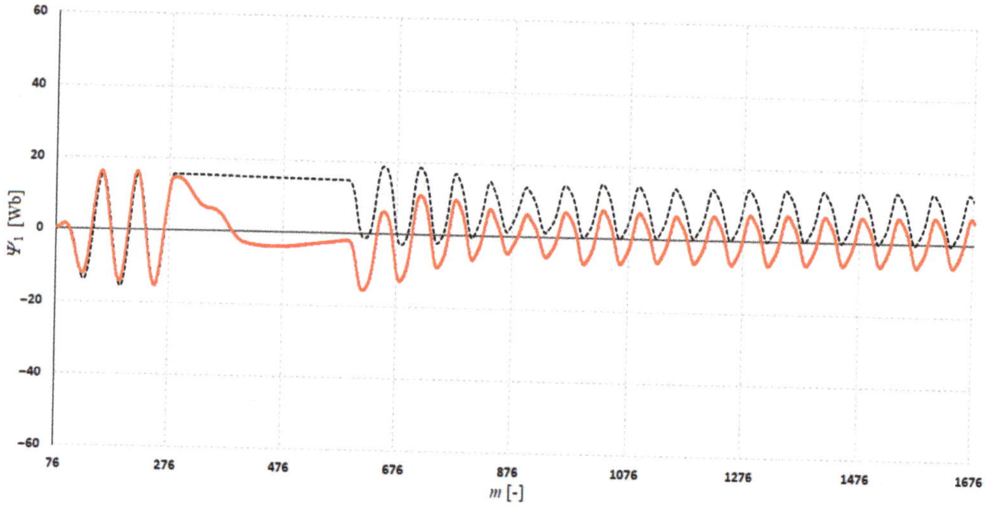

Figure 24. Comparison of the reference flux curve (grey, dashed) and the curve estimated with the proposed numerical integration algorithm with offset elimination (red) for the capacitance $C_0 = 100$ nF.

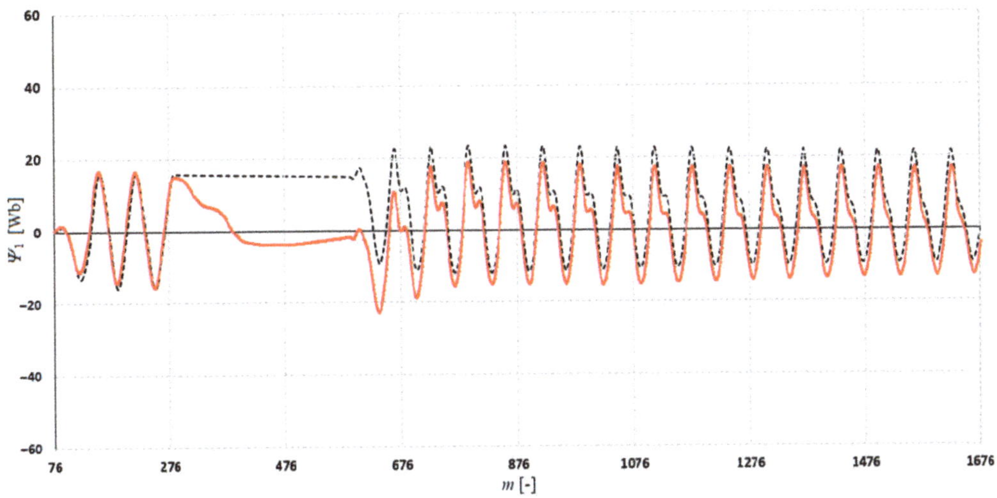

Figure 25. Comparison of the reference flux curve (grey, dashed) and the curve estimated with the proposed numerical integration algorithm with offset elimination (red) for the capacitance $C_0 = 9$ nF.

6.3. Comparison of the Results

After completing the research on both applied integration methods, the analogue and digital methods, aimed at comparing the estimated associated flux waveforms with the reference waveforms generated by simulation, an attempt was made to perform a comparative analysis of the results for both integration methods. Comparing the results of both methods, the accuracy (convergence) of the results, the speed of convergence and the stability of the solution were analysed. Comparing both methods with each other, as well as with the reference waveform, it was found that both methods do not allow for correct estimation of the constant component of the flux waveform. This is an expected consequence of using a differentiator and an additional resistor in the feedback loop of the differentiator of the analogue system. Similarly, for the digital method, this is a consequence of using mean value filters that eliminate the constant component, both at the input and output of the algorithm. Both methods allow for the estimation of the periodic component of the flux waveform but with different amplitude and angular accuracy. In the case of the analogue method, as the frequency of the input voltage signal decreases, the angular shift of the signal relative to the expected delay by 90° also decreases. Therefore, the accuracy of the integration operation decreases. Below the frequency of 10.26 Hz, the integration process stops completely, and the response of the analogue system is similar to the differentiation operation (the output signal leads the input signal in phase). This characteristic explains the change in the dynamics of the estimated slowly changing component in the flux course (Figure 20). The integrating term used in the digital method allows for the correct estimation of the periodic component for low frequencies, but the added average value filters, with the measurement window width set to 25 Hz, cause the estimated flux signals with a frequency lower than 25 Hz to be strongly distorted (Figure 25). This results from the oscillating responses of the average value filters at signal frequencies lower than the filter cut-off frequency (too narrow a measurement window of the filters). These oscillations, although with a much smaller amplitude, will also appear when the input signal frequency is not an integer multiple of the 25 Hz frequency. This feature is a source of estimation errors for the digital method.

The digital method was characterised by a faster, although nonlinear, elimination of the constant component (convergence to the steady state). The analogue method allows for a shorter elimination time of the constant component but at the cost of the angular accuracy of the integration operation.

Due to better integration properties for low frequencies, the applied analogue method allowed for a more accurate representation of the periodic components of the flux waveform. The digital method, although less accurate, turned out to be faster. The use of average value filters with a wider measurement window (e.g., for a frequency of 12.5 Hz) would improve the accuracy of the estimation but at the cost of extending its time.

7. Conclusions

The article presents the results of tests of two selected methods of integrating the secondary voltage waveforms of a voltage transformer, generated using a simulation model, in order to determine the linkage waveforms in the transformer core. The secondary voltage integration was performed using an analogue method on a prepared electronic integrator and a digital method using the proposed numerical integration algorithm (trapezoidal method) with the elimination of the constant component implemented in the STM32 microcontroller. The estimated flux waveforms were then compared with the reference flux waveforms generated by simulation in order to qualitatively assess the results obtained for the tested integration methods.

Based on the tests of selected integration methods, the following was found:

1. Both the analogue and digital methods are able to relatively accurately estimate the periodic component of the associated flux in steady states;
2. None of the applied integration methods is able to estimate the constant component of the associated flux in the core (magnetic remanence). This results from the necessity of eliminating the offset of the integration operation, both in the case of the analogue and digital methods and eliminating the constant component from the input signal;
3. For the adopted parameters of both applied integration methods, the elimination of the constant component is faster for the proposed digital method;
4. For the analogue method, the speed of eliminating the constant component depends on the adopted values of the parameters of the integrating element and the parameters of the differentiating element (high-pass filter used to eliminate the constant component of the input signal);
5. For the digital method, the speed of eliminating the constant component depends on the adopted widths of the measurement windows of the average value filters. Extending the width of the measurement window results in a slower filtration speed but improves the accuracy of estimating the periodic components of the slowly changing flux;
6. For a signal with a frequency of 25 Hz, the analogue method estimates the waveform of the linkage with a larger angular error than the proposed digital method. This results from the use of a differentiating term and the parameters of the integrating term. Reducing the angular error is possible by increasing the time constant and, therefore, by slowing down the dynamics of the system (slower elimination of the constant component);
7. The applied analogue method allowed for a more accurate estimation of the oscillatory decaying component compared to the proposed digital method. The errors in estimating slowly changing components result from the selected parameters and the properties of the mean value filters;
8. The advantage of the applied digital method is its flexibility due to its implementation in a microcontroller. This algorithm can be relatively easily modified, unlike the electronic system (analogue method) implemented in hardware;
9. Both the analogue and digital methods can be used as methods for estimating the linkage within the core in order to identify ferroresonance, provided, however, that the detection criterion is based only on measurements of the periodic component in the steady state;
10. Studies of the analogue input circuit have shown that the use of an operational amplifier operating in an inverting differential circuit allows for obtaining smaller interferences in the output signal than in the case of the used summation circuit. The

input signal should then first pass through the inverting amplifier and then be fed to the inverting (negative) input of the differential circuit. A constant offset voltage would be fed to the non-inverting (adding) input;
11. In the case of an attempt to estimate the flux waveform from the secondary voltage waveform, it is necessary not to use galvanic separation. Otherwise, the integration operation will, as it were, estimate the flux in the separating transformer and not in the core of the voltage transformer. In addition, the use of a separating transformer will result in an additional phase shift that is sensitive to the frequency of the input signal;
12. The proposed numerical integration algorithm with the elimination of the constant component (offset) implemented within the digital method requires further research.

8. Summary and Proposed Applications

As the main findings, it should be emphasised that both applied methods—analogue and digital—can be alternatively used to implement the integration operation and estimate the magnetic flux linkage in the core of a voltage transformer. Both methods allow for determining the periodic component of the flux course. Due to the construction of the proposed analogue electrical circuit and the offset elimination in the digital algorithm, it is not possible to estimate the magnetic remanence in the core. It is also worth noting that the problem of eliminating the offset of the numerical integration operation and making it insensitive to the constant component makes the digital algorithm quite complicated. This problem was addressed in the paper [15], where, in order to avoid this problem, it was decided to perform an approximate integration operation through a digital low-pass filter. Since this filter itself also suppresses the constant component, it also allows only for estimating the periodic component of the flux course (correctly only for a limited frequency range).

Potentially, both methods could be used to create a unique criterion for detecting ferroresonant oscillations in medium voltage networks. Phase voltages or zero sequence voltage could then be integrated. Magnetic fluxes calculated in this way could constitute an input signal for the excess element calculating the RMS value or the peak value of the periodic course. Measurements of both of these criteria quantities are, of course, associated with further problems (in particular, dependence on frequency). Nevertheless, even for a measurement window of constant width, the development of a new detection criterion using the estimated magnetic flux linkage is possible.

Another application could also be proposed as an attempt to estimate the location of the instantaneous operating point on the magnetisation characteristic of a voltage transformer. Assuming that the shape of the magnetisation characteristic is not known, an additional measurement of the current drawn by the voltage transformer is necessary. In combination with the estimated periodic component of the magnetic flux, this would allow for the estimation of the course of the magnetic hysteresis. The measured distorted current drawn by the transformer, which is almost equal to the magnetising current, could be the basis for reproducing the magnetic remanence in the transformer core. Of course, such an application requires further research and the development of a method for measuring the very small current drawn by the voltage transformer. Despite these difficulties, magnetic flux estimation could also be useful in this case.

Author Contributions: Conceptualization, P.S. and A.S.; methodology, P.S.; software, P.S. and A.S.; validation, P.S.; formal analysis, P.S. and A.S.; investigation, P.S. and M.O.; resources, P.S.; data curation, P.S.; writing—original draft preparation, P.S.; writing—review and editing, P.Ł., A.S., S.Ł., M.S., A.Ł. and Ł.K.; visualisation, P.S.; supervision, P.S. and A.S.; project administration, P.S.; funding acquisition, Ł.N. All authors have read and agreed to the published version of the manuscript.

Funding: This work was supported by Electrical Power Engineering Institute of Warsaw University of Technology within research subsidy, (ZPB program IE_ZPB_1_01_2022).

Institutional Review Board Statement: Not applicable.

Informed Consent Statement: Not applicable.

Data Availability Statement: The data presented in this study are available on request from the corresponding author. The data are not publicly available due to Mr. Suchorolski will be defending his doctorate on the subject. Until the defense, he does not want to disclose this information.

Conflicts of Interest: The authors declare no conflicts of interest.

References

1. Starczakow, W. *Przekładniki*; Państwowe Wydawnictwa Techniczne: Warszawa, Poland, 1959.
2. Minkner, R.; Schmid, J.; Däumling, H.; Prucker, U.; Bräunlich, R.; Hofstetter, M. *Ferroresonance Oscillations in Substations with Inductive Voltage Transformers in Medium and High Voltage Systems*; VDE VERLAG GmbH: Berlin, Germany, 2019.
3. Ferracci, P. *Ferroresonance, Cahier Technique No. 190*; Groupe Schneider: Rueil-Malmaison, France, 1998.
4. El-Shafhy, M.M.; Abdel-hamed, A.M.; Badran, E.A. Ferroresonance in Distribution Systems—State of the Art. *Przegląd Elektrotechniczny* **2022**, *1*, 3–17. [CrossRef]
5. Valverde, V.; Mazon, A.J.; Zamora, I.; Buigues, G. Ferroresonance in Voltage Transformers: Analysis and Simulations. *Renew. Energy Power Qual. J.* **2010**, *1*, 465–471. [CrossRef]
6. Emin, Z.; Martinez, M.; Val Escudero, M.; Adams, R.; De Souza Bronzeado, H.; Caillaut, C.; Chiesa, N.; Jacobson, D.; Kocis, L.; Martinich, T.; et al. *Resonance and Ferroresonance in Power Networks*; Power system technical performance (C4), WG C4.307; CIGRE: Paris, France, 2014.
7. Solak, K.; Rebizant, W. Modeling of Ferroresonance Phenomena in MV Networks. In Proceedings of the IEEE Electrical Power and Energy Conference (EPEC), Toronto, ON, Canada, 10–11 October 2018.
8. Wiśniewski, J.; Anderson, E.; Karolak, J. Sensitivity of Power Station Auxiliary Network to the Possibility of Ferroresonance Occurrence. *Acta Energetica* **2014**, *21*, 171–177. [CrossRef]
9. Piasecki, W.; Florkowski, M.; Fulczyk, M.; Mahonen, P.; Nowak, W. Mitigating Ferroresonance in Voltage Transformers in Ungrounded MV Networks. *IEEE Trans. Power Deliv.* **2007**, *22*, 2362–2369. [CrossRef]
10. Tokić, A.; Kasumović, M.; Demirovic, D.; Turkovic, I. Ferroresonance in 35 kV isolated networks: Causes and mitigations. *Elektrotehniski Vestn./Electrotech. Rev.* **2016**, *83*, 259–265.
11. Wagner, A.; Knauel, J.; Prochazka, R.; Tlusty, J. Ferroresonance Phenomena in Medium Voltage Systems. In Proceedings of the International Symposium on High Voltage Engineering, Pilsen, Czech Republic, 23–28 August 2015; ISH Collection.
12. Martínez, R.; Manana, M.; Rodríguez, J.I.; Álvarez, M.; Mínguez, R.; Arroyo, A.; Bayona, E.; Azcondo, F.; Pigazo, A.; Cuartas, F. Ferroresonance phenomena in medium-voltage isolated neutral grids: A case study. *IET Renew. Power Gener.* **2019**, *13*, 209–214. [CrossRef]
13. Zirka, S.E.; Moroz, Y.I.; Zhuykov, A.V.; Matveev, D.A.; Kubatkin, M.A.; Frolov, M.V.; Popov, M. Eliminating VT uncertainties in modeling ferroresonance phenomena caused by single phase-to-ground faults in isolated neutral network. *Int. J. Electr. Power Energy Syst.* **2021**, *133*, 107275. [CrossRef]
14. Kraszewski, W.; Syrek, P.; Mitoraj, M. Methods of Ferroresonance Mitigation in Voltage Transformers in a 30 kV Power Supply Network. *Energies* **2022**, *15*, 9516. [CrossRef]
15. Solak, K.; Rebizant, W.; Kereit, M. Detection of Ferroresonance Oscillations in Medium Voltage Networks. *Energies* **2020**, *13*, 4129. [CrossRef]
16. Kong, H.; Zhang, B. A novel ferroresonance and single-phase earth foult recognition method based on correlation analysis. In Proceedings of the 14th International Conference on Environment and Electrical Engineering, Krakow, Poland, 10–12 May 2014; pp. 426–430.
17. Rezaei, S. An intelligent algorithm for negative sequence directional element of DFIG during ferroresonance in smart grid. In Proceedings of the IEEE International Conference on Environment and Electrical Engineering and 2019 IEEE Industrial and Commercial Power Systems Europe (EEEIC/I&CPS Europe), Genova, Italy, 11–14 June 2019; pp. 1–6.
18. Sharbain, H.A.; Osman, A.; El-Hag, A. Detection and identification of ferroresonance. In Proceedings of the 7th International Conference on Modeling, Simulation, and Applied Optimization (ICMSAO), Sharjah, United Arab Emirates, 4–6 April 2017; pp. 1–4.
19. Arroyo, A.; Martinez, R.; Manana, M.; Pigazo, A.; Minguez, R. Detection of ferroresonance occurrence in inductive voltage transformers through vibration analysis. *Electr. Power Energy Syst.* **2019**, *106*, 294–300. [CrossRef]
20. Chwaleba, A.; Moeschke, B.; Płoszajski, G.; Majdak, P.; Świstak, P. *Podstawy Elektroniki*; Wydawnictwo Naukowe PWN: Warszawa, Poland, 2021.
21. Górecki, P. *Wzmacniacze Operacyjne*; Wydawnictwo BTC: Warszawa, Poland, 2004.
22. Carter, B.; Mancini, R. *Wzmacniacze Operacyjne Teoria i Praktyka*; Wydawnictwo BTC: Legionowo, Poland, 2011.
23. Markiewicz, T.; Szmurło, R.; Wincenciak, S. *Metody numeryczne. Wykłady na Wydziale Elektrycznym Politechniki Warszawskiej*; Oficyna Wydawnicza Politechniki Warszawskiej: Warszawa, Poland, 2014.
24. Wiszniewski, A. *Przekładniki w Elektroenergetyce*; Wydawnictwa Naukowo-Techniczne: Warszawa, Poland, 1982.
25. Tadeusiewicz, M. *Teoria Obwodów. Część I*; Wydawnictwo Politechniki Łódzkiej: Łodź, Poland, 2003.
26. Krakowski, M. *Elektrotechnika Teoretyczna. Obwody Liniowe i Nieliniowe*; Wydawnictwo Naukowe PWN: Warszawa, Poland, 1995.

27. Wiszniewski, A. *Algorytmy Pomiarów Cyfrowych w Automatyce Elektroenergetycznej*; Wydawnictwa Naukowo-Techniczne: Warszawa, Poland, 1990.
28. Marven, C.; Ewers, G. *Zarys Cyfrowego Przetwarzania Sygnałów*; Wydawnictwa Komunikacji i Łączności: Warszawa, Poland, 1999.

applied sciences

MDPI

Article

Two-Dimensional Scanning of Circularly Polarized Beams via Array-Fed Fabry–Perot Cavity Antennas

Mikhail Madji [1], Edoardo Negri [1,2], Walter Fuscaldo [2], Davide Comite [1], Alessandro Galli [1,*] and Paolo Burghignoli [1]

[1] Department of Information Engineering, Electronics and Telecommunications, Sapienza University of Rome, 00184 Rome, Italy; mikhail.madji@uniroma1.it (M.M.); edoardo.negri@uniroma1.it (E.N.); davide.comite@uniroma1.it (D.C.); paolo.burghignoli@uniroma1.it (P.B.)

[2] Istituto per la Microelettronica e Microsistemi, Consiglio Nazionale delle Ricerche, 00133 Rome, Italy; walter.fuscaldo@cnr.it

* Correspondence: alessandro.galli@uniroma1.it

Abstract: In this paper, we present an array-fed Fabry–Perot cavity antenna (FPCA) based on a partially reflecting sheet (PRS) capable of generating a circularly polarized (CP), highly directive, far-field radiation pattern in the 27–28.5 GHz frequency range. The PRS, the cavity, and the array of feeders serve to different purposes in this original structure. The PRS is engineered to produce a circular polarization from a linearly polarized source placed inside the cavity. The cavity is optimized to obtain a directive conical beam from the dipole-like pattern of the simple source, and allows for a frequency scan of the beam along the elevation plane. The array of feeders is designed to obtain a pencil beam whose azimuthal pointing direction can be controlled by properly phasing the sources. The radiation performance is studied with a specific application of the reciprocity theorem in a full-wave solver along with the pattern multiplication principle. A number of array-pattern configurations in terms of operation frequency and phase shift are investigated and presented to show the potential of the proposed solution in terms of design flexibility and radiation performance.

Keywords: Fabry–Perot cavity antennas; circular polarization; phased arrays; leaky-wave antennas

1. Introduction

Several applications areas, such as remote sensing, satellite communications, radar, and health engineering call for antenna solutions capable of realizing circularly polarized (CP) beams. No need for reciprocal alignment, improved resistance to multipath fading, and the capability to easily overcome obstacles on the data link confer an increased appeal to the CP regime [1–3]. With respect to other modern techniques, based on metasurfaces in transmitting or reflecting mode (see, e.g., [4–7]), CP leaky-wave antennas (LWAs), using a single-element structure, offer notable advantages in terms of compactness, planar geometries, and simple feeding schemes, critical for antennas in integrated complex systems. Two significant advantages of CP-LWAs compared to other techniques are represented by the inherent frequency-scanning property and the possibility to suitably engineer the radiating aperture to realize polarization-conversion metasurfaces. These two properties result in a significant simplification of the primary sources, which can, in turn, rely on simple, non-directive, dipole-like, linearly polarized elements [8–18].

Interestingly, attempts to exploit these two properties for obtaining scanning CP beams recently involved the use of 1-D LWAs based on substrate integrated waveguides (SIWs) [19,20]. While these solutions allow for radiating an elevation-directive CP fan beam from the backward to the forward quadrant through the broadside, they cannot reconfigure the beam over the azimuthal plane.

In this respect, Fabry–Perot cavity antennas (FPCAs) [21] offer a flexible and advantageous solution. As is well known [22], FPCAs can be modeled as 2-D LWAs, and are often designed to radiate either a linearly polarized (LP) pencil beam at the broadside, or an LP frequency-scannable (almost omnidirectional) conical beam [14]. Progress has recently been made in realizing CP beams, as well as in beam-shaping techniques.

Independent excitation of both a TM and a TE leaky wave has been proven as an effective technique in [23]. A way to ensure the two required modes consists of employing two distinct sources. A vertical electric dipole (VED) is obtained by the insertion of a coaxial cable through the ground plane to excite a TM leaky wave, whereas the TE counterpart can be excited by an equivalent vertical magnetic dipole (VMD) or, more practically, by a circular array of slots etched in the ground plane [24]. Considering a resonant cavity formed by a ground plane and a homogenized partially reflective surface (PRS), the proposed approach enables polarization control, easily switching from LP to CP beams. This feature is achieved through an antenna biasing system that equalizes the magnitudes of the vertical and horizontal far-field components and provides the desired phase shift in quadrature [23]. The antenna design in [23] demonstrates the flexibility in obtaining CP beams, once two complementary feeders are provided in the cavity. To reduce the complexity of the feeding structure, different antenna architectures for producing CP beams were explored.

Linear-to-circular polarization conversion has been investigated through different techniques. A self-polarizing FPCA architecture has been proposed in [25], employing a nonresonant frequency selective surface (FSS) to induce resonance and a further twisting surface to produce the desired feature of circular polarization. A simple LP feeder is employed to generate resonance inside the cavity, which enables partial power leakage towards a polarizing ground plane, producing the complementary field component. Accurate cavity optimization allows it to radiate a pure CP beam at the broadside.

Synthetic materials, given to their artificially derived properties, have extensively reshaped applications, including the sector of guiding and radiating systems.

Recent advancements in the development of metasurfaces inspired interesting designs that operate in both reflection and transmission modes, also including tunable properties [26–34].

The profitable use of a metasurface-based PRS has been further investigated to obtain compact planar geometries devoted to polarization conversion. In [35,36], the typical highly reflective PRS is designed as a layered superposition of dielectric substrates and metals. Specifically, in [36], two separated patches decoupled by a metallic plane are considered in a transmitting–receiving scheme, with the bottom one exhibiting a high reflectivity necessary for high elevation selectivity, and the upper shaped one responsible for polarization conversion.

On the other hand, electronic beam-control methods, as part of beam shaping, have been proposed in [37–40], where the dimensions of the design elements are tuned to adjust the modal features of the supported leaky-wave solutions. A classic strategy to perform electronic beam steering consists of exploiting the standard array theory. Simple free-space arrays may require a large number of elements to obtain a fine direction tuning, suffering from parasite cross-talk phenomena among elements, grating lobes, and requiring complex feeding systems [41]. Embedding multiple sources in resonant cavities has been proven effective in [42,43], in terms of array thinning, simplification of the feeding scheme, and grating lobes mitigation.

In this work, we combine the concepts of polarization conversion and electronic array-based beam steering to obtain a novel polarization-conversion metasurface (PCM) with an increased axial-ratio (AR) elevation stability and an enhanced azimuthal symmetry of the unit cell. The main goal of this study is to design an FPCA capable of radiating highly directive CP pencil beams in any desired direction within a certain angular range by exploiting both the leaky-wave frequency scanning behavior and the use of multiple feeders.

This paper is organized as follows. In Section 2, the theoretical background and the PCM design strategy are presented. The latter is exploited in Section 3, where the element patterns of an optimized, original unit cell are obtained through computationally efficient full-wave simulations based on the reciprocity theorem. The consequence of embedding multiple sources is then illustrated in Section 4 for a few case studies. The final remarks and future perspectives are discussed in Section 5.

2. Unit-Cell Design and Analysis Strategy

The antenna structure is presented in Figure 1, as well as a detailed zoom on the PCM unit cell. Three main components should be distinguished: the PCM, the ground plane, and a simple horizontal electric dipole (HED) oriented along the y axis and placed in the middle of the cavity to have maximum gain [44,45]. Here, we consider both the ground plane and the PCM of infinite extent without taking into account possible truncation effects, as is typical for leaky-wave antennas with high aperture efficiency [14]. As concerns the source, an FPCA is commonly fed by any LP dipole-like radiator [22]. The use of a horizontal magnetic dipole (HMD), typically implemented through a resonant slot on the ground plane [46], or an HED, usually in the form of an L-shaped probe [22], allows for obtaining the broadside pencil beam, which are instead not possible with vertical dipole sources [14].

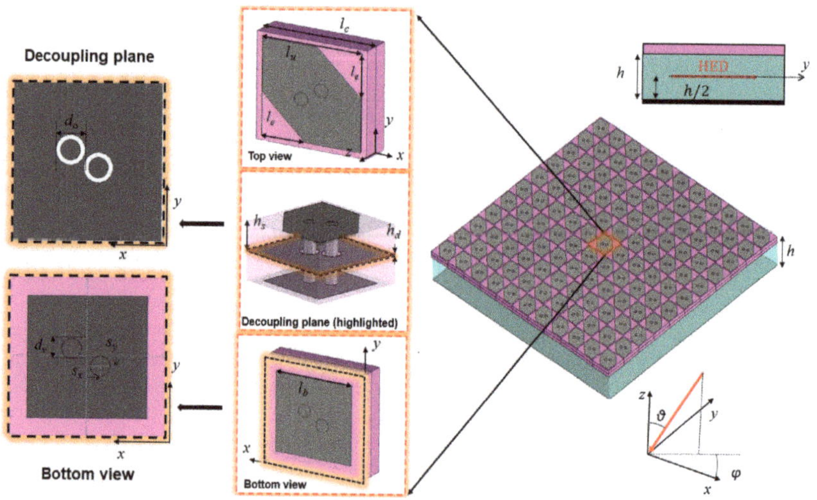

Figure 1. Pictorial representation of the proposed FPCA. The insets on the left show the PCM unit cell through different perspective views, indicating the main design parameters.

Concerning the PCM, this has been designed on the basis of the one proposed in [36], which has been suitably improved in order to ensure a good performance at different elevation and azimuth angles to allow for an efficient electronic scan of the beam. In particular, the PCM consists of three metallic patches sandwiching two square Rogers RO3203 dielectric substrates, whose dimensions are reported in Table 1. The bottom metallic square patch is responsible of field reflections inside the cavity [36], while the top metallic patch is shaped to obtain an LP-to-CP conversion [35]. The symmetry of the upper metallic patch with respect to the diagonal plane (see Figure 1) is instrumental to obtain the right-hand circular polarization (RHCP) [35,36]. The two top/bottom metallic sheets are separated by a further metallic layer located between them; the electrical coupling between the top and bottom layers is ensured by a pair (rather than a single, as in [36]) vertical via holes, whose symmetric location with respect to the center of the unit cell helps in improving the scanning performance of the resulting antenna.

As in [36], thanks to the stratified geometry of the PCM, one may optimize transmission features by tailoring the top patch without significantly affecting the reflection features, which are essentially established by the bottom patch. The central metallic patch that separates the dielectric substrates decouples the transmission and reflection patches so that their optimization can be carried out independently. Moreover, it has been shown that the position of the vias (see Figure 1), whose reciprocal distance accounts for the required phase quadrature between horizontal and vertical radiated components, does not modify the reflectivity of the bottom patch seen by the resonating field, both in terms of magnitude and phase. Hence, the phase of the reflection coefficient can be used, in particular, to design the cavity height h for maximum radiated power at broadside, according to von Trentini's formula [21], and it is not affected by further calibration steps.

In the case under analysis, a broadside pencil beam is obtained for $h = 3.5\,\text{mm}$.

Since typical multiple reflections inside an FPCA are supposed to modify the conversion properties of the free-standing PCM, we directly optimize the polarization-conversion properties of the latter in a reciprocity-based scenario. The latter accounts for multiple bounces that define the actual behavior of the device.

The optimization of the PCM top patch is performed by tuning the dimensions of its constituent elements on a given azimuthal plane, here the xz plane, such that the CP conditions are fulfilled, i.e., $|E_\theta|=|E_\phi|$, and $\angle E_\theta - \angle E_\phi = \pm 90°$.

The standard formulation based on the reciprocity theorem gives

$$\mathbf{J}_{\text{test}} \cdot \mathbf{E}_{\text{HED}} = \mathbf{J}_{\text{HED}} \cdot \mathbf{E}_{\text{test}} \tag{1}$$

where **J** and **E** represent the electric current density and the electric field, respectively, in the presence of the source (subscript 'HED') or of a test dipole in the far-field region producing an impinging plane wave (subscript 'test').

By reciprocity, the electric fields sampled by an ideal probe (oriented as the original HED), produced by plane waves impinging on the structure from different azimuthal and elevation angles, allow for recovering the overall 3-D far-field pattern for the E_ϕ and E_θ components from the incident TE and TM Floquet waves in the unit cell [47]. The CP components are finally obtained by the following transformation:

$$\begin{bmatrix} E_{\text{RHCP}} \\ E_{\text{LHCP}} \end{bmatrix} = \frac{1}{\sqrt{2}} \begin{bmatrix} 1 & j \\ 1 & -j \end{bmatrix} \begin{bmatrix} E_\theta \\ E_\phi \end{bmatrix} \tag{2}$$

with E_{RHCP} and E_{LHCP} being the right-hand and left-hand circular-polarization components, respectively.

The design parameters of the PCM are here optimized to have an RHCP broadside pencil beam at 27 GHz with low cross-polarization levels. Thanks to the aforementioned decoupling between the top and bottom layers of the PCM, the modifications introduced in the optimization of the top layer have very little impact on the reflection coefficient and hence on the cavity height. This concept is corroborated in Figure 2, where the reflection-coefficient phase is reported for different optimization steps showing a quasi-perfect superposition. The complete list of optimized unit-cell parameters is reported in Table 1, (see Figure 1 for the definition of the symbols).

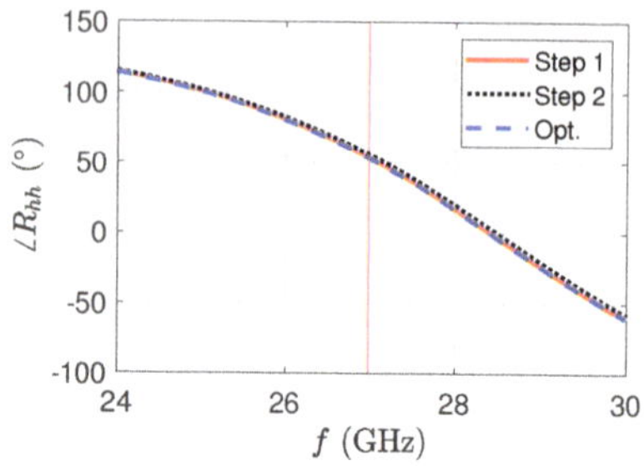

Figure 2. A comparison of the phases of the PCM reflection coefficient is presented. The blue dashed line represents the optimized configuration, while the red solid and black dotted lines correspond to sub-optimal cases, reflecting variations in the dimensions of the transmitting patch, the via holes, and their mutual distance.

Table 1. Unit -cell design parameters.

l_c (mm)	l_u (mm)	l_e (mm)	l_b (mm)	h_s (mm)
3.33	3	1.33	2.53	0.46
h_d (μm)	d_v (mm)	d_o (mm)	s_y (mm)	s_x (mm)
5	0.42	0.63	0.18	0.3

3. FPCA: Element Patterns and Far-Field Polarization

At this stage, one can evaluate the far-field components E_θ and E_ϕ over different directions and, thus, obtain the corresponding E_{RHCP} and E_{LHCP} quantities through (2). The desired co-polar, far-field pattern of the E_{RHCP} component is reported in Figure 3a–e for different frequencies in the overall 27–28.5 GHz range. As expected, in Figure 3a, a broadside pencil beam is observed at 27 GHz. The −3 dB gain and 3 dB AR isolines are reported with a dashed black line and solid magenta line, respectively. It is manifest that the design process effectively led to a CP narrow beam at broadside for 27 GHz.

As expected, as the frequency increases, the pencil beam turns into a conical beam, preserving its CP features. As shown in Figure 3b, at 27.3 GHz, an almost azimuthally symmetric beam pointing at $\theta = 12°$ is obtained with a half-power beamwidth (HPBW) well within the 3 dB AR range, thus demonstrating that the CP condition is maintained over the main beam. At higher frequencies, namely up to 28.2 GHz, one may observe from Figure 3c,d that a CP beam is maintained at elevation angle as large as $\theta = 32°$.

However, in this latter operating condition, the azimuthal symmetry of the beam is affected and the CP condition compromised around $\phi = -50°$ and $\phi = 130°$. Such behavior is more evident at even larger frequencies (see results for 28.5 GHz in Figure 3e), where the CP condition is compromised over larger azimuthal ranges, with the radiation maximum occurring for $\theta = 37°$.

An additional increase in frequency, although not shown, further enlarges the regions outside the CP regime, thus worsening the antenna radiation performance.

Finally, in Figure 3f, the importance of choosing the unit-cell design parameters in a *cavity* environment is stressed. The colormap shows the AR considering the PCM in a *free-standing* environment, after the reciprocity-driven optimization process. As is manifest, the AR levels are completely outside those limits that enclose the CP region, thus suggesting that the ground plane presence strongly modifies the PCM behavior. The *in-cavity* optimization procedure, while being uncommon for FPCA modeling, constitutes a simple and precise technique to account for multiple reflections, which otherwise would provide a detrimental effect on preserving satisfactory AR values.

Considered patterns of the co-polar right-hand component are also reported as 3-D radiation patterns in Figure 4a–e, where the elevation scan is evident as we depart from the broadside condition at 27 GHz in Figure 4a and approach an elevation angle of almost $\theta = 40°$, Figure 4e.

For comparison, at corresponding frequencies, the cross-polar E_{LHCP} component (normalized to the co-polar radiation maximum) is shown in Figure 5a–e to be -20 dB under the E_{RHCP} component.

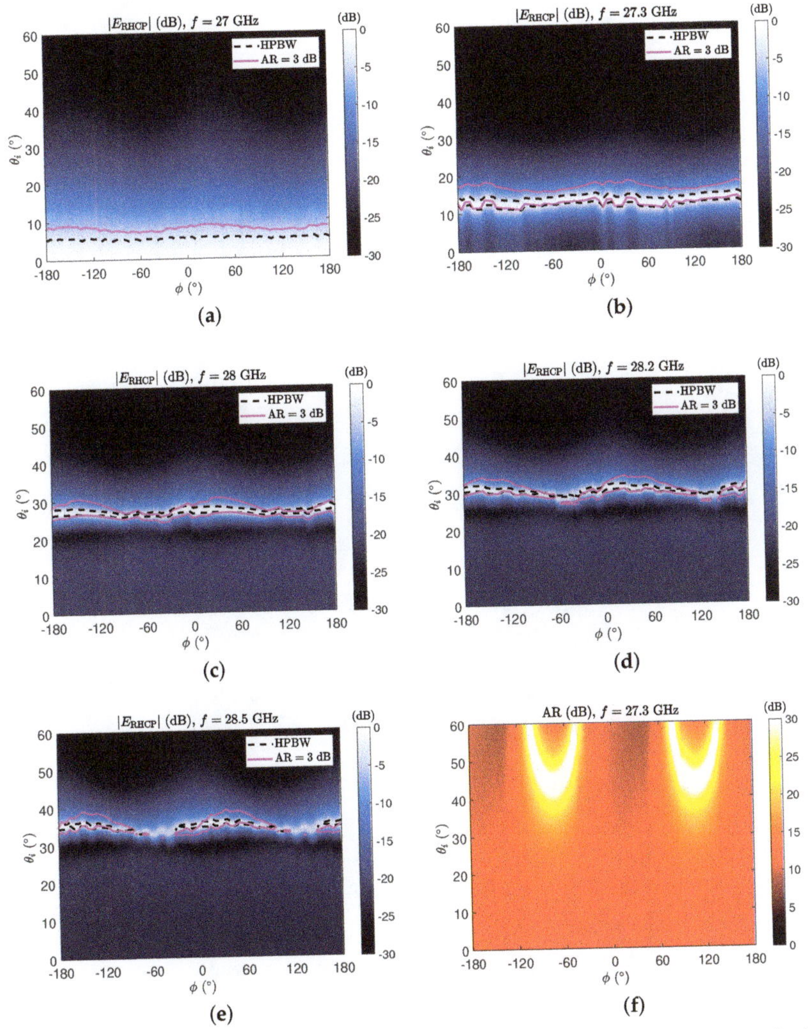

Figure 3. By exploiting the reciprocity theorem, the absolute value of the *cavity* antenna far-field component E_{RHCP} is reported in dB through a colormap normalized with respect to its maximum, for different elevation and azimuth angles at a working frequency f equal to **(a)** 27 GHz, **(b)** 27.3 GHz, **(c)** 28 GHz, **(d)** 28.2 GHz, and **(e)** 28.5 GHz. Magenta and black isolines represent the 3 dB axial-ratio (AR) level and the half-power beamwidth (HPBW) regions, respectively. **(f)** shows the different AR response of the PCM in a *free-standing* configuration (not placed above any cavity).

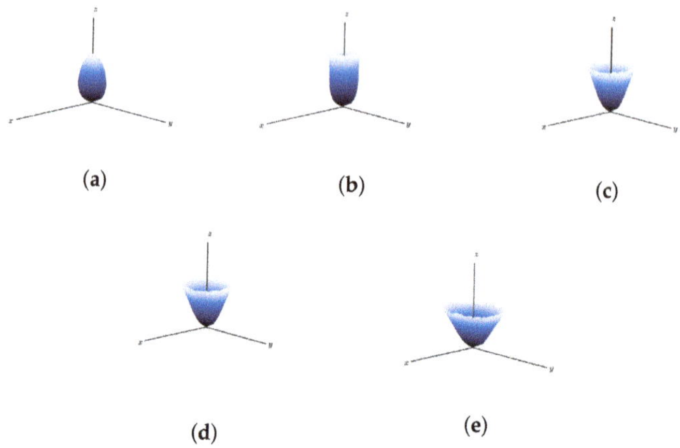

Figure 4. Pictorial representation of the co-polar, far-field component E_{RHCP}, in a 3-D format. From the broadside pencil beam starting condition in (**a**), by stepping up the operation frequency, the radiation pattern evolves to azimuthally invariant, conical patterns (**b**–**e**).

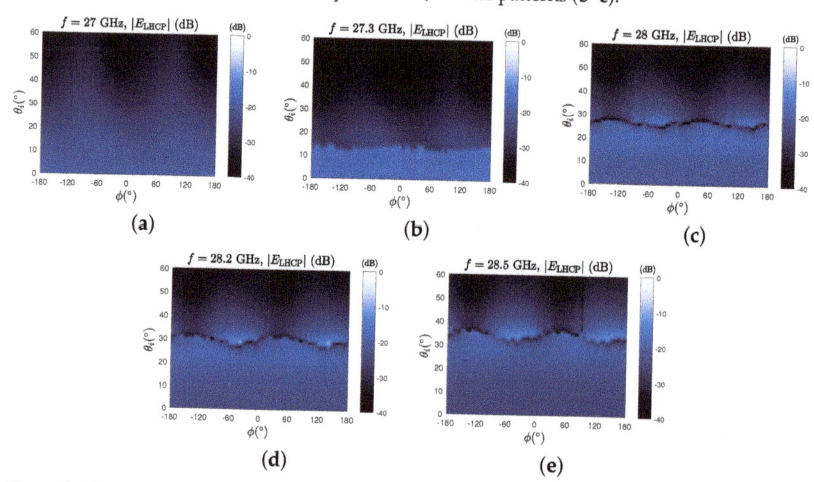

Figure 5. The cross-polar far-field component E_{LHCP} is reported after being normalized with respect to the E_{RHCP} maximum at each frequency. As it manifests, being on average −20 dB under the desired co-polar component within the main beam, its contribution to the far-field radiation is negligible.

4. FPCA: Array Feeding and Azimuth Scan

The presented FPCA results demonstrate the feasibility of frequency-based scanning of the elevation plane using a directive CP beam, enabled by the proposed PCM. However, this solution does not allow for both having a pencil beam off broadside and varying the azimuthal angle of the beam. For this purpose, a 2-D grid of sources can be used by exploiting the pattern multiplication principle of array theory. This idea has been demonstrated in [48] (an overview of array-fed 2-D LWAs is given in [49]) for LP beams using a planar array of feeders to gain further control of the beam features of an FPCA. In particular, the leaky-wave dispersion is exploited to scan by frequency the beam in elevation, whereas the phasing of the feeders allows for scanning in azimuth. This technique is here suitably modified for CP beams.

As is known from basic theory, the electric far-field pattern $\mathbf{E}_{\mathrm{AP}}$ radiated by the array is given by

$$\mathbf{E}_{\mathrm{AP}} = A_{\mathrm{F}} \mathbf{E}_{\mathrm{EP}} \tag{3}$$

where $\mathbf{E}_{\mathrm{EP}}$ is the element-pattern radiated when a single HED source is placed in the cavity and A_{F} is the relevant array factor. Here, the HEDs are arranged in a uniform planar 2-D array configuration so that the array factor is given by [41]

$$A_{\mathrm{F}} = \frac{1}{NM} \frac{\sin(N\frac{\psi_x}{2})}{\sin(\frac{\psi_x}{2})} \frac{\sin(M\frac{\psi_y}{2})}{\sin(\frac{\psi_y}{2})} \tag{4}$$

where N is the number of elements along the x axis, M is the number along the y axis, the quantities ψ_x and ψ_y depend on the spherical angles θ, ϕ, and the phase shifts $\Delta\phi_x, \Delta\phi_y$ along x, y through

$$\begin{aligned} \psi_x &= kd_x \sin\theta \cos\phi + \Delta\phi_x \\ \psi_y &= kd_y \sin\theta \sin\phi + \Delta\phi_y \end{aligned} \tag{5}$$

where k is the wavenumber, and d_x and d_y stand for inter-element spacing along x and y axes, respectively.

Here, we consider $N = 4$ and $M = 10$, for a total number of 40 elements. A common design criterion in standard antenna array theory consists of requiring the distance between adjacent elements to be lower than half a wavelength. This is to avoid grating lobes, specially if it is necessary to scan elevation angles far from the broadside, namely up to 60° and beyond. Here, the elevation angle is limited to approximately 40°, so grating lobes should not appear, even if such a condition is not strictly met. Additionally, possible unwanted lobes at different pointing angles are washed away due to high elevation selectivity of the element pattern, suggesting that sparser feeding grids can be considered [42]. Consequently, an equal inter-element spacing along the two directions, viz. $d_x = d_y$, has been chosen, setting a distance equal to twice the unit-cell periodicity, $d_x = d_y = 2l_c = 6.66$ mm. Since the lower frequency is 27 GHz, corresponding to $\lambda = 11.11$ mm, the element spacing is slightly higher than half a wavelength, but the results in Figure 6 confirm that we still manage to suppress all of the spurious lobes. In particular, in Figure 6, the ability of the proposed FPCA to radiate a CP pencil beam in any elevation direction (between $\theta = 0°$ and $\theta \simeq 40°$), as well as any azimuthal direction is demonstrated. Specifically, in Figure 6a, we show the possibility of producing a CP beam with the maximum at $\theta = 12°$ on the $\phi = -60°$ plane. The desired elevation angle is obtained by considering a 27.3 GHz working frequency, by exploiting the inherent frequency-scanning property of the LWA element pattern (see Figure 3b). For the azimuth-angle pointing direction $\phi = -60°$, the array theory [41] is applied to achieve the required inter-element phase difference values of $\Delta\phi_x = -22.68°$ and $\Delta\phi_y = 39.28°$, as derived from (5). In a similar manner, by fixing the working frequency at 28 GHz and setting $\Delta\phi_x = -105.05°$ and $\Delta\phi_y = 0°$, we ensure a perfect CP pencil-beam with the maximum on $\phi = 0°$ at $\theta = 28°$ (see Figure 6b). Similarly, by further increasing the frequency to 28.5 GHz, and thus considering the maximum of the element pattern at $\theta = 37°$, a perfectly CP pencil beam can be obtained on the $\phi = 30°$ plane imposing $\Delta\phi_x = -113.14°$ and $\Delta\phi_y = -65.32°$ (see Figure 6c).

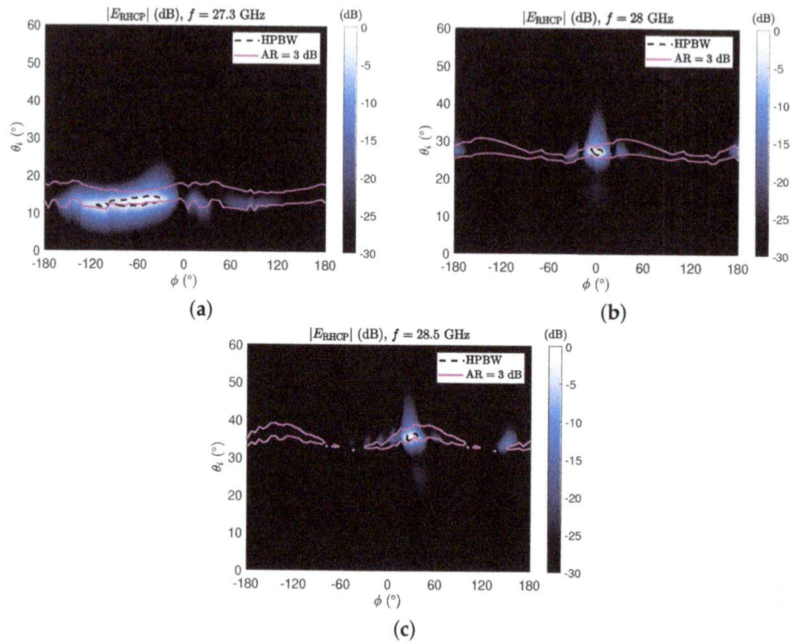

Figure 6. $|E_{\mathrm{RHCP}}|$ radiation-pattern colormaps obtained through the proposed array-fed FPCA pointing at (**a**) $\theta = 12^\circ$ and $\phi = -60^\circ$, (**b**) $\theta = 28^\circ$ and $\phi = 0^\circ$, and (**c**) $\theta = 38^\circ$ and $\phi = +30^\circ$. The black dashed and magenta solid lines represent the HPBW and AR $= 3$ dB boundaries, respectively.

We have thus demonstrated that the proposed array-fed FPCA is able to generate a pure CP pencil beam pointing at various directions. It is worthwhile to point out that the proposed approach does not consider the mutual coupling among the sources. However, as shown in [48], and experimentally validated in [50], this effect can be taken into account and easily mitigated, keeping cross-coupling scattering coefficients well under the threshold of -15 dB.

5. Conclusions

In this work, a compact, planar, Fabry–Perot cavity antenna is studied as a possible launcher for electronically steerable, circularly polarized pencil beams. A versatile and original application of the reciprocity theorem allowed for optimizing the unit-cell parameters. This latter strategy, though unusual for periodic metasurface design, constitutes a fast and effective way to account for multiple bounces, which otherwise may considerably affect the stability of the axial ratio.

Here, due to structure of the unit-cell, which is a multilayered stack of dielectrics and metallic patches, the in-cavity optimization process allows for evaluating and mitigating resonance effects on polarization degradation. The axial ratio is hence kept under the 3 dB threshold in the half-power beamwidth from 27 GHz corresponding to broadside radiation, to 28.5 GHz, where a conical, azimuthally invariant beam is obtained with the radiation maximum set on almost 40° off-broadside on the elevation plane.

Inserting a theoretical planar array of 40 equispaced, uniform sources accounting for horizontal electric dipoles, allows us to demonstrate that the associated array factor is capable of transforming the omnidirectional conically shaped element pattern to a circularly polarized pencil beam. Taking advantage of the frequency sweep and properly phasing the elements in the array, elevation and azimuth planes are scanned, respectively.

Obtained results clearly confirm that the reciprocity-based design is valid for dimensioning compact, planar, and electronically scanning CP pencil-beam launchers, with limitations appearing when the off-broadside angle steers to considerable values. Furthermore, this approach also demonstrates that, with respect to more classical solutions, based on free-space arrays, the problem of grating lobes appears to be considerably mitigated due to the directive nature of the element pattern.

Although the covered elevation angles are already sufficiently large for many practical applications, the obtained results clearly show that, in future works, further improvements in the unit-cell design could potentially extend the region in which elevation scan is possible in the CP regime.

Author Contributions: Conceptualization, M.M.; Methodology, E.N., W.F., D.C., A.G. and P.B.; Software, M.M.; Formal analysis, M.M., E.N., W.F., D.C., A.G. and P.B.; Writing—original draft, M.M.; Writing—review & editing, E.N., W.F., D.C., A.G. and P.B. All authors have read and agreed to the published version of the manuscript.

Funding: This work was supported by the European Union - Next Generation EU under the Italian National Recovery and Resilience Plan (NRRP), Mission 4, Component 2, Investment 1.3, CUP B53C22004050001, partnership on "Telecommunications of the Future" (PE00000001 - program "RESTART").

Institutional Review Board Statement: Not applicable.

Informed Consent Statement: Not applicable.

Data Availability Statement: The original contributions presented in this study are included in the article. Further inquiries can be directed to the corresponding author.

Conflicts of Interest: The authors declare no conflicts of interest.

References

1. Banerjee, U.; Karmakar, A.; Saha, A. A review on circularly polarized antennas, trends and advances. *Int. J. Microw. Wirel. Technol.* **2020**, *12*, 922–943. [CrossRef]
2. Nadeem, I.; Alibakhshikenari, M.; Babaeian, F.; Althuwayb, A.A.; Virdee, B.S.; Azpilicueta, L.; Khan, S.; Huynen, I.; Falcone, F.; Denidni, T.A.; et al. A comprehensive survey on 'circular polarized antennas' for existing and emerging wireless communication technologies. *J. Phys. D Appl. Phys.* **2021**, *55*, 033002. [CrossRef]
3. Balanis, C.A. *Antenna Theory: Analysis and Design*; John Wiley & Sons: Hoboken, NJ, USA, 2015.
4. Doumanis, E.; Goussetis, G.; Gomez-Tornero, J.L.; Cahill, R.; Fusco, V. Anisotropic impedance surfaces for linear to circular polarization conversion. *IEEE Trans. Antennas Propag.* **2012**, *60*, 212–219. [CrossRef]
5. Fonseca, N.J.G.; Mangenot, C. High-performance electrically thin dual-band polarizing reflective surface for broadband satellite applications. *IEEE Trans. Antennas Propag.* **2016**, *64*, 640–649. [CrossRef]
6. Mercader-Pellicer, S.; Goussetis, G.; Medero, G.M.; Legay, H.; Bresciani, D.; Fonseca, N.J. Cross-polarization reduction of linear-to-circular polarizing reflective surfaces. *IEEE Trans. Antennas Propag.* **2019**, *18*, 1527–1531. [CrossRef]
7. Costa, F.; Borgese, M. Systematic design of transmission-type polarization converters comprising multilayered anisotropic metasurfaces. *Phys. Rev. Appl.* **2020**, *14*, 034049. [CrossRef]
8. Marcuvitz, N. On field representations in terms of leaky modes or eigenmodes. *IRE Trans. Antennas Propag.* **1956**, *4*, 192–194. [CrossRef]
9. Goldstone, L.; Oliner, A.A. Leaky-wave antennas I: Rectangular Waveguides. *IRE Trans. Antennas Propag.* **1959**, *7*, 307–319. [CrossRef]
10. Goldstone, L.; Oliner, A.A. Leaky-wave antennas II: Circular Waveguides. *IRE Trans. Antennas Propag.* **1961**, *9*, 280–290. [CrossRef]
11. Hessel, A. General characteristics of traveling-wave antennas. In *Antenna Theory, Part 2*; Collin, R.E., Zucker, F.J., Eds.; McGraw-Hill: New York, NY, USA, 1969.
12. Tamir, T.; Oliner, A.A. Guided complex waves, Part 1: Fields at an interface Fields at an interface. *Proc. Inst. Electr. Eng.* **1963**, *110*, 310. [CrossRef]
13. Tamir, T.; Oliner, A.A. Guided complex waves, Part 2: Relation to radiation patterns. *Proc. Inst. Electr. Eng.* **1963**, *110*, 325. [CrossRef]
14. Ip, A.; Jackson, D.R. Radiation from cylindrical leaky waves. *IEEE Trans. Antennas Propag.* **1990**, *38*, 482–488. [CrossRef]
15. Burghignoli, P.; Fuscaldo, W.; Comite, D.; Baccarelli, P.; Galli, A. Higher-order cylindrical leaky waves–Part I: Canonical sources and radiation formulas. *IEEE Trans. Antennas Propag.* **2019**, *67*, 6735–6747. [CrossRef]
16. Fuscaldo, W.; Jackson, D.R.; Galli, A. General formulas for the beam properties of 1-D bidirectional leaky-wave antennas. *IEEE Trans. Antennas Propag.* **2019**, *67*, 3597–3608. [CrossRef]
17. Oliner, A.A.; Jackson, D.R.; Volakis, J.L. Leaky-wave antennas. *Antenna Eng. Handb.* **2007**, *4*, 12.

18. Tamir, T.; Collin, R.E.; Zucker, F.J. *Leaky-Wave Antennas*; Collin, R.E., Zucker, F.J., Eds.; McGraw-Hill: New York, NY, USA, 1969.
19. Sabahi, M.M.; Heidari, A.A.; Movahhedi, M. A compact CRLH circularly polarized leaky-wave antenna based on substrate-integrated waveguide. *IEEE Trans. Antennas Propag.* **2018**, *66*, 4407–4414. [CrossRef]
20. Chen, S.L.; Karmokar, D.K.; Li, Z.; Qin, P.Y.; Ziolkowski, R.W.; Guo, Y.J. Circular-polarized substrate-integrated-waveguide leaky-wave antenna with wide-angle and consistent-gain continuous beam scanning. *IEEE Trans. Antennas Propag.* **2019**, *67*, 4418–4428. [CrossRef]
21. von Trentini, G. Partially reflecting sheet arrays. *IRE Trans. Antennas Propag.* **1956**, *4*, 666–671. [CrossRef]
22. Burghignoli, P.; Fuscaldo, W.; Galli, A. Fabry–Perot cavity antennas: The leaky-wave perspective. *IEEE Antennas Propag. Mag.* **2021**, *63*, 116–145. [CrossRef]
23. Comite, D.; Baccarelli, P.; Burghignoli, P.; Galli, A. Omnidirectional 2-D leaky-wave antennas with reconfigurable polarization. *IEEE Antennas Wirel. Propag. Lett.* **2017**, *16*, 2354–2357. [CrossRef]
24. Negri, E.; Benassi, F.; Fuscaldo, W.; Masotti, D.; Burghignoli, P.; Costanzo, A.; Galli, A. Design of TE-polarized resonant Bessel-beam launchers for wireless power transfer links in the radiative near-field region. *Int. J. Microw. Wirel. Technol.* **2024**, 1–10. [CrossRef]
25. Muhammad, S.A.; Sauleau, R.; Valerio, G.; Le Coq, L.; Legay, H. Self-polarizing Fabry–Perot antennas based on polarization twisting element. *IEEE Trans. Antennas Propag.* **2012**, *61*, 1032–1040. [CrossRef]
26. Faenzi, M.; Minatti, G.; González-Ovejero, D.; Caminita, F.; Martini, E.; Della Giovampaola, C.; Maci, S. Metasurface antennas: New models, applications and realizations. *Sci. Rep.* **2019**, *9*, 10178. [CrossRef]
27. Noman, M.; Abutarboush, H.; Tahir, F. A.; Zahid, A.; Imran, M.; Abbasi, Q.H. A novel multifunctional chiral metasurface with asymmetric transmission. *Sci. Rep.* **2024**, *14*, 24681. [CrossRef] [PubMed]
28. Yin, T.; Ren, J.; Zhang, B.; Li, P.; Luan, Y.; Yin, Y. Reconfigurable transmission-reflection-integrated coding metasurface for full-space electromagnetic wavefront manipulation. *Adv. Opt. Mater.* **2024**, *12*, 2301326. [CrossRef]
29. Chen, L.; Ma, Q.; Luo, S.S.; Ye, F.J.; Cui, H.Y.; Cui, T.J. Touch-programmable metasurface for various electromagnetic manipulations and encryptions. *Small* **2022**, *18*, 2203871. [CrossRef]
30. Gao, X.; Ma, Q.; Gu, Z.; Cui, W.Y.; Liu, C.; Zhang, J.; Cui, T.J. Programmable surface plasmonic neural networks for microwave detection and processing. *Nat. Electron.* **2023**, *6*, 319–328. [CrossRef]
31. Wang, S.; Xu, H.; Wang, M.; Tang, S. A low-RCS, high-gain and polarization-insensitive FP antenna combing frequency selective rasorber and metasurface. *IEEE Open J. Antennas Propag.* **2024**, *5*, 1623–1628. [CrossRef]
32. Xu, H.; Sun, S.; Tang, S.; Ma, S.; He, Q.; Wang, G.; Cai, T.; Li, H.; Zhou, L. Dynamical control on helicity of electromagnetic waves by tunable metasurfaces. *Sci. Rep.* **2016**, *6*, 27503. [CrossRef] [PubMed]
33. Xu, H.; Tang, S.; Wang, G.; Cai, T.; Huang, W.; He, Q.; Sun, S.; Zhou, L. Multifunctional microstrip array combining a linear polarizer and focusing metasurface. *IEEE Trans. Antennas Propag.* **2016**, *64*, 3676–3682. [CrossRef]
34. Xu, J.; Xu, H.; Luo, H.; Wang, Y.; Wang, C. A low-RCS folded reflectarray combining dual-metasurface and rasorber. *IEEE Antennas Wireless Propag. Lett.* **2022**, *21*, 2462–2466. [CrossRef]
35. Huang, Y.; Yang, L.; Li, J.; Wang, Y.; Wen, G. Polarization conversion of metasurface for the application of wide band low-profile circular polarization slot antenna. *Appl. Phys. Lett.* **2016**, *109*. [CrossRef]
36. Xie, P.; Wang, G.; Li, H.; Liang, J.; Gao, X. Circularly polarized Fabry-Perot antenna employing a receiver–transmitter polarization conversion metasurface. *IEEE Trans. Antennas Propag.* **2019**, *68*, 3213–3218. [CrossRef]
37. Neto, A.; Llombart, N.; Gerini, G.; Bonnedal, M.D.; de Maagt, P. EBG enhanced feeds for the improvement of the aperture efficiency of reflector antennas. *IEEE Trans. Antennas Propag.* **2007**, *55*, 2185–2193. [CrossRef]
38. Neto, A.; Ettorre, M.; Gerini, G.; De Maagt, P. Leaky wave enhanced feeds for multibeam reflectors to be used for telecom satellite based links. *IEEE Trans. Antennas Propag.* **2011**, *60*, 110–120. [CrossRef]
39. Burghignoli, P.; Frezza, F.; Galli, A.; Schettini, G. Synthesis of broad-beam patterns through leaky-wave antennas with rectilinear geometry. *IEEE Antennas Wirel. Propag. Lett.* **2003**, *2*, 136–139. [CrossRef]
40. Gómez-Tornero, J.L.; Martinez, A.T.; Rebenaque, D.C.; Gugliemi, M.; Álvarez-Melcón, A. Design of tapered leaky-wave antennas in hybrid waveguide-planar technology for millimeter waveband applications. *IEEE Antennas Wirel. Propag. Lett.* **2005**, *53*, 2563–2577. [CrossRef]
41. Mailloux, R.J. *Phased Array Antenna Handbook*; Artech House: New York, NY, USA, 2017.
42. Borselli, L.; Di Nallo, C.; Galli, A.; Maci, S. Arrays with widely-spaced high-gain planar elements. In Proceedings of the IEEE Antennas and Propagation Society International Symposium. 1998 Digest. Antennas: Gateways to the Global Network. Held in Conjunction with: USNC/URSI National Radio Science Meeting (Cat. No.98CH36), Atlanta, GA, USA, 21–26 June 1998; pp. 1142–1145.
43. Gardelli, R.; Albani, M.; Capolino, F. Array thinning by using antennas in a Fabry—Perot cavity for gain enhancement. *IEEE Trans. Antennas Propag.* **2006**, *54*, 1979–1990. [CrossRef]
44. Jackson, D.R.; Oliner, A.A.; Ip, A. Leaky-wave propagation and radiation for a narrow-beam multiple-layer dielectric structure. *IEEE Trans. Antennas Propag.* **1993**, *41*, 344–348. [CrossRef]
45. Jackson, D.R.; Oliner, A.A. A leaky-wave analysis of the high-gain printed antenna configuration. *IEEE Trans. Antennas Propag.* **1988**, *36*, 905–910. [CrossRef]

46. Negri, E.; Fuscaldo, W.; Tofani, S.; Burghignoli, P.; Galli, A. An efficient and accurate semi-analytical matching technique for waveguide-fed antennas. *Sci. Rep.* **2024**, *14*, 3892. [CrossRef] [PubMed]
47. Zhao, T.; Jackson, D.R.; Williams, J.T.; Oliner, A.A. General formulas for 2-D leaky-wave antennas. *IEEE Trans. Antennas Propag.* **2005**, *53*, 3525–3533. [CrossRef]
48. Comite, D.; Burghignoli, P.; Baccarelli, P.; Galli, A. 2-D beam scanning with cylindrical-leaky-wave-enhanced phased arrays. *IEEE Trans. Antennas Propag.* **2019**, *67*, 3797–3808. [CrossRef]
49. Madji, M.; Negri, E.; Fuscaldo, W.; Comite, D.; Galli, A.; Burghignoli, P. The leaky-wave perspective for array-fed Fabry–Perot cavity and Bull's-Eye antennas. *Appl. Sci.* **2024**, *14*, 2076–3417. [CrossRef]
50. Comite, D.; Podilchak, S.K.; Kuznetcov, M.; Buendía, G.G.V.; Burghignoli, P.; Baccarelli, P.; Galli, A. Wideband array-fed Fabry-Perot cavity antenna for 2-D beam steering. *IEEE Trans. Antennas Propag.* **2021**, *69*, 784–794. [CrossRef]

applied sciences

MDPI

Article

High-Performance Digital Devices Design by the ASMD-FSMD Technique for Implementation in FPGA

Valery Salauyou *, Adam Klimowicz * and Tomasz Grzes

Faculty of Computer Science, Bialystok University of Technology, Wiejska 45A, 15-351 Bialystok, Poland; t.grzes@pb.edu.pl
* Correspondence: v.salauyou@pb.edu.pl (V.S.); a.klimowicz@pb.edu.pl (A.K.)

Abstract: The paper presents an application of the ASMD-FSMD technique for designing high-performance digital circuits on the example of an implementation of sequential multipliers in reconfigurable FPGA devices. The method primarily enables multiple operations on the same variable within a single clock cycle. The experiments were conducted using the QuartusPrime tool and Cyclone 10 LP devices, as well as Vivado tools and the Kintex UltraScale family device. The bit size of multiplicands varied from 4 to 128. A comparison of the ASMD-FSMD technique with the traditional approach using datapath with the controller has shown that the performance of the sequential multipliers increases by a factor of 2 and, for some examples, by a factor of 3. Practical recommendations for using the ASMD-FSMD technique to improve the performance of digital devices, as well as directions for further studies, are given in the conclusion.

Keywords: algorithmic state machine with datapath; finite state machine with datapath; high-level synthesis; performance; FPGA; Verilog HDL

1. Introduction

Typically, a digital device is designed and represented by an operational unit (datapath) and a control unit (controller). As a rule, these blocks are designed separately. The datapath is based on a set of standard functional units (registers, buses, multiplexers, etc.). The controller is implemented as a finite state machine (FSM).

The ASMD-FSMD method for creating digital devices involves describing the operation of the device as a diagram of an algorithmic state machine with datapath (ASMD) and coding the project in Verilog HDL as a finite state machine with datapath (FSMD).

Due to their clearness, algorithmic state machines (ASMs) are widely used to represent FSM behavior. The ASMs were first proposed in [1] as an alternative to automata graphs. In [2], it was proposed to use the ASM to describe the behavior of a control unit and operations performed in the datapath. Such ASM was called an ASMD. Recently, ASMD charts have been increasingly used in projects implemented in field programmable logic devices (FPGA): for the implementation of industrial control systems [3], to implement the asin function using the CORDIC (coordinate rotation digital computer) algorithm [4]; in the hardware implementation of the cryptographic algorithm AES (Advanced Encryption Standard) [5]; when designing a universal asynchronous receiver-transmitter (UART) [6]; in the hardware implementation of high-speed speech classifiers [7]; when designing a memory controller with high performance and low power consumption [8], etc.

In [9], it is proposed to combine the datapath and controller and represent them as a finite state machine with a datapath (FSMD). The FSMDs for synchronous and asynchronous projects are given in [10]. FSMDs are widely used in high-level synthesis: in the

https://doi.org/10.3390/app15010410

equivalence test method based on value propagation [11], for checking the correctness of translation of C/C++ descriptions into a register transfers level (RTL) [12], to solve the problem of global elimination of common subexpressions [13], etc.

The ASMD-FSMD technique for designing digital devices was first presented in [14]. In the ASMD-FSMD technique, it is proposed to describe the project code in Verilog HDL (hardware description language) directly according to the ASMD chart in the form of FSMD. A comparison of the ASMD-FSMD technique with the traditional approach in the case of using the Mealy FSM and the Moore FSM as a control unit is given in [15]. In [16], the ASMD-FSMD technique for designing digital signal processing devices is considered. The paper [17] presents the application of ASMD-FSMD methodology to the design of embedded processors on FPGA. The main advantage of the ASMD-FSMD technique is a significant reduction of design time (5–7 times). In addition, the use of the ASMD-FSMD technique, as compared to the traditional approach, allows, in most cases, the reduction of the implementation cost and increase in the speed of the devices.

Increasing the performance of digital devices and systems is always a topical problem. High performance is important in the design of the following devices and systems: adders [18,19], multipliers [20,21], frequency synthesizers [22], digital FIR filters [23,24], pipelines [25], accelerators [26], a datapath [27], memory access controllers [28,29], encoders/decoders for communication systems [30], programmable logic controllers [31], encryption systems [32], convolutional neural networks [33], finite state machines [34,35] as well as in high-level synthesis of digital systems [36,37]. It is also noticed in [38] that even slight variations in the description of devices using hardware description language (HDL) can result in notably distinct hardware implementations, affecting the final area usage, speed, and power consumption.

The proposed paper addresses the problem of increasing the performance of digital devices by applying the ASMD-FSMD technique. The main idea lies in the possibility of performing several operations on the same variable in one Verilog HDL procedural block. As a result, several operations can be executed during one clock cycle. It leads to an increase in device performance, as compared to the traditional approach. The proposed approach is demonstrated by an implementation in reconfigurable FPGA of sequential multipliers. Experimental studies have shown that using the ASMD-FSMD technique allows for increasing the performance of sequential multipliers on average by a factor of 2 and, for some examples, by a factor of 3.

The main contribution of this paper is the use of the ASMD-FSMD technique for designing high-performance digital devices. The novelty of the proposed technique is the execution of several operations with the same variable in one clock cycle, which leads to an increase in the performance of the device.

The main goal of the paper is to justify the increase in the performance of digital devices using the ASMD-FSMD technique, as well as provide practical recommendations for the design of high-performance digital devices by the ASMD-FSMD technique.

Summarizing the above, the originality and novelty of the proposed approach consist of the following key points:

- The use of the ASMD-FSMD technique for designing high-performance digital devices;
- The execution of several operations with the same variable in one clock cycle;
- The justification for the increase in the performance of digital devices using the ASMD-FSMD technique;
- The verification of the advantages of the ASMD-FSMD technique through implementations of the multiplier;
- The identification and summarization of practical recommendations for the design of high-performance digital devices using the ASMD-FSMD technique.

The paper is organized as follows. Section 2 presents the traditional approach to the design of sequential multipliers. Section 3 discusses the ASMD-FSMD technique and presents the main hypothesis of the work. Section 4 presents the results of the experimental studies. The conclusions in Section 5 give recommendations for the practical use of the ASMD-FSMD technique to increase the performance of digital devices, as well as indicate directions for further research of the ASMD-FSMD technique.

2. Traditional Approach to the Design of Sequential Multipliers

The following classical multiplication methods are known by which sequential multipliers are built:

- Algorithm *a*: the least significant bit of the multiplier is examined, the multiplier is shifted to the right, and the multiplicand to the left;
- Algorithm *b*: the most significant bit of the multiplier is examined, the multiplier is shifted to the left and the multiplicand to the right;
- Algorithm *c*: the most significant bit of the multiplier is examined, and the multiplier, along with the partial product, are shifted to the left;
- Algorithm *d*: the least significant bit of the multiplier is examined, and the multiplier, along with the partial product, is shifted to the right.

The datapath of the sequential multiplier c, as presented in Figure 1, consists of the following:

- A and B: the multiplicand and multiplier, respectively;
- Registers ra and rb for storing the multiplicand and multiplier, respectively;
- Register rp for storing the result;
- Counter cnt generates the done signal to indicate the end of the multiplication process and the internal signal roll that is used by the FSM.

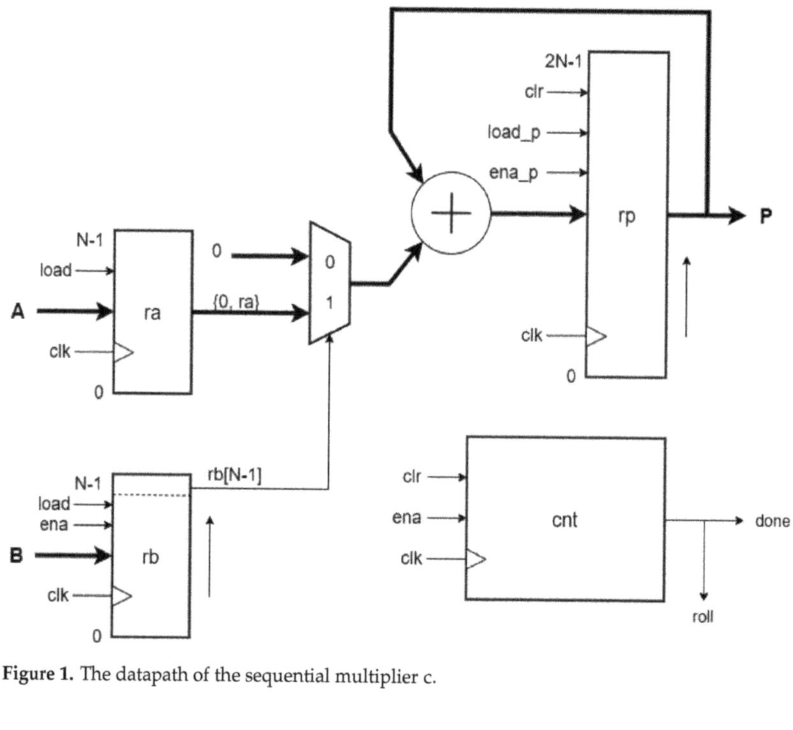

Figure 1. The datapath of the sequential multiplier c.

Input signals for every block are defined as follows:

- load: to load the values of multiplied words A and B into registers ra and rb;
- load_p: to load the result of addition into the register rp;
- clr: to reset the register rp and the counter cnt;
- ena: to allow the shift of the content of the register rb and the increase the counter cnt;
- ena_p: to allow the shift of the register rp;
- clk: clock signal;
- reset: reset signal;

The datapath of the sequential multiplier d presented in Figure 2 consists of:

- A and B: the multiplicand and multiplier, respectively;
- Registers ra and rb for storing the multiplicand and multiplier, respectively;
- Register rp for storing the result;
- Counter cnt, which generates the signal done to indicate the end of the multiplication process, and the internal signal roll, used by the FSM.

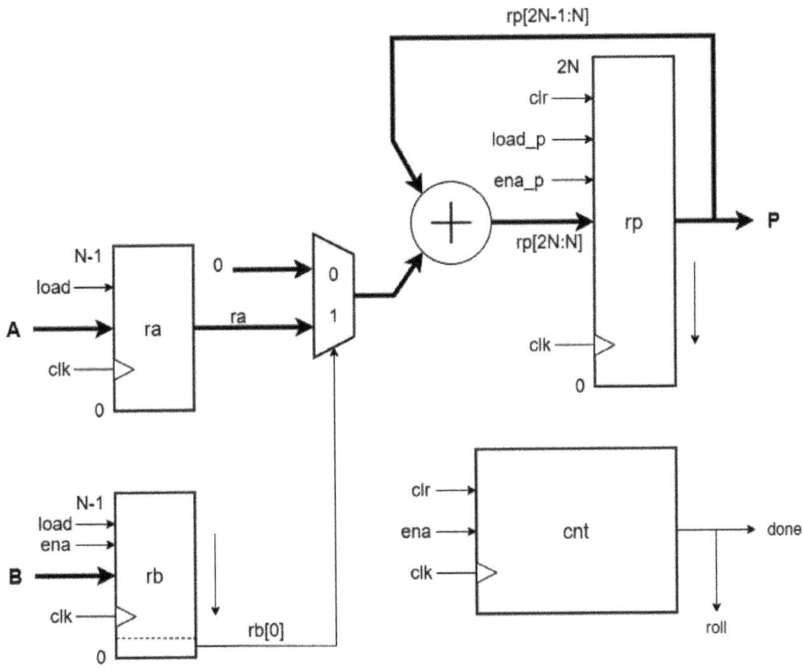

Figure 2. The datapath of the sequential multiplier d.

Input signals for every block are used for:

- load: to load the values of multiplied words A and B into registers ra and rb;
- load_p: to load the result of addition into the register rp;
- clr: to reset the register rp and the counter cnt;
- ena: to allow the shift of the content of the register rb and the increase the counter cnt;
- ena_p: to allow the shift of the register rp;
- clk: clock signal;
- reset: reset signal.

Using the ASMD-FSMD technique is the most efficient (in terms of speed) in designing multipliers c and d. So, consider the traditional approach in the design of multipliers c and

d. The datapath in the case of the traditional approach for both algorithms is shown in Figures 1 and 2, respectively.

The counter cnt generates the signal done, which indicates the end of the multiplication process and the internal signal roll that is used by the FSM. The process of multiplying the numbers A and B starts with the signal run.

The control functions identically for both algorithms (c and d). The FSM (Figure 3), based on the values of the signals run and roll, generates the necessary values for the control signals. These include load, which loads the values of multiplied words A and B into registers ra and rb; load_p, which loads the result of addition into the register rp; clr, which resets the register rp and the counter cnt; ena, which allows the shift of the content of the register rb and the increase the counter cnt; ena_p, which allows the shift of the register rp. Additionally, the multiplier is controlled by the clock signal clk and the reset signal reset.

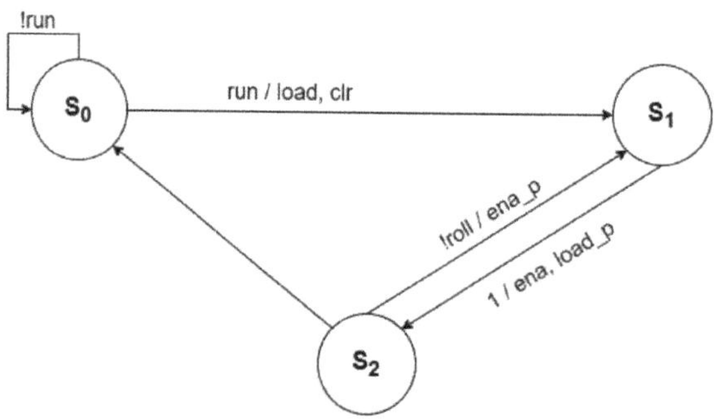

Figure 3. The control device of the sequential multipliers c and d in the form of Mealy's FSM.

In the state S_0, the FSM waits for the signal run, which starts the multiplication process by switching to the state S_1 and generating the signals load and clr. Since two clock cycles are required to load the results of the addition into the register rp and shift the content of the register rp, one multiplication cycle corresponds to two states, S_1 and S_2. When the FSM transitions from the state S_1 to the state S_2, the addition result is loaded into the register rp by the signal load_p, and the content shift of the register rb is performed by the signal ena. When the FSM transitions from state S_2 to state S_1 by the signal ena_p, the content of the register rp is shifted to the left. The multiplication process is terminated by the signal roll, and the FSM transitions to the state S_0. Thus, in the traditional approach, the multiplication of N-bit numbers A and B using the algorithm c is performed in $n = 2N + 1$ clock cycles.

3. The ASMD-FSMD Technique

The development of digital devices using the ASMD-FSMD technique consists of constructing the ASMD chart of device behavior and creating Verilog code in the form of the FSMD [14].

The ASMD chart consists of ASMD blocks (Figure 4). Every ASMD block represents the FSMD's behavior within a single state over one clock cycle. The ASMD block includes one state box (rectangle). Also, it may have several decision boxes (rhombuses) and conditional output boxes (ovals). The rhombuses may both precede ovals and follow ovals. The ASMD block has only one input, which is the input to the state box, and may have one or more outputs. The inputs and outputs of boxes are connected by arcs. Feedback loops are prohibited inside an ASMD block. Algorithm loops and wait states in the ASMD chart are implemented using external feedback (concerning the ASMD block).

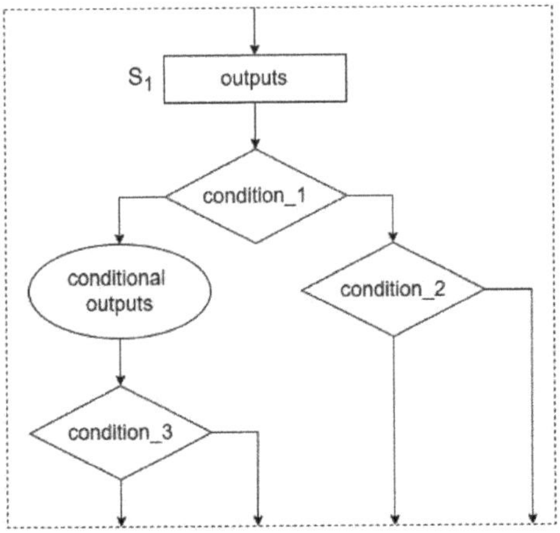

Figure 4. The ASMD block.

For the Moore FSMD, the operations performed in some states are written inside the state box. In the Mealy FSMD, the actions associated with transitions are noted within the conditional output boxes. Logical expressions are placed inside the decision boxes, with the decision block outputs being represented as either zero or one, indicating transitions based on whether the logical expression evaluates to false or true. Any operations written into either rectangles or ovals can be used if they are admissible in the Verilog HDL. The same is true for the logical expressions written down in rhombuses. The ASMD chart is a composition of connected ASMD blocks. Each output of any ASMD box can be connected to only one input of another box, i.e., branching of the algorithm is possible only in the decision boxes. The Verilog code of the design is built directly from the ASMD chart created before.

The ASMD-FSMD technique can be represented as the following Algorithm (Figure 5):

1. The FSMD states are determined.
2. The ASMD block is constructed for each FSMD state.
    a. Within the ASMD decision boxes, logical expressions are placed, and their values are evaluated in this state.
    b. In a Moore FSMD, the actions that are executed on the register content within this state are listed within the state box.
    c. In the Mealy FSMD, the operations carried out on the content of the registers during these transitions are placed in the conditional output box.
3. ASMD blocks are linked to one another following the device's operational algorithm. Each ASMD block's output may be connected to only one input of the same or a different ASMD block.
4. When needed, the ASMD is adjusted to enhance the device's performance or area. For instance, through analysis of the algorithm loops, the ASMD is altered to reduce the number of states within the loop.
5. The FSMD Verilog code is developed directly from the ASMD chart. Variables in the Verilog code are equivalent to the device registers. Logical statements in the **if** conditions align with those in the ASMD conditional boxes. Actions depicted in ASMD blocks are presented as procedural blocks enclosed between begin. . .end. For Moore FSMD, the operations conducted in the respective ASMD block are specified in the state box, and subsequent states are determined by ASMD transitions. In the case

of Mealy FSMD, every action performed in the associated ASMD block is presented in an algorithmic description format.

6. The FSMD is implemented using a suitable design tool.
7. End.

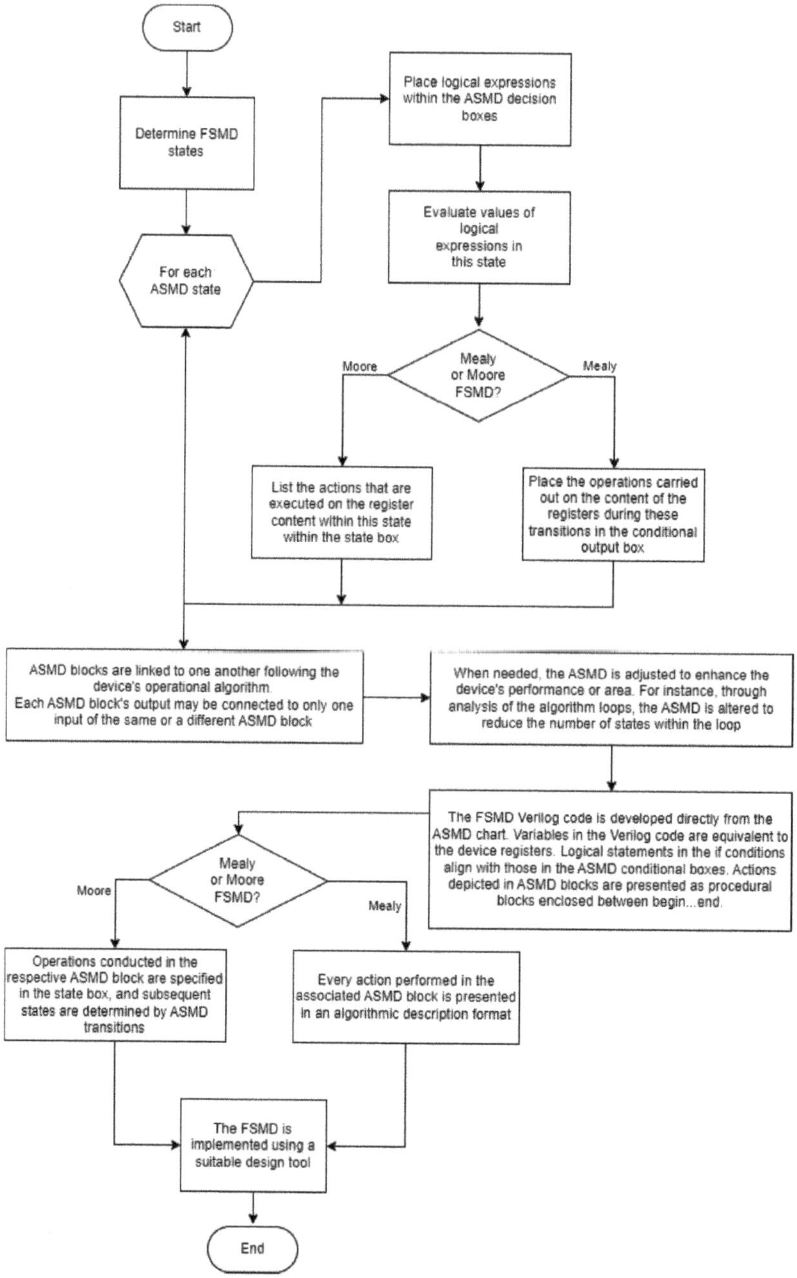

Figure 5. The ASMD-FSMD algorithm.

The primary distinction from traditional methods lies in combining two digital system description techniques within a single algorithm. An FSM described using ASMD is referred to as a state machine with a datapath (FSMD). The ASMD-based FSMD design methodology is called the ASMD-FSMD technique. Unlike traditional designs, the FSMD is not explicitly divided into a control unit (FSM) and a datapath. Instead, it more closely aligns with a behavioral or algorithmic representation of the device's operation. The central step in this design approach is creating an ASMD chart that represents the behavior or operational algorithm of the digital device. This approach avoids strict separation between the datapath and control unit. However, the ASMD chart establishes FSM states corresponding to the control unit's states. This linkage helps synchronize the device's operation with clock cycles, enabling developers to track the clock cycle count for each branch of the algorithm. Additionally, the ASMD chart does not directly specify the datapath's structure, leaving its implementation flexible.

Note that the ASMD language provides more possibilities for describing the behavior of the device than the traditional approach. For example, for a Mealy FSMD in one ASMD block, it is possible to perform various variable operations sequentially, compare the obtained values with each other or with constants, and, depending on the results of the comparison, perform some operations with the same variables. Moreover, all these operations are performed in one clock cycle. Thus, with ASMD, it is possible to describe a digital device on a behavioral level, which is impossible with the traditional approach.

Hypothesis 1. Using the ASMD-FSMD technique allows one to perform multiple operations on the same variable in a single clock cycle, which leads to an increase in device performance compared to the traditional approach.

Experience with the ASMD-FSMD technique [14–16] shows that the ASMDs of Mealy FSMDs are better suited for building high-performance digital devices. As an example, let us consider the ASMDs for the Mealy FSMD, which describes multipliers c and d (Figure 6).

The ASMD chart of the multiplication algorithm c (Figure 6, on the left) consists of two ASMD blocks, which correspond to the states S_0 and S_1 of Mealy's FSMD. State S_0 waits for the signal run, when run = 1 the variables are initialized. State S_1 corresponds to the multiplication loop. When rb[$N-1$] = 1, the multiplicand value is added to the content of the register rp; otherwise, nothing is added. The counter cnt value is then incremented, and the content of the register rb is shifted to the left. The value of the counter cnt is checked in the same ASMD block. If cnt = $N-1$, then the flag done is set, and the multiplication process ends. Otherwise, the content of the register rp is shifted to the left, and the multiplication cycle is repeated.

The ASMD chart of the multiplication algorithm d (Figure 6, on the right) is very similar to the ASMD of algorithm c. The differences are not significant, and they concern the register shift direction, the addition range, and the rb register bit, which should be checked. When rb[0] = 1, the multiplicand value is added to the content of the upper part ($2N-1:N$) of register rp; otherwise, nothing is added. During the incrementation of the counter cnt value, the content of the register rb is shifted to the right. If cnt is not equal to N-1, then the content of the register rp is shifted to the right, and the multiplication cycle is repeated.

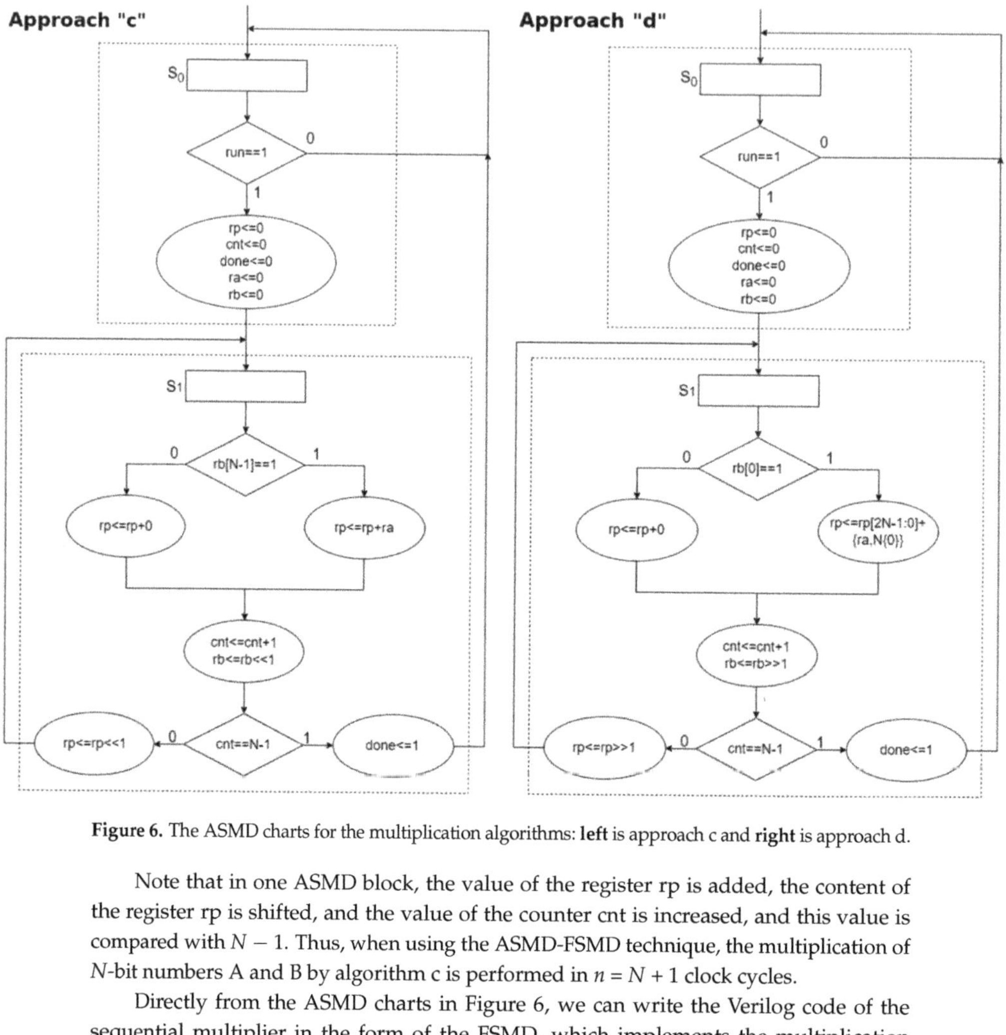

Figure 6. The ASMD charts for the multiplication algorithms: **left** is approach c and **right** is approach d.

Note that in one ASMD block, the value of the register rp is added, the content of the register rp is shifted, and the value of the counter cnt is increased, and this value is compared with $N - 1$. Thus, when using the ASMD-FSMD technique, the multiplication of N-bit numbers A and B by algorithm c is performed in $n = N + 1$ clock cycles.

Directly from the ASMD charts in Figure 6, we can write the Verilog code of the sequential multiplier in the form of the FSMD, which implements the multiplication algorithm c (Appendix A, module mult_c_Mealy_FSMD).

The variables in the ASMD charts for the multiplication algorithms presented in Figure 6 are described in the following:

- ra: multiplicand (value of register ra);
- rb: multiplier (value of register rb);
- rp: result (value of register rp);
- cnt: counter (value of register cnt);
- done: the value of the output signal done (from cnt).

The simulation results of the project mult_c_Mealy_FSMD in the tool Quartus Prime are shown in Figure 7. It shows that the multiplication of 4-bit numbers is performed in five clock cycles, i.e., the multiplication of N-bit numbers is performed in $N + 1$ clock cycles. For comparison, Figure 8 shows the simulation results of the synchronous multiplier, which implements the algorithm of multiplication c, which was designed by the traditional approach. Figure 8 shows that the multiplication of 4-bit numbers is performed in nine clock cycles.

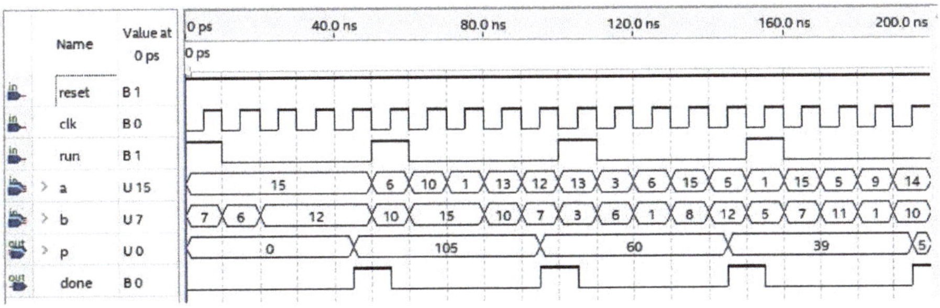

Figure 7. The simulation results of the multiplier (algorithm c) were designed using the ASMD-FSMD technique.

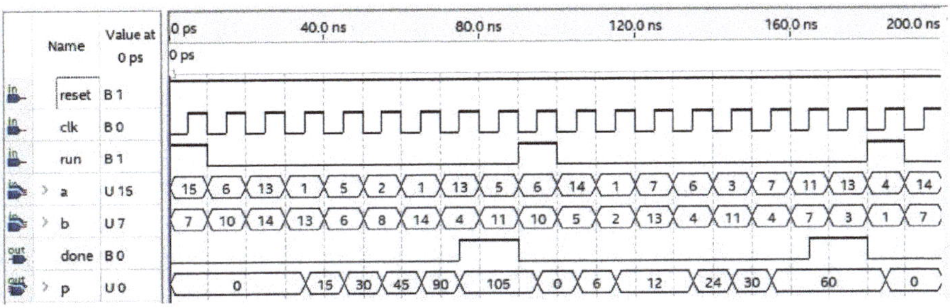

Figure 8. The simulation results of the multiplier (algorithm c) are built using the traditional approach.

Similarly to the project implementing algorithm c, we can describe algorithm d in the form of Verilog code. This code is shown in Appendix B (module mult_d_Mealy_FSMD). The simulation results of the project mult_d_Mealy_FSMD in the Quartus Prime are shown in Figure 9. It shows that the multiplication of 4-bit numbers is performed in five clock cycles. For comparison, Figure 10 shows the simulation results of the synchronous multiplier, which implements the algorithm of multiplication d, designed by the traditional approach. It shows that the multiplication of 4-bit numbers is performed in nine clock cycles.

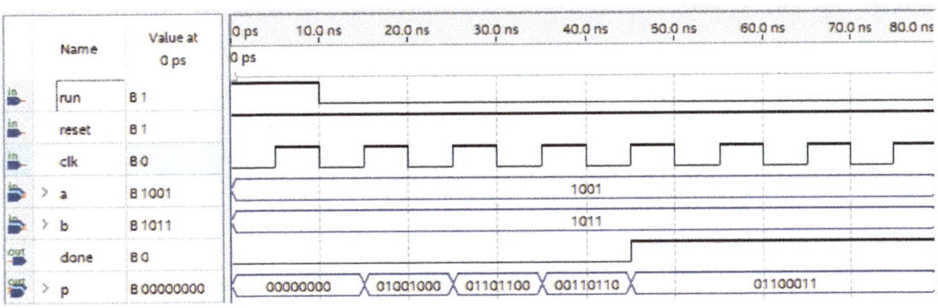

Figure 9. The simulation results of the multiplier (algorithm d) were designed using the ASMD-FSMD technique.

Thus, our hypothesis (that using the ASMD-FSMD technique allows multiple operations on the same variable in one clock cycle, resulting in increased device performance) is fully confirmed.

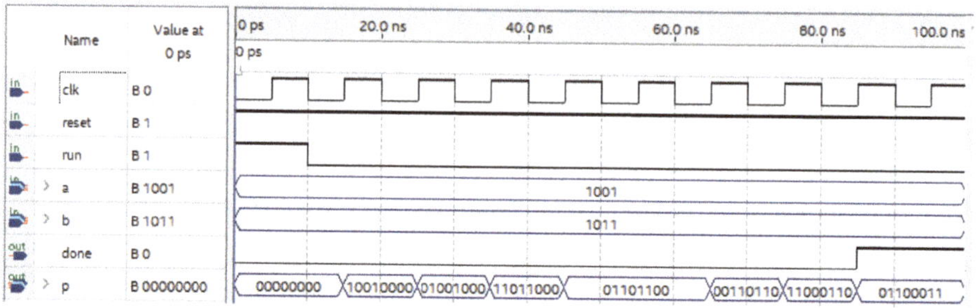

Figure 10. The simulation results of the multiplier (algorithm d) are built using the traditional approach.

4. Experiments and Discussion

The Quartus Prime 21.1 software tool was used for implementation in FPGA Cyclone 10 LP of the multipliers c and d. The multiplication algorithms c and d were implemented using the traditional approach in the form of the datapath and the FSM, as well as using the ASMD-FSMD technique. The designs were investigated with input word widths of 4, 8, 16, 32, 64, and 128 bits. The experimental results are shown in Table 1, where mult_c_*N* and mult_d_*N* are projects that implement multiplication algorithms c and d, respectively; *N* is the width of the input words A and B in bits; L_T and L_A are the numbers of used FPGA logic elements (the implementation cost) in case of the traditional approach and when using the ASMD-FSMD technique, respectively; t_T and t_A are the time of multiplication operation in nanoseconds in case of the traditional approach and when using the ASMD-FSMD technique with operating frequency 100 MHz; L_T/L_A and t_T/t_A are relations of corresponding parameters.

Table 1. The experimental results of the implementation of multipliers c and d by the Quartus tool.

Example	L_T	L_A	L_T/L_A	t_T	t_A	t_T/t_A
mult_c_4	35	35	1.00	40.25	20.22	1.99
mult_c_8	60	65	0.92	93.11	47.82	1.95
mult_c_16	112	138	0.81	183.55	97.72	1.88
mult_c_32	208	270	0.77	452.46	238.75	1.98
mult_c_64	405	540	0.75	1267.69	639.39	1.98
mult_c_128	793	1006	0.79	8216.11	4200.59	1.96
mult_d_4	32	29	1.10	41.77	20.67	2.02
mult_d_8	58	48	1.21	82.48	36.41	2.27
mult_d_16	98	75	1.31	159.26	53.86	2.96
mult_d_32	176	141	1.25	410.87	158.33	2.59
mult_d_64	338	271	1.25	940.51	355.62	2.64
mult_d_128	663	528	1.26	4851.80	2178.69	2.23

Table 1 shows that using the ASMD-FSMD technique allows, on average, to increase the performance of the algorithm c by a factor 1.96 (1.99, for example, mult_c_4) and the algorithm d by a factor of 2.45 (2.96, for example, mult_c_16). In addition, the ASMD-FSMD technique allows, on average, for algorithm d to reduce the implementation cost by a factor of 1.23 (for example, mult_c_16 by a factor of 1.31) [16]. A comparison of area (L_T/L_A) and time (t_T/t_A) ratios can also be seen in Figure 11.

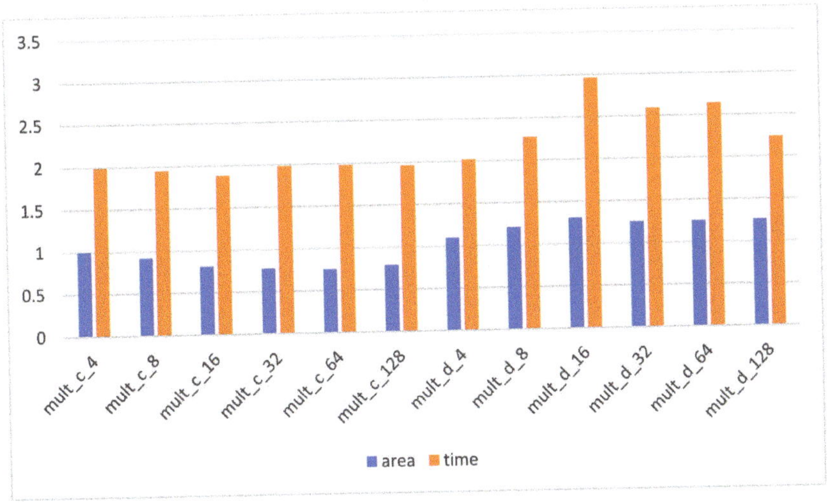

Figure 11. The comparison of L_T/L_A and t_T/t_A ratios for multipliers implemented by the Quartus tool.

Similar studies were also performed using the software tool Vivado 2021.1 in the implementation of multipliers in FPGAs of the family Kintex UltraScale. The experimental results are given in Table 2.

Table 2. The experimental results of the implementation of multipliers c and d by the Vivado tool.

Example	L_T	L_A	L_T/L_A	t_T	t_A	t_T/t_A
mult_c_4	19	23	0.83	74.56	38.30	1.95
mult_c_8	35	33	1.06	138.79	68.59	2.02
mult_c_16	66	65	1.02	275.55	145.52	1.89
mult_c_32	132	90	1.47	589.23	299.41	1.97
mult_c_64	267	171	1.56	1241.75	629.66	1.97
mult_c_128	528	462	1.14	2537.88	1239.05	2.05
mult_d_4	20	13	1.54	89.49	37.54	2.38
mult_d_8	36	24	1.50	157.24	69.26	2.27
mult_d_16	65	41	1.59	305.59	145.28	2.10
mult_d_32	124	90	1.38	619.21	307.82	2.01
mult_d_64	267	170	1.57	1216.07	629.85	1.93
mult_d_128	525	268	1.96	2466.98	1288.97	1.91

When implementing multipliers using the software tool Vivado, the ASMD-FSMD technique allows to increase the performance by a factor of 2.04 (2.38 for the example mult_d_4) and decrease the implementation cost by a factor of 1.39 (1.98 for the example mult_d_128). A comparison of area (L_T/L_A) and time (t_T/t_A) ratios can also be seen in Figure 12.

The results provided in Tables 1 and 2 and Figures 11 and 12 show that in most examples, the area and the time are decreasing significantly. The results obtained with the Vivado tool were better than the results from the Quartus tools according to area ratio (geometric mean equal to 1.35 for Vivado and 1.01 for Quartus), but according to time ratio, the Quartus tool was better (geometric mean equal to 2.18 for Quartus and 2.03 for Vivado).

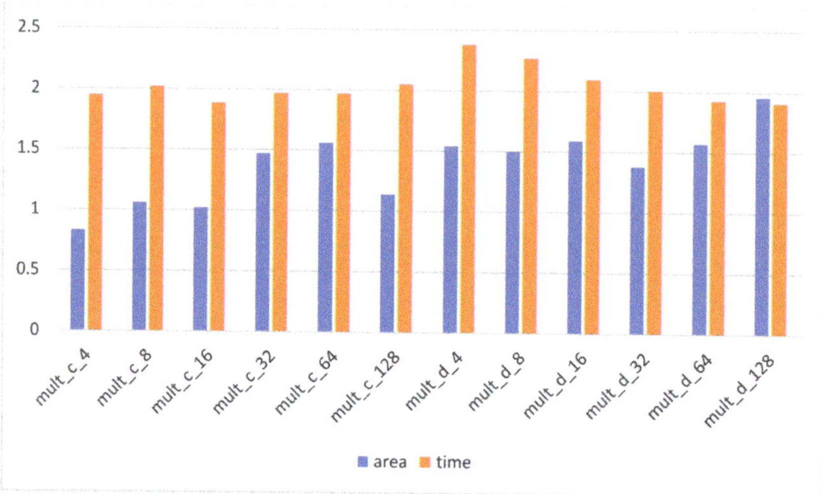

Figure 12. The comparison of L_T/L_A and t_T/t_A ratios for multipliers implemented by the Vivado tool.

Additionally, a comparison of the maximum clock signal frequency was performed for all tested systems. The results are shown in Table 3, where F_{TC} and F_{AC} are the maximum frequency of clock in MHz in case of the traditional approach and when using the ASMD-FSMD technique for Cyclone 10 LP device and Quartus tool; F_{TK} and F_{AK} are the maximum frequency of clock in MHz in case of the traditional approach and when using the ASMD-FSMD technique for Kintex Ultrascale device and Vivado tool; F_{AC}/F_{TC} and F_{AK}/F_{TK} are relations of corresponding parameters.

Table 3. Maximum operating frequency of the implemented multipliers.

Example	F_{TC}	F_{AC}	F_{AC}/F_{TC}	F_{TK}	F_{AK}	F_{AK}/F_{TK}
mult_c_4	177.75	190.55	1.07	120.71	130.57	1.08
mult_c_8	137.23	169.49	1.24	122.49	131.22	1.07
mult_c_16	130.4	142.96	1.10	119.76	116.82	0.98
mult_c_32	98.23	102.41	1.04	110.31	110.22	1.00
mult_c_64	64.94	65.65	1.01	103.89	103.23	0.99
mult_c_128	36.99	39.31	1.06	101.27	104.11	1.03
mult_d_4	194.78	209.38	1.07	122.93	133.19	1.08
mult_d_8	181.88	192.09	1.06	120.83	129.94	1.08
mult_d_16	156.99	197.94	1.26	114.53	117.01	1.02
mult_d_32	135.21	153.09	1.13	108.20	107.20	0.99
mult_d_64	97.05	125.6	1.29	107.72	103.20	0.96
mult_d_128	62.33	79.95	1.28	104.99	100.08	0.95

Table 3 shows that the maximum clock frequency for circuits described with the ASMD-FSMD technique in most cases was generally slightly higher than the maximum operation frequency of circuits developed with the traditional approach. It can also be seen that this frequency depends on the device and tool used. For the Cyclone device and Quartus tool, the advantage of the presented technique was higher than for the Kintex device and Vivado tool. This is the result of using different placing and routing algorithms in the design tools and differences in the architectures of the FPGA devices.

Note that the Quartus and Vivado software tools were used with the default synthesis parameters. Thus, the effectiveness of the ASMD-FSMD technique does not depend on the design tool used (Quartus or Vivado), and the effectiveness of the ASMD-FSMD technique is determined solely by describing the behavior of the digital device in the ASMD chart.

The improved performance of digital devices is due to the efficient implementation of Verilog compilers. However, in the traditional approach, when a device is presented as a datapath and an FSM, these capabilities of Verilog HDL compilers are simply not used. Thus, the advantage of the ASMD-FSMD technique over the traditional approach is to effectively use the capabilities of Verilog HDL compilers.

5. Conclusions

The following hypothesis was investigated in the paper: in the ASMD-FSMD technique, it is possible to perform several operations with the same variable in one clock cycle, which leads to an increase in the device performance compared to the traditional approach. This hypothesis was fully confirmed by the implementation of sequential multipliers in FPGA.

The presented approach is not limited only to multipliers; it can be applied to the design process of various devices, where control device and datapath are used. The multiplier design process is only an example of how this methodology was used to improve the implementation results. Of course, it cannot completely replace a variety of multipliers types. There are a lot of different approaches, mostly not sequential, such as Wallace, Booth, Dadd's, CSAM (Carry-Save Array Multiplier), and others. The user can also apply embedded MAC (multiply and accumulate) blocks of FPGA. The aim of this work was not to develop the best multiplier but to show how the presented technique can improve the results of sequential circuit synthesis by only changing the way the system is described in the HDL language. Our recommendations for the practical use of the ASMD-FSMD technique to implement high-performance digital devices are as follows:

- Use the ASMD chart for the Mealy FSMD;
- The cycles of the algorithm should be described by an ASMD chart with a minimum number of states (ASMD blocks), preferably using only one state;
- In one ASMD block, multiple operations can be applied to the same variable, and the results of those operations can be checked.

Future studies on enhancing the performance of the ASMD-FSMD technique should focus on the following:

- Determining subsets of Verilog HDL operations that can be executed with the same variable in one procedural block;
- Determining subsets of Verilog HDL operations that cannot be executed with the same variable in one procedural block;
- Determining by how much (in a number of clock cycles) the performance of a digital device increases when certain operations are combined in one procedural block.

Note that the ASMD-FSMD technique can also be used with other hardware description languages, such as VHDL and SystemVerilog, as well as in the design of digital devices not only on FPGA but also on ASICs (Application Specified Integrated Circuits).

The results of this experiment showed that the different factors of different tools (Vivado, Quartus) are better optimized. Thus, future work should also verify the impact of external factors on the results should be verified, including the following:

- Hardware description language used for implementation;
- Synthesis parameters are used in the Vivado and Quartus tools.

Author Contributions: Conceptualization, V.S.; methodology, V.S.; software, V.S.; validation, A.K. and T.G.; formal analysis, A.K.; investigation, A.K.; resources, A.K. and T.G.; writing—original draft preparation, V.S. and A.K.; writing—review and editing, A.K. and T.G.; visualization, A.K.; supervision, V.S.; project administration, A.K. and T.G.; funding acquisition, A.K. and T.G. All authors have read and agreed to the published version of the manuscript.

Funding: The work was supported by the WZ/WI-IIT/5/2023 and WZ/WI-IIT/3/2023 grants from the Bialystok University of Technology and funded with resources for research by the Ministry of Science and Higher Education in Poland.

Data Availability Statement: The original contributions presented in the study are included in the article, further inquiries can be directed to the corresponding author.

Conflicts of Interest: The authors declare no conflicts of interest.

Appendix A

This appendix presents an example of a Verilog code of the sequential multiplier in the form of the FSMD, which implements the multiplication algorithm c.

```
module mult_c_Mealy_FSMD
#(parameter N = 4)       //operand size
(input clk, reset, run,   //control signals
input [N – 1:0] a, b,   //multiplicand a and multiplier b
output reg [2*N-1:0] p,   //product p
output reg done);       //multiplication termination flag
reg [2*N – 1:0] rp;      //register declaration
reg [N – 1:0] ra, rb;
reg [N:0] cnt;       //counter
localparam [0:0] s0 = 0,s1 = 1;//states of FSMD
reg [0:0] state;      //state variable
//behavioral description of FSMD
always @(posedge clk, negedge reset)
    if(!reset)   state <= s0;   //reset of FSMD
    else
      case (state)
      s0:  if(run)
              begin //the first ASMD block
                rp = 0; cnt <= 0; done <= 0;
                ra <= a;
                rb <= b;
                state <= s1;
              end
              else   state <= s0;
      s1:  begin   //the second ASMD block
                if(rb[N – 1])rp = rp + ra;
                cnt <= cnt + 1'b1;
                rb <= rb << 1;
                if (cnt == N – 1)
                begin
                    done <= 1'b1;
                    p <= rp;
                    state <= s0;
                end
                else
```

```
                    begin
                        rp = rp << 1;
                        state <= s1;
                    end
                end
        default: state <= s0;
        endcase
endmodule
```

Appendix B

This appendix presents an example of a Verilog code of the sequential multiplier in the form of the FSMD, which implements the multiplication algorithm d.

```
module mult_d_Mealy_FSMD
#(parameter N = 4)
(input clk, reset, run,
input [N-1:0] a,b,
output [2*N-1:0] p,
output reg done);
reg [2*N:0] rp;
reg [N-1:0] ra,rb;
reg [N_cnt-1:0] cnt;
localparam N_cnt = clogb2(N – 1);
function integer clogb2(input [N – 1:0] v);
    for (clogb2 = 0; v > 0; clogb2 = clogb2 + 1)
      v = v >> 1;
endfunction
localparam [0:0] s0 = 0, s1 = 1;
reg [0:0] state;
always @(posedge clk, negedge reset)
    if(!reset)    state <= s0;
    else
      case (state)
      s0:  if(run)
           begin
             rp = 0; cnt <= 0; done <= 0;
             ra <= a;
             rb <= b;
             state <= s1;
           end
           else
             state <= s0;
      s1:  begin
             if(rb[0])   rp = rp[2*N – 1:0] + {ra,{N{1'b0}}};
             cnt <= cnt + 1'b1;
             rb <= rb >> 1;
             if (cnt == N – 1)
             begin
               rp = rp >> 1;
               done <= 1'b1;
               state <= s0;
```

```
                end
                else
                begin
                    rp = rp >> 1;
                    state <= s1;
                end
            end
        default: state <= s0;
        endcase
    assign p = rp[2*N − 1:0];
    endmodule
```

References

1. Clare, C.R. *Designing Logic Systems Using State Machines*; McGraw-Hill Book Company: New York, NY, USA, 1973.
2. Ciletti, M.D. *Advanced Digital Design With the Verilog HDL*; Prentice Hall of India: New Delhi, India, 2005.
3. Martín, P.; Bueno, E.; Rodríguez, F.J.; Sáez, V. A methodology for optimizing the FPGA implementation of industrial control systems. In Proceedings of the 35th Annual Conference of IEEE Industrial Electronics, Porto, Portugal, 3–5 November 2009; pp. 2811–2816.
4. Saha, A.; Ghosh, A.; Kumar, K.G. FPGA implementation of arcsine function using CORDIC algorithm. *AMSE J. AMSE IIETA Publ. 2017 Ser. Adv. A* **2017**, *54*, 197–202.
5. Burciu, P. An efficient (low resources) modular hardware implementation of the AES algorithm. *J. Electr. Eng. Electron. Control. Comput. Sci.* **2019**, *5*, 1–10.
6. Sowmya, K.B.; Gomes, S.; Tadiparthi, V.R. Design of UART module using ASMD technique. In Proceedings of the 2020 5th International Conference on Communication and Electronics Systems (ICCES), Coimbatore, India, 10–12 June 2020; pp. 176–181.
7. Srinivas, N.S.S.; Sugan, N.; Kumar, L.S.; Nath, M.K.; Kanhe, A. Digital Architecture for Instantaneous V/UV/S Classification of Noise Free Speech Segments. In Proceedings of the 2020 24th International Symposium on VLSI Design and Test (VDAT), Bhubaneswar, India, 23–25 July 2020; p. 1.
8. Sultana, J.; Alam, S.S. Performance Analysis and Implementation of SRAM Controller on Altera DE2 Board. In Proceedings of the 2021 International Conference on Electronics, Communications and Information Technology (ICECIT), Khulna, Bangladesh, 14–16 September 2021; p. 1.
9. Gajski, D.D.; Dutt, N.D.; Wu, A.C.; Lin, S.Y. *High-Level Synthesis: Introduction to Chip and System Design*; Kluwer: Boston, MA, USA, 1992.
10. Auletta, R.; Reese, B.; Traver, C. A comparison of synchronous and asynchronous FSMD designs. In Proceedings of the 1993 IEEE International Conference on Computer Design (ICCD'93), Cambridge, MA, USA, 3–6 October 1993; pp. 178–182.
11. Hu, J.; Wang, G.; Chen, G.; Wei, X. Equivalence checking of scheduling in high-level synthesis using deep state sequences. *IEEE Access* **2019**, *7*, 183435–183443. [CrossRef]
12. Chouksey, R.; Karfa, C. Verification of scheduling of conditional behaviors in high-level synthesis. *IEEE Trans. Very Large Scale Integr. (VLSI) Syst.* **2020**, *28*, 1638–1651. [CrossRef]
13. Hu, J.; Hu, Y.; Yu, L.; Yang, H.; Kang, Y.; Cheng, J. Validating GCSE in the scheduling of high-level synthesis. In Proceedings of the 2020 IEEE 29th Asian Test Symposium (ATS), Penang, Malaysia, 23–26 November 2020; p. 1.
14. Salauyou, V. Using ASMD-FSMD technique for digital device design. In Proceedings of the 2021 International Conference on Dependability and Complex Systems, Wrocław, Poland, 28 June–2 July 2021; pp. 391–401.
15. Salauyou, V.; Klimowicz, A. Digital Device Design by ASMD-FSMD Technique. In Proceedings of the 20th International Conference on Computer Information Systems and Industrial Management, Ełk, Poland, 24–26 September 2021; pp. 431–441.
16. Solov'ev, V.V. ASMD-FSMD technique in designing signal processing devices on field programmable gate arrays. *J. Commun. Technol. Electron.* **2021**, *66*, 1336–1345. [CrossRef]
17. Salauyou, V. Embedded Processor Design in FPGA by ASMD-FSMD and FSM-Single Techniques. In Proceedings of the 21st International Conference on Computer Information Systems and Industrial Management, Barranquilla, Colombia, 15–17 July 2022; pp. 374–389.
18. Naveen, G.; Rao, V.S.; Vijay, V.; Venkateswarlu, S.C.; Vallabhuni, R.R. Design of high-performance full adder using 20nm CNTFET technology. In Proceedings of the 2021 4th International Conference on Recent Trends in Computer Science and Technology (ICRTCST), Jamshedpur, India, 11–12 February 2022; pp. 192–196.

19. Manchala, V.S.; Sahoo, S.; Murthy, G.R. Design and analysis of 16-bit spares kogge stone adder with proposed 6T-XOR cell, 1-bit HFA design for high-speed arithmetic operations. In Proceedings of the 2022 International Conference on Communication, Computing and Internet of Things (IC3IoT), Chennai, India, 10–11 March 2022; p. 1.
20. Arunkumar, K.; Mangayarkarasi, P.; Jackson, B.; Juliette, A.A. Design of high speed, low power 16x16 vedic multiplier with adiabatic logic. In Proceedings of the 2022 8th International Conference on Smart Structures and Systems (ICSSS), Chennai, India, 21–22 April 2022; p. 1.
21. Kuo, C.-T.; Wu, Y.-C. FPGA Implementation of a Novel Multifunction Modulo (2n ± 1) Multiplier Using Radix-4 Booth Encoding Scheme. *Appl. Sci.* **2023**, *13*, 10407. [CrossRef]
22. Levantino, S. Recent Advances in High-Performance Frequency Synthesizer Design. In Proceedings of the 2022 IEEE Custom Integrated Circuits Conference (CICC), Newport Beach, CA, USA, 24–27 April 2022; p. 1.
23. Ye, J.; Yanagisawa, M.; Shi, Y. A high-performance symmetric hybrid form design for high-order FIR filters. In Proceedings of the 2020 IEEE Asia Pacific Conference on Circuits and Systems (APCCAS), Ha Long, Vietnam, 8–10 December 2020; pp. 121–124.
24. Chen, C.; Romashchenko, V.; Brutscheck, M.; Chmielewski, I. Performance Analysis and Optimization of Distributed Arithmetic-Based Convolutional Algorithms for FIR Filters on FPGA. In Proceedings of the 34th Irish Signals and Systems Conference (ISSC), Dublin, Ireland, 13–14 June 2023; p. 1.
25. Ayatollahi, F.S.; Ghaznavi-Ghoushchi, M.B.; Mohammadzadeh, N.; Ghamkhari, S.F. AMPS: An automated mesochronous pipeline scheduler and design space explorer for high performance digital circuits. *IEEE Trans. Circuits Syst. I Regul. Pap.* **2022**, *69*, 1681–1692. [CrossRef]
26. Muslim, F.B.; Ma, L.; Roozmeh, M.; Lavagno, L. Efficient FPGA implementation of OpenCL high-performance computing applications via high-level synthesis. *IEEE Access* **2017**, *5*, 2747–2762. [CrossRef]
27. Xydis, S.; Economakos, G.; Soudris, D.; Pekmestzi, K. High performance and area efficient flexible DSP datapath synthesis. *IEEE Trans. Very Large Scale Integr. (VLSI) Syst.* **2009**, *19*, 429–442. [CrossRef]
28. Chen, M.; Zhang, Z.; Ren, H. Design and verification of high performance memory interface based on AXI bus. In Proceedings of the 2021 IEEE 21st International Conference on Communication Technology (ICCT), Tianjin, China, 13–16 October 2021; pp. 695–699.
29. Kumar TR, D.; Babu, K.M.; Babu, S.S.; Reddy, S.N.; Sherrif, M.; Tharunkumar, A. High-Speed Communication in Memory Controller by Novel Pipeline Register Design. In Proceedings of the Second International Conference On Smart Technologies For Smart Nation (SmartTechCon), Singapore, 18–19 August 2023; pp. 600–604.
30. He, Z.; Roy, S.; Fortier, P. Powerful LDPC codes for broadband wireless networks: High-performance code construction and high-speed encoder/decoder design. In Proceedings of the 2007 International Symposium on Signals, Systems and Electronics, Iasi, Romania, 12–13 July 2007; pp. 173–176.
31. Milik, A.; Kubica, M.; Kania, D. Reconfigurable Logic Controller—Direct FPGA Synthesis Approach. *Appl. Sci.* **2021**, *11*, 8515. [CrossRef]
32. Wei, Y.; Li, B.; Zhang, B.; Yan, Y.; Zhou, Q. High-performance Data Hybrid Encryption Scheme Based on Mimic Defense. In Proceedings of the 3rd International Symposium on Computer Technology and Information Science (ISCTIS), Chengdu, China, 16–18 June 2023; pp. 114–121.
33. Mao, N.; Yang, H.; Huang, Z. A Parameterized Parallel Design Approach to Efficient Mapping of CNNs onto FPGA. *Electronics* **2023**, *12*, 1106. [CrossRef]
34. Barkalov, A.; Titarenko, L.; Krzywicki, K.; Saburova, S. Improving Characteristics of LUT-Based Mealy FSMs with Twofold State Assignment. *Electronics* **2021**, *10*, 901. [CrossRef]
35. Salauyou, V.; Bułatow, W. Optimized Sequential State Encoding Methods for Finite-State Machines in Field-Programmable Gate Array Implementations. *Appl. Sci.* **2024**, *14*, 5594. [CrossRef]
36. De Fine Licht, J.; Besta, M.; Meierhans, S.; Hoefler, T. Transformations of high-level synthesis codes for high-performance computing. *IEEE Trans. Parallel Distrib. Syst.* **2020**, *32*, 1014–1029. [CrossRef]
37. Xu, S.; Schafer, B.C. On the design of high performance hw accelerator through high-level synthesis scheduling approximations. In Proceedings of the 2020 Design, Automation & Test in Europe Conference & Exhibition (DATE), Grenoble, France, 9–13 March 2020; pp. 1378–1383.
38. Atwell, I.D.; Perera, D.G. HDL Code Variation: Impact on FPGA Performance Metrics and CAD Tools. In Proceedings of the IEEE Pacific Rim Conference on Communications, Computers and Signal Processing (PACRIM), Victoria, BC, Canada, 21–24 August 2024; p. 1.

applied sciences

Article

A Secure and Efficient Authentication Scheme for Fog-Based Vehicular Ad Hoc Networks

Sangjun Lee [1], Seunghwan Son [1], DeokKyu Kwon [1], Yohan Park [2] and Youngho Park [1,*]

1 School of Electronic and Electrical Engineering, Kyungpook National University, Daegu 41566, Republic of Korea; gumoning9010@knu.ac.kr (S.L.); sonshawn@knu.ac.kr (S.S.); kdk145@knu.ac.kr (D.K.)
2 School of Computer Engineering, Keimyung University, Daegu 42601, Republic of Korea; yhpark@kmu.ac.kr
* Correspondence: parkyh@knu.ac.kr

Abstract: Recently, the application of fog-computing technology to vehicular ad hoc networks (VANETs) has rapidly advanced. Despite these advancements, challenges remain in ensuring efficient communication and security. Specifically, there are issues such as the high communication and computation load of authentications and insecure communication over public channels between fog nodes and vehicles. To address these problems, a lightweight and secure authenticated key agreement protocol for confidential communication is proposed. However, we found that the protocol does not offer perfect forward secrecy and is vulnerable to several attacks, such as privileged insider, ephemeral secret leakage, and stolen smart card attacks. Furthermore, their protocol excessively uses elliptic curve cryptography (ECC), resulting in delays in VANET environments where authentication occurs frequently. Therefore, this paper proposes a novel authentication protocol that outperforms other related protocols regarding security and performance. The proposed protocol reduced the usage frequency of ECC primarily using hash and exclusive OR operations. We analyzed the proposed protocol using informal and formal methods, including the real-or-random (RoR) model, Burrows–Abadi–Nikoogadam (BAN) logic, and automated validation of internet security protocols and applications (AVISPA) simulation to show that the proposed protocol is correct and secure against various attacks. Moreover, We compared the computational cost, communication cost, and security features of the proposed protocol with other related protocols and show that the proposed methods have better performance and security than other schemes. As a result, the proposed scheme is more secure and efficient for fog-based VANETs.

Keywords: fog computing; vehicular ad hoc network; lightweight; key agreement; perfect forward secrecy; BAN logic; RoR model; AVISPA simulation

1. Introduction

The vehicular ad hoc network (VANET) [1] offers a promising approach to improving communication and data sharing between vehicles and infrastructure, transforming contemporary transportation. The VANET facilitates several applications, including road safety support, modernized traffic management, and improved driving experiences [2]. To provide these services, it is essential to handle the large amounts of traffic data generated by vehicles, which requires rapid data transmission and real-time data processing [3]. Traditional VANET architecture has used cloud computing technology for data storage and processing to satisfy these requirements. However, the cloud server is far from the vehicle; thus, processing the numerous data generated by a vehicle results in high latency and communication costs.

Fog computing [4] is a promising solution to improve the functionality of VANET environments, providing real-time processing and storage capabilities and using the communication and computing resources of each vehicle more efficiently. Furthermore, fog computing enables efficient data processing, enhanced scalability, and low-latency communication by extending the concept of cloud computing to the network edge in VANET environments [5]. Therefore, integrating fog computing with VANETs is necessary to improve the capabilities of autonomous vehicles.

However, fog-based VANETs encounter security challenges that threaten road safety and system integrity [6]. The interconnectedness of vehicles makes them vulnerable to cyberattacks, and messages transmitted over VANETs on public channels can be tampered with, replayed, intercepted, or deleted by an attacker. Moreover, the dynamic characteristics of fog nodes and reliance on wireless communication necessitate a robust authentication scheme to safeguard operations in fog-based VANETs [7]. Fog-based VANETs must satisfy certain security requirements, such as secure data transmission, privacy protection, and authentication.

Therefore, robust security protocols must be developed to authenticate entities and reduce potential threats. In 2024, Awais et al. [8] proposed a secure and lightweight authentication scheme to strengthen the security of fog-based VANETs. However, problems typically occur, such as session key exposure due to ephemeral secret leakage attacks and high communication costs due to the frequent use of public keys. Therefore, this paper proposes an improved protocol to address these security concerns effectively and enhance the overall reliability and efficiency of fog-based VANETs.

2. Related Works

This study introduces several papers that have described fog-based VANETs. Hou et al. [9] proposed a vehicular fog-computing architecture that uses vehicles as the infrastructures to improve communication and computational capacity. This architecture performs communication and computation by efficiently employing the resources of individual vehicles via a collaborative aggregation of end-user clients or nearby edge devices. Combining the resources of individual vehicles significantly improves the quality of vehicular applications and services. Peixoto et al. [10] proposed a framework for data clustering to reduce traffic data at the edge of vehicular networks using fog computing. The proposed framework for data clustering introduces two techniques to minimize the traffic information flow: a baseline technique that detects traffic congestion and two modified clustering techniques that order points to identify the clustering structure and density-based spatial clustering of applications with noise. This framework maintains high accuracy, even in highly congested vehicular traffic conditions, and reduces the communication costs in VANETs. Pereira et al. [11] introduced a framework for applying fog-computing technology in a VANET environment. Furthermore, they proposed a proof-of-concept system for data analyses in a fog-based VANET environment. Their study applied actual VANET data to demonstrate that fog computing is as effective as cloud computing. Their study demonstrated that distributed fog nodes can cooperate to process crucial data, quickly providing reliable data for smart city decision support systems. Farooqi et al. [12] designed a priority-based fog-computing model for smart-city vehicle transportation to reduce delays and latency. When the fog node was overloaded, they redirected high-priority requests to an adjacent node and transmitted low-priority requests to the cloud for additional processing. This technique reduced latency and delays by 20% and 35%, respectively, compared to the cloud computing architecture, allowing efficient communication between devices.

This research introduces several papers describing authentication protocols in wireless communication environments. For example, in 2017, Hamid et al. [13] proposed a triparty authenticated key agreement (AKA) protocol using a fog-computing facility in a healthcare environment. The proposed protocol uses bilinear pairing cryptography and decoy technology to access and store private healthcare data securely. In 2018, Jia et al. [14] proposed a triparty AKA protocol for fog-based healthcare systems. They employed an elliptic curve cryptosystem and bilinear pairing to guarantee the security of the session key. In 2018, Okay et al. [15] described a secure data aggregation protocol for smart grids using fog computing based on the additive privacy scheme proposed by Domingo-Ferrer. Moreover, in 2018, Lyu et al. [16] introduced an efficient and privacy-preserving aggregation scheme using fog-computing architecture to maintain aggregator anonymity. This protocol uses differential privacy and homomorphic encryption to safeguard aggregator obliviousness. In [13,14], computationally expensive cryptographic technology was used for the authentication phase. Bilinear pairing cryptography has high communication costs due to its computational complexity and the additional data required for key generation and data transmission. Moreover, precise data, such as healthcare information, demand high accuracy and reliability, increasing the latency. However, in fog-based VANETs, low latency is vital due to the importance of real-time data transmission and quick decision-making between vehicles. Therefore, the methods in [13,14] are inefficient and unsuitable for fog-based VANETs. In [15,16], the smart-grid environment is based on static data and designed without considering the dynamic network scalability, resulting in a lack of real-time data processing and responsiveness to dynamic situations. However, in fog-based VANETs, where many vehicles move simultaneously, real-time communication and data processing between vehicles and minimizing latency are essential. Therefore, the methods in [15,16] are unsuitable for fog-based VANETs.

Many researchers have studied effective and practical authentication schemes based on fog-based VANETs to address the security and privacy protection demands of vehicle communication. Ma et al. [17] proposed a novel AKA protocol without bilinear pairing to enable secure communication in fog-based VANETs. The protocol offers securely shared session keys, privacy protection, and mutual authentication. Eftekhari et al. [18] suggested a security-enhanced, three-party pairwise shared key agreement protocol for fog-based vehicular communication. They demonstrated that the protocol introduced by Ma et al. [17] does not satisfy several vital security requirements and is vulnerable to security attacks. To address these challenges, they reduced the communication costs compared to the protocol by Ma et al. [17] and improved security by defending against diverse attacks. Kumar et al. [19] introduced an authentication protocol based on fog nodes that adopts a multitrusted authority architecture, using operations based on ECC to achieve low communication and computational costs. They designed a robust and efficient authentication protocol using ECC and symmetric key encryption and decryption systems. Wu et al. [20] designed an authentication key exchange scheme that enhances secure communication in fog-based VANETs with fog nodes as relay nodes. This approach leads to a secure and efficient third-party authentication key exchange scheme. The proposed scheme uses only a few simple operations, including the cryptographic hash function, exclusive OR (XOR), and ECC, considering the restricted computing capabilities of vehicle users and fog nodes. Awais et al. [21] proposed a three-party AKA protocol for fog-based VANETs without depending on bilinear pairing. They used ECC to mitigate security threats in public wireless communication channels. Furthermore, they employed lightweight cryptographic operations for low computational and communication costs. Hedge et al. [8] introduced an efficient and secure authentication scheme using key agreement and management for a cloud–fog-device framework. This scheme applied symmetric trivariate polynomials, elliptic curve cryptography (ECC), and a fuzzy extractor for authentication. Awais et al. [22] proposed a novel four-party AKA protocol for fog-based VANETs using only lightweight cryptographic techniques and ECC without utilizing bilinear pairing technology. These protocols [8,17–22] proposed an authentication protocol for fog-based VANETs. However, these protocols require high computational and communication costs in order for them to be utilized in a fog-based VANET environment and do not meet several security requirements. Therefore, we proposed a secure and efficient authentication scheme for fog-based VANETs to address these issues.

3. Preliminaries

This section covers the concepts of ECC, the threat model, and the system model illustrated in Figure 1.

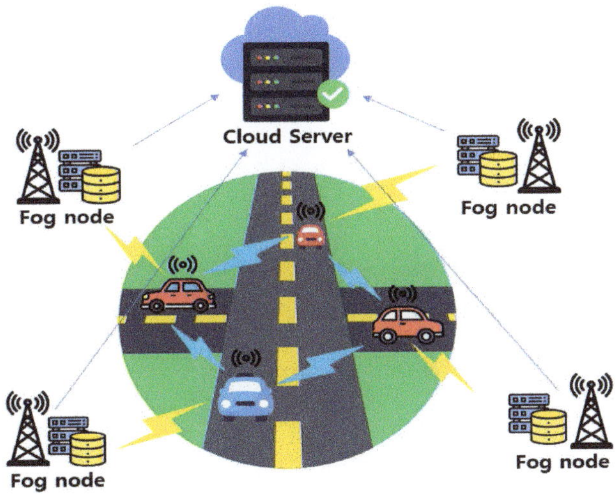

Figure 1. Fog-based VANET architecture.

3.1. Elliptic Curve Cryptography

Elliptic curve cryptography (ECC) [23] is a public key encryption method that applies the mathematical structure of elliptic curves. An elliptic curve, E, is defined as $E_q(a,b)$: $y^2 = x^3 + ax + b(modp)$, where $a, b \in F_p$, and p and q are large prime, and $4a^3 + 27b^2 \neq 0$. Then, we can select an additive cyclic elliptic curve group, G, with the order q and generator P. The properties of group G are listed below.

- Elliptic Curve Discrete Logarithm Problem: Given two random points, $A, B \in G$, calculating a random value k satisfying $A = k \cdot B$ in polynomial time is infeasible.
- Elliptic Curve Computational Diffie–Hellman (ECCDH) Problem: Given three random points, $A, M, N \in G$, calculating mnA satisfying $M = mA$ and $N = nA$ in polynomial time is infeasible.

3.2. Threat Assumption Model

This paper adopts the Dolev–Yao security model [24–26] and the Canetti and Krawczyk security model [27–29] as threat models for the proposed protocol. The capabilities of an adversary, A, are summarized as follows:

- A can intercept, modify, eavesdrop, and replay messages on public communication channels.

- A and vehicles know the identities of all fog nodes. A may be a legitimate vehicle user or a privileged insider on the cloud server.
- A can obtain the secret values of the smart card through power analysis attacks [30,31].
- A can obtain long- or short-term keys from the network and attempt to compute the session key. The long-term keys are the private keys of the network entities, and the short-term keys are the random values generated during the authentication process [32].

In a real VANET environment, the cloud server and fog nodes are securely connected, making it difficult for attackers to compromise them. However, vehicles can be captured or stolen by attackers, making them vulnerable targets. Therefore, we considered vehicles as insecure entities and assumed a threat model.

3.3. System Model

The system model includes the cloud server (CS), fog node (FN_j), and vehicle user (V_i).

- Cloud server (CS): The CS is a fully trusted entity that initializes the system setup and provides registration services for V_i and FN_j and stores the verification values derived from their identities for authentication.
- Fog Node (FN_j): FN_j is a semi-trusted entity in the protocol that has its own computing capabilities and storage capacity. The fog node mediates the authentication messages transmitted between CS and V_i. Once the authentication phase is complete, FN_j establishes a shared session key with CS and V_i. FN_j has data storage servers and is a wireless communication facility in VANET environments.
- Vehicles (V_i): Each V_i employs its on-board unit to communicate with other vehicles or infrastructure and collect real-time traffic information. In addition, V_i is considered untrustworthy in fog-based VANETs, so the adversary can perform attacks after registering as a legitimate user.

4. Proposed Protocol

This section introduces the proposed protocol comprising five phases: initialization, registration, login and authentication, password update, and user revocation and re-registration. Table 1 lists the notations for the proposed protocol.

Table 1. Notations of the proposed protocol.

Notation	Description
V_i	Vehicle user
FN_j	Fog node
CS	Cloud server
ID_i	Identity of vehicle user
ID_j	Identity of fog node
PID_i	Pseudo identity of vehicle user
RID_i	Secret pseudo identity of vehicle user
PSW_i	Password of vehicle user
N_i	Secret key of vehicle user
N_j	Secret key of fog node
s, x_i, y_j	Secret keys of cloud server
r_i	Set of random numbers
R_i	Set of public keys
SK_{i-j-cs}	Session keys of V_i, FN_j, and CS
$Auth_i, Auth_j$	A secret value needed for authentication
$h(\cdot)$	Cryptographic hash function
$\oplus$	Exclusive OR operation
$\|\|$	Concatenation operation

4.1. Initialization Phase

CS selects large prime numbers p, q and $a, b \in F_p$. Then, CS selects a secure elliptic curve, $E_q(a,b) : y^2 = x^3 + ax + b$ $(4a^3 + 27b^2 \neq 0)$, in a finite field, F_p, and $t = log_{2p}$ represents the security metrics. Moreover, G denotes a cyclic group with order q with a base point P. Then, CS randomly selects an integer, $s \in Z_q^*$, as a secret key and computes $P_{pub} = sP$. The public system parameters are released as (G, P, P_{pub}), whereas the value of s remains confidential. Then, CS selects secure one-way hash functions $h(.) : \{0,1\}^* \rightarrow \{0,1\}^{tn}$, generating a 256-bit output and a fuzzy verifier, $2^4 \leq s_0 \leq 2^8$. Finally, CS publishes system parameters $\{P_{pub}, E_q, P, h(.)\}$ and keeps s secret.

4.2. Vehicle Registration Phase

Each vehicle transmits a registration request to a fully trusted cloud server in this phase and receives a smart card.

Step 1: V_i inputs a user identity (ID_i) and password, PSW_i, and chooses an integer, $2^4 \leq s_0 \leq 2^8$. V_i computes $RPSW_i = h(ID_i \parallel PSW_i \parallel s_0)$ and $PID_i = h(ID_i \parallel RPSW_i \parallel s_0)$ and sends (ID_i) to CS in a secure manner.

Step 2: After responding to the request of V_i, CS randomly selects $x_i \in Z_p^*$ and calculates $N_i = h(PID_i \parallel s \parallel x_i)$. Then, CS stores N_i on a smart card and sends it to V_i through a secure channel. CS also stores the pair (PID_i, x_i) in a database.

Step 3: Then, V_i computes $M_i = h((h(ID_i) \oplus PSW_i) mod s_0)$ and $N_i^* = h(RPSW_i \parallel M_i) \oplus N_i$. V_i stores (N_i^*, M_i, s_0) on a smart card and deletes N_i.

Figure 2 presents the vehicle registration phase.

Vehicle user (V_i)		Cloud server (CS)
Inputs ID_i and PSW_i Chooses s_0 Computes $RPSW_i = h(ID_i \parallel PSW_i \parallel s_0)$ $PID_i = h(ID_i \parallel RPSW_i \parallel s_0)$		
	PID_i $\longrightarrow$ Secure channel	
		Selects $x_i \in Z_p^*$ Calculates $N_i = h(PID_i \parallel s \parallel x_i)$ Store N_i in smart card Stores the pair (PID_i, x_i)
	$\longleftarrow$ *Smartcard* Secure channel	
Computes $M_i = h((h(ID_i \oplus PSW_i) mod s_0)$ $N_i^* = h(RPSW_i \parallel M_i) \oplus N_i$ Stores (N_i^*, M_i, s_0) in smart card Deletes N_i in smart card		

Figure 2. Proposed vehicle registration phase.

4.3. Fog Node Registration Phase

FN_j is registered with CS before deployment. To achieve this, FN_j transmits its identity ID_j to CS, which randomly selects y_j from the set of integers, where $y_j \leq Z_p^*$. Afterward, CS computes $N_j = h(ID_j \parallel s \parallel y_j)$ and securely transmits N_j to FN_j and stores the pair (ID_j, y_j) in its database. Figure 3 presents the fog node registration phase.

Fog node (FN_j)		Cloud server (CS)
Selects ID_j		
	ID_j → Secure channel	
		Selects $y_j \in Z_p^*$ Calculates $N_j = h(ID_j \parallel s \parallel y_j)$ Stores the pair (ID_j, y_j)
	N_j ← Secure channel	

Figure 3. Proposed fog node registration phase.

4.4. Login and Authentication Phase

In this phase, CS, FN_j, and V_i authenticate each other using their secret values and agree on a shared session key for secure communication. Figure 4 presents their interactions, and the details are provided below.

Step 1: Insert ID_i and PSW_i and compute $M_i' = h((h(ID_i) \oplus PSW_i) mod s_0)$. After computing, check whether $M_i' = M_i$; if not true, V_i will terminate the session and notify the user of the login failure. Then, V_i request the user to retry the login process. If true, V_i computes $RPSW_i' = h(ID_i \parallel PSW_i \parallel s_0)$ and $N_i = N_i^* \oplus h(RPSW_i' \parallel M_i')$. Next, V_i selects a random number, $r_1 \leq Z_q^*$, and calculates $R_1 = r_1 P, \bar{R}_1 = r_1 P_{pub}, RID_i = PID_i \oplus h(\bar{R}_1)$, and $Q_i = h(\bar{R}_1 \parallel N_i \parallel ID_i \parallel ID_j)$, and V_i transmits $(D_1 = R_1, RID_i, Q_i, ID_j)$ to FN_j.

Step 2: FN_j verifies the freshness of the random number in D_1 from V_i and selects a random number, $r_2 \in Z_q^*$, to calculate $R_2 = r_2 P$ and $L_j = h(N_j \parallel ID_j \parallel Q_i)$. FN_j then transmits $(D_2 = R_1, RID_i, R_2, r_2 R_1, L_j, ID_j)$ to CS.

Step 3: After receiving the authentication request from FN_j, CS verifies the freshness of the random number in D_2 from FN_j and computes $\bar{R}_1' = sR_1$ and $PID_i' = RID_i \oplus h(\bar{R}_1')$. CS checks its database for items that correspond to (PID_i', x_i) and (ID_j', y_j). If CS does not find such items, it rejects the request and terminates the session. If CS finds the items, CS continues with additional computations as follows: - $N_i' = h(ID_i' \parallel s \parallel x_i)$ - $N_j' = h(ID_j \parallel s \parallel y_j)$ - $Q_i' = h(\bar{R}_1' \parallel N_i' \parallel ID_i' \parallel ID_j)$ - $L_j' = h(N_j \parallel ID_j \parallel Q_i')$. CS checks whether $L_j' = L_j$ is true, and if conditions are not true, CS will terminate the current session and request FN_j and V_i to retry the authentication process. Otherwise, CS randomly chooses $r_3 \in Z_q^*$, calculates $R_3 = r_3 P$, and computes the following: - $R_{i-j-cs} = r_3 \cdot (r_2 R_1)$ - $K_{ij} = h(N_i \parallel R_{i-j-cs}) \oplus h(N_j \parallel R_{i-j-cs})$ - $SK_{i-j-cs} = h(h(N_i \parallel R_{i-j-cs}) \parallel h(N_j \parallel R_i i - j - cs) \parallel R_{i-j-cs})$ - $Auth_j = h(h(N_i \parallel R_{i-j-cs}) \parallel R_{i-j-cs} \parallel SK_{i-j-cs})$. Then, CS transmits $(D_3 = K_{ij}, R_3, r_3 R_1, Auth_j)$ to FN_j.

Step 4: After receiving the response from CS, FN_j verifies the freshness of the random number in D_3 from CS and computes $R_{i-j-cs} = r_2 \cdot (r_3 R_1), h(N_i \parallel R_{i-j-cs}) = K_{ij} \oplus h(N_j \parallel R_{i-j-cs}), SK_{i-j-cs} = h(h(N_i \parallel R_{i-j-cs}) \parallel h(N_j \parallel R_{i-j-cs}) \parallel R_{i-j-cs})$, and $Auth_j' = h(h(N_i \parallel R_{i-j-cs}) \parallel R_{i-j-cs} \parallel SK_{i-j-cs})$. Then, FN_j verifies whether or not $Auth_j' = Auth_j$ is true, and if conditions are not true, FN_j will terminate the current session and notify CS of authentication failure. If true, FN_j computes $Auth_i = h(Auth_j \parallel h(N_j \parallel R_{i-j-cs}))$ and transmits $(D_4 = K_{ij}, r_2 R_3, Auth_i)$ to V_i.

Step 5: After receiving the response of FN_j, V_i verifies the freshness of the random number in D_4 from FN_j and computes $R_{i-j-cs} = r_1 \cdot (r_2 R_3), h(N_j \parallel R_{i-j-cs}) = K_{ij} \oplus h(N_i \parallel R_{i-j-cs}), SK_{i-j-cs} = h(h(N_i \parallel R_{i-j-cs}) \parallel h(N_j \parallel R_{i-j-cs}) \parallel R_{i-j-cs}), Auth_j' =$

$h(h(N_i \parallel R_{i-j-cs}) \parallel R_{i-j-cs} \parallel SK_{i-j-cs})$, and $Auth_i' = h(Auth_j' \parallel h(N_j \parallel R_{i-j-cs}))$. Then, V_i verifies whether or not $Auth_i' = Auth_i$; if conditions are not true, V_i will terminate the current session.

After the authentication phase is fully completed, a secure shared session key is established between V_i, FN_j, and CS.

Vehicle user (V_i)	Fog node (FN_j)	Cloud server (CS)

Vehicle user (V_i):

% Login
Inserts ID_i, PSW_i
Computes
$M_i' = h((h(ID_i) \oplus PSW_i) mod s_0)$
Checks $M_i' = M_i$
If not true, rejects login try;

% Generate authentication message
Otherwise, computes
$RPSW_i' = h(ID_i \parallel PSW_i \parallel s_0)$
$N_i = N_i^* \oplus h(RPSW_i' \parallel M_i')$
$r_1 \in Z_q^*, R_1 = r_1 P, \bar{R}_1 = r_1 P_{pub}$
$RID_i = PID_i \oplus h(\bar{R}_1)$
$Q_i = h(\bar{R}_1 \parallel N_i \parallel ID_i \parallel ID_j)$

$\xrightarrow{(D_1 = R_1, RID_i, Q_i, ID_j)}$

Fog node (FN_j):

% Relay authentication message
$r_2 \in Z_q^*, R_2 = r_2 P$
$L_j = h(N_j \parallel ID_j \parallel Q_i)$

$\xrightarrow{(D_2 = R_1, RID_i, R_2, r_2 R_1, L_j, ID_j)}$

Cloud server (CS):

% Verify authentication message
$\bar{R}_1' = sR_1$
Computes
$PID_i' = RID_i \oplus h(\bar{R}_1')$
Search the entire $(PID_i', x_i), (ID_j, y_j)$ in database
If not found, rejects the request and terminates the session
Otherwise, computes
$N_i' = h(ID_i' \parallel s \parallel x_i)$
$N_j = h(ID_j \parallel s \parallel y_i)$
$Q_i' = h(\bar{R}_1' \parallel N_i' \parallel ID_i' \parallel ID_j)$
$L_j' = h(N_j \parallel ID_j \parallel Q_i')$
Checks $L_j' = L_j$
If not true, terminates the session;

% Generate response message
Otherwise, chooses $r_3 \in Z_q^*, R_3 = r_3 P$
Computes $R_{i-j-cs} = r_3 \cdot (r_2 R_1)$
$K_{ij} = h(N_i \parallel R_{i-j-cs}) \oplus h(N_j \parallel R_{i-j-cs})$
$SK_{i-j-cs} = h(h(N_i \parallel R_{i-j-cs}) \parallel h(N_j \parallel R_{i-j-cs}) \parallel R_{i-j-cs})$
$Auth_j = h(h(N_i \parallel R_{i-j-cs}) \parallel R_{i-j-cs} \parallel SK_{i-j-cs})$

$\xleftarrow{(D_3 = K_{ij}, R_3, r_3 R_1, Auth_j)}$

Fog node (FN_j):

% Relay response message
Computes
$R_{i-j-cs} = r_2 \cdot (r_3 R_1)$
$h(N_i \parallel R_{i-j-cs}) = K_{ij} \oplus h(N_j \parallel R_{i-j-cs})$
$SK_{i-j-cs} = h(h(N_i \parallel R_{i-j-cs}) \parallel h(N_j \parallel R_{i-j-cs}) \parallel R_{i-j-cs})$
$Auth_j' = h(h(N_i \parallel R_{i-j-cs}) \parallel R_{i-j-cs} \parallel SK_{i-j-cs})$
Checks $Auth_j' = Auth_j$
If not true, terminates the session;
Otherwise, computes $Auth_i = h(Auth_j \parallel h(N_j \parallel R_{i-j-cs}))$

$\xleftarrow{(D_4 = K_{ij}, r_2 R_3, Auth_i)}$

Vehicle user (V_i):

% Verify response message
Computes
$R_{i-j-cs} = r_1 \cdot (r_2 R_3)$
$h(N_j \parallel R_{i-j-cs}) = K_{ij} \oplus h(N_i \parallel R_{i-j-cs})$
$SK_{i-j-cs} = h(h(N_i \parallel R_{i-j-cs}) \parallel h(N_j \parallel R_{i-j-cs}) \parallel R_{i-j-cs})$
$Auth_j' = h(h(N_i \parallel R_{i-j-cs}) \parallel R_{i-j-cs} \parallel SK_{i-j-cs})$
$Auth_i' = h(Auth_j' \parallel h(N_j \parallel R_{i-j-cs}))$
Checks $Auth_i' = Auth_i$
If not true, terminates the session;

Figure 4. Proposed authentication phase.

4.5. Password Update Phase

Vehicle users can update their passwords as often as desired, as follows:

Step 1: After entering ID_i and PSW_i in the smart card, V_i sends a password change request.

Step 2: The smart card computes $RPSW_i = h(ID_i \parallel PSW_i \parallel s_0)$ and $M_i = h(h(ID_i) \oplus PSW_i) mod s_0)$ and then checks whether or not $M_i' = M_i$ matches the stored M_i to verify the authenticity of M_i'. If the verification is confirmed, the smart card inputs ID_i and PSW_i.

Step 3: First, the new password, PSW_i^{new}, must be entered. Then, the smart card generates $2^4 \leq s_0^{new} \leq 2^8$ and calculates $RPSW_i^{new} = h(ID_i \parallel PSW_i^{new} \parallel s_0^{new})$ and $M_i^{new} = h(h(ID_i) \oplus PSW_i^{new}) mod s_0^{new})$. Finally, the smart card replaces (N_i^*, M_i, s_0) with $(N_i^{new}, M_i^{new}, s_0^{new})$.

4.6. User Revocation and Re-Registration

If V_i is compromised, CS deletes (ID_i, x_i) from its database. Then, login attempts with the previous smart card are rejected.

CS allows V_i to re-register through registration. V_i re-registers using the same identity and an updated password. Afterward, CS assigns a new random number, x_i^{new}, and stores it in the database with V_i's PID_i.

4.7. Fog Node Revocation

If FN_j is compromised, CS deletes (ID_j, y_j) from its database. Access requests from FN_j are denied afterward because the random number y_j is needed to verify authentication requests.

5. Security Analysis

This section analyzes the proposed protocol using formal and informal methods.

5.1. Formal Analysis

5.1.1. BAN Logic

This section presents the Burrows–Abadi–Nikoogadam (BAN) logic [33] of the proposed protocol. The BAN logic method is a formal approach used for analyzing and verifying the correctness of authentication protocols. Table 2 presents the notation and definitions, and the BAN logic rules are provided below.

Table 2. Burrows –Abadi–Nikoogadam (BAN) logic notation.

Notation	Description
θ_1, θ_2	Principals
σ_1, σ_2	Statements
$\theta_1 \mid\equiv \sigma_1$	θ_1 **believes** σ_1
$\theta_1 \mid\sim \sigma_1$	θ_1 once **said** σ_1
$\theta_1 \Rightarrow \sigma_1$	θ_1 **controls** σ_1
$\theta_1 \lhd \sigma_1$	θ_1 **receives** σ_1
$\#\sigma_1$	σ_1 is **fresh**
$(\sigma_1)_K$	σ_1 is **encrypted** by K
$\theta_1 \overset{K}{\leftrightarrow} \theta_2$	θ_1 and θ_2 have **shared** key K
SK	Session key

5.1.2. Burrows–Abadi–Nikoogadam (BAN) Logic Rules

1. Message meaning rule (MMR):

$$\frac{\theta_1 \Big| \equiv \theta_1 \overset{K}{\leftrightarrow} \theta_2, \quad \theta_1 \lhd (\sigma_1)_K}{\theta_1 | \equiv \theta_2 | \sim \sigma_1}$$

2. Nonce verification rule (NVR):

$$\frac{\theta_1 | \equiv \#(\sigma_1), \quad \theta_1 | \equiv \theta_2 \Big| \sim \sigma_1}{\theta_1 | \equiv \theta_2 | \equiv \sigma_1}$$

3. Jurisdiction rule (JR):

$$\frac{\theta_1 | \equiv \theta_2 | \Longrightarrow \sigma_1, \quad \theta_1 | \equiv \theta_2 | \equiv \sigma_1}{\theta_1 \Big| \equiv \sigma_1}$$

4. Belief rule (BR):

$$\frac{\theta_1 \Big| \equiv (\sigma_1, \sigma_2)}{\theta_1 \Big| \equiv \sigma_1}$$

5. Freshness rule (FR):

$$\frac{\theta_1 \Big| \equiv \#(\sigma_1)}{\theta_1 \Big| \equiv \#(\sigma_1, \sigma_2)}$$

5.1.3. Goals

The goals are to demonstrate that the vehicle user, V_i, fog node, FN_j, and cloud server, CS, all agree on the same session key, SK.

G 1: $V_i | \equiv V_i \overset{SK}{\longleftrightarrow} FN_j$

G 2: $V_i | \equiv FN_j | \equiv V_i \overset{SK}{\longleftrightarrow} FN_j$

G 3: $FN_j | \equiv V_i \overset{SK}{\longleftrightarrow} FN_j$

G 4: $FN_j | \equiv V_i | \equiv V_i \overset{SK}{\longleftrightarrow} FN_j$

G 5: $FN_j | \equiv CS \overset{SK}{\longleftrightarrow} FN_j$

G 6: $FN_j | \equiv CS | \equiv CS \overset{SK}{\longleftrightarrow} FN_j$

G 7: $CS | \equiv CS \overset{SK}{\longleftrightarrow} FN_j$

G 8: $CS | \equiv FN_j | \equiv CS \overset{SK}{\longleftrightarrow} FN_j$

5.1.4. Idealized Forms

The following idealized forms of each message are transmitted during the authentication phase:

D_1 : $V_i \rightarrow FN_j : (R_1, Q_i)_{N_i}$

D_2 : $FN_j \rightarrow CS : (R_1, R_2, r_2 R_1, L_j)_{N_j}$

D_3 : $CS \rightarrow FN_j : (R_3, r_3 R_1, h(N_i \parallel R_{i-j-cs}))_{h(N_j \| R_{i-j-cs})}$

D_4 : $FN_j \rightarrow V_i : (r_2 R_3, h(N_j \parallel R_{i-j-cs}))_{h(N_i \| R_{i-j-cs})}$

5.1.5. Assumptions

The assumptions of the proposed protocol are provided below.

A_1: $V_i| \equiv \#(r_2R_3)$

A_2: $FN_j| \equiv \#(R_1)$

A_3: $FN_j| \equiv \#(R_3)$

A_4: $CS| \equiv \#(R_2)$

A_5: $V_i| \equiv FN_j \Rightarrow (V_i \overset{SK}{\longleftrightarrow} FN_j)$

A_6: $FN_j| \equiv CS \Rightarrow (CS \overset{SK}{\longleftrightarrow} FN_j)$

A_7: $CS| \equiv FN_j \Rightarrow (CS \overset{SK}{\longleftrightarrow} FN_j)$

A_8: $FN_j| \equiv V_i \Rightarrow (V_i \overset{SK}{\longleftrightarrow} FN_j)$

A_9: $V_i| \equiv V_i \overset{h(N_i\|R_{i-j-cs})}{\longleftrightarrow} FN_j$

A_{10}: $FN_j| \equiv CS \overset{h(N_j)}{\longleftrightarrow} FN_j$

A_{11}: $CS| \equiv CS \overset{h(N_j)}{\longleftrightarrow} FN_j$

A_{12}: $FN_j| \equiv V_i \overset{h(N_i\|R_{i-j-cs})}{\longleftrightarrow} FN_j$

A_{13}: $V_i| \equiv V_i \overset{h(N_i)}{\longleftrightarrow} CS$

A_{14}: $CS| \equiv V_i \overset{h(N_i)}{\longleftrightarrow} CS$

5.1.6. Burrows–Abadi–Nikoogadam (BAN) Logic Proof

The BAN logic proof is based on the following assumptions and idealized forms:

S 1: FN_j receives D_1.

$$S_1\text{: } FN_j \lhd (R_1, Q_i)_{N_i}$$

S 2: CS receives D_2.

$$S_2\text{: } CS \lhd (R_1, R_2, r_2R_1, L_j)_{N_j}$$

S 3: Applying S_2 and A_{11} to the MMR yields S_3.

$$S_3 : CS| \equiv FN_j| \sim (R_1, R_2, r_2R_1, L_j)$$

S 4: Applying S_3 and A_4 to the FR yields S_8.

$$S_4 : CS| \equiv \#(R_1, R_2, r_2R_1, L_j)$$

S 5: Applying S_3 and S_4 to the NVR yields S_5.

$$S_5 : CS| \equiv FN_j| \equiv (R_1, R_2, r_2R_1, L_j)$$

S 6: We can obtain S_6 by applying S_5 to the BR.

$$S_6 : CS| \equiv FN_j| \equiv (r_2R_1)$$

S 7: FN_j receives D_3.

$$S_7\text{: } FN_j \lhd (R_3, r_3R_1, h(N_i \parallel R_{i-j-cs}))_{h(N_j \parallel R_{i-j-cs})}$$

S 8: Applying S_7 and A_{10} to the MMR yields S_8.

$$S_8 : FN_j| \equiv CS| \sim (R_3, r_3R_1, h(N_i \parallel R_{i-j-cs}))$$

S 9: Applying S_8 and A_3 to the FR yields S_9.

$$S_9 : FN_j| \equiv \#(R_3, r_3R_1, h(N_i \parallel R_{i-j-cs}))$$

S 10: Applying S_8 and S_9 to the NVR yields S_{10}.

$$S_{10} : FN_j| \equiv CS| \equiv (R_3, r_3R_1, h(N_i \parallel R_{i-j-cs}))$$

S 11: We can obtain S_{11} by applying S_{10} to the BR.

$$S_{11} : FN_j| \equiv CS| \equiv (r_3R_1)$$

S 12: V_i receives D_4.

$$S_{12}\text{: } V_i \lhd (r_2R_3, h(N_j \parallel R_{i-j-cs}))_{h(N_i \parallel R_{i-j-cs})}$$

S 13: Applying S_{12} and A_9 to the MMR yields S_{13}.

$$S_{13} : V_i| \equiv FN_j| \sim (r_2R_3, h(N_j \parallel R_{i-j-cs}))$$

S 14: Applying S_{13} and A_1 to the FR yields S_{14}.

$$S_{14} : V_i| \equiv \#(r_2R_3, h(N_j \parallel R_{i-j-cs}))$$

S 15: Applying S_{13} and S_{14} to the NVR yields S_{15}.

$$S_{15} : V_i| \equiv FN_j| \equiv (r_2R_3, h(N_j \parallel R_{i-j-cs}))$$

S 16: We can obtain S_{16} by applying S_{15} to the BR.

$$S_{16} : V_i| \equiv FN_j| \equiv (r_2R_3)$$

S 17: From S_6, S_{11}, and S_{16}, V_i, FN_j, and CS can compute the session key $SK_{i-j-cs} = h(h(N_i \parallel R_{i-j-cs}) \parallel h(N_j \parallel R_{i-j-cs}) \parallel R_{i-j-cs})$.

$$S_{17}\text{: } V_i| \equiv FN_j| \equiv V_i \overset{SK}{\longleftrightarrow} FN_j \quad \textbf{(Goal 2)}$$
$$S_{18}\text{: } FN_j| \equiv V_i| \equiv V_i \overset{SK}{\longleftrightarrow} FN_j \quad \textbf{(Goal 4)}$$
$$S_{19}\text{: } FN_j| \equiv CS| \equiv CS \overset{SK}{\longleftrightarrow} FN_j \quad \textbf{(Goal 6)}$$
$$S_{20}\text{: } CS| \equiv FN_j| \equiv CS \overset{SK}{\longleftrightarrow} FN_j \quad \textbf{(Goal 8)}$$

S 18: The JR can be applied to S_{21}, S_{22}, S_{23}, and S_{24} using A_5, A_8, A_6, and A_7, respectively.

$$S_{21}\text{: } V_i| \equiv V_i \overset{SK}{\longleftrightarrow} FN_j \quad \textbf{(Goal 1)}$$
$$S_{22}\text{: } FN_j| \equiv V_i \overset{SK}{\longleftrightarrow} FN_j \quad \textbf{(Goal 3)}$$
$$S_{23}\text{: } FN_j| \equiv CS \overset{SK}{\longleftrightarrow} FN_j \quad \textbf{(Goal 5)}$$
$$S_{24}\text{: } CS| \equiv CS \overset{SK}{\longleftrightarrow} FN_j \quad \textbf{(Goal 7)}$$

Finally, the vehicle user, fog node, and cloud server mutually authenticate each other.

5.1.7. Real-or-Random Model

The real-or-random (RoR) model [34] is a formal security analysis method that proves the semantic security of the session key in the authentication protocol. In the proposed protocol, the participants are the vehicle user, fog node, and cloud server: $Ta^{k_1}_{V_i}$, $Ta^{k_2}_{FN_i}$, and $Ta^{k_3}_{CS}$, respectively. In the RoR model, adversary A can intercept, eavesdrop, replay, and modify all insecure channel messages to determine the session key, SK. A can perform the queries $Execute(Ta^{k_1}_{V_i}, Ta^{k_2}_{FN_i}, Ta^{k_3}_{CS})$, $CorruptSC(Ta^{k_1}_{V_i})$, $Send(Ta^{k_n}_{x}, Msg)$, and $Test(Ta^{k_n}_{x})$. Table 3 presents the queries performed by A.

Table 3. Queries in the real-or-random (RoR) model.

Query	Description
$Execute(Ta^{k_1}_{V_i}, Ta^{k_2}_{FN_i}, Ta^{k_3}_{CS})$	A can eavesdrop messages transmitted via public channels between $Ta^{k_1}_{V_i}$, $Ta^{k_2}_{FN_i}$, and $Ta^{k_3}_{CS}$. A can perform passive attacks with these messages.
$CorruptSC(Ta^{k_1}_{V_i})$	A can obtain secret values stored in the stolen smart card of $Ta^{k_1}_{V_i}$ by performing this query.
$Send(Ta^{k_n}_{x}, Msg)$	By performing this query, A can send a message, Msg, to a participant, $Ta^{k_n}_{x}$. Furthermore, A can obtain a response message from a participant, $Ta^{k_n}_{x}$.
$Test(Ta^{k_n}_{x})$	In the last game, A performs this query. When this query is performed, an unbiased coin, c, is tossed. The head represents 1 and the tail represents 0. If $c = 1$, then $Ta^{k_n}_{x}$ returns the session key, SK; If $c = 0$, then $Ta^{k_n}_{x}$ returns a random number. In other cases, $Ta^{k_n}_{x}$ returns $NULL$. If A correctly guesses that the returned value is the session key, SK, A wins the game.

Theorem 1. *We define q_{ha}, $|Hash|$, q_{send}, and l as the number of hash queries performed by A, the range space of the hash function, the number of send queries performed by A, and the length of the identity V_i, respectively. Furthermore, the breaking possibility of the ECCDH problem is $Advp^{ECC}_{M}(A)$, and the Zipf parameters are C' and s'. When $Adv p(A)$ is the probability that A breaks the session key in polynomial time, we prove the following equation:*

$$Advp(A) \leq \frac{q^2_{ha}}{|Hash|} + 2Advp^{ECC}_{M}(A) + 2max\{C' q^{s'}_{send}, \frac{q_{send}}{2^l}\} \tag{1}$$

Proof. A plays five games, $GM_n (n = 0, 1, 2, 3, 4)$, based on the RoR model. $AVTG^{WIGM_n}(A)$ represents the advantage of A to break the session key after playing the game GM_n.

- GM_0: In the first game, A selects a random bit, r. A does not know any information required to calculate the session key, SK, and has no queries to perform. Thus, we derive the following equation:

$$Advp(A) = |2AVTG_{WIGM_0}(A) - 1|. \tag{2}$$

- GM_1: A performs the $Execute$ query to conduct an eavesdropping attack. From that query, A obtains all public channel messages $(D_1 = R_1, RID_i, Q_i, ID_j)$, $(D_2 = R_1, RID_i, R_2, r_2R_1, L_j, ID_j)$, $(D_3 = K_{ij}, R_3, r_3R_1, Auth_j)$, and $(D_4 = K_{ij}, r_2R_3, Auth_i)$. Afterward, A performs a $Test$ query to calculate the session key, SK. However, A

cannot calculate the session key, SK, because it is masked by long-term keys N_i and N_j and the short-term key R_{i-j-cs}. Thus, we obtain the following equation:

$$AVTG_{WIGM_1}(A) = AVTG_{WIGM_0}(A). \tag{3}$$

- GM_2: In this game, A performs the *Send* and *Hash* queries to calculate the session key, SK. To obtain the values needed for calculating the session key, SK, A must determine the hash collision using messages from the public channel. Thus, we obtain the following equation due to the birthday paradox [35]:

$$|AVTG_{WIGM_2}(A) - AVTG_{WIGM_1}(A)| \leq \frac{q_{ha}^2}{2|Hash|}. \tag{4}$$

- GM_3: In this game, A tries to compute SK with the messages $(D_1 = R_1, RID_i, Q_i, ID_j)$, $(D_2 = R_1, RID_i, R_2, r_2R_1, L_j, ID_j)$, $(D_3 = K_{ij}, R_3, r_3R_1, Auth_j)$, and $(D_4 = K_{ij}, r_2R_3, Auth_i)$. However, the session key, SK, consists of $R_{i-j-cs} = r_3 \cdot r_2 \cdot r_1 \cdot P$, derived from the ECCDH problem. Therefore, we obtain the following inequality:

$$|AVTG_{WIGM_3}(A) - AVTG_{WIGM_2}(A)| \leq Advp_M^{ECC}(A). \tag{5}$$

- GM_4: In the last game, A performs the *CorruptSC* query and extracts (N_i^*, M_i, s_0) from SC. However, A cannot compute the session key, SK, because the smart card values are masked with a hash function using ID_i and PSW_i. Thus, we obtain the following inequality using the Zipf law [36]:

$$|AVTG_{WIGM_4}(A) - AVTG_{WIGM_3}(A)| \leq max\{C'q_{send}^{s'}, \frac{q_{send}}{2^l}\}. \tag{6}$$

At the end of all games, A must guess whether or not r is correct from the *Test* query. Therefore, we obtain the following equation:

$$AVTG_{WIGM_4}(A) = \frac{1}{2}. \tag{7}$$

We derive the following equation from Equation (2) and (3):

$$\begin{aligned} \frac{1}{2}Advp(A) &= |AVTG_{WIGM_0}(A) - \frac{1}{2}| \\ &= |AVTG_{WIGM_1}(A) - \frac{1}{2}|. \end{aligned} \tag{8}$$

We also compute the following equation from Equations (7) and (8):

$$\frac{1}{2}Advp(A) = |AVTG_{WIGM_1}(A) - AVTG_{WIGM_4}(A)|. \tag{9}$$

We apply the triangular inequality to the Equation (9).

$$
\begin{aligned}
\frac{1}{2}Advp(A) &= |AVTG_{WIGM_1}(A) - AVTG_{WIGM_4}(A)| \\
&\leq |AVTG_{WIGM_1}(A) - AVTG_{WIGM_3}(A)| \\
&+ |AVTG_{WIGM_3}(A) - AVTG_{WIGM_4}(A)| \\
&\leq |AVTG_{WIGM_1}(A) - AVTG_{WIGM_2}(A)| \\
&+ |AVTG_{WIGM_2}(A) - AVTG_{WIGM_3}(A)| \\
&+ |AVTG_{WIGM_3}(A) - AVTG_{WIGM_4}(A)| \\
&\leq \frac{q_{ha}^2}{2|Hash|} + Advp_M^{ECC}(A) + max\{C' q_{send}^{s'}, \frac{q_{send}}{2^l}\}.
\end{aligned} \tag{10}
$$

By multiplying Equation (10) by two, we obtain the following result:

$$
Advp(A) \leq \frac{q_{ha}^2}{|Hash|} + 2Advp_M^{ECC}(A) + 2max\{C' q_{send}^{s'}, \frac{q_{send}}{2^l}\}. \tag{11}
$$

Finally, we prove the semantic security of our proposed protocol using the RoR model. □

5.1.8. AVISPA Simulation

In this section, we presents formal security verification of our proposed protocol using AVISPA [37]. AVISPA has been widely used to verify the security of authentication protocols, primarily to assess their resilience against man-in-the-middle and replay attacks. Moreover, AVISPA is a formal analysis tool that implements an authentication protocol using the High-Level Protocol Specification Language (HLPSL). In addition, AVISPA uses four back-end models: "on-the-fly model-checker (OFMC)", "constraint logic-based attack searcher (CL-AtSe)", "SAT-based model-checker (SATMC)", and "tree automata based on automatic approximations for the analysis of security protocols (TA4SP)". The back-end models evaluate the security features of an authentication protocol and generate the output format as a result. Since XOR operation is used in our proposed protocol, we only use OFMC and CL-AtSe back-end models. Figure 5 depicts the simulation results, and the proposed protocol is considered safe. Therefore, we can demonstrate that the proposed protocol resists replay and man-in-the-middle (MITM) attacks.

```
% OFMC
% Version of 2006/02/13
SUMMARY
  SAFE
DETAILS
  BOUNDED_NUMBER_OF_SESSIONS
PROTOCOL
  /home/span/span/testsuite/results/fogauthenti.if
GOAL
  as_specified
BACKEND
  OFMC
COMMENTS
STATISTICS
  parseTime: 0.00s
  searchTime: 0.00s
  visitedNodes: 8 nodes
  depth: 3 plies
```

```
SUMMARY
  SAFE
DETAILS
  BOUNDED_NUMBER_OF_SESSIONS
  TYPED_MODEL

PROTOCOL
  /home/span/span/testsuite/results/fogauthenti.if

GOAL
  as_specified

BACKEND
  OFMC

STATISTICS

  Analysed: 3 states
  Reachable: 0 states
  Translation: 0.00 seconds
  Computation: 0.00 seconds
```

Figure 5. Simulation results under OFMC and CL-AtSe.

5.2. Informal Analysis

This section demonstrates that the proposed protocol satisfies the security properties detailed below.

5.2.1. Anonymity and Untraceability

In the proposed protocol, the vehicle user performs the authentication step using the pseudo identity, PID_i, and the temporary identity, RID_i, ensuring the anonymity of the vehicle user. Furthermore, PID_i and RID_i change dynamically with each session due to timestamps and random values; hence, the attacker cannot track the vehicle user. Therefore, the proposed protocol guarantees the anonymity and untraceability of the vehicle user.

5.2.2. Perfect Forward Secrecy

If the long-term keys s, x_i, and y_j of the cloud server are exposed to an attacker, the attacker can compute the long-term keys of the vehicle and the fog node, N_i and N_j. However, the attacker cannot recognize both the long- and short-term keys of the network simultaneously (Section 3.2) because, even if the attacker knows the values of N_i and N_j, the attacker cannot determine the value of R_{i-j-cs}, consisting of the random values r_1, r_2, and r_3. Therefore, the attacker cannot calculate the session key, comprising the long-term keys N_i and N_j and short-term key R_{i-j-cs}. Therefore, the proposed protocol can safeguard perfect forward secrecy.

5.2.3. Stolen-Verifier Attack

If the cloud server database is leaked to the attacker, the attacker can obtain the pseudo identity and the random value x_i of the vehicle user and the identity and random value y_j of the fog node. The attacker may endeavor to calculate the session key using these values. However, without knowing the short-term keys r_1, r_2, and r_3, the attacker cannot compute the session key. Furthermore, the pseudo identity of the vehicle is masked with its identity, password, and s_0, and the attacker cannot derive sensitive information from the identity and the random values x_i and y_j of the fog node.

5.2.4. Stolen Smart Card Attack

The attacker can steal the vehicle's smart card to obtain the stored data (N_i^*, M_i, s_0). Based on these parameters, the attacker may attempt to impersonate the vehicle user and calculate the session key. However, all parameters are masked with the ID, password, and s_0 value of V_i. The attacker must guess the ID and password simultaneously, which is computationally infeasible. Therefore, the proposed protocol is resistant to stolen smart card attacks.

5.2.5. Session Key Disclosure Attack

The attacker may attempt to determine the session key using messages from the public channel and the obtained values. However, to compute the session key, the attacker must guess the values of N_i, N_j, and R_{i-j-cs}, which are masked in a hash function using s, xi, yj, and random values. The attacker cannot obtain these values; thus, the proposed protocol resists session key disclosure attacks.

5.2.6. Replay and Man-in-the-Middle Attacks

To attempt a replay attack, the attacker may intercept public channel messages D_1, D_2, D_3, and D_4. However, these messages contain timestamps T_1, T_2, T_3, and T_4 and verification parameters Q_i, L_j, $Auth_i$, and $Auth_j$, and each entity checks the freshness of the messages. Therefore, the network participants can confirm the secret parameter values. Thus, the proposed protocol resists replay and MITM attacks.

5.2.7. Ephemeral Secret Leakage Attack

If the temporary secret random values r_1, r_2, and r_3 are leaked, the attacker may attempt to calculate the value of R_{i-j-cs}. However, the attacker cannot know the long- and short-term keys of the network simultaneously (as seen in the threat model assumptions); thus, even if the attacker knows the random values r_1, r_2, and r_3, they cannot determine the values of N_i and N_j. Therefore, the attacker cannot compute the session key, comprising the long-term keys N_i and N_j and short-term key R_{i-j-cs}. Therefore, the proposed protocol resists ephemeral leakage attacks.

5.2.8. Privileged Insider Attack

If the attacker acquires all values used during the registration process, they may attempt to guess the ID and password of the vehicle user. However, the values used during the vehicle registration phase are masked in a hash function, including the ID, password, and s_0 values, making it impossible to guess them simultaneously. Therefore, the proposed protocol is resilient to privileged insider attacks.

6. Performance Analysis

In this section, the computational and communication cost of our protocol is compared to that of existing related protocols [18–21].

6.1. Computational Cost Analysis

This subsection compares the computational cost of our proposed protocol with [8,17–22]. We denoted the consumption time of the ECC scalar multiplication, hash operation, symmetric cryptography operation, and fuzzy extractor as T_{em}, T_h, $T_{e/d}$, and T_f. We used a cryptography library called MIRACL to measure all operations in these protocols. We conducted experiments in different environments, considering the computing performance of vehicles and fog nodes. First, we conducted an experiment on a desktop equipped with an i7-4790 intel CPU, 16 GB of RAM, and a Linux Ubuntu 20.04-desktop-amd64 operating system to reflect the high computing performance of the fog nodes. Moreover, we conducted the same experiment on a Raspberry PI 3B with an ARM Cortex-A53 and 1 GB of RAM to reflect the low computing performance of vehicles. We summarized the execution time for each operation in Table 4. We configured the PUF response produced by a fuzzy extractor to ensure noise resilience, assuming that the execution time is the same as that for ECC scalar multiplication. We investigated the computational costs deriving from all operations performed during the authentication phase of these protocols. In Ma et al.'s protocol [17], a vehicle performed three ECC scalar multiplications and four hash operations, so we calculated the computational cost of the vehicle as $3T_{em} + 4T_h = 4.479$ ms. A fog node performed four ECC scalar multiplications and four hash operations, so we calculated the computational cost of the fog node as $4T_{em} + 4T_h = 5.968$ ms. The cloud server performed eight ECC scalar multiplications and nine hash operations, so we calculated the computational cost of the cloud server as $8T_{em} + 9T_h = 11.939$ ms. Thus, the total cost of vehicle, fog node, and cloud server is $15T_{em} + 17T_h = 22.386$ ms.

Table 4. Execution time for each operation.

Notations	Descriptions	Desktop	Raspberry PI
T_{em}	ECC scalar multiplication	1.489 ms	2.579 ms
T_h	Hash operation	0.003 ms	0.021 ms
$T_{e/d}$	Symmetric cryptography operation	0.001 ms	0.013 ms
T_f	Fuzzy extractor	1.489 ms	2.579 ms

In Eftekhari et al.'s protocol [18], a vehicle performed three ECC scalar multiplication operations and fourteen hash operations, so we calculated the computational cost of the vehicle as $3T_{em} + 14T_h = 4.509$ ms. A fog node performed three ECC scalar multiplications and sixteen hash operations, so we calculated the computational cost of the fog node as $3T_{em} + 16T_h = 4.515$ ms. The cloud server performed three ECC scalar multiplications and seventeen hash operations, so we calculated the computational cost of the cloud server as $3T_{em} + 17T_h = 4.518$ ms. Thus, the total cost of vehicle, fog node, and cloud server is $9T_{em} + 47T_h = 13.542$ ms.

In Kumar et al.'s protocol [19], a vehicle performed five ECC scalar multiplications, eleven hash operations, and one symmetric cryptography operation, so we calculated the computational cost of the vehicle as $5T_{em} + 11T_h + 1T_{e/d} = 7.479$ ms. A fog node performed five ECC scalar multiplications, ten hash operations, and two symmetric cryptography operations, so we calculated the computational cost of the fog node as $5T_{em} + 10T_h + 2T_{e/d} = 7.477$ ms. The cloud server performed two ECC scalar multiplications, three hash operations, and three symmetric cryptography operations, so we calculated the computational cost of the cloud server as $2T_{em} + 3T_h + 3T_{e/d} = 2.99$ ms. Thus, the total cost of vehicle, fog node, and cloud server is $12T_{em} + 24T_h + 6T_{e/d} = 17.946$ ms.

In Wu et al.'s protocol [20], a vehicle performed two ECC scalar multiplications and eight hash operations, so we calculated the computational cost of the vehicle as $2T_{em} + 8T_h = 3.002$ ms. A fog node performed four ECC scalar multiplications and five hash operations, so we calculated the computational cost of the fog node as $4T_{em} + 5T_h = 5.971$ ms. The cloud server performed three ECC scalar multiplications and thirteen hash operations, so we calculated the computational cost of the cloud server as $3T_{em} + 13T_h = 4.506$ ms. Thus, the total cost of vehicle, fog node, and cloud server is $9T_{em} + 26T_h = 13.479$ ms.

In Awais et al.'s protocol [8], a vehicle performed three ECC scalar multiplications and six hash operations, so we calculated the computational cost of the vehicle as $3T_{em} + 6T_h = 3.002$ ms. A fog node performed four ECC scalar multiplications and four hash operations, so we calculated the computational cost of the fog node as $4T_{em} + 4T_h = 5.971$ ms. The cloud server performed four ECC scalar multiplications and nine hash operations, so we calculated the computational cost of the cloud server as $4T_{em} + 9T_h = 4.506$ ms. Thus, the total cost of vehicle, fog node, and cloud server is $11T_{em} + 19T_h = 16.436$ ms.

In Hedge et al.'s protocol [21], a smart device performed three ECC scalar multiplications and thirteen hash operations, so we calculated the computational cost of the vehicle as $3T_{em} + 13T_h = 4.506$ ms. A fog node performed five ECC scalar multiplications and ten hash operations, so we calculated the computational cost of the fog node as $5T_{em} + 10T_h = 7.475$ ms. The cloud server performed four ECC scalar multiplications and six hash operations, so we calculated the computational cost of the cloud server as $4T_{em} + 6T_h = 5.974$ ms. Thus, the total cost of smart device, fog node and cloud server is $12T_{em} + 29T_h = 17.955$ ms.

In Awais et al.'s protocol [22], we calculated the computational costs by combining those of the fog nodes and the RSUs. A vehicle performed three ECC scalar multiplications and three hash operations, so we calculated the computational cost of the vehicle as $3T_{em} + 3T_h = 4.476$ ms. A fog node performed five ECC scalar multiplications and five hash operations, so we calculated the computational cost of the fog node as $5T_{em} + 5T_h = 7.46$ ms. The cloud server performed six ECC scalar multiplications and ten hash operations, so we calculated the computational cost of the cloud server as $6T_{em} + 10T_h = 8.964$ ms. Thus, the total cost of vehicle, fog node and cloud server is $14T_{em} + 18T_h = 20.9$ ms.

In our proposed protocol, a vehicle performed three ECC scalar multiplications and fifteen hash operations, so we calculated the computational cost of the vehicle as $3T_{em} +$

$15T_h = 4.512$ ms. A fog node performed two ECC scalar multiplications and ten hash operations, so we calculated the computational cost of the fog node as $2T_{em} + 10T_h =$ 3.008 ms. The cloud server performed three ECC scalar multiplications and twelve hash operations, so we calculated the computational cost of the cloud server as $3T_{em} + 12T_h =$ 4.503 ms. Thus, the total cost of vehicle, fog node, and cloud server is $8T_{em} + 37T_h =$ 12.023 ms.

We show the comparison results of computational cost of our proposed protocol and other related protocols in Table 5 and Figure 6. The results show that our proposed protocol has a lower total computational cost, especially on the fog node side, than related protocols. Therefore, we can state that our proposed protocol has relatively higher computational efficiency than other related protocols.

Table 5. Comparison of computational costs.

Protocol	Vehicle User	Fog Node	Cloud Server	Total
[17]	4.479 ms	5.968 ms	11.939 ms	22.386 ms
[18]	4.509 ms	4.515 ms	4.518 ms	13.542 ms
[19]	7.479 ms	7.477 ms	2.99 ms	17.946 ms
[20]	3.002 ms	5.971 ms	4.506 ms	13.479 ms
[8]	4.485 ms	5.968 ms	5.983 ms	16.436 ms
[21]	4.506 ms	7.475 ms	5.974 ms	17.955 ms
[22]	4.476 ms	7.46 ms	8.964 ms	20.9 ms
Proposed	4.512 ms	3.008 ms	4.503 ms	12.023 ms

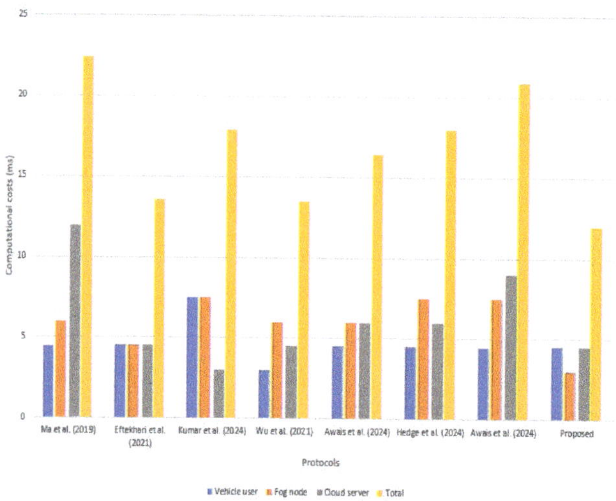

Figure 6. Visualization of computational costs comparison [8,17–22].

6.2. Communication Cost Analysis

This subsection compares the communication cost of our proposed protocol with [8,17–22]. We denoted that the ECC point, hash output, random nonce, identity, and timestamp were 320, 256, 256, 128, and 32 bits, respectively. In Ma et al.'s protocol [17], a vehicle transmitted $\{AID_{U_i}, T_{U_i}, R_1, \alpha\}$, so we calculated the communication cost of the vehicle as 864 bits. A fog node transmitted $\{AID_{U_i}, AID_{FN_j}, T_{U_i}, T_{FN_j}, R_1, R_2, \hat{R}_2, \alpha, \beta\}$ and $\{R_2, R_3, \hat{R}_3', T_{CS}, \bar{\gamma}\}$, so we calculated the communication cost of the fog node as 3296 bits. The cloud server transmitted $\{R_3, \hat{R}_3, \hat{R}_3', T_{CS}, \gamma, \bar{\gamma}\}$, so we calculated the communication cost of the cloud server as 1504 bits. Thus, the total cost of vehicle, fog node, and cloud server is 5664 bits.

In Eftekhari et al.'s protocol [18], a vehicle transmitted $\{RID_{DR}, X_{VE}, y_{VE}, h^{CS}_{VE}, T\}$, so we calculated the communication cost of the vehicle as 1120 bits. A fog node transmitted $\{RID_{FS}, RID_{DR}, X_{FS}, X_{VE}, y_{FS}, y_{VE}, h^{CS}_{FS}, T\}$ and $\{mRID^{DR_{new}}_{CS}, X_{FS}, X_{CS}, h^{VE}_{FS}\}$, so we calculated the communication cost of the fog node as 3104 bits. The cloud server transmitted $\{mRID^{DR_{new}}_{CS}, mRID^{FS_{new}}_{CS}, X_{CS}, h^{FS}_{CS}, h^{VE}_{CS}\}$, so we calculated the communication cost of the cloud server as 1344 bits. Thus, the total cost of vehicle, fog node, and cloud server is 5568 bits.

In Kumar et al.'s protocol [19], a vehicle transmitted $M_1 = \{PK_V, PIDV_i, V_1, T_1\}$ and $M_5 = \{PK_{V_1}, V_5, T_5\}$, so we calculated the communication cost of the vehicle as 1600 bits. A fog node transmitted $M_2 = \{M_1, PK_F, PIDFN_j, V_2, T_2\}$ and $M_4 = \{PK_{F_1}, V_4, T_4\}$, so we calculated the communication cost of the fog node as 2592 bits. The cloud server transmitted $M_3 = \{C_3, V_3, T_3\}$, so we calculated the communication cost of the cloud server as 544 bits. Thus, the total cost of vehicle, fog node, and cloud server is 4736 bits.

In Wu et al.'s protocol [20], a vehicle transmitted $M_1 = \{PID_i, N_i, B_2, B_3, T_v\}$, so we calculated the communication cost of the vehicle as 992 bits. A fog node transmitted $M_2 = \{M_1, PFSID_j, N_j, N_{ij}, B_5, B_6, T_f\}$ and $M_4 = \{K_{ij}, V_1, N_{jc}, T_c, T_{f2}\}$, so we calculated the communication cost of the fog node as 3200 bits. The cloud server transmitted $M_3 = \{K_{ij}, V_1, V_2, N_c, N_{ic}, T_c\}$, so we calculated the communication cost of the cloud server as 1440 bits. Thus, the total cost of vehicle, fog node, and cloud server is 5632 bits.

In Awais et al.'s protocol [8], a vehicle transmitted $D_1 = \{R_1, RID_i, Q_i\}$, so we calculated the communication cost of the vehicle as 832 bits. A fog node transmitted $D_2 = \{D_1, R_2, \hat{R}_2, RID_j, L_j\}$ and $D_4 = \{R_2, R_3, X_i, Auth_i\}$, so we calculated the communication cost of the fog node as 3136 bits. The cloud server transmitted $D_3 = \{R_3, Y_j, X_i, Auth_i, Auth_j\}$, so we calculated the communication cost of the cloud server as 1344 bits. Thus, the total cost of vehicle, fog node, and cloud server is 5312 bits.

In Hedge et al.'s protocol [21], a smart device transmitted $\{CID_s, RV_2, C_{sm}, T_1\}$, so we calculated the communication cost of the vehicle as 864 bits. A fog node transmitted $\{CID_s, CID_f, C_{sm}, C_f, F_c, FUID_i, RV_2, FV_2, T_1, T_2\}$ and $\{F_{sm}, T_4, FCSUID_i, T_3, CV_2\}$, so we calculated the communication cost of the fog node as 3136 bits. The cloud server transmitted $\{CV_2, T_3\}$, so we calculated the communication cost of the cloud server as 352 bits. Thus, the total cost of vehicle, fog node, and cloud server is 4352 bits.

In Awais et al.'s protocol [22], we calculated the computational costs by combining those of the fog nodes and the RSUs. A vehicle transmitted $M_1 = \{TID_{U_i}, R_1, \alpha\}$, so we calculated the communication cost of the vehicle as 704 bits. A fog node transmitted $M_2 = \{M_1, TID_{RSU_k}, R_2, \beta\}$, $M_3 = \{M_2, TID_{FN_j}, R_3, \gamma\}$, $M_5 = \{R_{10}, X_k\}$, and $M_6 = \{R_9, X_i\}$, so we calculated the communication cost of the fog node as 4672 bits. The cloud server transmitted $M_4 = \{R_7, R_8, R_9, X_j\}$, so we calculated the communication cost of the cloud server as 1344 bits. Thus, the total cost of vehicle, fog node, and cloud server is 6592 bits.

In our proposed protocol, a vehicle transmitted $D_1 = \{R_1, RID_i, Q_i, ID_j\}$, so we calculated the communication cost of the vehicle as 960 bits. A fog node transmitted $D_2 = \{R_1, RID_i, R_2, r_2R_1, L_j, ID_j\}$ and $D_4 = \{K_{ij}, r_2R_3, Auth_i\}$, so we calculated the communication cost of the fog node as 2432 bits. The cloud server transmitted $D_3 = \{K_{ij}, R_3, r_3R_1, Auth_j\}$, so we calculated the communication cost of the cloud server as 1152 bits. Thus, the total cost of vehicle, fog node, and cloud server is 4544 bits.

We show the comparison results of communication cost for our proposed protocol and other related protocols in Table 6 and Figure 7. In Table 6 and Figure 7, the results show that our proposed protocol has the lowest total communicational cost among other related protocols. Therefore, we can state that our proposed protocol has relatively higher communication efficiency than other related protocols.

Table 6. Comparison of communication costs.

Protocols	Communication Costs
[17]	5664 bits
[18]	5568 bits
[19]	4736 bits
[20]	5632 bits
[8]	5312 bits
[21]	4352 bits
[22]	6592 bits
Proposed	4544 bits

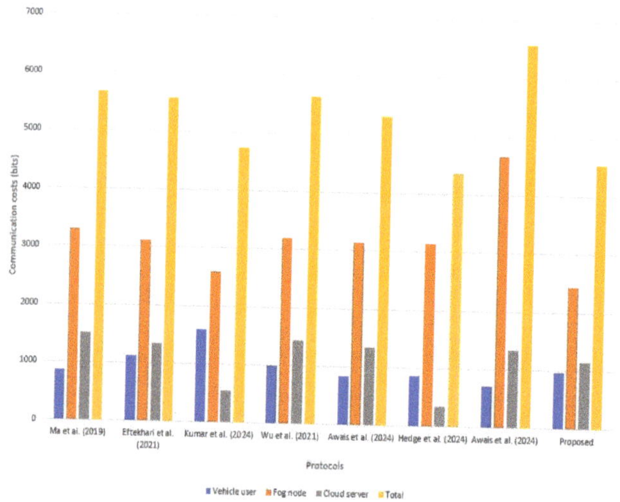

Figure 7. Visualization of communication costs comparison [8,17–22].

6.3. Security Features

We compared the security features of the proposed protocol with those of related protocols [8,17–22]. We considered (SF1) "preservation of anonymity", (SF2) "preservation of untraceability", (SF3) "preservation of perfect forward secrecy", (SF4) "resistance to stolen verifier attack", (SF5) "resistance to stolen smart card attack", (SF6) "resistance to session key disclosure attack", (SF7) "resistance to replay attack", (SF8) "resistance to MITM attack", (SF9) "resistance to ephemeral secret leakage attack", and (SF10) "resistance to privileged insider attack". Table 7 summarizes the comparison of security features. The results show that the proposed protocol has superior security than other related protocols in fog-based VANET environments.

Table 7. Comparison of security features.

Security Features	[17]	[18]	[19]	[20]	[8]	[21]	[22]	Proposed
SF1	O	O	O	O	O	O	O	O
SF2	O	O	O	O	O	O	O	O
SF3	O	O	O	O	X	-	O	O
SF4	O	O	O	-	O	-	O	O
SF5	O	O	-	-	X	O	-	O
SF6	O	-	-	-	O	-	O	O
SF7	O	O	O	O	O	O	O	O
SF8	O	O	O	O	O	O	O	O
SF9	X	O	O	O	X	O	O	O
SF10	X	-	-	-	-	O	-	O

-: Not considered. X: Insecure. O: Secure.

7. Conclusions

In this study, we proposed a lightweight and robust authentication protocol for securing fog-based VANETs. Considering the features of fog-based VANETs, we used the ECC system and fuzzy verifier to establish a session key securely and efficiently for vehicle-to-infrastructure communication. The proposed protocol provides perfect forward secrecy and resists various attacks, such as trace and ephemeral secret leakage attacks. Furthermore, we conducted informal and formal security analyses to demonstrate the efficiency and security robustness of our protocol. The informal security analysis demonstrated that our protocol satisfies security requirements and the formal security analysis using BAN logic, the AVISPA simulation tool, and the RoR model, demonstrating that our protocol offers mutual authentication and session key security. Finally, we compared the performance of our protocol with that of other related protocols to evaluate its efficiency. The results demonstrated that our protocol outperformed the compared protocols in computational and communication cost. In the future, we plan to assess our protocol's practical issues through simulations that consider actual VANET conditions. Moreover, future research will aim to expand this study to enable secure communication under various network conditions. Additionally, we plan to introduce outsourcing computing methods to lower the computational costs for vehicles, and these improvements will expand the potential applications of intelligent vehicle systems.

Author Contributions: Conceptualization, S.L.; methodology, S.L., S.S. and D.K.; software, S.S. and D.K.; validation, S.S., D.K., Y.P. (Yohan Park) and Y.P. (Youngho Park); investigation, S.L. and D.K.; formal analysis, S.L., S.S., D.K. and Y.P. (Yohan Park); writing—original draft, S.L.; writing—review and editing, S.S., D.K., Y.P. (Yohan Park) and Y.P. (Youngho Park); supervision, Y.P. (Youngho Park); project administration, Y.P. (Youngho Park). All authors have read and agreed to the published version of the manuscript.

Funding: This work was supported by the National Research Foundation of Korea (NRF) grant funded by the Korea government (Ministry of Science and ICT) (RS-2024-00450915).

Institutional Review Board Statement: Not applicable.

Informed Consent Statement: Not applicable.

Data Availability Statement: Data are contained within the article.

Conflicts of Interest: The authors declare no conflicts of interest.

References

1. Al-Sultan, S.; Al-Doori, M.M.; Al-Bayatti, A.H.; Zedan, H. A comprehensive survey on vehicular ad hoc network. *J. Netw. Comput. Appl.* **2014**, *37*, 380–392. [CrossRef]
2. Prajapat, S.; Gautam, D.; Kumar, P.; Jangirala, S.; Das, A.K.; Park, Y.; Lorenz, P. Secure lattice-based aggregate signature scheme for vehicular Ad Hoc networks. *IEEE Trans. Veh. Technol.* **2024**, *73*, 12370–12384. [CrossRef]
3. Yousefi, S.; Mousavi, M.S.; Fathy, M. Vehicular ad hoc networks (VANETs): Challenges and perspectives. In Proceedings of the 2006 6th International Conference on ITS Telecommunications, Chengdu, China, 21–23 June 2006; pp. 761–766.
4. Yi, S.; Li, C.; Li, Q. A Survey of Fog Computing. In Proceedings of the 2015 Workshop on Mobile Big Data-Mobidata '15, Hangzhou, China, 21 June 2015; pp. 37–42.
5. Sookhak, M.; Yu, F.R.; He, Y.; Talebian, H.; Safa, N.S.; Zhao, N.; Khan, M.K.; Kumar, N. Fog Vehicular Computing: Augmentation of Fog Computing Using Vehicular Cloud Computing. *IEEE Veh. Technol. Mag.* **2017**, *12*, 55–64. [CrossRef]
6. Huang, C.; Lu, R.; Choo, K.K.R. Vehicular fog computing: Architecture, use case, and security and forensic challenges. *IEEE Commun. Mag.* **2017**, *55*, 105–111. [CrossRef]
7. Stojmenovic, I.; Wen, S.; Huang, X.; Luan, H. An Overview of Fog Computing and Its Security Issues. *Concurr. Comput. Pract. Exp.* **2016**, *28*, 2991–3005. [CrossRef]
8. Awais, S.; Yucheng, W.; Mahmood, K.; Muhammad, H.; Badar, S.; Kharel, R.; Das, A. Provably secure fog-based authentication protocol for VANETs. *Comput. Netw.* **2024**, *246*, 110391. [CrossRef]

9. Hou, X.; Li, Y.; Chen, M.; Wu, D.; Jin, D.; Chen, S. Vehicular Fog Computing: A Viewpoint of Vehicles as the Infrastructures. *IEEE Trans. Veh. Technol.* **2016**, *65*, 3860–3873. [CrossRef]
10. Peixoto, M.L.M.; Maia, A.H.O.; Mota, E.; Rangel, E.; Costa, D.G.; Turgut, D.; Villas, L.A. A traffic data clustering framework based on fog computing for VANETs. *Veh. Commun.* **2021**, *31*, 100370.
11. Pereira, J.; Ricardo, L.; Luís, M.; Senna, C.; Sargento, S. Assessing the reliability of fog computing for smart mobility applications in VANETs. *Future Gener. Comput. Syst.* **2019**, *94*, 317–332. [CrossRef]
12. Farooqi, A.M.; Alam, M.A.; Hassan, S.I.; Idrees, S.M. A Fog Computing Model for VANET to Reduce Latency and Delay Using 5G Network in Smart City Transportation. *Appl. Sci.* **2022**, *12*, 2083. [CrossRef]
13. AlHamid, H.A.; Rahman, S.M.M.; Hossain, M.S.; Almogren, A.; Alamri, A. A Security Model for Preserving the Privacy of Medical Big Data in a Healthcare Cloud Using a Fog Computing Facility with Pairing-Based Cryptography. *IEEE Access* **2017**, *5*, 22313–22328. [CrossRef]
14. Jia, X.; He, D.; Kumar, N.; Choo, K.K.R. Authenticated key agreement scheme for fog-driven IoT healthcare system. *Wirel. Netw.* **2019**, *25*, 4737–4750. [CrossRef]
15. Okay, F.Y.; Ozdemir, S. A secure data aggregation protocol for fog computing based smart grids. In Proceedings of the 2018 IEEE 12th International Conference on Compatibility, Power Electronics and Power Engineering (CPE-POWERENG 2018), Doha, Qatar, 10–12 April 2018; pp. 1–6.
16. Lyu, L.; Nandakumar, K.; Rubinstein, B.; Jin, J.; Bedo, J.; Palaniswami, M. PPFA: Privacy preserving fog-enabled aggregation in smart grid. *IEEE Trans. Ind. Inform.* **2018**, *14*, 3733–3744. [CrossRef]
17. Ma, M.; He, D.; Wang, H.; Kumar, N.; Choo, K.K.R. An Efficient and Provably-Secure Authenticated Key Agreement Protocol for Fog-Based Vehicular Ad-Hoc Networks. *IEEE Internet Things J.* **2019**, *6*, 8065–8075. [CrossRef]
18. Eftekhari, S.A.; Nikooghadam, M.; Rafighi, M. Security-enhanced three-party pairwise secret key agreement protocol for fog-based vehicular ad-hoc communications. *Veh. Commun.* **2021**, *28*, 100306. [CrossRef]
19. Kumar,P.; Om, H. Multi-TA model-based conditional privacy-preserving authentication protocol for fog-enabled VANET. *Veh. Commun.* **2024**, *47*, 100785. [CrossRef]
20. Wu,T.Y.; Lee, Z.; Yang, L.; Luo, J.N.; Tso, R. Provably secure authentication key exchange scheme using fog nodes in vehicular ad hoc networks. *J. Supercomput.* **2021**, *77*, 6992–7020. [CrossRef]
21. Hegde, M.; Rao, R.R.; Bhat, R. Design of an Efficient and Secure Authentication Scheme for Cloud-Fog-Device Framework Using Key Agreement and Management. *IEEE Access* **2024**, *12*, 78173–78192. [CrossRef]
22. Awais, S.; Yucheng, W.; Mahmood, K.; Alenazi, M.; Bashir, A.; Das, A.; Lorenz, P. Provably secure and lightweight authentication and key agreement protocol for fog-based vehicular ad-hoc networks. *IEEE Trans. Intell. Transp. Syst.* **2024**, *25*, 21107–21116. [CrossRef]
23. Hankerson, D.; Menezes, A.J.; Vanstone, S. *Guide to Elliptic Curve Cryptography;* Springer: Berlin/Heidelberg, Germany, 2004.
24. Dolev, D.; Yao, A.C.-C. On the security of public key protocols. *IEEE Trans. Inf. Theory* **1983**, *29*, 198–207. [CrossRef]
25. Ryu, J.; Son, S.; Lee, J.; Park, Y.; Park, Y. Design of secure mutual authentication scheme for metaverse environments using blockchain. *IEEE Access* **2022**, *10*, 98944–98958. [CrossRef]
26. Yu, S.; Lee, J.; Sutrala, A.K.; Das, A.K.; Park, Y. LAKA-UAV: Lightweight authentication and key agreement scheme for cloud-assisted Unmanned Aerial Vehicle using blockchain in flying ad hoc networks. *Comput. Netw.* **2023**, *224*, 109612. [CrossRef]
27. Canetti, R.; Krawczyk, H. Analysis of Key-Exchange Protocols and Their Use for Building Secure Channels. In *EUROCRYPT 2001: Advances in Cryptology, Proceedings of the International Conference on the Theory and Applications of Cryptographic Techniques, Tallinn, Estonia, 15–19 May 2001;* Pfitzmann, B., Ed.; Lecture Notes in Computer Science; Springer: Berlin/Heidelberg, Germany, 2001; Volume 2045.
28. Wazid, M.; Bagga, P.; Das, A.K.; Shetty, S.; Rodrigues, J.J.; Park, Y. AKM-IoV: Authenticated Key Management Protocol in Fog Computing-Based Internet of Vehicles Deployment. *IEEE Internet Things J.* **2019**, *6*, 8804–8817. [CrossRef]
29. Das, A.K.; Wazid, M.; Yannam, A.R.; Rodrigues, J.J.; Park, Y. Provably secure ECC-based device access control and key agreement protocol for IOT environment. *IEEE Access* **2019**, *7*, 55382–55397. [CrossRef]
30. Kocher, P.; Jaffe, J.; Jun, B. Differential power analysis. In Proceedings of the Annual International Cryptology Conference, Santa Barbara, CA, USA, 15–19 August 1999; Springer: Berlin/Heidelberg, Germany, 1999; pp. 388–397.
31. Yu, S.; Park, Y. A robust authentication protocol for wireless medical sensor networks using blockchain and physically unclonable functions. *IEEE Internet Things J.* **2022**, *9*, 20214–20228. [CrossRef]
32. Son, S.; Kwon, D.; Lee, S.; Jeon, Y.; Das, A.K.; Park, Y. Design of secure and lightweight authentication scheme for UAV-enabled intelligent transportation systems using blockchain and PUF. *IEEE Access* **2023**, *11*, 60240–60253. [CrossRef]
33. Burrows, M.; Abadi, M.; Needham, R.M. A logic of authentication. *Proc. R. Soc. Lond. A. Math. Phys. Sci.* **1989**, *426*, 233–271.
34. Abdalla, M.; Fouque, P.A.; Pointcheval, D. Password-based authenticated key exchange in the three-party setting. In Proceedings of the 8th International Workshop on Public Key Cryptography, Les Diablerets, Switzerland, 23–26 January 2005; Volume 3386, pp. 65–84.

35. Boyko, V.; MacKenzie, P.; Patel, S. Provably secure password-authenticated key exchange using Diffie-Hellman. In Proceedings of the International Conference on the Theory and Applications of Cryptographic Techniques, Bruges, Belgium, 14–18 May 2000; pp. 156–171.
36. Wang,D.; Cheng, H.; Wang, P.; Huang, X.; Jian, G. Zipf's law in passwords. *IEEE Trans. Inf. Forensics Secur.* **2017**, *12*, 2776–2791. [CrossRef]
37. Vigano, L. Automated security protocol analysis with the AVISPA tool. *Electron. Notes Theor. Comput. Sci.* **2006**, *155*, 61–86. [CrossRef]

applied sciences

MDPI

Review

An Overview of Design Techniques for Two-Dimensional Leaky-Wave Antennas

Edoardo Negri [1,2], Walter Fuscaldo [2], Paolo Burghignoli [1] and Alessandro Galli [1,*]

[1] Department of Information Engineering, Electronics and Telecommunications, Sapienza University of Rome, 00184 Rome, Italy; edoardo.negri@uniroma1.it (E.N.); paolo.burghignoli@uniroma1.it (P.B.)
[2] Istituto per la Microelettronica e Microsistemi, Consiglio Nazionale delle Ricerche, 00133 Rome, Italy; walter.fuscaldo@cnr.it
* Correspondence: alessandro.galli@uniroma1.it

Abstract: Two-dimensional leaky-wave antennas offer effective, compact, single-feeder, easy-to-fabricate solutions to the longstanding problem of realizing a simultaneously directive and low-profile radiating device. These traveling-wave antennas have been thus proposed as wideband, reconfigurable, or frequency-scanning radiating structures in different application contexts, spacing from the microwave to terahertz frequency range. These diverse contexts call for a comprehensive guide to characterizing and designing two-dimensional leaky-wave antennas. In this work, a review of numerical techniques for the analysis of either quasi-uniform or radially periodic leaky-wave antennas is proposed in order to provide the reader with straightforward yet effective design guidelines. Theoretical results are corroborated through full-wave simulations of realistic three-dimensional models of the considered devices, thus demonstrating the effectiveness of the proposed methods.

Keywords: leaky-wave antennas; numerical methods; Fabry–Perot cavity antennas; radially periodic leaky-wave antennas; metasurfaces

1. Introduction

Leaky-wave antennas (LWAs) are radiating devices constituted by waveguiding structures which allow for continuous power radiation while propagating along their length [1–3]. Although the working principle is rather intuitive, the design of radiating devices by partially open waveguides found its mathematical and physical rigorous foundation only in the 1950s thanks to the famous work of N. Marcuvitz [4]. This paper, together with the works of T. Tamir and A. A. Oliner [5,6], had an important impact on the development of LWAs: thanks to an efficient and elegant theory, rather simple analytical procedures were outlined for designing such radiating devices, in a period when the computational resources were very limited. Nowadays, such a straightforward theoretical approach has been experimentally verified in different scenarios and with different radiating devices [7–15]. Moreover, this design method is still relevant and faster than full-wave optimization procedures [16].

It is well known that this kind of radiating devices shows many advantages since LWAs are simple and low-cost solutions able to generate highly directive beams pointing at almost arbitrary angles [17]. Moreover, they show a reconfigurability feature in terms of pointing angle since their beam naturally scans with frequency [18] or, if a fixed frequency is desired, they are able to scan electronically by incorporating tunable elements into the

 https://doi.org/10.3390/app15041854

design, such as varactor diodes [19], ferrites [20], microelectromechanical systems [21] based on micromachining technologies [22], graphene [23,24], or liquid crystals [25].

The main critical aspects of LWAs are typically related to the following trade-offs: pattern fractional bandwidth vs. directivity (leaky-wave antennas are usually highly directive but show a narrow bandwidth), reconfigurability vs. complexity (the higher the desired reconfigurability at a fixed frequency, the more complex the device architecture), and radiation efficiency vs. aperture size (a large radiating aperture is needed to achieve a highly directive antenna) [2]. Fortunately, various solutions have been proposed in recent years to address these challenges. For instance, to improve the figure of merit defined by the product of directivity with bandwidth, Fabry–Perot cavity antennas (FPCAs) incorporating a thick partially reflecting sheet (PRS) [26,27] or exhibiting high truncation effects [28,29] have been developed and studied through different techniques. As concerns, instead, reconfigurable leaky-wave antennas, different technological solutions have recently been addressed from the microwave to the terahertz frequency ranges [30–34]. Moreover, the longstanding problem of designing directive LWAs through compact devices has been solved by exploiting tapering techniques [35,36].

The effectiveness and the importance of LWAs from both a theoretical and a practical viewpoint are thus clear. However, a paper reviewing simple numerical techniques for characterizing LWAs and providing design guidelines for such radiators is still missing. This work aims to fill this gap by describing, step by step, the design workflow of uniform and radially periodic two-dimensional (2-D) LWAs which represent the common architectures of more sophisticated solutions, such as holographic [37] and modulated surface antennas [38–41], or even near-field focusing devices [42–44].

This manuscript is organized as follows. In Section 2, an established classification of LWAs is presented, highlighting the need for various approaches to analyze different kinds of these radiators. In Sections 3 and 4, the numerical techniques for the analysis and design of uniform and radially periodic 2-D LWAs are presented, respectively. Conclusions are finally drawn in Section 5.

2. Classification of Leaky-Wave Antennas

In this section, a widely accepted [1,18] classification of LWAs is provided with the aim of introducing the different working principles and radiating features of the devices discussed in this work.

The first distinction among LWAs is related to the *geometry* of the radiating device. Specifically, LWAs can be classified as one-dimensional (1-D) or two-dimensional (2-D), depending on whether the guiding structure is mainly linear or planar, respectively. In other words, a principal fixed direction of propagation can be easily identified in 1-D LWAs (see Figure 1a), whereas 2-D LWAs are, in general, radial devices commonly fed in the center, and are characterized by a partially guided wave propagating along a plane (see Figure 1b). This aspect influences the radiation properties of the device; a 1-D structure typically generates *fan beams*, whereas a 2-D structure produces *pencil beams* or *conical beams*, depending on the operating frequency [18].

The other classification concept, which affects the scanning behavior of the antenna, is related to the *working principle* of the device and it allows us to define uniform, quasi-uniform, and periodic LWAs. When the cross section of the radiator remains constant along the propagation direction, the structure is usually referred to as *1-D uniform LWA*. A classic historical example is a rectangular waveguide with a longitudinal slit (see Figure 2a), which enables power to leak as it propagates [45–47]. The radiation is usually related to the perturbation of the fundamental guided mode, which is, in general, a *fast wave*. In the *transmission* mode, 1-D LWAs are commonly fed from one side of the input waveguide launching the traveling leaky wave. By properly varying the working frequency, the main beam is scanned from nearly broadside to nearly endfire, with some intrinsic problems for the generation of a beam exactly at broadside or endfire [18]. It is worthwhile to point out that 1-D LWAs can also be fed in the center to generate leaky waves that propagate in both, opposite, directions. Such 1-D LWAs are commonly referred to as *bidirectional* [18].

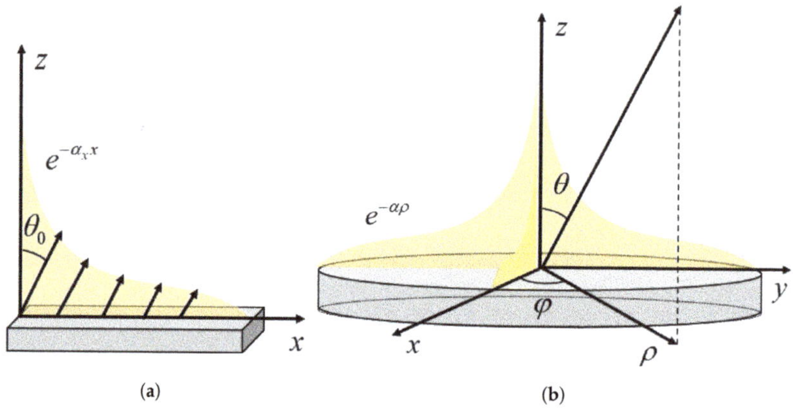

Figure 1. (**a**) Pictorial representation of a 1-D LWA. The electromagnetic field is partially guided in the x direction in the gray structure. The amount of transmitted power has an exponential decay due to radiation and expressed by the leakage constant α_x, generating a far-field radiation pattern pointing in the θ_0 direction. (**b**) Schematic view of a 2-D LWA. As in (**a**), the electromagnetic field is partially guided in the gray structure, undergoing an exponential decay of the transported power related to the leakage constant α in the radial direction.

When there is a periodic modulation of the geometry in the longitudinal direction of the radiating structure with a period d much lower than the operating wavelength λ, the device is referred to as *1-D quasi-uniform LWA*. The radiation properties of this kind of antenna are similar to those of 1-D uniform LWAs since both of them work with only the fundamental mode in propagation. The performance, however, can significantly be improved with respect to the uniform case by properly engineering the periodic modulation. For instance, the idea proposed in [48] to reduce the leakage rate and achieve a more directive antenna with respect to the uniform, slotted, rectangular waveguide was to consider closely placed holes rather than a continuous, longitudinal slit responsible for cutting the current lines on the metal walls of the guide (see Figure 2b).

When there is a periodic modulation of the geometry along the longitudinal direction of the radiating structure with a period p approximately larger than half of the operating wavelength λ, the device is referred to as *1-D periodic LWA*. The difference with respect to the 1-D quasi-uniform LWA is given by its working principle. While in the quasi-uniform case there is only the fundamental, basically *fast* mode in propagation, in 1-D *periodic* LWAs the guided wave is represented by an infinite number of *Floquet modes* (or *space harmonics*) due to the larger periodicity. A typical example of 1-D periodic LWAs is a dielectric waveguide or a microstrip that is loaded by perturbations with periodicity comparable to the wavelength [49] (see Figure 2c). As is common in this kind of structures, the fundamental Floquet mode is usually *slow*. For this reason, LWAs are typically designed so that the $n = -1$ harmonic is fast, enabling the device to radiate. A key advantage of 1-D periodic LWAs over the abovementioned types is their ability to scan from the backward to the forward quadrant. However, it is important to note that the antenna performance significantly deteriorates when the main beam approaches broadside. This issue, caused by the presence of an *open stopband*, has been extensively studied, and various strategies have been proposed to mitigate its negative effects (see, e.g., [41,50–52]).

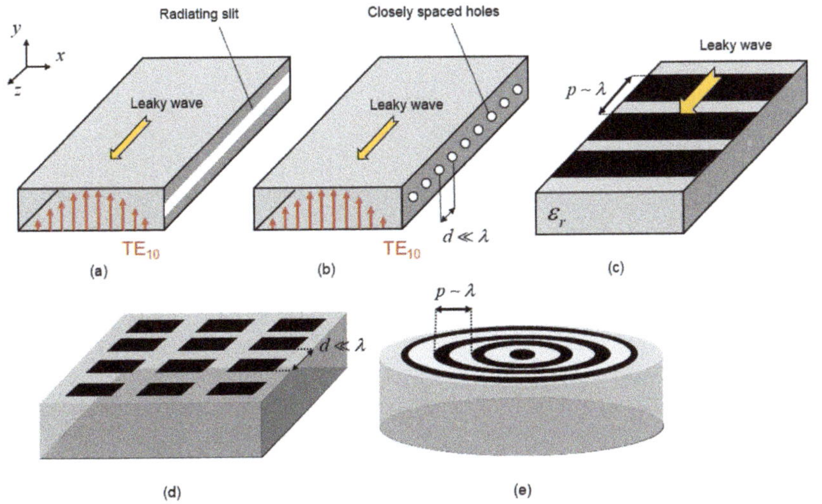

Figure 2. Pictorial representation of (**a**) a slitted rectangular waveguide (uniform 1-D LWA), (**b**) a rectangular waveguide with closely spaced holes (quasi-uniform 1-D LWA), (**c**) a grounded dielectric slab (GDS) with relative permittivity ε_r and with a metal strip grating supporting periodicity $p \sim \lambda$ on top (1-D periodic LWA), (**d**) a GDS supporting a 2-D periodic screen with periodicity $d \ll \lambda$ (quasi-uniform 2-D LWA), and (**e**) a GDS supporting annular concentric microstrip rings (radially periodic 2-D LWA).

The definition of LWAs based on the working principle of 1-D structures can be extended to the 2-D case. Two-dimensional *uniform* and *quasi-uniform* LWAs are indeed 2-D partially open waveguiding structures able to support a *cylindrical leaky wave* which radially propagates outward from the central source [53]. This type of LWA can, typically by varying the frequency, generate a directive pencil beam at broadside or a conical beam with its axis aligned with the vertical direction. Interestingly, by considering an array feeding scheme, a directive pencil beam can be achieved off broadside [54], even with a circular polarization if a proper polarization-conversion metasurface is employed [55–57]. As for their 1-D counterpart, the radiation features of 2-D uniform and *quasi-uniform* LWAs are commonly related to the fundamental leaky mode, which is a *fast wave*. One of the most important examples of 2-D uniform LWAs is a grounded dielectric slab (GDS) with a PRS on top, constituting an FPCA (see Figure 2d) [16].

Similarly to the distinction among 1-D *periodic* and *uniform* or *quasi-uniform* LWAs, it is possible to define a *2-D periodic leaky-wave antenna* when a 2-D partially open waveguiding structure presents a periodic modulation capable of propagating higher-order Floquet modes. If the periodicity occurs in only one dimension, which is a common case study, the radiating device is referred to as a *1-D periodic 2-D LWA*. A typical example in this context, which corresponds to the structure analyzed in this work, is the case of an annular metal strip grating printed on top of a GDS (see, e.g., [7]) where the periodicity is only present in the radial direction (see Figure 2e). If the periodicity occurs in two directions, as in the case of a metal-patch array printed on a GDS studied in [58], the radiating device is referred to as a *2-D periodic 2-D LWA*.

This work deals with the numerical methods and the design rules that can be efficiently used for characterizing 2-D uniform and quasi-uniform LWAs (FPCAs) and 1-D periodic

2-D LWAs. These approaches can also be profitably exploited for the design of their 1-D counterparts [43,59].

3. Fabry–Perot Cavity Antennas

This section deals with the design of FPCAs. While the theoretical working principles and design workflow for these radiating devices are presented in Section 3.1, the numerical techniques needed for describing such FPCAs are reported in Sections 3.2 and 3.3. The possible realizations of a feeder for such devices are then reported in Section 3.4 and the implementation of an efficient and fast full-wave simulation of FPCAs is shown in Section 3.5.

3.1. Theoretical Background

Fabry–Perot cavity antennas are constituted by a grounded dielectric slab with a partially reflecting sheet on top. These devices are usually fed through dipole-like sources in the center (see Figure 3a). If a vertical electric dipole (VED)—which can be easily implemented through a coaxial cable [60,61]—or a vertical magnetic dipole (VMD)—commonly realized through a loop antenna [62,63]—is exploited, a cylindrical leaky wave with a pure transverse magnetic (TM) or electric (TE) polarization is excited, thus generating an omnidirectional conical beam (see the results shown in Section 3.5). However, radiation at broadside is prevented in this case by the null enforced by the source geometry [16]. With the aim of achieving a broadside pencil beam, a horizontal magnetic dipole (HMD)—commonly implemented through a slot on the ground plane excited by a microstrip [17] or a rectangular waveguide [64–66]—or a horizontal electric dipole (HED)—typically realized through an L-probe, bent coaxial feed [67,68]—has to be employed. Such sources excite both TE and TM cylindrical leaky waves [53] and, thus, some difficulties in producing omnidirectional conical beams may arise due to possible TE–TM disequalization [16].

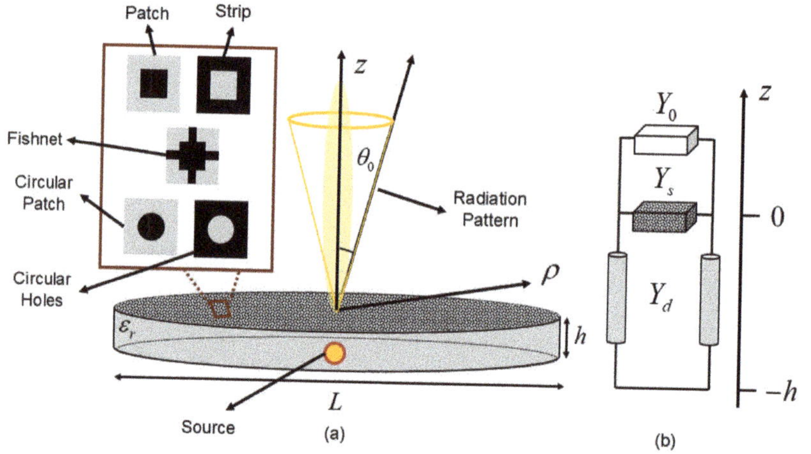

Figure 3. (**a**) Schematic representation of an FPCA (constituted by a grounded dielectric slab—in gray—with a PRS on top), its source (realized through dipole-like feeders), and its far-field radiation pattern (which can be a broadside pencil beam or a scanned conical beam). The red box on the left represents the possible implementations of the PRS unit cells through simple isotropic metasurfaces based on metallic lattices (black regions) printed on top of the dielectric slab (gray areas). (**b**) Transverse equivalent network of the FPCA. Y_0 and Y_d represent the wave admittances of the free space and the dielectric constituting the cavity, respectively, and Y_s is the equivalent sheet admittance of the PRS.

Once the feeder has been properly chosen, physically implemented, and matched (as discussed in the following, Section 3.4), the goal is to properly design the FPCA to achieve the desired performance in terms of directivity, pointing angle, working frequency, bandwidth, and efficiency. This objective can be achieved by simultaneously designing the PRS with the GDS characteristics, viz., the cavity height h, the lateral dimension L, and the dielectric-filling permittivity ε_r (see Figure 3a). On the one hand, the electrical thickness of the cavity mainly determines the beam angle [69]. On the other hand, the reflectivity of the PRS controls how much power leaks during propagation. For this reason, the beamwidth mainly depends on the PRS design [1]. These intuitive physical concepts can be rigorously described through the *leaky-wave theory* [16] or the *reciprocity approach* [70], obtaining, in both cases, closed-form design equations for FPCAs.

The first parameter which can be easily chosen is the minimum lateral dimension L of the FPCA (see Figure 3a). This parameter has to be designed to ensure that the radiating characteristics of an infinite structure remain nearly unchanged when implemented in a practical device, thereby achieving high radiation efficiency (assuming the structure has low material losses). In other words, this means that L has to be designed to avoid significant edge effects. The design goal to achieve a very high aperture efficiency is thus to reach the lateral aperture with the power as low as possible or, in other terms, to let almost all the transmitted power radiate before reaching the FPCA's lateral boundaries. In *lossless* FPCAs, the radiation efficiency is given by [1,18]

$$\eta_L = 1 - e^{-\alpha L} \tag{1}$$

A simple design equation for L is thus found for a desired value of the aperture efficiency (a typical minimum lower bound is set at $\eta_L = 90\%$ [16]):

$$L = -\frac{\ln(1-\eta_L)}{\alpha} \tag{2}$$

Thus, the importance of accurately evaluating the leaky attenuation constant α for the correct design of the device is clear. Such a parameter not only affects the aperture efficiency, but also the beamwidth, the directivity, and the fractional bandwidth (FBW).

On the other hand, the leaky phase constant β mainly determines the pointing angle of the device at a given frequency. (provided the attenuation constant is small, as commented next.) For this reason, in general, the correct evaluation of the leaky wavenumber $k_\rho = \beta - j\alpha$—with β and α being the leaky phase and attenuation constants, respectively—plays a fundamental role. For this reason, simple yet effective methods for the evaluation of k_ρ are reported both in the case of FPCAs and radially periodic LWAs in this work. While a Bloch analysis is needed for the latter [7], this procedure is addressed through the *transverse resonance technique* in the former case, as discussed in detail in Section 3.2. This method requires the representation of the FPCA through a transverse equivalent network (see Figure 3b): the GDS is considered to be a transmission-line section whose dimension and characteristic impedance depend on the cavity height, the considered polarization, and the dielectric permittivity of the material (assuming $\mu_r = 1$ for simplicity); the PRS, if lossless (the lossy case is a natural evolution of this analysis and it is discussed in [71]), is commonly well represented through a purely imaginary impedance sheet $Z_s = jX_s$ [72,73] (see, e.g., the inset on the left in Figure 3a,b).

In the leaky-wave perspective, the radiation features of the FPCAs are known once the leaky-wave wavenumber is correctly evaluated. By assuming that the feeder launches an omnidirectional cylindrical leaky wave with small attenuation constant $\alpha \ll k_0$ (where k_0 is the vacuum wavenumber), the latter provides the main contribution to the field on the antenna aperture plane at $z = 0$ (see Figure 3a) [5,6]. These cylindrical leaky waves are known in closed formulas (reported for the first time in [53]) and they can be used to evaluate the far-field radiation pattern through a simple Fourier transform, thus obtaining the following (assuming an infinite aperture):

$$\mathrm{SF}(\theta) = \frac{4|k_\rho|^2}{|k_\rho^2 - k_0^2 \sin^2\theta|^2} \tag{3}$$

where SF stands for space factor.

From the far-field radiation pattern in (3), one can easily retrieve important design relations [53]. For instance, the maximum value of SF for different θ angles is obtained by minimizing the denominator in (3). It is thus clear that the pointing angle for the FPCA is given by

$$\theta_0 = \arcsin\left[\sqrt{\left(\frac{\beta}{k_0}\right)^2 - \left(\frac{\alpha}{k_0}\right)^2}\right] \tag{4}$$

Since $\alpha \ll k_0$ in order to have a dominant leaky-wave contribution to the leaky-wave aperture [5,6], Equation (4) reveals that β mainly determines the pointing angle θ_0. Starting from Equation (3), one can also easily derive the half-power beamwidth (HPBW) $\Delta\theta$ as [16]

$$\Delta\theta = 2\frac{\alpha}{k_0}\sec\theta_0 \tag{5}$$

Also, Equation (5) reveals an important result. The beamwidth, which is strictly related to the directivity, mainly depends on the attenuation constant α. The lower α is, the narrower the beamwidth is and, in turn, the pattern peaks in the pointing-angle direction. Therefore, the more reflective the PRS is and, in turn, the lower α is (since the PRS reactance controls the amount of power which leaks out), the more directive the antenna is. This relation between the directivity D and the attenuation constant α is expressed in a closed formula for an FPCA radiating at broadside as [16]

$$D \simeq \frac{k_0^2\pi^2}{8\alpha^2} \tag{6}$$

It is worthwhile to point out that the attenuation constant is also strictly related to the bandwidth. In particular, it has been shown in [74] that, when broadside radiation is considered, the fractional bandwidth (FBW)—defined as the frequency range, normalized with respect to the central frequency, over which the power density at broadside decreases by less than 3 dB [70]—can be computed as [16]

$$\mathrm{FBW} = \frac{2\alpha^2}{k_0^2\varepsilon_r} \tag{7}$$

By observing Equations (6) and (7), an evident *trade-off* between directivity and fractional bandwidth appears. The figure of merit (FoM) given by the product $D \cdot \mathrm{FBW}$ for an FPCA based on a single thin PRS is constant and equal to

$$\mathrm{FoM} = D \cdot \mathrm{FBW} \simeq \frac{2.47}{\varepsilon_r} \tag{8}$$

It is thus clear that low-permittivity and low-loss materials are the best choice for maximizing this figure of merit.

With these formulas in mind, one can easily find three different working conditions for FPCAs depending on the mutual comparison of β and α. When $\beta < \alpha$, the FPCA radiates at broadside [74] in the so-called *reactive* region. A deep analysis of FPCAs radiating in this frequency range has been presented in [75]. The condition $\beta \simeq \alpha$ provides, instead, the best working point to maximize the radiated power at broadside [74]. In this context, a broadside pencil beam is produced by the FPCA with a beamwidth which depends on the X_s or, similarly, on the α value. Finally, by increasing the frequency, the condition $\beta > \alpha$ is reached. In this working region, FPCAs generate a scanning conical beam whose pointing angle mainly depends on the β value through (4) and the beamwidth on the α value through (5) (and, in turn, on the X_s value). These aspects, along with additional design formulas, are rigorously addressed by exploiting the *transverse resonance technique* discussed in the following subsection.

3.2. Evaluation of the Dispersion Curves

The standard procedure for determining the eigenvalues in waveguiding structures requires one to solve Maxwell's equations in any homogeneous region of the domain of interest and then apply the appropriate boundary conditions [76]. A nontrivial solution is then obtained by discretizing the problem, thus reducing it to a linear algebraic system, and enforcing the determinant of the coefficient matrix to be equal to zero. The complex roots of the resulting determinantal equation—which is commonly referred to as a *dispersion equation*—are the desired eigenvalues. This approach enables the expression of any solution to the problem in terms of its eigenvalue (the waveguide mode) and eigenfunction (the modal field), up to a multiplicative constant that depends on the excitation. This procedure, however, could be lengthy for devices with different media and complicated structures. Since, in the leaky-wave perspective, we are usually interested only in the evaluation of the eigenvalues, a faster approach is given by the *transverse resonance technique* [77]. It is indeed well known [78] that the eigenvalues of a waveguide problem correspond to the pole singularities of an appropriate characteristic Green's function in the k_z complex plane, which represents the voltage (or current) in a transmission line along one of the transverse directions of the waveguide [5,6]. In this network formalism, the pole singularities correspond to the resonances of the transverse equivalent network (TEN) model, which can be effectively calculated using both analytical and numerical methods.

Since FPCAs are constituted by a grounded dielectric slab with a PRS on top, their TEN is formed by a transmission-line segment—with characteristic admittance Y_d and transverse number $k_{zd} = \sqrt{k_0^2\varepsilon_r - k_\rho^2}$—terminated, on one side, on the equivalent sheet admittance of the PRS Y_s, and, on the other side, on a short circuit representing the ground plane (see Figure 3b). The term PRS generally denotes any type of screen that provides partial shielding of the radiation emitted by the primary dipole-like source located within the cavity [16]. For this reason, PRSs may take various forms that are conveniently categorized into three different classes [16] (see Figure 4):

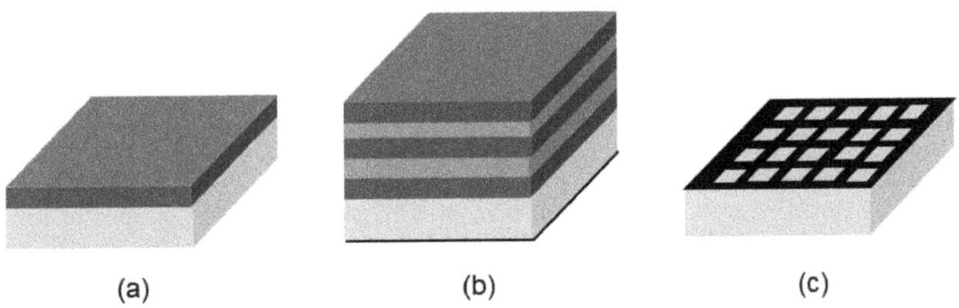

Figure 4. Schematic representation of Fabry–Perot cavity antennas with different physical implementation of their partially reflecting screen: (**a**) single-layer superstrate, (**b**) dielectric multilayer, and (**c**) homogenized metasurface. Different gray-scale colors represent different dielectric relative permittivities, while the black color represents metal areas.

- Single-layer dielectric covers which are typically implemented through a quarter-wavelength-thick high-permittivity slab [79,80];
- Dielectric multilayers consisting of alternating quarter-wavelength-thick slabs of high and low permittivity to realize a distributed Bragg reflector [81];
- Homogenized metasurfaces which are realized through subwavelength (with period $p \ll \lambda_0$) periodic planar arrangements of metal scatterers [82].

The last class is the most common at microwave frequencies and beyond to reduce dielectric losses [82]. This kind of PRS is rigorously represented by an equivalent impedance $\underline{\mathbf{Z}}_s$ with a tensor-like form and a spatially and frequency-dispersive model. However, since PRSs with simple geometries are commonly implemented in FPCAs that are typically required to operate over a narrow FBW and/or at a fixed beam angle (or over a small angular variation) [82], the model of the PRS is usually constituted by a single, scalar, generally complex, sheet impedance $Z_s = R_s + jX_s$, with R_s and X_s being the equivalent sheet resistance and reactance of the PRS, respectively. For lossless isotropic metasurfaces, this contribution is given by a scalar, purely imaginary, sheet impedance $Z_s = jX_s$. This assumption is valid for a large class of metasurfaces, even in the terahertz frequency range [82]. Typical examples, shown in Figure 3a, are 2-D patch arrays, metal strip gratings, and fishnet-like metasurfaces [72,73,82]. A method for the evaluation of such equivalent impedance value is shown in the following, Section 3.3.

Depending on the nature of the PRS (viz., if the metasurface is mainly inductive or capacitive) and on the considered polarization, a variety of modes (i.e., surface, leaky, or plasmonic) can be generated. The generation of the different kinds of waves and their nature is discussed in depth in [83]. In this manuscript, we are just interested in leaky-wave modes for achieving an effective, compact, and directive radiating device. The application of the transverse resonance techniques [77] to the TEN implies equating to zero the sum of the input impedance or admittance looking downward and looking upward at an arbitrary cross section of the equivalent transmission line. In this case study, it is convenient to assume $z = 0$ as a reference plane where the PRS is present (see Figure 3). In this manner, on the one side (the upper), there is the free-space characteristic admittance Y_0, and, on the other side (the lower), there is the parallel admittance of the equivalent PRS admittance $Y_s = 1/Z_s$ (which is purely imaginary if the PRS is lossless, obtaining $Y_s = jB_s$, with $B_s = -1/X_s$) and of the short-circuited transmission-line section $Y_{sc} = -jY_d \cot(k_{zd}h)$. Therefore, the *dispersion equation* of the FPCA in the presence of a lossless PRS reads:

$$Y_0 + Y_{sc} = Y_0 + jB_s - jY_d \cot(k_{zd}h) = 0 \tag{9}$$

It is worthwhile to point out that, in FPCAs able to produce a broadside pencil beam, by exciting the structure through an HED or an HMD both TE and TM modes are excited. It is thus important to report here the different quantities that appear in (9) for both polarizations, indicating with the hat $\hat{\cdot}$ the normalization with respect to the free-space wavenumber k_0 and with $\eta_0 = 120\pi\ \Omega$ the vacuum characteristic impedance.

$$Y_0^{\mathrm{TE}} = \frac{\hat{k}_{z0}}{\eta_0},\ Y_d^{\mathrm{TE}} = \frac{\hat{k}_{zd}}{\eta_0\mu_r},\ \hat{k}_{z0} = \sqrt{1-\hat{k}_\rho^2},\ \hat{k}_{zd} = \sqrt{\varepsilon_r\mu_r - \hat{k}_\rho^2} \tag{10}$$

$$Y_0^{\mathrm{TM}} = \frac{1}{\hat{k}_{z0}\eta_0},\ Y_d^{\mathrm{TM}} = \frac{\varepsilon_r}{\eta_0\hat{k}_{zd}},\ \hat{k}_{z0} = \sqrt{1-\hat{k}_\rho^2},\ \hat{k}_{zd} = \sqrt{\varepsilon_r\mu_r - \hat{k}_\rho^2} \tag{11}$$

By considering a nonmagnetic material ($\mu_r = 1$) and by substituting Equations (10) or (11) in (9), the dispersion equation for TE,

$$\sqrt{1-\hat{k}_\rho^2} + jB_s\eta_0 - j\sqrt{\varepsilon_r - \hat{k}_\rho^2}\cot\left(k_0 h\sqrt{\varepsilon_r - \hat{k}_\rho^2}\right) = 0 \quad (12)$$

or TM,

$$\left(\sqrt{1-\hat{k}_\rho^2}\right)^{-1} + jB_s\eta_0 - j\varepsilon_r\left(\sqrt{\varepsilon_r - \hat{k}_\rho^2}\right)^{-1}\cot\left[k_0 h\sqrt{\varepsilon_r - \hat{k}_\rho^2}\right] = 0 \quad (13)$$

modes are achieved, respectively. The zeros in Equations (12) and (13) can numerically be found efficiently through the *Padé* algorithm [84]. In particular, by searching for the complex *improper* roots (i.e., with $\mathrm{Im}[k_z] > 0$), the dispersion curves of the *leaky-wave modes* can be found and one can predict the radiating performance of the FPCAs under analysis.

3.3. Evaluation of the Equivalent Sheet Impedance of a Partially Reflecting Sheet

The evaluation of the equivalent sheet impedance Z_s for a homogenized metasurface is a crucial step in the design of the realistic devices for FPCAs. A scalar sheet impedance Z_s, which generally depends on the polarization, can represent a planar patterned metal sheet if its periodicity p is much lower than the operative wavelength λ. This assumption, which corresponds to the *homogenization principle*, is needed to let only the fundamental $n = 0$ Floquet harmonic propagate.

In order to evaluate the Z_s value, the unit cell of the homogenized metasurface is implemented on a commercial solver (such as CST Microwave Studio [85] or HFSS [86]) in a periodic environment (which means the application of *phase-shift* walls as boundary conditions on the periodicity directions). On top of the patterned metal, an air block is considered and, at the bottom, a grounded dielectric slab, where the metasurface lies, is assumed. In Figure 5, for instance, the case of a fishnet-like metasurface printed on top of a grounded dielectric slab of thickness h is considered.

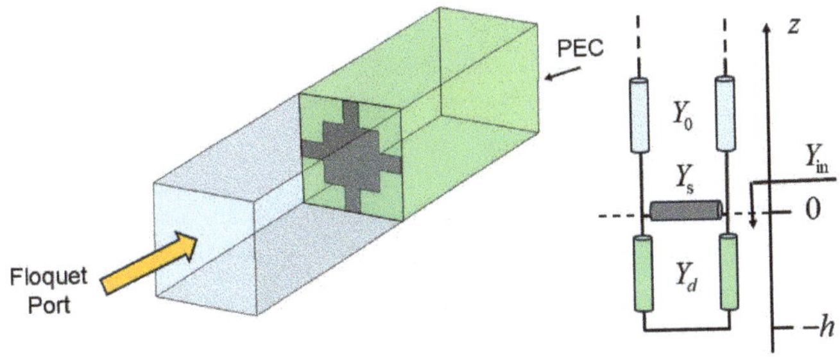

Figure 5. Full-wave model of a fishnet-like metasurface unit cell in a periodic environment on the left. A wave port is considered on top and it impinges on the homogenized-metasurface unit cell, taking into account the substrate effect. On the bottom, a perfect-electric-conductor (PEC) condition is considered in order to represent the ground plane of the dielectric slab. On the right, the equivalent transmission-line model of the problem is shown.

By de-embedding the reference plane for the wave port shown in Figure 5 at the metasurface level ($z = 0$), the reflection coefficient S_{11} at the air–PRS interface is retrieved from the full-wave solver. At this point, one can easily evaluate the input admittance Y_{in} (see Figure 5) as

$$Y_{\mathrm{in}} = Y_0\frac{1-S_{11}}{1+S_{11}} \quad (14)$$

where Y_0 is the vacuum wave admittance of the mode in propagation.

By observing the equivalent circuit in Figure 5, it is clear that $Y_{\rm in}$, evaluated through a full-wave simulation, is given by the parallel of the homogenized-metasurface admittance Y_s and the input admittance of an h-thick, short-circuited, transmission-line segment with the dielectric characteristic admittance Y_d and propagation constant k_{zd}. Therefore, the desired Y_s value is straightforwardly evaluated as

$$Y_s = Y_{\rm in} - jY_d \cot(k_{zd}h) \tag{15}$$

Once the equivalent admittance is known, the evaluation of the equivalent sheet impedance of the homogenized metasurface is trivial:

$$Z_s = R_s + jX_s = 1/Y_s \tag{16}$$

with R_s the equivalent resistance (which takes into account ohmic and dielectric losses) and X_s the equivalent sheet reactance (in lossless material, one commonly has $Z_s = jX_s$). The reactance sign can be either positive or negative, representing an inductive- or capacitive-like metasurface, respectively.

In order to corroborate the proposed approach, an inductive-like partially reflecting sheet with X_s closed-form homogenization expressions is considered. In particular, a metal strip grating printed on an air-like grounded dielectric slab with strip width w and periodicity p is assumed (see Figure 6). For this kind of unit cell, it has been demonstrated in [72] that

$$X_s = \frac{\eta_0 k_0 p}{2\pi} \ln\left(\csc\frac{\pi w}{2p}\right) \tag{17}$$

In Figure 6, for a fixed working frequency and periodicity, the equivalent reactance computed through full-wave simulations and theoretical formulas for different w/p filling factors are in a perfect agreement, thus corroborating the proposed approach.

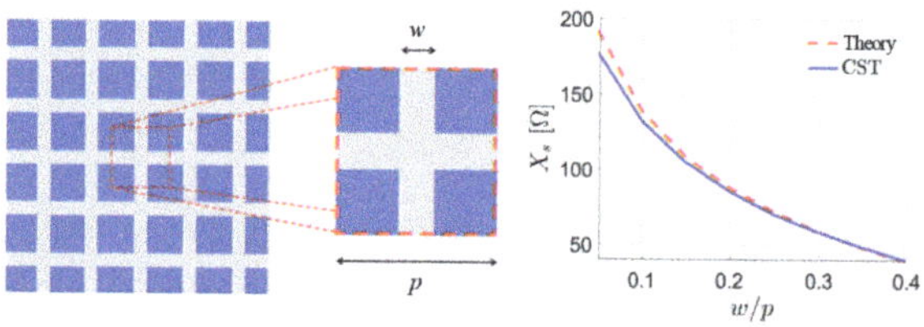

Figure 6. A schematic representation of a metal strip grating is reported on the left (metal and air are described in gray and blue, respectively). The equivalent sheet reactance of the homogenized metasurface is reported on the right, showing a remarkable agreement between the numerical analysis furnished in [72] and the proposed full-wave approach.

3.4. Feeding Schemes and Matching Networks

In this subsection, the physical implementation of the feeders of FPCAs is discussed. So far, ideal, dipole-like sources have been assumed. From a practical viewpoint, these kinds of feeders do not exist but they can be realized through devices with similar radiating features. Moreover, in order to avoid return-loss effects, which have been completely neglected so far, the feeding schemes have to be properly engineered to be adequately matched. Such a goal is addressed in different manners depending on the considered source.

In the case of a VED-like feeder, a coaxial cable is commonly employed. The latter can be matched e.g., by efficiently choosing the penetration depth of its inner conductor and/or its dielectric filling in the FPCA. Moreover, a circular metallic patch can be properly designed in the center of the PRS as an additional element of the matching network. These parameters are usually optimized through parametric full-wave simulations [60,61,87]. Additionally, a similar approach is commonly employed for HED- and VMD-like sources, since they are implemented through bent coaxial cables in the FPCA, viz. an L-probe [67] and a loop antenna [62,63], respectively. Particular attention is needed for HMDs. The latter are implemented through rectangular slots on the ground plane and, depending on their feeding scheme, they can be matched in different manners. For subresonant slots, a microstrip feeding network is commonly employed and it can be matched through standard transmission-line techniques [88,89]. In the case of quasi-resonant slots, the device can be fed through rectangular waveguides [44,66] whose return loss can be improved with different techniques [88]. In particular, an efficient transmission-line-based method that requires a single full-wave simulation to design capacitive irises has been proposed and validated in [64].

3.5. Full-Wave Validation of the Theoretical Model

This subsection simultaneously provides a rapid full-wave simulation setup for FPCAs and a validation of the theoretical leaky-wave model and of the correct antenna design. In order to carry this out, a case study is considered with an equivalent sheet impedance $X_s = 30\ \Omega$ and a dielectric slab with negligible losses (lossy cases are thoroughly discussed in [71]), thickness $h = 2.77$ mm, and relative permittivity $\varepsilon_r = 3$. It is worthwhile to point out that the X_s, ε_r, and h values can be properly designed to achieve the desired radiating features at a certain frequency f_0, as previously discussed in Section 3.1.

Once the design parameters of the proposed FPCA are fixed, one can easily evaluate the leaky-wave dispersion curves through the transverse resonance technique applied to the TEN of the device, as thoroughly discussed in Section 3.2. In this manner, the profile of the phase and attenuation constant normalized with respect to the vacuum wavenumber k_0, viz. $\hat{\beta} = \beta/k_0$ and $\hat{\alpha} = \alpha/k_0$, respectively, are retrieved vs. frequency f, as shown in Figure 7a. From the dispersion curves, it is clear that the proposed device is able to generate a pencil beam with a maximum radiated power at broadside at $f_c = 29.88$ GHz, when $\beta^{\mathrm{TE}} \simeq \alpha^{\mathrm{TE}} \simeq \beta^{\mathrm{TM}} \simeq \alpha^{\mathrm{TM}}$ [74]. Moreover, as previously discussed in Section 3.2, one can assert that the device is working in the reactive regime for $f < f_c$ [75] and it is generating a conical beam for $f > f_c$. By exploiting the evaluation of the dispersion curves, it is also possible to choose the lateral extension of the device to achieve a radiation efficiency of, at least, 90 % at a certain working frequency $f_w = 33$ GHz. In particular, by considering $\alpha = \min\{\alpha^{\mathrm{TE}}(f_w), \alpha^{\mathrm{TM}}(f_w)\}$, the minimum extension of the radiating device is set at $L = 38.96$ mm through (2).

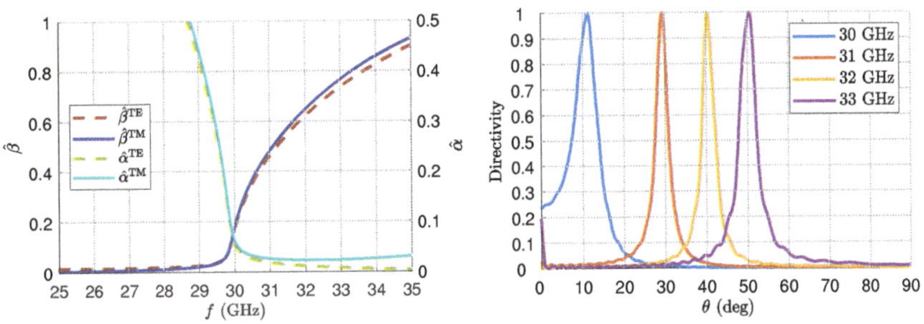

(a) (b)

Figure 7. (**a**) Dispersion curves of both the TE and TM modes of the phase and attenuation constants normalized with respect to the vacuum wavenumber k_0, viz. $\hat{\beta} = \beta/k_0$ and $\hat{\alpha} = \alpha/k_0$, respectively. (**b**) Radiation patterns, normalized with respect to their maximum on a linear scale, of the simulated FPCA at different frequencies.

Once the minimum lateral dimension of the FPCA has been found, the device is ready to be simulated on a commercial full-wave solver to verify its radiation property. In order to perform that and to strongly reduce the computational effort, one can implement the source as an ideal dipole (its physical implementation and matching techniques are discussed in Section 3.4) and the PRS through a surface impedance boundary condition (SIBC)—the design of the real reflecting layer can be addressed through a homogenized metasurface designed with the approach shown in Section 3.3. It is worthwhile to point out that the SIBC has to be described with a frequency-dispersive behavior which respects the Foster's reactance theorem [90]. Therefore, depending on the inductive-like or capacitive-like nature of the PRS, one has to enforce $Z_s = j\omega L$ or $Z_s = -j/\omega C$, respectively, on the full-wave solver. Specifically, the lumped inductance L and capacitance C value are fixed so as to match the desired X_s value at the working frequency of the design.

By applying the simulation guidelines discussed so far, a three-dimensional (3-D) model of the proposed FPCA has been implemented on CST Microwave Studio [85] through a *transparent* SIBC on top of a cylindrical grounded dielectric slab with height $h = 2.77$ mm, aperture diameter $L = 40$ mm, and relative permittivity $\varepsilon_r = 3$. By exciting the device through an HED in the middle of the cavity [55], the far-field radiation patterns for $f > f_c$ reported in Figure 7b were achieved. The generation of conical beams, with a scanning pointing angle θ_0 which varies as the frequency increases through (4), is thus demonstrated.

4. Radially Periodic Leaky-Wave Antennas

This section deals with the analysis of radially periodic LWAs. Since the latter are constituted by two-dimensional, leaky-wave, radiating devices, the design rules in terms of directivity and fractional bandwidth as a function of the leaky phase and attenuation constants are the same as those presented in Section 3.1. The main difference lies in the evaluation method of β and α. In FPCAs, it is indeed possible to consider the PRS in the homogenization regime and, thus, to exploit the transverse resonance technique applied to the TEN of the device. In radially periodic LWAs, the periodicity of the annular metal strip grating printed on top of the GDS is instead comparable to the operating wavelength λ and the radiation is usually related to the first-order, fast, Floquet–Bloch mode in propagation [43,87]. Here, we provide a simple technique for the Bloch analysis in Section 4.1 and validate it in Section 4.2 through a full-wave simulation of the entire structure.

4.1. A Simple Technique for the Bloch Analysis

As mentioned above, a two-dimensional radially periodic LWA is constituted by a subwavelength-thick grounded dielectric slab with an annular metal strip on top (see Figure 2e) [7]. By considering an azimuthally symmetric source, such as a VED, it is possible to locally linearize the radial structure as a 1-D periodic metal strip grating, which can be conveniently described in terms of space harmonics [7]. The radial leaky-wave propagation over an annular metal strip grating can indeed be seen as a 1-D propagation over an infinite metal strip grating with phase advance normal to the printed strips thanks to the azimuthal symmetry of the device [7]. This aspect is well explained in Figure 8, where the linearization process for an azimuthally symmetric radial periodicity on a 2-D structure is reported straightforwardly.

The device can thus be analyzed as a 1-D periodic LWA. In this context, the generic m-th Floquet space harmonic (with $m = 0, \pm 1, \pm 2, \dots$) has a dispersive behavior related to the fundamental harmonic wavenumber $k_{\rho 0} = \beta_0 - j\alpha$ and a periodicity (along the radial direction) p as follows:

$$k_{\rho m} = \beta_0 + \frac{2\pi m}{p} - j\alpha \quad (18)$$

The structure is usually designed to let the $m = -1$ harmonic propagate in the working bandwidth. Thus, it is manifest that, in this case too, it is crucial to accurately determine the leaky wavenumber for the theoretical design and performance assessment of the LWA. In this context, the possibility to describe the device through its linearized counterpart [7] (see Figure 8) is crucial for the evaluation of the leaky radial wavenumber. This is because different techniques have been already proposed for retrieving the dispersion diagram of leaky modes propagating in 1-D periodic LWAs (see, e.g., [91–94] and the references therein).

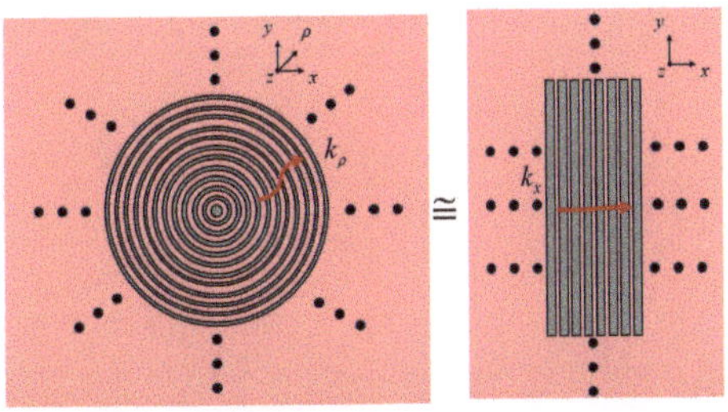

Figure 8. The complex leaky radial wavenumber, k_ρ, of the radially periodic LWA (represented on the **left**) can be approximately seen as the complex leaky longitudinal wavenumber k_x of an infinite, linear, metal strip grating with phase advance normal to the printed strips (as shown on the **right**) [7].

In this paper, in order to avoid the implementation of an ad hoc method-of-moments (MoM) approach for the considered structures [91], the need for complicated numerical routines [93], or the correct selection of higher-order modes in the simulation model [92], a method originally proposed for the analysis of *frozen* modes is exploited [95].

In order to corroborate the proposed approach, the reference case in [87] is considered since the dispersion curves are retrieved through an MoM [91]. While, in [87], the radially periodic device was considered to be a wideband Bessel-beam launcher (BBL) in the near-field region, the same structure will be considered here as an LWA in the far-field region. The wideband BBL proposed in [87] works with a central frequency $f_0 = 23$ GHz through a GDS with relative permittivity $\varepsilon_r = 2.2$ and thickness $h = 3.14$ mm perturbed by a metal strip grating with periodicity $p = 10$ mm and slot width $s = 6$ mm (see Figure 9a).

In order to apply the approach proposed in [95], two waveguide ports are defined here in the periodic direction with a height $h_{\text{port}} = 3.5$ h and lateral dimension $w_{\text{port}} = \lambda_0/4$ to ensure the correct representation of the fundamental TM_0 surface wave of the grounded dielectric slab. Moreover, as shown in Figure 9a, perfect-magnetic-conductor (PMC) boundaries and an open boundary condition are assigned along y and z, respectively.

At this stage, the transfer matrix of a single unit cell is obtained through CST full-wave simulations [85] by multiplying the transfer matrix obtained considering $N + 1$ unit cells with the inverse of the one with N unit cells [95]. The T matrix of the single unit cell, which takes into account the mutual coupling of adjacent cells, can thus be found. Then, the leaky phase and attenuation constants can be derived through well-known formulas [88,92,94]. As shown in Figure 9b (for the two case studies $N = 6$ and $N = 7$) and Figure 9c (for the two case studies $N = 15$ and $N = 16$), this method perfectly evaluates the phase constant β regardless of the number of periods utilized in the analysis. This is not the case for the evaluation of the leakage constants as shown in Figure 9d,e, since the evaluation of α is typically more difficult [94]. By adding unit cells in the CST simulation, indeed, the only effect is to introduce additional numerical noise. This is due to the fact that α represents an amplitude decay and, by considering high values of N, the evaluation of this parameter is performed over distances at which most of the power has already been radiated by the equivalent 1-D periodic LWA implemented on CST. On the other hand, a small number of periods does not suitably represent the mutual coupling among unit cells.

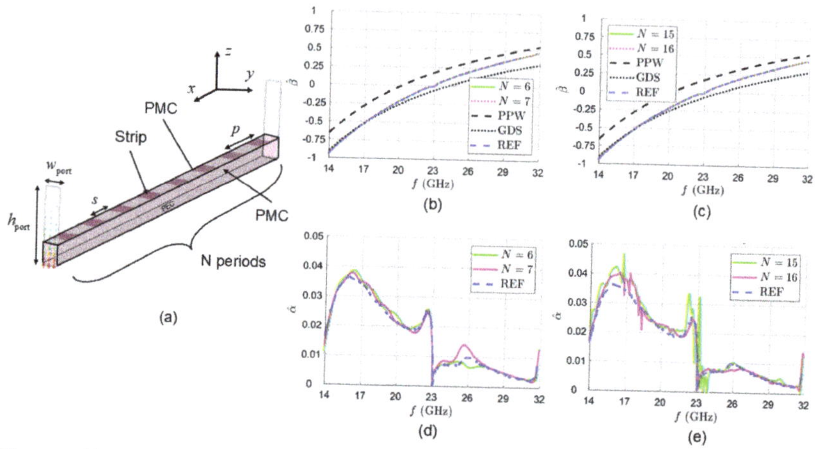

Figure 9. (**a**) Schematic representation of the full-wave model of the linearized counterpart of the radially periodic 2-D LWA constituted by a grounded dielectric slab (pink solid) with N unit cells of a metal strip grating on top (dark areas). The two rectangular areas delimited by light-gray lines represent the two considered waveguide ports. In one of them, the modal field distribution is reported through lines of force, showing the correct excitation of the TM_0 mode in the device. (**b–e**) Dispersion diagrams of the normalized leaky (**b**,**c**) phase $\hat{\beta}$ and (**d**,**e**) attenuation $\hat{\alpha}$ constants. While the blue dashed lines represent the reference case obtained through an MoM approach [87], black dashed and dotted lines represent the limiting, unperturbed cases of a parallel-plate waveguide (PPW) and of a grounded dielectric slab (GDS) structure, respectively. The green and magenta colors represent two subsequent case studies: $N = 6$ and $N = 7$ for (**b**,**d**), and $N = 15$ and $N = 16$ for (**c**,**e**).

By observing the dispersion curves of the leaky phase and attenuation constants, the presence of the open-stopband phenomenon, which is related to the contradirectional coupling between two Floquet–Bloch harmonics, is clear [41]. When β tends to zero, indeed, the value of α varies quickly, preventing the proper generation of a beam at broadside [41]: initially, it shows a sharply peaked behavior due to the accumulation of reactive energy, and then it drops to zero at the broadside frequency [3]. Although this aspect goes beyond the interest of this paper, it is worthwhile to point out that different techniques were proposed to mitigate or suppress the open stopband, thereby improving the near-field [96] and far-field radiating properties of 1-D and 2-D LWAs [97,98].

4.2. Full-Wave Validation of the Theoretical Model

In this subsection, the 3-D model of the radially periodic LWA studied in [87] is simulated in CST Microwave Studio with the aim of deriving its far-field radiation pattern. The results are reported in Figure 10 through 3-D radiation patterns normalized with respect to their maximum in a linear scale. As expected, the device generates a conical beam in the far-field region pointing at θ_0, which decreases as the frequency increases from 17 GHz to 20 GHz. This aspect is in perfect agreement with the dispersion curves reported in Figure 9 since the absolute value of β decreases in that frequency range and, thus, θ_0 decreases, as expected from (4).

Figure 10. Three-dimensional radiation pattern of the considered radially periodic LWA in a linear scale at (**a**) 17 GHz, (**b**) 18 GHz, (**c**) 19 GHz, and (**d**) 20 GHz.

5. Conclusions

This paper provides guidelines for the characterization and design of uniform, quasi-uniform, and radially periodic two-dimensional leaky-wave antennas from theoretical, numerical, and simulative viewpoints.

In particular, as concerns the analysis of Fabry–Perot leaky-wave antennas, different techniques and methods are reviewed: the leaky-wave approach for predicting and designing the performance of the radiating device, the application of the transverse resonance technique to the transverse equivalent network of the antenna, the evaluation and design of a desired equivalent sheet impedance through homogenized metasurfaces, and the correct choice and implementation of a realistic feeder. As concerns radially periodic leaky-wave antennas, a simple technique for the Bloch analysis is proposed and corroborated. Moreover, all the considered designs are verified through full-wave simulations, confirming the validity of the proposed approaches for a simple, effective, and fast design of different kinds of leaky-wave antennas.

Author Contributions: Conceptualization, E.N. and W.F.; methodology, E.N. and W.F.; software, E.N. and W.F.; validation, E.N.; formal analysis, E.N., W.F., P.B. and A.G.; investigation, E.N.; resources, E.N. and W.F.; data curation, E.N.; writing—original draft preparation, E.N.; writing—review and editing, E.N., W.F., P.B. and A.G.; visualization, E.N.; supervision, W.F., P.B. and A.G.; project administration, W.F., P.B. and A.G.; funding acquisition, W.F. and A.G. All authors have read and agreed to the published version of the manuscript.

Funding: This work was supported by the European Union—Next Generation EU under the Italian National Recovery and Resilience Plan (NRRP), Mission 4, Component 2, Investment 1.3, CUP B53C22004050001, partnership on "Telecommunications of the Future" (PE00000001—program "RESTART").

Institutional Review Board Statement: Not applicable.

Informed Consent Statement: Not applicable.

Data Availability Statement: The original contributions presented in this study are included in the article. Further inquiries can be directed to the corresponding author.

Conflicts of Interest: The authors declare no conflicts of interest.

Abbreviations

The following abbreviations are used in this manuscript:

1-D	One Dimensional
2-D	Two Dimensional
3-D	Three Dimensional
BBL	Bessel-Beam Launcher
FBW	Fractional Bandwidth
FoM	Figure of Merit
FPCA	Fabry–Perot Cavity Antenna

GDS	Grounded Dielectric Slab
HED	Horizontal Electric Dipole
HMD	Horizontal Magnetic Dipole
HPBW	Half-Power Beamwidth
LWA	Leaky-Wave Antenna
MoM	Method of Moments
PEC	Perfect Electric Conductor
PMC	Perfect Magnetic Conductor
PPW	Parallel-Plate Waveguide
PRS	Partially Reflecting Sheet
TEN	Transverse Equivalent Network
VED	Vertical Electric Dipole
VMD	Vertical Magnetic Dipole

References

1. Jackson, D.R.; Caloz, C.; Itoh, T. Leaky-wave antennas. *Proc. IEEE* **2012**, *100*, 2194–2206. [CrossRef]
2. Monticone, F.; Alù, A. Leaky-Wave Theory, Techniques, and Applications: From Microwaves to Visible Frequencies. *Proc. IEEE* **2015**, *103*, 793–821. [CrossRef]
3. Oliner, A.A.; Jackson, D.R.; Volakis, J. Leaky-Wave Antennas. *Antenna Engineering Handbook*; McGraw-Hill Education: New York, NY, USA, 2007; Volume 4, p. 12.
4. Marcuvitz, N. On field representations in terms of leaky modes or eigenmodes. *IRE Trans. Antennas Propag.* **1956**, *4*, 192–194. [CrossRef]
5. Tamir, T.; Oliner, A.A. Guided complex waves. Part 1: Fields at an interface. *Proc. IEE* **1963**, *110*, 310–324. [CrossRef]
6. Tamir, T.; Oliner, A.A. Guided complex waves. Part 2: Relation to radiation patterns. *Proc. IEE* **1963**, *110*, 325–334. [CrossRef]
7. Podilchak, S.K.; Baccarelli, P.; Burghignoli, P.; Freundorfer, A.P.; Antar, Y.M.M. Analysis and design of annular microstrip-based planar periodic leaky-wave antennas. *IEEE Trans. Antennas Propag.* **2014**, *62*, 2978–2991. [CrossRef]
8. Sengupta, S.; Jackson, D.R.; Almutawa, A.T.; Kazemi, H.; Capolino, F.; Long, S.A. A cross-shaped 2-D periodic leaky-wave antenna. *IEEE Trans. Antennas Propag.* **2020**, *68*, 1289–1301. [CrossRef]
9. Sengupta, S.; Jackson, D.R.; Almutawa, A.T.; Kazemi, H.; Capolino, F.; Long, S.A. Radiation properties of a 2-D periodic leaky-wave antenna. *IEEE Trans. Antennas Propag.* **2019**, *67*, 3560–3573. [CrossRef]
10. Askarian, A.; Yao, J.; Lu, Z.; Wu, K. Extremely low-profile periodic 2-D leaky-wave antenna: An optimal solution for antenna-frontend integration. *IEEE Trans. Antennas Propag.* **2022**, *70*, 7798–7812. [CrossRef]
11. Wei, B.; Li, Z.; Ma, Y.; Wang, Z.; Wang, J. A two-dimensional fixed-frequency beam-scanning leaky-wave antenna array for millimeter-wave application. *IEEE Trans. Antennas Propag.* **2024**, *72*, 4888–4899. [CrossRef]
12. Xu, F.; Wu, K.; Zhang, X. Periodic leaky-wave antenna for millimeter wave applications based on substrate integrated waveguide. *IEEE Trans. Antennas Propag.* **2009**, *58*, 340–347.
13. Rahmani, M.H.; Deslandes, D. Backward to forward scanning periodic leaky-wave antenna with wide scanning range. *IEEE Trans. Antennas Propag.* **2017**, *65*, 3326–3335. [CrossRef]
14. Vadher, P.; Sacco, G.; Nikolayev, D. Meandering microstrip leaky wave antenna with dual-band linear–circular polarization and suppressed open stopband. *IEEE Trans. Antennas Propag.* **2024**, *72*, 375–386. [CrossRef]
15. Neto, A.; Bruni, S.; Gerini, G.; Sabbadini, M. The leaky lens: A broad-band fixed-beam leaky-wave antenna. *IEEE Trans. Antennas Propag.* **2005**, *53*, 3240–3246. [CrossRef]
16. Burghignoli, P.; Fuscaldo, W.; Galli, A. Fabry–Perot cavity antennas: The leaky-wave perspective. *IEEE Antennas Propag. Mag.* **2021**, *63*, 116–145. [CrossRef]
17. Balanis, C.A. *Antenna Theory: Analysis and Design*; Wiley: Hoboken, NJ, USA, 2015.
18. Galli, A.; Baccarelli, P.; Burghignoli, P. Leaky-Wave Antennas. In *Wiley Encyclopedia of Electrical and Electronics Engineering*; Wiley: Hoboken, NJ, USA, 2016; pp. 1–20.
19. Wang, M.; Ma, H.F.; Zhang, H.C.; Tang, W.X.; Zhang, X.R.; Cui, T.J. Frequency-fixed beam-scanning leaky-wave antenna using electronically controllable corrugated microstrip line. *IEEE Trans. Antennas Propag.* **2018**, *66*, 4449–4457. [CrossRef]
20. Kodera, T.; Caloz, C. Uniform ferrite-loaded open waveguide structure with CRLH response and its application to a novel backfire-to-endfire leaky-wave antenna. *IEEE Trans. Microw. Theory Tech.* **2009**, *57*, 784–795. [CrossRef]
21. Chang, L.; Zhang, Z.; Li, Y.; Wang, S.; Feng, Z. 60-GHz air substrate leaky-wave antenna based on MEMS micromachining technology. *IEEE Trans. Compon. Packag. Manuf. Technol.* **2016**, *6*, 1656–1662. [CrossRef]

22. Buzzin, A.; Asquini, R.; Caputo, D.; de Cesare, G. Sensitive and compact evanescent-waveguide optical detector for sugar sensing in commercial beverages. *Sensors* **2023**, *23*, 8184. [CrossRef] [PubMed]
23. Fuscaldo, W.; Burghignoli, P.; Baccarelli, P.; Galli, A. Graphene Fabry–Perot cavity leaky-wave antennas: Plasmonic versus nonplasmonic solutions. *IEEE Trans. Antennas Propag.* **2017**, *65*, 1651–1660. [CrossRef]
24. Wang, X.C.; Zhao, W.S.; Hu, J.; Yin, W.Y. Reconfigurable terahertz leaky-wave antenna using graphene-based high-impedance surface. *IEEE Trans. Nanotechnol.* **2015**, *14*, 62–69. [CrossRef]
25. Jiang, D.; Li, X.; Fu, Z.; Ran, P.; Wang, G.; Zheng, Z.; Zhang, T.; Wang, W.Q. Liquid crystal-based Wideband reconfigurable leaky wave X-band antenna. *IEEE Access* **2019**, *7*, 127320–127326. [CrossRef]
26. Almutawa, A.T.; Hosseini, A.; Jackson, D.R.; Capolino, F. Leaky-wave analysis of wideband planar Fabry–Pérot cavity antennas formed by a thick PRS. *IEEE Trans. Antennas Propag.* **2019**, *67*, 5163–5175. [CrossRef]
27. Al-Tarifi, M.A.; Anagnostou, D.E.; Amert, A.K.; Whites, K.W. Bandwidth enhancement of the resonant cavity antenna by using two dielectric superstrates. *IEEE Trans. Antennas Propag.* **2013**, *61*, 1898–1908. [CrossRef]
28. Baba, A.A.; Hashmi, R.M.; Esselle, K.P. Achieving a large gain-bandwidth product from a compact antenna. *IEEE Trans. Antennas Propag.* **2017**, *65*, 3437–3446. [CrossRef]
29. Baba, A.A.; Hashmi, R.M.; Esselle, K.P.; Weily, A.R. Compact high-gain antenna with simple all-dielectric partially reflecting surface. *IEEE Trans. Antennas Propag.* **2018**, *66*, 4343–4348. [CrossRef]
30. Karmokar, D.K.; Esselle, K.P.; Hay, S.G. Fixed-frequency beam steering of microstrip leaky-wave antennas using binary switches. *IEEE Trans. Antennas Propag.* **2016**, *64*, 2146–2154. [CrossRef]
31. Javanbakht, N.; Syrett, B.; Amaya, R.E.; Shaker, J. A review of reconfigurable leaky-wave antennas. *IEEE Access* **2021**, *9*, 94224–94238. [CrossRef]
32. Negri, E.; Fuscaldo, W.; Burghignoli, P.; Galli, A. Reconfigurable THz leaky-wave antennas based on innovative metal–graphene metasurfaces. *J. Phys. D Appl. Phys.* **2024**, *57*, 485102. [CrossRef]
33. Gu, Z.; Ma, Q.; Gao, X.; You, J.W.; Cui, T.J. Direct electromagnetic information processing with planar diffractive neural network. *Sci. Adv.* **2024**, *10*, 3937. [CrossRef]
34. Gao, X.; Ma, Q.; Gu, Z.; Cui, W.Y.; Liu, C.; Zhang, J.; Cui, T.J. Programmable surface plasmonic neural networks for microwave detection and processing. *Nat. Electron.* **2023**, *6*, 319–328. [CrossRef]
35. Gómez-Tornero, J.; Martinez, A.; Rebenaque, D.; Gugliemi, M.; Alvarez-Melcón, A. Design of tapered leaky-wave antennas in hybrid waveguide-planar technology for millimeter waveband applications. *IEEE Trans. Antennas Propag.* **2005**, *53*, 2563–2577. [CrossRef]
36. Gómez-Tornero, J.L. Analysis and design of conformal tapered leaky-wave antennas. *IEEE Antennas Wirel. Propag. Lett.* **2011**, *10*, 1068–1071. [CrossRef]
37. Fong, B.; Colburn, J.S.; Ottusch, J.J.; Visher, J.; Sievenpiper, D. Scalar and tensor holographic artificial impedance surfaces. *IEEE Trans. Antennas Propag.* **2010**, *58*, 3212–3221. [CrossRef]
38. Minatti, G.; Caminita, F.; Casaletti, M.; Maci, S. Spiral leaky-wave antennas based on modulated surface impedance. *IEEE Trans. Antennas Propag.* **2011**, *59*, 4436–4444. [CrossRef]
39. Minatti, G.; Faenzi, M.; Martini, E.; Caminita, F.; De Vita, P.; González-Ovejero, D.; Sabbadini, M.; Maci, S. Modulated metasurface antennas for space: Synthesis, analysis and realizations. *IEEE Trans. Antennas Propag.* **2014**, *63*, 1288–1300. [CrossRef]
40. Faenzi, M.; Caminita, F.; Martini, E.; De Vita, P.; Minatti, G.; Sabbadini, M.; Maci, S. Realization and measurement of broadside beam modulated metasurface antennas. *IEEE Antennas Wirel. Propag. Lett.* **2015**, *15*, 610–613. [CrossRef]
41. Giusti, F.; Maci, S.; Martini, E. Complete open-stopband suppression using sinusoidally modulated anisotropic metasurfaces. *IEEE Trans. Antennas Propag.* **2023**, *71*, 8537–8547. [CrossRef]
42. Ettorre, M.; Pavone, S.C.; Casaletti, M.; Albani, M.; Mazzinghi, A.; Freni, A. Near-field focusing by non-diffracting Bessel beams. In *Aperture Antennas for Millimeter and Sub-Millimeter Wave Applications*; Springer: Cham, Switzerland, 2018; pp. 243–288.
43. Negri, E.; Fuscaldo, W.; González-Ovejero, D.; Burghignoli, P.; Galli, A. TE-polarized leaky-wave beam launchers: Generation of Bessel and Bessel–Gauss beams. *Appl. Phys. Lett.* **2024**, *125*, 181703. [CrossRef]
44. Negri, E.; Fuscaldo, W.; Burghignoli, P.; Galli, A. Leaky-wave analysis of TM-, TE-, and hybrid-polarized aperture-fed Bessel-beam launchers for wireless power transfer links. *IEEE Trans. Antennas Propag.* **2023**, *71*, 1424–1436. [CrossRef]
45. Hansen, W.W. Radiating Electromagnetic Wave Guide. US Patent 2,402,622, 25 June 1946.
46. Goldstone, L.; Oliner, A.A. Leaky-wave antennas I: Rectangular waveguides. *IRE Trans. Antennas Propag.* **1959**, *7*, 307–319. [CrossRef]
47. Goldstone, L.; Oliner, A.A. Leaky-wave antennas II: Circular waveguides. *IRE Trans. Antennas Propag.* **1961**, *9*, 280–290. [CrossRef]
48. Hines, J.N.; Rumsey, V.H.; Walter, C.H. Traveling-wave slot antennas. *Proc. IRE* **1953**, *41*, 1624–1631. [CrossRef]
49. Collin, R.E.; Zucker, F.J. *Antenna Theory*; McGraw-Hill: New York, NY, USA, 1969.

50. Rezaee, S.; Memarian, M. Analytical study of open-stopband suppression in leaky-wave antennas. *IEEE Antennas Wirel. Propag. Lett.* **2020**, *19*, 363–367. [CrossRef]
51. Otto, S.; Al-Bassam, A.; Rennings, A.; Solbach, K.; Caloz, C. Transversal asymmetry in periodic leaky-wave antennas for Bloch impedance and radiation efficiency equalization through broadside. *IEEE Trans. Antennas Propag.* **2014**, *62*, 5037–5054. [CrossRef]
52. Otto, S.; Al-Bassam, A.; Rennings, A.; Solbach, K.; Caloz, C. Radiation efficiency of longitudinally symmetric and asymmetric periodic leaky-wave antennas. *IEEE Antennas Wirel. Propag. Lett.* **2012**, *11*, 612–615. [CrossRef]
53. Ip, A.; Jackson, D.R. Radiation from cylindrical leaky waves. *IEEE Trans. Antennas Propag.* **1990**, *38*, 482–488. [CrossRef]
54. Madji, M.; Negri, E.; Fuscaldo, W.; Comite, D.; Galli, A.; Burghignoli, P. The leaky-wave perspective for array-fed Fabry-Perot cavity and bull's-eye antennas. *Appl. Sci.* **2024**, *14*, 6775. [CrossRef]
55. Madji, M.; Negri, E.; Fuscaldo, W.; Comite, D.; Galli, A.; Burghignoli, P. Two-dimensional scanning of circularly polarized beams via array-fed Fabry–Perot cavity antennas. *Appl. Sci.* **2024**, *14*, 12058. [CrossRef]
56. Xie, P.; Wang, G.; Li, H.; Liang, J.; Gao, X. Circularly polarized Fabry-Perot antenna employing a receiver–transmitter polarization conversion metasurface. *IEEE Trans. Antennas Propag.* **2019**, *68*, 3213–3218. [CrossRef]
57. Huang, Y.; Yang, L.; Li, J.; Wang, Y.; Wen, G. Polarization conversion of metasurface for the application of wide band low-profile circular polarization slot antenna. *Appl. Phys. Lett.* **2016**, *109*, 054101. [CrossRef]
58. Sengupta, S.; Jackson, D.R.; Long, S.A. Modal analysis and propagation characteristics of leaky waves on a 2-D periodic leaky-wave antenna. *IEEE Trans. Microw. Theory Tech.* **2018**, *66*, 1181–1191. [CrossRef]
59. Fuscaldo, W.; Galli, A.; Jackson, D.R. Optimization of 1-D unidirectional leaky-wave antennas based on partially reflecting sheets. *IEEE Trans. Antennas Propag.* **2022**, *70*, 7853–7868. [CrossRef]
60. Ettorre, M.; Grbic, A. Generation of propagating Bessel beams using leaky-wave modes. *IEEE Trans. Antennas Propag.* **2012**, *60*, 3605–3613. [CrossRef]
61. Ettorre, M.; Rudolph, S.M.; Grbic, A. Generation of propagating Bessel beams using leaky-wave modes: Experimental validation. *IEEE Trans. Antennas Propag.* **2012**, *60*, 2645–2653. [CrossRef]
62. Lu, P.; Bréard, A.; Huillery, J.; Yang, X.S.; Voyer, D. Feeding coils design for TE-polarized Bessel antenna to generate rotationally symmetric magnetic field distribution. *IEEE Antennas Wirel. Propag. Lett.* **2018**, *17*, 2424–2428. [CrossRef]
63. Lu, P.; Voyer, D.; Bréard, A.; Huillery, J.; Allard, B.; Lin-Shi, X.; Yang, X.S. Design of TE-polarized Bessel antenna in microwave range using leaky-wave modes. *IEEE Trans. Antennas Propag.* **2017**, *66*, 32–41. [CrossRef]
64. Negri, E.; Fuscaldo, W.; Tofani, S.; Burghignoli, P.; Galli, A. An efficient and accurate semi-analytical matching technique for waveguide-fed antennas. *Sci. Rep.* **2024**, *14*, 3892. [CrossRef]
65. Feresidis, A.; Vardaxoglou, J. High gain planar antenna using optimised partially reflective surfaces. *IEE Proc. Microwaves Antennas Propag* **2001**, *148*, 345–350. [CrossRef]
66. Scattone, F.; Ettorre, M.; Sauleau, R.; Nguyen, N.T.; Fonseca, N.J. Optimization procedure for planar leaky-wave antennas with flat-topped radiation patterns. *IEEE Trans. Antennas Propag.* **2015**, *63*, 5854–5859. [CrossRef]
67. Guo, Y.X.; Chia, M.; Chen, Z.N.; Luk, K.M. Wide-band L-probe fed circular patch antenna for conical-pattern radiation. *IEEE Trans. Antennas Propag.* **2004**, *52*, 1115–1116. [CrossRef]
68. Mateo-Segura, C.; Feresidis, A.P.; Goussetis, G. Bandwidth enhancement of 2-D leaky-wave antennas with double-layer periodic surfaces. *IEEE Trans. Antennas Propag.* **2013**, *62*, 586–593. [CrossRef]
69. Von Trentini, G. Partially reflecting sheet arrays. *IRE Trans. Antennas Propag.* **1956**, *4*, 666–671. [CrossRef]
70. Zhao, T.; Jackson, D.; Williams, J.; Oliner, A. General formulas for 2-D leaky-wave antennas. *IEEE Trans. Antennas Propag.* **2005**, *53*, 3525–3533. [CrossRef]
71. Fuscaldo, W. Rigorous evaluation of losses in uniform leaky-wave antennas. *IEEE Trans. Antennas Propag.* **2020**, *68*, 643–655. [CrossRef]
72. Luukkonen, O.; Simovski, C.; Granet, G.; Goussetis, G.; Lioubtchenko, D.; Raisanen, A.V.; Tretyakov, S.A. Simple and accurate analytical model of planar grids and high-impedance surfaces comprising metal strips or patches. *IEEE Trans. Antennas Propag.* **2008**, *56*, 1624–1632. [CrossRef]
73. Tretyakov, S. *Analytical Modeling in Applied Electromagnetics*; Artech House: Norwood, MA, USA, 2003.
74. Lovat, G.; Burghignoli, P.; Jackson, D.R. Fundamental properties and optimization of broadside radiation from uniform leaky-wave antennas. *IEEE Trans. Antennas Propag.* **2006**, *54*, 1442–1452. [CrossRef]
75. Fuscaldo, W.; Burghignoli, P.; Galli, A. The transition between reactive and radiative regimes for leaky modes in planar waveguides based on homogenized partially reflecting surfaces. *IEEE Trans. Microw. Theory Tech.* **2020**, *68*, 5259–5269. [CrossRef]
76. Balanis, C.A. *Advanced Engineering Electromagnetics*; Wiley & Sons: New York, NY, USA, 2012.
77. Sorrentino, R.; Mongiardo, M. *Transverse Resonance Techniques*; John Wiley & Sons: New York, NY, USA, 2005. [CrossRef]
78. Felsen, L.B.; Marcuvitz, N. *Radiation and Scattering of Waves*; John Wiley & Sons: Hoboken, NJ, USA, 1994; Volume 31.
79. Jackson, D.R.; Oliner, A.A. A leaky-wave analysis of the high-gain printed antenna configuration. *IEEE Trans. Antennas Propag.* **1988**, *36*, 905–910. [CrossRef]

80. Jackson, D.R.; Alexopoulos, N.G. Gain enhancement methods for printed circuit antennas. *IEEE Trans. Antennas Propag.* **1985**, *33*, 976–987. [CrossRef]
81. Jackson, D.R.; Oliner, A.A.; Ip, A. Leaky-wave propagation and radiation for a narrow-beam multiple-layer dielectric structure. *IEEE Trans. Antennas Propag.* **1993**, *41*, 344–348. [CrossRef]
82. Fuscaldo, W.; Tofani, S.; Zografopoulos, D.C.; Baccarelli, P.; Burghignoli, P.; Beccherelli, R.; Galli, A. Systematic design of THz leaky-wave antennas based on homogenized metasurfaces. *IEEE Trans. Antennas Propag.* **2018**, *66*, 1169–1178. [CrossRef]
83. Fuscaldo, W.; Burghignoli, P.; Galli, A. Genealogy of leaky, surface, and plasmonic modes in partially open waveguides. *Phys. Rev. Appl.* **2022**, *17*, 34–38. [CrossRef]
84. Galdi, V.; Pinto, I.M. A simple algorithm for accurate location of leaky-wave poles for grounded inhomogeneous dielectric slabs. *Microw. Opt. Technol. Lett.* **2000**, *24*, 135–140. [CrossRef]
85. CST Products Dassault Systèmes, France. Version 2021. Available online: https://www.3ds.com/products/simulia/cst-studio-suite (accessed on 5 February 2025).
86. Ansys Corporation, Ansys HFSS Version 16.0, 1984–2016. Available online: https://www.ansys.com/it-it/products/electronics/ansys-hfss (accessed on 5 February 2025).
87. Comite, D.; Fuscaldo, W.; Podilchak, S.K.; Hílario-Re, P.D.; Gómez-Guillamón Buendía, V.; Burghignoli, P.; Baccarelli, P.; Galli, A. Radially periodic leaky-wave antenna for Bessel beam generation over a wide-frequency range. *IEEE Trans. Antennas Propag.* **2018**, *66*, 2828–2843. [CrossRef]
88. Pozar, D.M. *Microwave Engineering: Theory and Techniques*; John Wiley & Sons: Hoboken, NJ, USA, 2021.
89. Konstantinidis, K.; Feresidis, A.P.; Hall, P.S. Dual-slot feeding technique for broadband Fabry–Perot cavity antennas. *IET Microw. Antennas Propag.* **2015**, *9*, 861–866. [CrossRef]
90. Foster, R.M. A reactance theorem. *Bell Sys. Tech. J.* **1924**, *3*, 259–267. [CrossRef]
91. Baccarelli, P.; Burghignoli, P.; Di Nallo, C.; Frezza, F.; Galli, A.; Lampariello, P.; Ruggieri, G. Full-wave analysis of printed leaky-wave phased arrays. *Int. J. RF Microw. Comput.-Aided Eng.* **2002**, *12*, 272–287. [CrossRef]
92. Giusti, F.; Chen, Q.; Mesa, F.; Albani, M.; Quevedo-Teruel, O. Efficient Bloch analysis of general periodic structures with a linearized multimodal transfer-matrix approach. *IEEE Trans. Antennas Propag.* **2022**, *70*, 5555–5562. [CrossRef]
93. Valerio, G.; Paulotto, S.; Baccarelli, P.; Burghignoli, P.; Galli, A. Accurate Bloch analysis of 1-D periodic lines through the simulation of truncated structures. *IEEE Trans. Antennas Propag.* **2011**, *59*, 2188–2195. [CrossRef]
94. Mesa, F.; Valerio, G.; Rodríguez-Berral, R.; Quevedo-Teruel, O. Simulation-Assisted Efficient Computation of the Dispersion Diagram of Periodic Structures: A comprehensive overview with applications to filters, leaky-wave antennas and metasurfaces. *IEEE Antennas Propag. Mag.* **2021**, *63*, 33–45. [CrossRef]
95. Apaydin, N.; Zhang, L.; Sertel, K.; Volakis, J.L. Experimental validation of frozen modes guided on printed coupled Transmission Lines. *IEEE Trans. Microw. Theory Tech.* **2012**, *60*, 1513–1519. [CrossRef]
96. Negri, E.; Giusti, F.; Fuscaldo, W.; Burghignoli, P.; Martini, E.; Galli, A. Generation of a Long-Nondiffractive-Range Leaky-Wave Bessel Beam through an Open-Stopband Mitigation Technique. In Proceedings of the Int. Symp. Antennas Propag. (ISAP) 2024, Incheon, Republic of Korea, 5–8 November 2024; pp. 1–2.
97. Liu, J.; Zhou, W.; Long, Y. A simple technique for open-stopband suppression in periodic leaky-wave antennas using two nonidentical elements per unit cell. *IEEE Trans. Antennas Propag.* **2018**, *66*, 2741–2751. [CrossRef]
98. Al-Bassam, A.; Otto, S.; Heberling, D.; Caloz, C. Broadside dual-channel orthogonal-polarization radiation using a double-asymmetric periodic leaky-wave antenna. *IEEE Trans. Antennas Propag.* **2017**, *65*, 2855–2864. [CrossRef]

applied sciences

MDPI

Systematic Review

Comparative Study of Minimally Invasive Microwave Ablation Applicators

Nikolaos Karkanis [1], Theodoros N. F. Kaifas [1], Theodoros Samaras [2] and George A. Kyriacou [1,*]

[1] Department of Electrical and Computer Engineering, Democritus University of Thrace, 67100 Xanthi, Greece; nkarkani@ee.duth.gr (N.K.); tkaifas@ee.duth.gr (T.N.F.K.)
[2] Department of Physics, Aristotle University of Thessaloniki, 54124 Thessaloniki, Greece; theosama@auth.gr
* Correspondence: gkyriac@ee.duth.gr

Abstract: This work presents a comparative analysis of microwave ablation applicators, including both antenna-based and open waveguide designs, which are guided and inserted into tumors via catheters. Applicators previously proposed in the literature are evaluated through both electromagnetic and thermal simulations. The objective is to assess temperature distribution within the tumor and surrounding healthy tissues; with a focus on identifying patterns of heat diffusion. Although a variety of applicators have been designed, each typically operates at different central frequency or targets specific tumor shapes and tissue types. In this study, we standardize conditions by analyzing multiple applicators' designs for the same tumor type. The results highlight the shape of the ablation zone and corresponding temperature distribution, offering insights into potential healthy tissue damage. This comparative analysis provides critical information for optimizing microwave ablation applicators for more precise and effective treatment.

Keywords: microwave ablation; Specific Absorption Rate (SAR); temperature distribution; ablation zone; aspect ratio

1. Introduction

Microwave ablation (MWA) has emerged as a prominent thermal therapy technique for the treatment of tumors. As a minimally invasive procedure, it offers a promising alternative to traditional surgical methods, providing the benefits of reduced recovery time, lower risk of complications and side effects and the potential for outpatient treatment. Therefore, MWA is a powerful tool in the fight against cancer, a disease that has plagued humanity from its emergence and is one of the leading causes of death worldwide. The primary mechanism of MWA involves the use of microwave energy to generate heat, inducing localized coagulative necrosis of tumor cells. This procedure has been effectively applied to a range of cancers, including liver, lung, kidney, bone tumors etc., making it a versatile tool in the oncological arsenal [1–5].

The efficacy and safety of microwave tumor ablation heavily depends on the design and performance of the microwave applicator and the device responsible for delivering microwave energy to the targeted tissue [6]. Various microwave applicators have been developed, each with unique characteristics that influence their heating patterns, penetration depth, and overall ablation efficiency. The fundamental designs for antennas include monopole, dipole, and slot antennas [6–11]. These antennas typically generate "comet-shaped" ablation zones due to backward heating along the antenna shaft, that in turn is caused by leaking currents mainly resulting from the unbalanced structure of the antennas. This leads to the unintended burning of not only the tumor but also of healthy tissue. To address this issue, modified antennas have been proposed through the incorporation of chokes or sleeves [6,7,12–18]. These modifications improve the radiation pattern and reduce the backward heating effect, thereby minimizing the tail of the comet-shaped ablation zones.

Initially, chokes and sleeves were added externally to the antenna, but more recent designs have integrated these components within the antenna structure to reduce invasiveness [6,7,19,20]. Additionally, backward heating has been mitigated by incorporating more slots into the antenna design [6,7,21–26] or by employing cooling systems (water-cooled antennas [27–31], gas-cooled antennas [32–34]). Alternative designs include helix and spiral antennas [7,35–41] and flexible antennas as well [42]. Finally, in case it is not possible to achieve the desired efficiency when optimizing the structural/electrical parameters of the antenna alone, an impedance matching network can be introduced into the design to further enhance the antenna's performance [6,35].

Another solution to achieve impedance matching and improve the antenna's performance is a balun (balanced-to-unbalanced transformer). This is a critical component in antenna systems to transition between balanced and unbalanced circuits while preserving the desired signal characteristics. Balanced systems, such as dipole antennas, have two symmetrical conductors with equal and opposite currents, while unbalanced systems, such as coaxial cables, consist of a single conductor with a return path through a ground plane. Without a balun, the unbalanced nature of the feed line can induce undesired currents on the outer surface of the coaxial cable, leading to distortions in the radiation pattern, increased reflections, and unwanted heating along the feed line. Various balun designs have been developed to address these issues, including $\lambda/4$ sleeves, choke baluns, and tapered-slot configurations. These designs introduce high-impedance points or suppress surface currents, ensuring effective impedance matching and minimizing interference. The choice of balun modification depends on the specific application, bandwidth requirements, and physical constraints, making it a versatile solution for achieving efficient and reliable antenna performance in diverse scenarios.

Therefore, the choice of applicator plays a crucial role in achieving optimal therapeutic outcomes. Factors such as the geometry of the applicator, operating frequency and cooling mechanisms can significantly affect the precision of energy delivery and the extent of the ablation zone.

The designed applicators include the monopole (initial design) [43], capacitive capped monopole antenna [44], dual-slot antenna [45], multi-slot antenna [21], floating sleeve dipole (FSD) antenna [46], choke dipole antenna [47], triaxial antenna [47], balun-free base-fed monopole (balun-free helical antenna) [47], balun-free helical dipole antenna [48], and a helical open waveguide structure (featuring a helix with an increasing radius starting at the end of the outer conductor of the coaxial cable) [41]. The selection of these designs is deliberate. The basic monopole design was initially implemented to observe the comet-shaped ablation zone, followed by the dual-slot antenna, a modified design intended to address the backward heating issue. The triaxial and choke dipole antennas, along with the FSD dipole antenna, were incorporated because they are utilized in commercial MWA systems approved by the U.S. Food and Drug Administration (FDA) [47]. According to [21,44], multi-slot antenna and capacitive capped monopole antenna provide more spherical ablation zones than others. Moreover, the FSD antenna was implemented on the grounds that it provides similar results to the balun-free helical antenna. Finally, all helical designs were included to compare them with our recent work [41].

The first part of this study concerns the benefits of helical open waveguide structure and the comparison with monopole. Then, the work focuses on the precise simulation of all these designs as presented in previous works. To ensure accuracy, the dimensions, lengths, boundaries, frequency, properties, and materials used were closely aligned with those in the corresponding papers. This alignment is essential for conducting a fair and valid comparison of all indicative applicators considered. After performing the simulations and confirming that the results, specifically the temperature distribution, closely match those of the corresponding parsing studies, the final part of the study is undertaken. This involves implementing all designs within a two-compartment model (tumor and healthy tissue), which provides a reasonably accurate representation of anatomical geometry [49].

This paper aims at comparing the different microwave applicators used in microwave tumor ablation, focusing on their design principles and studying for the same tumor. These published studies have mainly focused on the liver using a two-compartment model, which applies different properties to tumor and healthy tissue. A two-compartment model is already a good approximation in terms of anatomical geometry. However, it is crucial to use accurate tissue properties for each compartment, as the predicted treatment outcome is highly sensitive to these parameters. Ultimately, this study compares the temperature distribution of different applicators when applied to the same tumor models as well as the shape of the ablated region and its impact on healthy tissue.

To sum up, this work provides the first comparative study where multiple, published, microwave applicators are simulated under unified conditions. The novelty of this study lies in its approach: simulations are conducted under standardized conditions, including a two-compartment model that better approximates real experimental results.

2. Materials and Methods

2.1. Applicators Structure: Geometrical Characteristics

The applicators to be examined herein (the authors made any possible effort to comply with the PRISMA process [50]) are illustrated in Figure 1 and are proposed in [21,41,43–48]. The complete flow diagram detailing the PRISMA screening and selection process is provided in the Supplementary Materials (see Supplementary Figure S1).

The triaxial, choke dipole, balun-free base-fed monopole, balun-free helical dipole, and multi-slot antennas are all constructed out of UT-085C. The FSD antenna (Figure 1g) was fabricated using 50 Ω UT-085C-LL semi-rigid coaxial cable from Micro-Coax (Pottstown, PA, USA). The monopole antenna (Figure 1) was constructed out of RG-405. The dimensions of the coaxial cable of the capacitive capped monopole, dual-slot antennas, and helical open waveguide were specifically defined by authors for their optimal applicators' performance. Furthermore, all the applicators with their geometrical parameters are presented at Figure 1 and enlisted with detail in accompanying Tables, (Tables 1 and 2).

Table 1. Coaxial cable dimensions of the designs under study.

Coaxial Cable Dimensions	Outer Conductor Diameter (mm)	Inner Conductor Diameter (mm)	Center Conductor Diameter (mm)	Commercial Coaxial Cables	Figure, References
Monopole	2.18	1.68	0.51	RG-405	Figure 1a, [43]
Capacitive capped monopole	2.197	1.676	0.511	NA	Figure 1b, [44]
Multi-slot	2.2	1.68	0.51	UT-085C	Figure 1c, [21]
Dual-slot	0.86	0.66	0.2	NA	Figure 1d, [45]
Triaxial	2.2	1.68	0.51	UT-085C	Figure 1e, [47]
Choke dipole	2.2	1.68	0.51	UT-085C	Figure 1f, [47]
Balun-free base-fed monopole	2.2	1.68	0.51	UT-085C	Figure 1g, [47]
FSD	2.2	1.676	0.515	UT-085C-LL	Figure 1h, [46]
Balun-free helical dipole	2.38	1.67	0.51	UT-085C	Figure 1i, [48]
Helical open waveguide	7.96	6.36	1.9	NA	Figure 1j, [41]

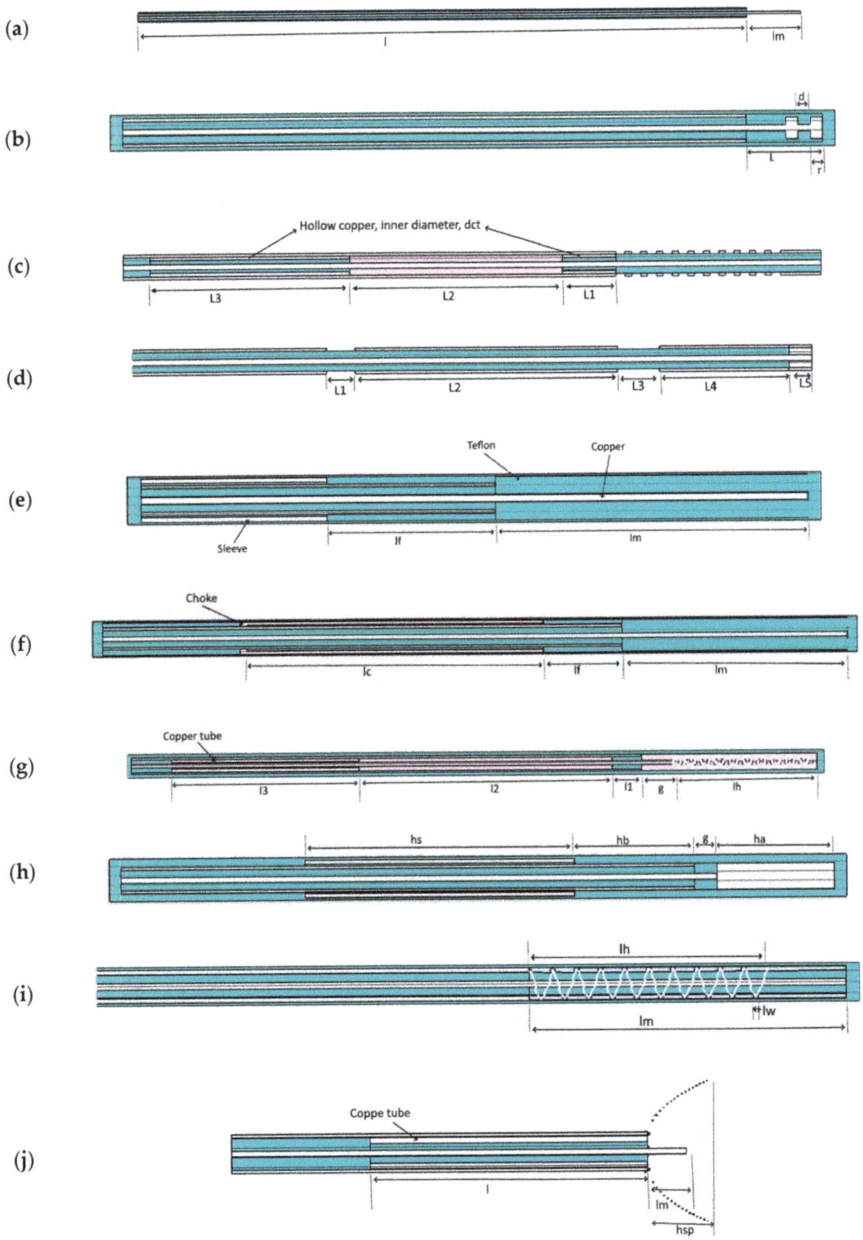

Figure 1. Topology of all designs considered in this work. The above figures represent: Monopole [43] (**a**), Capacitive capped monopole antenna [44] (**b**), Multi-slot antenna [21] (**c**), Dual-slot antenna [45] (**d**), Triaxial antenna [47] (**e**), Choke antenna [47] (**f**), Balun-free base-fed monopole antenna [47] (**g**), Floating sleeve dipole (FSD) antenna [46] (**h**), Balun-free helical dipole antenna [48] (**i**), and Helical open waveguide structure [41] (**j**). The light blue, purple, and white colors indicate Teflon, air, and copper, respectively.

Table 2. Details of the designs' parameter values (all parameters listed in Table 2 correspond to magnitudes depicted in Figure 1 for the respective applicators).

Design	Values of Parameters (mm)	Overall Diameter (mm)	Frequency (GHz)	Power (W)
Monopole	l = 140, lm = 12.7	2.18	2.45	40
Capacitive capped monopole	L = 6.2, r = 1, d = 1	2.797	5.8	10
Multi-slot	L1 = 4.8,L2 = 19,L3 = 18,dct = 1.1, N = 10, s = 0.8, w = 0.6	2.6	2.45	30
Dual-slot	L1 = 1, L2 = 9, L3 = 1.44, L4 = 4.5, L5 = 0.8	1	2.45	NA
Triaxial	lf = 12.5, lm = 23.5, inner and outer diameter of sleeve = 2.5 and 3.2	3.5	1.9	40
Choke dipole	lc = 30, lf = 8, lm = 23, inner and outer diameter of choke = 2.5 and 3.2	3.5	1.9	40
Balun-free base-fed monopole	l3 = 26, l2 = 35, l1 = 4, g = 4, lh = 20, N = 10 number of turns of helix, inner diameter of copper tube = 0.876	3.1	1.9	40
FSD	hs = 23.5, hb = 10.4, g = 2, ha = 10.4, inner and outer diameter of sleeve = 2.5 and 3.2	3.5	1.9	42
Balun-free helical dipole	lm = 24, lh = 18, N = 9.9 number of turns of helix	2.8	1.9	42
Helical open waveguide	lm = 7.61, N = 4 number of spirals, hsp = 12 mm, l = 56.56 mm, inner diameter of copper tube = 2.546 mm	7.96	0.915	25

2.2. Comparison Criteria Definition

In microwave ablation (MWA), an optimal antenna is characterized by minimal invasiveness to the patient, high energy transmission efficiency, and the ability to achieve a target ablation zone with precision in both size and shape [6]. Additional important criteria include the antenna's peak temperature, deposited power, temperature distribution, insertion depth, and the control of heat dispersion within healthy tissue.

The evaluation and comparison of antenna and waveguide designs are based on these essential criteria. In the following sections, the applicators' dimensions are detailed, and simulations verifying existing studied designs are presented. Additionally, the Specific Absorption Rate (SAR) and temperature distribution at a standardized insertion depth and deposited power are analyzed. Finally, the dimensions of the ablation zone and the aspect ratio are presented to enable a thorough comparison and analysis.

2.3. Simulation Framework and Methods for Applicator Analysis

Microwave ablation (MWA) involves the absorption of electromagnetic energy by biological tissues, leading to localized heating. The electromagnetic field distribution is governed by Maxwell's equations:

$$\nabla \mathrm{x} \vec{\mathrm{E}} = -j\omega\mu\vec{\mathrm{H}} \tag{1}$$

$$\nabla \mathrm{x} \vec{\mathrm{H}} = \vec{\mathrm{J}} + j\omega\varepsilon\vec{\mathrm{E}} \tag{2}$$

where $\vec{\mathrm{E}}$ and $\vec{\mathrm{H}}$ are the electric and magnetic fields, ε is the electrical permittivity, μ is the magnetic permeability, ω is the angular frequency and $\vec{\mathrm{J}}$ is the current density.

These equations are coupled with tissue dielectric properties to calculate the power deposition in tissues, quantified as Specific Absorption Rate (SAR) [51]:

$$\mathrm{SAR} = \frac{\sigma}{2\rho}||\vec{\mathrm{E}}||^2 \tag{3}$$

where σ is the tissue conductivity $\overrightarrow{E}$ is the electric field strength and ρ is the tissue density. The resultant heat diffusion in the tissue is governed by the Penne's bioheat equation:

$$\rho c \frac{dT}{dt} = \nabla \cdot k \nabla T + Q - \omega_{bl} c_{bl} (T - T_{bl}) + Q_{meta} \tag{4}$$

where ρ and c are the tissue density and specific heat, T is the temperature, k is the thermal conductivity, Q represents the heat generated by electromagnetic absorption (SAR), the perfusion term accounts for cooling by blood flow $\omega_{bl} c_{bl} (T - T_{bl})$, and Q_{meta} reflects tissue metabolism.

In the electromagnetic simulations, boundary conditions of Perfectly Matched Layers (PMLs) are applied at the computational domain boundaries to absorb outgoing waves and prevent artificial reflections. For thermal boundary conditions, a constant temperature is assumed at the tissue surface, set to body temperature (37 °C). This assumption simplifies the modeling while aligning with the study's focus on standardized comparisons across applicator designs.

These equations and conditions provide the foundation for accurate modeling of electromagnetic and thermal fields, enabling the standardized comparison of applicator designs in this study. By incorporating realistic material properties and boundary conditions, this approach ensures that simulation results are closely aligned with experimental and clinical scenarios. Herein, a commercial electromagnetic simulator (CST) is utilized which incorporates the above equations and reliably solves both the electromagnetic and thermal problems.

2.4. *Verification of Already Existed Designs*

We present the verification of existing designs as modeled herein by comparing them with those reported in the literature. The purpose of this section is to ensure that the applicators are correctly constructed as intended by the proposing researchers. The temperature profiles, power settings, and material properties (both dielectric and thermal) used in the simulations are aligned with or closely matched to those in the referenced studies. In cases where certain values were not explicitly provided—for instance, power is not specified in reference [45], and precise dielectric properties are absent in references [21,43,46–48]—we have approximated these parameters as closely as possible. This verification is illustrated in Figure 2.

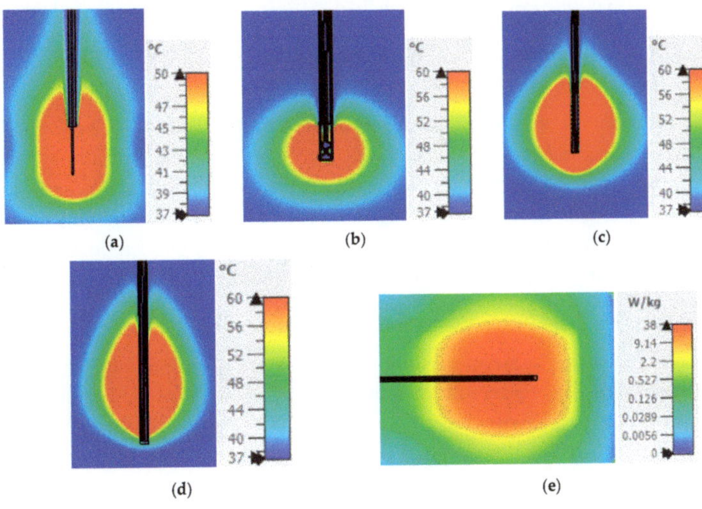

Figure 2. *Cont.*

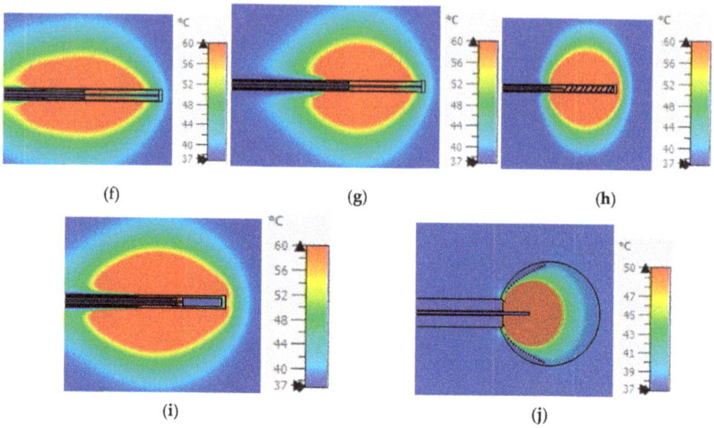

Figure 2. SAR of dual-slot and temperature distribution (ablation zone) of all the other designs and comparison with the figures (experiments or simulations) in their corresponding references. (**a**) Monopole → Figure 6 in [43]; (**b**) Capacitive capped monopole → Figure 4 in [44]; (**c**) Multi-slot → Figures 2 and 7 in [21]; (**d**) Balun-free helical dipole → Figures 5 and 7 in [48]; (**e**) Dual-slot → Figure 12 in [45]; (**f**) Triaxial → Figures 4 and 5 in [47]; (**g**) Choke → Figures 4 and 5 in [47]; (**h**) Balun-free base-fed monopole → Figures 4 and 5 in [47]; (**i**) FSD → Figures 4 and 9 in [46]; (**j**) Helical open waveguide → Figure 7 in [41].

Although all the applicators reviewed in this work were previously simulated, designed, and tested in their respective publications [21,41,43–48], it was deemed necessary to repeat the simulations using the same phantom model utilized in the corresponding trials to ensure a reliable and fair comparison. Initially, a simulation replicating the original model and conditions was conducted to verify the reported performance. Subsequently, each applicator was inserted into a tumor and simulated to evaluate its SAR and temperature distribution. These results are compared according to the criteria defined above.

The applicators in Figure 2a,c,d,f,g,i retain the comet-tail shape of ablation area, which causes difficulties in ensuring the safe exposure of healthy tissues on the back side of the applicators. On the contrary, the treated area is closer to a spherical shape in Figure 2b,h. However, it is only in Figure 2j that the ablation area is restricted inside the tapered spiral providing the means to control the exposure of the healthy tissue.

3. Results

This section presents a comparative analysis of the simulation results for the applicators, focusing on Specific Absorption Rate (SAR) and temperature distribution. First, the simulation results are provided for all designs using identical parameters as reported by the original authors. Subsequently, simulations are presented for both a homogeneous model and a two-compartment model, each with consistent power deposition, identical healthy tissue and tumor properties, and the same placement insertion depth.

3.1. Performance of the Homogeneous Model for All Designs

In this part of the paper, simulation results for Specific Absorption Rate (SAR) and temperature distribution are presented for all designs within a homogeneous model corresponding to a mean biological tissue with $\varepsilon_r = 46.8$ and $\sigma = 0.861$ at 915 MHz [52]. The simulations were conducted with consistent power deposition and the same insertion depth across all designs. Explicit comparisons follow in the two next subsections.

3.1.1. Specific Absorption Rate (SAR) of the Homogeneous Model for All Designs

In this analysis, we examine the SAR distribution of all applicators using the same homogeneous model (Figure 3). According to IEEE norm [51], SAR should be measured or defined as a mean value averaged over either 1 g or 10 g of mass, namely, corresponding to 1 cm^3 or 10 cm^3 of tissue. However, the numerical simulator estimates the "point SAR" in order to be accurately transferred to the Pennes bioheat diffusion equation solver. This approach may involve overestimation of point defined power absorption around metallic edges and particularly near metallic tips and corners. In turn, this may yield unexpected, overestimated local temperatures. In Figure 3, we present SAR contours at levels of 2.5, 5, 7.5, and 10 W/kg.

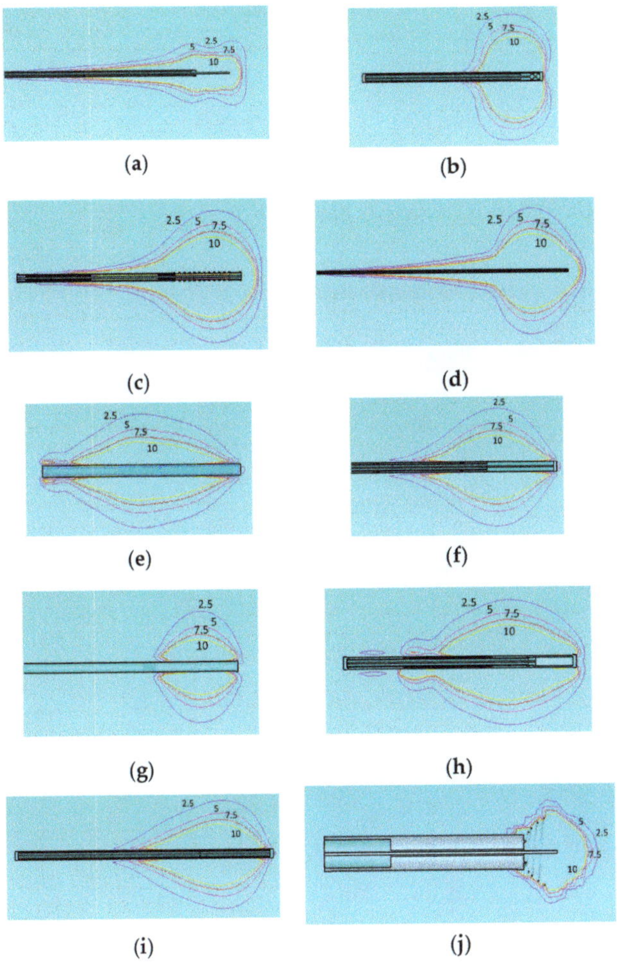

Figure 3. Specific Absorption Rate (SAR) of the different applicators embedded in a homogeneous tissue with ε_r = 46.8, σ = 0.861 at 915 MHz. Monopole antenna (**a**), capacitive capped monopole antenna (**b**), multi-slot coaxial antenna (**c**), dual-slot antenna (**d**), triaxial antenna (**e**), choke dipole antenna (**f**), balun-free base-fed monopole (**g**), floating sleeve dipole antenna (FSD) (**h**), balun-free helical dipole antenna (**i**), helical open waveguide structure (**j**) at one model (healthy tissue). The blue, purple, red, and yellow colors indicate SAR contours of 2.5, 5, 7.5, and 10 W/kg, respectively.

The 2.5 W/kg contour represents a low exposure level, generally regarded as safe according to norm [51]. The 5 W/kg contour indicates moderate exposure, which may still fall within safe limits for healthy tissue. The 7.5 W/kg contour approaches levels where caution may be necessary, depending on the duration of exposure. Finally, the 10 W/kg contour reflects a high exposure level that could increase the risk of thermal damage, particularly with prolonged exposure. Regarding the shape of the treated area, the same observation noted for Figure 2 also applies to Figure 3 exhibiting comet-tail, nearly spherical, or nearly rectangular shapes.

3.1.2. Temperature Distribution of the Homogeneous Model for All Designs

We examine the temperature distribution in Figure 4 of all the above applicators using the same homogeneous model.

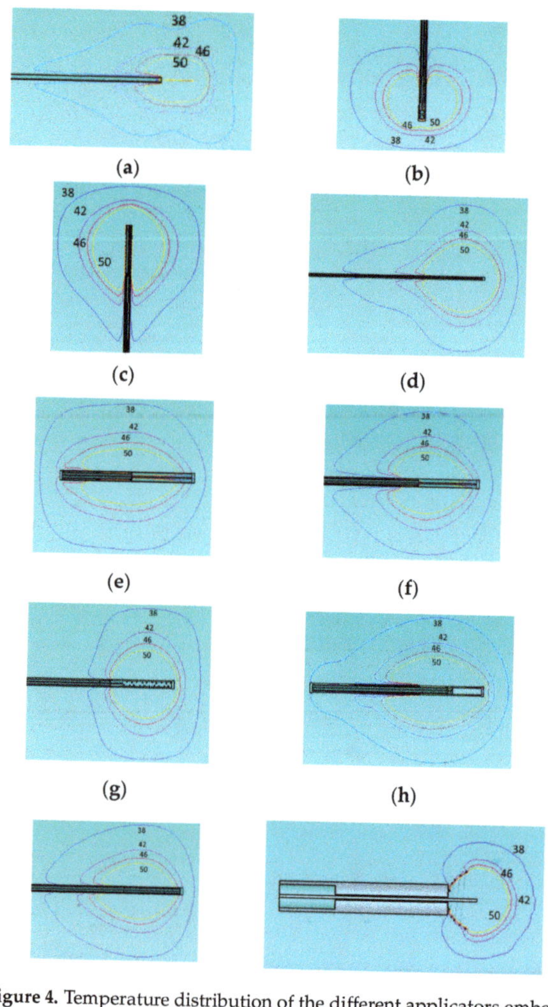

Figure 4. Temperature distribution of the different applicators embedded in a homogeneous tissue with $\varepsilon_r = 46.8$, $\sigma = 0.861$ at 915 MHz. Monopole antenna (**a**), capacitive capped monopole antenna (**b**), multi-slot coaxial antenna (**c**), dual-slot antenna (**d**), triaxial antenna (**e**), choke dipole antenna (**f**), balun-free base-fed monopole (**g**), floating sleeve dipole antenna (FSD) (**h**), balun-free helical dipole antenna (**i**), and helical open waveguide structure (**j**). The blue, purple, red, and yellow colors indicate temperature contours of 38 °C, 42 °C, 46 °C, and 50 °C, respectively.

We present the temperature contours of 38, 42, 46, and 50 degrees Celsius. We examine especially these contours on the grounds that irreversible changes start at 38 °C and beyond, the possibility of cell necrosis starts at 42 °C, the cancer cells are destroyed into few hours at 46 °C and into few minutes at 50 °C. The shapes of the temperature equi-level lines follow that of the SAR. The desired spherical or rectangular shapes, assumed more adaptable to tumor ones, are supported again by capacitive capped (b), multi-slot coaxial (c), balun-free (g), and open helical (j) cases. However, only the last one is promising to control-restrict the area above 42 °C inside the tumor. As we can see from Figure 4, the results of our simulations for the homogeneous model are close to what depicted in the corresponding papers [21,41,43–48]. However, as shown next in Section 3.3.2, the behavior of temperature distribution changes when we are using a more realistic two-compartment model for the tumor.

3.2. Temperature Distribution of Helical Open Waveguide Structure vs. Monopole for the Two-Compartment Model

The helical open waveguide structure [41] is discussed here, with simulation results presented to demonstrate its flexibility in producing various ablation zone shapes.

Figure 5 presents two designs in which the spirals are arranged in a suboptimal configuration, reducing their effectiveness in containing the electromagnetic field within the tumor. This arrangement results in unintended exposure of surrounding healthy tissue to potentially harmful levels of electromagnetic energy. Figure 5a depicts a helical open waveguide structure consisting of three spirals, while Figure 5b shows a structure with two spirals. Both configurations share a height of 12 mm and a monopole length of 7.61 mm.

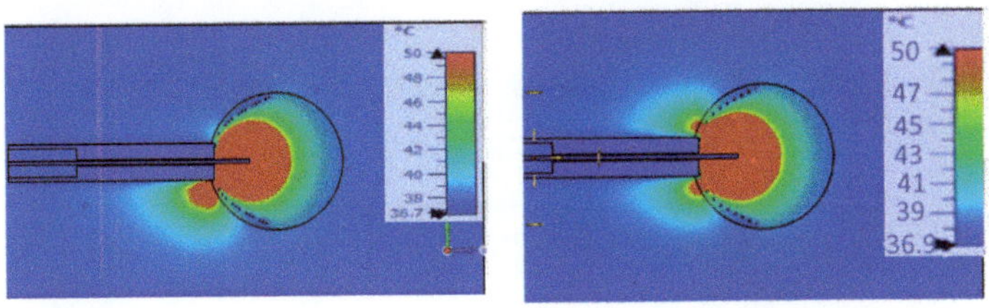

(a) (b)

Figure 5. Temperature distribution of suboptimum designs of the helical open waveguide structure: (a) with 3 spirals, (b) with 2 spirals.

The adjustment of the number of spirals, in combination with their opening (e.g., different openings for tumors with diameters of 3 cm and 2 cm) and the dimensions of the coaxial cable, play a crucial role in mitigating the issue of backward heating. This issue can be effectively addressed by increasing the number of spirals, as demonstrated in Figure 6. Figure 6 illustrates the ablation zones produced under different configurations.

These results demonstrate that by adjusting the power of the generator and altering the monopole length and spiral height, it is possible to produce various ablation zone shapes. In the first two images (a, b), the ablation zone assumes a spherical shape. In images (c, d), simulations present an ellipsoid-shaped ablation zone. In images (e–g), the simulations depict a bell-shaped ablation zone. These simulations were conducted on a large intestine model with a tumor diameter of 3 cm and power source 25 W, with the properties of both the large intestine and tumor taken from [41], as large intestine $\varepsilon_r = 57$, $\sigma = 1.09$, and tumor $\varepsilon_r{}^t = 60$, $\sigma^t = 0.67$. The tissue and tumor model in this section is placed in the large intestine, consistent with [41], which initially analyzed the helical open waveguide structure under these conditions. This study extends the findings of [41] by performing a parametric analysis of the same antenna, varying the monopole length and spiral height to optimize its performance in the large intestine model. In contrast, for simulations in other sections, we employed a liver model to provide a unified evaluation framework for comparing different designs. This approach ensures both consistency with prior studies and meaningful cross-design comparisons.

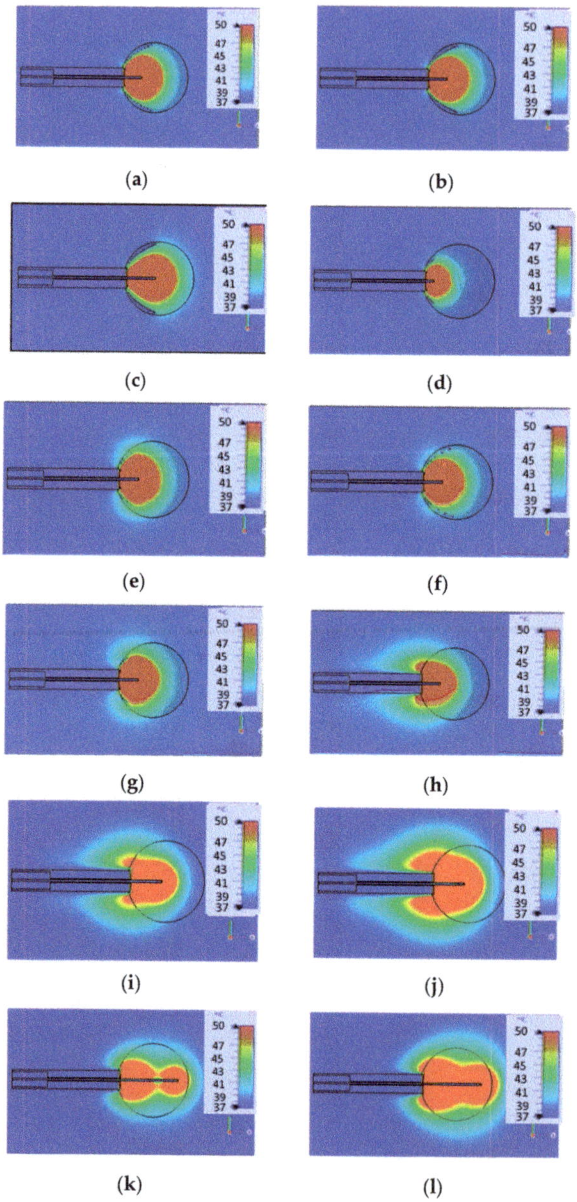

Figure 6. Parametric analysis of helical open waveguide structure (**a–g**) and design of monopole (**h–l**): 2 spirals with height = 3 mm and 2 spirals with height = 12 mm (**a**), 4 spirals with height = 12 mm (**b**), 4 spirals with height = 12 mm (**c**), 4 spirals with height = 3 mm (**d**), 2 spirals with height = 1 mm and 2 spirals with height = 4.5 mm (**e**), 3 spirals with height = 3 mm and 1 spiral with height = 12 mm (**f**), 4 spirals with height = 3 mm (**g**). The length of monopole is 7.61 mm at (**a**,**b**,**e–h**), 12 mm at (**c**,**i**,**j**), 3 mm at (**d**), and 24 mm at (**k**,**l**).

In the final images (h–l), the monopole design is depicted for different lengths (7.61 cm: h, 12 cm: i, j and 24 cm: k, l) and different source powers (25 W: images h, i, k, and 50 W: j, l). For (h, i, j) cases, the backward heating problem persists, resulting in a comet-shaped ablation zone that leads to the burning of healthy tissue. In contrast, in all other simulations, the backward heating issue is eliminated by properly adjusting the number and the density of the helices, confining the heat to the tumor and leaving the surrounding healthy tissue unaffected.

The results of Figure 6 indicate that the spirals function as a shield, effectively trapping the electromagnetic field within the spiral structure, and consequently within the tumor. To achieve this desired outcome, extensive simulations and careful refinements are required.

In summary, the number of spiral turns and their configuration play a critical role in achieving the desired outcome: eliminating backward heating and ensuring that only the tumor is ablated. Additionally, the open and tapered helical structure provides flexibility in shaping ablation zones, enhancing the safety and precision of microwave ablation as a treatment modality.

3.3. Performance of the Two-Compartment Model for All Designs

In this segment of the study, simulation results for Specific Absorption Rate (SAR) and temperature distribution are presented for all designs within a two-compartment model corresponding to a mean biological tissue $\varepsilon_r = 46.8$ and $\sigma = 0.861$ and tumor with $\varepsilon_r = 57.09$ and $\sigma = 1.05$ at 915 MHz [52,53]. The simulations were conducted with consistent power deposition and the same insertion depth across all designs. Explicit comparisons follow in the two next subsections.

3.3.1. Specific Absorption Rate (SAR) of the Two-Compartment Model for All Designs

Figure 7 presents the SAR distribution of a two-compartment model across all designs.

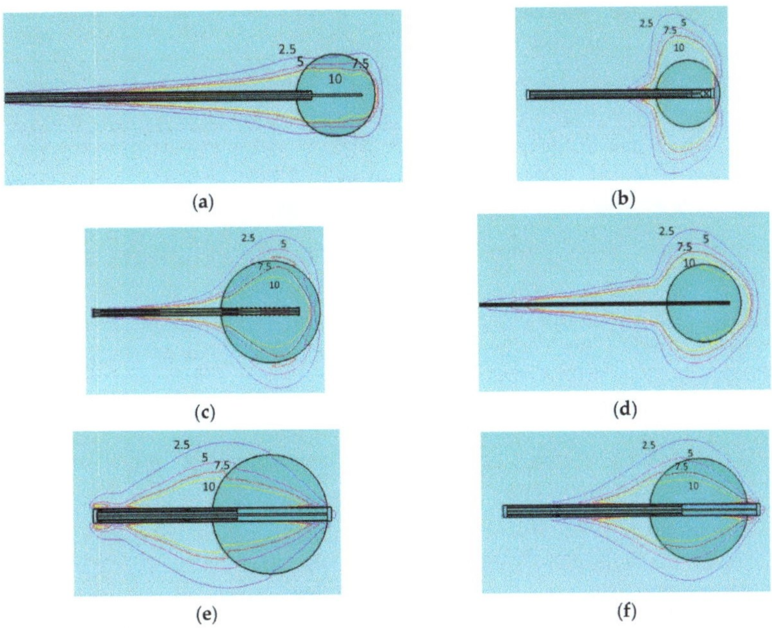

Figure 7. *Cont.*

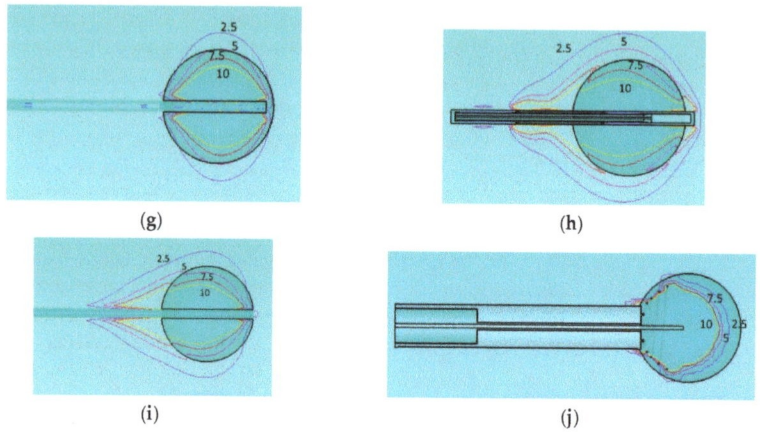

Figure 7. Specific Absorption Rate (SAR) with a deposited power of 40 W of monopole antenna (**a**), capacitive capped monopole antenna (**b**), multi-slot coaxial antenna (**c**), dual-slot antenna (**d**), triaxial antenna (**e**), choke dipole antenna (**f**), balun-free base-fed monopole (**g**), floating sleeve dipole antenna (FSD) (**h**), balun-free helical dipole antenna (**i**), and helical open waveguide structure (**j**) in the two-compartment model (healthy tissue and tumor). The blue, purple, red, and yellow colors indicate SAR contours of 2.5, 5, 7.5, and 10 W/kg, respectively.

All simulations were conducted using the same tumor type with consistent properties. It is obvious that only two applicators restrict the electromagnetic energy within the tumor. These are the balun-free base-fed monopole (Figure 7g) and the helical open waveguide (Figure 7j). Explicitly, one may see that the 7.5 W/kg contour lies entirely inside the tumor only for these two cases.

3.3.2. Temperature Distribution of the Two-Compartment Model for All Designs

This part of the results addresses the temperature distribution across all designs within a two-compartment model. The corresponding results are displayed in Figure 8. It is again clear that only the two applicators Figure 8g,j show the temperature contours above 42 °C restricted inside or slightly outside the tumor boundary. Since it is desired to cauterize a ring of about 1 cm beyond the tumor boundary, Figure 8g is obtained for the appropriate deposited power of 40 W. However, the applicator of Figure 8j allows for an additional small increase of the source power.

We analyze the temperature distribution of all the, aforementioned, applicators using both a simple model and a two-compartment model. The temperature contours at 38 °C, 42 °C, 46 °C, and 50 °C are presented. As mentioned before, these specific contours are of particular interest because irreversible changes in tissue begin at 38 °C, cell necrosis becomes possible at 42 °C, and cancer cells are destroyed within a few hours at 46 °C and within a few minutes at 50 °C.

The tumor diameter was set to 3 cm for the multi-slot, triaxial, choke, FSD, balun-free base-fed monopole, and balun-free helical dipole antennas, and 2 cm for the monopole, capacitive monopole, dual-slot antennas, and helical open waveguide. This variation is based on the ablation zone dimensions reported in the literature and the attempt to confine the treatment temperature (50 °C) within the tumor. Both tumor models were assumed to be perfectly spherical. As observed, there are notable differences between the homogeneous model and the two-compartment model.

A comparative description of Figures 2–7 is given next in the discussion section.

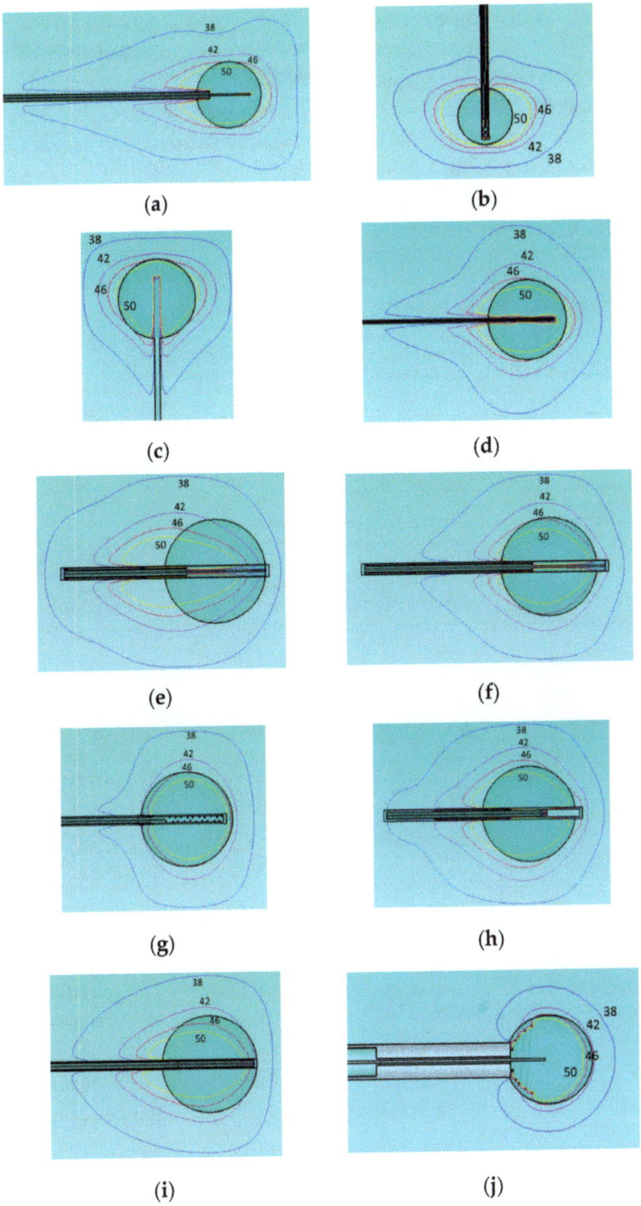

Figure 8. Temperature distribution with a deposited power of 40 W of monopole antenna (**a**), capacitive capped monopole antenna (**b**), multi-slot coaxial antenna (**c**), dual-slot antenna (**d**), triaxial antenna (**e**), choke dipole antenna (**f**), balun-free base-fed monopole (**g**), floating sleeve dipole antenna (FSD) (**h**), balun-free helical dipole antenna (**i**), and helical open waveguide structure (**j**) in the two-compartment model (healthy tissue and tumor). The blue, purple, red, and yellow colors indicate temperature contours of 38 °C, 42 °C, 46 °C, and 50 °C, respectively.

3.4. Quantitative Comparison of Ablation Performance Across Applicators Under Standardized Conditions

The final focus of the results is to provide a quantitative comparison of all designs. To ensure consistency, each applicator design is initially positioned within healthy tissue (homogeneous model—HM) and subsequently within healthy tissue with tumor (two-compartment model—TCM) at the same insertion depth, with all configurations set to receive an identical power level (same deposited power equal to 40 W). Comparison criteria include maximum temperature, ablation zone dimensions (diameter and length), aspect ratio, and dimensions penetration of the 38 °C zone into healthy tissue. The outcomes of this comparison are summarized in Table 3. It is observed that the maximum temperature is too high for the applicators; Figure 1g,j presented the best energy concentration inside the tumor.

Table 3. Comparison of all designs as aware of maximum temperature, ablation zone, and aspect ratio (in all cases, the absorbed power deposited in the tissues was the same and equal to 40 W).

Design	Maximum Temperature (°C)		Ablation Diameter/d_1 (mm)		Ablation Length/d_2 (mm)		Aspect Ratio (d_2/d_1)		Figure, References
	HM	TCM	HM	TCM	HM	TCM	HM	TCM	
Monopole	142	160.7	18.3	18.4	28	30.6	1.53	1.66	Figure 1a, [43]
Capacitive capped monopole	145.1	117.1	30.3	34.8	22.1	21.2	0.73	0.61	Figure 1b, [44]
Multi-slot	84.8	79.45	26.9	31.4	32.8	29.6	1.22	0.94	Figure 1c, [21]
Dual-slot	143.9	96.9	22	18.8	25.5	25.5	1.16	1.36	Figure 1d, [45]
Triaxial	76.8	68.6	23.2	23.7	40.6	38.7	1.75	1.63	Figure 1e, [47]
Choke dipole	86.1	79.7	26.3	26.6	32.2	32.2	1.22	1.21	Figure 1f, [47]
Balun-free base-fed monopole	121.3	124.6	27.9	28.1	26.4	26.2	0.95	0.93	Figure 1g, [47]
FSD	95.2	74.1	24.4	27.4	35.8	31.3	1.47	1.14	Figure 1h, [46]
Balun-free helical dipole	116.2	98.1	22.9	28.4	32.6	33.8	1.42	1.19	Figure 1i, [48]
Helical open waveguide	187	150.3	18.9	19	17.5	16.9	0.93	0.89	Figure 1j, [41]

However, this can be reduced by lowering the microwave source power without any compromise in the ablation zone shape. Besides that, this maximum temperature value may be fictitiously caused by the high values of the considered point SAR. In turn, excessive SAR values are related to field singularities at metallic edges. In any case, this issue needs further examination through careful research. Table 4 illustrates the performance metrics of applicators after power reduction to achieve safe maximum temperature. We consider values close to 100 °C as the maximum temperature, where the water starts to boil and evaporate.

Although water evaporation may seem to involve major complications, there is no clear relevance in the standards, e.g., Ref. [51], denoting a maximum allowable temperature. Notably, the deposited power was reduced as shown in Table 4 to 10–30 W to maintain a maximum temperature close to 100 °C. The highest reduction was observed in the most focusing applicator of helical open waveguide. The question is whether, in most cases where the deposited energy is restricted within the tumor, the entire tumor is uniformly covered/ablated. To examine this option, the corresponding temperature distribution is depicted in Figure 9.

Table 4. Comparison of applicators with adjusted power to maintain safe maximum temperature limits (HM = homogeneous model, TCM = two compartment model).

Design	Deposited Power (W)		Maximum Temperature (°C)		Ablation Diameter/d_1 (mm)		Ablation Length/d_2 (mm)		Aspect Ratio (d_2/d_1)		Figure, References
	HM	TCM	HM	TCM	HM	TCM	HM	TCM	HM	TCM	
Monopole	25	20	102.5	98.4	14.9	12.9	22.4	20.3	1.5	1.57	Figure 1a, [43]
Capacitive capped monopole	20	30	93.3	100.4	23.7	31.5	17.3	18.3	0.73	0.58	Figure 1b, [44]
Dual-slot	25	-	103.8	-	19.6	-	23.9	-	1.22	-	Figure 1d, [45]
Balun-free base-fed monopole	30	30	100.2	103	24.4	25.5	25	24.8	1.02	0.97	Figure 1g, [47]
Balun-free helical dipole	30	-	96.8	-	21.9	-	31.6	-	1.44	-	Figure 1i, [48]
Helical open waveguide	10	15	103	93.7	14.5	14.9	14.8	14.5	1.02	0.97	Figure 1j, [41]

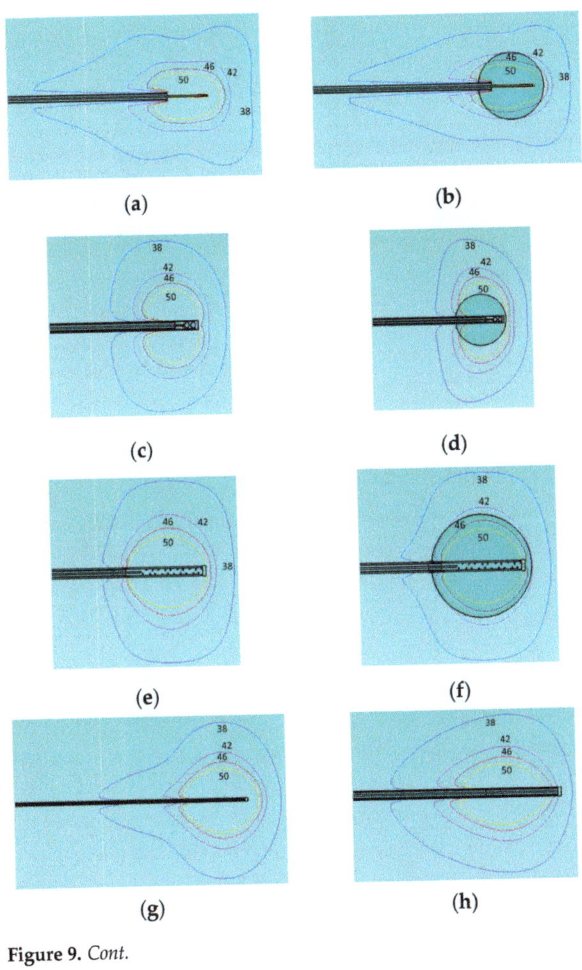

Figure 9. *Cont.*

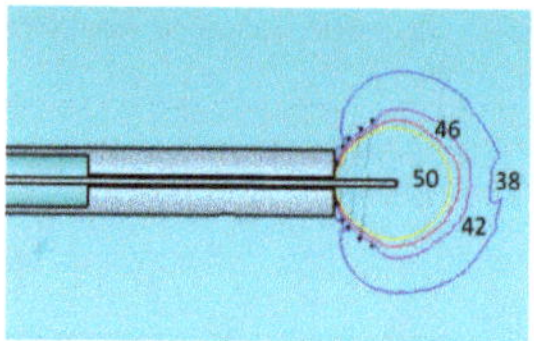

(i)

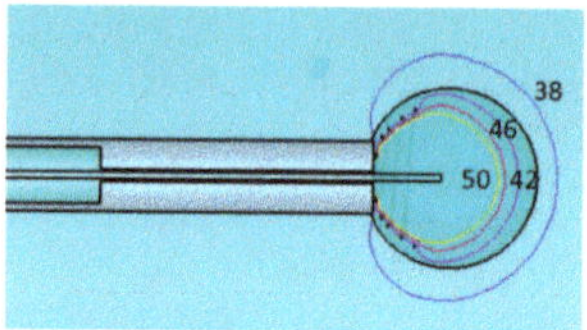

(j)

Figure 9. Temperature distribution for applicators of Table 4 and deposited power levels: (**a**) monopole antenna with 25 W deposited power, (**b**) monopole antenna with tumor and 20 W deposited power, (**c**) capacitive-capped monopole antenna with 20 W deposited power, (**d**) capacitive-capped monopole antenna with tumor and 30 W deposited power, (**e**) balun-free base-fed monopole antenna with 30 W deposited power, (**f**) balun-free base-fed monopole antenna with tumor and 30 W deposited power, (**g**) dual-slot antenna with 25 W deposited power, (**h**) balun-free helical dipole antenna with 30 deposited power, (**i**) helical open waveguide structure with 10 W deposited power, and (**j**) helical open waveguide structure with tumor 15 W deposited power. Temperature contours are indicated by colors: blue (38 °C), purple (42 °C), red (46 °C), and yellow (50 °C).

Figure 9 illustrates, through schematic representations, the results presented in Table 5. It is observed that the 50 °C isothermal line encloses the 3 cm or 2 cm tumor diameter in all cases. However, only the open waveguide (Figure 9j) restricts the 38 °C isothermal to only 1 cm beyond the tumor boundary as desired to avoid healthy tissue damage.

Table 5. Comparison of all designs with respect to the 38 °C penetration zone. The two rightmost columns denote the depth g (mm) that the 38 °C isothermal extends beyond the tumor boundary.

Design	38 °C Penetration Zone						Figure, References
	Diameter/d_1 (mm)		Length/d_2 (mm)		Extension Beyond the 3 mm or 2 mm Diameter Tumor (mm)		
	HM	TCM	HM	TCM	Diameter/d_{1TCM}-d_{tumor} = Extension Ring g (mm)	Length/d_{2TCM}-d_{tumor} = Extension Ring g (mm)	
Monopole	48.4	45.4	80.8	85	25.4	65	Figure 1a, [43]
Capacitive capped monopole	58.2	66.4	40	39.4	44.4	19.4	Figure 1b, [44]
Multi-slot	51.9	56.4	53	54.1	26.4	24.1	Figure 1c, [21]
Dual-slot	46.3	47.1	49.2	55.3	27.1	35.3	Figure 1d, [45]
Triaxial	54	55.1	70.8	69.8	25.1	39.8	Figure 1e, [47]
Choke dipole	55.1	56.6	65.2	63.5	26.6	33.5	Figure 1f, [47]
Balun-free base-fed monopole	56.2	56.1	43.8	50.4	26.1	20.4	Figure 1g, [47]
FSD	51.7	55.9	63.5	68	25.9	38	Figure 1h, [46]
Balun-free helical dipole	53.3	55.1	63.1	63.7	25.1	33.7	Figure 1i, [48]
Helical open waveguide	30.8	29.9	25.1	24.2	9.9	4.2	Figure 1j, [41]

Finally, Table 5 presents the 38 °C penetration zone for all applicators and the deviation of this zone from the tumor, providing a quantitative assessment of the uncontrolled temperature distribution. Specifically, the extension of the 38 °C isothermal beyond the tumor's diameter (2 cm or 3 cm) is calculated by subtracting the tumor's dimensions from the isothermal's length (horizontal axis) and diameter (vertical axis).

4. Discussion

Our objective was to replicate all designs proposed in the literature, with implementations closely following those reported in previous studies, using the data provided in the respective publications. Figures 2–4 (results for the homogeneous model) show favorable comparisons with simulation and experimental results reported in the literature for the homogeneous model. However, when a tumor model volume of 2 cm or 3 cm, with distinct dielectric properties from healthy tissue (two-compartment model), is introduced (Figures 7 and 8), the shape and form of the temperature distribution are significantly altered and deformed. Similar observations are evident from the SAR distribution, shown in Figures 3 and 7.

As demonstrated in Figures 2–8 and Table 3, some applicators produce nearly spherical ablation zones, indicating a uniform distribution of electromagnetic energy into the region of interest. However, there is a notable lack of control over temperature distribution (examine the temperature contours at 38 °C and 42 °C), which becomes particularly critical when the tumor is located near sensitive biological structures, such as blood vessels. This issue is partially mitigated by the balun-free, base-fed monopole antenna and fully addressed only by the helical open waveguide structure. As shown in Table 4, the 38 °C penetration zone exceeds the tumor dimensions by less than 1 cm in both diameter and length only for the helical open waveguide structure. This, combined with the safety margin of approximately 1 cm, makes this applicator the most secure and ideal choice for tumors located near vulnerable biological tissues. The main drawback of this helical open waveguide is its challenging construction and placement. Our group is brainstorming on this issue, where a convenient and practical solution is found that will be presented in a follow-up paper. In any case, other researchers are welcome to propose appropriate mechanical solutions.

Additionally, precise power calibration is essential to achieve spherical ablation zones; deviations in power can lead to elliptical ablation zones. Accurate applicator positioning is also critical, as the design directly affects its efficacy in ablating the tumor. The applicator must be inserted into the tumor before the microwave ablation (MWA) process begins, which may risk the dissemination of tumor cells. Positioned at the tumor periphery, the applicator initiates ablation immediately upon insertion, a critical step to prevent metastasis that can occur if cancer cells enter the bloodstream during treatment. The helical open waveguide structure, for instance, could address this concern by initiating MWA immediately upon insertion, thereby reducing the risk of tumor cell dissemination and enhancing treatment outcomes.

In the helical open waveguide design, spirals serve as a protective shield, enabling precise control of the electromagnetic field and allowing flexibility in adjusting the shielding based on the clinical context. For example, if the tumor is adjacent to sensitive biological tissues and no safety margin exists, a stronger shield can be applied. Conversely, if a safety margin is present, the shielding can be adjusted to a lower intensity.

As MWA is an image-guided treatment modality, the helical open waveguide design further enhances precision by encapsulating the target tumor with minimal operator error when guided by imaging techniques, thus increasing the safety of the procedure. However, given that MWA is a minimally invasive treatment, the size of the helical open waveguide is a primary limitation compared to existing applicators and other designs analyzed here. Additionally, it appears to create a smaller ablation zone than other designs. However, the ablation zone coincides with the tumor volume; thus, different sizes can be utilized in each case so as to exactly fit each tumor.

It is important to note that several designs in this analysis—including the capacitive capped monopole antenna, dual-slot antenna (as referenced in [45]), and helical open waveguide—have not yet been physically constructed. While this may limit direct experimental validation, the computational model provides an initial assessment of each design's theoretical performance relative to existing designs.

Moreover, it is important to address the management and control of maximum temperature during therapy. The simulator utilizes the point-wise Specific Absorption Rate (SAR) as the thermal source point, which may occasionally lead to an overestimation of maximum temperature levels. Despite this, it is essential to continuously monitor temperature throughout the therapy to ensure it remains within a safe range. Temperature control can be achieved using sensors that provide real-time temperature measurements. Additionally, regulating the microwave source power or employing cooling mechanisms can help maintain safe temperature levels. Notably, the designs in Figure 1e,f mentioned above are already in clinical use and have received FDA approval, ensuring consistent temperature control for patient safety. However, for designs that have not yet been constructed or approved by the FDA, it is crucial to prioritize patient safety by implementing these temperature control measurements rigorously.

Recall that this study is a computational comparative analysis. The simulations do not account for changes in tissue properties that occur during ablation, such as temperature-dependent dielectric properties, nor do they incorporate thermodynamic mechanisms like the latent heat of water vaporization. These factors inevitably introduce some discrepancies between simulation results and ex vivo ablation experiments. A challenging next step is to encourage researchers to carry out the corresponding simulation studies. Nonetheless, the presented simplified simulations offer valuable insights into the relative performance of these designs in ablation scenarios.

5. Conclusions

This study presents the first comparative analysis of microwave ablation (MWA) applicators under standardized conditions, utilizing both homogeneous and two-compartment models. It also evaluates the safety aspects of MWA by investigating not only the temperature thresholds for effective treatment (50 °C and 60 °C) but also the isothermal contours at 42 °C and 38 °C. These contours are critical to ensuring the safety of MWA, a key factor in advancing this therapeutic modality. To achieve this, a two-compartment model, incorporating both tumor and healthy tissue, is employed. This model provides a robust framework for validating the performance of MWA applicators under these critical conditions.

This comparative analysis was conducted between previously developed microwave ablation applicators. Initially, various applicators were modeled, including the monopole, capacitive-fed monopole antenna, floating sleeve dipole antenna, dual-slot antenna, multi-slot antenna, triaxial antenna, choke antenna, balun-free base-fed monopole antenna, balun-free helical dipole antenna, and the helical open waveguide structure.

Following the simulation phase, our results show strong alignment with those reported in the literature. We subsequently tested the applicators using (i) a homogenous tissue and (ii) a two-compartment model, incorporating a tumor with a diameter of 3 cm or 2 cm. This model differentiated between healthy tissue and the tumor by assigning distinct electrical properties, offering a reliable approximation of anatomical geometry.

The results revealed notable differences in the behavior of the electromagnetic field between the homogeneous model and the two-compartment model. Notably, all applicators except for helical open waveguide failed to confine the temperature field within the tumor, resulting in unintended damage to surrounding healthy tissue. In contrast, helical open waveguide demonstrated the capability to limit the ablation zone effect to the tumor region, thereby enhancing the safety and precision of the microwave ablation process. However, its current size is unsuitable for an immediate exploitation as a minimally invasive microwave ablation (MWA) applicator, even though a plethora of folding techniques exist that may devise a mechanism to compress the spirals inside the catheter. These can be unfolded to form the proper shape after the insertion of the catheter inside the tumor.

Supplementary Materials: The following supporting information can be downloaded at: https://www.mdpi.com/article/10.3390/app15042142/s1, The flow diagram illustrating the PRISMA screening and selection process is available as Supplementary Figure S1 online.

Funding: This research received no external funding.

Conflicts of Interest: The authors declare no conflicts of interest.

References

1. Afaghi, P.; Lapolla, M.A.; Ghandi, K. Percutaneous microwave ablation applications for liver tumors: Recommendations for COVID-19 patients. *Heliyon* **2021**, *7*, e06454. [CrossRef]
2. Brace, C.L. Microwave Tissue Ablation: Biophysics, Technology, and Applications. *Crit. Rev. Biomed. Eng.* **2010**, *38*, 65–78. [CrossRef] [PubMed]
3. Simon, C.J.; Dupuy, D.E.; Mayo-Smith, W.W. Microwave Ablation: Principles and Applications. *RadioGraphics* **2005**, *25* (Suppl. S1), S69–S83. [CrossRef] [PubMed]
4. Lubner, M.G.; Brace, C.L.; Hinshaw, J.L.; Lee, F.T. Microwave Tumor Ablation: Mechanism of Action, Clinical Results, and Devices. *J. Vasc. Interv. Radiol.* **2010**, *21*, S192–S203. [CrossRef] [PubMed]
5. Brace, C.L. Radiofrequency and Microwave Ablation of the Liver, Lung, Kidney, and Bone: What Are the Differences? *Curr. Probl. Diagn. Radiol.* **2009**, *38*, 135–143. [CrossRef] [PubMed]
6. Huang, H.; Zhang, L.; Moser, M.A.J.; Zhang, W.; Zhang, B. A review of antenna designs for percutaneous microwave ablation. *Phys. Medica* **2021**, *84*, 254–264. [CrossRef] [PubMed]
7. Fallahi, H.; Prakash, P. Antenna Designs for Microwave Tissue Ablation. *Crit. Rev. Biomed. Eng.* **2018**, *46*, 495–521. [CrossRef]
8. Bertram, J.M.; Yang, D.; Converse, M.C.; Webster, J.G.; Mahvi, D.M. A Review of Coaxial-Based Interstitial Antennas for Hepatic Microwave Ablation. *Crit. Rev. Biomed. Eng.* **2006**, *34*, 187–213. [CrossRef] [PubMed]
9. Hurter, W.; Reinbold, F.; Lorenz, W.J. A dipole antenna for interstitial microwave hyperthermia. *IEEE Trans. Microw. Theory Tech.* **1991**, *39*, 1048–1054. [CrossRef]
10. Mohtashami, Y.; Hagness, S.C.; Behdad, N. A Hybrid Slot/Monopole Antenna With Directional Heating Patterns for Microwave Ablation. *IEEE Trans. Antennas Propag.* **2017**, *65*, 3889–3896. [CrossRef]
11. Karampatzakis, A.; Kühn, S.; Tsanidis, G.; Neufeld, E.; Samaras, T.; Kuster, N. Antenna design and tissue parameters considerations for an improved modelling of microwave ablation in the liver. *Phys. Med. Biol.* **2013**, *58*, 3191–3206. [CrossRef] [PubMed]
12. Bertram, J.M.; Yang, D.; Converse, M.C.; Webster, J.G.; Mahvi, D.M. Antenna design for microwave hepatic ablation using an axisymmetric electromagnetic model. *BioMed Eng. OnLine* **2006**, *5*, 15. [CrossRef] [PubMed]
13. Nevels, R.D.; Arndt, G.D.; Raffoul, G.W.; Carl, J.R.; Pacifico, A. Microwave catheter design. *IEEE Trans. Biomed. Eng.* **1998**, *45*, 885–890. [CrossRef] [PubMed]
14. Cavagnaro, M.; Amabile, C.; Bernardi, P.; Pisa, S.; Tosoratti, N. A Minimally Invasive Antenna for Microwave Ablation Therapies: Design, Performances, and Experimental Assessment. *IEEE Trans. Biomed. Eng.* **2011**, *58*, 949–959. [CrossRef] [PubMed]
15. Brace, C.L.; Laeseke, P.F.; Van Der Weide, D.W.; Lee, F.T. Microwave ablation with a triaxial antenna: Results in ex vivo bovine liver. *IEEE Trans. Microw. Theory Tech.* **2005**, *53*, 215–220. [CrossRef] [PubMed]
16. Wakaki, T.; Michiyama, T.; Kuwano, S. A new interstitial choke embedded antenna for microwave ablation. *IEICE Commun. Express* **2017**, *6*, 435–438. [CrossRef]
17. Longo, I.; Gentili, G.B.; Cerretelli, M.; Tosoratti, N. A coaxial antenna with miniaturized choke for minimally invasive interstitial heating. *IEEE Trans. Biomed. Eng.* **2003**, *50*, 82–88. [CrossRef] [PubMed]
18. Pisa, S.; Cavagnaro, M.; Bernardi, P.; Lin, J.C. A 915-MHz antenna for microwave thermal ablation treatment: Physical design, computer modeling and experimental measurement. *IEEE Trans. Biomed. Eng.* **2001**, *48*, 599–601. [CrossRef]
19. Luyen, H.; Hagness, S.C.; Behdad, N. Reduced-Diameter Designs of Coax-Fed Microwave Ablation Antennas Equipped With Baluns. *IEEE Antennas Wirel. Propag. Lett.* **2017**, *16*, 1385–1388. [CrossRef]
20. Luyen, H.; Hagness, S.C.; Behdad, N. A Minimally Invasive Coax-Fed Microwave Ablation Antenna With a Tapered Balun. *IEEE Trans. Antennas Propag.* **2017**, *65*, 7280–7287. [CrossRef]
21. Ge, M.; Jiang, H.; Huang, X.; Zhou, Y.; Zhi, D.; Zhao, G.; Chen, Y.; Wang, L.; Qiu, B. A multi-slot coaxial microwave antenna for liver tumor ablation. *Phys. Med. Biol.* **2018**, *63*, 175011. [CrossRef] [PubMed]

22. Aziz, S.B.; Kaysir, M.R.; Jahirul Islam, M.; Islam, T.; Rahman, M. Effect of the antenna slot numbers and position on the performance of microwave ablation. *Med. Nov. Technol. Devices* **2023**, *20*, 100271. [CrossRef]
23. Wang, T.; Zhao, G.; Qiu, B. Theoretical evaluation of the treatment effectiveness of a novel coaxial multi-slot antenna for conformal microwave ablation of tumors. *Int. J. Heat Mass Transf.* **2015**, *90*, 81–91. [CrossRef]
24. Wu, C.; Huang, H.; Liu, Y.; Chen, L.; Yu, S.; Moser, M.A.J.; Zhang, W.; Fang, Z.; Zhang, B. Optimal design of aperiodic tri-slot antennas for the conformal ablation of liver tumors using an experimentally validated MWA computer model. *Comput. Methods Programs Biomed.* **2023**, *242*, 107799. [CrossRef] [PubMed]
25. Ibitoye, Z.A.; Nwoye, E.O.; Aweda, M.A.; Oremosu, A.A.; Annunobi, C.C.; Akanmu, O.N. Optimization of dual slot antenna using floating metallic sleeve for microwave ablation. *Med. Eng. Phys.* **2015**, *37*, 384–391. [CrossRef]
26. Xu, Y.; Moser, M.A.J.; Zhang, E.; Zhang, W.; Zhang, B. Large and round ablation zones with microwave ablation: A preliminary study of an optimal aperiodic tri-slot coaxial antenna with the π-matching network section. *Int. J. Therm. Sci.* **2019**, *140*, 539–548. [CrossRef]
27. Blain, M.; Narayanan, G.; Ricoeur, A.; Kobe, A.; Mahendra, A.M.; Jacks, B.; Letty, Q.; Bonnet, B.; Tselikas, L.; Deschamps, F.; et al. Safety and Efficacy of Percutaneous Liver Microwave Ablation Using a Fully Water-Cooled Choke Ring Antenna: First Multicenter Clinical Report. *CardioVascular Interv. Radiol.* **2023**, *46*, 1086–1091. [CrossRef]
28. Fallahi, H.; Clausing, D.; Shahzad, A.; O'Halloran, M.; Dennedy, M.C.; Prakash, P. Microwave antennas for thermal ablation of benign adrenal adenomas. *Biomed. Phys. Eng. Express* **2019**, *5*, 025044. [CrossRef]
29. Wang, Y.; Sun, Y.; Feng, L.; Gao, Y.; Ni, X.; Liang, P. Internally cooled antenna for microwave ablation: Results in ex vivo and in vivo porcine livers. *Eur. J. Radiol.* **2008**, *67*, 357–361. [CrossRef]
30. Kuang, M.; Lu, M.D.; Xie, X.Y.; Xu, H.X.; Mo, L.Q.; Liu, G.J.; Xu, Z.F.; Zheng, Y.L.; Liang, J.Y. Liver Cancer: Increased Microwave Delivery to Ablation Zone with Cooled-Shaft Antenna—Experimental and Clinical Studies. *Radiology* **2007**, *242*, 914–924. [CrossRef] [PubMed]
31. Zhou, Q.; Jin, X.; Jiao, D.-C.; Zhang, F.-J.; Zhang, L.; Han, X.-W.; Duan, G.-F.; Han, J.-J.; Li, C.-X. Microwave ablation: Results in ex vivo and in vivo porcine livers with 2450-MHz cooled-shaft antenna. *Chin. Med. J.* **2011**, *124*, 3386–3393.
32. Horn, J.C.; Patel, R.S.; Kim, E.; Nowakowski, F.S.; Lookstein, R.A.; Fischman, A.M. Percutaneous Microwave Ablation of Renal Tumors Using a Gas-Cooled 2.4-GHz Probe: Technique and Initial Results. *J. Vasc. Interv. Radiol.* **2014**, *25*, 448–453. [CrossRef]
33. Ziemlewicz, T.J.; Hinshaw, J.L.; Lubner, M.G.; Brace, C.L.; Alexander, M.L.; Agarwal, P.; Lee, F.T. Percutaneous Microwave Ablation of Hepatocellular Carcinoma with a Gas-Cooled System: Initial Clinical Results with 107 Tumors. *J. Vasc. Interv. Radiol.* **2015**, *26*, 62–68. [CrossRef]
34. Leapman, M.; Jayadevan, R.; Phillips, C.; Hall, S.J.; Palese, M.A.; Fischman, A.M. V5-14 Percutaneous Gas-Cooled Microwave Ablation for Small Renal Masses: The Mount Sinai Experience. *J. Urol.* **2014**, *191*, e620. [CrossRef]
35. Luyen, H.; Hagness, S.C.; Behdad, N. A Balun-Free Helical Antenna for Minimally Invasive Microwave Ablation. *IEEE Trans. Antennas Propag.* **2015**, *63*, 959–965. [CrossRef]
36. Lee, M.; Son, T. Helical Slot Antenna for the Microwave Ablation. *Int. J. Antennas Propag.* **2019**, *2019*, 1–9. [CrossRef]
37. Maini, S.; Shekhawat, D.S. Analysis of Copper Tube Sleeve Coaxial Spiral Antenna for Interstitial Hepatic Microwave Ablation. In Proceedings of the 2018 Eighth International Conference on Information Science and Technology (ICIST), Cordoba, Spain, 30 June–6 July 2018; pp. 31–34. [CrossRef]
38. Mohtashami, Y.; Behdad, N.; Hagness, S.C. Ex Vivo Performance of a Flexible Microwave Ablation Antenna. *IEEE Trans. Biomed. Eng.* **2021**, *68*, 1680–1689. [CrossRef]
39. Gu, Z.; Rappaport, C.M.; Wang, P.J.; VanderBrink, B.A. A 2 1/4-turn spiral antenna for catheter cardiac ablation. *IEEE Trans. Biomed. Eng.* **1999**, *46*, 1480–1482. [CrossRef] [PubMed]
40. Satoh, T.; Stauffer, P.R. Implantable helical coil microwave antenna for interstitial hyperthermia. *Int. J. Hyperth.* **1988**, *4*, 497–512. [CrossRef]
41. Karkanis, N.; Kyriakou, G.; Psomas, M.; Samaras, T.; Kaifas, T.N.F. Helical Open Waveguide Structure for Optimization of Microwave Ablation. In Proceedings of the 2024 Panhellenic Conference on Electronics & Telecommunications (PACET), Thessaloniki, Greece, 28–29 March 2024; pp. 1–4. [CrossRef]
42. He, Z.; Lin, X.; Yang, X.; Li, C. A Flexible Microwave Ablation Antenna for Lung Cancer Treatment. *IEEE Antennas Wirel. Propag. Lett.* **2023**, *22*, 3147–3151. [CrossRef]
43. Cilia, F.; Farrugia, L.; Bonello, J.; Farhat, I.; Sammut, C.V.; Joe Dimech, E. Design of an uncooled microwave monopole antenna for tissue ablation at 2.45 GHz. In Proceedings of the 2021 15th European Conference on Antennas and Propagation (EuCAP), Dusseldorf, Germany, 22–26 March 2021; pp. 1–5. [CrossRef]
44. Yassin, M.M.; Tammam, E.; Ibrahim, A.A.; Said, A.M.; Galal, A.I. A Dual Ring Interstitial Monopole Antenna with Spherical Heating Pattern for Hepatic Tumor Microwave Ablation. In Proceedings of the 2019 36th National Radio Science Conference (NRSC), Port Said, Egypt, 16–18 April 2019; pp. 425–430. [CrossRef]

45. Aparna, V.C.; Gandhi, A.S.; Naik, S.B.; Harsh, R. Minimally Invasive Microwave Ablation Antenna Designs at 915 MHz and 2.45 GHz. In Proceedings of the 2022 National Conference on Communications (NCC), Online, 24 May–27 May 2022; pp. 280–284. [CrossRef]
46. Hung, L.; Gao, F.; Hagness, S.C.; Behdad, N. Microwave Ablation at 10.0 GHz Achieves Comparable Ablation Zones to 1.9 GHz in Ex Vivo Bovine Liver. *IEEE Trans. Biomed. Eng.* **2014**, *61*, 1702–1710. [CrossRef] [PubMed]
47. Mohtashami, Y.; Luyen, H.; Sawicki, J.F.; Shea, J.D.; Behdad, N.; Hagness, S.C. Tools for Attacking Tumors: Performance Comparison of Triaxial, Choke Dipole, and Balun-Free Base-Fed Monopole Antennas for Microwave Ablation. *IEEE Antennas Propag. Mag.* **2018**, *60*, 52–57. [CrossRef]
48. Mohtashami, Y.; Behdad, N.; Hagness, S.C. Toward Flexible Microwave Ablation Antennas With a Balun-Free Helical Dipole Design. *IEEE Trans. Antennas Propag.* **2020**, *68*, 5052–5060. [CrossRef]
49. Zorbas, G.; Samaras, T. Simulation of radiofrequency ablation in real human anatomy. *Int. J. Hyperth.* **2014**, *30*, 570–578. [CrossRef] [PubMed]
50. Page, M.J.; McKenzie, J.E.; Bossuyt, P.M.; Boutron, I.; Hoffmann, T.C.; Mulrow, C.D.; Shamseer, L.; Tetzlaff, J.M.; Akl, E.A.; Brennan, S.E.; et al. The PRISMA 2020 statement: An updated guideline for reporting systematic reviews. *BMJ* **2021**, *372*, n71. [CrossRef]
51. IEEE. *Standard for Safety Levels with Respect to Human Exposure to Radio Frequency Electromagnetic Fields, 3 kHz to 300 GHz*; IEEE: New York, NY, USA, 1992. [CrossRef]
52. IT'IS Foundation, «TISSUE PROPERTIES». Available online: https://itis.swiss/virtual-population/tissue-properties/database/database-summary/ (accessed on 4 February 2025).
53. O'Rourke, A.P.; Lazebnik, M.; Bertram, J.M.; Converse, M.C.; Hagness, S.C.; Webster, J.G.; Mahvi, D.M. Dielectric properties of human normal, malignant and cirrhotic liver tissue: In vivo and ex vivo measurements from 0.5 to 20 GHz using a precision open-ended coaxial probe. *Phys. Med. Biol.* **2007**, *52*, 4707–4719. [CrossRef]

applied sciences

MDPI

Article

Denoising-Autoencoder-Aided Euclidean Distance Matrix Reconstruction for Connectivity-Based Localization: A Low-Rank Perspective

Woong-Hee Lee [1], Mustafa Ozger [2], Ursula Challita [3] and Taewon Song [4,*]

1 Division of Electronics and Electrical Engineering, Dongguk University-Seoul, Seoul 04620, Republic of Korea; woongheelee@dongguk.edu
2 Department of Electronic Systems, Aalborg University, 2450 Copenhagen, Denmark; mozger@es.aau.dk
3 Ericsson AB, 16440 Stockholm, Sweden; ursula.challita@ericsson.com
4 Department of Internet of Things, Soonchunhyang University, Asan 31538, Republic of Korea
* Correspondence: twsong@sch.ac.kr

Abstract: In contrast to conventional localization methods, connectivity-based localization is a promising approach that leverages wireless links among network nodes. Here, the Euclidean distance matrix (EDM) plays a pivotal role in implementing the multidimensional scaling technique for the localization of wireless nodes based on pairwise distance measurements. This is based on the representation of complex datasets in lower-dimensional spaces, resulting from the mathematical property of an EDM being a low-rank matrix. However, EDM data are inevitably susceptible to contamination due to errors such as measurement imperfections, channel dynamics, and clock asynchronization. Motivated by the low-rank property of the EDM, we introduce a new pre-processor for connectivity-based localization, namely denoising-autoencoder-aided EDM reconstruction (DAE-EDMR). The proposed method is based on optimizing the neural network by inputting and outputting vectors of the eigenvalues of the noisy EDM and the original EDM, respectively. The optimized NN denoises the contaminated EDM, leading to an exceptional performance in connectivity-based localization. Additionally, we introduce a relaxed version of DAE-EDMR, i.e., truncated DAE-EDMR (T-DAE-EDMR), which remains operational regardless of variations in the number of nodes between the training and test phases in NN operations. The proposed algorithms show a superior performance in both EDM denoising and localization accuracy. Moreover, the method of T-DAE-EDMR notably requires a minimal number of training datasets compared to that in conventional approaches such as deep learning algorithms. Overall, our proposed algorithms reduce the required training dataset's size by approximately one-tenth while achieving more than twice the effectiveness in EDM denoising, as demonstrated through our experiments.

Keywords: connectivity-based localization; denoising autoencoder; Euclidean distance matrix; multidimensional scaling; neural networks

1. Introduction

To configure, monitor, and control many applications in Internet of Things (IoT) networks, accurate localization of every sensor will be a key enabling technology for private 5G applications and beyond, especially for industries [1]. Many systems with localization algorithms have been developed by means of wireless sensor networks for both indoor and outdoor environments. To achieve a higher localization accuracy, additional hardware implementations are utilized by most of the existing localization solutions, which increase the cost and considerably limit location-based applications. Consequently, conventional localization methods such as global positioning systems (GPSs) are not suitable, as their direct implementation in IoT networks involves prohibitive demands for sophisticated equipment and substantial energy consumption and cannot meet the required accuracy level, for instance, in industrial setups. These limitations have significantly restricted the practical scalability of IoT networks. To overcome these challenges, massive wireless connections in IoT networks are leveraged for the cooperative location estimation of IoT devices, which is called connectivity-based localization [2–9]. This approach not only tackles the limitations of the conventional localization methods but also enhances the localization accuracy, resulting in more robust and energy-efficient localization within IoT networks.

From an algorithmic standpoint, multidimensional scaling (MDS) is a widely employed collection of statistical methods which are extensively utilized to create mappings of items based on their distance, i.e., dissimilarity [10–15]. MDS methods are able to represent complex datasets in spaces with lower dimensions; meanwhile, they maintain the dissimilarity relations among the items in the original datasets. Here, the Euclidean distance matrix (EDM) is the key information for implementing the MDS technique, which is constructed using pairwise distance measurements. The EDM serves as a useful description of the point sets and a solid foundation for localization algorithm design due to its effective description of the point sets. However, in real-world environments, EDM data are inevitably prone to contamination due to errors resulting from different sources, such as the measurement resolution, signal quality, network asynchronization, non line-of-sight (NLoS) conditions, and so on. In fact, the contamination in the EDM degrades the localization performance of the MDS, particularly in large-scale IoT networks. Errors in the EDM may lead to inaccurate and imprecise location estimations, which will result in a less reliable and robust connectivity-based localization process. Hence, it is critical to address the EDM contamination issue to ensure accurate and efficient localization in large-scale IoT networks.

To mitigate the effects of noisy measurements on the EDM, denoising techniques have been extensively utilized, and they aim to denoise a noisy EDM by resolving properly designed optimization problems such as semi-definite relaxation [16,17] and low-rank tensor completion [18]. However, they rely on solving complex optimization problems, which may limit their efficiency and effectiveness. Developments in artificial intelligence (AI) methods, particularly neural network (NN)-based denoising methods such as [19–22], have become promising in leveraging statistical inference as a novel and potentially more robust alternative for dealing with noisy measurements in EDM-based localization.

The existing NN-based EDM denoising techniques require computations that scale with the square of the total number of nodes since both the input and output of the NN framework are based on pairwise distances. This is due to the combinatorial nature of measuring and generating the distances between node pairs. As the number of nodes increases, the computational complexity grows quadratically, leading to the need for a large training dataset size and extensive NN models.

In addition, the existing NN-based denoising methods may not be suitable for IoT networks due to their resource limitations. Although major research efforts have focused on big data analysis and deep neural networks, it is crucial to consider that most IoT devices face severe limitations in terms of their data acquisition capabilities, computational power, and memory size. Hence, the successful implementation of efficient NN-based algorithms that can handle big data while considering the resource limitations of IoT devices is a critical challenge to address.

In this paper, we propose a novel denoiser for a noisy EDM, referred to as DAE-EDMR (Readers can understand our framework more easily by referring to Figure 1. Our method is based on the mathematical fact that the EDM measured from N nodes in a k-dimensional space must have a rank of at most $k+2$. Abstractly, this implies that N-choose-2 pairwise distances can be rearranged into a k-dimensional structure. Consequently, if the pairwise distances are not accurately measured, reconstructing these segments would require embedding them into a higher-dimensional space. Using this concept, we optimize the NN model for EDM denoising by utilizing the eigenvalues to capture how the nodes are volumetrically distributed. A detailed explanation is given in Section 2), which leverages a denoising autoencoder (DAE). To increase the efficiency of the NN operations, we exploit the low-rank property of the EDM, which is bounded to only a $k+2$ number of eigenvalues, where k is the dimension of the Euclidean space, independent of the number of sensor nodes [23]. Leveraging this valuable mathematical observation, we design our NN model by inputting and outputting vectors of the eigenvalues of the noisy and original EDMs, respectively. Through these inputting/outputting rules, the proposed scheme achieves remarkable denoising results, even with a relatively small training dataset. The efficiency of the proposed denoiser is attributed to the utilization of the low-rank property of the EDM, which helps the NN model to establish better inference with limited training data. In fact, the combination of the DAE and EDM is highly attractive due to the complementary features of these two techniques. On the one hand, the DAE is a powerful NN framework for manifold learning, which enables it to effectively capture intricate data patterns and facilitate efficient denoising. On the other hand, the EDM exhibits an extremely-low-rank property, contributing to the dimensionality reduction. Regarding the online complexity, the proposed method requires eigenvalue decomposition (EVD) of the EDM as a pre-processing step for the NN operations.

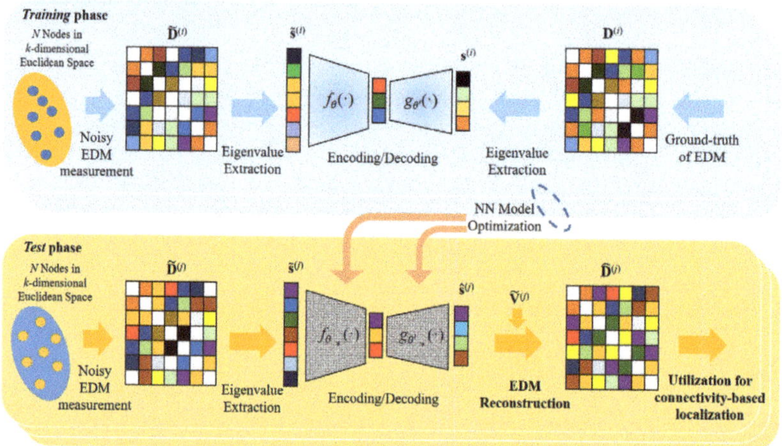

Figure 1. An illustration of an example of the proposed DAE-EDMR (Additionally, truncated DAE-EDMR (T-DAE-EDMR) is presented as a relaxed version of DAE-EDMR. This additional work is carried out to make the optimized NN model more efficient by using the dominant $k+2$ eigenvalues as the input data. Details can be found in Section 2.3).

In addition, we propose a technique called truncated DAE-EDMR, i.e., *T-DAE-EDMR*, to enhance the robustness of DAE-EDMR to diverse environments conditions, such as changes in the number of nodes, even after NN optimization. In other words, T-DAE-EDMR offers the flexibility to be utilized in scenarios where the number of nodes varies between the training and test phases. The T-DAE-EDMR scheme involves feeding $k+2$

eigenvalues from the noisy EDM to the NN, which are extracted through $(k+2)$-truncated EVD. In contrast, DAE-EDMR inputs N eigenvalues, making T-DAE-EDMR more versatile in accommodating different environments and simultaneously reducing the online complexity. Hence, T-DAE-EDMR is envisioned to demonstrate its superior effectiveness in environments characterized by a large number of nodes or frequent topology changes, such as vehicle-to-everything (V2X) systems.

To summarize, the main contributions of the proposed algorithms to denoising the noisy EDMs and enhancing the localization accuracy are four-fold:

- **Minimizing the reconstruction errors for the EDM through the mix-up of mathematical evidence and NNs**: We reveal the potential to reconstruct the EDM according to the low-rank property of the ground-truth EDM and the low-dimensional representations of the NN operation, which is robust to various noise models in distance measurements.
- **Reducing the size of the training dataset and NN model**: We develop an efficient NN framework requiring a small-sized training dataset and NN model. This is based on the novel inputting and outputting for the NN model, which consist of the eigenvalues of the noisy EDM and the ground-truth EDM, respectively.
- **Assisting the existing connectivity-based localization algorithms as a pre-processor**: We combine our proposed scheme with the connectivity-based localization technique to validate its utility in various environments. It is verified that these joint frameworks show a superior performance compared to that of the conventional approaches. This achievement is highly remarkable, as we only need to extract the eigenvalues of an EDM, requiring marginal online complexity.
- **Making the NN model robust to the dynamics of wireless networks**: By additionally presenting a modified model of our proposed model, we introduce an NN that can be robust to the variability in wireless networks, e.g., the number of nodes in the test phase is changed after NN optimization.

The remainder of this paper is organized as follows: Section 2 presents the system model, the problem design, and the method for the proposed algorithms. In Section 3, we provide numerical results to demonstrate the superiority of our proposed algorithms compared to other schemes even given the aspects of various environments. Finally, Section 4 presents the concluding remarks.

2. The Proposed Schemes: DAE-EDMR and T-DAE-EDMR

2.1. The System Model and Problem Formulation

Consider a collection of N nodes in a k-dimensional Euclidean space, $\mathbf{X} = [\mathbf{x}_1, \cdots, \mathbf{x}_N] \in \mathbb{R}^{k\times N}$, where the positions of all N nodes, $\mathbf{x}_1, \cdots, \mathbf{x}_N \in \mathbb{R}^k$, are randomly distributed. With the knowledge of the positions of $P(> k)$ reference nodes, we estimate the positions of the remaining N-P nodes. To accomplish this, we will utilize the concept of an EDM denoted by $\mathbf{D} \in \mathbb{R}_+^{N\times N}$. It is a symmetric matrix whose (i,j)-element can be represented as follows:

$$\mathbf{D}(i,j) = d_{ij}^2 = ||\mathbf{x}_i - \mathbf{x}_j||_2^2 =< \mathbf{x}_i - \mathbf{x}_j, \mathbf{x}_i - \mathbf{x}_j >, \tag{1}$$

where d_{ij} is the true distance between nodes i and j.

To model practical measurements, we first consider three types of random variables due to the environment as follows:

- B_N: ranging errors dependent on the signal quality;
- B_U: ranging errors due to clock asynchronization;
- B_{NLoS}: non line-of-sight (NLoS) events.

We assume that B_N, B_U, and B_{NLoS} follow normal, uniform, and Bernoulli distributions, respectively. Hence, we can define the random variable for the bias, B_{bias}, as follows:

$$B_{bias} = B_N + B_U + R_{NLoS}B_{NLoS}, \quad (2)$$

where R_{NLoS} is the distance bias in the event of NLoS conditions. Note that B_{bias} does not follow any known probability distribution, as it is a convolution of three different distributions.

Second, we assume that the distance is measured using a grid consisting of measurement resolutions, which is determined by the ranging configuration, e.g., the time of arrival (ToA). Thus, we define the quantization function $\mathcal{Q}_G$ to represent the measured distance with a resolution of G, e.g., $\mathcal{Q}_{10}(23) = 20$.

Third, we formulate a function to indicate whether the distance is measured or not, based on the communication capability between nodes i and j, as follows:

$$\delta_{ij} = \begin{cases} 1 & \text{if } d_{ij} \text{ is measured,} \\ 0 & \text{otherwise.} \end{cases} \quad (3)$$

Thus, the noisy measurement of the distance between the i-th and the j-th nodes is defined as follows:

$$\tilde{d}_{ij} = \delta_{ij} \cdot \mathcal{Q}_G(d_{ij} + e_{ij}), \quad (4)$$

where e_{ij} is the realization of B_{bias}. Then, we can define the noisy EDM using the following expression:

$$\tilde{\mathbf{D}} = [\tilde{d}_{ij}^2]_{i,j=1}^N \in \mathbb{R}_+^{N \times N}. \quad (5)$$

Finally, the objective of this paper is to find the denoising function $\mathcal{H}$, which is formulated as

$$\min_{\mathcal{H}} ||\mathbf{D} - \mathcal{H}(\tilde{\mathbf{D}})||_F^2. \quad (6)$$

2.2. Method I: DAE-EDMR

In the conventional approaches, the denoising function was set as $\mathcal{H}$: $\mathbb{R}_+^{N\times N} \mapsto \mathbb{R}_+^{N\times N}$, more specifically $\mathcal{H}$: $\tilde{\mathbf{D}} \mapsto \mathbf{D}$, such as in semi-definite relaxation and nonlocal patch tensor-based methods. These techniques require high computational complexity, as they perform iterative matrix multiplication operations while solving high-order optimization problems. In order to overcome this problem, NN-based techniques have recently been proposed. However, the dimension of the input and output data is large, which are the entire elements of the EDM. As a result, they exhibit low performance and require a large amount of training data and a large-sized neural network.

Considering the above problems, we propose a new method, namely DAE-EDMR, to denoise the noisy EDM in an efficient way.

2.2.1. A Denoising Process

Before describing the framework of DAE-EDMR, we will revisit the low-rank property of an EDM [23].

Property 1. *The rank* $(\mathbf{D})$*, corresponding to the points in* $\mathbb{R}^k$*, is at most* $k+2$.

This is based on the following equality:

$$\mathbf{D} = \mathbf{1}_N \text{diag}(\mathbf{X}^T\mathbf{X})^T - 2\mathbf{X}^T\mathbf{X} + \text{diag}(\mathbf{X}^T\mathbf{X})\mathbf{1}_N^T, \quad (7)$$

where $\mathbf{1}_N$ is the one-vector of size N. According to rank characteristics, the rank of $\mathbf{D}$ is bounded to the summation of the ranks of each term, i.e., $\text{rank}(\mathbf{D}) \leq \text{rank}(\mathbf{1}_N \text{diag}(\mathbf{X}^T\mathbf{X})^T) +$

$\text{rank}(\mathbf{X}^T\mathbf{X}) + \text{rank}(\text{diag}(\mathbf{X}^T\mathbf{X})\mathbf{1}_N^T) = 1 + k + 1$. This determines the rank of an EDM as extremely low, i.e., $\text{rank}(\mathbf{D}) \leq k + 2$, regardless of the number of nodes. It implies that it is effective to perform denoising given the small dimension of the (potential) latent space of an NN model, i.e., the similar level of the rank of the EDM, rather than treating the distance information as a whole.

Now, let $\mathbf{s} \in \mathbb{R}^{k+2}$ and $\tilde{\mathbf{s}} \in \mathbb{R}^N$ denote the vectors whose elements are the descending-order eigenvalues of $\mathbf{D}$ and $\tilde{\mathbf{D}}$, respectively. Thus, the optimal denoising function $\mathcal{H}^*\colon \mathbb{R}^N \mapsto \mathbb{R}^{k+2}$ can be constructed as follows:

$$\mathcal{H}^* = \underset{\mathcal{H}}{\text{argmin}}\, ||\mathbf{s} - \mathcal{H}(\tilde{\mathbf{s}})||_2^2. \tag{8}$$

Here, we design a fully connected NN framework denoted by $\mathcal{H}^{\text{NN}}$ to approximate $\mathcal{H}^*$. To this end, we will define the required terms as follows:

- N': The dimension of the latent space.
- $\mathbf{W} \in \mathbb{R}^{N' \times N}, \mathbf{W}' \in \mathbb{R}^{(k+2) \times N'}$: The weight matrices for encoding and decoding, respectively.
- $\mathbf{b} \in \mathbb{R}^{N'}, \mathbf{b}' \in \mathbb{R}^{k+2}$: The bias vectors for encoding and decoding, respectively.
- $\mathcal{S}$: The activation function for neural networks. At the propagation between the final hidden layer and the output layer, $\mathcal{S}(a) = a$, i.e., an identity function. For other types of propagation between adjacent layers, $\mathcal{S}(a) = \frac{e^a - e^{-a}}{e^a + e^{-a}}$, i.e., a hyperbolic tangent function. And $\mathcal{S}(\mathbf{a}) = (\mathcal{S}(\mathbf{a}[1]), \cdots, \mathcal{S}(\mathbf{a}[P]))^T$ where $\mathbf{a} \in \mathbb{R}^P$ is an arbitrary input vector.

With these terms (For simplicity, the description of the NN model design throughout this article is based on a single hidden layer; however, it is obvious that deeper hidden layers can be made using multiple encoding/decoding function parameters, i.e., $\{\theta_i\}_{i=1}^I$ and $\{\theta_i'\}_{i=1}^I$, where I, θ_i, and θ_i' are the depth of the NN model and the i-th encoding and decoding function parameters), we define f_θ as the encoding function where the parameter θ is $\{\mathbf{W}, \mathbf{b}\}$, i.e., $f_\theta(\tilde{\mathbf{s}}) = \mathcal{S}(\mathbf{W}\tilde{\mathbf{s}} + \mathbf{b})$. In addition, we define $g_{\theta'}$ as the decoding function where the parameter θ' is $\{\mathbf{W}', \mathbf{b}'\}$, i.e., $g_{\theta'}(f_\theta(\tilde{\mathbf{s}})) = \mathcal{S}(\mathbf{W}' f_\theta(\tilde{\mathbf{s}}) + \mathbf{b}')$.

Finally, we can define $\mathcal{H}^{\text{NN}}$ consisting of the optimal encoding and decoding functions, denoted by $f_{\theta*}$ and $g_{\theta'*}$, respectively, as follows:

$$\mathcal{H}^{\text{NN}} = \{f_{\theta*}, g_{\theta'*}\} = \underset{f_\theta, g_{\theta'}}{\text{argmin}}\, \frac{1}{M} \sum_{i=1}^{M} ||\mathbf{s}^{(i)} - g_{\theta'}(f_\theta(\tilde{\mathbf{s}}^{(i)}))||_2^2, \tag{9}$$

where M is the number of training datasets. Let Θ be all of the model parameters, i.e., $\Theta := \theta \cup \theta' = \{\mathbf{W}, \mathbf{W}', \mathbf{b}, \mathbf{b}'\}$; then, it simultaneously updates every parameter in Θ at each iteration toward the direction of the steepest descent as follows:

$$\Theta^{(n+1)} = \Theta^{(n)} - \eta \nabla_\Theta \Big(\frac{1}{M} \sum_{i=1}^{M} ||\mathbf{s}^{(i)} - g_{\theta'}(f_\theta(\tilde{\mathbf{s}}^{(i)}))||_2^2 \Big), \tag{10}$$

where ∇_Θ is the gradient operator with respect to Θ and η is the learning rate related to the step size. Through this procedure, we can optimize the fully connected NN model $\mathcal{H}^{\text{NN}}$ for denoising the eigenvalues.

Next, in the test phase, let $\hat{\mathbf{s}}^{(j)}$ denote the j-th denoised eigenvalues with the optimized $\mathcal{H}^{\text{NN}}$, and this can be obtained as follows:

$$\hat{\mathbf{s}}^{(j)} = \mathcal{H}^{\text{NN}}(\tilde{\mathbf{s}}^{(j)}) = g_{\theta'*}(f_{\theta*}(\tilde{\mathbf{s}}^{(j)})). \tag{11}$$

Finally, the denoised EDM $\hat{\mathbf{D}}^{(j)}$ can be reconstructed as follows:

$$\hat{\mathbf{D}}^{(j)} = \tilde{\mathbf{V}}^{(j)}\text{diag}(\hat{\mathbf{s}}^{(j)})[\tilde{\mathbf{V}}^{(j)}]^T, \quad (12)$$

where $\tilde{\mathbf{V}}^{(j)} \in \mathbb{R}^{N\times(k+2)}$ is the matrix consisting of $k+2$ eigenvectors of $\tilde{\mathbf{D}}^{(j)}$.

2.2.2. The Connectivity-Based Localization Process

To obtain an estimate of $\mathbf{X}$, which is denoted by $\hat{\mathbf{X}} \in \mathbb{R}^{k\times N}$, based on the classical MDS method, we first define the geometric centering matrix as follows:

$$\mathbf{C} = I_N - \frac{1}{N}\mathbf{1}_N\mathbf{1}_N^T \in \mathbb{R}^{N\times N}, \quad (13)$$

where I_N is the identity matrix N by N in size. Next, the estimated centered Gram matrix (GM) is obtained as

$$\hat{\mathbf{G}}_c = -\frac{1}{2}\mathbf{C}\hat{\mathbf{D}}\mathbf{C} \in \mathbb{R}^{N\times N}. \quad (14)$$

Recalling the fact that $\hat{\mathbf{G}}_c = \hat{\mathbf{X}}_c^T\hat{\mathbf{X}}_c$, where $\hat{\mathbf{X}}_c$ is the centered $\hat{\mathbf{X}}$, we can easily obtain $\hat{\mathbf{X}}_c$ through the k-truncated EVD of $\hat{\mathbf{G}}_c$. Based on this, we can finally obtain $\hat{\mathbf{X}}$ through a rigid linear transform, i.e., rotation and translation, of $\hat{\mathbf{X}}_c$ with the pre-knowledge of $[\mathbf{x}_1, \cdots, \mathbf{x}_P] \in \mathbb{R}^{k\times P}$, which are the positions of the reference nodes.

2.3. Method II: Truncated DAE-EDMR (T-DAE-EDMR)

This subsection introduces T-DAE-EDMR, which is the relaxed version of DAE-EDMR. From the previous subsection, the low-rank property of the EDM can be used more efficiently from the NN training/test point of view. Assume that the NN model is optimized in a network with N nodes. Here, we consider a scenario where the number of nodes changes at the test phase, which is frequently shown in wireless networks. If the NN model can be used flexibly under this kind of environment change, it will be a more efficient utilization.

For this reason, we newly define the optimal denoising function $\mathcal{H}_T^*$: $\mathbb{R}^{k+2} \mapsto \mathbb{R}^{k+2}$, which can be formulated as follows:

$$\mathcal{H}_T^* = \underset{\mathcal{H}}{\text{argmin}}\,||\mathbf{s} - \mathcal{H}(\tilde{\mathbf{s}}_T)||_2^2, \quad (15)$$

where $\tilde{\mathbf{s}}_T \in \mathbb{R}^{k+2}$ is the $(k+2)$-truncated vector of $\tilde{\mathbf{s}}$ in descending order.

Again, we can design T-DAE-EDMR denoted by $\mathcal{H}_T^{\text{NN}}$ with a new $\{f_{\theta*}, g_{\theta'*}\}$ as $\{f_{\theta_T*}, g_{\theta'_T*}\}$. In order to construct T-DAE-EDMR, we only need to change the dimension of the weight matrix for encoding to $\mathbf{W} \in \mathbb{R}^{N'\times(k+2)}$, and all the other configurations are the same as for $\mathcal{H}^{\text{NN}}$. Now, $\mathcal{H}_T^{\text{NN}}$ can be obtained through the M training dataset as follows:

$$\mathcal{H}_T^{\text{NN}} = \{f_{\theta_T*}, g_{\theta'_T*}\} = \underset{f_\theta, g_{\theta'}}{\text{argmin}}\,\frac{1}{M}\sum_{i=1}^{M}||\mathbf{s}^{(i)} - g_{\theta'}(f_\theta(\tilde{\mathbf{s}}_T^{(i)}))||_2^2. \quad (16)$$

Next, in the test phase, let $\hat{\mathbf{s}}_T^{(j)}$ denote the j-th denoised eigenvalues with the optimized $\mathcal{H}_T^{\text{NN}}$, and this can be written as

$$\hat{\mathbf{s}}_T^{(j)} = \mathcal{H}_T^{\text{NN}}(\tilde{\mathbf{s}}_T^{(j)}) = g_{\theta'_T*}(f_{\theta_T*}(\tilde{\mathbf{s}}_T^{(j)})). \quad (17)$$

Finally, in the test phase, we can again obtain the j-th denoised EDM $\hat{\mathbf{D}}_T^{(j)}$ as follows:

$$\hat{\mathbf{D}}_T^{(j)} = \tilde{\mathbf{V}}^{(j)}\text{diag}(\hat{\mathbf{s}}_T^{(j)})[\tilde{\mathbf{V}}^{(j)}]^T. \quad (18)$$

After obtaining $\hat{\mathbf{D}}_T$, performing connectivity-based localization involves repeating the work in Section 2.2.2 but replacing $\hat{\mathbf{D}}$ with $\hat{\mathbf{D}}_T$.

Overall, Algorithms 1 and 2 describe the processes of DAE-EDMR and T-DAE-EDMR, respectively.

Algorithm 1 The `DAE-EDMR` process

1: [*The training phase* (M: number of training datasets)]
2: Collect the training dataset of true and noisy EDMs, i.e., $\mathbf{D}^{(i)}$ and $\tilde{\mathbf{D}}^{(i)}$, for all $i \in \{1, \cdots, M\}$.
3: **for** $i \leftarrow 1$ to M, **do**
4: Extract the vectors of the eigenvalues of $\mathbf{D}^{(i)}$ and $\tilde{\mathbf{D}}^{(i)}$, i.e., $\mathbf{s}^{(i)}$ and $\tilde{\mathbf{s}}^{(i)}$.
5: **end for**
6: Optimize the NN-based denoiser consisting of encoding/decoding functions based on (9), i.e., $\mathcal{H}^{\text{NN}}(= \{f_{\theta*}, g_{\theta'*}\})$, by inputting and outputting $\tilde{\mathbf{s}}^{(i)}$ and $\mathbf{s}^{(i)}$, respectively.
7: [*The test phase* (L: number of test datasets)]
8: Collect the test dataset of true and noisy EDMs, i.e., $\mathbf{D}^{(j)}$ and $\tilde{\mathbf{D}}^{(j)}$, for all $j \in \{1, \cdots, L\}$.
9: **for** $j \leftarrow 1$ to L, **do**
10: Make the input vector $\tilde{\mathbf{s}}^{(j)}$ referring to step 4.
11: Generate $\hat{\mathbf{s}}^{(j)}$ by passing $\tilde{\mathbf{s}}^{(j)}$ to $\mathcal{H}^{\text{NN}}$.
12: Obtain the denoised EDM, i.e., $\hat{\mathbf{D}}^{(j)}$, based on (12).
13: Implement the classical MDS with $\hat{\mathbf{D}}^{(j)}$ to obtain the estimate of $\mathbf{X}^{(j)}$.
14: **end for**

Algorithm 2 The `T-DAE-EDMR` process

1: [*The training phase* (M: number of training datasets)]
2: Collect the training dataset of true and noisy EDMs, i.e., $\mathbf{D}^{(i)}$ and $\tilde{\mathbf{D}}^{(i)}$, for all $i \in \{1, \cdots, M\}$.
3: **for** $i \leftarrow 1$ to M **do**
4: Extract the eigenvalues of $\mathbf{D}^{(i)}$, i.e., $\mathbf{s}^{(i)}$.
5: Select the dominant $k+2$ eigenvalues of $\tilde{\mathbf{D}}^{(i)}$, i.e., $\tilde{\mathbf{s}}_T^{(i)}$.
6: **end for**
7: Optimize the NN-based denoiser consisting of encoding/decoding functions based on (16), i.e., $\mathcal{H}_T^{\text{NN}}(= \{f_{\theta_T*}, g_{\theta'_T*}\})$, by inputting and outputting $\tilde{\mathbf{s}}_T^{(i)}$ and $\mathbf{s}^{(i)}$, respectively.
8: [*The test phase* (L: number of test datasets)]
9: Collect the test dataset of true and noisy EDMs, i.e., $\mathbf{D}^{(j)}$ and $\tilde{\mathbf{D}}^{(j)}$, for all $j \in \{1, \cdots, L\}$.
10: **for** $j \leftarrow 1$ to L, **do**
11: Make the input vector $\tilde{\mathbf{s}}_T^{(j)}$ by referring to step 5.
12: Generate $\hat{\mathbf{s}}_T^{(j)}$ by passing $\tilde{\mathbf{s}}_T^{(j)}$ to $\mathcal{H}_T^{\text{NN}}$.
13: Obtain the denoised EDM, i.e., $\hat{\mathbf{D}}_T^{(j)}$, based on (18).
14: Implement the classical MDS with $\hat{\mathbf{D}}_T^{(j)}$ to obtain the estimate of $\mathbf{X}^{(j)}$.
15: **end for**

2.4. *Computational Complexity and Memory Utilization of DAE-EDMR and T-DAE-EDMR*

Since the training process is performed offline and will not affect the online denoising overhead, we mainly consider the complexity of online denoising. Recalling the dimension of the latent space N' and the depth of the NN model I, FLOPs of $\mathcal{O}(IN'N)$ and $\mathcal{O}(IN'(k+2))$ are basically required in DAE-EDMR and T-DAE-EDMR, respectively, in terms of the online complexity for the fully connected NN model's operation. The proposed DAE-EDMR requires an additional online complexity of $\mathcal{O}(N^3)$ FLOPs [24] for EVD of the noisy EDM $\tilde{\mathbf{D}} \in \mathbb{R}_+^{N \times N}$ compared to conventional NN-based works requiring online complexity for matrix multiplications (As is generally known, the FLOPs required to extract the eigenvalues are $4N^3/3$. Additionally, in the case of the extraction of the eigenvalues and eigenvectors together, the required FLOPs are $8N^3/3$. In our work, we only take the eigenvalues because these alone are sufficient for denoising and reducing the number of FLOPs required in offline training. Furthermore, since EDMs are inherently symmetric matrices, extracting the eigenvalues can be performed more efficiently. Investigating this aspect further could be an intriguing direction of future work, potentially leading to more computationally efficient approaches to EDM-based processing.). Additionally, T-DAE-EDMR can reduce the online complexity of DAE-EDMR to $\mathcal{O}((k+2)N^2)$ FLOPs regarding the truncated eigenproblem. Furthermore, in contrast to traditional EDM-based NNs, which require a memory storage proportional to $\mathcal{O}(N^2)$ due to their pairwise distance representations, our proposed model significantly reduces the memory usage by limiting the input and output dimensions to $k+2$. This allows for a more scalable and efficeint implementation, making it particularly suitable for large-scale networks.

3. Simulation Results

In this section, we analyze the effect of DAE-EDMR and T-DAE-EDMR from various perspectives. We compare the performance of our proposed methods with that of the conventional algorithms, which are semi-definite relaxation [16], the nonlocal patch tensor-based method [18], and conventional NN-based methods referred to as deep-learning-based methods A [19] and B [22]. We also provide the result for the undenoised EDM to show the denoising performance of each algorithm. Overall, we will demonstrate the effectiveness of each scheme in denoising the noisy EDM and assess its impact on the localization performance.

3.1. The Simulation Setup

The performance of the proposed algorithms is evaluated via 5000 episodes. We define two error metrics: the EDM error and the localization error. The EDM error quantifies the deviation between the denoised EDM and the original EDM. Specifically, it is computed by first taking the Frobenius norm of their difference and then normalizing it by the Frobenius norm of the original EDM, with the final result averaged over all experimental trials. This metric provides a measure of the accuracy of the denoised pairwise distances. Meanwhile, the localization error represents the average localization error across all experimental trials, capturing the overall accuracy of the proposed method in reconstructing spatial coordinates.

In the simulations, N is set to 30, and the entire nodes are randomly distributed over a 100×100-sized space. Furthermore, the resolution of the distance measurements is assumed to be 10. Next, we set the variables of the noisy measurements, which are defined in Section 2 A, as follows: $B_N \sim \mathcal{N}(0,5), B_U \sim \mathcal{U}(0,10), B_{NLoS} \sim \text{Ber}(0.5)$ (except for Section 3C), and $R_{NLoS} = 25$. In addition, δ_{ij} in (3) follows $\text{Ber}(0.9)$ for all i, j, i.e., 10% of the distance measurements are missed on average. To clearly confirm the performance in EDM denoising, all of the EDM measurements follow the above assumptions in terms of the statistical parameters for error modeling and the resolution of the distance measurements, irrespective of whether the pair measuring their distance contains the reference/target node. Additionally, except for Table 1a, the number of reference nodes (P) is 18. The classical MDS [23] is utilized as the localization method to estimate the position of the target nodes.

Throughout all cases for NN optimization, the squared error and the scaled conjugate gradient are applied as the loss function and the optimization method, respectively. We consider a fully connected NN model. Furthermore, the depth of the hidden layer and the number of perceptrons per hidden layer are 2 and 450, respectively. With the exception of Figure 2, the size of the training dataset (M) was 10,000 for all experiments. We tested on NVIDIA RTX A2000 GPU machines (Santa Clara, CA, USA).

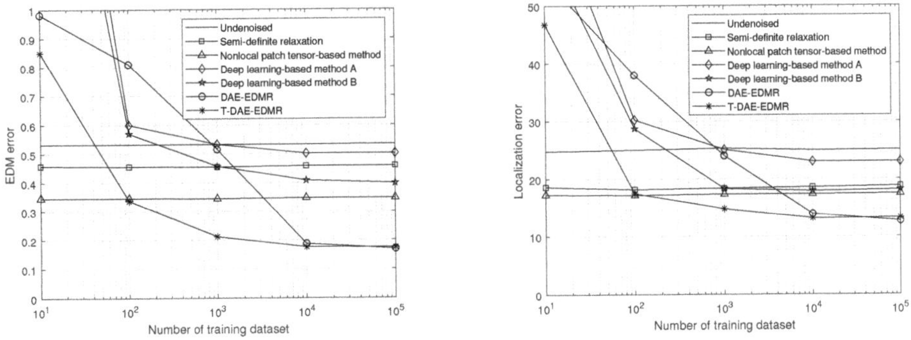

(a) (b)

Figure 2. Performance comparison according to the number of training datasets. (**a**) NMSE between ground-truth and denoised EDMs and (**b**) localization error in meters.

Table 1. The performance of each scheme under varying cardinalities of the sensor network (left: NMSE between ground-truth and denoised EDMs; right: Localization error in meters).

(a) In Cases of Variation in the Number of Reference Nodes (*P*) Where the Number of Reference and Target Nodes (*N*) is Fixed to 30.

Algorithms \ Variations	$P = 5$	$P = 10$	$P = 15$	$P = 20$	$P = 25$
None (undenoised)	0.532 \ 31.69	0.554 \ 26.41	0.539 \ 25.28	0.535 \ 25.01	0.538 \ 24.31
Semi-definite relaxation	0.466 \ 24.70	0.458 \ 20.21	0.457 \ 18.69	0.470 \ 18.31	0.477 \ 18.10
Nonlocal patch tensor-based method	0.321 \ 24.31	0.326 \ 19.46	0.328 \ 18.12	0.330 \ 17.78	0.325 \ 17.36
Deep-learning-based method A	0.530 \ 29.65	0.527 \ 25.65	0.522 \ 22.82	0.533 \ 22.91	0.539 \ 22.91
Deep-learning-based method B	0.334 \ 24.64	0.323 \ 19.71	0.328 \ 18.29	0.325 \ 18.04	0.326 \ 17.90
DAE-EDMR	0.180 \ 17.57	0.176 \ 15.72	0.178 \ 13.92	0.177 \ 13.81	0.172 \ 12.03
T-DAE-EDMR	0.183 \ 18.62	0.183 \ 14.89	0.183 \ 13.59	0.178 \ 12.94	0.176 \ 12.42

(b) In Cases of Variation in the Number of Nodes After NN Optimization Where the Number of Reference Nodes is Fixed to 18.

Algorithms \ Variations	$N_{new} - N = -10$	$N_{new} - N = -5$	$N_{new} = N$	$N_{new} - N = 5$	$N_{new} - N = 10$
None (undenoised)	0.552 \ 24.32	0.540 \ 22.80	0.533 \ 21.57	0.525 \ 20.48	0.521 \ 20.01
Semi-definite relaxation	0.482 \ 21.37	0.472 \ 20.04	0.465 \ 18.51	0.456 \ 17.99	0.451 \ 17.89
Nonlocal patch tensor-based method	0.332 \ 19.06	0.325 \ 18.11	0.320 \ 17.12	0.316 \ 16.89	0.314 \ 16.51
Deep-learning-based method A	N/A	N/A	0.531 \ 24.12	N/A	N/A
Deep-learning-based method B	N/A	N/A	0.327 \ 18.91	N/A	N/A
DAE-EDMR	N/A	N/A	0.177 \ 13.22	N/A	N/A
T-DAE-EDMR	0.491 \ 20.21	0.219 \ 15.77	0.179 \ 13.47	0.185 \ 14.17	0.323 \ 17.78

3.2. Simulation Results According to the Number of Training Datasets

Figure 2 shows the performance of each algorithm with respect to the size of the training dataset used in the NN optimization process. Only the NN-based methods show variation in their performance with the size of the training dataset.

Despite the large size of the training dataset, such as 10^5, the conventional deep-learning-based methods are not able to surpass the performance of the nonlocal patch tensor-based method.

This can be attributed to the challenge of extracting valuable information from the raw and unrefined training dataset. Remarkably, the T-DAE-EDMR technique outperforms the other techniques even when M is just 10^2. In addition, DAE-EDMR shows a noticeable improvement when M is increased to 10^3. It is noteworthy that when M is 10^5, DAE-EDMR shows a slightly better performance than that of T-DAE-EDMR. This observation implies that extracting information from N contaminated eigenvalues, instead of solely relying on the $k + 2$ highest values among them, can yield advantages when a large training dataset is available.

3.3. Simulation Results According to NLoS Probability

Figure 3 illustrates the impact of the NLoS probability on the EDM and localization errors. It is assumed that the NLoS probability follows a Bernoulli distribution. As the NLoS probability increases, the error for distance measurements naturally increases, resulting in a worse localization performance. Therefore, the non-NN-based techniques are in line with this general situation. On the other hand, a different phenomenon appears from the information-theoretic perspective. In the NN-based methods, i.e., deep-learning-based methods A and B, DAE-EDMR, and T-DAE-EDMR, the EDM error takes the form of a concave function for the NLoS probability. This is related to the fact that the variance in and the entropy of $\text{Ber}(p)$ are $p(1-p)$ and $-p\log(p)-(1-p)\log(1-p)$, respectively, which are in the form of concave functions. Interestingly, our proposed methods show a superior localization performance in the extreme case where the NLoS probability is 1 and can therefore be effectively applied in environments where NLoS conditions occur frequently. For future work, an interesting denoising task may involve modeling the distance measurement error due to NLoS conditions as a joint random variable, considering both the event occurrence and distance biasing. This approach could provide valuable insights into further enhancing the denoising techniques in the presence of errors due to NLoS conditions.

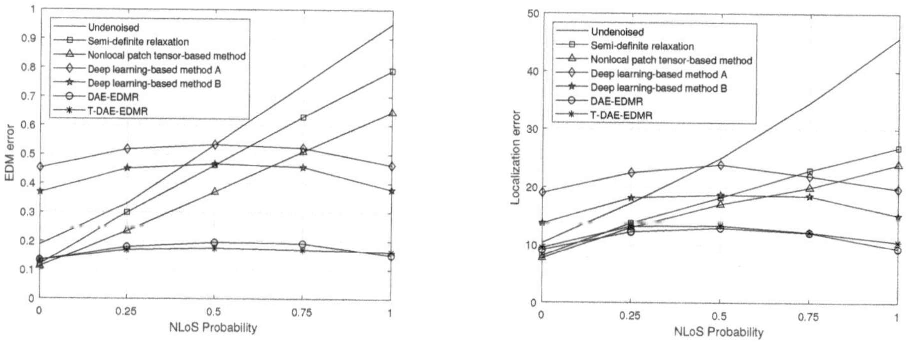

(a) (b)

Figure 3. Performance comparison according to the NLoS probability. (**a**) NMSE between ground-truth and denoised EDMs and (**b**) localization error in meters.

3.4. Simulation Results According to the Variation in the Cardinality of the Sensor Network

In this subsection, we deal with the dynamics of the sensor nodes. Table 1a shows the EDM and localization errors for a case where only P is changed while keeping N constant ($N = 30$). Since the EDM measurements are independent of P, only the denoising performance of each algorithm affects the EDM error. In the case of localization errors, it can be seen that the performance improves as P increases for all algorithms, and the two algorithms we propose show an excellent performance overall.

Table 1b shows the impact of the change in the number of nodes after NN optimization is performed, with N equal to 30. In other words, this experiment serves to verify the flexibility of T-DAE-EDMR when the number of nodes, N, changes between the training and test phases. For convenience, we will refer to the changed value of N as N_{new}. In the undenoised scenario, as N_{new} increases, the possibility of cooperation between the nodes increases; consequently, it can be seen that the performance marginally improves. As expected, T-DAE-EDMR shows its denoising capability well when N_{new} is equal to N. In addition, since the model is optimized based on the information for a situation where N is 30, the performance of T-DAE-EDMR deteriorates as the value of $|N_{new} - N|$

increases. Nevertheless, our proposed T-DAE-EDMR can be considered an effectively designed algorithm that can adapt robustly to a change in the number of nodes between the training and test phases. Due to its potential, T-DAE-EDMR could be very useful in highly time-varying networks.

3.5. Simulation Results According to the Utilized Matrices

Figure 4 shows the results of applying our techniques to both an EDM and a GM, where a GM has a sharper condition in terms of its low-rank property. Under this setting, the EDM error and the localization error are investigated with respect to the size of the training dataset. A GM is created by multiplying the centering matrix on both sides of the EDM, and it is clear that it has a sharper condition than that of the EDM. In other words, rank(GM) $\leq k$ where k is the dimension of the Euclidean space. As can be seen in Figure 4, both tests show a mostly similar performance when the size of the training dataset is large enough since they contain essentially the same information. However, in cases where the training dataset is insufficient, a slight deterioration in performance is observed when the GM is applied. This can be inferred because when the GM is created through the multiplication of the EDM and the centering matrix, then some useful information is contaminated during this procedure, as the centering matrix is a singular matrix.

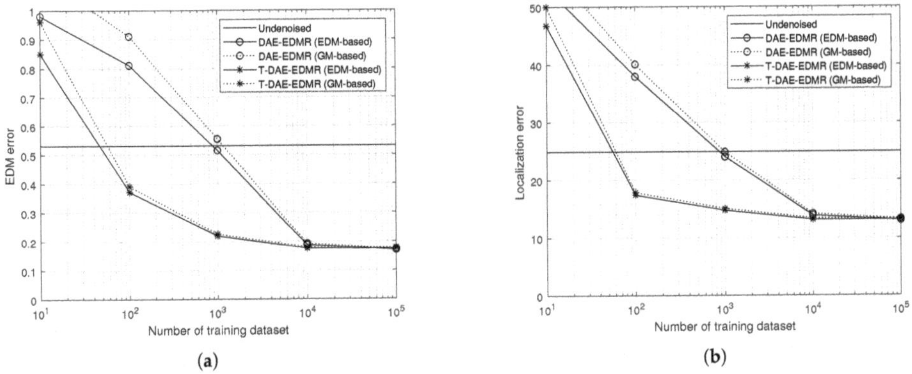

Figure 4. Performance comparison according to the utilized matrices. (**a**) NMSE between ground-truth and denoised EDMs and (**b**) localization error in meters.

4. Discussion and Conclusions

In this paper, we investigated the problem of denoising a contaminated Euclidean distance matrix (EDM) for high-accuracy connectivity-based localization based on the mathematical fact of an EDM, i.e., its low-rank property. Compared to conventional neural network (NN)-based algorithms with large-scale frameworks, we proposed two efficient algorithms, called denoising-autoencoder-aided EDM reconstruction (DAE-EDMR) and truncated DAE-EDMR (T-DAE-EDMR), which show a superior EDM denoising performance. Notably, the latter is designed within the NN framework, enabling it to achieve a robust performance even with a limited number of training datasets. Our contributions stem from the concept of inputting N (or $k + 2$ dominant) eigenvalues of the noisy EDM into the NN model, with the addition of marginal online complexity for eigenvalue decomposition (EVD) of the EDMs. Furthermore, T-DAE-EDMR reinforces the robustness of DAE-EDMR to variations in the number of nodes between the training and test phases. T-DAE-EDMR inputs the $k + 2$ dominant eigenvalues of the noisy EDM into the NN, extracted through $(k + 2)$-truncated EVD. This approach, as opposed to inputting N eigenvalues into DAE-EDMR, enhances the robustness to changing environments while reducing the required training dataset and off/online complexity. The proposed approach effectively leverages the linear algebraic properties of wireless localization. In particular, the use of eigenvalues to optimize the NN model for EDM denoising suggests that the volume of the convex hull formed by the distributed nodes can be interpreted as the crucial information. Our experimental results demonstrate that the proposed algorithms reduce the required training dataset's size to nearly one-tenth of its original size while achieving more than twice the effectiveness in EDM denoising. Given the suitability of the proposed methods for massive connectivity scenarios, our approach offers useful advantages for practical deployment. Furthermore, there is an opportunity to further enhance the EDM denoising performance by incorporating deeper mathematical insights, considering not only eigenvalues but also eigenvectors. Building on these strengths, future research will focus on extending our proposed schemes to localization and tracking techniques that can more robustly adapt to time-varying environments, making them even more applicable to large-scale implementations.

Author Contributions: Conceptualization: W.-H.L. and T.S. Methodology: W.-H.L. Software: W.-H.L.. Validation: M.O. and U.C. Formal analysis: M.O. Investigation: U.C. Resources: W.-H.L. Data curation: W.-H.L. Writing—original draft preparation: W.-H.L. Writing—review and editing: W.-H.L., M.O., U.C., and T.S. Visualization: W.-H.L. Supervision: T.S. Project administration: T.S. Funding acquisition: W.-H.L. and T.S. All authors have read and agreed to the published version of the manuscript.

Funding: This work was supported in part by an Institute of Information & Communications Technology Planning & Evaluation (IITP) grant funded by the Korean government (MSIT) (No. RS-2023-00217885, Development of integrated interference analysis technology for improving frequency utilization efficiency) and in part by the Soonchunhyang University Research Fund.

Institutional Review Board Statement: Not applicable.

Informed Consent Statement: Not applicable.

Data Availability Statement: The data supporting the reported results in this study can be shared upon reasonable request. Interested researchers should contact the corresponding author to discuss access. Please note that data sharing may be subject to restrictions due to privacy, ethical considerations, or intellectual property agreements with funders.

Conflicts of Interest: Author Ursula Challita was employed by the company Ericsson AB. The remaining authors declare that the re-search was conducted in the absence of any commercial or financial relationships that could be construed as a potential conflict of interest.

References

1. Li, Y.; Zhuang, Y.; Hu, X.; Gao, Z.; Hu, J.; Chen, L.; He, Z.; Pei, L.; Chen, K.; Wang, M.; et al. Toward Location-Enabled IoT (LE-IoT): IoT Positioning Techniques, Error Sources, and Error Mitigation. *IEEE Internet Things J.* **2021**, *8*, 4035–4062. [CrossRef]
2. Yao, Y.; Zhang, H.; Lin, L.; Lin, G.; Shibasaki, R.; Song, X.; Yu, K. Internet of Things Positioning Technology Based Intelligent Delivery System. *IEEE Trans. Intell. Transp. Syst.* **2022**, *24*, 12862–12876. [CrossRef]
3. Farahsari, P.S.; Farahzadi, A.; Rezazadeh, J.; Bagheri, A. A survey on indoor positioning systems for IoT-based applications. *IEEE Internet Things J.* **2022**, *9*, 7680–7699. [CrossRef]
4. Alrajeh, N.A.; Bashir, M.; Shams, B. Localization techniques in wireless sensor networks. *Int. J. Distrib. Sens. Netw.* **2013**, *9*, 304628. [CrossRef]
5. Chen, R.; Liu, M.; Hui, Y.; Cheng, N.; Li, J. Reconfigurable intelligent surfaces for 6G IoT wireless positioning: A contemporary survey. *IEEE Internet Things J.* **2022**, *9*, 23570–23582. [CrossRef]
6. Shyam, S.; Juliet, S.; Ezra, K. An Emerging Paradigm in IoT-Based Indoor Positioning System. In *Disruptive Technologies for Big Data and Cloud Applications: Proceedings of ICBDCC 2021*; Springer Nature: Berlin/Heidelberg, Germany, 2022; pp. 613–620.
7. Sneha, V.; Nagarajan, M. Localization in wireless sensor networks: A review. *Cybern. Inf. Technol.* **2020**, *20*, 3–26. [CrossRef]
8. Chen, Z.; Xia, F.; Huang, T.; Bu, F.; Wang, H. A localization method for the Internet of Things. *J. Supercomput.* **2013**, *63*, 657–674. [CrossRef]

9. Lin, X.; Bergman, J.; Gunnarsson, F.; Liberg, O.; Razavi, S.M.; Razaghi, H.S.; Rydn, H.; Sui, Y. Positioning for the Internet of Things: A 3GPP perspective. *IEEE Commun. Mag.* **2017**, *55*, 179–185. [CrossRef]
10. Shang, Y.; Ruml, W.; Zhang, Y.; Fromherz, M.P. Localization from mere connectivity. In Proceedings of the 4th ACM International Symposium on Mobile ad Hoc Networking & Computing, Annapolis, MD, USA, 1–3 June 2003; pp. 201–212.
11. Costa, J.A.; Patwari, N.; Hero III, A.O. Distributed weighted-multidimensional scaling for node localization in sensor networks. *ACM Trans. Sens. Netw. (TOSN)* **2006**, *2*, 39–64. [CrossRef]
12. Lee, W.H.; Choi, J.; Lee, J.H.; Kim, Y.H.; Kim, S.C. Distributed power control-based connectivity reconstruction game in wireless localization. *IEEE Commun. Lett.* **2016**, *21*, 334–337. [CrossRef]
13. Jin, M.; Xia, S.; Wu, H.; Gu, X. Scalable and fully distributed localization with mere connectivity. In Proceedings of the 2011 Proceedings IEEE INFOCOM, Shanghai, China, 10–15 April 2011; pp. 3164–3172.
14. Shang, Y.; Rumi, W.; Zhang, Y.; Fromherz, M. Localization from connectivity in sensor networks. *IEEE Trans. Parallel Distrib. Syst.* **2004**, *15*, 961–974. [CrossRef]
15. Kang, I.; Nam, H. Robust Localization System Using Vector Combination in Wireless Sensor Networks. *IEEE Access* **2022**, *10*, 73437–73445. [CrossRef]
16. Alfakih, A.Y.; Khandani, A.; Wolkowicz, H. Solving Euclidean distance matrix completion problems via semidefinite programming. *Comput. Optim. Appl.* **1999**, *12*, 13–30. [CrossRef]
17. Krislock, N.; Wolkowicz, H. Euclidean distance matrices and applications. In *Handbook on Semidefinite, Conic and Polynomial Optimization*; Springer: Berlin/Heidelberg, Germany, 2012; pp. 879–914.
18. Zhang, L.; Song, L.; Du, B.; Zhang, Y. Nonlocal low-rank tensor completion for visual data. *IEEE Trans. Cybern.* **2019**, *51*, 673–685. [CrossRef] [PubMed]
19. Njima, W.; Chafii, M.; Nimr, A.; Fettweis, G. Deep learning based data recovery for localization. *IEEE Access* **2020**, *8*, 175741–175752. [CrossRef]
20. Zou, H.; Chen, C.L.; Li, M.; Yang, J.; Zhou, Y.; Xie, L.; Spanos, C.J. Adversarial learning-enabled automatic WiFi indoor radio map construction and adaptation with mobile robot. *IEEE Internet Things J.* **2020**, *7*, 6946–6954. [CrossRef]
21. Lee, W.H.; Ozger, M.; Challita, U.; Sung, K.W. Noise learning-based denoising autoencoder. *IEEE Commun. Lett.* **2021**, *25*, 2983–2987. [CrossRef]
22. Kim, S.; Nguyen, L.T.; Kim, J.; Shim, B. Deep learning based low-rank matrix completion for IoT network localization. *IEEE Wirel. Commun. Lett.* **2021**, *10*, 2115–2119. [CrossRef]
23. Dokmanic, I.; Parhizkar, R.; Ranieri, J.; Vetterli, M. Euclidean distance matrices: Essential theory, algorithms, and applications. *IEEE Signal Process. Mag.* **2015**, *32*, 12–30. [CrossRef]
24. Demmel, J.W. *Applied Numerical Linear Algebra*; SIAM: Philadelphia, PA, USA, 1997.

applied sciences

MDPI

Article

Multi-Channel Speech Enhancement Using Labelled Random Finite Sets and a Neural Beamformer in Cocktail Party Scenario

Jayanta Datta [1,*], Ali Dehghan Firoozabadi [2,*], David Zabala-Blanco [3] and Francisco R. Castillo-Soria [4]

1 Department of Electrical Engineering, Universidad de Chile, Santiago 8370451, Chile
2 Department of Electricity, Universidad Tecnológica Metropolitana, Av. José Pedro Alessandri 1242, Santiago 7800002, Chile
3 Department of Computing and Industries, Universidad Católica del Maule, Talca 3466706, Chile; dzabala@ucm.cl
4 Faculty of Science, Universidad Autónoma de San Luis Potosí, San Luis Potosí 78295, Mexico; ruben.soria@uaslp.mx
* Correspondence: ch_12321@yahoo.co.in (J.D.); adehghanfirouzabadi@utem.cl (A.D.F.); Tel.: +56-2-2787-7117 (A.D.F.)

Abstract: In this research, a multi-channel target speech enhancement scheme is proposed that is based on deep learning (DL) architecture and assisted by multi-source tracking using a labeled random finite set (RFS) framework. A neural network based on minimum variance distortionless response (MVDR) beamformer is considered as the beamformer of choice, where a residual dense convolutional graph-U-Net is applied in a generative adversarial network (GAN) setting to model the beamformer for target speech enhancement under reverberant conditions involving multiple moving speech sources. The input dataset for this neural architecture is constructed by applying multi-source tracking using multi-sensor generalized labeled multi-Bernoulli (MS-GLMB) filtering, which belongs to the labeled RFS framework, to obtain estimations of the sources' positions and the associated labels (corresponding to each source) at each time frame with high accuracy under the effect of undesirable factors like reverberation and background noise. The tracked sources' positions and associated labels help to correctly discriminate the target source from the interferers across all time frames and generate time–frequency (T-F) masks corresponding to the target source from the output of a time-varying, minimum variance distortionless response (MVDR) beamformer. These T-F masks constitute the target label set used to train the proposed deep neural architecture to perform target speech enhancement. The exploitation of MS-GLMB filtering and a time-varying MVDR beamformer help in providing the spatial information of the sources, in addition to the spectral information, within the neural speech enhancement framework during the training phase. Moreover, the application of the GAN framework takes advantage of adversarial optimization as an alternative to maximum likelihood (ML)-based frameworks, which further boosts the performance of target speech enhancement under reverberant conditions. The computer simulations demonstrate that the proposed approach leads to better target speech enhancement performance compared with existing state-of-the-art DL-based methodologies which do not incorporate the labeled RFS-based approach, something which is evident from the 75% ESTOI and PESQ of 2.70 achieved by the proposed approach as compared with the 46.74% ESTOI and PESQ of 1.84 achieved by Mask-MVDR with self-attention mechanism at a reverberation time (RT60) of 550 ms.

Keywords: SRP-PHAT; deep learning; microphone array; MS-GLMB filtering; beamforming

 https://doi.org/10.3390/app15062944

1. Introduction

Speech enhancement is generally performed as a front-end signal processing procedure in a speech processing pipeline, whose primary objective is to improve the intelligibility and quality of target speech under noisy, reverberant conditions. A common example of an indoor acoustic environment is the so-called "cocktail party" scenario [1], where multiple speech sources are speaking at the same time. Unlike conventional approaches [1–7], contemporary research has treated speech enhancement as a supervised learning problem from the context of deep learning (DL) [8–30]. Among these works [8–26] are those that outline DL-based speech enhancement methodologies, where convolutional and recurrent neural architectures have been utilized to combine spectral and spatial features for target speech enhancement, while the works outlined in [27–30] utilize graph neural architectures to perform speech enhancement. Among the DL-based speech enhancement approaches, mask-based beamformers [8,13] and neural spectro-spatial filtering [14,15] are two prominent approaches which provide excellent performance even under high reverberation and low acoustic signal-to-noise ratio (SNR). While the mask-based beamforming approach outlined in [8] provides a DL-based time-varying (TV) beamformer to enhance the target speech, the neural spectro-spatial filtering approach presented in [14] performs complex spectral mapping (CSM), which involves the mapping of real and imaginary components of an input mixture spectrogram to those of a target speech spectrogram by a DL architecture. Despite their advantages, both these methods suffer from a common drawback due to their apparent failure to consider the random nature of the cardinality of the speech sources in motion, something which is attributed to the disappearance of existing sources as well as the appearance of new sources inside the acoustic environment. A failure to account for sources' appearances and disappearances directly impacts the performance of speech enhancement.

The multi-sensor generalized labelled multi-Bernoulli (MS-GLMB) [6,31,32] filtering algorithm within the labelled random finite sets (RFS) framework offers a flexible mechanism by which to address the problem of the unknown and time-varying cardinality of the speech sources in a Bayesian setting and helps to resolve the space-time permutation ambiguity by jointly estimating the sources' positions and labels. The space-time permutation problem, also referred to as the data association problem, addresses the uncertainty about which measurement is associated to which source in space, as well as the uncertainty about associations between different measurements and sources across different time frames [6]. A solution to space-time permutation ambiguity leads to better source tracking and hence to improved target speech enhancement in the presence of reverberation, noise and motion of the sources.

In this work, MS-GLMB filtering is applied within the dynamic speech enhancement framework during training time, in order to assist the deep neural architecture to learn, within each time frame, the mapping from a reverberant mixture of speech signals belonging to mobile sources located at different spatial positions to the desired mask specific to the target source. This approach differs from the approach in [26], as, during test time, the proposed neural architecture presented in this work directly predicts the desired source-specific mask from the input magnitude spectrogram, without the need for additional MS-GLMB filtering. The contemporary research works on MS-GLMB filtering-assisted speech enhancement do not focus on the use of multi-source tracking based on MS-GLMB filtering to create datasets for training DL architectures for target speech enhancement under reverberant conditions [6,26,31]. An interesting research work in this direction can be found in [33], where it has been demonstrated through computer simulation results that the utilization of the outputs of the GLMB-based multi-target tracking filter by the subsequent deep reinforcement learning (RL) module leads to better tracking performance.

The overall system proposed in [33] utilizes the observations from the GLMB filter to learn the system dynamics and the reward function and ultimately leads to the prediction of each target's next states. However, the domain of application of the methodology presented in [33] is different from acoustic domain, and the application area is different from speech enhancement.

In this article, we have utilized the MS-GLMB filter to assist in the construction of training label sets for the subsequent neural target speech enhancement module. The training procedure considers the relative motion of the different acoustic sources within the indoor environment, as well as the effects of reverberation and noise, which leads to improved training of the neural architecture. As such, the proposed system is capable of dynamically enhancing the target speech in the cocktail party scenario.

In some previous works, an angular/directional feature was used to assist neural speech enhancement [13,15–18,20] by using visual information, and was utilized to construct a directional feature which can lead to robust performance. However, in situations where visual information suffers from impairments, such as low light ambient conditions, camera jitters, or obstruction in the field of view (FoV) of the camera due to motion of the sources, the acoustic information, such as the speech signal, is the only source of information which needs to be exploited by the neural beamformer to perform target speech enhancement. In the approach presented in this article, the impact of reverberation and the sources' motion at each time frame are considered by the MS-GLMB filtering to provide estimates of the sources' positions at each time frame as well as their associated labels, which in turn help to train the subsequent neural architecture to predict the desired mask corresponding to the target speech source even in the presence of reverberation, noise and the motion of the sources. In other words, the MS-GLMB filtering assists the neural architecture to discriminate the target source from the interfering sources and to learn the mapping from the input features to the target source-specific mask with higher accuracy, leading to improved target speech enhancement performance.

The neural architecture used in this work to model the beamformer operation is a residual dense convolutional U-Net framework with a graph convolutional recurrent neural network (GCRNN) [34] module embedded within the bottleneck and the skip connection layers. The neural framework can be referred to as a residual dense graph-U-Net (RD-graph-U-Net) applied in a generative adversarial network (GAN) [35,36] setting. Details about the neural architecture are presented in Section 3. While traditional supervised techniques based on deep convolutional neural frameworks have demonstrated good speech enhancement performance, they are prone to unseen adversarial conditions, which can render the overall neural framework incapable of discriminating between the original desired signal and noisy received signal at the input. The mask estimation framework based on GAN [21–25] is an alternative to the conventional CNN-based framework, whereby the GAN learns a mapping function from the noisy received signal to the time–frequency (T-F) mask by undergoing a discriminative process involving minimization of the distributional divergence between the model and data distribution. A GAN-based T-F mask estimation framework can lead to considerable improvement in speech intelligibility under noisy acoustic conditions while being flexible in application to real-time implementations and also generalizable to different T-F representations. On the contrary, non-GAN framework approaches to learning the mapping function may be incapable of enhancing noisy speech with improvements in intelligibility and auditory perception as compared with a GAN-based T-F masking approach.

Prior research works on GNN-based target speech enhancement are presented in [27–30]. More information about graph signal processing concepts and applications of graph neural frameworks can be found in [37–39]. As the name indicates, the proposed deep neural architecture is actually a U-Net framework [40], which incorporates residual dense network (RDN) [41–43] modules in the encoder and decoder pathways. The residual block in the RDN module improves the generalization capability of the network architecture, while the dense convolutional module [44] within the RDN facilitates feature re-use, promotes gradient flow among the neural layers and reduces the number of parameters, leading to an overall improvement in accuracy and reduction in computational complexity. The presence of a GCRNN module in the bottleneck and skip-connection layers improves the feature extraction capability of the overall architectural framework. Due to the presence of the GCRNN module, the multi-channel latent space of the signals is transformed into a graph domain, resulting in an increase in the flexibility in exploitation of spatiotemporal and spectral information. The neural architecture for speech enhancement used in this work combines the advantageous features of both GANs and GCRNNs to provide good performance under noisy acoustic conditions. The overall GAN-based setting can help the architecture to undergo a discriminative process involving minimization of the distributional divergence between the model and data distribution, while the GCRNN embedded within the bottleneck layer can facilitate exploitation of the implicit information (i.e., spatial and spectro-temporal information) through transformation of the multi-channel latent space at the end of the encoder path to graph domain. Consequently, the overall speech intelligibility is improved under noisy acoustic conditions as compared with existing approaches. While the work presented in this article attempts to present an innovative speech enhancement methodology with the help of MS-GLMB filtering and neural architecture-assisted beamforming, it utilizes an acoustic parameter setup such as microphone array geometry and positions as well as room dimensions which have been already utilized in prior research works [6,26,31,45]. While some of the simulation parameters might be similar, the approach presented in this article differs from the works in [6,26,31,45] due to the utilization of MS-GLMB filtering to create the datasets (incorporating the effects of sources' motion and reverberation) that are used to train the neural architecture.

The contributions of this paper are two-fold:

i. Construction of label-set data for training a neural architecture for target speech enhancement with the help of MS-GLMB filtering-based multi-source tracking and a time-varying MVDR beamformer, one which takes into account the effect of reverberation, noise and motion of the sources at each time frame. While the GLMB-assisted tracking relies on initial location information provided by steered response power phase transform (SRP-PHAT) [46], the inclusion of the tracking framework within the neural training procedure helps to develop the knowledge of spectro-spatial information of the moving sources within the neural architecture, so that it is able to generalize to "unseen" acoustic conditions as well and directly predict the desired T-F mask.
ii. Construction of a residual dense convolutional U-Net architecture with an embedded GCRNN module, referred to as RD-graph-U-Net, which is applied in a GAN setting to predict the target source-specific mask.

The proposed approach is tested on publicly available datasets [47–51] using speech quality evaluation metrics [52–54]. The image source method (ISM) [55] is used to generate the room impulse response (RIR) between the source speaker and receiver microphone array. Adaptive momentum estimation (ADAM) [56] is selected as the optimization strategy to train the proposed neural architecture. Based on computer simulation results, it can be inferred that the proposed methodology improves the intelligibility of the speech corresponding to target source in motion, under noisy reverberant conditions involving multiple moving speech sources. The proposed approach is also tested with recorded RIRs obtained from Aachen impulse response (AIR) [57] database, where it shows good results.

This is largely because of the signal discriminative capability of the proposed neural approach, which it acquires due to the training procedure outlined in Section 3. The proposed approach can be applicable in many practical scenarios such as conferencing [58], assistive listening devices [59] and speech transcription systems [60]. The remainder of the article is arranged as follows. Section 2 describes the system model of the overall methodology; Section 3 describes the proposed neural architecture-based speech enhancement module; Section 4 provides a brief discussion about the proposed approach; Section 5 presents some future research directions in this area; and, finally, Section 6 concludes this article.

2. System Model

Similar to magnitude–domain spectra, which are widely used in mono-aural speech enhancement, both real and imaginary spectrograms exhibit a spectro-temporal structure, which is useful for training the deep neural algorithm. While the complex spectrograms provide spectral cues, the spatial cues are obtained from the directional feature as well as inter-microphone phase difference (IPD). The combination of spectral and spatial cues can be referred to as spectro-spatial features, and it enables the neural beamformer to learn to suppress the interfering signals arriving from directions other than the target speech signal. In this section, the overall procedure of MS-GLMB filtering-assisted spectro-spatial feature construction is described, followed by the minimum variance distortionless response (MVDR) beamforming. While Sections 2.1–2.3 highlight the operations of SRP-PHAT for the localization of sources, MS-GLMB filtering for tracking of sources and exploitation of spectro-spatial information for guiding the T-F masking-based speech enhancement, the operation of the beamformer is described in Section 2.4. The beamformer selected for this work is GSC-MVDR of a time-varying nature, which exploits the spatial information of the sources and dynamically enhances the speech signal corresponding to the target source.

2.1. Steered Response Power Phase Transform (SRP-PHAT)

The SRP method, $P_{SRP}(\boldsymbol{X})$, can be treated as the output power of a filter-and-sum (F-S) beamformer, one which is steered to a set of source positions defined under a spatial grid. $\boldsymbol{X} = [x, y]^T$ is a vector, and represents the (x, y) position coordinates of the target acoustic source [46].

The phase transform (PHAT) is a weighting technique whose inclusion in the formulation of SRP helps to emphasize the phase information of the involved signals, thereby avoiding peak spreading [46]. For a microphone array with N elements, $P_{SRP}(\boldsymbol{X})$ can be expressed as the summation of individual generalized cross correlation (GCC) functions, $R_{nm}^{GCC}(\tau(\boldsymbol{X}))$:

$$P_{SRP}(\boldsymbol{X}) = \sum_{n=0}^{N-1} \sum_{m=0}^{N-1} R_{nm}^{GCC}(\tau(\boldsymbol{X})) \quad (1)$$

Unlike simplified scenarios, in realistic acoustic propagation environments, the signals received from different microphone elements do not simply differ from each other because of the delay that is dependent on the relative position of the source with respect to other microphone elements. This is due to the impairments caused by multipath effects like reverberation as well as the presence of ambient and diffuse noise. Hence, the mapping from SRP-PHAT to 3D positional coordinates using simple regression methods suffers from inaccuracies.

2.2. MS-GLMB Filtering

Multi-sensor (MS) RFS filtering-based tracking provides superior performance than single sensor tracking when multiple acoustic sources are in motion [6,31,32]. MS-GLMB filtering is applied in this work, whereby the propagation of the filtering density is achieved through a recursive procedure comprising two steps, namely the time update and the data update. In this work, the time-updated and data-updated filtering densities can be expressed in closed-form via the GLMB density [6,31,32]:

$$\pi(\mathbf{X}_k) = \Delta(\mathbf{X}_k)\sum_{\theta_{1:k}\in\boldsymbol{\theta}_{1:k}} \omega^{(\theta_{1:k})}(\mathcal{L}(\mathbf{X}_k))\prod_{x_k\in\mathbf{X}_k} p^{(\theta_{1:k})}(x_k) \tag{2}$$

In (2), $\theta_{1:k} \in \boldsymbol{\theta}_{1:k}$ represents the history of multi-array association mappings up to frame 'k', i.e., $\theta_{1:k} \triangleq (\theta_1,\ \theta_2 \ldots \theta_k)$. The term $\mathcal{L}(\mathbf{X}_k)$ can be further expressed as follows:

$$\mathcal{L}(\mathbf{X}_k) \triangleq \{l : (x_k, l) \in \mathbf{X}_k\} \tag{3}$$

Furthermore, in (2), the term $\Delta(.)$ denotes a distinct label indicator where $\Delta(\mathbf{X}_k) = 1$ if and only if the cardinality of the label set denoted by $|\mathcal{L}(\mathbf{X}_k)|$ equals the cardinality of $\mathbf{X}_k$ denoted by $|\mathbf{X}_k|$. Each weight term $\omega^{(\theta_{1:k})}(\mathcal{L}(\mathbf{X}_k))$ in (2) is a non-negative weight, such that their sum equals 1:

$$\sum_{L\subseteq\mathbb{L}_{0:k}} \sum_{\theta_{1:k}\in\boldsymbol{\theta}_{1:k}} \omega^{(\theta_{1:k})}(L) = 1 \tag{4}$$

Each of the non-negative weights in (3) and (4), represented by $\omega^{(\theta_{1:k})}(\mathcal{L}(\mathbf{X}_k))$, can be interpreted as a probability of the sources with label set $\mathcal{L}(\mathbf{X}_k)$ being active, while at the same time being associated with the detections indicated by the history of multi-array association mappings up to the frame 'k', denoted by $\theta_{1:k}$. Finally, the term $p^{(\theta_{1:k})}(x_k)$ in (2) represents the probability density of the source (with label 'l') that is located at the state $x_k = \left(\alpha_k^{pos}, \alpha_k^{vel}\right)$. A detailed explanation of the terms in (2) can be found in [6,31,32]. The estimated position and label corresponding to the sources at each frame 'k' can be expressed as follows:

$$X_k^{est} = \left\{\left(\alpha_{k,1,est}^{pos}, l_1^{est}\right), \left(\alpha_{k,2,est}^{pos}, l_2^{est}\right) \ldots \left(\alpha_{k,N_k,est}^{pos}, l_{N_k}^{est}\right)\right\} \tag{5}$$

In (5), the term $N_k = \left|X_k^{est}\right|$ denotes the estimated number of sources at the kth frame. The estimated position and its corresponding label $\left(\alpha_{k,i,est}^{pos}, l_i^{est}\right), i = 1, 2 \ldots N_k$ can be used to construct the steering vector corresponding to the direction of the target source represented by the position–label pair $(\alpha_{k,d,est}^{pos}, l_d^{est})$ while directing spectral nulls in the directions of the interfering sources denoted by the position–label pairs, $\left(\alpha_{k,i,est}^{pos}, l_i^{est}\right)$, $\forall i \neq d$. As reported in [6], such a beamformer can dynamically enhance the speech corresponding to the target acoustic source by utilizing the estimates from the GLMB filter. In this work, we focus on utilizing MS-GLMB filtering to assist the construction of the target label set (in this case, the T-F mask specific to the target speech source) for the neural architecture. Due to the association of a unique label with every speech source within the environment, the MS-GLMB filtering helps to correctly discriminate between the target source and the interfering sources, which helps to train the subsequent deep neural architecture with an appropriately constructed label set specifically to the target source in motion under noisy reverberant conditions. The following sub-section provides more details on the role of MS-GLMB filtering in the overall target speech enhancement procedure.

2.3. Spectro-Spatial Information-Guided T-F Domain Masking for GSC-MVDR Beamformer

In prior state-of-the-art research works on neural network-assisted target speech enhancement [11–13], the angular feature (AF) was computed and used to construct an input feature set for the subsequent DL architecture, which predicts the target label (e.g., a mask specific to the target source). While the works outlined in [11–13] use AF as input feature for transformer- and recurrent neural network (RNN)-based deep neural architectures, the work outlined in [26] applies the feature set constructed using AF to a fully convolutional neural architecture arranged in a U-Net structure. The input feature set in all of these works comprised a concatenation of magnitude spectrogram, IPD, and AF. In addition, the works in [6,31,32] involve MS-GLMB filtering to compute the labels distinguishing the target source from the interfering sources at every time frame, which were also instrumental in constructing T-V beamformer weights. The overall procedure outlined in [26] is expressed in Figure 1, for reference.

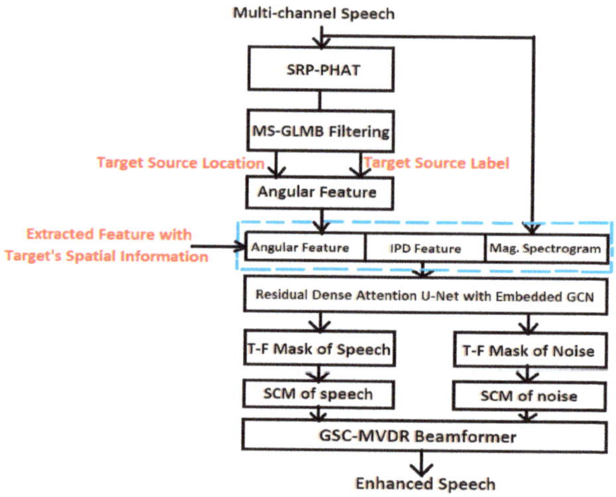

Figure 1. Target speech enhancement with MS-GLMB filtering-assisted covariance mask prediction and GSC-based D-S beamformer [26].

Within the indoor environment, the area of potential target locations is divided into multiple angular sectors, each of which corresponds to an angular position of the target source at any time frame. The labelled RFS framework is helpful to demarcate the potential locations of the target speech source at different time frames from those of the interfering sources. This, in turn, helps to generate the training input dataset for the DL architecture, where the generated dataset reflects the effect of reverberation as well as the activity status of the target source. As the target and the interferers can be in different states of motion at different time frames, the dataset generated using the labelled RFS framework will reflect the state of the sources at different instants of time, which in turn helps to train the DL architecture more efficiently to predict the mask in a dynamic manner. The overall procedure can also be referred to as a form of beam zooming [20], where the applied DL architecture facilitates beam zooming on the potential location of the target source at each time frame.

In this work, the angular location information of the target source is utilized to create the training dataset on which the proposed neural architecture is trained. The dataset is constructed from the magnitude spectrogram, while the label set (T-F mask specific to target source) to train the neural architecture is constructed from the spatial information of the target source estimated by the MS-GLMB filter. The procedure is depicted in Figure 2.

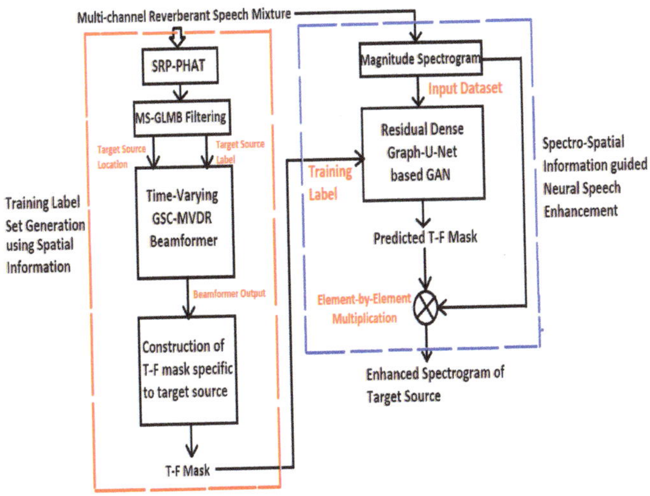

Figure 2. T-F mask prediction using a spectro-spatial feature set (constructed from input multichannel spectrogram and location information obtained by MS-GLMB filtering) and proposed residual dense convolutional graph-U-Net framework (training phase).

While the AF used in previous works [11–13] is instrumental in achieving good target speech enhancement performance due to the construction of a feature set comprising spectro-spatial features corresponding to the target source, it may be helpful to use a simpler feature set (such as magnitude spectrogram) as input to the deep neural architecture, while still leveraging the spatial information of the moving target source at each frame to construct a suitable target label set to train the neural architecture. Hence, in this work, the proposed deep neural architecture is trained on the magnitude spectrograms of the received multichannel reverberant mixture with the target source-specific T-F masks generated as labels, the latter having been generated by utilizing the spatial information of the multiple sources in motion. While direct estimation of a T-F mask from the complex spectra of received multichannel speech, as reported in [14,15], can also lead to dereverberation, speaker separation and noise cancellation, the exploitation of speaker-dependent spatial features for the generation of a label set for the deep neural architecture can lead to improvement in signal selectivity, which in turn can improve the performance of the beamformer.

Figure 3 shows the operation of the proposed neural framework during testing phase. The sequence of blocks at the lower half of this figure illustrates the implicit dependence of the neural processing on the spatial information of the target source. As the spatial information corresponding to the target source is utilized in the training of the proposed neural framework, the trained neural model incorporates the spatial information in addition to the spectral information. As such, the overall neural speech enhancement can be described as a spectro-spatial information processing framework. Hence, this methodology can also be referred to as spectro-spatial neural speech enhancement. Beamforming leads to an improvement in the SNR of the source-of-interest (SOI), resulting in a subsequent improvement in intelligibility under noisy and reverberant conditions. With the inclusion of T-F masking, a further improvement in the intelligibility of the SOI is achievable even in the presence of multiple interfering speakers. The training label generation procedure can be compactly explained in terms of subsections *A* and *B*.

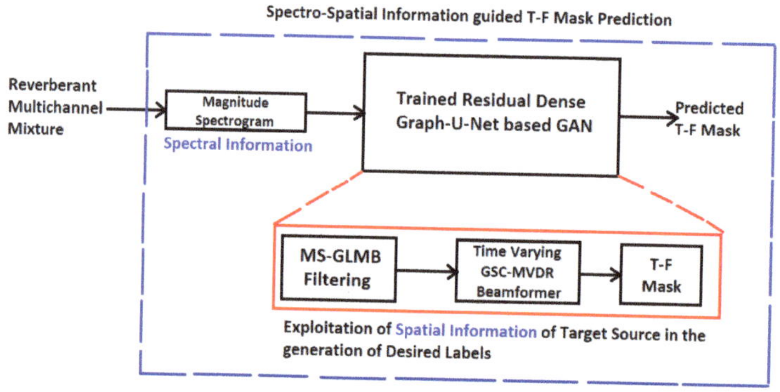

Figure 3. T-F mask by the proposed residual dense convolutional graph-U-Net framework (testing phase).

2.4. TV-GSC-MVDR Beamformer

In this sub-section, the TV-MVDR beamformer based on a GSC structure, referred to as TV-GSC-MVDR, is described, and is utilized in the T-F mask generation process as part of the neural network training.

The MVDR beamformer can be formulated by the following constrained optimization problem:

$$min_{w}\boldsymbol{w}^{H}\boldsymbol{R}_{n}\boldsymbol{w}\ s.t.\boldsymbol{w}^{H}.\boldsymbol{d}_{steer}=1 \tag{6}$$

The optimal solution to (6) is given as follows:

$$\boldsymbol{w}_{opt}=\frac{(\boldsymbol{R}_{n})^{-1}.\boldsymbol{d}_{steer}}{(\boldsymbol{d}_{steer})^{H}(\boldsymbol{R}_{n})^{-1}.\boldsymbol{d}_{steer}} \tag{7}$$

In Equations (6) and (7), the term $\boldsymbol{d}_{steer}$ denotes the beam-steering vector which is computed from the TDOA (alternatively, DOA). The term $\boldsymbol{R}_n$ denotes the noise covariance matrix, while the terms $\boldsymbol{w}$ and $\boldsymbol{w}_{opt}$ refer to MVDR beamformer weights and optimal MVDR beamformer weights, respectively. The selection of the steering vector for the kth frame (denoted by $\boldsymbol{d}_k$) is achieved by exploiting the source state and corresponding label predicted by the MS-GLMB filter. As pointed out in [6], the steering vector can be selected by choosing the column vector from the steering matrix $D^{(q)}_{k,\boldsymbol{x}_k^{est}}(f)$ for the kth time frame, where $D^{(q)}_{k,\boldsymbol{x}_k^{est}}(f)$ can be expressed as follows:

$$D^{(q)}_{k,\boldsymbol{x}_k^{est}}(f)=\begin{bmatrix} e^{j\omega_f(\tau(\alpha^{pos}_{k,1},u^{(q,1)}))} & \cdots & e^{j\omega_f(\tau(\alpha^{pos}_{k,N_k^{est}},u^{(q,1)}))} \\ \vdots & \ddots & \vdots \\ e^{j\omega_f(\tau(\alpha^{pos}_{k,1},u^{(q,M_q)}))} & \cdots & e^{j\omega_f(\tau(\alpha^{pos}_{k,N_k^{est}},u^{(q,M_q)}))} \end{bmatrix} \tag{8}$$

In (8), the terms $\alpha^{pos}_{k,1}\ldots\alpha^{pos}_{k,N_k^{est}}$ denote the positions of sources indexed $1\ldots N_k^{est}$ at frame 'k', $u^{(q,1)}\ldots u^{(q,M_q)}$ denote the positions of microphones indexed $(q,1)\ldots(q,M_q)$ for the qth array and microphone elements $(1\ldots M_q)$, respectively. The term $\tau\left(\alpha^{pos}_{k,\mathrm{n}},u^{(q,\mathrm{m})}\right)$, $\mathrm{n}=1\ldots N_k^{est}$, $m=1\ldots M_q$ represents the time delay between nth source located at position $\alpha^{pos}_{k,\mathrm{n}}$ and the mth microphone element of the qth array represented by the position $u^{(q,\mathrm{m})}$. The term ω_f denotes the angular frequency. Finally, the term N_k^{est} denotes the estimated number of sources in the acoustic environment.

The steering vector selection is achieved by the following operation:

$$d^{(q)}_{k,l_i^{est}}(f) = \left((D^{(q)}_{k,x_k^{est}}(f))^H\right)^{\#} . r_{N_k^{est}}(l_i^{est}) \quad (9)$$

In (9), as described in [8], the term $r_{N_k^{est}}(l_i^{est})$ denotes the selection operator, which selects the steering vector for the target speaker. The dimension of $r_{N_k^{est}}(l_i^{est})$ depends on the number of estimated sources. The term $d^{(q)}_{k,l_i^{est}}(f)$ denotes the steering vector selected by the operation in (9) for the T-F point (k, f), where the suffix l_i^{est} denotes the label of the source estimated by the MS-GLMB filtering algorithm, which helps to demarcate the target source from the interfering sources within the time frame. Thus, the dynamic MVDR beamformer weight for the *k*th frame can be expressed as follows:

$$\boldsymbol{w}_{k,l_i^{est}}{}^{(q)} = \frac{\boldsymbol{R}_n{}^{-1}.\boldsymbol{d}^{(q)}_{k,l_i^{est}}(f)}{\left(\boldsymbol{d}^{(q)}_{k,l_i^{est}}(f)\right)^H .\boldsymbol{R}_n{}^{-1}.\boldsymbol{d}^{(q)}_{k,l_i^{est}}(f)} \quad (10)$$

A. *T-F Mask Generation for constructing label set for training neural architecture.*

The beamformer output is utilized to compute the T-F mask corresponding to the target source at each time frame, which can lead to dynamic speech enhancement. Let the output of the beamformer at the T-F point (*f*, *k*) be denoted by $s^{MVDR}_{k,l_i^{est}}(f)$. As pointed out in [7], while the beamforming gain for the location of the target source might be higher than for the locations of interferers, the power spectrum in each T-F window may be dominated by interfering sources, in addition to noise and reverberation, during periods of inactivity of the target source or loud speech from the interfering sources. A spectral power ratio is computed to determine the T-F locations, which are dominated by the target speech and interference, respectively. This spectral power ratio can be expressed as follows:

$$G^{MVDR}_{k,l_i^{est}}(f) = \frac{|s^{MVDR}_{k,l_i^{est}}(f)|^2}{|s^{MVDR}_{k,l_j^{est}}(f)|^2}, \; i \neq j \quad (11)$$

In (11), while the numerator represents the power of the target signal (also referred to as SOI) in the spectral domain, the denominator also represents the power of the interferer source, $s^{MVDR}_{k,l_j^{est}}(f)$, identified by the estimated label l_j^{est}, in the spectral domain. The binary mask can be selected as:

$$\mathcal{M}_{k,\,l_i^{est}}(f) = \begin{cases} 1, \; if \; G^{MVDR}_{k,l_i^{est}}(f) \geq 1 \\ 0, \; if \; G^{MVDR}_{k,l_i^{est}}(f) < 1 \end{cases} \quad (12)$$

Using the mask in (12), the enhanced speech corresponding to the target source can be obtained as follows:

$$S^{TF}_{k,l_i^{est}}(f) = \mathcal{M}_{k,\,l_i^{est}}(f).s^{MVDR}_{k,l_j^{est}}(f) \quad (13)$$

By masking out those T-F bins, where the SOI is overwhelmed by speech from interfering sources as well as background noise, the intelligibility of the SOI can be considerably improved. The binary masks $\mathcal{M}_{k,l_i^{est}}(f)$ are generated from the label set for training the proposed residual dense Graph-U-Net-based GAN, as pictorially depicted in Figures 2 and 3.

B. *Dataset Construction*

The steps involved in the construction of the dataset for training the neural architecture are mentioned in this subsection, as follows:

(i) Selection of clean speech signals corresponding to three speakers from publicly available speech databases such as LibriSpeech and WSJ0mix. This is also mentioned in Section 4 on experimental results.
(ii) Generation of acoustic room impulse responses (RIRs) using the image source method (ISM).
(iii) Selection of reverberation times—RT60 of 550 ms, 250 ms and 50 ms—in three rooms of different dimensions.
(iv) Generation of noise samples at different acoustic SNRs.
(v) Creation of reverberant, noisy mixture of speech signals by convolution of clean speech signals with generated RIRs, with the addition of reverberation and noise samples.
(vi) Estimation of position coordinates and label of each source using MS-GLMB filtering algorithm.
(vii) Enhanced speech signal corresponding to target source across different time frames using GSC-MVDR beamforming.
(viii) Construction of T-F mask from the output of beamformer as explained in Section 2.4 A.
(ix) Creation of training dataset (to train the neural architecture) comprising the reverberant speech mixtures as input data and T-F masks as corresponding labels. In addition, the dataset is split into training, validation and testing datasets. This is further elaborated in quantitative terms in Section 4, where the experimental setup is described.

3. Residual Dense Convolutional Graph-U-Net-Based GAN for Target Speech Enhancement

Before discussing the overall neural architecture with the embedded graph convolutional network (GCN) module, the following subsections will present preliminaries on graph signal processing (GSP) [37] concepts and GAN operations [35,36].

3.1. Graph Signal Processing: Basic Concepts

Graph neural networks (GNNs) comprise a new class of neural architecture, which operates on graph-structured data. GNNs are capable of aggregating information from neighboring nodes of the graph, which help these neural architectures to encode structural–relational information into the overall representation. Consider $\mathcal{G}$ as a graph where the set of nodes is represented by $\mathcal{V}$ and the set of edges is represented by $\mathcal{E}$. Mathematically, this can be expressed as follows:

$$\mathcal{G} = (\mathcal{V}, \mathcal{E}) \tag{14}$$

The GCN applies a non-linear transformation on the input $\mathcal{X} \in \mathbb{R}^{|\mathcal{V}| \times N}$, where $|\mathcal{V}|$ denotes the cardinality of the nodes of the graph and N denotes the node feature size. The operation of the GCN can be mathematically represented as follows:

$$\mathcal{H}^{(l)} = g(\mathcal{D}^{-\frac{1}{2}} \mathcal{A} \mathcal{D}^{-\frac{1}{2}} \mathcal{H}^{(l-1)} \mathcal{W}^{(l-1)}) \tag{15}$$

where $\mathcal{D} \in \mathbb{R}^{|\mathcal{V}| \times |\mathcal{V}|}$ is a diagonal matrix, $\mathcal{A} \in \mathbb{R}^{|\mathcal{V}| \times |\mathcal{V}|}$ is the adjacency matrix, $\mathcal{H}^{(l)} \in \mathbb{R}^{|\mathcal{V}| \times K}$ is the lth hidden layer with K hidden features, $\mathcal{W}^{(l-1)}$ is the set of trainable parameters at the (l-1)-*th* layer and $g(.)$ denotes the non-linear activation function. The term $\mathcal{H}^{(0)}$ represents the input $\mathcal{X}$ to the GCN.

3.2. Generative Adversarial Network: Basic Concepts

GAN was proposed by Goodfellow et al. in 2014 [35]. Its ability to generate realistic images and generalize well to pixel-wise, complex distributions has led to its widespread use in numerous applications in image restoration, computer vision, speech processing, wireless communications, etc. In speech enhancement, GAN architecture is capable of providing fast enhancement performance due to the absence of any recursive operation like RNN. Moreover, GAN architecture is able to learn from different speakers and noise types, which renders it capable of providing good target speech enhancement performance under noisy conditions. A GAN includes two models, the generator (*G*) and the discriminator (*D*). The generator (*G*)'s main task is to learn an effective mapping, which can imitate the real data distribution to generate novel samples related to those of the training set. This is achieved by G when it solely maps the data distribution characteristics to the manifold defined in the prior distribution, without memorizing input–output pairs. The GAN operates through an adversarial process which can be formulated as a mini–max game between *G* and *D*. The objective function of the mini–max game can be expressed as follows:

$$min_G max_D V(D, G) = E_{x\sim p_{data}}[\log(D(x))] + E_{z\sim p_z(z)}[\log(1 - D(G(z)))] \quad (16)$$

Several GAN architectures have been applied to target speech enhancement [21–25], where most of these are based on the conditional GAN (c-GAN) approach [24]. While traditional GAN can generate realistic samples, there is no control on the data being generated in such as an unconditional generative architecture. For speech enhancement tasks, it is necessary to control the generated data samples based on the noisy input samples (for e.g., received multi-channel speech mixture). This issue is addressed by the c-GAN framework, where the neural architecture is conditioned to control the data generation process based on the input data. c-GANs have demonstrated promising performance in noise suppression. The c-GAN architecture is trained to generate the spectrogram of clean speech given the noisy speech spectrogram; however, it ignores the phase mismatch problem.

3.3. Architecture of Residual Dense-U-Net with Embedded GCRNN

In prior research works involving graph convolutional blocks embedded in U-Net's bottleneck layer [27–29], residual dense blocks were not explicitly applied in encoder and decoder parts of the architecture. In this article, a residual dense-U-Net architecture with a GCRNN embedded within the bottleneck layer (i.e., the GCRNN acts as the core embedding layer) is used as the neural framework of choice, and processes the spectro-spatial features to predict the target source-specific T-F mask. In addition, the skip connections also include GCRNN blocks. As mentioned earlier, neural architecture is applied in a GAN setting. In the generator, the embedded GCRNN's nodes are set equal to the number of channels that are also referred to as kernels of the last RDN layer in the encoder part of the U-Net architecture. The generator and discriminator network's operations are based on mini–max principles.

The encoder is composed of a stack of residual, densely connected convolutional blocks, whereas the decoder is composed of a stack of residual, densely connected deconvolutional blocks. Each densely connected block is a stack of four convolutional layers, with dense connections between layers. The output of each densely connected block in the encoder is passed through a GCRNN block-based skip pathway and then concatenated with the features of the corresponding residual densely connected de-convolutional block in the decoder.

A residual dense block (RDB) is a set of neural architecture, which can not only obtain the state from the preceding RDB via a contiguous memory (CM) mechanism but can also fully utilize all of the layers via local dense connections [41–43]. It contains densely connected layers, local feature fusion (LFF) and local residual learning together to lead to the CM mechanism. While residual learning modules, as in Res-Net architecture, can lead to better generalization capability of the model, they lack the dense concatenation of previous convolutional outputs to successive feature maps. Due to the presence of dense connectivity, a dense convolutional network, such as DenseNet [44], is able to utilize information from all previous convolutional operations, which allows the gradients to flow through several paths and thus enables richer information to be combined for feature extraction in consecutive layers. While the combination of residual and dense modules has been proposed in contemporary research works, their application in the domain of target speech enhancement for sources in motion seems limited. In the following subsections, the operation of the residual dense Graph-U-Net in a GAN setting is explained.

3.3.1. Generator Network: Residual Dense Graph-U-Net

The generator is a U-Net structure whose encoder is responsible for extracting the local and structural features. It halves the size of the feature maps using the convolutional kernel (whose stride is 2) instead of using pooling mechanism. Each convolutional layer is sequentially followed by one rectified linear unit (ReLU) and one instance normalization (IN) layer, which leads to significant reduction in the computational load. The process increases the receptive field of the network, which in turn improves model robustness.

The skip connections in the U-Net bypass the intermediate compression stages and directly pass fine-grained information to the decoder. As their presence facilitates flow of gradients through deeper layers of the overall network architecture, the skip connections can lead to better training performance by the network.

The operations of the generator network can be expressed in terms of hierarchical feature extraction and down-sampling at the encoder, the transformation of the multi-channel latent space of signals to the graph domain by the GCRNN module (embedded in the bottleneck layer), which leads to exploitation of spatio-temporal as well as spectral information in a more flexible manner, and up-sampling at the decoder. The operations of the residual dense blocks at the encoder part can be expressed as follows:

$$F_d = H^d_{RDB}(F_{d-1}) = H^d_{RDB}(H^{d-1}_{RDB}(\ldots(H^1_{RDB}(F_0)))) \tag{17}$$

In Equation (17), the term $H^d_{RDB}(.)$ represents the composite operation of convolution and ReLU at the RDB. As pointed out in [42,43], the residual dense block implements a CM mechanism by passing the state of the preceding residual dense block to each layer of the current residual dense block. The operation of the c-th convolution layer within the d-th residual dense block can be expressed in terms of the concatenation of the feature maps provided by the $(d-1)$th residual dense block as well as the (c − 1) convolutional layers $1,2\ldots(c-1)$ belonging to the d-th residual dense block, which results in $(G_0 + (c-1).\ G_0)$ feature maps. G_0 is the number of output feature maps, also referred to as growth rate. This is the dense connectivity, which helps to preserve the feed-forward nature. The overall operation can be expressed as follows:

$$F^c_d = ReLU(W^c_d[F_{d-1}, F^1_d, F^2_d \ldots F^{c-1}_d]) \tag{18}$$

In Equation (18), W^c_d represents the weights of the c-th convolutional layer, whereas F^c_d represents the output of the c-th convolution layer within the d-th residual dense block. The operation of the LFF component of the residual dense block can be expressed as follows:

$$H^{LF}_d = H^{LFF}_d([F_{d-1}, F^1_d \ldots, F^c_d, \ldots F^C_d]) \tag{19}$$

In Equation (19), $H_d^{LFF}(.)$ represents the 1-by-1 convolutional operation in the d-th RDB. Finally, the output of the RDB can be expressed as the output of local residual learning operation, as follows:

$$F_d = F_{d-1} + F_d^{LF} \tag{20}$$

The RDB employed in this work is pictorially depicted in Figure 4.

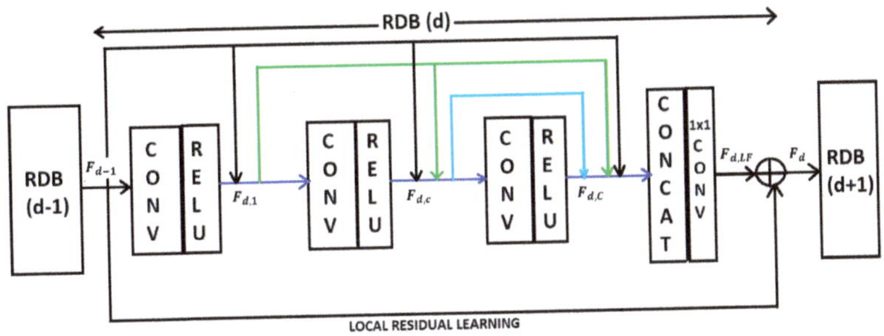

Figure 4. Architecture of the RDB utilized within each layer of encoder and decoder of the residual dense Graph-U-Net (The different colors denote the dense interconnections between convolutional layers within the dth residual block).

The last RDB of the encoder produces representations of dimension H-by-T′-by-F′, where H denotes the number of filters in the last residual dense convolutional layer of the encoder. As shown in Figure 5, the representations obtained at the last residual dense convolutional layer of the encoder parts are used to construct a graph with H nodes.

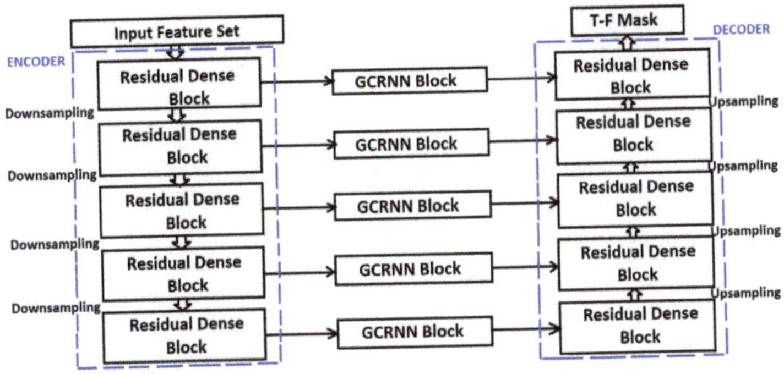

Figure 5. Prediction of T-F mask using the residual dense convolution-based Graph-U-Net framework for speech enhancement.

A. *Graph Construction*

In this article, the graph neural architecture is presented based on a message passing neural network, which operates through two phases, namely the message passing phase and the read-out phase [34,39]. The operations of these two steps for graph construction are expressed in terms of feature aggregation and update. The k-nearest neighbors (k-NN) [34] aggregation is utilized for graph construction, whereby it is possible to acquire k-NN by computing the Euclidean feature distance matrix, $D \in \mathbb{R}^{TF \times TF}$, formulated as follows:

$$d_{mn} = \sqrt{\sum_{D}(v_m - v_n)^2} \tag{21}$$

In (21), the term $d_{mn} \in$ D denotes the distance from node v_m to node v_n. A graph is constructed by applying k-NN to every node where the resultant graph is of shape

$D \times F \times T \times k$, for which $F \times T$ nodes with D features are linked by directed edges. More specifically, each node in the constructed graph points to an edge feature set of size k which contains k neighbor nodes. A self-loop is also represented by pointing a node to itself. The graph convolution operation can be represented as a sequence of aggregation and update operations which can be expressed as follows:

$$\mathcal{G}' = \mathcal{F}(\mathcal{G}, \mathcal{W}) \tag{22}$$

$$= Update(Aggregate(\mathcal{G}, W_{agg}),\ W_{update}) \tag{23}$$

In Equations (22) and (23), $\mathcal{G}$ denotes the input graph of a specific GCN layer, $\mathcal{G}'$ denotes the output graph of a specific GCN layer, W_{agg} denotes the learnable weights of the aggregation operator and W_{update} denotes the learnable weights of the update operator. The operation described in Equations (22) and (23) can be further elaborated with the help of Equations (24)–(27). If the set of neighbor nodes of the *i-th* node v_i is represented by $\mathcal{N}(v_i)$, the graph convolution operation represented by Equations (22) and (23) can be re-expressed as follows:

$$v_i' = h(v_i, g(v_i, \mathcal{N}(v_i), W_{agg}), W_{update}) \tag{24}$$

While in the graph convolutional layer, the aggregate operator can be either of the permutation-invariant operators, such as mean, sum, max, attention etc., the max-relative operator is applied in Equation (24) for the aggregate operation, which can be expressed by Equations (25) and (26), as follows:

$$\Psi_{ji} = v_j - v_i \ s.t.\ v_j \in \mathcal{N}(v_i) \tag{25}$$

$$g(.) = v_i' = [v_i, \max\{\Psi_{ji}\}] \tag{26}$$

The update operation in Equation (24) is implemented by a multi-layer perception (MLP), as follows:

$$h(.) = MLP(Concat(v_i, v_i')) \tag{27}$$

B. Operation of the GCRNN module

The output of the last RDB, denoted by F_d of dimensions H-by-T′-by-F′, is treated as a graph signal with H nodes and feature size T′*F′. The construction of the graph is mentioned in subsection A. The thus-constructed graph is processed by the GCRNN module embedded in the bottleneck layer, which acts as a bridge between the encoder and decoder. This bottleneck layer is responsible for capturing all of the critical features while maintaining spatial information. The output of the GCRNN layer is forwarded through the different residual dense convolutional layers of the decoder part, as a result of which the hidden features are transformed to the original dimension at the output of the decoder of the overall U-Net architecture. Each skip connection pathway connecting an encoder layer with the corresponding decoder layer in the U-Net architecture is also considered by a GCRNN block. In this work, the GCRNN is a GCN for feature extraction and is selected together with long short-term memory (LSTM) for sequence learning. The overall operations of the GCRNN module can be expressed as follows:

$$F_t^{GCN} = CNN_{\mathcal{G}}(F_{d,t}) \tag{28}$$

$$i_t = \sigma(W_{xi}.F_t^{GCN} + W_{hi}.h_{t-1} + W_{ci} \odot c_{t-1} + b_i) \quad (29)$$

$$f_t = \sigma(W_{xf}.F_t^{GCN} + W_{hf}.h_{t-1} + W_{cf} \odot c_{t-1} + b_f) \quad (30)$$

$$c_t = f_t \odot c_{t-1} + i_t \odot \tanh(W_{xc}.F_t^{GCN} + W_{hc}.h_{t-1} + b_c) \quad (31)$$

$$o_t = \sigma(W_{xo}.F_t^{GCN} + W_{ho}.h_{t-1} + W_{co} \odot c_t + b_o) \quad (32)$$

$$h_t = o_t \odot \tanh(c_t) \quad (33)$$

In (28), the term $F_{d,t}$ represents the input to the GCN denoted by the expression $CNN_{\mathcal{G}}(.)$, whereas the term F_t^{GCN} represents the output of the GCN gate. As evident from the above discussion, the input $F_{d,t} \in \mathbb{R}^{H \times T\prime.F\prime}$ is the output of the encoder with H nodes and T′*F′ features.

3.3.2. Discriminator Network

The discriminator is similar to the encoding stage of the generator network. Thus, it consists of a series of densely connected residual convolution blocks. Leaky ReLU (lReLU) is applied following the convolutional layers in the discriminator. After the down sampling process, the feature maps will pass through a fully connected layer whose output is a confidence value representing the similarity between the generated mask and true mask.

The functionalities of the generator and discriminator can be concisely expressed by the following steps:

Update discriminator such that (x, y)-pairs are classified as real i.e., $D(x, y) = 1$.

Update discriminator such that the pair comprising generated samples x_{pred} and true labels y are classified as fake i.e., $D(x_{pred}, y) = 0$.

Freeze the discriminator and update the generator such that the discriminator classifies the (x_{pred}, y)-pair as real i.e., $D(x_{pred}, y) = 1$.

3.3.3. Loss Function Used in Residual Dense Graph-U-Net GAN

For updating the generator and discriminator networks, the least-squares (LS) cost function is utilized in this work, and substitutes the conventional cross-entropy loss function of the binary classifier in the discriminator by an LS-based loss function. Furthermore, the application of the LS-based loss function can lead to improvements in the quality of the generated samples in the generator network and, due to increased stability, improvements in the training performance of the generator network. Moreover, an additional loss function term is also used in the GAN network, which minimizes the L1 distance between the generated samples and the clean samples. The L1 term is controlled by a hyper-parameter term, λ. The loss functions corresponding to the discriminator and generator networks are given by (28) and (29) respectively:

$$Discriminator: min_D \mathcal{L}(D) = \frac{1}{2}\mathbb{E}_{x,y \sim p_{data}(x,y)}[D(x,y) - 1]^2 + \frac{1}{2}\mathbb{E}_{z \sim Z, y \sim p_{data}(y)}\left[D(x^{est}, y)\right]^2 \quad (34)$$

$$Generator: min_G \mathcal{L}(G) = \mathbb{E}_{z \sim Z, y \sim p_{data}(y)}\left[D(x^{est}, y) - 1\right]^2 + \lambda.||x^{est} - y||_1 \quad (35)$$

3.4. Loss Function

In most works on speech enhancement using DL, the mean square error (MSE)-based loss function is used as the criterion for training the neural architecture. In addition to MSE, the scale invariant signal-to-noise ratio (SI-SNR) can also be incorporated within the loss function as a training criterion. A loss function combining the SI-SNR and MSE for better training of the neural architecture has been applied in [27], leading to good speech enhancement performance under low SNR conditions. Following [27], we also apply the combination of SI-SNR and MSE as the loss function in this work, whereby the formulation of the loss function can be explained by (36)–(40), as follows:

$$x_{target} = \frac{< x_{enh}, x_{clean} > .x_{clean}}{||x_{clean}||_2^2} \tag{36}$$

$$z_{noise} = x_{enh} - x_{clean} \tag{37}$$

$$\mathcal{L}_{SI-SNR}(x_{clean}, x_{enh}) = 10.log_{10}(\frac{||x_{target}||_2^2}{||z_{noise}||_2^2}) \tag{38}$$

In (36)–(38), the terms x_{enh} and x_{clean} represent the enhanced and clean target speech signals in the time domain, respectively. The operation $< .,. >$ denotes the dot product operation between any two vectors. In (38), $||.||_2^2$ denotes the L2 (or Euclidean) norm. The SI-SNR-based loss function is denoted by $\mathcal{L}_{SI-SNR}(.)$. If the true mask and estimated mask are denoted by M_{clean} and M_{est} (where $M_{est} \in \{M_s^{DL}, M_{int+noise}^{DL}\}$), respectively, then the MSE loss function can be expressed as follows:

$$\mathcal{L}_{MSE}(M_{clean}, M_{est}) = \sum_{t,f}[(Re(M_{clean}) - Re(M_{est}))^2 + (Im(M_{clean}) - Im(M_{est}))^2] \tag{39}$$

In (39), $Re(.)$ and $Im(.)$ denote the real and imaginary parts, respectively. Based on (38) and (39), the combined loss function can be expressed as follows:

$$\mathcal{L}(x_{clean}, x_{enh}) = \mathcal{L}_{SI-SNR}(x_{clean}, x_{enh}) + \log(\mathcal{L}_{MSE}(M_{clean}, M_{est})) \tag{40}$$

4. Computer Simulation Results

4.1. Experimental Dataset

4.1.1. Speech Source Parameters

In order to evaluate the effectiveness of the proposed methodology, in this work we have constructed a new dataset of simulated speech sources in motion under noisy, reverberant conditions. Speech signals corresponding to the sources have been selected from the WSJ0mix [46] and LibriSpeech [47] speech corpuses, while the noise samples were selected from CHiME-3 [48], the diverse environments multichannel acoustic noise database (DEMAND) [49] and environment sound classification (ESC-50) [50] databases.

The signals from WSJ0mix and CHiME-3 are randomly selected and mixed for SNRs between 2 dB and 10 dB. The selected noise samples from the DEMAND database correspond to noise signals recorded in diverse acoustic environments such as a busy subway station, an office cafeteria, and a university restaurant. Fifteen noises were selected for training and validation sets, whereas three noises were selected for the testing set. The SNR selected for training and validation sets were randomly sampled between −5 dB and 0 dB. However, for the testing set, different SNR values of −5 dB, 0 dB and 5 dB were used. ESC-50 is a dataset for environment sound samples, one which contains a total of 2000 environmental sound recordings organized into 5 primary classes, namely animal, natural, human, interior/domestic and exterior. The dataset is labelled with 50 classes and is also available with noise added to the audio signals. Therefore, the ESC-50 dataset also provides a plethora of sound waveforms which can be added to speech waveforms in the indoor environment to illustrate the target speech waveform enhancement task. In this work, a training set comprising 7000 speech mixtures was created for training the proposed neural architecture, whereas a validation set comprising 1000 speech mixture signals for validation and a testing set comprising 1000 speech signal mixtures for testing the proposed neural architecture were also created. MATLAB 2024b is used to generate the reverberant speech signals, whereas Tensorflow 2.11 is used with Python version 3.9 to train and test the proposed neural approach. The signals were sampled at 16 KHz. In addition, a Hamming window of a duration of 20 ms was utilized to segment the waveforms into a set of time frames, whereby an overlap of 50% between adjacent frames is applied. The size of the DFT applied to each time frame of received speech signal mixture is therefore of a length of 320 points.

The room impulse response (RIR) between the source speaker and the receiving microphone array is generated using the ISM [55] approach. The acoustic scene parameters used for this simulation are tabulated in Table 1. For each simulated RIR, the room geometry, array position and start and end coordinates of the source speakers are randomly selected. Similar parameters of acoustic scenes and microphone array configurations have also been considered in [6,26,31]. However, this work involves a DL-based combined approach of tracking and enhancement, and the DL parameters used in this work are mentioned in Section 4.3. The speech signals corresponding to the 3 speakers are simulated inside a room with the dimensions of 10 m by 18 m by 6 m, where the reverberation times denoted by RT60 are considered as 50 ms, 250 ms and 550 ms, respectively. During the training phase, RT60 values of 50 ms, 250 ms and 550 ms are chosen, whereas during the testing phase, RT60 values of 550 ms are chosen to test the performance of the DL architecture. A single microphone array with 6 sensors is simulated. The maximum number of speakers chosen is 3. The RIRs were generated using ISM [54] at the above-mentioned reverberation times. The sampling frequency is taken to be 16,000 Hz.

Table 1. Acoustic scene parameters.

Room Dimensions in x,y Coordinates (in m)	X (14 m)	Y (22 m)
SNR (in dB)	0–60 (training)	15, 35, 80 (testing)
Reverberation time, T60 (in ms)	50, 250, 550	550
Microphone array	Linear	6 sensors per array
Number of speakers	3 (training)	3 (testing)

In the simulation setting, a maximum number of 3 speakers is selected, and these are placed in continuous motion inside the room. The different microphone sensors 'coordinates are taken to be (7.11, 6.0), (7.11, 5.55), (7.11, 5.10), (7.11, 4.65), (7.11, 4.20) and (7.11, 3.75). The motion of the speakers is modelled by the Langevin model. Details about the Langevin model can be found in [6] and the references therein. The state equations governed by the Langevin model can be expressed as follows:

$$\alpha_{k+1}^{pos} = \alpha_k^{pos} + \varnothing.\alpha_k^{vel} \tag{41}$$

$$\alpha_{k+1}^{vel} = e^{-\beta\varnothing}.\alpha_k^{vel} + \vartheta.\sqrt{1-e^{-2\beta\varnothing}}.\Sigma_k \tag{42}$$

In (41) and (42), α_k^{pos} and α_k^{vel} represent the 3D position vector and velocity vector of the target speaker in motion. The terms β, ϕ and Σ_k represent the rate constant which controls the rate of decay of velocity, discretization time step interval, and process noise, respectively. The process noise Σ_k is a 3D Gaussian vector with mean zero and covariance, $\sigma_\Sigma.\sigma_\Sigma^T$, where σ_Σ represents the standard deviation of the process noise. The Langevin model parameters used for the simulation are included in Table 2.

Table 2. Parameters of the Langevin model.

Parameters	Values
β (in s^{-1})	10
ϑ (in ms^{-1})	1
ϕ (in ms)	32
σ_Σ (in ms^{-1})	$[4.5,\ 4.5,\ 4.5]^T$

4.1.2. MS-GLMB Filtering Parameters

The 3D coordinates of the target source are obtained from the SRP-PHAT data. These 3D coordinates are used to construct the measurement set for the MS-GLMB filter. Table 3 outlines the parameters corresponding to the MS-GLMB filter. In this work, the same parameters of MS-GLMB filter are used as used in [6].

Table 3. Parameters of the MS-GLMB filter.

$r_B(l_1)$	0.005
$r_B(l_2)$	0.005
$r_B(l_3)$	0.005
$\mu_B^{(1)}$	$[5.0\ 1.0\ 1.8\ 0\ 0\ 0]^T$
$\mu_B^{(2)}$	$[4.0\ 3.0\ 1.5\ 0\ 0\ 0]^T$
$\mu_B^{(3)}$	$[2.5\ 0.5\ 1.5\ 0\ 0\ 0]^T$
$P_B^{(1)}$	$\mathrm{diag}([0.15; 0.15; 0.15; 0.15; 0.15; 0.15]^T)$
$P_B^{(2)}$	$\mathrm{diag}([0.15; 0.15; 0.15; 0.15; 0.15; 0.15]^T)$
$P_B^{(3)}$	$\mathrm{diag}([0.15; 0.15; 0.15; 0.15; 0.15; 0.15]^T)$

The birth parameters of the 3 speakers can be denoted by $\left\{r_B(l_i), p_B(.,l_i) \triangleq \mathcal{N}(.; \mu_B^{(i)}, P_B^{(i)})\right\}_{i=1}^{3}$, where $r_B(l_i)$ denotes the birth probability of the ith speaker with label l_i and $p_B(.,l_i)$ denotes the birth probability density of the ith speaker, which is a Gaussian with mean $\mu_B^{(i)}$ and covariance $P_B^{(i)}$. The Gaussian mean $\mu_B^{(i)}$ represents a vector which contains the expected location of the birth of the ith speaker with label l_i. The covariance $P_B^{(i)}$ signifies the spatial uncertainty associated with the ith speaker. The estimated label corresponding to the target speaker is obtained by MS-GLMB filtering. The label information is helpful in demarcating the trajectories corresponding to the different speech sources within the environment, which in turn helps the algorithm to track the sources in motion across all the time frames.

4.2. MS-GLMB Filtering Based Multi-Source Tracking Filter

As mentioned earlier, the multi-array measurements are processed by the MS-GLMB filter at each frame, whereby the source tracks comprising positions and labels are estimated. In this regard, it is useful to mention that a track can be considered as a function whose domain comprises the set of time instants at which the source exists. In general, a track corresponding to a particular source exists when the estimated positions of that source across the time frames can be associated with a common label. In practical scenarios, such as online multi-object tracking, the source may intermittently speak or disappear from the scene, giving rise to fragmented (or broken) tracks. Another scenario which frequently happens in online multi-object tracking is that which, when multiple sources are in very close proximity, the associated labels and their tracks may interchange. Figure 6 depicts the prediction of the (x-, y-) coordinates across all of the time frames by the MS-GLMB filtering at RT60 = 550 ms and compares against the ground truth positions.

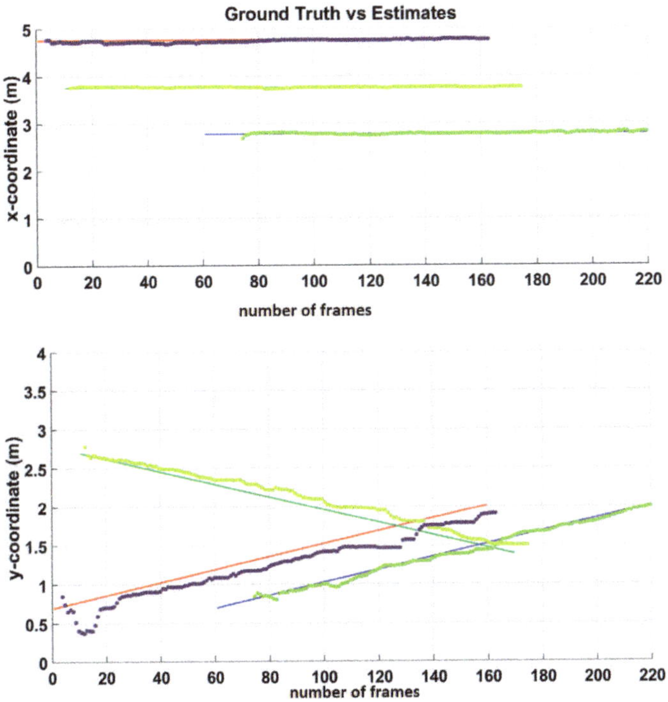

Figure 6. Plot of estimated (x-, y-) coordinates by MS-GLMB filter across all time frames at reverberation time RT60 = 550 ms and acoustic SNR = 35 dB. The colored tracks in the form of straight lines indicate the original i.e., ground truth trajectories corresponding to 3 speech sources, whereas the colored tracks with dots indicate estimates of the source trajectories obtained by the MS-GLMB filter.

As observed from Figure 6, the application of MS-GLMB filtering to multi-source tracking in the acoustic domain leads to estimation of source tracks, which can still closely resemble the ground-truth tracks under the effects of noise and reverberation. This is due to the ability of the MS-GLMB filter to resolve the space-time permutation problem by jointly estimating the source labels and positions. This framework can account for noise, false positives and false negatives in the multi-array measurements (in this case, SRP-PHAT-based acoustic measurement at each array). Furthermore, source motions, labels as well as their appearances and disappearances are also incorporated into the formulation of the MS-GLMB filter for multi-source tracking. Because of these advantages, the MS-GLMB filter can guide the construction of input features in order to train the proposed neural framework, whereby the input feature set includes the directional information of the target source provided by the MS-GLMB filter.

4.3. Experimental Setup for the Residual Dense Graph-U-Net

In order to evaluate the extent to which the proposed methodology works under different acoustic environments, the proposed approach is subject to different room environments where the room dimensions are different from those of the original environment. The room dimensions considered for evaluating the proposed approach under different acoustic conditions are chosen as 5.80 m by 3.30 m by 2.00 m, 7.50 m by 3.50 m by 2.80 m and 10.50 m by 6.50 m by 3.40 m. The rooms corresponding to these three different room dimensions are designated as 'Test Room I', 'Test Room II', and 'Test Room III', respectively. Table 4 presents the overall summary of experimental conditions, while Table 5 depicts the test rooms' dimensions. Table 6 presents the positions of microphone elements within each test room.

Table 4. Summary of experimental conditions.

Configuration of Mask Estimation Network (Generator)	
ENCODER	
Number of down-sampling layers	5
Number of RDBs in each encoder layer	1
Kernels of CNN layers in each encoder block	{64, 128, 128, 128, 32}
Kernel sizes of CNN layers	3 × 3
Stride	2 × 2
Padding	0
DECODER	
Number of up-sampling layers	5
Number of RDBs in each decoder layer	5
Kernels of CNN layers in each decoder block	{32, 128, 128, 128, 64}
Kernel sizes of CNN layers	3 × 3
Stride	2 × 2
Padding	0
Loss Function	MSE
Optimization criterion	ADAM
Learning rate	10^{-4}
Batch size	32

Table 5. Test room dimensions.

Test Room I	5.80 m by 3.30 m by 2.00 m
Test Room II	7.50 m by 3.50 m by 2.80 m
Test Room III	10.50 m by 6.50 m by 3.40 m

Table 6. Microphone positions for Test Room I, Test Room II and Test Room III.

Position 1	[(2.40, 0.3), (2.60, 0.3), (2.80, 0.3), (3.0, 0.3), (3.20, 0.3), (3.40, 0.3)]
Position 2	[(4.00, 0.3), (4.20, 0.3), (4.40, 0.3), (4.60, 0.3), (4.80, 0.3), (5.00, 0.3)]
Position 3	[(3.6, 3.11), (3.4, 3.11), (3.2, 3.11), (3.0, 3.11), (2.8, 3.11), (2.6, 3.11)]

The reverberation time used for these environments is RT60 = 550 ms. The microphone sensors' coordinates are varied so that the positions of the array elements are different from those placed in the room in which the algorithm was originally trained. The different positions of the microphone sensors in the array in the test environments are tabulated in Table 6. The configurations selected in Tables 5 and 6 have also been applied in prior research works and are included in [31,45]. In particular, the research work presented in [45] utilized a Dense-U-Net architecture, which performs localization of acoustic sources in motion. The training procedure involved in that research work involved training and testing the Dense-U-Net architecture using three test rooms as well as a six-element linear microphone array whose positions were varied in the three rooms to effectively train the neural architecture to predict the locations of the sources with high accuracy in the presence of acoustic impairments like reverberation as well as sources' motion. Motivated by the results presented in [45], the work presented in this article also utilizes the same test room dimensions and microphone array positions as in [45] for testing the proposed speech enhancement approach.

In the test environments, apart from varying the microphone sensors' positions, the SNR is varied such that the selected acoustic SNRs fall in the set [0 dB, 10 dB, 20 dB, 30 dB, 40 dB, 50 dB, 60 dB]. To test the proposed approach, an SNR value is randomly selected from the above set of SNRs, whereby the test room dimensions and positions of the microphone array sensors are also randomly selected from Tables 5 and 6 respectively.

4.4. Evaluation Metrics

The proposed methodology is compared with other methodologies which have also been applied to the moving speech sources scenario. As evaluation metrics, enhanced short-time objective intelligibility (ESTOI) [51], perceptual evaluation of speech quality (PESQ) [52], SI-SNR [18] and signal-to-distortion ratio (SDR) [53] are used for performance comparison in this work. In this section, the spectrograms of the clean target speech, reverberant mixture and enhanced speech are first presented for comparison. Second, the proposed approach is evaluated against other state-of-the-art neural speech enhancement approaches in terms of some established evaluation metrics. Figure 7a–c depict the spectrograms of clean target, reverberant mixture, and enhanced speech corresponding to waveforms selected from the LibriSpeech dataset.

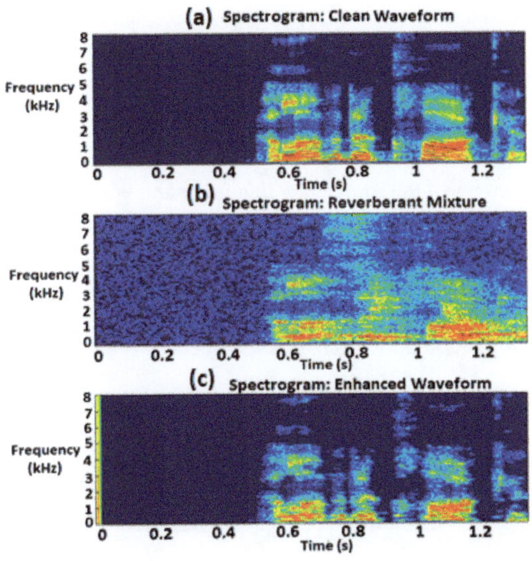

Figure 7. (**a**) Spectrogram of the clean speech signal belonging to the target source, (**b**) spectrogram of the reverberant mixture of speech signals corresponding to 3 sources, (**c**) spectrogram of the enhanced speech signal corresponding to target source. The colored portion of the spectrograms between 0.5 s and 1.3 s denote the presence of speech (*All speech signals belong to LibriSpeech dataset*).

Figure 8a–c depict the spectrograms of the clean target, reverberant mixture, and enhanced speech corresponding to the waveforms selected from the Ws2J0mix dataset.

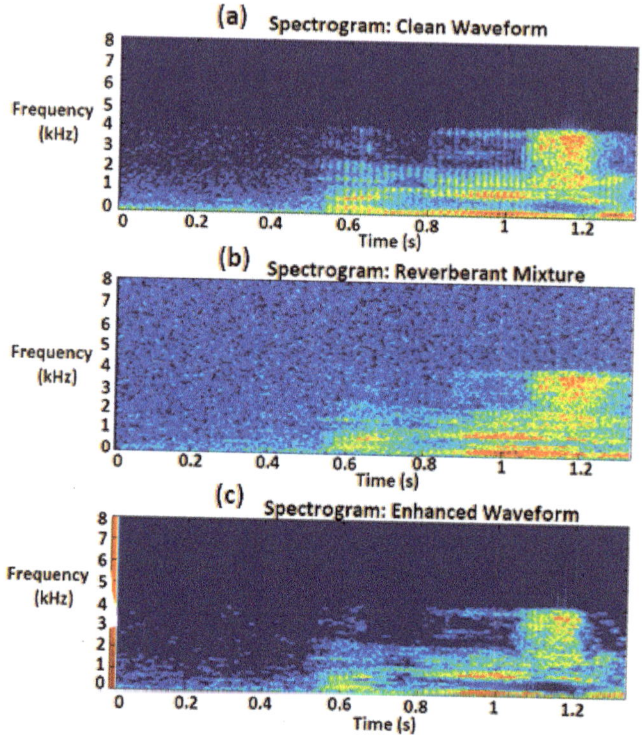

Figure 8. (**a**) Spectrogram of the clean speech signal belonging to the target source, (**b**) spectrogram of the reverberant mixture of speech signals corresponding to 3 sources, (**c**) spectrogram of enhanced speech signal corresponding to the target source. The colored portion of the spectrograms between 0.5 s and 1.3 s denote the presence of speech (*All speech signals belong to WS2J0 dataset*).

As evident from the spectrograms presented in Figures 7 and 8, the proposed neural approach of speech enhancement successfully cancels the background noise and reverberation to enhance the target speech, even when the sources are in motion and intermittently speaking. This is evident from Figures 7c and 8c. Next, Table 7 shows a performance comparison in terms of objective metrics such as PESQ and SI-SNR between the proposed approach and other state-of-the-art approaches at three different RT60 values (550 ms, 250 ms and 50 ms), which tackle the problem of speech enhancement including speech dereverberation and interference cancellation under dynamic scenarios.

Table 7. Performance comparison of different state-of-the-art approaches for speech dereverberation under dynamic conditions at 3 different reverberation times.

Method	RT60 = 550 ms		RT60 = 250 ms		RT60 = 50 ms	
	PESQ	SI-SNR (dB)	PESQ	SI-SNR (dB)	PESQ	SI-SNR (dB)
MS-GLMB filter-assisted DS	2.41	4.42	2.79	10.73	2.91	13.94
TI-MVDR	2.43	2.35	2.73	4.42	2.76	5.13
Online-MVDR	3.22	4.85	3.38	5.62	3.45	6.52

Table 7. *Cont.*

Method	RT60 = 550 ms		RT60 = 250 ms		RT60 = 50 ms	
	PESQ	SI-SNR (dB)	PESQ	SI-SNR (dB)	PESQ	SI-SNR (dB)
MS-GLMB filter-assisted MVDR	3.28	5.65	3.44	6.55	3.51	7.66
DOA-MVDR	3.43	8.85	3.49	9.75	3.55	10.36
Mask-MVDR with self-attention	3.57	10.37	3.60	10.55	3.65	12.66
U-Net with embedded GCN	3.56	10.54	3.65	11.66	3.67	12.78
RD-GAN	3.58	10.58	3.67	11.72	3.69	12.82
RD-Graph-U-Net-GAN (proposed approach)	3.60	10.77	3.70	11.88	3.85	12.86

4.4.1. Beamformer Baselines for Performance Comparison

In this section, an overview of the state-of-the-art beamformer approaches is presented. The proposed approach is compared with these approaches for target speech enhancement under reverberant conditions involving moving sources. The evaluated baseline beamformers can be denoted by time invariant MVDR (TI_MVDR), online MVDR (online_ MVDR) involving online computation of SCM, block MVDR (BLK_ MVDR) involving block-wise processing of time-varying SCM, direction-of-arrival (DOA)-based MVDR (DOA_MVDR) baseline, mask-based MVDR using attention mechanism (ATT_MASK_ MVDR), residual dense GAN-based beamformer (RD-GAN) [25] and GCN-based MVDR (GCN_ MVDR). Outlines of such beamformer baselines can be obtained from [8,25,29].

TI-MVDR Beamformer Baseline

The TI_MVDR system computes the SCM in a time-invariant fashion, where the assumption is that the transfer function is static within an utterance. The time-invariant SCMs can be computed as follows:

$$\boldsymbol{\Phi}_f^v = \sum\nolimits_{\tau=1}^{T} \frac{1}{\sum\nolimits_{\tau'=1}^{T} m_{\tau',f}^v} m_{\tau,f}^v . Y_{\tau,f} . Y_{\tau,f}^T \tag{43}$$

In (43), the term $Y_{\tau,f}.Y_{\tau,f}^T$ can be represented by $\boldsymbol{\Psi}_{\tau,f}^v$, which can be referred to as an instantaneous SCM (ISCM) at the T-F bin. The term $m_{\tau',f}^v \in [\mathbf{0},\ \mathbf{1}]$ represents the T-F mask. In (43), the superscript $v \in \{S, N\}$ denotes the indices of speech (S) and noise (N).

Online MVDR Beamformer Baseline

The online_MVDR system involves the application of a recursive approach to compute a time-varying (T-V) SCM, $\boldsymbol{\Phi}_{t,f}^v$. Such an approach can lead to the computation of SCMs for the MVDR beamformer in an online manner. The recursive computation of the online SCMs can be expressed as follows:

$$\boldsymbol{\Phi}_{t,f}^v = \alpha.\boldsymbol{\Phi}_{t-1,f}^v + \boldsymbol{\Psi}_{t,f}^v = \sum\nolimits_{\tau=1}^{t} \alpha^{t-\tau}.\boldsymbol{\Psi}_{\tau,f}^v \tag{44}$$

The online_MVDR approach enables the computation of SCMs as well as MVDR beamformer weights at each time frame, which in turn allows for the tracking of a speech source.

Block MVDR Beamformer Baseline

The BLK_MVDR system involves the computation of SCM corresponding to each time block of the signal into which it is divided. The block-wise computation of the time-varying SCMs can be expressed as follows:

$$\boldsymbol{\Phi}_{t,f}^v = \sum\nolimits_{\tau=t-L}^{t+L} \frac{1}{\sum\nolimits_{\tau'=t-L}^{t+L} m_{\tau',f}^v} . \boldsymbol{\Psi}_{\tau,f}^v \tag{45}$$

In (45), the term L denotes the block-size parameter and $(2L + 1)$ frames were utilized for the computation of SCM for each block.

DOA-Based MVDR Beamformer Baseline

The DOA_MVDR system computes the steering vector from the DOA information which can be expressed as follows:

$$h_{t,f} = \left[e^{j\frac{2\pi f}{v}\tau_1}, e^{j\frac{2\pi f}{v}\tau_2} \ldots e^{j\frac{2\pi f}{v}\tau_C}\right]^T \quad (46)$$

In (46), $h_{t,f}$ denotes the beam steering vector, v the speed of sound waves, and τ_C the propagation delay w.r.t origin for microphone indexed C. The steering vector is constructed from the DOA information and can be used to construct SCM corresponding to speech signal, which can be utilized in the MVDR beamformer formulation. A baseline beamformer can be constructed utilizing the a priori known DOA information with which performance of other beamformers may be compared in acoustic scenarios involving speech sources in motion.

Mask-Based MVDR Beamformer Baseline Based on Attention Mechanism

The details of this work can be obtained from [8]. In this sub-section, a brief overview of the approach behind this baseline beamformer is included. The baseline beamformer in [8] involves a generalized approach to the computation of SCMs for moving speech sources, which can be interpreted as the weighted sum of ISCMs, weighted by attention weights. A self-attention-based neural architecture is utilized to predict these attention weights. The procedure to compute the attention weights involves processing the vectorized ISCMs by a neural network architecture, which can be expressed as follows:

$$\{c_v^t\}_{t=1}^T = \mathcal{F}^v(\{\Upsilon_{t,f}^v\}_{t=1}^T; \mathcal{P}_v) \quad (47)$$

In (47), $\{c_v^t\}_{t=1}^T$ represents the attention weights, $\mathcal{F}^v(.)$ the neural architecture operation, $\left\{\Upsilon_{t,f}^v\right\}_{t=1}^T$ the ISCMs and $\mathcal{P}_v$ the parameters of the neural architecture. Once the attention weights are constructed, they are utilized to compute the SCMs which then help to compute the MVDR beamformer weights. In [8], it has been pointed out that the efficacy of this approach lies in the ability of the self-attention-based neural architecture to predict the attention weights which facilitate the accumulation of ISCMs from a similar direction while making it possible to track a speech source.

Apart from the abovementioned baseline beamformers, the 'gcn_mvdr' baseline beamformer is presented in [29], which involves the incorporation of a GCN module within the neural architecture. Such an approach helps in the exploitation of spatio-temporal and spectral information in a flexible manner.

Performance comparisons between the proposed approach and other state-of-the-art neural approaches on simulated RIRs are presented in Tables 7 and 8. Table 7 presents the performance comparison in terms of speech dereverberation, whereas Table 8 presents the performance comparison in terms of speech separation on simulated RIRs. Moreover, evaluation of the proposed approach on recorded RIRs is also presented in Table 9.

Table 8. Performance comparison of different approaches for speaker separation under 3 different levels of reverberation.

Method	RT60 = 550 ms				RT60 = 250 ms				RT60 = 50 ms			
	ESTOI (%)	PESQ	SI-SNR (dB)	SDR (dB)	ESTOI (%)	PESQ	SI-SNR (dB)	SDR (dB)	ESTOI (%)	PESQ	SI-SNR (dB)	SDR (dB)
MS-GLMB filter-assisted DS	47.63	1.81	−2.60	1.40	63.88	2.23	3.71	6.27	68.80	2.32	5.96	8.06
TI-MVDR	40.53	1.74	−5.42	0.24	40.77	1.89	−2.87	2.71	41.95	1.89	−3.49	2.28
Online-MVDR	45.20	1.79	−4.06	1.00	55.57	2.05	−0.89	4.14	52.78	1.99	−1.85	3.47
MS-GLMB filter-assisted MVDR	56.80	2.02	0.46	3.76	79.23	2.75	8.31	10.86	79.71	2.75	7.95	10.72
DOA-MVDR	40.70	1.76	−4.68	0.94	54.91	2.26	−1.44	4.28	50.00	2.16	−2.14	3.55
Mask-MVDR with self-attention	46.74	1.84	−3.48	1.61	59.59	2.25	−0.22	5.02	54.00	2.10	−1.82	3.54
U-Net with embedded GCN	72.32	2.56	2.03	5.97	75.10	2.67	3.36	7.58	78.71	2.78	5.87	9.44
RD-GAN	46.99	1.87	−3.14	1.40	58.22	2.16	−1.19	3.06	60.65	2.24	0.25	3.96
RD-Graph-U-Net (proposed approach)	75.00	2.70	2.16	6.12	79.60	2.88	3.77	7.80	80.50	2.90	5.96	9.66

Table 9. Evaluation of proposed approach on recorded RIRs.

Method	Office Room (RT60 = 0.52 s)		Corridor (RT60 = 1.25 s)	
	PESQ	ESTOI (%)	PESQ	ESTOI (%)
RD-Graph-U-Net (proposed approach)	3.06	77.40	2.56	75.58
MS-GLMB filter-assisted MVDR	2.77	74.46	2.25	72.23
Mask-MVDR with self-attention	2.85	75.56	2.36	73.39
U-Net with embedded GCN	2.84	75.32	2.29	72.78

4.4.2. Performance Comparison of Proposed Approach on Simulated and Recorded RIRs

From Table 7, it is evident that the proposed approach of the residual dense Graph-U-Net, assisted by MS-GLMB filtering, outperforms the other state-of-the-art approaches of target speech enhancement under reverberant conditions, when the sources are in motion with intermittent speech activity. This is because the spectro-spatial features extracted by the MS-GLMB filtering framework provides training data for the proposed neural architecture by incorporating the effects of reverberation and motion of the sources, which helps the proposed neural architecture to learn the mapping from input spectro-spatial features to the target source-specific mask better than other approaches where a motion model of the speech sources is not considered.

In Table 8, ESTOI, PESQ, SI-SNR and SDR are used as the evaluation metrics of choice. Compared with STOI, ESTOI provides a more comprehensive assessment of the intelligibility of enhanced speech by considering additional factors such as additive and convolutional distortions that are commonly encountered in real-world scenarios.

As observed from Table 8, the TI_MVDR cannot handle the moving sources well because the estimated SCMs by TI_MVDR are time-invariant in nature, which causes the beamforming filter coefficients to also be time invariant. The online_MVDR method does appear to track moving sources but, in this approach, the tracking seems to depend on the forgetting factor that is responsible for providing exponentially less weight to the older ISCMs. Therefore, it is cumbersome to tune this parameter in order to offer optimal performance for various acoustic conditions that may arise during movements of the speech sources. The BLK_MVDR approach also suffers from sub-optimal performance due to the challenge involved in tuning the block sizes during online SCM computation. Because, during online operation, the objective is to perform beamforming based on an adequate number of signal samples received within a short time interval, it is challenging to tune the block size of received signals so as to provide optimal performance with this approach. The DOA_MVDR baseline approach serves as a benchmark for evaluating the performance of other beamforming approaches whereby an 'oracle' approach is designed with a priori knowledge of the DOAs. While it helps in performance evaluation, in practical scenarios, perfect knowledge of the DOAs cannot be obtained a priori because the estimated DOA information will be contaminated by noise imperfections. Finally, the mask-based MVDR beamformer approach with self-attention neural architecture seems to provide good performance under source movements due to the capability of the self-attention-based neural architecture to focus on a particular DOA direction. However, all of these beamforming approaches suffer from the assumption of a fixed cardinality of the sources, whereas the cardinality of the speech sources may vary due to the appearance and disappearances of the sources at different time frames within the acoustic environment. Due to the random nature of the cardinality, the MVDR beamformer needs to be dynamic in nature in order to be able to accurately steer the beam towards the target source while directing nulls towards the interfering sources at different time frames. In this regard, the proposed approach seems to outperform other state-of-the-art approaches of speech enhancement using DL techniques under reverberant conditions when all the sources are in motion. While the MS-GLMB-assisted source tracking helps in target source tracking across the time frames, the presence of dense convolutions with residual blocks in the neural architecture helps to cancel the noise better than conventional convolutional modules in the U-Net architecture. Moreover, the presence of GCRNN in the bottleneck of the overall U-Net helps to exploit the implicit information, such as spatial and temporal-spectral information, in a more flexible manner as compared with conventional methodologies. Speech enhancement methods based on conventional beamforming are sensitive to the motion of acoustic sources, which explains why the performance of the conventional GSC-based beamformer degrades in dynamic conditions. Estimation of the time-varying statistics, using labelled RFS-based algorithms and DL architectures, within the conventional beamforming pipeline (such as GSC-MVDR) lead to improved speech intelligibility and speech quality than the approaches without labelled RFS and DL methodology. This can be attributed to the fact that the labelled RFS-based algorithms provide a powerful framework to model the motion of the sources, which in turn leads to better construction of the dataset by considering the effects of time-varying interference and multipath impairments such as reverberation with higher accuracy. From Tables 7 and 8, it is evident that the performance of the integrated MS-GLMB filtering-assisted neural beamforming is superior to other neural speech enhancement methods under reverberant conditions when the sources are in motion.

Unlike the results in Tables 7 and 8, which were based on simulated RIRs, in this subsection, we outline the results of the application of the proposed approach to recorded RIRs. The Aachen impulse response (AIR) [57] database is used for selecting the recorded RIRs, in this case two RIRs, recorded from office and corridor environments and with RT60 = 0.52 s and 1.25 s respectively. Moreover, noise samples from the DEMAND database were added to these RIRs to create a noisy, reverberant dataset at a low acoustic SNR of 0 dB.

As observed from Table 9, the proposed neural approach also outperforms other methods of speech enhancement in terms of objective quality metrics under recorded RIRs. This indicates that the proposed method is also able to generalize well to recorded RIRs, under noisy conditions.

4.4.3. ANOVA Analysis

In this sub-section, we confirm the significance of the results achieved using the proposed speech enhancement approach over other methods using the analysis-of-variance (ANOVA) approach. The statistical tests were conducted at a 95% confidence interval. The differences between achieved ESTOI and PESQ using the proposed method and other approaches are considered to be significant if the probability value denoted by the *p*-value is less than 0.05 and if the *F*-value of the Fisher–Snedecor distribution (also referred to as the F-distribution) is higher than its critical value (*F*-critical). Table 10 presents the results of the statistical test at a 95% confidence interval with the value of *F*-critical at 4.10.

Table 10. ANOVA analysis of speech enhancement methods at 95% confidence interval.

Speech Enhancement Approach	PESQ		ESTOI	
	p-Value	F-Value	*p*-Value	F-Value
Proposed approach -> noisy speech	0.001	50.25	0.001	54.24
Proposed approach -> MS-GLMB filtering-assisted MVDR beamformer	0.023	12.17	0.042	09.45
Proposed approach -> mask MVDR with self-attention	0.021	20.07	0.031	15.15
Proposed approach -> U-Net with embedded GCN	0.012	14.76	0.039	12.15

From the results presented in Table 10, it is clear that the results are statistically significant, and that the proposed approach consistently outperforms prior state-of-the-art approaches in terms of speech intelligibility and quality (represented by ESTOI and PESQ metrics, respectively).

4.4.4. Ablation Study

In order to investigate the contribution of different components in the proposed neural speech enhancement architecture, in this sub-section we conduct an ablation study. In this study, we compare variants of the proposed speech enhancement approach whereby the results are presented in Table 11.

Table 11. Results of ablation study.

Method	RT60 = 550 ms		RT60 = 250 ms		RT60 = 50 ms	
	PESQ	ESTOI	PESQ	ESTOI	PESQ	ESTOI
Proposed approach	2.70	75.00%	2.88	79.60%	2.90	80.50%
w/o GCRNN block in skip connections	2.65	72.60%	2.84	76.70%	2.87	78.40%
w/o Residual block in encoder and decoder	2.57	69.50%	2.75	72.22%	2.78	76.32%
w/o Discriminator	2.67	74.43%	2.85	77.45%	2.89	79.20%

In Table 11, the PESQ and ESTOI values corresponding to variants of the proposed approach are listed, and these clearly demonstrate the superior performance achieved by the proposed approach. The entry 'w/o GCRNN block in skip connections' indicates that the GCRNN blocks were removed from the skip connections of the overall U-Net architecture, while including the GCRNN in the bottleneck layer of the U-Net. There is a decrease in PESQ value by 0.05 for the reverberation time RT60 of 550 ms after the removal of the GCRNN blocks from the skip connections, which is due to reduction in feature extraction capability of the neural architecture. As the GCRNN block in the bottleneck layer is still left unchanged, some degree of flexibility in the exploitation of spatiotemporal and spectral information is still maintained. There is also a slight reduction in ESTOI value due to removal of the GCRNN blocks from the skip connections, which indicates a slight reduction in speech intelligibility. The entry 'w/o Residual block in Encoder and Decoder' in Table 11 indicates the removal of residual blocks from the encoder and decoder pathways of the U-Net architecture while keeping other components intact. It is evident that the removal of residual blocks leads to loss of feature preservation in the overall neural architecture, which is why the PESQ and ESTOI values become diminished. The entry 'w/o Discriminator' refers to the case in which the discriminator of the GAN framework is removed. As expected, the PESQ and ESTOI values are reduced as compared with the original proposed approach, as the non-GAN neural framework is incapable of discriminating between the original desired signal and the noisy received signal at the input and is also prone to adversarial conditions.

5. Discussion

The MS-GLMB filtering can solve the space-time permutation problem. Hence, its application in the source tracking-assisted beamforming procedure is useful to generate the labels (i.e., identities) of the multiple sources, along with their location estimates, across all of the time frames, with high accuracy even under low SNR and high reverberation and while sources change their positions and speak intermittently. The estimated labels are instrumental in correctly discriminating between the target speech source and interferers, which facilitate the construction of time-varying MVDR beamformers and subsequent T-F mask corresponding to the target source. This in turn can enhance the target speech in a dynamic manner within each time frame, even under the combined effect of imperfections caused by the sources' motion, reverberation and background noise. The T-F masks thus generated form an effective target label set for the proposed neural architecture, which is robust to imperfections caused by background noise, reverberation and motion of the sources. As an appropriate motion model such as the Langevin model is considered in modelling the motion of the sources while implementing the MS-GLMB filter, the dynamic changes in positions of the mobile sources are accounted for, which is reflected in the training procedure of the proposed residual dense Graph-U-Net-based neural speech enhancement model. In prior works concerning speech enhancement using deep neural architectures [8–30], the dynamics of the sources in motion using appropriate motion models were not considered, which is why the state-of-the-art deep neural architectures employed in prior research works may not provide satisfactory performance under the combined effect of imperfections caused by reverberation, noise and interfering sources. As evident in this work, the label generation procedure for training the neural architecture considers the sources' motion, whose trajectories possess different start and termination points as well as different velocities. Moreover, the circumvention of the space-time permutation problem by the MS-GLMB filtering leads to correct discrimination between the target source and the interfering sources across all of the time frames, which in turn assists the training label generation procedure to generate the T-F masks with high accuracy. The proposed neural framework effectively learns the mapping from the spectrograms corresponding to a received multichannel reverberant mixture of speech signals belonging to the multiple sources at different spatial positions to the T-F mask corresponding to the target source. Through this overall procedure, the knowledge about the sources' spatial information, as well as the dynamic beamformer's operation within each time frame, are implicitly included within the training procedure of the proposed neural framework, which enables the trained version to generalize to unseen conditions such as different RIRs, SNRs and variations in the sources' motion. While the research work outlined in [18–20], relying on "complex spectral mapping," as well as the research works in [14,15], aim to predict the target source-specific mask to enhance the target speech, as mentioned earlier they do not consider the motion of the sources, nor do they consider the random nature of the cardinality of the sources while training the respective neural architectures. Hence, compared with those approaches, the approach presented in this article performs better under dynamic conditions.

As pointed out in [19,25,42,43], the goal of dense connections is to maximize the information processing from all layers, whereas the inclusion of residual connections leads to an improved utilization of information as well as preservation of signal integrity. The combination of dense and residual connections leads to the formation of the residual dense block which improves the network efficiency. This in turn ensures an enhancement in the fusion of feature information. While similar approaches of target speech enhancement using GCN have been reported, this work embeds a GCRNN module in a residual dense convolutional U-Net framework, which is different from the neural architectures adopted in [27–29].

6. Application Scenarios of the Proposed Approach

In this sub-section, we outline a few applications for which the proposed speech enhancement approach can be leveraged.

6.1. Applications in Conferencing Scenarios

During video conferencing, the quality of speech can become severely degraded due to background noise, reverberation, the number of recording microphones, the geometry of the microphone array, the acoustic and circuit design of the microphone arrays, the interference due to speakers, etc. [58]. Therefore, speech enhancement is a critical component of the overall speech processing system and plays an important role in video conferencing applications. As compared with a microphone placed very close to a speaker, microphone arrays offer better speech intelligibility by offering significant directional gain as well as effective noise reduction, thereby leading to an improvement in overall audio experience for the participants in the conference. Due to the motion of the speakers, it is necessary to track them and switch the focus towards the desired speaker in a dynamic manner. For this reason, microphone array-based speech enhancement techniques which incorporate localization and tracking methods are ideal for ensuring clear and intelligible communication in conference rooms, rooms which involve participants changing their positions or intermittently speaking from different locations. The proposed approach in this paper involves multiple microphone arrays with an MS-GLMB filtering algorithm to track the speakers and deep neural architecture-based speech enhancement. Such an approach can be leveraged to dynamically enhance the targeted speech in a conference environment.

6.2. Applications in Assistive Listening Devices

The proposed approach can be leveraged to assistive listening devices such as hearing aids in order to improve the overall audio experience of the listener. Due to the distributed nature of the multi-microphone array configuration used in this work, it possesses the advantages of spatial diversity, enhanced noise reduction performance, and flexibility of placement. Spatial diversity indicates the placement of microphones at different positions which can enable the speech enhancement system to distinguish between the speech emanating from the target source and interfering signals and noise arriving from different directions. This can, in turn, help the system to isolate and enhance the desired speech signal while suppressing undesired components. The enhanced noise reduction performance can be attributed to beamforming, which helps to focus on a speech signal arriving from a specific direction while suppressing other directions. Finally, owing to its distributed nature, the microphone array elements can be flexibly placed across the user's clothing, or they can be distributed across the indoor environment, so as to effectively capture the acoustic signals from different directions [59]. The proposed approach, if leveraged to a distributed microphone array-based hearing aid application, can localize the speech source-of-interest at each time frame and improve the intelligibility of speech by performing dynamic beamforming-based target speech enhancement.

6.3. Applications in Automatic Speech Recognition for Speakers in Motion

Automatic speech recognition is a crucial step in the overall speech processing pipeline, one which requires the application of appropriate speech enhancement technique to improve speech intelligibility. This is most critical in scenarios involving moving speakers who change their positions across different time frames while speaking intermittently. The movement of speakers introduces additional challenges, such as changing acoustics, noise, as well as motion-induced acoustic impairments which hamper accurate recognition of the received speech signal. Automatic speech recognition is an important procedure in speech transcription systems [60]. The proposed technique can be leveraged to such scenarios where the source tracking assisted neural beamformer can effectively isolate the desired speech component from the interference signals, thereby leading to better recognition of the target speech as well as better transcription.

7. Conclusions

In this research work, a deep neural architecture for enhancing the target speech under reverberant conditions is proposed, whereby the training labels are created by exploiting the spatial information of the sources across all of the time frames using MS-GLMB filtering. Such an approach helps to correctly discriminate between the target source and interfering sources and the overall methodology demonstrates better performance in scenarios in which the sources are in motion than state-of-the-art neural speech enhancement methods which do not employ MS-GLMB filtering. The positive outcome of the proposed methodology lies in the incorporation of the spectro-spatial information within the training procedure of the neural architecture, which enables the trained neural architecture to directly predict the desired T-F masks from the input magnitude spectrograms even under "un-seen" acoustic conditions, such as different RIRs, SNRs and sources' motion, which were not included in the training phase.

8. Future Work

As mentioned in the article, the methodology exploits the SRP-PHAT-based acoustic measurements for constructing the measurement set for the MS-GLMB filter. While the tracking performance is generally good in the presence of noise and reverberation, it can be further improved by modeling the SRP-PHAT computation by a suitable deep neural architecture. Such a neural SRP approach can provide increased noise immunity to the localization and tracking procedure, which can lead to improved reliability under sources' motions as well as background noise and reverberation. This in turn can lead to better target source separation by the MVDR beamformer module.

The proposed neural architecture can be leveraged in audio-visual information-guided target speech enhancement, where the visual tracking of the target speech source can be assisted by a neural acoustic localization. Such a neural localization framework can benefit from the residual dense convolutional Graph-U-Net applied in this work. Moreover, the proposed neural framework can also be incorporated within the audio-visual speech enhancement module.

Author Contributions: Conceptualization, J.D.; methodology, J.D.; software, J.D.; validation, J.D., A.D.F., D.Z.-B. and F.R.C.-S.; formal analysis, J.D.; investigation, J.D.; resources, J.D.; data curation,

J.D.; writing—original draft preparation, J.D.; writing—review and editing, A.D.F., D.Z.-B. and F.R.C.-S.; visualization, J.D.; supervision, A.D.F.; project administration, J.D.; funding acquisition, A.D.F. All authors have read and agreed to the published version of the manuscript.

Funding: The authors acknowledge the financial support from Projects ANID/FONDECYT Iniciación No. 11230129, and the Competition for Research Regular Projects, year 2021, code LPR21-02; Universidad Tecnológica Metropolitana.

Institutional Review Board Statement: Not applicable.

Informed Consent Statement: Not applicable.

Data Availability Statement: The raw data supporting the conclusions of this article will be made available by the authors on request.

Conflicts of Interest: The authors declare no conflict of interest.

Abbreviations

DL	Deep learning
MVDR	Minimum variance unbiased response
GAN	Generative adversarial network
MS-GLMB	Multi-sensor generalized labeled multi-Bernoulli
RFS	Random finite set
T-F	Time–frequency
SNR	Signal-to-noise ratio
CSM	Complex spectral mapping
FoV	Field of view
GCRNN	Graph convolutional recurrent neural network
RDN	Residual dense network
SRP-PHAT	Steered response power phase transform
IPD	Inter-microphone phase difference
TV	Time-varying
GSC	Generalized side-lobe canceller
GSP	Graph signal processing
GCN	Graph convolutional network
CM	Contiguous memory
LFF	Local feature fusion
ReLU	Rectified linear unit
IN	Instance normalization
k-NN	k-nearest neighbors
LSTM	Long short-term memory
SI-SNR	Scale invariant signal-to-noise ratio
MSE	Mean square error
ISM	Image source method
RIR	Room impulse response
ESTOI	Enhanced short time objective intelligibility
PESQ	Perceptual evaluation of speech quality
SDR	Signal-to-distortion ratio
TI-MVDR	Time invariant minimum variance unbiased response
SCM	Signal covariance matrix
ISCM	Instantaneous signal covariance matrix
AIR	Aachen impulse response
ANOVA	Analysis-of-variance

References

1. Brendel, A.; Haubner, T.; Kellermann, W. A Unifying View on Blind Source Separation of Convolutive Mixtures Based on Independent Component Analysis. *IEEE Trans. Sig. Proc.* **2023**, *71*, 816–830. [CrossRef]
2. Wang, T.; Yang, F.; Yang, J. Convolutive Transfer Function-Based Multichannel Nonnegative Matrix Factorization for Overdetermined Blind Source Separation. *IEEE/ACM Trans. Audio Speech Lang. Proc.* **2022**, *30*, 802–815. [CrossRef]
3. Nionm, D.; Mokios, K.N.; Sidiropoulos, N.D.; Potamianos, A. Batch and Adaptive PARAFAC-based Blind Separation of Convolutive Speech Mixtures. *IEEE Trans. Audio Speech Lang. Proc.* **2010**, *18*, 1193–1207. [CrossRef]
4. Gannot, S.; Vincent, E.; Markovich-Golan, S.; Ozerov, A. A consolidated perspective on multimicrophone speech enhancement and source separation. *IEEE/ACM Trans. Audio Speech Lang. Proc.* **2017**, *25*, 692–730. [CrossRef]
5. Markovich-Golan, S.; Gannot, S.; Kellermann, W. Combined LCMV-TRINICON Beamforming for Separating Multiple Speech Sources in Noisy and Reverberant Environments. *IEEE/ACM Trans. Audio Speech Lang. Proc.* **2016**, *25*, 320–332. [CrossRef]
6. Ong, J.; Vo, B.T.; Nordholm, S. Blind Separation for Multiple Moving Sources with Labeled Random Finite Sets. *IEEE/ACM Trans. Audio Speech Lang. Proc.* **2021**, *29*, 2137–2151. [CrossRef]
7. Morgan, J.P. Time-Frequency Masking Performance for Improved Intelligibility with Microphone Arrays. Master's Thesis, University of Kentucky, Lexington, KY, USA, 2017.
8. Ochiai, T.; Delcroix, M.; Nakatani, T.; Araki, S. Mask-Based Neural Beamforming for Moving Speakers with Self-Attention-Based Tracking. *IEEE/ACM Trans. Audio Speech Lang. Proc.* **2023**, *31*, 835–848. [CrossRef]
9. Tammen, M.; Ochiai, T.; Delcroix, M.; Nakatani, T.; Araki, S.; Doclo, S. Array Geometry-Robust Attention-Based Neural Beamformer for Moving Speakers. *arXiv* **2024**, arXiv:2402.03058.
10. Wang, Y.; Politis, A.; Virtanen, T. Attention-Driven Multichannel Speech Enhancement in Moving Sound Source Scenarios. In Proceedings of the 2024 IEEE International Conference on Acoustics, Speech and Signal Processing (ICASSP), Seoul, Republic of Korea, 14–19 April 2024.
11. Xu, Y.; Yu, M.; Zhang, S.; Chen, L.; Weng, C.; Liu, J.; Yu, D. Neural Spatio-Temporal Beamformer for Target Speech Separation. In Proceedings of the INTERSPEECH 2020, Shanghai, China, 25–29 October 2020.
12. Xu, Y.; Zhang, Z.; Yu, M.; Zhang, S.-X.; Yu, D. Generalized Spatio-Temporal RNN Beamformer for Target Speech Separation. In Proceedings of the INTERSPEECH 2021, Brno, Czech Republic, 30 August–3 September 2021.
13. Guo, A.; Wu, J.; Gao, P.; Zhu, W.; Guo, Q.; Gao, D.; Wang, Y. Enhanced Neural Beamformer with Spatial Information for Target Speech Extraction. In Proceedings of the 2023 Asia Pacific Signal and Information Processing Association Annual Summit and Conference (APSIPA ASC) 2023, Taipei, Taiwan, 31 October–3 November 2023.
14. Tan, K.; Wang, Z.-Q.; Wang, D. Neural spectrospatial filtering. *IEEE/ACM Trans. Audio Speech Lang. Proc.* **2022**, *30*, 605–621. [CrossRef]
15. Wang, Z.-Q.; Wang, D. Combining spectral and spatial features for deep learning based blind speaker separation. *IEEE/ACM Trans. Audio Speech Lang. Proc.* **2019**, *27*, 457–468. [CrossRef]
16. Zhang, Z.; Xu, Y.; Yu, M.; Zhang, S.-X.; Chen, L.; Yu, D. ADLMVDR: All deep learning MVDR beamformer for target speech separation. In Proceedings of the 2021 IEEE International Conference on Acoustics, Speech and Signal Processing (ICASSP), Toronto, ON, Canada, 6–11 June 2021.
17. Gu, R.; Chen, L.; Zhang, S.-X.; Zheng, J.; Xu, Y.; Yu, M.; Su, D.; Zou, Y.; Yu, D. Neural spatial filter: Target speaker speech separation assisted with directional information. In Proceedings of the INTERSPEECH 2019, Graz, Austria, 15–19 September 2019.
18. Luo, Y.; Mesgarani, N. Conv-TasNet: Surpassing ideal time-frequency magnitude masking for speech separation. *IEEE/ACM Trans. Audio Lang. Proc.* **2019**, *27*, 1256–1266. [CrossRef]
19. Tolooshams, B.; Giri, R.; Song, A.H.; Isik, U.; Krishnaswamy, A. Channel-Attention Dense U-Net for Multichannel Speech Enhancement. In Proceedings of the 2020 IEEE International Conference on Acoustics, Speech and Signal Processing (ICASSP), Barcelona, Spain, 4–8 May 2020.
20. Nair, A.A.; Reiter, A.; Zheng, C.; Nayar, S. Audiovisual Zooming: What You See Is What You Hear. In Proceedings of the 27th ACM International Conference on Multimedia, Nice, France, 21–25 October 2019.
21. Soni, M.H.; Shah, N.; Patil, H.A. Time-Frequency Masking-Based Speech Enhancement Using Generative Adversarial Network. In Proceedings of the 2018 IEEE International Conference on Acoustics, Speech and Signal Processing (ICASSP), Calgary, AB, Canada, 15–20 April 2018.
22. Baby, D. iSEGAN: Improved Speech Enhancement Generative Adversarial Networks. *arXiv* **2020**, arXiv:2002.08796v1. [CrossRef]
23. Michelsanti, D.; Tan, Z.-H. Conditional Generative Adversarial Networks for Speech Enhancement and Noise-Robust Speaker Verification. In Proceedings of the INTERSPEECH 2017, Stockholm, Sweden, 20–24 August 2017.
24. Pascual, S.; Bonafonte, A.; Serrà, J. SEGAN: Speech Enhancement Generative Adversarial Network. *arXiv* **2017**, arXiv:1703.09452v3. [CrossRef]
25. Zhou, L.; Zhong, Q.; Wang, T.; Lu, S.; Hu, H. Speech Enhancement via Residual Dense Generative Adversarial Network. *Comp. Sys. Sci. Eng.* **2021**, *38*, 279–289. [CrossRef]

26. Datta, J.; Firoozabadi, A.D.; Zabala-Blanco, D.; Soria, F.R.C.; Adams, M.; Perez, C. Multi-channel Target Speech Enhancement using Labeled Random Finite Sets and Deep Learning under Reverberant Environments. In Proceedings of the 2023 IEEE 5th Eurasia Conference on IOT, Communication and Engineering (ECICE), Yunlin, Taiwan, 27–29 October 2023.
27. Binh, N.H.; Hai, D.V.; Dat, B.T.; Chau, H.N.; Cuong, N.Q. Multi-channel speech enhancement using a minimum variance distortionless response beamformer based on graph convolutional network. *Int. J. Adv. Comput. Sci. Appl.* **2022**, *13*, 739–747. [CrossRef]
28. Chau, H.N.; Bui, T.D.; Nguyen, H.B.; Duong, T.T.H.; Nguyen, Q.C. A Novel Approach to Multi-Channel Speech Enhancement Based on Graph Neural Networks. *IEEE/ACM Trans. Audio Speech Lang. Proc.* **2024**, *32*, 1133–1144. [CrossRef]
29. Tzirakis, P.; Kumar, A.; Donley, J. Multi-channel speech enhancement using graph neural networks. Proceedings of 2021 the IEEE International Conference on Acoustics, Speech and Signal Processing (ICASSP), Toronto, ON, Canada, 6–11 June 2021.
30. Zhang, C.; Xiang, P. Single-channel speech enhancement using Graph Fourier Transform. In Proceedings of the INTERSPEECH 2022, Incheon, Republic of Korea, 18–22 September 2022.
31. Ong, J.; Vo, B.T.; Nordholm, S.; Vo, B.-N.; Moratuwage, D.; Shim, C. Audio-Visual Based Online Multi-Source Separation. *IEEE/ACM Trans. Audio. Speech. Lang. Proc.* **2022**, *30*, 1219–1234. [CrossRef]
32. Vo, B.-N.; Vo, B.-T.; Beard, M. Multi-sensor multi-object tracking with the generalized labeled multi-bernoulli filter. *IEEE Trans. Signal Process.* **2019**, *67*, 5952–5967. [CrossRef]
33. Thomas, R.W.; Larson, J.D. Inverse Reinforcement Learning for Generalized Labeled Multi-Bernoulli Multi-Target Tracking. In Proceedings of the 2021 IEEE Aerospace Conference (50100), Big Sky, MT, USA, 6–13 March 2021.
34. Jiang, D.; Qu, H.; Zhao, J. Multi-level graph convolutional recurrent neural network for semantic image segmentation. *Telecom. Sys.* **2021**, *77*, 563–576. [CrossRef]
35. Goodfellow, I.J.; Abadie, J.P.; Mirza, M.; Xu, B.; Farley, D.W.; Ozair, S.; Courville, A.; Bengio, Y. Generative Adversarial Networks. *arXiv* **2014**, arXiv:1406.2661v1. [CrossRef]
36. Pan, Z.; Yu, W.; Yi, X.; Khan, A.; Yuan, F.; Zheng, Y. Recent Progress on Generative Adversarial Networks (GANs): A Survey. *IEEE Access.* **2019**, *7*, 36322–36333. [CrossRef]
37. Marques, A.G.; Kiyavash, N.; Moura, J.M.F.; Van De Ville, D.; Willett, R. Graph Signal Processing: Foundations and Emerging Directions [From the Guest Editors]. *IEEE Sig. Proc. Mag.* **2020**, *37*, 11–13. [CrossRef]
38. Li, G.; Muller, M.; Thabet, A.; Ghanem, B. DeepGCNs: Can GCNs go as deep as CNNs? In Proceedings of IEEE/CVF International Conference on Computer Vision, Seoul, Republic of Korea, 27 October–2 November 2019.
39. Seo, Y.; Defferrard, M.; Vandergheynst, P.; Bresson, X. Structured Sequence Modeling with Graph Convolutional Recurrent Networks. *arXiv* **2016**, arXiv:1612.07659. [CrossRef]
40. Ronneberger, O.; Fischer, P.; Brox, T. U-Net: Convolutional Networks for Biomedical Image Segmentation. In *Medical Image Computing and Computer-Assisted Intervention–MICCAI 2015, Proceedings of the MICCAI 2015, Munich, Germany, 5–9 October 2014*; Navab, N., Hornegger, J., Wells, W., Frangi, A., Eds.; Lecture Notes in Computer Science 9351; Springer: Cham, Switzerland, 2014. [CrossRef]
41. He, K.; Zhang, X.; Ren, S.; Sun, J. Deep Residual Learning for Image Recognition. *arXiv* **2015**, arXiv:1512.03385v1. [CrossRef]
42. Zhang, Z.; Liu, Q.; Wang, Y. Road Extraction by Deep Residual U-Net. *IEEE Geosci. Remote Sens. Lett.* **2018**, *15*, 749–753. [CrossRef]
43. Yang, X.; Li, X.; Ye, Y.; Zhang, X.; Zhang, H.; Huang, X. Road Detection via Deep Residual Dense U-Net. In Proceedings of the 2019 International Joint Conference on Neural Networks (IJCNN), Budapest, Hungary, 14–19 July 2019.
44. Huang, G.; Liu, Z.; van der Laurens, M.; Weinberger, K.Q. Densely connected convolutional networks. In Proceedings of the 2017 IEEE Conference on Computer Vision and Pattern Recognition, Piscataway, NJ, USA, 21–26 July 2017.
45. Datta, J.; Adams, M.; Perez, C. Dense-U-Net assisted Localization of Speech Sources in Motion under Reverberant conditions. In Proceedings of the 2023 12th International Conference on Control, Automation and Information Sciences (ICCAIS), Hanoi, Vietnam, 27–29 November 2023. [CrossRef]
46. Do, H.; Silverman, H.F.; Yu, Y. A real-time SRP-PHAT source location implementation using stochastic region contraction (SRC) on a large-aperture microphone array. In Proceedings of the 2007 IEEE International Conference on Acoustics, Speech, and Signal Processing (ICASSP), Honolulu, HI, USA, 16–20 April 2007.
47. Paul, D.B.; Baker, J. The design for the wall street journal-based CSR corpus. In Proceedings of the 1992 Workshop on Speech and Natural Language, Harriman, NY, USA, 23–26 February 1992.
48. Panayotov, V.; Chen, G.; Povey, D.; Khudanpur, S. Librispeech: An ASR corpus based on public domain audio books. In Proceedings of the 2015 IEEE International Conference on Acoustics, Speech and Signal Processing (ICASSP), South Brisbance, QLD, Australia, 19–24 April 2015.
49. Barker, J.; Marxer, R.; Vincent, E.; Watanabe, S. The third 'CHiME' speech separation and recognition challenge: Dataset, task and baselines. In Proceedings of the 2015 IEEE Workshop on Automatic Speech Recognition and Understanding (ASRU), Scottsdale, AZ, USA, 13–17 December 2015.

50. Thiemann, J.; Ito, N.; Vincent, E. The diverse environments multichannel acoustic noise database: A database of multichannel environmental noise recordings. *J. Acoust. Soc. Am.* **2013**, *133*, 3591. [CrossRef]
51. Piczak, K.J. ESC: Dataset for Environmental Sound Classification. In Proceedings of the 23rd Annual ACM Conference on Multimedia, Brisbane, Australia, 26–30 October 2015.
52. Jensen, J.; Taal, C.H. An algorithm for predicting the intelligibility of speech masked by modulated noise maskers. *IEEE/ACM Trans. Audio Speech Lang. Proc.* **2016**, *24*, 2009–2022. [CrossRef]
53. Rix, A.W.; Beerends, J.G.; Hollier, M.P.; Hekstra, A.P. Perceptual evaluation of speech quality (PESQ)-a new method for speech quality assessment of telephone networks and codecs. In Proceedings of the 2001 IEEE International Conference on Acoustics, Speech, Signal Processing, Salt Lake City, UT, USA, 7–11 May 2001.
54. Le Roux, J.; Wisdom, S.; Erdogan, H.; Hershey, J.R. SDR–half-baked or well done? In Proceedings of 2019 IEEE International Conference on Acoustics, Speech, Signal Processing (ICASSP), Brighton, UK, 12–17 May 2019.
55. Lehmann, E.A.; Johansson, A.M.; Nordholm, S. Reverberation-time prediction method for room impulse responses simulated with the image source model. In Proceedings of the 2007 IEEE Workshop on Applications of Signal Processing to Audio and Acoustics, New Paltz, NY, USA, 21–24 October 2007.
56. Kingma, D.P.; Ba, J. Adam: A method for stochastic optimization. *arXiv* **2014**, arXiv:1412.6980.
57. Jeub, M.; Sch¨afer, M.; Kr¨uger, H.; Nelke, C.; Beaugeant, C.; Vary, P. Do we need dereverberation for hand-held telephony? In Proceedings of 2010 International Congress on Acoustics (ICA), Sydney, Australia, 23–27 August 2010.
58. Rao, W.; Fu, Y.; Hu, Y.; Xu, X.; Jv, Y.; Han, J.; Jiang, Z.; Xie, L.; Wang, Y.; Watanabe, S.; et al. Conferencingspeech Challenge: Towards Far-Field Multi-Channel Speech Enhancement for Video Conferencing. In Proceedings of the 2021 IEEE Automatic Speech Recognition and Understanding Workshop (ASRU), Cartagena, Colombia, 13–17 December 2021; IEEE: Piscataway, NJ, USA, 2021; pp. 679–686. [CrossRef]
59. Pasha, S.; Lundgren, J.; Ritz, C.; Zou, Y. Distributed Microphone Arrays, Emerging Speech and Audio Signal Processing Platforms: A Review. *Adv. Sci. Technol. Eng. Syst. J.* **2020**, *5*, 331–343. [CrossRef]
60. Audhkhasi, K.; Georgiou, P.G.; Narayanan, S.S. Analyzing quality of crowd-sourced speech transcriptions of noisy audio for acoustic model adaptation. In Proceedings of the 2012 IEEE International Conference on Acoustics, Speech and Signal Processing (ICASSP), Kyoto, Japan, 25–30 March 2012; IEEE: Piscataway, NJ, USA, 2012; pp. 4137–4140. [CrossRef]

applied sciences

MDPI

Article

A Fast, Simple, and Approximate Method for a Minimal Unit Cell Design of Glide-Symmetric Double-Corrugated Parallel-Plate Waveguides

Fatih Çolak [1,†] and Agah Oktay Ertay [2,*,†]

1 Graduate School of Natural and Applied Sciences, Erzincan Binali Yildirim University, Yalnizbag Campus, Erzincan 24002, Türkiye; fatih.colak@ogr.ebyu.edu.tr

2 Faculty of Engineering and Architecture, Department of Electrical and Electronics Engineering, Erzincan Binali Yildirim University, Yalnizbag Campus, Erzincan 24002, Türkiye

* Correspondence: aoertay@erzincan.edu.tr

† These authors contributed equally to this work.

Abstract: Glide-symmetric double-corrugated parallel-plate waveguides (GS-DCPPWs) have essential technical properties such as an electromagnetic bandgap, lower dispersion, and the ability to control the equivalent refractive index. For this reason, a fast and simple analysis and design of GS-DCPPW structures have great importance to improve related microwave systems. This paper introduces a novel design methodology based on the auxiliary functions of generalized scattering matrix (AFGSM) for the dimensional synthesis of GS-DCPPWs. We test the applicability of the AFGSM method on a variety of numerical examples to determine the passband/stopband regions of single and GS-DCPPWs before applying the design procedure. Certain design specifications are chosen, and unit cell dimensions are constructed in accordance with the proposed design technique. Three design scenarios are considered to assess the success of how well the design criteria can be met with the proposed method. The designed unit cells have been periodically connected in a various finite numbers to create periodic filters as a test application for adjusting the electromagnetic bandgap. The success of the periodic GS-DCPPW filters obtained with the proposed design strategy in meeting the specified design requirements has been tested using full-wave electromagnetic simulators (CST Microwave Studio and HFSS). The results indicate that the combined use of the equivalent transmission line circuit and the root-finding routine provided by the proposed method facilitates rapid, efficient, versatile, and approximate designs for corrugated parallel-plate waveguides. Moreover, the design methodology provides the viability of developing a minimal unit cell and a compact periodic filter performance with respect to the literature counterparts.

Keywords: corrugated parallel-plate waveguides; dimensional synthesis; glide symmetry; periodic filter design

1. Introduction

Electromagnetic propagation properties of periodic structures have been the subject of extensive investigation for decades [1–10]. These structures include properties like how waves move forward and backward and how fast and slow they are, as well as the presence and effect of bandgaps [11–14]. The examination and elucidation of these characteristics of periodic structures across many geometric models maintain the relevance of this subject [5,7,9,11–13]. These significantly higher technical properties have established their role in critical applications, which include antennas, frequency-selective surfaces, filters, and metasurfaces [14–19]. Essentially, periodic structures can be employed in filters to establish stopbands and attain multiple pass and stopband characteristics through the exploitation of degrees of freedom [14–16]; in antennas to facilitate wide-angle scanning and enhance radiation efficiency across an extensive frequency range [17]; in metasurfaces to direct electromagnetic waves and transform them into various wave configurations with specified attributes [18]; and in frequency-selective surfaces to generate passband and stopband regions, expand operational bandwidth, and improve polarization converter performance [19]. These components are indispensable to various devices utilized in microwave and millimeter-wave applications.

In recent years, the analysis, design, and investigation of periodic structures with higher symmetries in microwave applications have gained prominence [20–25]. The utilization of these symmetries in periodic structures began 50–60 years ago [1,26–28]. Glide-symmetric periodic structures, applicable to various geometries [21,26,29–37], have been extensively studied by researchers due to their outstanding performance in reducing dispersion, controlling bandgaps and bandwidth, and adjusting the equivalent refractive index for particular applications [22,27]. One of the geometries that implement glide symmetry comprise corrugated parallel-plate waveguides (CPPWs). These structures are frequently employed in the development of broadband microwave devices [17,28,38,39]. When making microwave devices with CPPW periodic structures that have glide-symmetric corrugations, it is important to first figure out the structure's dispersion diagram. A dispersion diagram provides critical insights into the attenuation and phase connection of the structure [40].

Recent analyses of dispersion diagrams for these structures have been extensively performed through mode-matching techniques, method of moments, frequency domain, and eigenmode solvers of full-wave electromagnetic simulators, as well as their corresponding designs [29,32,36,41–44]. Mode-matching formulations have been used in [29,41] to investigate the dispersion characteristics of glide-symmetric periodic structures. Conversely, these methodologies are inadequate for elucidating the physical comprehension of the impact of glide symmetry on the periodic structure. In frequency domain solvers, network parameters (scattering (S)-parameters, ABCD parameters) of the unit cell of the periodic structure are determined using multimodal excitation, and the dispersion diagram of the periodic structure is derived by substituting the obtained parameters into the eigenvalue equation [4,5,45]. Despite the complex geometry of the periodic structure, it is feasible to precisely derive the dispersion diagram by analyzing the behavior of the eigenvalues using these methods. Nevertheless, full-wave simulators result in excessively prolonged calculation durations. Consequently, investigating and proposing the bandgap characteristics of glide-symmetric parallel plate waveguides using simple and effective computational techniques can drastically reduce design time.

An equivalent circuit model has been recently introduced for the analysis of CPPWs featuring glide-symmetric corrugations [36]. This equivalent circuit model allows for the assumption that in the regions excited by discontinuities, only the dominant mode is propagated inside a periodic structure among an infinite set of higher-order modes [46]. This circuit model is a rapid and effective method that calculates the ABCD parameters of the unit cell and produces dispersion results that are comparable to those of full-wave simulators for a broad spectrum of geometrical parameters [36]. By deriving the circuit model of this structure [36] and obtaining the ABCD or S-parameters from the circuit model, the dispersion diagram of the model can only be obtained by solving the eigenvalue equations specified in [5,36]. Moreover, the auxiliary functions of generalized scattering matrix (AFGSM) method [5] is an extremely successful alternative technique that identifies passband and stopband regions of periodic structures by analyzing the zero crossings of auxiliary functions. This method, explained in detail in [5], does not need to solve the eigenvalue equation (EE). A significant reduction in computation load can be achieved in this way for controlling bandgaps of periodic structures. It has been previously applied in numerous applications, including rectangular waveguides [5,14], photonic crystals [47], and helix slow-wave structures [14,48], to determine the passband/stopband regions of periodic structures and unit cell designs. To the best of our knowledge, the AFGSM method has not been applied to the analysis, design, and investigation of CPPW structures with glide-symmetric corrugations.

This study proposes a novel design procedure for one-dimensional glide-symmetric double CPPW structures based on the AFGSM method in the open literature. Firstly, we performed analyses to test the effectiveness of the AFGSM method in determining the passband/stopband regions in the considered structures. We compared the results of each analysis with the eigenvalue equation. The next stage involved selecting design requirements and obtaining unit cell designs through dimensional synthesis using the proposed method. This method can yield numerous unit cell dimensions that align with the same design requirements. We evaluated the filtering performances of final designs using finite periodic implementations to understand whether optimal unit cell dimensions determined by the AFGSM method meet the design requirements. The full-wave electromagnetic simulators (HFSS and CST Microwave Studio) were used for testing the filtering performances of unit cells designed with the AFGSM method. We compared the performance of filters designed using the proposed design procedure with the reported literature. One of the main contributions is that we provide here a different perspective to gather network parameters of CPPW structures by using the equivalent transmission line model with their scattering matrices. Graphical illustrations of EE and AFGSM methods of single and glide-symmetric double CPPW structures were compared for the analysis and design stages. Other contributions can be explained from the analysis and design results, demonstrating that the presented method can be efficiently utilized for observing the electromagnetic bandgap of CPPWs. The proposed design method that obtains the unit cell's S-parameters using an equivalent circuit model is more fruitful than those in the literature, which utilize full-wave electromagnetic solvers for gathering S-parameters [44,45]. Another important contribution in this study is providing the ability to minimize the glide-symmetric DCPPW unit cell design for compactness via the AFGSM method. Additionally, the auxiliary functions provide a fast design advantage in determining the passband/stopband regions in the structures under examination. The next sections present important information about how to easily use single and glide-symmetric double CPPW periodic structures to find the electromagnetic bandgap and bandwidth using the AFGSM method. The sections also discuss the use of these structures to create a periodic filter using the proposed method as an example application.

2. Materials and Methods

Theory and Design Strategy

Figure 1 demonstrates single and glide-symmetric double CPPW structures. As mentioned in [36], if $h_2 = h_3$ and $m = p/2$, the unit cell has glide symmetry, as demonstrated in Figure 1. Full-wave electromagnetic simulators are capable of modeling these structures to derive their dispersion characteristics. On the other hand, the longitudinal transmission line model for these geometries is presented using the circuit model described in [36], as shown in Figure 2. The circuit approach developed by Marcuvitz, with detailed information provided in Appendix A and in [49], was utilized for the circuit structure pertinent to this problem. This methodology combines the circuit model from Figure 2 with the necessary parameters from Appendix A, resulting in terminals for single and double corrugations with a short circuit configuration. The phase constant of single Floquet mode supported by the unit cell of the periodic structure under consideration can be determined using the following equation [36]:

$$\cos(\beta_x p) = \frac{A(f) + D(f)}{2} = A(f). \tag{1}$$

The parameters β_x, p, $A(f)$, and $D(f)$ in Equation (1) represent the Floquet phase constant associated with the periodic structure with respect to the x direction, the unit cell's period, and the matrix elements A and D, which is a function of frequency and of the $ABCD$ matrix referring to the unit cell, respectively. This study will investigate the scattering matrix representation of the unit cell in both the input and output reference planes. We will determine the scattering matrix for each structure in the circuit model inside the unit cell, as illustrated in Figure 2. As shown in Figure 1, the next step is to stack the scattering matrices of these structures on top of each other to get the full set of S-parameters for the corrugated waveguides' periodic structure. Figure 2 demonstrates the representations of subcircuits. The scattering matrices of the block structures can be seen to cascade from the first block (S1) to the last block (S5), ending with the scattering matrix of the whole structure. S matrices of all models given in Figure 2a,b are explained in the Appendix A. The phase constant for the structure's dominant mode can be found using the eigenvalue equation given below [5] after obtaining the unit cell's S-parameters:

$$\cos(\beta_x p) = \frac{1 + S_{11}^2 + S_{21}^2}{2S_{21}}. \tag{2}$$

The two parameters S_{11} and S_{21} in Equation (2) indicate the scattering parameter components of the unit cell. Full-wave simulators can accomplish multimodal excitation for the unit cell. We can utilize the generalized scattering matrix elements from full-wave simulators to determine the passband and stopband regions of the periodic structure within the following equation [5]:

$$\begin{bmatrix} \mathbf{I} & -\mathbf{S}_{11} \\ \mathbf{0} & -\mathbf{S}_{12} \end{bmatrix} \begin{bmatrix} \mathbf{b}_1 \\ \mathbf{a}_1 \end{bmatrix} + \lambda \begin{bmatrix} -\mathbf{S}_{12} & \mathbf{0} \\ -\mathbf{S}_{22} & \mathbf{I} \end{bmatrix} \begin{bmatrix} \mathbf{b}_1 \\ \mathbf{a}_1 \end{bmatrix} = 0. \tag{3}$$

The AFGSM method can be used for finding band edge frequencies in a symmetric unit cell structure in the case of multimode excitation, and it is described in the literature with the equation below [5]:

$$X_{\pm}^{full} = 2\,\mathrm{Im}(S_{n,n} \pm S_{n,n+P}) - \sum_{k=M+1}^{P} |S_{n,k} \pm S_{n,k+P}|^2 = 0. \tag{4}$$

There are a total of P modes, with M and $P - M$ being the number of propagating and non-propagating modes in the waveguide used in Equation (4). $S_{i,j}$ is the generalized scattering matrix element, and n is the input port that corresponds to the dominant propagating waveguide mode. Single-mode propagation can occur when using the circuit model of the CPPW structure given in Figure 2. Furthermore, the reduced form of Equation (4) can be written taking into account the equivalent transmission line model only for $P = M = 1$ and $n = 1$ [5]:

$$X_{\pm} = 2\,\mathrm{Im}(S_{1,1} \pm S_{1,2}) = 0. \tag{5}$$

All notations are listed in Appendix B. Equation (5) can only be used for the dominant mode, not including higher-order mode interaction. Despite the fact that some deviations from the design objectives can occur in periodic filter design [50], the circuit model can be utilized for rapidly computing the dimensions of unit cells. The designer can significantly reduce computational burden by solving Equation (5) using the root-finding routine, as opposed to using the fine frequency sweeps of Equation (2) to derive the dispersion diagram of glide-symmetric double CPPWs. This fast approach reduces the size of the design space and provides a simple and approximate design method. Unit cell analysis is important for analyzing the dispersion diagram of the periodic structure and establishing approximate solutions. In addition, the finite number of unit cells examined gives the designer an important insight into the compatibility of the passband/stopband regions of the periodic structure and its filtering behavior. Based on this information, the applicability of the AFGSM method for the unit cell analysis of corrugated PPW structures and the dimensional synthesis of such filters will be tested. Firstly, Equation (5) is applied to determine the passband/stopband regions of a single corrugated PPW, and then the dimensional synthesis of the same structure in accordance with the design requirements is performed. A similar process will be applied for the analysis and dimensional design of glide-symmetric CPPWs. In this context, the following design strategy has been established:

- Step 1: Select single/glide-symmetric double CPPW model and start appropriate unit cell configuration.
- Step 2: Constrain the design space so that the dimensional parameters of the unit cell based on the circuit model given in Figure 2 are in the appropriate range.
- Step 3: Modify the dimensions in the limited design space obtained in Step 2, and determine the appropriate unit cell parameters satisfying the given design requirements employing Equation (5).
- Step 4: Connect the designed unit cells back-to-back a finite number of times to meet the design requirements and obtain the filter responses with full-wave simulators.

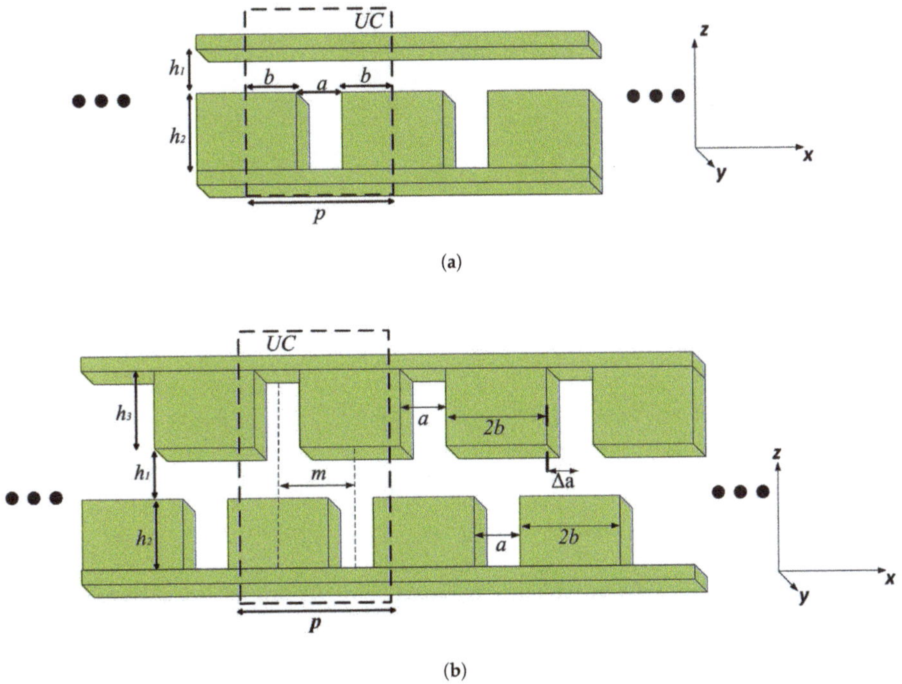

Figure 1. Unit cell geometries of 1D corrugated parallel-plate waveguides. (**a**) single CPPW ; (**b**) glide-symmetric DCPPW.

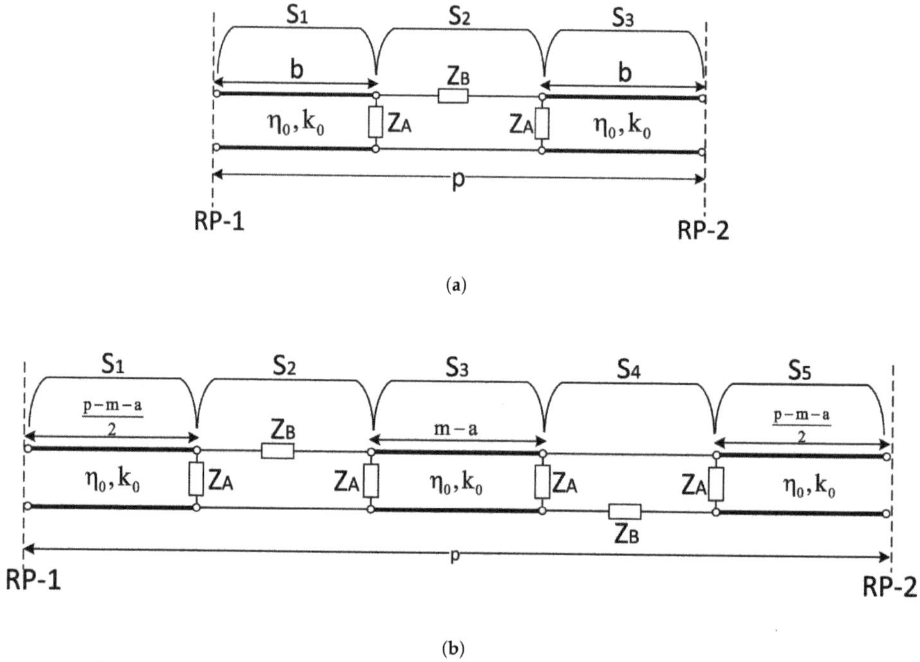

Figure 2. Equivalent circuit model of (**a**) single-corrugated and (**b**) glide-symmetric double-corrugated PPW structures.

3. Results and Discussion

3.1. Numerical Examples

We first investigate the applicability of the AFGSM method for determining the passband and stopband regions of corrugated PPW structures. The final phase is dimensional synthesis in accordance with the design objectives. Figures 3 and 4 serve as analysis examples to evaluate the efficacy of the AFGSM method in distinguishing passband and stopband regions including not only wide but also narrow stopbands inside single and glide-symmetric double-corrugated PPW structures. Parametric details of Figure 3a,b are given with $\varepsilon_r = 1$, $p = 6$ mm, $h_1 = 3.5$ mm, $h_2 = 4.33$ mm, $a = 5.1$ mm, and $b = 0.45$ mm and $\varepsilon_r = 1$, $p = 9$ mm, $h_1 = 6$ mm, $h_2 = 1$ mm, $a = 1$ mm, and $b = 4$ mm, respectively. All parameter values of Figure 4a,b are taken as $\varepsilon_r = 1$, $p = 6$ mm, $h_1 = 3.5$ mm, $h_2 = h_3 = 15$ mm, $a = 3$ mm, and $b = 1.5$ mm and $\varepsilon_r = 1$, $p = 9$ mm, $h_1 = 10$ mm, $h_2 = h_3 = 1$ mm, $a = 0.5$ mm, and $b = 4.25$ mm, respectively. The first and second stopbands of the periodic structure are obtained by applying the eigenvalue equation to the wide stopband example in Figure 3. These stopbands are located within the ranges of 12.14–19.58 GHz and 29.89–37.26 GHz, respectively. The AFGSM method yields the band edge frequencies of 12.136 GHz, 19.584 GHz, 29.881 GHz, and 37.263 GHz, respectively. The AFGSM method identified the band edges with a maximum difference of 6 MHz, which coincides with the results derived from the eigenvalue equation. Figure 3b presents a narrowband example, indicating the first and second stopband edges at nearly 16.33 GHz, 16.71 GHz, 32.29 GHz, and 33.43 GHz for AFGSM and EE. We achieved band edges near the eigenvalue equation in the narrow stopband scenario, with a maximum deviation of 7 MHz.

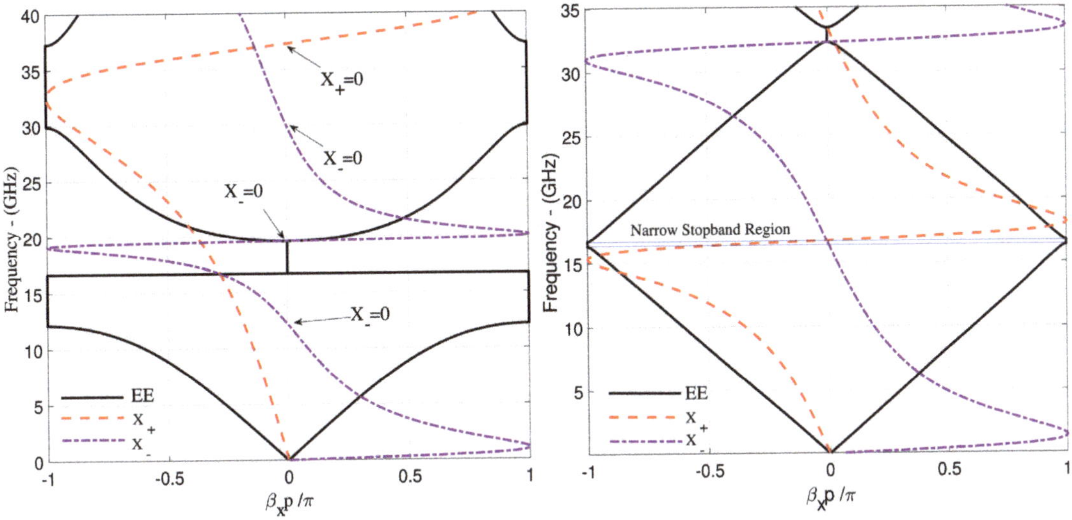

(a) (b)

Figure 3. Dispersion diagram and X_+ , X_- frequency behavior of single-corrugated PPW for (**a**) wide and (**b**) narrow stopband region analysis.

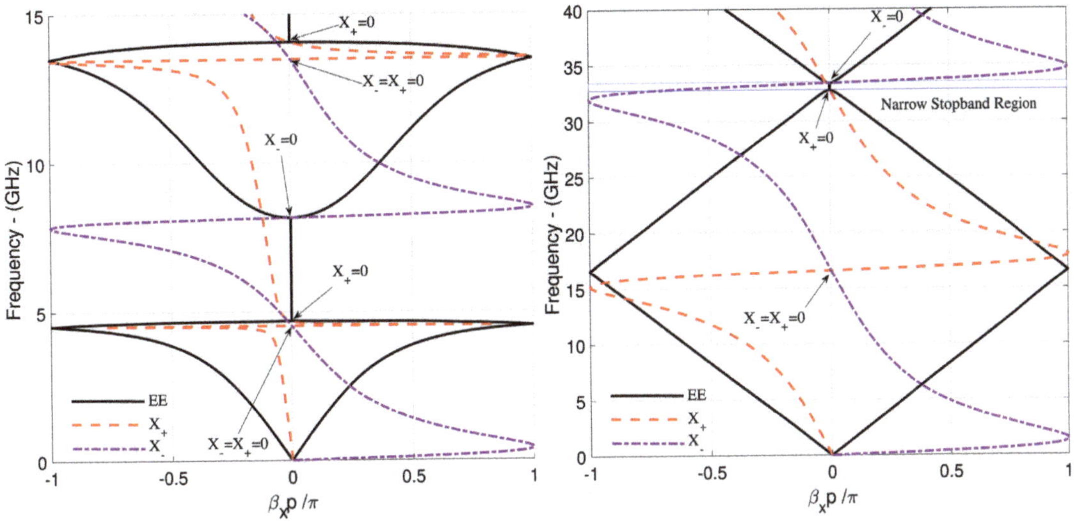

(a) (b)

Figure 4. Dispersion diagram and X_+ , X_- frequency behavior of glide-symmetric double-corrugated PPW for (**a**) wide and (**b**) narrow stopband region analysis.

Figure 4a,b demonstrates that the zero crossings of the X_+ and X_- functions in the AFGSM method consistently align closely with the band edge frequencies in the dispersion diagrams derived from the eigenvalue equation solutions. Floquet mode transitions are observed in certain regions of the dispersion diagrams without stopbands in Figure 4a,b, with transitions occurring at 4.52 GHz and 13.49 GHz, respectively, and 16.57 GHz in Figure 4b. In these regions, the zero crossings of the X_+ and X_- functions occur at identical frequencies. Table 1 presents the band edge frequency results associated with Figure 4a,b.

Based on all these analysis results, it is possible to say that Equation (5) provides an alternative method to determine the passband/stopband regions of one-dimensional corrugated PPW structures. Furthermore, the AFGSM functions clearly demonstrate the separation of the band edges, even if the stop bandwidth is narrow. The interval division root-finding routine determines the roots of the X_+ and X_- functions, eliminating the need for fine frequency sweeps and reducing the computation time by a factor of six compared to the eigenvalue equation. Figures 5 and 6 illustrate the dispersion diagrams and the characteristics of auxiliary functions for single and glide-symmetric double-corrugated PPW unit cells with varying dielectric constants. Parameter values of Figure 5a,b are given as $\varepsilon_r = 1$, $\varepsilon_r = 2.25$, and $\varepsilon_r = 3$, $\varepsilon_r = 11.2$ with $p = 12$ mm, $h_1 = 3$ mm, $h_2 = 0.5$ mm, $a = 5$ mm, and $b = 3.5$ mm for all cases, respectively. Details of the parameters in Figure 6a,b are taken as $\varepsilon_r = 1$, $\varepsilon_r = 2.25$, and $\varepsilon_r = 3$, $\varepsilon_r = 11.2$ with $p = 16$ mm, $h_1 = 4$ mm, $h_2 = h_3 = 8$ mm, $a = 4$ mm, and $b = 6$ mm for all cases, respectively. The variations in the dielectric constant have evidently induced adjustments in the passband and stopband regions of the structure, and the auxiliary functions effectively demonstrate the band separation via zero crossings. We have modeled the single-corrugated and glide-symmetric double-corrugated PPW unit cell for multimode excitation (ten waveguide modes for each geometry) using the CST frequency domain solver. In the CST frequency domain solver, the S-parameters associated with the dominant mode of multimode excitation have been extracted and included in the eigenvalue equation shown in Equation (2). Furthermore, all S-parameters derived from CST have been included in Equation (4). Figures 7 and 8a illustrate the dispersion diagrams for all operations and the characteristics of the auxiliary functions. These results indicate that the simulator-assisted AFGSM functions are indistinguishably identical to the eigenvalue equations derived from CST and the equivalent circuit (EC) at the band edges. In Figure 8a, the band edge frequency derived from the eigenvalue equation of EC at about 12 GHz seems higher. This variation is due to a limited level of high-order mode interaction inside the circuit model. Parametric details of Figures 7 and 8 are given as $\varepsilon_r = 1$, $p = 8.28$ mm, $h_1 = 1$ mm, $h_2 = 1.8$ mm, $a = 1.08$ mm, and $b = 3.6$ mm and $\varepsilon_r = 1$, $p = 26.5$ mm, $h_1 = 0.5$ mm, $h_2 = h_3 = 2$ mm, $a = 1.5$ mm, and $b = 12.5$ mm, respectively. Figure 7b demonstrates that the stopband of the structure extends exclusively owing to the gradual increase in h_2. We investigated manufacturing tolerances in Figure 8b by slowly changing the glide symmetry of the structure. The offset or gradual breaking of the glide symmetry of one corrugation results in the broadening of the structure's stopband.

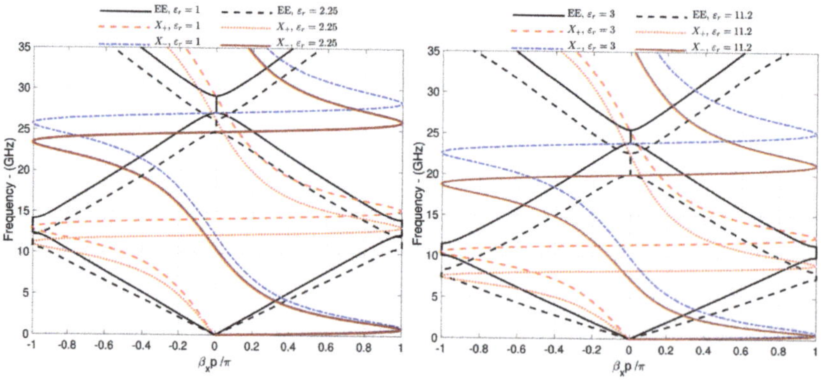

(a) (b)

Figure 5. Dispersion diagram and X_+, X_- frequency behavior of single-corrugated PPW for different dielectric loading for (**a**) $\varepsilon_r = 1$, $\varepsilon_r = 2.25$ (**b**) $\varepsilon_r = 3$, $\varepsilon_r = 11.2$.

In order to apply the dimensional design approach, the following two design objectives were identified:

- (a) Ku-band filter design with a suppression level of more than −50 dB in the 15.20–17.78 GHz range for a single CPPW.
- (b) X-band filter design with a suppression level of more than −60 dB in the 8.27–10.91 GHz range for glide-symmetric double CPPWs.

Table 1. Band edge frequency results for the frequency behaviors of the EE and AFGSM methods in Figure 4a,b.

Figures	X_+ [GHz]	X_- [GHz]	EE [GHz]	$X_+ = X_- = 0$ [GHz]
Figure 4a	4.681	8.157	4.69–8.15	4.52, 13.49
Figure 4b	32.729	33.364	32.73–33.363	16.57

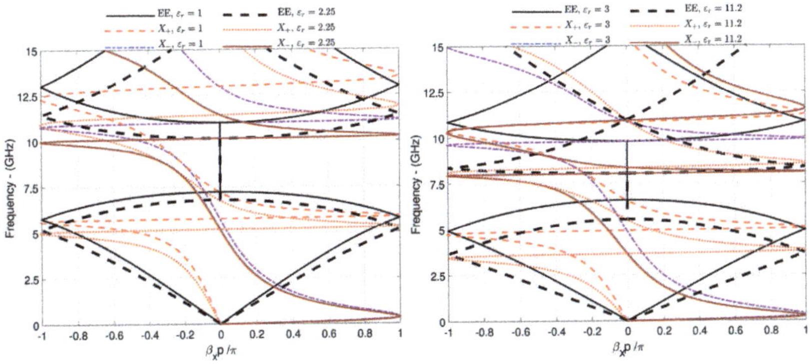

(a) (b)

Figure 6. Dispersion diagram and X_+ and X_- frequency behavior of glide-symmetric double-corrugated PPW for different dielectric loading for (**a**) $\varepsilon_r = 1$, $\varepsilon_r = 2.25$ (**b**) $\varepsilon_r = 3$, $\varepsilon_r = 11.2$.

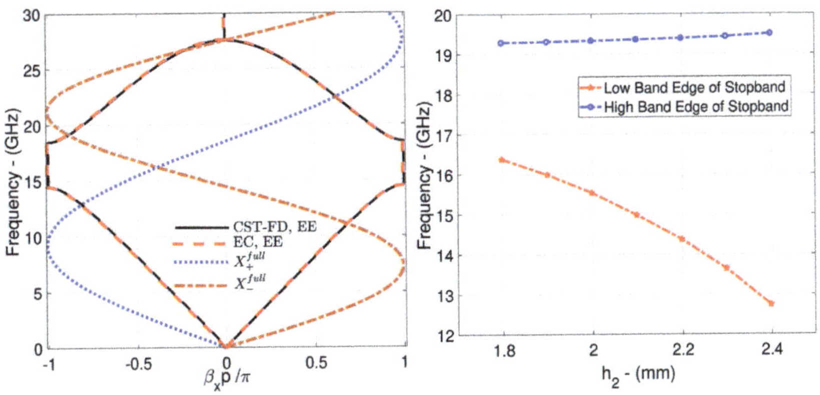

(a) (b)

Figure 7. (**a**) CST-FD dispersion diagram. X_+^{full}, X_-^{full} frequency behavior of the dominant mode of a single CPPW unit cell, and the dispersion diagram of the equivalent circuit model geometry under multimode excitation. (**b**) Tolerance analysis of single CPPW unit cell with h_2 variation using full-wave simulator assisted X_+^{full}, X_-^{full}.

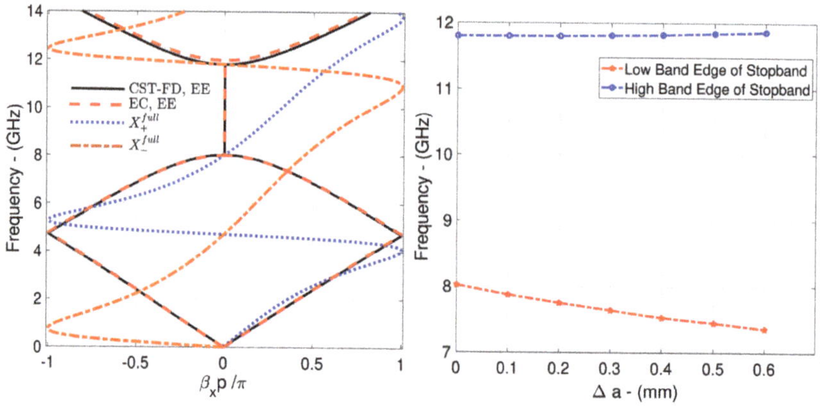

(a) (b)

Figure 8. (**a**) CST-FD dispersion diagram. X_+^{full}, X_-^{full} frequency behavior of the dominant mode of a single CPPW unit cell, and the dispersion diagram of the equivalent circuit model geometry under multimode excitation. (**b**) Tolerance analysis of glide-symmetric DCPPW unit cell with Δa variation using full-wave simulator assisted X_+^{full}, X_-^{full}.

3.2. Design of Unit Cell and Cascade Connection Analysis of Corrugated PPW Structures

The design phase begins with the selection of an appropriate unit cell model. We select the initial parameters $h_1 = 1$ mm, $h_2 = 1.8$ mm, $a = 0.8\ h_2$, and $b = 2.2\ h_2$ for the air-filled single-corrugated PPW model. This selection implements the design procedure as outlined in the initial step. At this point, the design of the unit cell transitions to the determination of the critical parameters of the design geometry. Figure 9 illustrates the relationship between the geometrical parameters of the AFGSM functions and the zero crossings across various frequencies. In the second step, the design procedure maintains the constrained design spaces (with respect to h_1 and h_2 for $h_1 = 1$ mm and $h_2 = 1.8$ mm) while restricting a and b to specific ranges, as illustrated in Figure 9. The variations given in this figure provide a solution for obtaining the parameters corresponding to the targeted stopband bandwidth for the parameters under investigation.

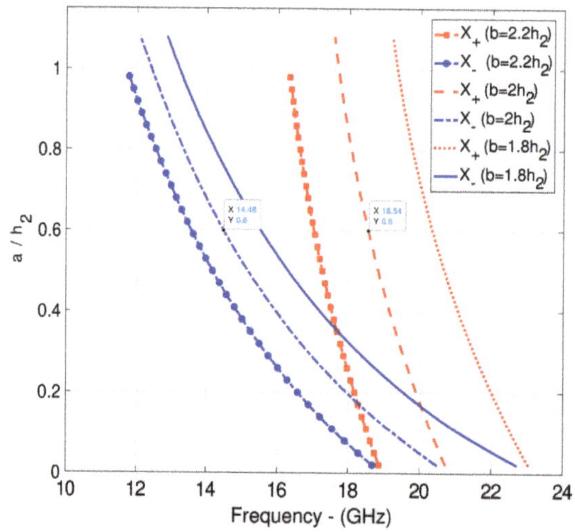

Figure 9. Frequency dependence of bandgap on a/h_2 and b/h_2 computed via AFGSM functions X_+ and X_-.

Step 3 investigates the variation in X_+ and X_- functions for the dimensions in the limited design space obtained in step 2. Figure 9 illustrates that the X_+ and X_- functions for the lines $b = 2\,h_2$ and $a = 0.6\,h_2$ possess a stopband that satisfies the design requirements, as depicted for X and Y point pairs. The AFGSM method enables the initial selection and simultaneous modelling of specific geometric parameters within the frequency range that meets design criteria, offering the designer precise alternatives for determining the optimal geometry of the unit cell, as demonstrated in Figure 9. In the final step, Figure 10a shows the dispersion diagram of the designed unit cell, satisfying the suppression-level design criterion. We obtained a unit cell design with a stopband of 4.06 GHz bandwidth and a center frequency of 16.51 GHz. To test the band properties, we connected unit cells back to back in varying numbers, as illustrated in Figure 10b. Figure 10b shows that the full-wave electromagnetic solver results are quite compatible. The $|S_{21}|$-dB results of the EC model for the cascade-connected single-corrugated PPW unit cells exhibit a less deep stopband region in contrast to the $|S_{21}|$-dB results from the full-wave electromagnetic model of the structure. The EC model is inadequate for accurately representing the discontinuities in the cross-sections for this structure. Discontinuities in the sections result in the excitation of high-order modes. Only the reactive components on the junction planes receive evaluation for high-order mode interactions in the circuit model [36]. Mode-matching methods may be used on these structures to obtain results comparable to full-wave electromagnetic simulation outcomes [31]. As it is well-known in periodic structures, increasing the number of unit cells leads to a deeper stopband in single CPPWs. In this example, we ensured adequate design requirements by increasing the number of unit cells (N) to 10.

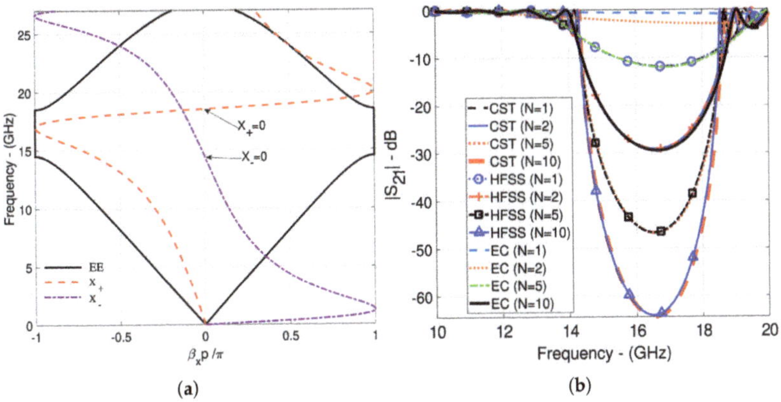

Figure 10. (**a**) Designed bandgap via AFGSM functions. (**b**) Amplitude–frequency characterization of cascading different numbers of the designed single C-PPW unit cell via CST, HFSS, and EC results.

For glide-symmetric double CPPW structures, we set the parameters to $a = 1$ mm, $h_1 = 0.5$ mm, $h_2 = h_3 = 1$ mm, and $b = 12.4$ mm. This selection implements the design procedure as outlined in the initial step. We limited the a and $h_2 = h_3$ parameters to 1–2.5 mm and b to 12.4–13.6 mm at intervals of 0.1 mm by creating multiple design spaces and preserving the glide-symmetry case. This limitation significantly reduces the computational burden in achieving the design requirements. In the design space, the stopband edges of the first stopband region for each parameter are found and recorded using X_+ and X_- functions. We obtained a significant dataset on a large scale, determining the band edge frequencies determined by the AFGSM functions in the constrained design space. The dataset contains a variety of selectable stopband frequencies and the stopband widths situated at these centers. We have selected a center frequency in this context that can cover the targeted stopband. From this set of data, Equation (5) pulls out the values for different dimensions with a center frequency of 10 GHz, different stop bandwidth values, and a certain frequency deviation (δ), as shown in Table 2. The AFGSM method offers various design dimensions for identifying appropriate unit cell parameters via multi-geometric parameter optimization, as illustrated in Table 2. The crucial aspect prior to dimensional design, as illustrated in the dataset of the second example, is to restrict the design area to a defined region. In this case, the AFGSM approach guarantees the quick and precise operation of the design algorithm. At this point, three scenarios, bold and italicized in Table 2, have been selected to meet the design requirements of the dimensional design applicability of Equation (5) for the same and different stop bandwidths.

Table 2. Width of stopbands ($\Delta f = f_1 - f_2$) centered 10 GHz versus a, $h_2 = h_3$, and b for $h_1 = 0.5$ mm and $\varepsilon_r = 1$ with a certain frequency deviation (δ). Frequency deviation is a quantity dependent upon the identification of band edge frequencies within a certain error frequency range and divergence from the expected center frequency.

Δf [GHz]	δ [MHz]	a [mm]	$h_2 = h_3$ [mm]	b [mm]
1.8	30	1.1	1.1	13.6
2	10	1.2	1.1	13.5
2.7	10	***1.5***	***1.2***	***13.2***
		1.7	1	13.3
3	10	1.2	1.8	12.9
3.2	10	1.5	1.5	12.9
3.6	10	1.7	1.5	12.8
		2.1	1.1	13.1
3.8	10	1.3	2.2	12.5
		1.7	1.6	12.7
		2.2	1.1	13.1
4	***20***	***1.5***	***2***	***12.5***
		1.9	1.5	12.7
		2	1.4	12.8
		2.1	1.3	12.9
		2.2	1.2	13
		2.3	***1.1***	***13.1***
4.4	10	2	1.6	12.6
	10	2.4	1.2	13
4.8		2.4	1.4	12.8

The bold & italics cases shows selected different scenarios.

Figures 11–13 illustrate dispersion diagrams and the dominant mode of the $|S_{21}|$ frequency characteristics derived from various finite periodic configurations of designed unit cells throughout three selected scenarios. All AFGSM function behaviors and dispersion characteristics of all scenarios given in Figures 11a, 12a, and 13a indicate that the roots of the AFGSM functions can efficiently seperate passband/stopband regions. The analysis of the filtering characteristics obtained by cascading the unit cells was performed in CST Microwave Studio and HFSS simulation environments. In order to model one-dimensional corrugated PPWs in CST and HFSS, it was necessary to assign appropriate boundary conditions. For this purpose, in CST, electric ($E_t = 0$) and magnetic ($H_t = 0$) conditions were used; in HFSS, perfect E and perfect H boundary conditions were assigned to the top, bottom, and side walls of the considered structures, respectively. The same computer was used to run the simulations of CST, HFSS, and our code of the proposed method. The ordinary laptop had an Intel (R) Core (TM) i7-6700HQ CPU@2.6 GHz with 16 GB RAM. In the examined structures, the first ten dominant waveguide modes of excitation were satisfied to perform with the waveguide port in CST and with the waveport in HFSS, and the frequency characteristics of the first dominant mode of $|S_{21}|$ were investigated. Obtaining the dataset in the given limited design space took 360 h with CST Eigen Mode Solver, while solving the eigenvalue equation based on the circuit model took 612 s. The same dataset was generated in 20 s using the AFGSM method. We observe from Figure 11a that Scenario 1's band edges were 8.648 GHz and 11.344 GHz. In the first scenario, we selected a stop bandwidth of 2.7 GHz and determined the dimensions using the AFGSM functions, with a deviation of 10 MHz. The filtering characteristics of the unit cell designed in Scenario 1 with different numbers of finite periodic arrays are given in Figure 11b. The periodic arrangement of the geometry considered in Scenario 1 significantly increased the passband fluctuation levels, as shown in Figure 11b. However, it is evident that the design specifications have not yet reached their target. Selecting unit cell parameters with a broader stopband would prove beneficial in terms of both size and design goals. Figure 12b unequivocally illustrates that a periodic arrangement with $N = 10$ adequately fulfills the design specifications, and the passband ripple levels are considerable. The specified design requirements primarily provide the starting stopband frequency for the suppression level but do not determine the required stop bandwidth in Figure 13b.

Figures 11 and 12b illustrate that the results of the full-wave electromagnetic simulation and the EC model converge with an increasing number of unit cells. In Figure 13b, although an EC simulation result that aligned with the required stopband was achieved, it was noted that the full-wave electromagnetic simulation results yielded a smaller and less deep stopband region. The discrepancies occur due to the placement of the anticipated stopband region in the upper modes of the dispersion diagram, the prominence of discontinuity regions inside the structure, and the resultant increase in higher-order mode interactions. The single-corrugated and glide-symmetric double-corrugated PPW designed bandstop filters for two examples exhibit ripples outside the band. Figures 10b–13b indicate that these ripples are at lower levels in the substantially single-corrugated PPW filter. In the X-band filter designs, significant ripples have been observed, particularly in the low passbands. The characteristics of the periodic arrangement anticipate these ripples. Furthermore, Figures 11–13 clearly demonstrate that the use of glide symmetry enhances the ripples generated by the periodic design. In this situation, passband ripples can be managed using a different design method that employs the AFGSM algorithm, either by adjusting the unit cell parameters of the broken glide symmetry [15,27,37,42,51–53] or by examining each unit cell parameter with tapering technology [15,54]. These solutions are not investigated here due to the stopband characteristics of the periodic arrangements of the GS-DCPPW unit cell only being taken into account for testing purposes. The frequency characteristics of $|S_{21}|$, with a constant unit cell count of $N = 10$ for all selected scenarios, are presented in Figure 14.

Table 3 presents the design unit cell parameter values for all scenarios and the overall filter dimensions achieved for $N = 10$. Currently, there are trade-offs regarding filter performance and dimensions for the scenarios given in Figure 14 and Table 3. Initially, fulfilling the design specifications of Scenario 1 will evidently necessitate an increased number of unit cells. This circumstance will lead to a substantial increase in passband ripple levels. Consequently, Scenario 1 fails to satisfy the design specifications. Scenario 2 satisfies the design specifications with an identical quantity of unit cells, in contrast to the other two scenarios, which utilize varying sizes yet yield the same stopband width. Furthermore, the overall filter length of Scenario 2 is shorter than that of Scenario 3, presenting a compact design possibility. Conversely, while Scenario 3 does not entirely fulfill the design specifications, its ripple levels in the passband surpass those of Scenario 2, thereby providing a design advantage to Scenario 3. Table 3 shows that Scenario 3 provides a compact design that is advantageous in terms of filter height. In glide-symmetrical double

CPPWs, the frequency characteristics of $|S_{21}|$, illustrated by the finite periodic combinations in Figures 11b, 12b, and 13b, indicate that frequency behaviors of the cascaded unit cell begin to approach the center frequency of the stopband depicted in Table 2 as the number of unit cells increases. The situation is important to consider in ascertaining the designer's requirements. Utilizing this knowledge, the designer begins the design by selecting a higher stopband center frequency, extracting the unit cell design parameters from the AFGSM functions and trying to ascertain the design requirements. The AFGSM method finds different solutions that meet the same design criteria. These solutions allow you to choose the unit cell with the smallest dimension possible, which makes it easier to create small designs.

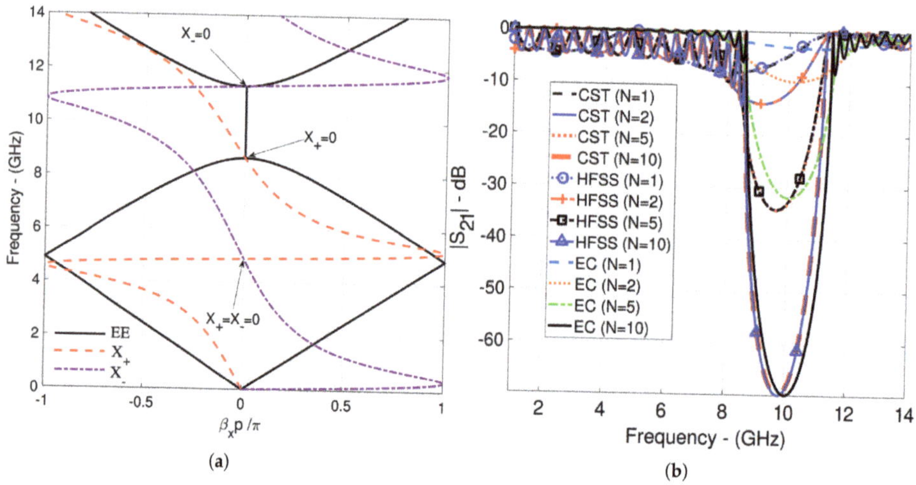

Figure 11. (**a**) Obtained passband–stopband characterization of designed glide-symmetric DCPPW with AFGSM functions and other computation methods for Scenario 1. (**b**) $|S_{21}|$ frequency characterization of cascading different numbers of the designed GS-DCPPW unit cell of Scenario 1 via CST, HFSS, and equivalent circuit results.

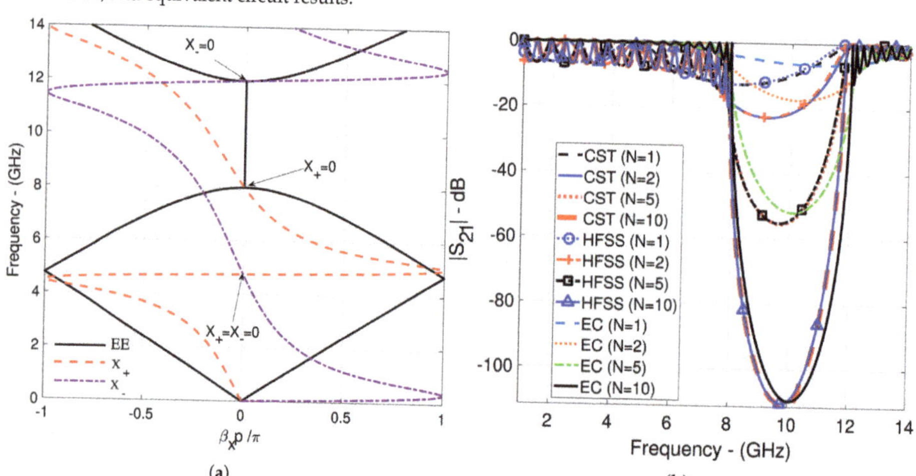

Figure 12. (**a**) Obtained passband–stopband characterization of designed glide-symmetric DCPPW with AFGSM functions and other computation methods for Scenario 2. (**b**) $|S_{21}|$ frequency characterization of cascading different numbers of the designed GS-DCPPW unit cell of Scenario 2 via CST, HFSS, and EC results.

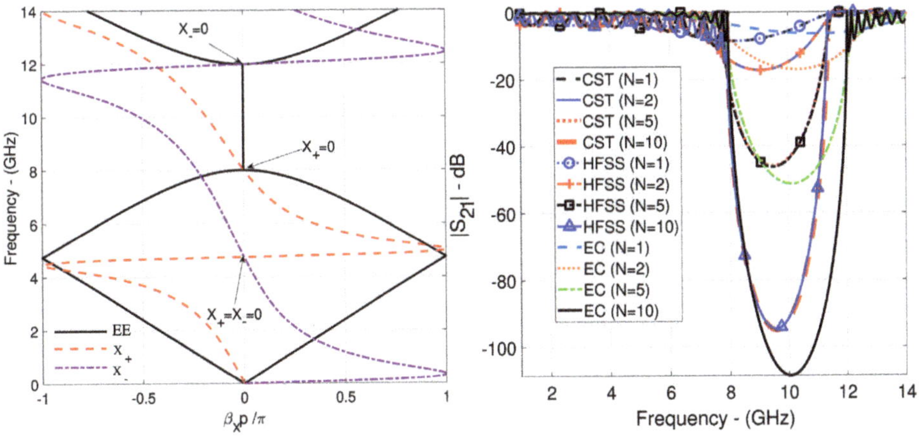

(**a**) (**b**)

Figure 13. (**a**) Obtained passband–stopband characterization of designed glide-symmetric DCPPW with AFGSM functions and other computation methods for Scenario 3. (**b**) $|S_{21}|$ frequency characterization of cascading different numbers of the designed GS-DCPPW unit cell of Scenario 3 via CST, HFSS, and EC results.

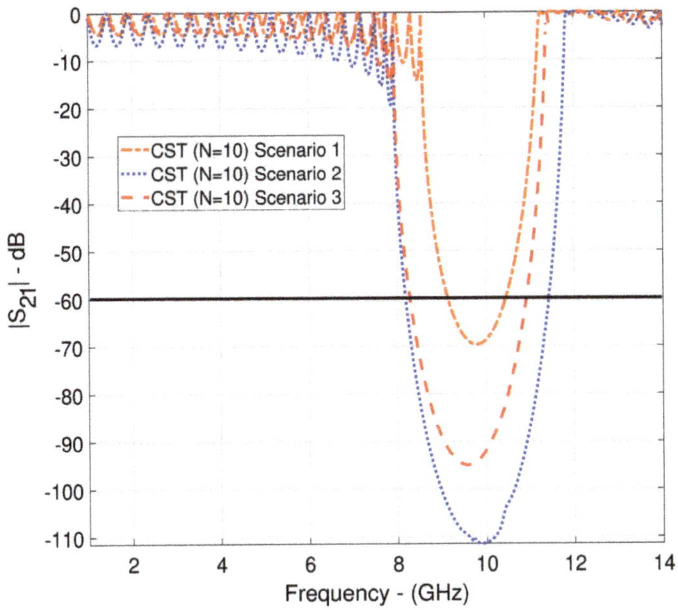

Figure 14. Comparison of Scenario 1, Scenario 2, and Scenario 3 for obtaining design objectives.

Table 3. Designed unit cell parameters for all scenarios and total filter dimensions (TFDs) for $N = 10$.

Studies	a [mm]	b [mm]	h_1 [mm]	$h_2 = h_3$ [mm]	p [mm]	$h_1 + h_2 + h_3$ [mm]	TFD [mm]
Scenario 1	1.5	13.2	0.5	1.2	27.9	2.9	279
Scenario 2	1.5	12.5	0.5	2	26.5	4.5	265
Scenario 3	2.3	13.1	0.5	1.1	28.5	2.7	285

Table 4 compares the performance of designed periodic bandstop filters with similar performances reported in the open literature. The designed filter exhibits a broader suppression level bandwidth (SLBW) and achieves more compact design according to [5]. Bandstop filter designs based on microstrip technology given in [55–57] have notably compact configurations. Ref. [55] has a similar suppression level as Scenario 2, whereas the designed filter demonstrates a wider stopband bandwidth. However, Refs. [56,57] show higher suppression characteristics and narrow bandwidths with respect to the developed filter. One clearly states that despite the conventional cavity BPF design given in [58] having small dimensions, the suppression level bandwidth could not be as wide as the designed filter. It can be revealed that although the BPF design based on hybrid (microstrip–stripline) technology [58] depicts compact dimensions, the developed filter has a wider suppression level. A major drawback of the developed filter is its very high fluctuation levels in the passband. Conversely, we note that the stopband slope is superior to other designs except [5,58] for the upper transition band, respectively. However, regarding the normalized circuit size, the performance of the proposed filter is slightly lower compared to other designs.

Table 4. A comparison table for designed bandstop fiter via the AFGSM method with the literature studies.

Works	f_0, *Technology* [GHz]	PR_1 * [dB]	PR_2 * [dB]	*SLBW* [GHz]	SS_1 * dB/GHz	SS_2 * dB/GHz	Physical Dimensions [mm × mm × mm]	NCS * $\lambda_g \times \lambda_g \times \lambda_g$
[5], Figure 10, MM-GSM	9, Waveguide	~1	~1	@-60 dB, 0.1	~370	~370	1120.14 × 22.86 × 10.16	Not given
[55], Figure 6, SONNET	9.7, Microstrip	~0.1	~0.1	@-60 dB, 1	~33.04	~20.56	12.87 × 7.04 × 0.25	0.65 × 0.36 × 0.01
[58], Figure 9, Conv. BSF	9.3, Waveguide	~0.6	~0.6	@-60 dB, 1.23	~10.57	~37	86 × 74 × 18	Not given
[58], Figure 9, Prop. BSF	9.35, Hybrid	~0.6	~0.6	@-55.5 dB, 2.67	~61.67	~370	15 × 8 × 1	0.5 × 0.25 × 0.04
[56], Figure 10a, State (01)	10.3, Microstrip	~0.15	~0.56	@-20 dB, 0.215	~92.5	~46.25	7.3 × 7.5 × 0.508	0.4 × 0.42 × 0.03
[56], Figure 10a, State (10)	10.2, Microstrip	~0.15	~0.51	@-20 dB, 0.22	NA *	NA *	7.3 × 7.5 × 0.508	0.4 × 0.42 × 0.03
[56], Figure 14a, V_b=25V	9.56, Microstrip	~0.10	~0.16	@-20 dB, 0.192	~119.35	~84.09	7.3 × 7.5 × 0.508	0.38 × 0.39 × 0.03
[57], Table 5, Open-short	9, Microstrip	~0.5	~0.5	@-10 dB, 0.7	NA *	NA *	6.1 × 6.2 × 0.4	0.51 × 0.52 × 0.03
This work, Scenario 2, Figure 14, CST	9.59, Waveguide	~6.6	~2.5	@-60 dB, 2.64	~148	~185	265 × 26.5 × 4.5	8.47 × 0.85 × 0.85

* PR_1: lower region passband ripple; PR_2: upper region passband ripple; SS_1: low-frequency stopband slope; SS_2: high-frequency stopband slope; NCS: normalized circuit size; NA: not available, λ_g has been determined based on the frequency f_0 in this table.

The AFGSM approach relies on the S-parameters of the unit cell, which emphasize the need to ascertain the S-parameters of the structure. One of the easiest ways to carry these calculations out is by utilizing the equivalent circuit model of the investigated periodic structure. Ref. [36] provides that the impact of glide symmetry is obviously identical to merely reducing the spatial period by half. This equivalent circuit model addresses the impact of the glide symmetry of the periodic structure within the AFGSM approach. The demonstrated equivalent circuit model, if it supports multimode excitation, enables the extraction of precise information on the passband/stopband regions of the studied geometry via Equation (4). If the model supports single-mode excitation, we can derive comprehensive information using Equation (5). Adapting the multimode equivalent circuit model [19] to glide-symmetric periodic structures like GS-DCPPWs and, in this direction, modeling 1D and 2D periodic structures such as frequency-selective surfaces [19], holey metasurfaces [29], tapered/non-tapered corrugated planar transmission lines [31,59,60], and composite FHMSIW/SSPP waveguides [61–63] for determining band edges using reformulated or novel AFGSM functions and comparing the results with full-wave simulators could be an important future study. Furthermore, using full-wave electromagnetic simulators provides the ability to gather scattering characteristics for all structures analyzed under multimode excitation via frequency domain analysis of the unit cell. Incorporating the scattering parameters derived from this point of origin into Equation (4) establishes the full-wave simulation-assisted AFGSM method. The investigation or design of the complex periodic structures described in [59–63] may be performed using the AFGSM methodology. In this context, the inclusion of higher-order modes enhances the precision of the resulting analysis or design results. This condition results in an increase in computation time. The mode-matching methodology yields the S-parameters of the unit cell, and when included in the AFGSM method, it may decrease computing time.

4. Conclusions

This study aimed to investigate the potential of the AFGSM method in analyzing and designing corrugated parallel-plate waveguide unit cells. The AFGSM method made it simple to find the passband and stopband regions of single and glide-symmetric double CPPW periodic structures. This method led to the development of a novel design procedure for filter designs with CPPW structures. We demonstrate that we can design glide-symmetric double CPPW filters using the AFGSM method. The design procedure demonstrates the ability to determine the minimum unit cell size. The proposed method and design procedure yield a bandstop filter characteristic that is more compact and has a high degree of suppression bandwidth. The AFGSM method allows for thorough studies of the bandgap in corrugated parallel-plate waveguides, no matter the mode number, and it also helps in checking initial manufacturing tolerances.

Author Contributions: Conceptualization, F.Ç. and A.O.E.; methodology, F.Ç. and A.O.E.; software, F.Ç. and A.O.E.; validation, F.Ç. and A.O.E.; analysis, F.Ç. and A.O.E.; investigation, F.Ç. and A.O.E.; resources, F.Ç. and A.O.E.; writing—original draft preparation, F.Ç.; writing—review and editing, A.O.E.; visualization, F.Ç. and A.O.E.; supervision, A.O.E.; project administration, A.O.E. All authors have read and agreed to the published version of the manuscript.

Funding: This research received no external funding.

Institutional Review Board Statement: Not applicable.

Informed Consent Statement: Not applicable.

Data Availability Statement: The data that support the findings of this study are available from the corresponding author upon request.

Conflicts of Interest: The authors declare no conflicts of interest.

Abbreviations

The following abbreviations are used in this manuscript:

MM-GSM	Mode Matching–Generalized Scattering Matrix
BSF	Band Stop Filter
HFSS	High-Frequency Structure Simulator
CST	Computer Simulation Technology
FHMSIW	Folded Half-Mode Substrate Integrated Waveguide
SSPP	Spoof Surface Plasmon Polaritons
UC	Unit Cell

Appendix A. Network Representation Explanation of Expanded Version of Equivalent Circuit of Corrugations and Obtaining S-Parameters of Unit Cell with All Definitions

To find the scattering matrices of all structures belonging to the unit cells given in Figure 2, it is necessary to find the scattering matrix of each block element S_i $(i = 1, 2, \ldots, 5)$. Since blocks S1, S3, and S5 in Figure 2 are conventional transmission lines, the scattering parameters of a lossless transmission line of length l are defined as follows:

$$\left[S^{TL}\right] = \begin{bmatrix} 0 & e^{-jk_0 l} \\ e^{-jk_0 l} & 0 \end{bmatrix}. \tag{A1}$$

By replacing l and $k_0 = 2\pi f / c$ (where f and c are the frequency and speed of light) with the length and phase constant of the block under consideration, the scattering parameters for blocks S1, S3, and S5 can be found. In this case, l is b for S1 and S3 in a single-corrugated PPW; in a glide-symmetric double-corrugated PPW, it is $(p - m - a)/2$ for S1 and S5 and $(m - a)$ for S3. S2 and S4 circuits play a crucial role in determining the scattering parameters of the unit cells in the corrugated PPW structures under study. To clarify this situation, the open forms of the π circuits (S2 and S4) are given in Figure A1a,b, with series stubs reduced in Figure 2.

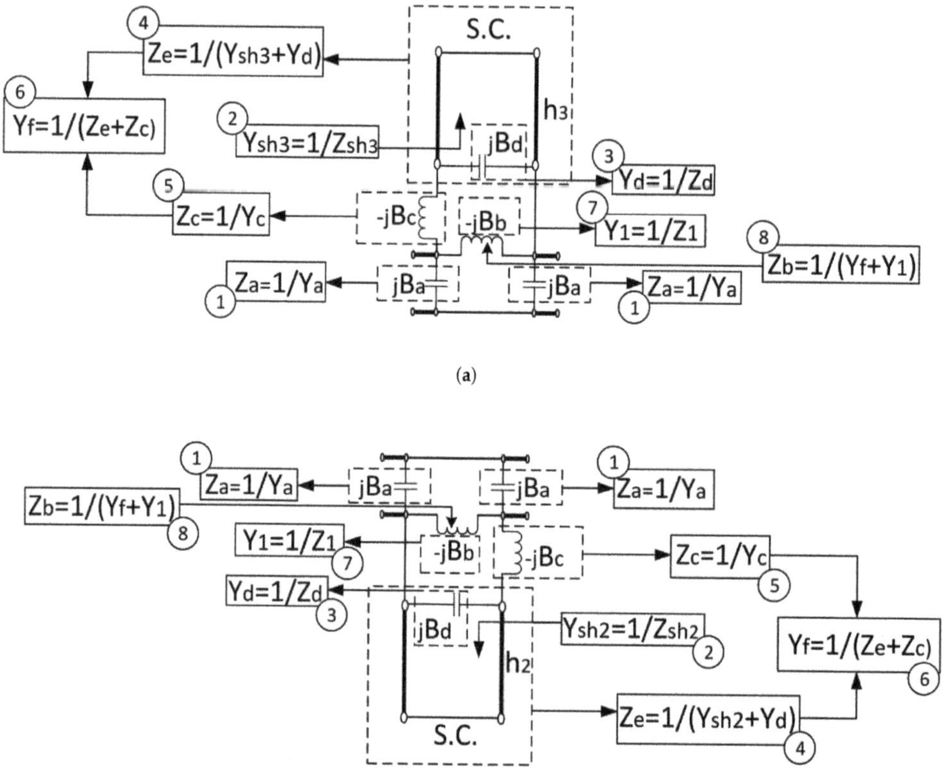

(a)

(b)

Figure A1. Full view of π circuit in (a) S2 and (b) S4 blocks given in Figure 2.

The reactive elements indicated in Figure A1a,b are located at the junctions to account for higher-order mode interactions [36]. The corrugations consist of a series of stubs terminated with a short circuit. Impedance expressions (Z_A and Z_B) for the reduced forms of the π circuits mentioned in this work are given. Figure A1 presents the derivation of Z_A and Z_B in a sequentially numbered format. In step 1, Y_A is first derived using the provided equality $Y_A = jB_a$, followed by the calculation of Z_A as $Z_A = 1/Y_A$ [49].

$$B_a = \frac{2a}{\lambda_0 \eta_0}\left[\tan^{-1}(1/\alpha) + \frac{\ln(\sqrt{1+\alpha^2})}{\alpha}\right] \tag{A2}$$

The equality in Equation (A2) is represented by α, λ_0, and η_0, corresponding to $a/2h_1$, $2\pi/k_0$, and 120π, respectively. In step 2, the impedance of the transmission line $Z_{shi}(i=2,3) = j\eta_0^{'} \tan(k_0 h_i)(i=2,3)$, which is terminated by a short circuit, is considered. The admittance of this structure $Y_{shi}(i=2,3) = 1/Z_{shi}$ is derived from this point. Here, $\eta_0^{'}$ is equal to $\eta_0 \frac{a}{h_1}$ [49,64]. In step 3, the admittance $Y_d = jB_d$ of the capacitor linked to Y_{shi} is determined using the equations shown below [49]:

$$B_d = \frac{h_1}{\lambda_0 \eta_0}\left(\frac{\pi}{3\alpha} + A_2\right) \tag{A3}$$

$$A_2 = 2\left[\alpha \tan^{-1}(1/\alpha) + \frac{\tan^{-1}(\alpha)}{\alpha} + \ln(\frac{1+\alpha^2}{4\alpha}) - \frac{\pi(1+\alpha^2)}{6\alpha}\right] - A_1 \tag{A4}$$

$$A_1 = -\frac{2\alpha}{\pi} e^{\left(-\frac{2\tan^{-1}(\alpha)}{\alpha}\right)}\left[1 + \frac{5+\alpha^2}{4(1+\alpha^2)} e^{\left(-\frac{2\tan^{-1}(\alpha)}{\alpha}\right)} + \left[\frac{4}{1+\alpha^2} + \left(\frac{5-\alpha^2}{1+\alpha^2}\right)^2\right] \frac{e^{\left(-\frac{4\tan^{-1}(\alpha)}{\alpha}\right)}}{9}\right] \tag{A5}$$

In step 4, Z_e may be computed using Y_d and Y_{shi} derived in steps 2 and 3, as $Z_e = 1/(Y_{shi} + Y_d)$. The admittance of the inductance specified in step 5, $Y_c = -jB_c$, is calculated using the given equation, and $Z_c = 1/Y_c$ is found [49].

$$B_c = \frac{\lambda_0}{(2\pi a \eta_0)} \tag{A6}$$

In step 6, the admittance $Y_f = 1/(Z_e + Z_c)$ is found using the impedances Z_c and Z_e obtained in steps 4 and 5. In step 7, the admittance of the inductance specified is found using the following equation [49]:

$$B_b = \frac{\left[B_a - \left[\left(\frac{2h_1}{\lambda_0 \eta_0}\right)\left(\frac{\pi\alpha}{3} + A_1\right)\right]\right]}{2} \tag{A7}$$

In step 8, using the admittances Y_f and Y_1 found in steps 6 and 7, $Z_B = 1/(Y_f + Y_1)$ is obtained. Thus, all the Z_A and Z_B impedances given in Figure 2 can be easily determined. The π circuits given in Figure A1a,b are symmetrical circuits, and the scattering parameters are defined below:

$$S_{11}^{\pi} = S_{22}^{\pi} = \frac{\{[(\eta_0||Z_A) + Z_B]||Z_A\} - \eta_0}{\{[(\eta_0||Z_A) + Z_B]||Z_A\} + \eta_0} \tag{A8}$$

$$S_{21}^{\pi} = S_{12}^{\pi} = (1 + S_{11})\frac{\eta_0||Z_A}{(\eta_0||Z_A) + Z_B} \tag{A9}$$

After the scattering matrices of each S_i $(i = 1, 2, ..., 5)$ block circuit are found, the scattering matrices of the blocks are cascaded as $[S_A]$ and $[S_B]$, respectively, by the following equations, and the scattering parameters of the unit cell are obtained:

$$S_{11} = S_{11}^A + \frac{S_{12}^A S_{11}^B S_{21}^A}{1 - S_{22}^A S_{11}^B} \tag{A10}$$

$$S_{12} = \frac{S_{12}^A S_{12}^B}{1 - S_{11}^B S_{22}^A} \tag{A11}$$

$$S_{21} = \frac{S_{21}^B S_{21}^A}{1 - S_{22}^A S_{11}^B} \tag{A12}$$

$$S_{22} = S_{22}^B + \frac{S_{21}^B S_{22}^A S_{12}^B}{1 - S_{11}^B S_{22}^A} \tag{A13}$$

Appendix B. Notation List

$A(f), D(f)$	The A and D elements of ABCD parameters
a	The corrugate width of single and glide-symmetric double CPPW
a_1, b_1	The normalized power waves used in scattering parameters
b	The length of half of each ridge in the CPPW
β_x	The Floquet phase factor propagating in the x direction
δ	The frequency deviation
Δ_f	The width of the stopband
ε_r	The dielectric constant of the material loaded in the CPPW
E_t	The tangential component of the electric field
f	The frequency
f_1	The last frequency of the stopband
f_2	The first frequency of the stopband
h_1	The height between corrugated parallel plates
h_2	The height of the bottom section of corrugated parallel plates
h_3	The height of the top section of corrugated parallel plates
H_t	The tangential component of the magnetic field
$\mathbf{I}$	The block identity matrix
l	The length of any transmission line
λ	The eigenvalue
m	The gliding operator
N	The number of unit cells
p	The period of the periodic structure
$S_{11}, S_{12}, S_{21}, S_{22}$	The elements of a classical scattering matrix of a two-port network
$\mathbf{S_{11}}, \mathbf{S_{12}}, \mathbf{S_{21}}, \mathbf{S_{22}}$	The block submatrices of the generalized scattering matrix
$X_{\pm}^{full}$	The complete form of auxiliary functions
$X_{\pm}$	The reduced form of auxiliary functions

References

1. Hessel, A.; Chen, M.H.; Li, R.C.; Oliner, A.A. Propagation in periodically loaded waveguides with higher symmetries. *Proc. IEEE* **1973**, *61*, 183–195. [CrossRef]
2. Navarro, M.S.; Rozzi, T.E.; Lo, Y.T. Propagation in a rectangular waveguide periodically loaded with resonant irises. *IEEE Trans. Microw. Theory Tech.* **1980**, *8*, 857–865. [CrossRef]
3. Amari, S.; Vahldieck, R.; Bornemann, J.; Leuchtmann, P. Spectrum of corrugated and periodically loaded waveguides from classical matrix eigenvalues. *IEEE Trans. Microw. Theory Tech.* **2000**, *3*, 453–460. [CrossRef]

4. Lech, R.; Mazur, J. Propagation in rectangular waveguides periodically loaded with cylindrical posts. *IEEE Microw. Wirel. Compon. Lett.* **2004**, *14*, 177–179. [CrossRef]
5. Simsek, S.; Topuz, E. Some properties of generalized scattering matrix representations for metallic waveguides with periodic dielectric loading. *IEEE Trans. Microw. Theory Tech.* **2007**, *11*, 2336–2344. [CrossRef]
6. Othman, M.A.K.; Pan, X.; Atmatzakis, G.; Christodoulou, C.G.; Capolino, F. Experimental demonstration of degenerate band edge in metallic periodically loaded circular waveguide. *IEEE Trans. Microw. Theory Tech.* **2017**, *11*, 4037–4045. [CrossRef]
7. Ertay, A.O.; Simsek, S. Detection of band edge frequencies in symmetric/asymmetric dielectric loaded helix slow-wave structures. *Int. J. Circuit Theory Appl.* **2022**, *50*, 507–524. [CrossRef]
8. Petek, M.; Rico-Fernández, J.; Vásquez, J.A.T.; Valerio, G.; Mesa, F.; Quevedo-Teruel, O.; Vipiana, F. Numerical Modelling of Higher-Symmetric Periodic Structures with Hexagonal Lattice. *IEEE Trans. Antennas Propag.* **2025**, *73*, 1650–1661. [CrossRef]
9. Tahir, G.; Hassan, A.; Ali, S.; Bermak, A. Unit Cell Optimization of Groove Gap Waveguide for High Bandwidth Microwave Applications. *Appl. Sci.* **2024**, *14*, 10891. [CrossRef]
10. Jimenez-Suarez, J.M.; Mesa, F.; Quevedo-Teruel, O. A Symmetry-Based Multimodal Transfer-Matrix Method for the Analysis of 2D-Periodic Structures. *IEEE Trans. Microw. Theory Tech.* **2025**, 1–11. [CrossRef]
11. Şimşek, S.; Topuz, E.; Niver, E. A novel design method for electromagnetic bandgap based waveguide filters with periodic dielectric loading. *AEU-Int. J. Electron. Commun.* **2012**, *66*, 228–234. [CrossRef]
12. Coves, A.; San-Blas, A.A.; Bronchalo, E. Analysis of the dispersion characteristics in periodic Substrate Integrated Waveguides. *AEU-Int. J. Electron. Commun.* **2021**, *139*, 153914. [CrossRef]
13. Mesa, F.; Rodríguez-Berral, R.; Medina, F. On the computation of the dispersion diagram of symmetric one-dimensionally periodic structures. *Symmetry* **2018**, *10*, 307. [CrossRef]
14. Ertay, A.O.; Şimşek, S. A comprehensive auxiliary functions of generalized scattering matrix (AFGSM) method to determine bandgap characteristics of periodic structures. *AEU-Int. J. Electron. Commun.* **2018**, *94*, 139–144. [CrossRef]
15. Karamirad, M.; Pouyanfar, N.; Alibakhshikenari, M.; Ghobadi, C.; Nourinia, J.; See, C.H.; Falcone, F. Low-loss and dual-band filter inspired by glide symmetry principle over millimeter-wave spectrum for 5G cellular networks. *Iscience* **2023**, *26*, 1–14. [CrossRef]
16. Xu, S.; Wu, J.; Chen, X. Design of Broadband Highly Efficient Power Amplifier Based on Low-Pass Filtering Network with Periodic Structure. *Int. J. Circuit Theory Appl.* **2024**. [CrossRef]
17. Liu, Z.; Lu, H.; Liu, J.; Yang, S.; Liu, Y.; Lv, X. Compact fully metallic millimeter-wave waveguide-fed periodic leaky-wave antenna based on corrugated parallel-plate waveguides. *IEEE Antennas Wirel. Propag. Lett.* **2020**, *19*, 806–810. [CrossRef]
18. Maci, S.; Minatti, G.; Casaletti, M.; Bosiljevac, M. Metasurfing: Addressing waves on impenetrable metasurfaces. *IEEE Antennas Wirel. Propag. Lett.* **2011**, *10*, 1499–1502. [CrossRef]
19. Alex-Amor, A.; Mesa, F.; Palomares-Caballero, Á.; Molero, C.; Padilla, P. Exploring the potential of the multi-modal equivalent circuit approach for stacks of 2-D aperture arrays. *IEEE Trans. Antennas Propag.* **2021**, *69*, 6453–6467. [CrossRef]
20. Quevedo-Teruel, O.; Valerio, G.; Sipus, Z.; Rajo-Iglesias, E. Periodic structures with higher symmetries: Their applications in electromagnetic devices. *IEEE Microw. Mag.* **2020**, *21*, 36–49. [CrossRef]
21. Palomares-Caballero, Á.; Alex-Amor, A.; Padilla, P.; Valenzuela-Valdés, J.F. Dispersion and filtering properties of rectangular waveguides loaded with holey structures. *IEEE Trans. Microw. Theory Tech.* **2020**, *68*, 5132–5144. [CrossRef]
22. Quevedo-Teruel, O.; Chen, Q.; Mesa, F.; Fonseca, N.J.; Valerio, G. On the benefits of glide symmetries for microwave devices. *IEEE J. Microwaves* **2021**, *1*, 457–469. [CrossRef]
23. Ghasemifard, F.; Norgren, M.; Quevedo-Teruel, O. Twist and polar glide symmetries: An additional degree of freedom to control the propagation characteristics of periodic structures. *Sci. Rep.* **2018**, *8*, 11266. [CrossRef] [PubMed]
24. Dahlberg, O.; Mitchell-Thomas, R.; Quevedo-Teruel, O. Reducing the dispersion of periodic structures with twist and polar glide symmetries. *Sci. Rep.* **2017**, *7*, 10136. [CrossRef]
25. Arnberg, P.; Barreira Petersson, O.; Zetterstrom, O.; Ghasemifard, F.; Quevedo-Teruel, O. High refractive index electromagnetic devices in printed technology based on glide-symmetric periodic structures. *Appl. Sci.* **2020**, *10*, 3216. [CrossRef]
26. Ebrahimpouri, M.; Quevedo-Teruel, O.; Rajo-Iglesias, E. Design guidelines for gap waveguide technology based on glide-symmetric holey structures. *IEEE Microw. Wirel. Compon. Lett.* **2017**, *27*, 542–544. [CrossRef]
27. Tamayo-Dominguez, A.; Fernandez-Gonzalez, J.M.; Quevedo-Teruel, O. One-plane glide-symmetric holey structures for stop-band and refraction index reconfiguration. *Symmetry* **2019**, *11*, 495. [CrossRef]
28. Quevedo-Teruel, O.; Ebrahimpouri, M.; Kehn, M.N.M. Ultrawideband metasurface lenses based on off-shifted opposite layers. *IEEE Antennas Wirel. Propag. Lett.* **2015**, *15*, 484–487. [CrossRef]
29. Ghasemifard, F.; Norgren, M.; Quevedo-Teruel, O.; Valerio, G. Analyzing glide-symmetric holey metasurfaces using a generalized Floquet theorem. *IEEE Access* **2018**, *6*, 71743–71750. [CrossRef]
30. Herran, L.F.; Chen, Q.; Mesa, F.; Quevedo-Teruel, O. Electromagnetic Bandgap Based on a Compact Three-Hole Double-Layer Periodic Structure. *IEEE Trans. Antennas Propag.* **2023**,*72*, 1045–1050. [CrossRef]

31. Ghasemifard, F.; Norgren, M.; Quevedo-Teruel, O. Dispersion analysis of 2-D glide-symmetric corrugated metasurfaces using mode-matching technique. *IEEE Microw. Wirel. Components Lett.* **2017**, *28*, 1–3. [CrossRef]
32. Valerio, G.; Ghasemifard, F.; Sipus, Z.; Quevedo-Teruel, O. Glide-symmetric all-metal holey metasurfaces for low-dispersive artificial materials: Modeling and properties. *IEEE Trans. Microw. Theory Tech.* **2018**, *66*, 3210–3223. [CrossRef]
33. Fischer, B.; Valerio, G. Dispersion properties of glide-symmetric corrugated metasurface waveguides. *Int. J. Microw. Wirel. Technol.* **2024**, *16*, 13–20. [CrossRef]
34. Memeletzoglou, N.; Sanchez-Cabello, C.; Pizarro-Torres, F.; Rajo-Iglesias, E. Analysis of periodic structures made of pins inside a parallel plate waveguide. *Symmetry* **2019**, *11*, 582. [CrossRef]
35. Chen, Q.; Mesa, F.; Yin, X.; Quevedo-Teruel, O. Accurate characterization and design guidelines of glide-symmetric holey EBG. *IEEE Trans. Microw. Theory Tech.* **2020**, *68*, 4984–4994. [CrossRef]
36. Valerio, G.; Sipus, Z.; Grbic, A.; Quevedo-Teruel, O. Accurate equivalent-circuit descriptions of thin glide-symmetric corrugated metasurfaces. *IEEE Trans. Antennas Propag.* **2017**, *65*, 2695–2700. [CrossRef]
37. Ertay, A.O. Modeling, Analysis, and Comparison of Rectangular Waveguide Structures Having Glide Symmetrical Step Discontinuity with Periodic Dielectric Loading. *Erzincan Univ. J. Sci. Technol.* **2024**, *17*, 826–839. [CrossRef]
38. Fischer, B.; Valerio, G. Quasi-static homogenization of glide-symmetric holey parallel-plate waveguides with ultra-wideband validity. *IEEE Trans. Antennas Propag.* **2022**, *70*, 10569–10582. [CrossRef]
39. Lai, W.Y.; Kehn, M.N.M. Analysis of Rotated Corrugated Parallel Plate Waveguide Using Asymptotic Corrugation Boundary Conditions. In Proceedings of the 2019 IEEE International Symposium on Antennas and Propagation and USNC-URSI Radio Science Meeting, Atlanta, GA, USA, 7–12 July 2019; pp. 837–838.
40. Mesa, F.; Valerio, G.; Rodriguez-Berral, R.; Quevedo-Teruel, O. Simulation-assisted efficient computation of the dispersion diagram of periodic structures: A comprehensive overview with applications to filters, leaky-wave antennas and metasurfaces. *IEEE Antennas Propag. Mag.* **2020**, *63*, 33–45. [CrossRef]
41. Petek, M.; Rivero, J.; Vásquez, J. A. T.; Valerio, G.; Quevedo-Teruel, O.; Vipiana, F. Method of Moments for the Dispersion Modeling of Glide-Symmetric Periodic Structures. *IEEE Trans. Antennas Propag.* **2024**, *72*, 756–766. [CrossRef]
42. Castillo-Tapia, P.; Mesa, F.; Yakovlev, A.; Valerio, G.; Quevedo-Teruel, O. Study of forward and backward modes in double-sided dielectric-filled corrugated waveguides. *Sensors* **2021**, *21*, 6293. [CrossRef] [PubMed]
43. Castillo-Tapia, P.; Mesa, F.; Quevedo-Teruel, O. Multimodal Transfer Matrix Approach for the Analysis and Fundamental Understanding of Periodic Structures with Higher Symmetries. In Proceedings of the 2022 16th European Conference on Antennas and Propagation (EuCAP), Madrid, Spain, 27 March–1 April 2022; pp. 1–5.
44. Bagheriasl, M.; Quevedo-Teruel, O; Valerio, G. Bloch analysis of artificial lines and surfaces exhibiting glide symmetry. *IEEE Trans. Microw. Theory Tech.* **2019**, *67*, 2618–2628. [CrossRef]
45. Castillo-Tapia, P. The Multimodal Transfer Matrix Method: And Its Application to Higher-Symmetric Periodic Structures. Ph.D. Thesis, KTH Royal Institute of Technology, Stockholm, Sweden, 2022.
46. Mesa, F.; Rodriguez-Berral, R.; Medina, F. Unlocking complexity using the ECA: The equivalent circuit model as an efficient and physically insightful tool for microwave engineering. *IEEE Microw. Mag.* **2018**, *19*, 44–65. [CrossRef]
47. Şimşek, S. A fast and accurate design method for broad omnidirectional bandgaps of one dimensional photonic crystals. *AEU-Int. J. Electron. Commun.* **2014**, *68*, 865–868. [CrossRef]
48. Ertay, A.O.; Şimşek, S. Determination of stopband characteristics of asymmetrically loaded helix slow wave structures with Auxiliary Functions of Generalized Scattering Matrix (AFGSM) method. *AEU-Int. J. Electron. Commun.* **2018**, *95*, 271–278. [CrossRef]
49. Marcuvitz, N. *Waveguide Handbook*; P. Peregrinus on Behalf of the Institution of Electrical Engineers: London, UK, 1986.
50. Şimşek, S.; Rezaeieh, S.A. A design method for substrate integrated waveguide electromagnetic bandgap (SIW-EBG) filters. *AEU-Int. J. Electron. Commun.* **2013**, *67*, 981–983. [CrossRef]
51. Padilla, P.; Herran, L.; Tamayo-Dominguez, A.; Valenzuela-Valdes, J.; Quevedo-Teruel, O. Glide symmetry to prevent the lowest stopband of printed corrugated transmission lines. *IEEE Microw. Wirel. Components Lett.* **2018** *28*, 750–752. [CrossRef]
52. Padilla, P.; Palomares-Caballero, A.; Alex-Amor, A.; Valenzuela-Valdes, J.; Fernández-Gonzalez, J.; Quevedo-Teruel, O. Broken glide-symmetric holey structures for bandgap selection in gap-waveguide technology. *IEEE Microw. Wirel. Compon. Lett.* **2019** *29*, 327–329. [CrossRef]
53. Monje-Real, A.; Fonseca, N.; Zetterstrom, O.; Pucci, E.; Quevedo-Teruel, O. Holey glide-symmetric filters for 5G at millimeter-wave frequencies. *IEEE Microw. Wirel. Components Lett.* **2019** *30*, 31–34.
54. Zhu, H.; Mao, J. Miniaturized tapered EBG structure with wide stopband and flat passband. *IEEE Antennas Wirel. Propag. Lett.* **2012**, *11*, 314–317.
55. Ertay, A.O.; Şimşek, S. A compact bandstop filter design for X-band applications. In Proceedings of the 2016 International Symposium on Fundamentals of Electrical Engineering (ISFEE), Bucharest, Romania, 30 June–2 July 2016; pp. 1–6.

56. Reines, I.; Park, S.J.; Rebeiz, G.M. Compact low-loss tunable X-band bandstop filter with miniature RF-MEMS switches. *IEEE Trans. Microw. Theory Tech.* **2010**, *58*, 1887–1895. [CrossRef]
57. Zheng, G.; Papapolymerou, J. Monolithic reconfigurable bandstop filter using RF MEMS switches. *Int. J. RF Microw. Comput.-Aided Eng.* **2004**, *14*, 373–382. [CrossRef]
58. Hou, F.; Li, L.; Shen, Y.; Sun, C.; Luan, H.; Hu, S. Wideband switchable sharp-rejection filter in compact 3-D heterogeneous integration. *IEEE Trans. Compon. Packag. Manuf. Technol.* **2022**, *12*, 1583–1590. [CrossRef]
59. Cabello-Sánchez, J.; Drakinskiy, V.; Stake, J.; Rodilla, H. Analysis of the electromagnetic interaction between periodically corrugated transmission lines through the mutual capacitance and mutual inductance. *IEEE Access.* **2022**, *10*, 15818–15834.
60. Wu, C.H.; Zhou, G.; Ma, P.; Wu, Y.; Li, K.; Shen, L.; Shen, Q.; Zhang, H.; Yan, J.; You, Y.; et al. A corrugated planar-Goubau-line termination for terahertz waves. *IEEE Microw. Wirel. Technol. Lett.* **2023**, *33*, 643–646.
61. Wang, S.; Chung, K.L.; Du, L.; Kong, F.; Li, K. Design and analysis of a compact frequency beam-scanning antenna based on composite FHMSIW/SSPP waveguide. *IEEE Antennas Wirel. Propag. Lett.* **2021**, *21*, 546–550. [CrossRef]
62. Yan, X.T.; Tang, W.; Liu, J.F.; Wang, M.; Gao, X.X.; Cui, T.J. Glide symmetry for mode control and significant suppression of coupling in dual-strip SSPP transmission lines. *Soc. Photo-Opt. Instrum. Eng.* **2021**, *3*, 026001. [CrossRef]
63. Wang, S.; Chung, K.L.; Kong, F.; Du, L.; Li, K. A simple circularly polarized beam-scanning antenna using modulated slotline-spoof surface plasmon polariton slow-wave transmission line. *IEEE Antennas Wirel. Propag. Lett.* **2023**, *22*, 1109–1113. [CrossRef]
64. Pozar, D.M. *Microwave Engineering: Theory and Techniques*; John Wiley & Sons: Hoboken, NJ, USA, 2021.

applied sciences

MDPI

Article

Performance Analysis of Data-Driven and Deterministic Latency Models in Dynamic Packet-Switched Xhaul Networks

Mirosław Klinkowski * and Dariusz Więcek

National Institute of Telecommunications, Szachowa 1, 04-894 Warsaw, Poland; d.wiecek@il-pib.pl
* Correspondence: m.klinkowski@il-pib.pl

Abstract: Accurate prediction of maximum flow latency is crucial for ensuring the efficient transport of latency-sensitive fronthaul traffic in packet-switched Xhaul networks while maintaining the reliable operation of 5G and beyond Radio Access Networks (RANs). Deterministic worst-case (WC) models provide strict latency guarantees but tend to overestimate actual delays, resulting in resource over-provisioning and inefficient network utilization. To address this limitation, this study evaluates a data-driven Quantile Regression (QR) model for latency prediction in Time-Sensitive Networking (TSN)-enabled packet-switched Xhaul networks operating under dynamic traffic conditions. The proposed QR model estimates high-percentile (tail) latency values by leveraging both deterministic and queuing-related data features. Its performance is quantitatively compared with the WC estimator across diverse network topologies and traffic load scenarios. The results demonstrate that the QR model achieves significantly higher prediction accuracy—particularly for midhaul flows—while still maintaining compliance with latency constraints. Furthermore, when applied to dynamic Xhaul network operation, QR-based latency predictions enable a reduction in active processing-node utilization compared with WC-based estimations. These findings confirm that data-driven models can effectively complement deterministic methods in supporting latency-aware optimization and adaptive operation of 5G/6G Xhaul networks.

Keywords: 5G; 6G; Xhaul; packet-switched network; latency modeling; machine learning; quantile regression; time-sensitive networking; network optimization

1. Introduction

The evolution toward the fifth- and sixth-generation (5G/6G) mobile networks, increasingly based on centralized (C-RAN) and virtualized (vRAN) radio access architectures, brings unprecedented performance demands to the underlying transport layer, commonly referred to as the fronthaul (FH) or converged Xhaul [1,2]. A major challenge in these new mobile networks is the support of ultra-reliable low-latency communications (URLLC), where the overall end-to-end delay must be kept within the order of a millisecond—or even less—while maintaining reliability levels approaching 99.999% [3]. Within the transport segment, stringent constraints apply in particular to high-priority FH user-plane traffic, for which standardized profiles typically assume a maximum one-way latency budget targeted at or below 100 μs [4,5]. Under these conditions, the ability to accurately predict network latency becomes essential for ensuring the expected Quality of Service (QoS) levels. Reliable latency prediction under time-varying traffic loads enables intelligent routing, adaptive resource allocation across network slices, and effective admission control, thereby ensuring Service Level Agreement (SLA) compliance and stable network performance [6–10].

Ethernet-based, packet-switched Xhaul networks have emerged as a cost-effective and scalable solution for transporting heterogeneous radio data flows between distributed radio and processing elements in 5G/6G RANs [4,11–13]. However, their operation is inherently affected by non-deterministic delays resulting from packet buffering and contention in Ethernet switches (bridges), which make it challenging to provide the strict delay guarantees required by latency-sensitive FH traffic. To meet these demands, packet-switched Ethernet Xhaul networks have been enhanced with Time-Sensitive Networking (TSN) mechanisms, standardized for fronthaul applications in IEEE 802.1CM [11]. The TSN suite of IEEE standards specifies traffic classes, scheduling profiles, and mechanisms such as time-aware shaping and frame preemption that enable deterministic, bounded transmission delays [14,15]. While TSN significantly improves delay determinism, its guarantees can degrade under high and bursty FH loads, where contention among high-priority flows still leads to excessive buffering and increased queuing delays [16,17]. Consequently, maintaining predictable latency requires not only TSN mechanisms but also accurate latency models that capture the buffering behavior of packet flows and enable real-time prediction and control of delay during dynamic network operation.

Traditional queuing-theory models are primarily intended to estimate average delays [18]. Although these models can be extended to approximate high-percentile delay values [17,19], such formulations remain approximations that, while useful for FH link dimensioning [17], cannot ensure the strict maximum latency guarantees required in 5G RANs. To achieve strict delay compliance, deterministic worst-case (WC) latency models, often derived using Network Calculus [20] or related analytical frameworks [11,21], are typically employed to establish upper bounds that flow latencies cannot exceed. However, the main drawback of WC estimates lies in their pessimistic nature, as they remain accurate under low traffic conditions but become increasingly conservative as congestion builds up in multi-hop networks [20]. This conservatism leads to resource over-provisioning and, consequently, inefficient utilization of network capacity [22].

To overcome the limitations of conservative WC modeling and enable more efficient resource utilization, data-driven modeling approaches have gained increasing attention. Machine Learning (ML) and Deep Learning (DL) methods are now increasingly applied to capture network performance dynamics, often framing latency estimation as a time-series prediction [7,8] or as a regression problem [9,22]. However, data-driven techniques have rarely been applied to predict maximum flow latencies in packet-switched Xhaul networks, with only a few studies addressing this topic. Among these, ref. [22] focuses on TSN-based Ethernet Xhaul networks, employing a linear regression (LR) model to predict maximum flow latencies and thereby refine the estimates produced by a deterministic WC model. In contrast, the authors of [19] investigate a different transport technology—namely, time-slotted FlexE—which follows a circuit-style transmission paradigm rather than packet switching. Consequently, the applicability of data-driven latency prediction methods to TSN-enabled packet-switched Xhaul networks, as defined in the IEEE 1914.1 standard [4] and referenced in Open RAN (O-RAN) specifications [12], remains largely unexplored.

In this study, we evaluate the effectiveness of a regression-based approach for predicting maximum flow latencies in TSN-enabled packet-switched Xhaul networks. The analysis focuses on the Xhaul network operating under dynamic conditions, as expected in 5G/6G environments, where both traffic loads and flow configurations may change over time. Specifically, we employ a Quantile Regression (QR) model [23], which is well suited for this task as it estimates high-percentile delay values and thus effectively captures the tail behavior of latency distributions under variable traffic conditions. The model is trained using a comprehensive data set generated for multiple Xhaul topologies and diverse traffic load scenarios, ensuring broad representativeness of network states. Its performance is then evaluated in a dynamic network environment, where both traffic configurations and load levels vary over time. The predictive accuracy and robustness of the QR model are compared against the deterministic WC estimator, providing quantitative insights into the potential of data-driven methods to complement analytical latency modeling in future 5G/6G transport networks.

The main contributions of this study are summarized as follows:

- A regression-based approach is proposed to predict maximum flow latencies in dynamic TSN-enabled packet-switched Xhaul networks.
- The performance of the proposed QR predictor is evaluated and compared with deterministic WC latency estimations in a dynamic Xhaul scenario characterized by varying traffic loads and changing Xhaul flow configurations.
- The accuracy and applicability of the QR model, trained on a comprehensive data set generated under diverse network configurations and load conditions, are validated across a wide range of evaluation scenarios.
- The impact of data-driven latency prediction on overall network performance is analyzed, demonstrating its potential to enhance deterministic latency modeling in dynamic Xhaul operation.

The novelty of this work lies in the quantitative comparison of a data-driven QR model against a deterministic WC model for latency prediction of traffic flows in complex Xhaul topologies (mesh and ring). We demonstrate that the improved accuracy of the QR model yields measurable, multi-percent gains in resource efficiency during network operation, thereby providing a practical, data-driven solution to mitigate the over-provisioning inherent in conservative WC estimations.

The remainder of this paper is organized as follows. Section 2 reviews the related literature. Section 3 introduces the main assumptions of the considered network and traffic models. Section 4 presents the deterministic WC and data-driven QR latency models analyzed in this study. Section 5 outlines the data generation workflow for ML analysis, including the details of the network scenarios and evaluation tools. Section 6 describes the dynamic packet-switched Xhaul network scenario used for model evaluation. Section 7 reports the results of simulation experiments, while Section 8 provides their interpretation and discussion. Finally, Section 9 concludes the paper and summarizes the main findings.

2. Related Works

Latency management in TSN-based packet-switched networks focuses on mitigating the non-deterministic delays caused by packet buffering and contention in Ethernet bridges (switches). Solutions defined within the IEEE TSN family of standards, including IEEE 802.1CM, dedicated to fronthaul networks [11], as well as IEEE 802.1Qbv scheduled traffic [14] and IEEE 802.1Qbu frame preemption [15], aim to provide the deterministic transmission guarantees required by latency-sensitive services. In particular, IEEE 802.1CM explicitly defines the individual latency components, including queuing delays, and specifies a reference latency model for the calculation of worst-case delay in TSN-enabled packet-switched fronthaul networks [11].

Early research efforts concentrated on implementing and evaluating standards-based fronthaul solutions such as Common Public Radio Interface over Ethernet (CoE) and enhanced CPRI (eCPRI), in conjunction with TSN mechanisms defined in IEEE 802.1CM [16]. Several studies investigated whether TSN techniques, including IEEE 802.1Qbv scheduled traffic and IEEE 802.1Qbu frame preemption, are capable of satisfying the stringent delay and jitter requirements imposed on fronthaul traffic [24]. Additionally, advanced scheduling algorithms aimed at jitter minimization, such as exhaustive-search or the proposed Comb-Fitting scheduling methods, were introduced to maintain packet delay variation within the required strict limits [16].

Deterministic analytical approaches, particularly those based on Network Calculus (NC) [20], have been extensively applied to estimate worst-case upper bounds on end-to-end latency [21,25]. NC is widely used for worst-case delay analysis in TSN networks, especially for time-triggered or other latency-critical traffic classes [26]. While NC provides formal bounds, these bounds often overestimate actual latencies, potentially leading to the over-dimensioning of network resources [22].

Queuing theory models [18] are widely employed to analyze latencies in packet-switched networks. Classical models such as M/M/1 and G/G/1 are, however, primarily intended for estimating mean delays and thus insufficient to guarantee the strict maximum latency requirements imposed by 5G/6G systems [19,27]. Nevertheless, several extensions and more sophisticated models have proven effective. For instance, the N*D/D/1 model has been successfully applied to estimate extreme queuing delay percentiles-such as the 99.9999999th percentile corresponding to a Frame Loss Ratio (FLR) target of 10^{-7}-for aggregated eCPRI high-priority FH flows in 5G New Radio (NR) networks [17]. This approach enables maximizing link lengths while maintaining compliance with IEEE 802.1CM latency constraints. Furthermore, a queuing-based model combining a Quasi-Birth-Death (QBD) process for centralized unit (CU) and distributed unit (DU) nodes with Open Jackson Network theory for the packet-switched fronthaul segment has been proposed to evaluate end-to-end delays under flexible functional split configurations [27]. In more general Deterministic Networking (DetNet) scenarios, the M/M/1 envelope model has been introduced as a simple yet effective methodology for obtaining tight upper bounds on delay percentiles, providing a practical tool for network planning and dimensioning [28].

To achieve higher accuracy than deterministic bounds and enable proactive network management, recent studies have increasingly adopted data-driven modeling approaches. ML and DL techniques are applied to predict network latency, typically formulated as time-series forecasting or regression problems, which are particularly relevant for URLLC scenarios [9]. Linear Regression (LR) has been employed to refine deterministic WC latency estimates by training on simulated data, thereby improving prediction accuracy and mitigating the risk of resource over-dimensioning [22]. More advanced Neural Network (NN) architectures—such as Feedforward Neural Networks (FNN), Convolutional Neural Networks (CNN), Recurrent Neural Networks (RNN), and Long Short-Term Memory (LSTM) models—have been explored to forecast network latency based on historical measurement data [29]. Graph Neural Network (GNN) models, including RouteNet and GraphSAGE, have also been applied to predict per-flow end-to-end delays by leveraging network topology, flow configuration, and dynamic indicators such as queue utilization [25]. A lightweight Multi-Layer Perceptron (MLP) model for accurate Round-Trip Time (RTT) prediction in 5G NSA edge networks was proposed in [30] and validated using real-world measurement data collected across diverse mobility scenarios. The authors of [8] introduced an adaptive contrastive learning framework that employs a dilated-convolution encoder and a hierarchical contrastive loss function to predict network latency in 5G URLLC scenarios, using real-world data collected along the entire communication path. Hybrid approaches that integrate analytical latency bounds from NC (e.g., Total Flow Analysis or Separate Flow Analysis) as input features for GNNs have been shown to further enhance the prediction of high-latency quantiles [25].

5G/6G networks built upon O-RAN architectures are expected to increasingly rely on Artificial Intelligence (AI) and ML for dynamic spectrum management, resource allocation, and real-time network control and optimization [31,32]. Within this context, several recent studies have applied AI/ML techniques to enhance latency management in next-generation RANs. In [33], the authors proposed an O-RAN-compliant mathematical framework for 6G networks supporting multiple URLLC services, incorporating a Stochastic Network

Calculus (SNC)-based controller that allocates guaranteed radio resources and ensures that packet delay violation probabilities remain within prescribed service-level tolerances. In a related line of work, ref. [34] presented an AI-driven latency forecasting system, implemented and validated within a functional 5G O-RAN hardware prototype, which leverages a bidirectional LSTM model for real-time prediction of air-interface delay and link quality to support adaptive, latency-aware decision-making.

Despite increasing interest in data-driven latency modeling, only a few studies explicitly address the prediction of maximum one-way latencies in packet-switched Xhaul networks. In [19], a Deep-Q learning approach was proposed to forecast input traffic patterns and optimize resource allocation, using the 99.9th percentile delay along Xhaul paths as a strict performance constraint. However, that study focused on a time-slotted FlexE-based Xhaul network, which follows a circuit-style transmission paradigm and thus differs from the non-deterministic packet-switching behavior defined in IEEE 802.1CM TSN networks. In contrast, ref. [22] examined a TSN-based Ethernet Xhaul network and introduced an LR model to refine deterministic WC latency estimates. While the LR approach improved average prediction accuracy, it inherently estimates conditional means rather than high-percentile values, and therefore requires additional engineering to capture tail latency behavior, limiting its applicability in practice.

To the best of our knowledge, no prior work has investigated a regression-based approach employing a QR model specifically designed to predict high-percentile latencies in dynamic TSN-enabled packet-switched Xhaul networks, where both traffic loads and flow configurations vary over time.

3. Network Model

The study considers a packet-switched Xhaul network that interconnects the functional components of a RAN [4]. The assumptions regarding the network, traffic, and latency models follow those adopted in our previous works [10,35,36]. The architecture consists of three main entities: (i) radio units (RUs) located at antenna sites, (ii) distributed units (DUs) that perform part of the baseband processing and can be virtualized at processing-pool (PP) nodes, and (iii) centralized units (CUs) positioned at a hub node to complete the radio processing chain. The RUs, PPs, and the hub are interconnected through an Ethernet-based transport infrastructure that multiplexes and routes data flows among these entities [11].

The considered network supports two categories of traffic. Fronthaul (FH) flows connect the RUs with their assigned PP nodes hosting DUs, whereas midhaul (MH) flows connect PPs with the hub node performing CU functions. Communication occurs in both directions: uplink (UL, RU $\rightarrow$ PP $\rightarrow$ hub) and downlink (DL, hub $\rightarrow$ PP $\rightarrow$ RU), resulting in four flow types: FH-UL, FH-DL, MH-UL, and MH-DL. Each flow type is characterized by distinct bit-rate and latency requirements. The RUs attached to a common access switch are assumed to form a cluster that may require joint DU processing for multi-cell coordination. Consequently, all FH flows originating from the same cluster are routed to a common DU node.

All flows are transmitted as periodic bursts of Ethernet frames that encapsulate radio data [17,37]. Bursts are forwarded end-to-end without fragmentation, following a store-and-forward policy at each switch. Traffic scheduling follows a strict-priority discipline [11], where FH bursts have higher priority than MH bursts, and bursts of the same priority are served in the first-in–first-out (FIFO) order. Each burst consists of a fixed number of Ethernet frames, and the time interval between consecutive bursts, referred to as the transmission window, depends on the applied 5G numerology [38]. For numerology index $\mu \in [0, 4]$, the subcarrier spacing equals $15 \times 2^{\mu}$ kHz, resulting in a transmission window of $66.\bar{6} \times 2^{-\mu}$ µs [17,38]. Each network instance defined in Section 5 and evaluated in

Section 7 assumes a fixed numerology to examine its impact on latency modeling and overall network performance.

Figure 1 shows an example of FH and MH packet burst transmission and buffering in both UL and DL directions of the packet-switched Xhaul network. The figure illustrates the periodic generation of bursts, their traversal through consecutive switching nodes, and the operation of TSN mechanisms that apply strict-priority burst scheduling.

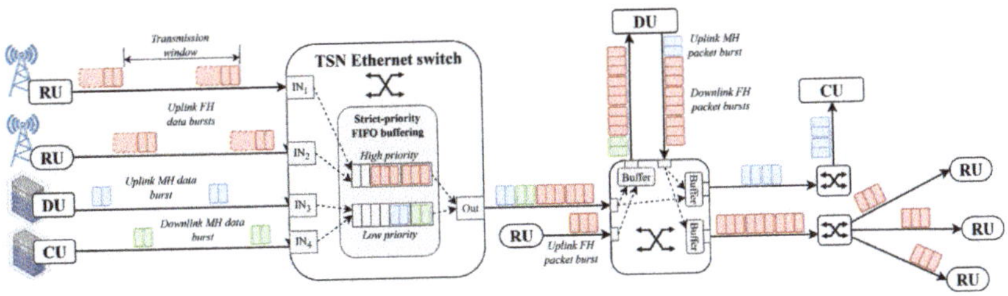

Figure 1. Transmission and buffering of FH and MH packet bursts in uplink and downlink directions in a packet-switched Xhaul network.

Although the network illustrated in Figure 1 ensures that latency-sensitive FH traffic is prioritized over MH traffic, contention among bursts of the same priority may still lead to considerable queuing delays. Because reliable RAN operation requires that the one-way latencies of FH and MH flows remain within predefined limits [4,5], predicting maximum burst delays accurately becomes critical for ensuring service-level compliance. This study therefore investigates the Xhaul transport network under these latency constraints, using analytical and data-driven latency models described in the next section.

4. Latency Models

The Xhaul transport network must ensure that the one-way latency experienced by any packet flow remains within predefined limits [4,5]. In the considered packet-switched Xhaul network scenario, this requirement implies that the delay of any burst belonging to a flow cannot exceed a specified maximum value. In this section, we present two latency models used to estimate or predict these delays: a deterministic worst-case (WC) estimator and a data-driven quantile regression (QR) predictor.

4.1. Worst-Case Model

The considered worst-case latency model was introduced in [11] for estimating packet delays in TSN packet-switched fronthaul networks, where flows of different priorities coexist. It accounts for static delays caused by signal propagation in links (L_f^{P}), packet store-and-forward operations in switches (L_f^{SF}), and transmission times of packet bursts over links (L_f^{T}), as well as for buffering delays that occur at switch output ports (L_f^{B}). For a given flow f, the total latency is expressed as

$$L_f^{\mathrm{WC}} = L_f^{\mathrm{P}} + L_f^{\mathrm{SF}} + L_f^{\mathrm{T}} + L_f^{\mathrm{B}}, \tag{1}$$

where the first three components represent static delays, and the last term corresponds to buffering delays accumulated along the path.

The WC model assumes worst-case buffering delays. In particular, L_f^{B} is estimated as an upper bound on the queuing latency of bursts served under the strict-priority scheduling algorithm (adopted in this study), derived using the principles of network calculus theory, as discussed in [21]. These buffering delays arise from two sources:

- bursts belonging to other flows of equal or higher priority that may be transmitted before the burst of the considered flow, and
- the largest burst of a lower-priority flow that may already be in transmission and is not preempted.

For a flow f routed through buffered links e along path p, the buffering latency L_f^{B} is calculated as

$$L_f^{\mathrm{B}} = \sum_{e \in p} \left(\sum_{q \in \mathcal{H}(f,e)} L(q,e) + \max_{q \in \mathcal{L}(f,e)} L(q,e) \right), \tag{2}$$

where $\mathcal{H}(f,e)$ denotes the set of flows with equal or higher priority than f that share link e, $\mathcal{L}(f,e)$ represents the set of lower-priority flows interfering with f, and $L(q,e)$ is the latency contribution of an interfering flow q on link e, corresponding to the transmission delay of the burst of flow q in that link. The first term in (2) aggregates the delays caused by all higher- or equal-priority flows, while the second term accounts for the largest delay that can be introduced by a lower-priority flow already in transmission.

4.2. Quantile Regression Model

The quantile regression model provides a data-driven alternative to deterministic latency estimation by learning the conditional distribution of flow latency from observed data. Unlike ordinary least-squares regression, which estimates the conditional mean of a dependent variable, QR predicts a specific quantile (e.g., 0.95 or 0.99) of the latency distribution, thereby capturing high-percentile delay behavior. This capability makes QR particularly suitable for packet-switched Xhaul networks, which must comply with strict one-way latency limits and where queuing effects produce long-tailed latency distributions that are not well characterized by mean-based models. The concept of quantile regression was first introduced in [39] and has since been widely adopted in predictive modeling, including recent applications to delay forecasting in packet networks [40].

From a theoretical viewpoint, QR extends classical linear regression by replacing the mean-squared loss with an asymmetric quantile (pinball) loss, which penalizes underestimation more heavily for higher quantiles [23]. Given a flow f described by a vector of features $\mathbf{x}_f = [x_{f,1}, x_{f,2}, \ldots, x_{f,n}]$, the QR-predicted latency is expressed as:

$$L_f^{\mathrm{QR}} = \beta_0 + \sum_{i=1}^{n} \beta_i x_{f,i}, \tag{3}$$

where β_0 is the intercept and β_i are regression coefficients. The coefficient values β_i $(0 \le i \le n)$ are obtained by minimizing the quantile loss function

$$\mathcal{L}_Q(y,\hat{y}) = \begin{cases} Q\,(y-\hat{y}), & \text{if } y \ge \hat{y}, \\ (1-Q)\,(\hat{y}-y), & \text{otherwise.} \end{cases} \tag{4}$$

where Q is the desired quantile level $(0 < Q < 1)$, and y and $\hat{y}$ are the actual and predicted latency values, respectively. This asymmetric loss function enforces conservative predictions for high quantiles (e.g., $Q \ge 0.99$), thereby reducing the risk of underestimating latency values.

In this study, the feature set combines descriptors that represent both static path properties and dynamic queuing interactions of packet flows. The complete feature set used for each flow f includes:

- Routing path characteristics: hop count N_f^{hops}, the number of buffered links along the path N_f^{buffers}, and the static latency L_f^{stat}, representing the sum of propagation, store-and-forward, and transmission delays, i.e., $L_f^{\text{stat}} = L_f^{\text{P}} + L_f^{\text{SF}} + L_f^{\text{T}}$;
- Deterministic latency bound: the worst-case latency estimate L_f^{WC}, which serves as a baseline input linking the QR model to analytical latency bounds;
- Queuing-related indicators:
  - $L_f^{\text{EP,same}}$—buffering contribution from equal-priority (EP) flows entering the same switch input port g. It captures the overlap between the reception delay of the burst of flow f ($L(f,g)$) and the transmission delay of a burst of another EP flow q at the switch output port e ($L(q,e)$). If $L(q,e) \leq L(f,g)$, the burst of flow q is completely transmitted before the burst of flow f is fully received, and no buffering delay is introduced. Otherwise, a partial buffering delay occurs, which is reduced proportionally to the difference between the burst reception and transmission times.
  - $L_f^{\text{EP,other}}$—buffering contribution from EP flows arriving from other input ports. It accounts for the longest EP burst from each such port, and is calculated as the sum of their respective delay contributions.
  - $L_f^{\text{HP,sum}}$—aggregated buffering impact from higher-priority (HP) flows, calculated as the total delay induced by all such flows contending for transmission at the same output port.

This combination of deterministic and empirical features enables the QR model to learn both the structural characteristics of the routing path and the stochastic variability caused by packet contention.

5. Data Generation

This section describes the methodology used to generate the data sets used in the ML analysis and training of the QR latency prediction model. The data generation process integrates optimization-based flow allocation and packet-level network simulations to produce representative latency measurements under diverse Xhaul configurations. The following subsections outline the main network and system assumptions, the workflow for building the data sets for ring and mesh topologies, the underlying MILP optimization used to obtain feasible flow allocations, and the simulation framework used for latency measurements and feature extraction.

5.1. Main Assumptions

The study considers two representative Xhaul transport topologies: ring and mesh networks [10,41,42]. In the case of ring networks (RING-N), the number of switching nodes (N) ranges from 5 to 10, whereas for mesh (MESH-N), two larger networks are analyzed, with $N \in \{20, 38\}$. The corresponding topologies are shown in Figure 2.

For each topology, network scenarios were generated with varying numbers of RUs (R), randomly attached to the switching nodes. In RING-N networks, we consider $R \in \{10, 20, 30\}$, while in MESH-N networks the range extends to $R \in \{10, 20, 30, 40, 50\}$. The parameters of the network links, including capacities and lengths, are shown in Table 1 [10], where the actual link lengths are randomly selected within given ranges. Propagation delays are derived assuming a transmission speed of 2×10^5 km/s, which reflects the typical velocity factor of optical fiber (≈0.67c). Each switch introduces a store-and-forward latency of 5 µs, corresponding to the forwarding delay value used for latency analysis in Annex B of the IEEE 802.1CM standard [11].

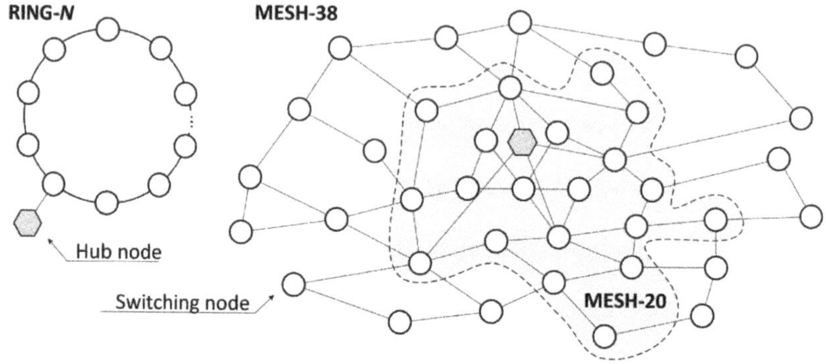

Figure 2. Xhaul transport network topologies assumed in analysis: RING-N and MESH-N.

Table 1. Parameters of network links.

Link	Bit-Rate [Gbit/s]	Length [km]
switch–RU	25	$[0.2 \ldots 0.5]$
switch–switch	100	$[1 \ldots 3]$
switch–PP	400	$[0.2 \ldots 0.5]$
switch–hub	400	$[10 \ldots 15]$

In the analysis, we assume a radio system configured with eight MIMO layers, 32 antenna ports, and 100 MHz channels [43]. The functional split adopts Option 7.2 for FH and Option 2 for MH [44]. The corresponding maximum radio data flow rates, derived from the model in [43], are 21.624 Gbps and 22.204 Gbps for FH uplink and downlink, and 3.024 Gbps and 4.016 Gbps for MH uplink and downlink, respectively. Two numerologies are considered, $\mu \in \{1,2\}$. The Ethernet frame size is fixed at 1542 bytes, consistent with the assumptions adopted in [11]. The burst size for each flow follows directly from the radio bit-rate, the Ethernet frame size, the applied numerology, and the periodic traffic generation model proposed in [17] and described in detail in [35]. Flow routing is determined using the k-shortest path algorithm.

5.2. Data Generation Workflow

Two independent data sets were created for the ML analysis, one for the ring and the other for the mesh topology, using the network scenarios and system parameters defined in Section 5.1 within the procedure illustrated in Figure 3.

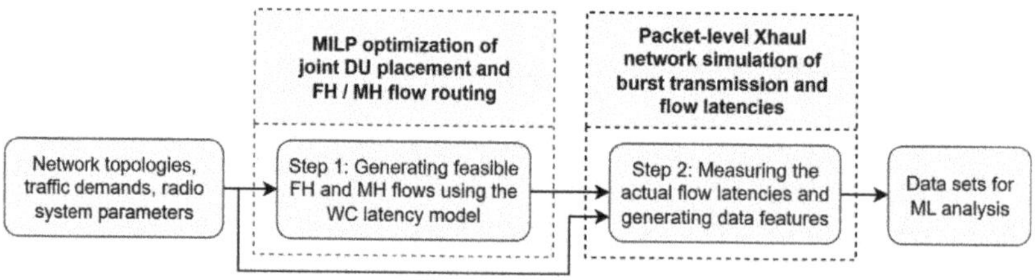

Figure 3. Data set generation workflow.

The data generation workflow in Figure 3 consists of the following two steps.

Step 1: Generating feasible flows—feasible FH and MH flows satisfying capacity and latency constraints were generated for each network scenario. For this purpose, a mixed-integer linear programming (MILP) optimization method, discussed in Section 5.3, was applied

assuming maximum Xhaul flow bit-rates ($\rho = 1.0$) and latency estimation based on the WC model.
Step 2: Generating data features—the goal of this step was to generate the data features, including the measurement of the actual latencies, for each individual data flow produced in Step 1. To this end, packet-level Xhaul network simulations were executed for each network scenario and data were gathered, as described in Section 5.4.

For the ring topology, a total of 7200 network scenarios were processed. Specifically, six networks with different numbers of switching nodes (N) were considered, each combined with three RU counts (R), according to the assumptions in Section 5.1. Every configuration was repeated ten times with random RU-to-switch assignments and evaluated under two radio numerologies (μ). For each flow, the one-way latency limit was set either as a random value between 50 µs and 150 µs in the case of FH, or as a fixed 1 ms for MH flows [4]. Traffic load levels $\rho \in \{0.1, 0.25, 0.5, 0.75, 1.0\}$ were considered, where ρ denotes the fraction of the maximum radio flow bit-rates (see Section 5.1) allocated to corresponding flow types (FH/MH in both uplink and downlink). To introduce variability, the bit rate of each flow was further perturbed by a random deviation bounded by $\delta \in \{0, 0.1, 0.2, 0.5\}$, while ensuring that the resulting load remained within $0.01 \leq \rho \leq 1.0$. Assuming on average 20 RUs per scenario and four flows per RU, the resulting ring data set contains 576,000 labeled flow samples.

The data set for the mesh topology was derived from 12,000 distinct scenarios. It comprises two networks with different numbers of switching nodes (N), each combined with five RU counts (R) as defined in Section 5.1. Every configuration was evaluated under ten random RU-to-switch assignments and two numerologies. For each case, three FH latency limits were applied: (a) a fixed 75 µs, (b) a fixed 100 µs, and (c) a randomly chosen value between 50 µs and 150 µs, independently assigned per flow. The same sets of ρ and δ as in the ring scenarios were considered. Assuming an average of 30 RUs per scenario and four flows per RU, the mesh data set comprises 1,440,000 labeled flow samples.

The generated data sets were used in the ML analysis to train and test the QR latency prediction model with the quantile parameter set to $Q = 0.9999$. The model was implemented using the `QuantileRegressor` class from the scikit-learn Python library and trained separately for each data flow type (FH-UL, FH-DL, MH-UL, MH-DL), numerology, and network topology (ring or mesh). In the training process, the regularization coefficient was set to $\alpha = 0$, and the `highs` solver was used as the underlying optimization method. All remaining optimization settings followed their default values, and no additional parameter tuning was applied.

Figures 4 and 5 illustrate the relationship between the measured maximum one-way flow latencies and the corresponding values estimated using the WC model (left) and predicted by the QR model (right). Dedicated plots for individual flow types and network topologies are presented, covering the complete RING-N and MESH-N data sets and both numerologies, $\mu \in \{1, 2\}$. Each point represents a pair of measured and modeled latency values, with color intensity reflecting sample density, where darker regions indicate areas of higher concentration. These plots show how closely the QR-based predictions align with the actual flow latencies compared to the more conservative WC estimates.

To quantitatively assess model performance, the coefficient of determination (R^2) metric available in the Python scikit-learn library was used. The R^2 score ranges from $-\infty$ to 1, with higher values indicating better model accuracy. Table 2 summarizes the R^2 results obtained for the evaluated models across different network scenarios—RING-N and MESH-N—and numerologies $\mu \in \{1, 2\}$. Results are reported separately for FH and MH flows in both uplink (UL) and downlink (DL) directions.

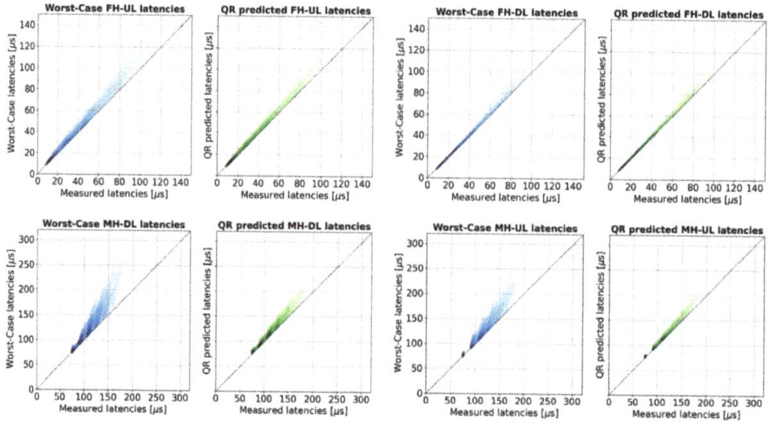

Figure 4. Flow latencies in RING-N networks: measured, WC-estimated, and QR-predicted.

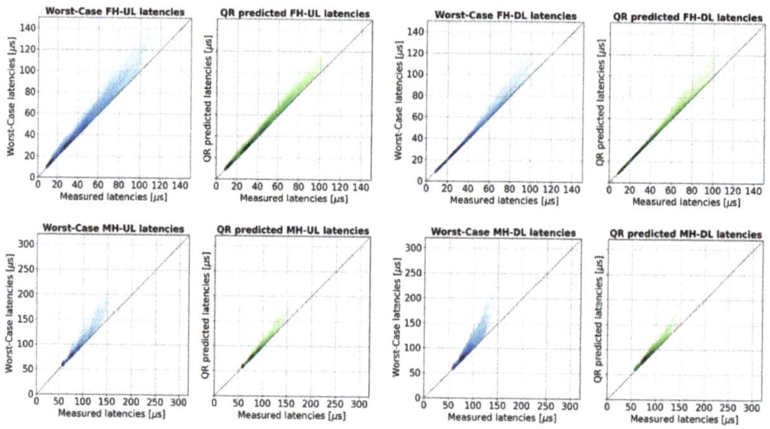

Figure 5. Flow latencies in MESH-N networks: measured, WC-estimated, and QR-predicted.

The results in Table 2 show that the WC model performs very well for FH flows, achieving R^2 values of 0.918–0.96 for FH-UL and up to about 0.98–0.991 for FH-DL. However, its accuracy declines noticeably for MH flows, leading to less reliable latency estimates for this flow type. In all cases, the QR model provides more accurate latency predictions than the WC model, with particularly large improvements observed for MH flows.

Table 2. Comparison of the R^2 score of WC and QR latency models in networks RING-N and MESH-N for numerologies $\mu \in \{1,2\}$.

			R^2 Score			
			FH		MH	
Network	μ	Model	UL	DL	UL	DL
RING-N	1	WC	0.952	0.990	0.633	0.012
		QR	0.980	0.993	0.952	0.864
	2	WC	0.956	0.991	0.823	0.516
		QR	0.986	0.995	0.972	0.929
MESH-N	1	WC	0.960	0.990	0.754	0.381
		QR	0.984	0.993	0.944	0.873
	2	WC	0.918	0.980	0.884	0.480
		QR	0.974	0.991	0.963	0.853

5.3. MILP Optimization

Feasible allocations of FH and MH flows, necessary for conducting the network simulations, were obtained using the MILP optimization model introduced in [35]. For clarity and brevity, only the main modeling assumptions are summarized below, while the full mathematical formulation can be found in [35].

The MILP models a problem of planning a packet-switched Xhaul network, jointly finding the placement of DUs at selected PP nodes and the routing of FH and MH flows between RUs, PPs, and the hub. The formulation includes constraints ensuring that each cluster of RUs is assigned to a common PP location, that the link utilization does not exceed available capacity, and that individual flow latencies remain within the imposed limits. The objective is to minimize the number of active PPs required to satisfy these constraints. The MILP problem is solved using the CPLEX v.12.9 optimizer [45].

5.4. Network Simulations

The transmission and routing of packet flows between Xhaul network elements were emulated using an event-driven simulator developed in the OMNeT++ v.5.6.1 environment [46]. For each network scenario, the simulations provided measurements of actual flow latencies and feature values associated with individual flows. The simulator emulates the operation of packet switches, including output-buffer queuing and prioritized handling of fronthaul packets. The main assumptions adopted in the simulator implementation are summarized below.

- Packet bursts from each flow source are transmitted periodically within a transmission window defined by the 5G radio numerology, as detailed in Section 3, following the traffic model described in [17].
- To introduce variability and avoid repetitive buffering patterns, the departure time of each burst (i.e., its offset relative to the start of the transmission window) is randomly modified every two transmission periods. Furthermore, the simulation enforces that all bursts complete their transmission within each two-window cycle, preventing temporal congestion caused by overlapping bursts from the same source.
- A store-and-forward switching mechanism without cut-through is assumed, meaning that each burst is fully received at the input port before transmission begins at the output port.
- Packet bursts are queued in a first-in–first-out (FIFO) manner and transmitted as complete units, without fragmentation or interleaving.
- Switches operate according to the strict-priority algorithm [11], which ensures that high-priority (HP) latency-sensitive FH bursts are always served before lower-priority (LP) MH bursts.
- Profile A of operation, as defined in [11], is applied, guaranteeing that an LP burst already being transmitted cannot be preempted by an HP burst.
- The latency of a flow, defined as the maximum one-way delay, is taken as the largest delay value measured among all bursts of that flow transmitted during the entire simulation.
- Each simulation assumes the transmission of 10^7 bursts, after which the simulation terminates.

6. Evaluation Scenario

The latency models are evaluated in a dynamic network scenario illustrated in Figure 6.

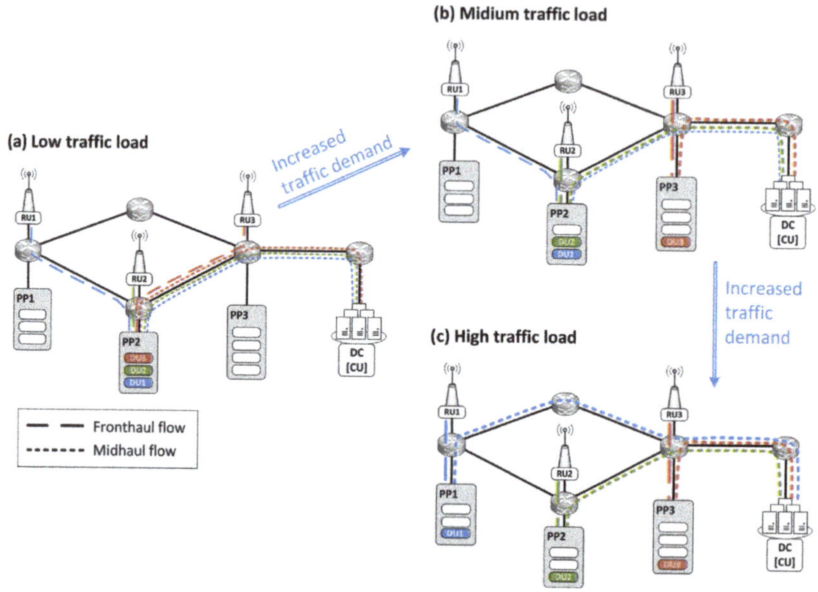

Figure 6. Evaluation scenario illustrating the reallocation of DUs and the adaptation of FH and MH routing paths as traffic load increases.

The network evaluation scenario assumes a progressive increase in network traffic load—from low to high levels—accompanied by dynamic reallocation of DU units among PP nodes and the adaptation of FH and MH routing paths. At low load conditions (see Figure 6a), DU units are aggregated into a smaller number of active PPs, allowing the remaining PPs to enter a sleep mode and thereby improving energy efficiency [47]. As the traffic load (ρ) increases, and either link utilization approaches capacity limits or flow latencies become excessive, DUs are gradually reallocated to PPs located closer to their corresponding RUs to satisfy capacity and latency constraints (see Figure 6b,c).

The implemented DU reallocation mechanism consists of the following two stages.

Stage 1: Selection of PP nodes—In an offline preprocessing stage, a pair of PP nodes, denoted as PP^{min} and PP^{max}, is determined for each RU by solving the MILP optimization model described in Section 5.3 for two extreme network load conditions, namely the minimum ($\rho = 0.1$) and maximum ($\rho = 1.0$) traffic levels.

Stage 2: DU reallocation—During the network simulation, whenever a change in traffic load is detected, the system verifies whether the current DU allocation satisfies the transmission capacity and latency constraints of all flows. If these conditions are not met, an inactive PP^{max} node hosting the largest number of DUs is activated, and the corresponding DUs are reallocated to this node. The reallocation is carried out only to the minimum extent required to restore feasibility, ensuring that the number of active PP nodes remains as small as possible throughout the simulation.

The network simulations start with the traffic load set to $\rho = 0.1$, with all DUs initially allocated to their corresponding PP^{min} nodes. At each simulation step, the traffic load is incremented by $\Delta\rho = 0.05$, and network reconfiguration is performed when required, following the procedure described above. The simulations continue until the traffic load reaches $\rho = 1.0$.

The considered dynamic network scenario effectively reflects the adaptive nature of packet-switched Xhaul networks, which can reconfigure flow allocations in response to varying traffic conditions, making it well suited for evaluating latency models across a wide range of traffic loads. It is essential to note that the latency constraints verified during traffic-load variations in the network simulations are evaluated using one of the latency models introduced in Section 4, namely the WC or QR model, depending on the case under analysis. Simultaneously, the actual flow latencies are measured in the simulator and used as a reference to assess the accuracy of the employed model and to validate its reliability, as discussed in the next section.

7. Results

In this section, the QR and WC latency models are numerically evaluated in dynamic packet-switched Xhaul networks, using the evaluation scenario introduced in Section 6. We begin by validating the maximum FH latencies predicted by the QR model against the given latency limits, and by comparing them with WC estimations and simulation outcomes for ring and mesh topologies. Next, we assess the prediction accuracy of both models for FH and MF flows under different traffic loads, latency limits, and numerologies. Finally, we analyze the impact of latency prediction accuracy on network performance in terms of PP utilization, considering the number of RUs, traffic load, latency limits, and numerologies as evaluation parameters. These results provide an overview of how model choice influences latency estimation, SLA compliance, and resource efficiency in packet-switched Xhaul networks.

7.1. Validation of QR Model

Here, we examine the reliability of the QR model, specifically verifying whether its maximum latency estimates remain within the imposed latency limits. Figures 7 and 8 present the maximum one-way FH latencies in RING-N and MESH-N networks, respectively, as functions of traffic load (ρ). Simulation results (denoted as Sim) are compared with the quantile regression predicted values (QR) and the worst-case estimated values (WC), assuming FH latency limits of 75 µs and 100 µs. For each load level, the reported value corresponds to the maximum latency across all analyzed scenarios, i.e., different network instances and parameter settings, assuming $N \in \{6, 8, 10\}$ for RING-N and $N \in \{20, 38\}$ for MESH-N topologies, $R \in \{10, 20, 30\}$ RUs, and numerologies $\mu \in \{1, 2\}$, with 10 random RU placements considered for each network setting. The results were obtained for the networks using the QR model.

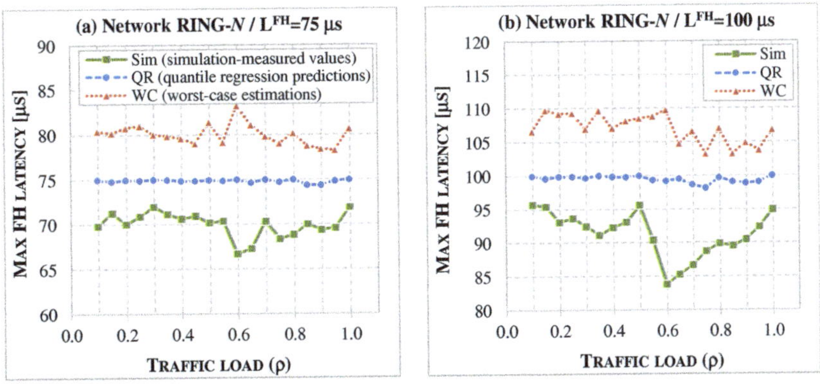

Figure 7. Maximum fronthaul latencies in RING-N networks under varying traffic load (ρ), obtained for networks utilizing the QR model, assuming FH latency limits of (**a**) 75 µs and (**b**) 100 µs, compared with simulation results (Sim) and WC estimates.

The results in Figures 7 and 8 show that the QR predictions remain below the latency limits across the entire range of ρ, confirming QR as a reliable model for one-way latency estimation in dynamic packet-switched Xhaul networks with varying traffic loads. The reported maximum predicted values are also close to the corresponding simulated latencies—particularly in MESH-N networks—with deviations typically within a few microseconds. In contrast, the WC estimates consistently exceed the FH latency limits, reflecting their conservative, overestimation approach. It is worth noting that these results correspond to networks optimized using the QR model, which explains why the WC estimates may lie above the limits.

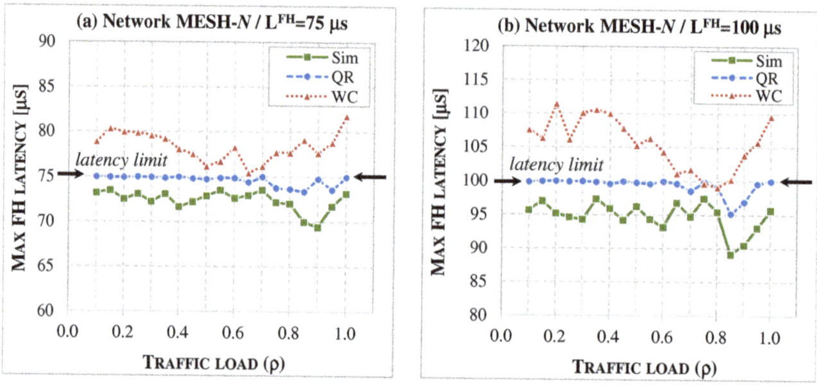

Figure 8. Maximum fronthaul latencies in MESH-N networks under varying traffic load (ρ), obtained for networks utilizing the QR model, assuming FH latency limits of (**a**) 75 μs and (**b**) 100 μs, compared with simulation results (Sim) and WC estimates.

7.2. Accuracy of Latency Models

Next, we analyze the accuracy of latency predictions (Δ), defined as the relative difference between estimated or predicted latencies and the simulation results, where lower values of Δ indicate higher accuracy.

Figure 9 shows the average prediction accuracy of the WC and QR models for FH flows in RING-N and MESH-N networks, evaluated over the same set of scenarios as in Section 7.1. The values of Δ are plotted as functions of traffic load (ρ) for FH latency limits $L^{FH} = 75$ μs and 100 μs, illustrating how both models behave under different load conditions.

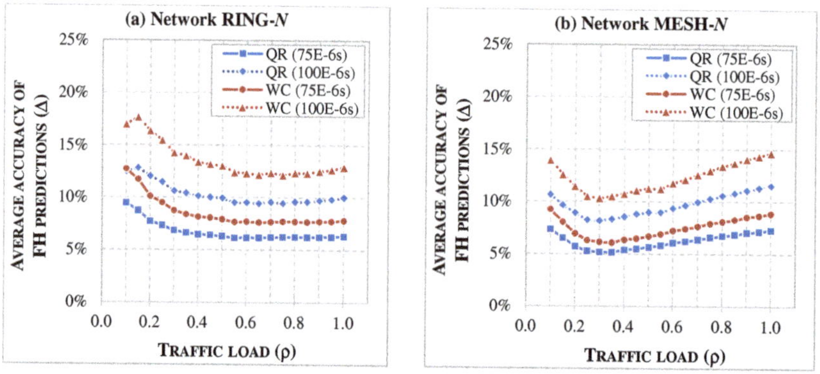

Figure 9. Average prediction accuracy of FH latencies as a function of traffic load (ρ), obtained with the WC and QR models for FH latency limits of 75 μs and 100 μs in (**a**) RING-N and (**b**) MESH-N networks.

In Figure 9, the average accuracy results for FH flows indicate that QR achieves higher accuracy than WC, with Δ ranging from about 5% (for $L^{FH} = 75$ μs in MESH-*N*) to 13% (for $L^{FH} = 100$ μs in RING-*N*), compared to WC, where Δ varies between 6% (for $L^{FH} = 75$ μs in MESH-*N*) and up to 18% (for $L^{FH} = 100$ μs in RING-*N*). Accuracy for both models is generally higher across the entire range of ρ when lower latency limits are imposed. In RING-*N* networks, both models exhibit reduced accuracy at low loads, which improves as ρ increases and stabilizes beyond $\rho \geq 40\%$. The highest accuracy in MESH-*N* is observed at moderate loads ($20\% \leq \rho \leq 40\%$), while performance deteriorates at both very low and very high load conditions.

Figure 10 extends the accuracy analysis to MH flows in RING-*N* and MESH-*N* networks, again as a function of traffic load (ρ) for latency limits $L^{FH} \in 75, 100$ μs. Compared to FH flows, a different trend can be observed: in RING-*N* networks, the accuracy of both models decreases as ρ increases. Moreover, while the QR model maintains a level of accuracy comparable to that for FH flows, the accuracy of the WC model deteriorates sharply at higher loads in RING-*N*, with Δ exceeding 22% on average.

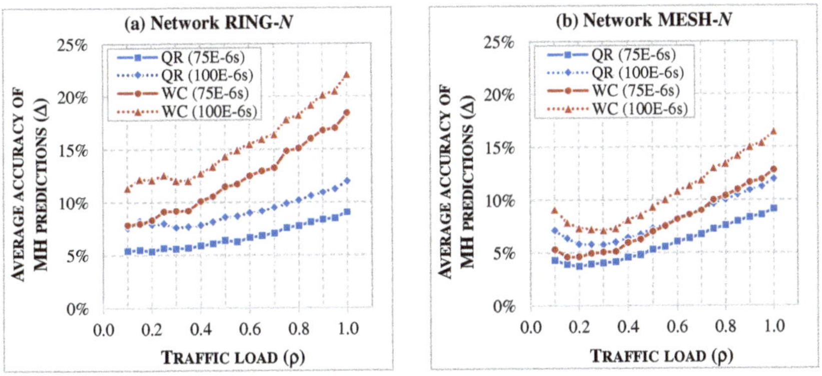

Figure 10. Average prediction accuracy of MH latencies as a function of traffic load (ρ), obtained with the WC and QR models for FH latency limits of 75 μs and 100 μs in (a) RING-*N* and (**b**) MESH-*N* networks.

Table 3 reports the average prediction accuracy of the WC and QR latency models for both FH and MH flows. The values are averaged over RING-*N* and MESH-*N* scenarios for traffic loads ρ ranging from 0.1 to 1.0 (step 0.05), with FH latency limits $L^{FH} \in \{75, 100\}$ μs and numerologies $\mu \in \{1, 2\}$

Table 3. Average prediction accuracy (Δ) of the WC and QR latency models for FH and MH flows in RING-*N* and MESH-*N* networks, evaluated for FH latency limits $L^{FH} \in \{75, 100\}$ μs and numerologies $\mu \in \{1, 2\}$.

			Model WC		Model QR		Absolute Difference	
Network	L^{FH} **[μs]**	μ	**FH**	**MH**	**FH**	**MH**	**FH**	**MH**
RING-*N*	75	1	7%	14%	6%	8%	1%	6%
		2	10%	10%	7%	5%	3%	5%
	100	1	13%	19%	11%	12%	2%	7%
		2	14%	12%	10%	7%	4%	5%
MESH-*N*	75	1	6%	8%	5%	6%	1%	2%
		2	9%	7%	7%	5%	2%	2%
	100	1	10%	12%	9%	9%	2%	3%
		2	14%	9%	11%	7%	4%	2%

The results in Table 3 confirm the trends shown in Figures 9 and 10, with QR reducing the average prediction error by several percentage points (pp) compared to WC, as summarized in the last two columns of the table. For FH flows, predictions are generally more accurate (lower values of Δ) for the lower numerology ($\mu = 1$), particularly in the case of WC. In contrast, for MH flows, both models perform better at the higher numerology ($\mu = 2$). Another observation is that prediction accuracy decreases when the FH latency limit (L^{FH}) is increased.

Concluding this subsection, QR predictions achieve consistently higher accuracy than WC estimations for both FH and MH flows. Nevertheless, the error of QR predictions still ranges from a few to several percent depending on the network scenario and traffic load, which motivates further exploration of alternative ML models that may deliver additional improvements in prediction accuracy.

7.3. Impact on Network Performance

Finally, we assess the impact of latency prediction models on network performance in terms of processing resource utilization.

Figure 11 presents the average number of active PPs (bars) and the relative reduction in PPs (lines) achieved with QR predictions compared to WC estimates in RING-N and MESH-N networks. The results are averaged over the network instances considered in the previous subsection—covering different traffic loads, latency limits, and numerologies—and are reported for scenarios with varying numbers of RUs, $R \in \{10, 20, 30\}$. The use of QR predictions consistently reduces the number of required active PPs compared with WC-based estimates, with the relative savings most pronounced in MESH-N networks and increasing with the number of RUs, reaching nearly 10% in some scenarios.

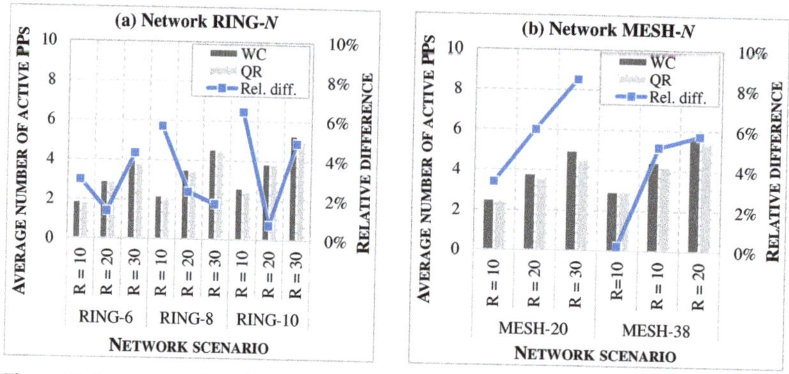

Figure 11. Average number of active PPs (bars) and relative reduction of PPs (lines) achieved with the QR model compared to the WC model in (**a**) RING-N and (**b**) MESH-N networks scenarios with different numbers of RUs (R).

Figure 12 presents a similar analysis of PP utilization gains, this time as a function of traffic load (ρ). QR-based latency predictions require fewer active PPs than WC, with average reductions ranging from about 2% to more than 6%. The relative difference between the models remains relatively stable across the entire load range in MESH-N networks, whereas in RING-N networks it decreases with increasing traffic load.

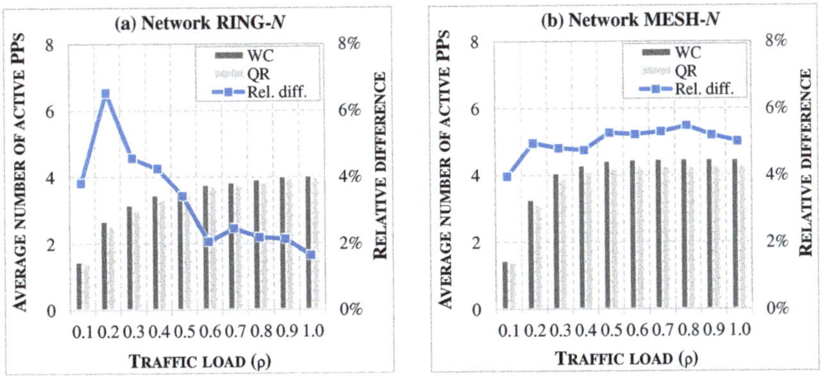

Figure 12. Average number of active PPs (bars) and relative reduction of PPs (lines) achieved with the QR model compared to the WC model under different traffic loads (ρ) in (**a**) RING-*N* and (**b**) MESH-*N* networks.

Table 4 reports the average performance gains obtained by using QR instead of WC for different FH latency limits (L^{FH}) at specific traffic loads in RING-*N* and MESH-*N* networks. Gains are evident for both latency limits, with savings in active PPs typically ranging from 2% to 11%, and the highest values observed in lightly loaded networks ($\rho = 0.2$) with the higher latency limit of 100 µs.

Table 4. Average performance gain, expressed as the reduction in active PPs achieved with the QR model compared to the WC model, in RING-*N* and MESH-*N* networks under different traffic loads (ρ) and FH latency limits $L^{FH} \in \{75, 100\}$ µs.

		Traffic Load (ρ)									
Network	L^{FH} **[µs]**	**0.1**	**0.2**	**0.3**	**0.4**	**0.5**	**0.6**	**0.7**	**0.8**	**0.9**	**1.0**
RING-*N*	75	4%	3%	3%	4%	3%	2%	2%	3%	3%	2%
	100	4%	11%	6%	5%	4%	2%	3%	2%	1%	2%
MESH-*N*	75	3%	3%	5%	5%	6%	6%	6%	6%	6%	6%
	100	5%	8%	4%	4%	4%	4%	4%	4%	4%	4%

Furthermore, Table 5 presents similar results, but this time for different numerologies, $\mu \in 1, 2$. In MESH-*N* networks, QR shows consistently larger benefits at $\mu = 2$ compared with $\mu = 1$ for almost all traffic loads ($\rho \geq 0.2$), whereas in RING-*N* networks the results are more variable across load levels.

Table 5. Average performance gain, expressed as the reduction in active PPs achieved with the QR model compared to the WC model, in RING-*N* and MESH-*N* networks under different traffic loads (ρ) and numerologies $\mu \in \{1, 2\}$.

		Traffic Load (ρ)									
Network	μ	**0.1**	**0.2**	**0.3**	**0.4**	**0.5**	**0.6**	**0.7**	**0.8**	**0.9**	**1.0**
RING-*N*	1	6%	5%	4%	4%	3%	1%	1%	2%	3%	2%
	2	1%	9%	5%	4%	4%	3%	4%	3%	1%	1%
MESH-*N*	1	5%	2%	2%	3%	5%	4%	4%	4%	4%	3%
	2	3%	9%	10%	8%	7%	8%	8%	8%	8%	8%

8. Discussion

This Section provides concluding remarks on the analysis presented in Section 7 and discusses the applicability of the QR-based latency predictor.

1. The comparison presented in Section 7 shows that deterministic WC estimation, while ensuring that latency limits are not violated, is overly conservative. WC values often exceed the actual latencies observed in simulations, which may lead to rejecting feasible configurations and allocating more network resources than necessary. In contrast, the QR-based predictions remain within acceptable limits and closely approximate the measured latencies, making them a more accurate approach for estimating maximum one-way delays.
2. The accuracy analysis confirms that the QR model consistently reduces prediction errors for both FH and MH flows. Although the absolute error still reaches a few percent in some cases, it represents a clear improvement over the WC estimator, especially in mesh topologies and at higher traffic loads. The results also show that tighter latency limits improve the accuracy of both models and that the impact of numerology differs between FH and MH flows. These observations highlight the need for parameter-aware adaptation of predictors and motivate the exploration of more advanced ML models.
3. At the network level, more accurate latency prediction translates directly into improved resource efficiency. When QR-based estimates are applied during network operation, a decrease of 1–11% in active processing nodes is observed on average, depending on the scenario. Although these gains may seem modest, they become significant in large-scale deployments, where even small efficiency improvements yield noticeable reductions in energy consumption and operational costs. Importantly, this effect is consistent across different network sizes, traffic loads, and RU configurations, confirming the robustness of the QR approach.
4. An important consideration regarding the applicability of the QR model is the range of network sizes and traffic loads represented in the training data. In this study, the maximum load level was limited to $\rho = 1.0$, corresponding to the full radio-flow bit-rate defined for each RU, and therefore representing the intended maximum Xhaul traffic. Scenarios with $\rho > 1.0$—i.e., exceeding the nominal RU capacity—were not considered. While the QR predictor may still produce reasonable outputs under such conditions, proper training for these extreme loads would require incorporating corresponding samples into the dataset. Similarly, although the training data cover a diverse set of topologies, including ring networks with up to 10 switches and mesh networks with up to 50 RUs, applying the model to significantly larger or structurally different networks would likely require extending the training dataset to ensure robust generalization.
5. The QR model is well suited for packet-switched Xhaul networks because it focuses on conservatively predicting high-quantile latency values. In this study, the QR predictor incorporates worst-case latency estimations as one of its input features. If analogous WC estimations can be formulated for scenarios with additional traffic classes or more advanced QoS differentiation schemes, the same QR-based methodology could be extended to those settings as well. Extending the approach to multi-class priority scheduling or differentiated QoS policies therefore constitutes a promising direction for future research.
6. While the evaluation considers a broad range of traffic loads and dynamically changing flow configurations, it does not explicitly address extreme operating conditions such as sudden traffic surges or link failures. The analysis assumes that traffic remains within the SLA-compliant maximum bit-rate levels defined for the flows. Nevertheless, the simulations include scenarios with varying routing configurations and time-varying loads, suggesting that the QR model may retain applicability in situations where flows must be rerouted following a link failure. A systematic investigation

of such extreme network states, particularly those involving abrupt congestion spikes or partial network outages, remains an important topic for future research.

7. An additional consideration concerns the computational complexity of the QR model in the context of dynamic network operation. Although the model is intended for real-time use, its training is performed entirely offline using large data sets that cover diverse traffic loads and routing configurations. For the mesh topology, training on the complete dataset of up to 1.44 million labeled samples, corresponding to 360,000 samples per flow type, required approximately 1.5–2 h per flow type on a standard laptop. Once trained, the model can be deployed without further retraining, even under dynamically changing flow configurations. Inference is lightweight (sub-millisecond), as it involves only simple linear operations on features such as WC and other latency-related components, which are dynamically computed through iterative summation of per-link latency values along each flow's routing path. These properties make the QR predictor entirely suitable for real-time network control. While a formal complexity analysis of the underlying optimization solver is beyond the scope of this work, the empirical results indicate that the approach is computationally efficient and practically deployable.
8. Overall, the obtained results show that applying the QR model in latency-sensitive packet-switched Xhaul networks improves efficiency without violating SLA constraints. By mitigating conservatism in WC estimates, the QR approach enables more effective use of network resources. These findings support the integration of data-driven latency predictors into future network control and management systems, including those operating within the O-RAN architecture, enabling proactive and automated network optimization.

9. Conclusions

This study addressed the problem of accurate latency prediction in dynamic TSN-enabled packet-switched Xhaul networks that transport fronthaul and midhaul traffic in 5G and beyond RANs. Two latency modeling approaches were considered and compared: a deterministic worst-case model derived from network calculus principles, and a data-driven quantile regression model designed to predict high-percentile (tail) flow latencies. The WC model provides strict upper bounds on transmission delays, ensuring network reliability but often resulting in overly conservative (overestimated) latency values.

In contrast, the QR model estimates conditional quantiles of latency distributions, leveraging both deterministic and queuing-related data features.

The results demonstrate that the QR model significantly improves the accuracy of latency prediction—particularly for midhaul flows—while maintaining compliance with stringent latency limits required by 5G/6G RANs. When applied in a dynamic network operation scenario, the QR-based predictions translate into measurable resource savings, reducing the number of active processing nodes by several percent compared with WC-based estimations.

These findings confirm that data-driven models can effectively complement deterministic latency models, offering a practical means to mitigate the over-provisioning effects typical of conservative WC calculations.

Future work will focus on further improving latency prediction accuracy beyond the results achieved with the QR model by exploring alternative, more advanced ML and DL models. In addition, the data-driven modeling framework will be extended toward hybrid learning approaches that combine analytical latency bounds with real-time telemetry data, enabling continuous model adaptation during network operation. These developments are expected to further enhance the predictive reliability of latency models in evolving 6G Xhaul systems and facilitate their integration into digital-twin-based network management platforms.

Author Contributions: Conceptualization, M.K.; methodology, M.K.; software, M.K.; validation, D.W.; investigation, M.K. and D.W.; resources, M.K.; data curation, M.K.; writing—original draft preparation, M.K.; writing—review and editing, M.K. and D.W.; visualization, M.K.; supervision, M.K.; project administration, M.K.; funding acquisition, M.K. All authors have read and agreed to the published version of the manuscript.

Funding: This research was supported by National Science Centre, Poland, under grant number 2024/53/B/ST7/02482.

Institutional Review Board Statement: Not applicable.

Informed Consent Statement: Not applicable.

Data Availability Statement: The raw data used in this study are available from the corresponding author upon request.

Conflicts of Interest: The authors declare no conflicts of interest.

References

1. Alimi, I.A.; Teixeira, A.; Monteiro, P. Towards an Efficient C-RAN Optical Fronthaul for the Future Networks: A Tutorial on Technologies, Requirements, Challenges, and Solutions. *IEEE Commun. Surv. Tutor.* **2018**, *20*, 708–769. [CrossRef]
2. Chih-Lin, I.; Li, H.; Korhonen, J.; Huang, J.; Han, L. RAN Revolution with NGFI (xhaul) for 5G. *IEEE J. Lightw. Technol.* **2018**, *36*, 541–550.
3. Abdullah, M.; Elayoubi, S.E.; Chahed, T.; Lisser, A. Performance Modeling and Dimensioning of Latency-Critical Traffic in 5G Networks. In Proceedings of the GLOBECOM 2023—2023 IEEE Global Communications Conference, Kuala Lumpur, Malaysia, 4–8 December 2023.
4. *1914.1-2019*; IEEE Standard for Packet-Based Fronthaul Transport Networks. IEEE: New York, NY, USA, 2019.
5. Common Public Radio Interface: eCPRI V1.2 Requirements for the eCPRI Transport Network. 2018. Available online: https://www.cpri.info/downloads/Requirements_for_the_eCPRI_Transport_Network_V1_2_2018_06_25.pdf (accessed on 14 October 2025).
6. O-RAN Alliance. O-RAN Control, User and Synchronization Plane Specification, v18.0. Available online: https://www.o-ran.org/ (accessed on 14 October 2025).
7. Skocaj, M.; Conserva, F.; Grande, N.S.; Orsi, A.; Micheli, D.; Ghinamo, G.; Bizzarri, S.; Verdone, R. Data-driven Predictive Latency for 5G: A Theoretical and Experimental Analysis Using Network Measurements. In Proceedings of the 2023 IEEE 34th Annual International Symposium on Personal, Indoor and Mobile Radio Communications (PIMRC), Toronto, ON, Canada, 5–8 September 2023.
8. Cai, Y.; Li, W.; Meng, X.; Zheng, W.; Chen, C.; Liang, Z. Adaptive Contrastive Learning Based Network Latency Prediction in 5G URLLC Scenarios. *Comput. Netw.* **2024**, *240*, 110185. [CrossRef]
9. Zhang, L.; Fu, J.; He, Y.; Jiang, X. Toward Deterministic Wireless Communication: Latency Prediction Using Network Measurement Data. In Proceedings of the 2024 IEEE 35th International Symposium on Software Reliability Engineering Workshops (ISSREW), Tsukuba, Japan, 28–31 October 2024.
10. Klinkowski, M. Optimized Planning of DU/CU Placement and Flow Routing in 5G Packet Xhaul Networks. *IEEE Trans. Netw. Serv. Manag.* **2024**, *21*, 232–248. [CrossRef]
11. *802.1CM-2018*; IEEE Standard for Local and Metropolitan Area Networks—Time-Sensitive Networking for Fronthaul. IEEE: New York, NY, USA, 2018.
12. O-RAN Alliance. Xhaul Packet Switched Architectures and Solutions. Tech. Spec. v8.0. 2025. Available online: https://specifications.o-ran.org/specifications (accessed on 14 October 2025).
13. Bertin, E.; Crespi, N.; Magedanz, T. *Shaping Future 6G Networks: Needs, Impacts, and Technologies*; John Wiley & Sons: Hoboken, NJ, USA, 2021.
14. *802.1Qbv-2015*; IEEE Standard for Local and Metropolitan Area Networks—Bridges and Bridged Networks—Amendment 25: Enhancements for Scheduled Traffic. IEEE: New York, NY, USA, 2015.
15. *802.1Qbu-2016*; IEEE Standard for Local and Metropolitan Area Networks—Bridges and Bridged Networks—Amendment 26: Frame Preemption. IEEE: New York, NY, USA, 2016.

16. Chitimalla, D.; Kondepu, K.; Valcarenghi, L.; Tornatore, M.; Mukherjee, B. 5G Fronthaul–Latency and Jitter Studies of CPRI over Ethernet. *J. Opt. Commun. Netw.* **2017**, *9*, 172–182. [CrossRef]
17. Perez, G.O.; Larrabeiti, D.; Hernandez, J.A. 5G New Radio Fronthaul Network Design for eCPRI-IEEE 802.1CM and Extreme Latency Percentiles. *IEEE Access* **2019**, *7*, 82218–82229. [CrossRef]
18. Kleinrock, L. *Queueing Systems Volume 1: Theory*; John Wiley & Sons: Hoboken, NJ, USA, 1975.
19. Chughtai, M.N.; Noor, S.; Laurinavicius, I.; Assimakopoulos, P.; Gomes, N.J.; Zhu, H.; Wang, J.; Zheng, X.; Yan, Q. User and Resource Allocation in Latency Constrained Xhaul via Reinforcement Learning. *J. Opt. Commun. Netw.* **2023**, *15*, 219–228. [CrossRef]
20. Boudec, J.Y.L.; Thiran, P. *Network Calculus—A Theory of Deterministic Queuing Systems for the Internet*; Lecture Notes in Computer Science (2050); Springer: Berlin/Heidelberg, Germany, 2001.
21. Zhang, J.; Wang, T.; Finn, N. Bounded latency calculating method, using network calculus. In Proceedings of the IEEE 802.1 Working Group Interim Session, Hiroshima, Japan, 14–17 January 2019.
22. Klinkowski, M.; Perello, J.; Careglio, D. Application of Linear Regression in Latency Estimation in Packet-Switched 5G xHaul Networks. In Proceedings of the 2023 23rd International Conference on Transparent Optical Networks (ICTON), Bucharest, Romania, 2–6 July 2023.
23. Koenker, R. *Quantile Regression*; Econometric Society Monographs; Cambridge University Press: Cambridge, UK, 2005.
24. Wan, T.; Ashwood-Smith, P. A performance Study of CPRI over Ethernet with IEEE 802.1Qbu and 802.1Qbv Enhancements. In Proceedings of the 2015 IEEE Global Communications Conference (GLOBECOM), San Diego, CA, USA, 6–10 December 2015.
25. Helm, M.; Carle, G. Predicting Latency Quantiles Using Network Calculus-assisted GNNs. In Proceedings of the GNNet '23: Proceedings of the 2nd on Graph Neural Networking Workshop 2023, Paris, France, 8 December 2023.
26. Zhao, L.; Pop, P.; Craciunas, S.S. Worst-Case Latency Analysis for IEEE 802.1Qbv Time Sensitive Networks Using Network Calculus. *IEEE Access* **2018**, *6*, 41803–41815. [CrossRef]
27. Diez, L.; Alba, A.M.; Kellerer, W.; Agüero, R. Flexible functional split and fronthaul delay: A queuing-based model. *IEEE Access* **2021**, *9*, 151049–151066. [CrossRef]
28. Koneva, N.; Sánchez-Macián, A.; Hernández, J.A.; Arpanaei, F.; González de Dios, O. On Finding Empirical Upper Bound Models for Latency Guarantees in Packet-Optical Networks. In Proceedings of the 2025 International Conference on Optical Network Design and Modeling (ONDM), Pisa, Italy, 6–9 May 2025.
29. Elgcrona, E. Latency Prediction in 5G Networks by Using Machine Learning. Master's Thesis, Lund University, Lund, Sweden, 2023.
30. Zinno, S.; Navarro, A.; Rotbei, S.; Pasquino, N.; Botta, A.; Ventre, G. A Lightweight Deep Learning Approach for Latency Prediction in 5G and Beyond. In Proceedings of the 2025 21st International Conference on Network and Service Management (CNSM), Bologna, Italy, 27–31 October 2025.
31. Agarwal, B.; Irmer, R.; Lister, D.; Muntean, G.M. Open RAN for 6G Networks: Architecture, Use Cases and Open Issues. *IEEE Commun. Surv. Tutor.* **2025**. [CrossRef]
32. Brik, B.; Chergui, H.; Zanzi, L.; Devoti, F.; Ksentini, A.; Siddiqui, M.S.; Costa-Pérez, X.; Verikoukis, C. Explainable AI in 6G O-RAN: A Tutorial and Survey on Architecture, Use Cases, Challenges, and Future Research. *IEEE Commun. Surv. Tutor.* **2025**, *27*, 2826–2859. [CrossRef]
33. Adamuz-Hinojosa, O.; Zanzi, L.; Sciancalepore, V.; Garcia-Saavedra, A.; Costa-Pérez, X. ORANUS: Latency-tailored Orchestration via Stochastic Network Calculus in 6G O-RAN. In Proceedings of the IEEE INFOCOM 2024—IEEE Conference on Computer Communications, Vancouver, BC, Canada, 20–23 May 2024; pp. 61–70.
34. Garcia-Saavedra, A.; Costa-Perez, X.; Leith, D.J.; Iosifidis, G. Enhancing 5G O-RAN Communication Efficiency Through AI-Based Latency Forecasting. In Proceedings of the IEEE INFOCOM 2025—IEEE Conference on Computer Communications Workshops (INFOCOM WKSHPS), London, UK, 19 May 2025; pp. 1–2.
35. Klinkowski, M. Optimization of Latency-Aware Flow Allocation in NGFI Networks. *Comp. Commun.* **2020**, *161*, 344–359. [CrossRef]
36. Klinkowski, M. Latency-Aware DU/CU Placement in Convergent Packet-Based 5G Fronthaul Transport Networks. *Appl. Sci.* **2020**, *10*, 7429. [CrossRef]
37. Common Public Radio Interface: eCPRI V1.2 Interface Specification. 2018. Available online: https://www.cpri.info/downloads/eCPRI_v_1_2_2018_06_25.pdf (accessed on 14 October 2025).
38. Esmaeily, A.; Mendis, H.V.K.; Mahmoodi, T.; Kralevska, K. Beyond 5G Resource Slicing With Mixed-Numerologies for Mission Critical URLLC and eMBB Coexistence. *IEEE Open J. Comm. Soc.* **2023**, *4*, 727–747. [CrossRef]
39. Koenker, R.; Bassett, G.J. Regression Quantiles. *Econometrica* **1978**, *46*, 33–50. [CrossRef]
40. Skocaj, D.; Dincic, M.; Bennesby, T.; Vukadinovic, V. TAILING: Tail Distribution Forecasting of Packet Delays Using Quantile Regression Neural Networks. In Proceedings of the ICC 2023—IEEE International Conference on Communications, Rome, Italy, 28 May–1 June 2023.

41. ITU-T Technical Report. Transport Network Support of IMT-2020/5G. 2018. Available online: https://www.itu.int/hub/publication/t-tut-home-2018/ (accessed on 14 October 2025).
42. Khorsandi, B.M.; Raffaelli, C. BBU location algorithms for survivable 5G C-RAN over WDM. *Comput. Netw.* **2018**, *144*, 53–63. [CrossRef]
43. Lagen, S.; Giupponi, L.; Hansson, A.; Gelabert, X. Modulation Compression in Next Generation RAN: Air Interface and Fronthaul Trade-offs. *IEEE Comm. Mag.* **2021**, *59*, 89–95. [CrossRef]
44. 3GPP. Study on New Radio Access Technology: Radio Access Architecture and Interfaces. Tech. Rep. TR 38.801, v14.0.0. 2017. Available online: https://portal.3gpp.org/desktopmodules/Specifications/SpecificationDetails.aspx?specificationId=3056 (accessed on 14 October 2025).
45. IBM. CPLEX Optimizer. Available online: https://www.ibm.com/products/ilog-cplex-optimization-studio (accessed on 14 October 2025).
46. Varga, A. OMNeT++ Discrete Event Simulator. Available online: https://omnetpp.org/ (accessed on 14 October 2025).
47. Innovative Optical Wireless Network Global Forum. PoC Reference of Mobile Fronthaul over APN (ver. 2.0). 2024. Available online: https://iowngf.org/wp-content/uploads/2025/02/IOWN-GF-RD-PoC_Reference_of_MFH_over_APN-2.0.pdf (accessed on 14 October 2025).

MDPI AG
Grosspeteranlage 5
4052 Basel
Switzerland
Tel.: +41 61 683 77 34

Applied Sciences Editorial Office
E-mail: applsci@mdpi.com
www.mdpi.com/journal/applsci

www.ingramcontent.com/pod-product-compliance
Lightning Source LLC
Chambersburg PA
CBHW061807210926
51850CB00006B/636
* 9 7 8 3 7 2 5 8 7 5 7 9 5 *